Introduction to Islamic Economics and Finance

INTRODUCTION TO ISLAMIC ECONOMICS AND FINANCE

Editor

M Kabir Hassan
University of New Orleans, USA

World Scientific

NEW JERSEY • LONDON • SINGAPORE • BEIJING • SHANGHAI • TAIPEI • CHENNAI

Published by

World Scientific Publishing Co. Pte. Ltd.
5 Toh Tuck Link, Singapore 596224
USA office: 27 Warren Street, Suite 401-402, Hackensack, NJ 07601
UK office: 57 Shelton Street, Covent Garden, London WC2H 9HE

British Library Cataloguing-in-Publication Data
A catalogue record for this book is available from the British Library.

INTRODUCTION TO ISLAMIC ECONOMICS AND FINANCE

Copyright © 2025 by World Scientific Publishing Co. Pte. Ltd.

All rights reserved. This book, or parts thereof, may not be reproduced in any form or by any means, electronic or mechanical, including photocopying, recording or any information storage and retrieval system now known or to be invented, without written permission from the publisher.

For photocopying of material in this volume, please pay a copying fee through the Copyright Clearance Center, Inc., 222 Rosewood Drive, Danvers, MA 01923, USA. In this case permission to photocopy is not required from the publisher.

ISBN 978-981-98-1372-8 (hardcover)
ISBN 978-981-98-1373-5 (ebook for institutions)
ISBN 978-981-98-1374-2 (ebook for individuals)

For any available supplementary material, please visit
https://www.worldscientific.com/worldscibooks/10.1142/14330#t=suppl

Desk Editors: Eshak Nabi Akbar Ali/Yulin Jiang

Typeset by Stallion Press
Email: enquiries@stallionpress.com

About the Editor

Mohammad Kabir Hassan is Professor of Finance at the Department of Economics and Finance at the University of New Orleans. He currently holds four Endowed Professorships and the Moffett Chair in World Resources, Prices, and Economic Development at the University of New Orleans. *Professor Hassan won the 2016 Islamic Development Bank (IDB) Prize in the Islamic Banking and Finance category.* Professor Hassan is in the top 2% of cited authors, according to a 2024 Standford University Survey. According to the 2024 ScholarGPS rankings, Dr. Hassan's research publications rate him #1 in the Islam, #110 in the Economics, and #343 in the Social Sciences categories worldwide. Professor Hassan is the recipient of the 2019 University of Louisiana System Outstanding Educator Award, the 2019 Life-long Research Achievement Award, and the 2018 UNO Nick Mueller International Leadership Medallion Award. Professor Hassan is the Editor-in-Chief of several scholarly journals published by reputable publishers. Dr. Hassan has won numerous awards from professional academic societies for research and innovative teaching. Hassan was a Senior Fulbright Scholar from 2022 to 2024. He has served on the AAOIFI AGEB Board since 2020 and is Chairman of the AAOFIF Education Board. Professor Hassan has recently been named the Hamid D. Habib Chair of Finance at the Institute of Business Administration, Karachi, Pakistan. Professor Hassan has recently been named Honorary Professor at the University of Jordan, Jordan.

Contents

About the Editor		v
Introduction		ix
Chapter 1	Building Trust in *Waqf* Management — Implications of Good Governance and Transparent Reporting *Rashedul Hasan, Abu Umar Faruq Ahmad and Siti Alawiah Bt. Siraj*	1
Chapter 2	Impact of Non-Intermediation Activities of Banks on Economic Growth and Volatility: An Evidence from OIC *Mohsin Ali, Mansor H. Ibrahim and Mohamed Eskandar Shah*	19
Chapter 3	Competition-Stability Relationship in Dual Banking Systems: Evidence from Efficiency-Adjusted Market Power *Mudeer Ahmed Khattak, Omar Alaeddin and Moutaz Abojeib*	35
Chapter 4	*Shari'ah* Oriented Precious Metal Backed Cryptocurrency: From *Shari'ah* Advisors' and Financial Experts' Perceptions *Mousa Ajouz, Adam Abdullah and Salina Kassim*	59
Chapter 5	Individual's Behavior and Access to Finance: Evidence from Palestine *Fadi Hassan Shihadeh*	79
Chapter 6	Impact of Islamic Finance on Economic Growth: An Empirical Analysis of Muslim Countries *Syeda Arooj Naz and Saqib Gulzar*	101
Chapter 7	Determinants of Credit Risk: A Comparative Analysis between Islamic and Conventional Banks in Bangladesh *Md. Nurul Kabir, Mohammad Dulal Miah and Rubaiya Nadia Huda*	123
Chapter 8	Comparative TFP Growth between GCC Conventional and Islamic Banks before and after the 2008 Financial Crisis *Azzeddine Azzam and Belaid Rettab*	155
Chapter 9	Does Foreign Aid Help or Hinder the Institutional Quality of the Recipient Country? New Evidence from the OIC Countries *Mohammad Ashraful Ferdous Chowdhury, Mohamed Ariff, Mansur Masih and Izlin Ismail*	175

Chapter 10	The Investment Account Holders Disclosure Level in the Annual Reports of Islamic Banks: Construction of IAHs Disclosure Index *Raoudha Saidani, Neila Boulila Taktak and Khaled Hussainey*	205
Chapter 11	AAOIFI Accounting Standards and a Theory of Interest-Free Banking *Assyad Al-Wreiket, Ali Ashraf, Ola Al-Sheyab, M. Kabir Hassan and Ivan Julio*	231
Chapter 12	Domains and Motives of *Musharakah* Spur in the Islamic Banking Industry of Pakistan *Muhammad Nouman, Karim Ullah and Shafiullah Jan*	273
Chapter 13	Financial Inclusion, Institutional Quality, and Financial Development: Empirical Evidence from OIC Countries *Minhaj Ali, Muhammad Imran Nazir, Shujahat Haider Hashmi and Wajeeh Ullah*	303
Chapter 14	Does Financial Inclusion Drive the Islamic Banking Efficiency? A Post-Financial Crisis Analysis *Hasanul Banna, Md. Rabiul Alam, Rubi Ahmad and Norhanim Mat Sari*	331
Chapter 15	Low-Frequency Volatility and Macroeconomic Dynamics: Conventional Versus Islamic Stock Markets *Hong-Bae Kim and A.S.M. Sohel Azad*	357
Chapter 16	Does Islamic Finance Follow Financial Hierarchy? Evidence from the Malaysian Firms *Mamoru Nagano*	385
Chapter 17	The Economic Cost of Revolution: The Iranian Case. A Synthetic Control Analysis *Serhat Hasancebi*	415
Chapter 18	Islamic Blended Finance for Circular Economy Impactful SMEs to Achieve SDGs *Tariqullah Khan and Fatou Badjie*	437
Chapter 19	Hybrid Review of Islamic Pricing Literature *Md. Abdullah Al Mamun, M. Kabir Hassan, Md. Abul Kalam Azad and Mamunur Rashid*	463
Chapter 20	A Contemporary Review of Islamic Finance and Accounting Literature *M. Kabir Hassan, Sirajo Aliyu and Mumtaz Hussain*	497

Introduction to Special Issue on Islamic Economics and Finance

M. Kabir Hassan

Professor of Finance, University of New Orleans
New Orleans, Louisiana, USA
mhassan@uno.edu

The special issue on Islamic Economics and Finance (IEF) — published in the *Singapore Economic Review* — focuses on providing financial services to the growing Muslim population based on Islamic principles, particularly the prohibition of interest-based transactions. The IEF industry has seen significant growth over the last two decades, primarily driven by the growth of Islamic banking. However, it has faced various challenges, including competition from traditional finance, regulatory and accounting issues, harmonization of practices, and the impact of global crises.

The special issue highlights inconsistent findings between the performances of Islamic and conventional financial institutions; and recommends new advents in Islamic banks and alternative Islamic institutions. The advancements will fuel the necessary growth in Islamic finance to diversify, beyond solely banking — Islamic banking contributes over 70% of contemporary Islamic Economic and Finance activities — rather leveraging fintech, automation, and blockchain into the industry. The twenty chapters within this issue can be divided into the following themes: (1) Islamic finance and disclosure governance, (2) market volatility linkages in OIC nations and institutions, (3) financial inclusion, efficiency, and growth in Islamic banks, (4) risk metrics of novel Islamic finance instruments, and (5) contemporary research applications.

Chapter 1, "Building Trust in *Waqf* Management — Implications of Good Governance and Transparent Reporting," highlights the implications of governance and reporting practices in ensuring accountability and building donors' trust in Bangladesh's Waqf Institutions (WIs). Board ability and voluntary information disclosure have a significant positive impact on accountability. Accountability has a significant impact on building trust in Waqf management. The study also discusses recent policies and necessary forthcoming amendments to ensure good governance and Waqf reporting within Bangladesh and other nations.

Chapter 2, "Impact of Non-Intermediation Activities of Banks on Economic Growth and Volatility: Evidence from OIC," investigates the impact of the non-intermediation activities of OIC banks on economic growth and volatility. Findings show non-intermediation income to be insignificant within OIC member countries' growth and volatility, but significant in GCC countries where it reduces volatility. OIC intermediation activities are found to be insignificantly related to growth, but interestingly reduce volatility.

Chapter 3, "Competition-Stability Relationship in Dual Banking Systems: Evidence from Efficiency-Adjusted Market Power," explores the impact of banking competition on financial stability and Hindered by lower market power to conventional counterparts, Islamic banks show lower stability and higher default vulnerability, thus supporting the *competition–fragility view*. Since the evidence from this research suggests no difference in the relationship between Islamic banks and conventional banks, a uniform competition strategy can be formed to govern both banking models within the sampling countries.

Chapter 4, "Shari'ah Oriented Precious Metal Backed Cryptocurrency: From Shari'ah Advisors' and Financial Experts' Perceptions," investigates the perceptions of Shari'ah-compliant precious metal-backed cryptocurrency (PMC). Although Shari'ah advisors and financial experts have differing views on assets-backed money; they agree on the desirability of cryptocurrency and technological advancement. PMC needs to be checked by financial regulation and should endorse blockchain technology to increase transparency. The informants agreed that PMC can definitely have a place in the future of Shari'ah-compliant instruments.

Chapter 5, "Individual's Behavior and Access to Finance: Evidence from Palestine," delves into whether individual socioeconomic characteristics influence financial inclusion in Palestine. While formal institutions have made remarkable efforts to develop an inclusive financial infrastructure in Palestine, the country's unstable political climate impedes economic stability and individuals' motivation to use formal financial resources, such as credit. The results also indicated that females were less likely to be included in financial transactions, primarily involving borrowing and formal accounts. More efforts to specifically encourage youth, the poor, and women to use formal banking could enhance their access to financial services (Islamic financial services, online banking platforms, etc.).

Chapter 6, "Impact of Islamic Finance on Economic Growth: An Empirical Analysis of Muslim Countries," provides insight into how Islamic finance and relevant intermediaries have developed economies, improved infrastructure, and fostered development in human capital. The results show the bidirectional contribution of the Islamic banking system and Islamic bonds to the economic growth and, in the long run, the economic welfare of Muslim countries. As such, policymakers should prioritize policies to ensure the stability of this sector.

Chapter 7, "Determinants of Credit Risk: A Comparative Analysis between Islamic and Conventional Banks in Bangladesh," shows that among several macroeconomic variables, GDP growth decreases credit risk, whereas real interest rate and inflation increase credit risk. Bank-specific variables prove that both clusters of banks suffer from adverse selection and moral hazard problems. Results also indicate that competition has a risk-enhancing effect on banks, which supports the *competition–fragility nexus*. Further analysis shows that board size and board independence affect the credit risk of both clusters of banks. The findings of this study suggest some policy implications from the macro, bank, and governance perspectives and can be generalized for other emerging economies.

Chapter 8, "Comparative TFP Growth between GCC Conventional and Islamic Banks before and after the 2008 Financial Crisis," measures and compares conventional and Islamic banks in terms of total factor productivity growth (TFPG) – based on technical change, economy size, and asset growth. The results show that Islamic banks outperformed conventional banks overall in size-based subsamples and the whole sample. Regarding the product and process innovation provisions of TFPG, Islamic banks weathered the 2008 financial crisis by being more innovative than conventional banks.

Chapter 9, "Does Foreign Aid Help or Hinder the Institutional Quality of the Recipient Country? New Evidence from the OIC Countries," reviews Muslim countries' aid practices and IQ. This study finds that the overall impact of aid flows on IQ is negative. Aid flows dictate worsening political and governance corruption indicators. Additionally, aid volatility adversely affects the IQ of aid-dependent countries. The negative effect of aid volatility on institutions may increase through rent-seeking and corruption. The results suggest that the effect or magnitude of the negative impact of aid on IQ is manifested, especially in countries with weak institutions rather than in countries with strong institutions.

Chapter 10, "The Investment Account Holders Disclosure Level in the Annual Reports of Islamic Banks: Construction of IAHs Disclosure Index," develops a specific IAH disclosure index based on the Accounting and Auditing Organization for Islamic Financial Institutions (AAOIFI) standards. The sample includes 49 Islamic banks across 10 countries. The findings show an overall level of 28% disclosure. Indeed, the sampled Islamic banks provide fewer disclosures related to IAHs. This study can help regulators in different countries understand and strengthen the IAH disclosure practices in Islamic banks by imposing AAOIFI disclosure requirements in terms of IAH reporting.

Chapter 11, "AAOIFI Accounting Standards and a Theory of Interest-Free Banking," obtains the cost of contract financing. The results reveal that Islamic bank profit rates and conventional bank interest rates are correlated in an economic environment where conventional and Islamic banks dwell under the same regulatory framework. Fixed and predetermined interest rates charged by traditional commercial banks create a fixed financial burden for the participating firm or the business, as the business is obliged to make interest payments no matter the business situation. On the other hand, a client of an Islamic bank in a profit/loss sharing arrangement has less financial burden, as an Islamic bank shares the risk of loss and the firm is not obliged to pay a fixed profit rate.

Chapter 12, "Domains and Motives of *Musharakah* Spur in the Islamic Banking Industry of Pakistan," explores the contemporary shift toward participatory financing, which is primarily characterized by an increase in working capital financing and commodity operations financing through *Musharakah* mode Islamic banks. Moreover, five factors contribute to the spur of participatory financing: (i) introducing varieties in *Musharakah*, (ii) enhanced applicability, (iii) high-volume projects, (iv) government interventions, and (v) the regulator's role. The framework can significantly advance understanding with respect to the implementation theory of participation financing within Islamic banking and related Shariah compliance and regulation.

Chapter 13, "Financial Inclusion, Institutional Quality, and Financial Development: Empirical Evidence from OIC Countries," examines the moderation effect of institutional quality (IQ) on the relationship between financial inclusion (FI) and financial development (FD) of 45 Organization of Islamic Cooperation (OIC) countries. The empirical results confirm the significant positive relationship between FI, IQ, and FD. Interestingly, IQ moderates FI and has a significant positive impact on FD. Policymakers must sensibly understand the pivotal role of FI and IQ in establishing sustainable future development in OIC countries.

Chapter 14, "Does Financial Inclusion Drive the Islamic Banking Efficiency? A Post-Financial Crisis Analysis," estimates both the non-bias-corrected and bias-corrected efficiency in examinations of how financial inclusion impacts Islamic banks. This study finds that most of the countries, except some Asian and Middle Eastern countries, have inconsistent efficiency trends in the Islamic banking sector. Additionally, financial inclusion is significantly allied with Islamic banking efficiency. The results propose that Islamic banks bearing recessionary consequences should focus on financial inclusion.

Chapter 15, "Low-Frequency Volatility and Macroeconomic Dynamics: Conventional Versus Islamic Stock Markets," investigates the relationship between macroeconomic risk and the low-frequency volatility of conventional and Islamic stock markets. It finds that low-frequency market volatility is lower for Islamic countries and markets with a greater number of listed companies, higher market capitalization relative to GDP, and larger variability in industrial production. The study also finds that the low-frequency component of volatility is greater when the macroeconomic factors of GDP, unemployment, short-term interest rates, inflation, money supply, and foreign exchange rates are more volatile. The findings imply that religiosity has an influence on the correction of market volatility and diversification opportunities.

Chapter 16, "Does Islamic Finance Follow Financial Hierarchy? Evidence from the Malaysian Firms," estimates the degree and influences of informaiton asymmetry in Sukuk issuance. First, a cost-plus-sales-based Murabahah, sukuk is available for all sukuk issuers, even though the degree of information asymmetry is high. Second, a lease-based Ijarah sukuk can be chosen by high-information-asymmetric firms only when the firm has qualified collateral assets. Third, only a low-information-asymmetric firm can choose a profit-and-loss-sharing based Musyarakah sukuk. The paper concludes that sukuk issuance also follows a financial hierarchy in accordance with the agency costs of each financial methodology required when a specific sukuk is chosen.

Chapter 17, "The Economic Cost of Revolution: The Iranian Case. A Synthetic Control Analysis," investigates the economic cost of the revolution using the synthetic control method. Estimates conclude that after the emergence of the revolution, the annual real gross domestic product (GDP) per capita in Iran declined by about 20.15% on average relative to its synthetic counterpart without the revolution in the period 1978–1980. If Iran had not faced such a revolution, the accumulated per capita GDP would have been $6,479 higher, which amounts to an average annual loss of about

$2,159 over that period. The research provides valuable case study material on the economic shocks of a revolution.

Chapter 18, "Islamic Blended Finance for Circular Economy Impactful SMEs to Achieve SDGs," presents a blended Islamic finance framework for small and medium enterprises (SMEs) to achieve sustainable development goals (SDGs). In essence, the financial contracts would tie in ESG incentives. In the contract design, the private sector provides finance, the philanthropist pays the costs of funds, the public sector facilitates, and the impactful SME receives subsidized financing. Blending Islamic finance offers additional avenues to attract capital and resources for developmental intentions. Through the philanthropic component, SMEs may access the source of social subsidy, thus reducing risk perception and spurring growth.

Chapter 19, "Hybrid Review of Islamic Pricing Literature," critically examines IP literature boom. The bibliometric results show that IP literature demonstrates a low productivity, low citations ratio, and high research collaboration. The content analysis identifies that pricing methods and operational mechanisms are under-researched in industries outside of Islamic finance. This study is of critical importance because it simultaneously shows the evolution of IP.

Chapter 20, "A Contemporary Review of Islamic Finance and Accounting Literature," reviews the new body of emerging empirical literature on Islamic finance focusing on corporate finance, Takaful, and Islamic accounting. The literature review provides a mixed summary into Islamic financial markets and the various instruments. The story delves into both optimal and sub-optimal periods, measuring and comparing performance between Islamic and conventional institutions. This paper discusses issues that are relevant to Islamic finance and identifies avenues for future research and policy implications.

The following table shows a snippet of the findings.

Theme	Takeaways	Policy Implications	Future Research
ISLAMIC FINANCE (GENERAL)	Islamic finance must expand beyond the banking sector (dominates 80% of its assets). Movement toward debt-driven contracts. Capital market instruments are utilized for infrastructure and sovereign finance, which have examinable impacts on overall economic growth and development.	Regulations allow avenues for developing new risk and reward-sharing products, as well as functional incentives. Preset benchmarks for risk minimization on (permissible) debts. Regulators must expand auditing and enforcement of adherence to Shariah.	Empirical investigation and surveys of literature regarding Islamic social finance initiatives and legislations. Extent to which Islamic financial institutions are minimizing risk on their permissible debt contracts. Paradigm shifts in the Islamic finance.

(*Continued*)

Theme	Takeaways	Policy Implications	Future Research
ISLAMIC CORPORATE FINANCE	Islamic financial institutions are designed to share profit and loss with a broad range of transactional restrictions which include interest, gambling, complex derivatives, and extreme uncertainty. Therefore, Sharia-compliant firms are largely asset-based, with an ownership legitimacy share of the investment account holder in other cases.	Regulators of Shariah-compliant firms must control earnings manipulation and promote corporate social responsibility. Earn-out agreements contradict essential principles and demand attention. The transfer of managers' services within and outside the Islamic financial industry affects financial decisions.	Suitable corporate measurements and contractual procedures complying with Sharia law. Optimal capital structure and dividend activity promoting profit and risk sharing, sustainable wealth creation and redistribution, and cost reduction. Managers' movements and their effect on firm value and efficiency maximization.
TAKAFUL	Income/education levels, Muslim proportion, and development all influence Takaful insurance demand. The size of the board and firm influences cost efficiency, whereas splitting the top management does not affect efficiency. Limited Takaful empirical literature regarding determination, efficiency, and performance.	Takaful investments require efficient services that can compete with conventional insurance companies. Regulators have to detail the percentage of acceptable product combinations between mutuality and proprietary entities to avoid conflicts of interest. Policy arrangement is required to accommodate ideal practices and the required corporate governance structure of Takaful.	The effect of deviating from the mutuality principle in the capital structure as well as the policyholders' benefits. Limited literature on Takaful neglects areas such as corporate structure, accountability, consumer protections, insolvency, disclosure, and capital regulations.

(Continued)

Theme	Takeaways	Policy Implications	Future Research
ISLAMIC ACCOUNTING	Islamic accounting techniques are consistent with Sharia. IFRS standards (over FAS) are used for Islamic finance institutions. The significant differences between conventional and Islamic accounting treatment lie in the "form above substance" claim and the reflection of the time value of money in some Sharia-based transactions.	Regulators have to engage in providing a comprehensive procedure for Islamic accounting to note distinctions from conventional principles. Extending grants, conferences, and seminars to Muslim minority countries will contribute toward understanding the nature of the Islamic finance practices, particularly in the financially developed nations.	Studies on Islamic accounting are qualitative with few empirical investigations. Explore the form and substance issues regarding accounting techniques for treating unresolved Islamic financial transactions. Cross-country comparisons.

© 2025 World Scientific Publishing Company
https://doi.org/10.1142/9789819813735_0001

Chapter 1

Building Trust in *Waqf* Management — Implications of Good Governance and Transparent Reporting[#]

Rashedul Hasan[*]

Faculty of Business, Communication and Law
INTI International University, Malaysia
hasanaiub05@gmail.com

Abu Umar Faruq Ahmad

Islamic Economics Institute, King Abdulaziz University
Kingdom of Saudi Arabia
aufahmad@gmail.com

Siti Alawiah Bt. Siraj

Department of Accounting
International Islamic University, Malaysia
s.alawiah@iium.edu.my

This study seeks to highlight the implications of governance and reporting practices in ensuring accountability and building donors trust in *Waqf* Institutions (WIs). Data gathered through the survey are analyzed using PLS-SEM technique. The conceptual model was developed based on the critical review of the past literature. Among the three proxies of board attributes, only board ability has a significant positive impact on accountability. Voluntary information disclosure has a significant positive impact on accountability. Accountability has a significant impact on building trust in *waqf* management. Results provided by the study advocate for the adoption of formal reporting and improved governance mechanisms to enhance donors' trust in WIs.

Keywords: *Waqf*; trust; governance; reporting; accountability; Shari'ah.

1. Introduction

Poverty has been identified as one of the critical challenges for Bangladesh since the country achieved its independence in 1971. Like other developing countries, poverty has imposed challenges on resource allocations for the government of the People's Republic of Bangladesh (Ahmad and Karim, 2019). Like other developing countries, Bangladesh has adopted the Millennium Development Goals (MDGs) with a target to achieve all MDGs' milestone by 2015. It has made significant progress to reduce extreme poverty. Such

---
[*]Corresponding author.
[#]This Chapter first appeared in the *Singapore Economic Review*, Vol. 67, No. 1, doi: 10.1142/S0217590820420059. © 2022 World Scientific Publishing.

progress was possible due to the efforts taken by both governments (such as Palli Karma Sahayak Foundation (PKSF) and non-government organizations (NGOs) (such as BRAC) (Mobin and Ahmad, 2017). Microfinance institutions (MFIs) (such as the Grameen Bank) have contributed toward poverty alleviation in Bangladesh by promoting entrepreneurial activity among the rural population. According to the World Bank, the percentage of the population living below the upper poverty line reduced to 12.9% in 2019 from 24.3% in 2016.[1]

Microfinance has been gaining momentum over the past four decades around the world due to its long-run impacts on poverty alleviation and household consumption. The success of MFIs in poverty-stricken Asian countries, such as Bangladesh has attracted attention from various parts of the globe with similar demographics (Mobin and Ahmad, 2017) MFIs provide loans to micro-enterprises. According to the World Bank, enterprises with up to 10 employees or total assets up to USD 10,000 or total annual turnover of USD 100,000 are micro-enterprise. Micro-enterprise often finds it difficult to access credit through the traditional banking channels due to inadequate assets for collateral (Demirgüç-Kunt *et al.*, 2008).

Bangladesh is considered as the pioneer of microfinance scheme and the Grameen Bank, established by Noble laureate Dr Muhammad Yunus, has made significant efforts to improve the living standards of rural women living below the poverty line in Bangladesh (Rahman, 2019). Grameen Bank has been extending microcredits to poor borrowers, the majority of them are women, without any collateral since 1976. The microcredit model introduced by Muhammad Yunus through the Grameen Bank has become a model of poverty alleviation and sustainable development in Asia (Khan and SR Khan, 2016) and Africa (Buchenrieder *et al.*, 2019). The microfinance program introduced by Muhammad Yunus attempted to highlight the crucial role of women in managing credit and allow entrepreneurs with insufficient credit history to access finance from traditional banking channels.

In Bangladesh, the expansion of microfinance has three phases (Khandker *et al.*, 2016). First, we observe the limited expansion of microfinance firms that focused on the rural non-farms' activities before 1994. Second, public and private microfinance entities expanded between 1995–2004 to provide lending opportunities to microenterprises. Third, the post-2004 phase, which witnessed fierce competition among the MFIs for survival and market expansion.

MFIs are facing difficulties to reach the poor (Hickson, 2001). Bateman (2010) has criticized the profit-oriented operations of MFIs, drawing the example of Grameen Bank, which supports the findings of Morduch (1998) that states that MFIs do not make a significant contribution to reducing poverty in developing countries. Faruqee and Khalily (2011) report that interest rates charged by MFIs in Bangladesh range between 28.11–35.75% for rural micro-credit and between 28.00–34.73% for urban microcredit, which is higher than the 10–13% interest rate charged by the commercial banks. The interest rate charged by MFIs in Bangladesh have not dropped significantly, rather remained lower than credit cards' interest rate. This is unlike the case for MFIs operating in

---

[1] "Poverty and Equity Brief", accessed on 18 April, 2020 at: https://databank.worldbank.org/data/download/poverty/33EF03BB-9722-4AE2-ABC7-AA2972D68AFE/Archives-2019/Global_POVEQ_BGD.pdf.

Cameroon, Morocco, Peru, Senegal, Tanzania, Uzbekistan and Zambia as interest rates charged by MFIs in those countries are higher than the credit card or consumer interest rates (see Appendix A). In addition to charging high-interest rates, MFI managers in Bangladesh report high levels of multiple indebtedness.[2] Inability to repay microfinance loans has resulted in some suicide incidents and organ trafficking, which emphasizes the criticisms of Bateman (2010). It also poses serious doubt on the ability of microfinance to alleviate poverty (Banerjee and Jackson, 2017).

Karim *et al.* (2008) argue that religious beliefs play a vital role among large numbers of poverty-stricken demographic in developing countries while deciding to reject the Grameen bank style MFIs offering microcredit at high-interest rates. In the absence of robust governance mechanisms and limited public resources for long-term development plans (Hasan and Siraj, 2017), academic interest has delved into the application of the Shari'ah principles to curb excess interest and reduce the debt burden of micro-enterprises. Past studies have proposed *Waqf* based Islamic microfinance models (Ahmed, 2007; Haneef *et al.*, 2015) as Shari'ah compliant alternatives to conventional MFIs.

Waqf has a widespread presence in Bangladesh. *Waqf* properties in Bangladesh have two groups, registered and unregistered *Waqf* properties. The Ministry of Religious Affairs (MoRA) has the responsibility to administer all registered waqf properties. In the case of the unregistered *Waqf*, *Waqif* (donor) takes the responsibility to administer such private *Waqf* properties. MoRA has established the Office of the Administrator of *Waqf*s Bangladesh to administer all registered *Waqf* properties under the legal framework prescribed in the *Waqf Ordinance, 1962* (Ahmad and Karim, 2017). Registered *Waqf* properties in Bangladesh are subject to a breach of trust, mismanagement, malfeasance and misappropriation (Ahmed, 2007). Inadequate workforce, misappropriation of *Waqf* properties, operational inefficiency, old legal framework and low integrity among *Mutawalli*s (administers) has resulted into lack of motivation among independent *Mutawalli*s to register *Waqf* properties (Hasan and Siraj, 2016) under the supervision of 'the Administrators of Waqf Bangladesh'. Therefore, more than one-third of the *Waqf* properties in Bangladesh remain unregistered (Karim, 2009).

The lack of skilled employees (Chowdhury *et al.*, 2012), reduced level of governance (Kasim et al., 2016) and reporting practices (Hamdan *et al.*, 2013) affect the efficient utilization of registered *Waqf* properties. Alpay and Haneef (2015) recommended maintaining transparency and accountability between funding and implementing agencies to achieve the goal of poverty reduction through the utilization of *Waqf* donations. Ihsan and Ibrahim (2011) report that WIs ensure better accountability through transparent reporting. Sargeant and Lee (2004) and Torres-Moraga *et al.* (2010) conclude that poor quality of governance and reporting practices might affect accountability and reduce donors' trust in charitable organizations. Such findings cannot be generalized for WIs due to the lack of empirical evidence which forms the primary objective of this study.

---

[2] "The new moneylenders: are the poor being exploited by high microcredit interest rates?", accessed on 18 April, 2020 at: https://www.cgap.org/sites/default/files/CGAP-Occasional-Paper-The-New-Moneylenders-Are-the-Poor-Being-Exploited-by-High-Microcredit-Interest-Rates-Feb-2009.pdf.

Lack of governance and transparency contributes to lack of stakeholder trust in public *Waqf* management in Pakistan (Shirazi, 2006). Similar conclusions are presented by Ihsan and Ibrahim (2011) for Indonesian and Malaysian WIs. Ahmad and Safiullah (2012) report that the *Waqf* administration in Bangladesh is interested in approving the transfer of *Waqf* properties through sale or lease. The public perception about *Waqf* is that the *Waqf* fund is useful for building mosques and operating religious and educational institutions for the poor. Given that, it is vital to assess the governance structure of WIs to establish excellent governance standards that can revitalize their importance of *Waqf* for economic development among the stakeholders.

According to World Bank, the member countries of Organization of Islamic Cooperation (OIC) have inferior governance performance and low scores in accountability and regulatory authority. However, empirical evidence on the role of governance toward ensuring accountability and trust among donors of WIs is limited in supply. Therefore, this study aims to provide empirical evidence on the influence of governance and reporting practices in building donors' trust in Public *Waqf* management in Bangladesh, being a member country of OIC. The principal objective of this study is to focus and concentrate on establishing governance and disclosure as a tool to enhance transparency that could lead to an increase in donors' trust in the public management of *Waqf* properties.

In the process, the study seeks to attempt to provide a critical review of the literature (in Section 2) by reviewing the *Waqf* fund management practices in selected OIC member countries. The literature review section highlights several problems in *Waqf* fund management and reflects on the importance of good governance and transparent reporting to improve accountability among charitable institutions. The study develops the conceptual framework in Section 3, which includes a brief description of methodological issues. Section 4 presents the structural equation modeling (SEM) results. Finally, results derived from the SEM analysis are related to the objective of the paper in a manner that allows regulators and practitioners to understand the significance of proper governance and reporting practices to ensure donor trust in the administration of WIs to achieve good governance.

2. Literature Review and Hypothesis Development

Sadeq (2002) defined *Waqf* as a perpetual and voluntary charitable act, which can provide equitable and just distribution of wealth. *Waqf* can harness the potential of charitable giving as it provides the owner with the opportunity to dedicate an asset for the permanent social benefits. One of the essential features of *Waqf*, as pinpointed by Shaikh *et al.* (2017), The World Bank (2015) are that it provides flexibility in fund utilization as compared to *Zakah*. Efficient management of *Waqf* fund has attracted research attention, and past studies (e.g., Cizakca, 2002) have highlighted the importance of professional management and transparent administration. Ambrose *et al.* (2018) explored the ability of *Waqf* for financing public goods in Malaysia and suggested for a uniformed *Waqf* law to manage *Waqf* estates under a sole trustee.

Iqbal and Lewis (2009) found that governance plays a vital role in establishing accountability from an Islamic perspective. Agency theory provides a framework of governance for a profit-making organization. According to agency theory (Jensen and Meckling, 1976), the opportunistic behavior of the managers of an organization requires effective governance mechanisms that will positively affect the disclosure quality and reduce information asymmetry between managers and shareholders. Previous studies report that agency theory is applicable in organizational scenarios where governance quality positively affect disclosure quality (Kelton and Yang, 2008; Lokman *et al.*, 2011; Arshad *et al.*, 2013). Such findings justify the opportunistic behavior of managers in profit-making organizations.

The inefficient and unsystematic management of WIs has triggered recent studies to explore the existence of agency conflict in WIs (Zeni and Sapuan, 2017). Past studies (Ihsan and Ibrahim, 2007; Chowdhury *et al.*, 2012) have also reflected on the conflict of interest between donors and *Mutawallis*. Siswantoro *et al.* (2018) argued that the principal-agent relationship exists in the accountability dimension for WIs when administered by individual *Mutawalli*. (Abdullah, 2015) further asserted that the principal-agency problem is inherent in individual *Mutawalli* to a greater extent than in the institutional *Mutawalli*. The agency conflict among institutional *Mutawalli* requires enhanced reporting and monitoring (Hashim, 2013).

While a plethora of empirical evidence exists on the governance practices of Islamic financial institutions, evidence on the governance structure for WIs is limited in supply. Alnasser and Muhammed (2012) highlighted the importance of establishing Shari'ah governance based on the principles stated in the Qur'an and concluded that the governance structure should ensure that financial transactions in the Muslim community are compatible with the tenets of Islamic law. Iqbal and Mirakhor (2004) viewed that the structure of Islamic corporate governance closely resembles the stakeholder model of corporate governance, which focuses on the fiduciary duty of the managers and promotes stakeholders' rights to participate in corporate decision making. In the process, managers can stimulate truthfulness, justice and contribute their knowledge.

Drawing from agency and stewardship theory, Franco-Santos *et al.* (2017) emphasized the role of performance measurement to monitor the performance of governance mechanism. Noordin *et al.* (2017) provide similar emphasis for WIs. de Waal *et al.* (2011) reported that performance management has an impact on the results of non-profit organizations and the establishment of critical success factors (CSFs) and key performance indicators (KPIs) can assist in performance measurement for non-profit organizations. Siraj (2012) reaffirms the importance of KPIs for the performance measurement of WIs operating in Malaysia.

The composition of committee members often determines the quality of governance. A positive influence of committee composition on disclosure for both non-profit organizations (Zainon *et al.*, 2014) and profit-making organizations (Fathi, 2013) indicates opportunistic behavior among managers, as proposed by agency theory. Hassan and Shahid (2010) argued that professional business management would improve the effective delegation of responsibility and ease accountability for WIs. Application of professional management among WIs can attract broader public participation to attract a higher degree of confidence among stakeholders (Noordin *et al.*, 2017).

The stakeholder theory provides the notion that there are many groups in the society to whom an organization is responsible, and the organization can only achieve its objectives by balancing the interests of these different groups that are often conflicting. A competent board can assist in resolving such conflict and improve coordination for the organization and enables a party to influence within some specific domain. Magalhães and Al-Saad (2013) identified seven qualities of a competent board of Islamic financial institutions in their proposed theoretical corporate governance model. The governance model provided in the King Report on Corporate Governance (from now on referred to as King Report, 2002), which include fairness, responsibility, accountability, independence, transparency and discipline as core the requirements of effective governance. Their proposed model shows the interconnection between these qualities to implement a successful business model from an Islamic perspective.

Fairness or benevolence is one of the main pillars of Islamic finance practice which respects the rights of the stakeholders and creates a culture of accountability. The King Report (2002) defines 'discipline' as a commitment by a company's senior management to adhere to behavior that is universally recognized and acceptable to be correct and proper. The definition of 'discipline' states in this report matches the definition of 'integrity' was provided earlier by Mayer and Davis (1999) in the conceptual model of organizational trust. Researchers have explored these measures of board governance (Torres-Moraga *et al.*, 2010; Mustafa *et al.*, 2013; Hasan and Siraj, 2017) in previous literature. However, empirical evidence on the influence of board attributes in ensuring accountability for WIs is not yet available. Thus, we formulate the following hypotheses:

- **H_{1a}**: Boards' ability has a positive impact on the accountability of WIs.
- **H_{1b}**: Boards' benevolence has a positive impact on the accountability of WIs.
- **H_{1c}**: Boards' integrity has a positive impact on the accountability of WIs.

Sargeant and Lee (2004) have empirically tested the impact of disclosure practices on donors' trust on charities operating in the United Kingdom. Communication is the strongest predictor of donors' commitment. Torres-Moraga *et al.* (2010) also tested the impact of communication on donors' trust for charities operating in Chili and found communication effectiveness to have an indirect effect on donors' trust. However, Ihsan and Ibrahim (2011) found that the presence of committed professionals with Islamic principles can lead to increased transparency, which ultimately leads to greater accountability for WIs in Indonesia. Ibrahim (2000) established reporting practices as the central element for achieving dual accountability, i.e., accountability to Allah and the *Waqif* (the donor of *Waqf* estate).

Rokyah (2005) examined the financial reports of WIs in Malaysia and reported a low level of disclosure in their annual reports. Yaacob (2006) made a similar attempt employing qualitative research method and discovered a minimal improvement in the record-keeping among WIs in the Federal Territories (Wilayah Persekutuan) in Malaysia. Such evidence is non-existent in the context of Bangladesh. The *Waqf Ordinance 1962* discloses financial information to the donors' voluntary. Accounting plays an essential role in ensuring the accountability of the management responsible for entrusted properties by the donor (Iqbal and Lewis, 2009) Ramli *et al.* (2015) explored the importance of governance in discharging accountability for WIs in Indonesia and recommended to follow the uniform accounting standards that could enhance the accountability of the *Mutawallis*' managing *Waqf* estates. Therefore, we formulate the following hypothesis by examining the importance of proper disclosure practice in WIs to ensure accountability.

- **H$_2$**: Communication has a positive impact on the accountability of WIs.

The concept of accountability in Islam differs to some extent, from that of conventional understanding (Lewis, 2006). In Islam, human beings are *Khalifah* (stewards) of all the resources entrusted to them by Allah. The concept of ownership of property provides the notion of the primary difference between Islamic and conventional concept of accountability from the premises that the conventional view of accountability recognizes individuals as owners of the resources. Such accountability relationships require the stewards to be accountable primarily to those individuals as owners (Nahar and Yaacob, 2011). From this point of view, accountability from an Islamic perspective should relate to the *Maqasid al-Shari'ah* or the underlying objectives of the Shari'ah, which covers five aspects of human beings — namely the maintenance and preservation of faith, life, intellect, progeny and property.

Ihsan and Ibrahim (2007) demonstrated a two-dimensional accountability relationship served by WIs through the application of Islamic accounting system. Siswantoro *et al.* (2018), drawing from the pluralism concept defined by Coule (2013), state that it is difficult to restrict accountability among a specific group of people. Coule (2013) demonstrated a direct relationship between donation and accountability of religious non-profit organizations. Accountability can enhance the credibility of WIs and enhance trust among stakeholders, which can spread to others to donate Kearns *et al.* (2005). Such claims have been re-examined by Noordin *et al.* (2017) as their study relates the Islamic perspective of accountability with the concept of *Amanah* (trust) and *Khilafah* (viceregency). Therefore, the we formulate the following hypothesis:

- **H$_3$**: Accountability has a positive impact on donors' trust of WIs.

3. Research Methodology

Partial least square structural equation modeling (PLS-SEM) technique is used in this study to assess the relationship between the exogenous and endogenous variables. PLS is gaining popularity in analyzing empirical data and has been used in the field of Islamic finance. Moreover, PLS provides a unique advantage to test a complicated relationship with a small sample and does not require data normality (Hair *et al.*, 2014). It also allows simultaneous analysis of the entire set of variables to establish a fundamental structure.

The study population consists of *Waqifin* (*Waqf* providers) who have registered their *Waqf* donations with Waqf Bangladesh. Hair *et al.* (2017) suggest the minimum sample size to be 10 times the number of the variable of the study. At the time of this study, a comprehensive list of *Waqf* donors is not available. Therefore, we adopt the Respondent-Driven Sampling (RDS) technique for the selection of respondents in this study following (Opawole and Jagboro, 2017). RDS sampling technique implements a snowball sampling approach to identify respondents in a study that involves an unknown population. The RDS sampling method can overcome bias by utilizing network-based methods with the statistical validity of standard probability (Salganik and Heckathorn, 2004). The RDS sampling technique requires the identification of one known respondent who becomes the driver-respondent and assists in the recruitment of his peers. For this study, *Waqif* who has registered their donation with Waqf Bangladesh have assisted in building the referral chain of respondents. Overall, we manage to contact 95 respondents representing all divisions of Bangladesh. The sample size is sufficient in the context of the study as Hackshaw (2008) recommended testing a new research hypothesis in a small number of the subject.

The survey instrument used in the study consists of 30 items. The measurement items are adopted from previously conducted studies. Table 1 provides the operational definition of variables and their sources. Except for demographic variables, all items are measured on a five-point Likert scale, from strongly disagree (1) to strongly agree (5). Questionnaire

Table 1. Measurement Instrument

Latent Construct	Abbreviation	Operationalization	Source
Board Benevolence	BB	The extent to which a board member is believed to be seeking to do good to the trustor.	Adapted from Mayer and Davis (1999)
Board Ability	BA	Group of skills, competencies and characteristics that enable board members responsible for *Waqf* management to influence within some specific domains.	Adapted from Mayer and Davis (1999)
Board Integrity	BI	Donors' perception that board members adhere to a set of principles that the trustor finds acceptable, i.e., *Waqf* deeds, and *Waqf* ordinance.	Adapted from Mayer and Davis (1999)
Communication	COM	Voluntary disclosure of financial and non-financial information related to *Waqf* endowments.	Adapted from Torres-Moraga *et al.* (2010)
Accountability	ACC	Accountability is related to the ethical contents of the practice carried out by the managers of *Waqf* endowments.	Adapted from Bennett and Barkensjo (2005)
Donor Trust	TRUST	The willingness of the donors to trust WIs.	Adapted from Bennett and Barkensjo (2005)

Source: Authors' own.

items contain accountability, trust, board attributes and trust that are adopted from Bennett and Barkensjo (2005) Mayer and Davis (1999) and Torres-Moraga et al. (2010), respectively. The items are adapted for the context of the study following the suggestions of Saunders et al. (2012)

Mayer et al. (1995) have developed initially the measures of board attributes to reflect ability, benevolence and integrity of the management team followed by the developed by Rotter (1967). In a later study, Mayer and Davis (1999) altered the original items to reflect top management. The authors have adopted the items from Mayer and Davis (1999) as this study has also focused on the ability, benevolence and ability of the top management responsible for *Waqf* management in Bangladesh. The study of Torres-Moraga et al., (2010) is unique in the sense that it has focused on exploring the influence on the communication of the charity sector to ensure donors' trust. The authors have adopted the communication items from Torres-Moraga et al. (2010) as it reflects the context of this study. Bennett and Barkensjo (2005) introduced accountability and trust as causes that could influence the level and frequency of donations. Authors have adopted the measures of accountability and trust used by Bennett and Barkensjo (2005) as they allowed us to explore the influence of accountability on trust which has not been examined in other studies and has been conceptualized by Seal and Vincent-Jones (1997). Reliability and validity of the questionnaire items are discussed in the following section of the study along with the structural equation modeling results.

4. Results and Analysis

So far, the gender affiliation of the respondents is concerned the majority of them are male (75%) with at least a high school degree (58.93%). As far as the area of the study is concerned, it covers seven divisions in Bangladesh. However, the highest number of respondents hail from Dhaka, the capital city of the country (33.9%), followed by Chittagong metropolitan city (30.4%). We evaluate PLS-SEM results in two stages. First, we examine the measurement model for reliability, convergent and discriminant validity. The second stage of the analysis involves the examination of the structural model to determine the significance of the structural relationship and test the developed hypotheses.

The measurement model analysis consists of convergent and discriminant validity. It is achieved when the items of a construct are in harmony, not contrasting each other and contributing to building a conceptual meaning to the construct Hair et al. (2014). In this regard, Table 2 provides the loadings, cross-loadings, composite reliability and average variance extracted for the measurement model.

Hair et al., (2014) recommend a loading value of 0.70 that allows the construct to explain the indicator's variance. A score of 0.50 can be accepted provided its average variance extracted (AVE) value is above 0.50. We use Cronbach's alpha values to determine internal consistency reliability. George and Mallery (2003) stated that an alpha value of less than 0.50 is unacceptable, while a value higher than 0.70 is acceptable. Table 2 provides the results of convergent validity. Loadings for all items are above the threshold of 0.70 except for B4, C2 and T3. However, their AVE score is between the acceptable range

Table 2. Summary of the Measurement Model

Latent Variable	Items	Loadings	CR	Cronbach's Alpha	AVE
Board benevolence	B1	0.699	0.814	0.651	0.595
	B2	0.760			
	B4	0.848			
Board ability	A1	0.804	0.773	0.866	0.500
	A3	0.704			
	A4	0.562			
	A5	0.630			
Board integrity	I4	0.894	0.781	0.781	0.645
	I5	0.700			
Communication	C1	0.897	0.764	0.840	0.529
	C2	0.678			
	C3	0.566			
Accountability	AC1	0.849	0.851	0.869	0.589
	AC2	0.737			
	AC3	0.751			
	AC4	0.727			
Donor trust	T1	0.889	0.879	0.725	0.784
	T2	0.881			

of 0.60–0.70 (Hair *et al.*, 2014). Composite reliability scores are above the recommended score of 0.70 and AVE score for all items are above 0.50. These scores provide statistical validity for all the constructs used in this study. We measure discriminant validity using the correlations of measures of potential overlapping variables. Items should load more strongly on their constructs in the model, and the average variance shared between each construct and its measure should be higher than the variance shared between the construct and another construct. The squared correlations of each construct provided in Table 3 indicate that the results have exceeded the intercorrelations of constructs with other constructs of the proposed model, indicating adequate discriminant validity.

Table 3. Discriminant Validity

	BA	ACC	BB	COM	BI	TRUST
BA	**0.681**					
ACC	0.477	**0.768**				
BB	0.568	0.367	**0.771**			
COM	0.306	0.513	0.345	**0.727**		
BI	0.475	0.457	0.385	0.389	**0.803**	
T	0.248	0.520	0.291	0.434	0.401	**0.885**

Table 4. Structural Model (Bootstrapping Result)

Hypothesis	Path Coefficient	Beta	Standard Deviation	p-Value	t-Value	Decision
H_{1a}	BB→ACC	0.021	0.112	0.852	0.187	Not supported
H_{1b}	BA→ACC	0.270	0.105	0.010**	2.575	Supported
H_{1c}	BI→ACC	0.184	0.112	0.102	1.636	Not supported
H_2	COM→ACC	0.351	0.096	0.000*	3.668	Supported
H_3	ACC→TRUST	0.520	0.087	0.000*	5.962	Supported

Note: * and ** indicates significance at 1% and 5%, respectively.
Source: Authors' own.

To assess the structural model, authors first look at the R^2, beta and the corresponding t-values via a bootstrapping procedure with 5,000 resamples. Hair *et al.* (2014) suggested R^2 of 0.70, 0.50 and 0.25 of endogenous latent variables as substantial, moderate and weak, respectively. The R^2 value of the study ranges from 0.284 to 0.429 and thus moderately explains the variation in accountability and trust in WIs through boards' attributes and communications. Table 4 provides the regression statistics for each hypothesis drawn earlier in this study.

The study hypothesizes that the inclusion of benevolent board members would lead to an increased level of accountability among WIs. Board benevolence does not have a significant impact on accountability. We conclude that board members can actively resolve conflict and enhance the accountability of WIs toward various groups in society. Results provided in Table 4 indicate the statistical validity of H_{1b} as ability positively affects accountability. Such results indicate that donors perceive board members with increased educational and practical experiences who might engage in fraudulent activities while managing endowed properties. Board ability does not have a significant positive impact on accountability. Therefore, only H_{1b} is supported.

We reject H_{1a} and H_{1c} as results provided in Table 4 do not establish a statistically significant relationship between board benevolence and accountability; board integrity and accountability. In the context of this study, WIs under public administration in Bangladesh, these findings indicate that donors did not perceive that a benevolent board with integrity could further enhance accountability for *Waqf* institution. We accept H_2 as communication has a positive impact on accountability and complements the results of Ramli *et al.* (2015). Finally, accountability was found to have a significant positive impact on donors' trust and complements the results provided by Kearns *et al.* (2005). Thus, H_3 is accepted. Board ability is the most significant predictor of accountability for WIs.

5. Discussion, Implication and Conclusion

Ahmed *et al.* (2015) and Hasan *et al.* (2017) reported that the lack of public trust in *Waqf* management results from the absence of good governance mechanisms, transparent reporting and accountability relationships. Studies conducted on *Waqf* management in South Asian context also report similar conclusions (Rani and Aziz, 2010; Ihsan and

Ibrahim, 2011; Hamdan *et al.*, 2013; Ramli *et al.*, 2015). Therefore, our study contributes to establishing the importance of improved governance and reporting practices for publicly managed WIs. The trust exists when one party has the confidence that the other party is caring, honest and competent. Findings of the study contribute to the existing body of literature by highlighting the importance of competent members of the board of public WIs toward maintain accountability relationships and enhance public trust towards *Waqf*. Similar views are provided by other previous studies and empirically tested in them (Kahf, 2007, Ahmed *et al.*, 2015). Results provided by this study extend the validity of the evidence provided by Ihsan and Ibrahim (2011). Also, this study validates the propositions of the stakeholder theory. It highlights the importance of competent board members to achieve the objectives of balancing the interest of various groups in society.

Both formal and informal communication from the WIs has a significant impact on accountability and building trust among donors. The WIs explored in this study is not required to provide any formal reports to the donors, nor does it to the MoRA. The absence of proper accounting and reporting mechanisms might lead to an insignificant relationship which was found significant in countries with improved regulations for WIs (Ihsan and Ibrahim, 2011; Masruki and Shafii, 2013). Such findings are valid in the context of Bangladesh as this study reports the significant positive impact of formal and informal communication on accountability. Results provided by the study validates the qualitative findings presented by Yaacob (2006) and the theoretical Islamic accountability framework provided by Ibrahim (2000).

This study has introduced the importance of governance in maintaining accountability relationships which can contribute to building trust among donors of WIs. Dimensions of governance introduced in this study expects to contribute to the existing literature by highlighting the importance of including benevolent and capable members of the board of *Waqf* management with a high level of integrity. The problem of governance with *Waqf* management is due to the lack of an independent regulatory framework and the non-existence of any reporting standards. *The Waqf Ordinance 1962* provides detailed instructions relating to the remuneration and power and constitution of the committee for *Waqf* management. However, it provides minimal instructions on the composition, independence and auditing of WIs. The issue of competence of the *Waqf* administrators is not present in the ordinance. Thus, regulators are required to review the inclusivity of the ordinance to ensure effective *Waqf* management in Bangladesh. Subsequently, some amendments have been made in the ordinance through appropriate steps need to be taken towards good governance and reporting practices to ensure accountability and building trust in *Waqf* management in Bangladesh. The Codes of Corporate Governance issued by the Bangladesh Securities and Exchange Commission in June 2018 can be a starting point for the MoRA as these codes provide important guidelines for board composition and financial reporting for state-owned enterprises. The relevant regulatory authority in Bangladesh can explore some guidelines to develop reporting standards for WIs in line with the Statement of Recommended Practices (SORP) that have been suggested by Ihsan and Ibrahim (2011) for Malaysian WIs.

The experience in some countries proved that *Waqf* could play a very significant role in socio-economic developments of a country by redesigning the function of the third sector of the economy. Historically, *Waqf* funds can finance all governmental expenditures. The role of *Waqf* in sustainable economic developments and poverty alleviation cannot be overlooked in a Muslim majority country like Bangladesh. The government would immensely benefit from an operational *Waqf*-based micro-finance model which requires public trust on the *Waqf* management. The ability of *Waqf* administrators to serve their accountability relationships with various stakeholders could play a vital role in enhancing public trust in the ability of *Waqf*. The regulatory authority needs to bring more amendments to the present *Waqf* laws to ensure the good governance and develop reporting systems that can increase credibility and transparency of WIs.

Appendix A

A.1. Average Real Interest Rates of MFIs Weighted by Number of Borrowers

Country	Borrowers (in Millions)	Average Interest Rate (%)
Bangladesh	8.8	20.1
Bolivia	0.5	20
Cambodia	0.4	27.6
India	1.8	24.5
Indonesia	3.3	22.2
Mexico	1.1	46.6
Morocco	0.6	29.4
Peru	1.3	32.8
Philippines	0.7	46.7

Source: Rosenberg *et. al.* (2007).

References

Abdullah, M (2015). A new framework of corporate governance for waqf: A preliminary proposal. *Islam and Civilisational Renewal*, 274(2625), 1–18.

Ahmad, AUF and MFK Karim (2019). Opportunities and challenges of *waqf* in Bangladesh: The way forward to socio-economic development. In *Revitalization of Waqf for Socio-Economic Development*, Vol. I, pp.193–212, Mohammad Ali Khalifa, MK Hassan and ASA Elzahi (eds.), doi: https://doi.org/10.1007/978-3-030-18445-2_10.

Ahmad, AUF and MFK Karim (2017). Issues deterring the continued growth of *awqaf* in Bangladesh: The way forward to its development and widening the scope of its benefits. In *Islamic Economies: Stability, Markets and Endowments*, N Alam and SAR Rizvi (eds.), pp. 79–98, doi: https://doi.org/10.1007/978-3-319-47937-8.

Ahmad, MM and M Safiullah (2012). Management of waqf estates in Bangladesh: Towards a sustainable policy formulation. In *Waqf Laws and Management* (with special reference to Malaysia), pp. 229–262.

Ahmed, H (2007). *Waqf*-based microfinance: Realizing the social role of Islamic finance. In *International Seminar on Integrating Awqaf in the Islamic Financial Sector*, pp. 1–22. Singapore: World Bank.

Ahmed, U, Momoa Faosiy and NM Daud (2015). Investigating the influence of public trust on the revival of *waqf* institution in Uganda. *Middle-East Journal of Scientific Research*, 23(6), 1165–1172.

Alnasser, SAS and J Muhammed (2012). Introduction to corporate governance from Islamic perspective. *Humanomics*, 28(3), 220–231.

Alpay, S and MA Haneef (2015). *Integration of Waqf and Islamic Microfinance for Poverty Reduction: Case Studies of Malaysia.*

Ambrose, AHA, MAG Hassan and H Hanafi (2018). A proposed model for *waqf* financing public goods and mixed public goods in Malaysia. *International Journal of Islamic and Middle Eastern Finance and Management.*

Arshad, R, AN Bakar, FH Sakri and N Omar (2013). Organizational characteristics and disclosure practices of non-profit organizations in Malaysia. *Asian Social Science*, 9(1), 209–217.

Banerjee, SB and L Jackson (2017). Microfinance and the business of poverty reduction: Critical perspectives from rural Bangladesh. *Human Relations*, 70(1), 63–91.

Bateman, M (2010). *Why Doesn't Microfinance Work?: The Destructive Rise of Local Neoliberalism.* Zed Books Ltd, London.

Bennett, R and A Barkensjo (2005). Causes and consequenc of donor perceptions of quality of the relationshi marketing activities of charitable organisations. *Journal of Targeting, Measurement and Analysis for Marketing*, 13(2), 122–139.

Buchenrieder, G, GJ Nguefo and E Benjamin (2019). Poverty alleviation through microcredit in Sub-Saharan Africa revisited: New evidence from a Cameroonian village bank, the Mutuelle Communautaire de Croissance. *Agricultural Finance Review*, 79(3), 386–407, Doi: 10.1108/AFR-03-2018-0019.

Chowdhury, IA, MSR Chowdhury and MR Yasoa' (2012). Problems of *waqf* administration and proposals for improvement: A study in Malaysia. *Journal of Internet Banking and Commerce*, 17(1).

Cizakca, M (2002). Latest developments in the western non-profit sector and the implications for Islamic *awqaf. Islamic Economics and the Elimination of Poverty.*

Coule, TM (2013). Nonprofit governance and accountability: Broadening the theoretical perspective. *Nonprofit and Voluntary Sector Quarterly*, 20(10), 1–23.

Demirgüç-Kunt, A, P Honohan and T Beck (2008). Finance for all? Policies and pitfalls in expanding access, *World Bank Policy Research Report.* Washington, DC.

Faruqee, R and M Khalily (2011). *Interest Rates in Bangladesh Microcredit Market.*

Fathi, J (2013). The determinants of the quality of financial information disclosed by french listed companies. *Mediterranean Journal of Social Sciences*, 4(2), 319–336. Accessed on 18 April, 2020 at: http://www.scopus.com/inward/record.url?eid=2-s2.0-84892593763&partnerID=tZOtx3y1.

Franco-Santos, M, M Nalick, P Rivera-Torres and L Gomez-Meji (2017). Governance and well-being in academia: Negative consequences of applying an agency theory logic in higher education. *British Journal of Management*, 28(4), 711–730.

George, D and M Mallery (2003). *Using SPSS for Windows Step by Step: A Simple Guide and Reference.*

Hackshaw, A (2008). Small studies: Strengths and limitations'. *European Respiratory Journal*, 32(5), 1141–1143.

Hair, J, CL Hollingsworth, AB Randolph and AYL Chong (2017). An updated and expanded assessment of PLS-SEM in information systems research. *Industrial Management & Data Systems*, 117(3), 442–458.

Hair, J, GTM Hult, CM Ringle and M Sarstedt (2014). *Primer on Partial Least Squares Structural Equation Modeling (PLS-SE)*, 1st edition. Wasington, DC: Sage Publications, Inc.

Hamdan, N, AM Ramli, A Jalil and A Haris (2013). Accounting for *waqf* institutions?: A review on the adaptation of fund accounting in developing the Shariah compliant financial reports for mosque. In *Transforming Islamic Philanthropy For Ummah Excellence*, UITM and IKAZ (eds.), pp. 1–10. UITM.

Haneef, MA, AH Pramanik, MO Mohammed, F Amin and AD Muhammad (2015). Integration of *waqf*-Islamic microfinance model for poverty reduction: The case of Bangladesh. *International Journal of Islamic and Middle Eastern Finance and Management*, 8(2), 246–270, doi: dx.doi.org/10.1108/IMEFM-03-2014-0029.

Hasan, R and SA Siraj (2016). Complexities of *waqf* development in Bangladesh. *Journal of Emerging Economies and Islamic Research*, 4(3).

Hasan, R and SA Siraj (2017). Toward developing a model of stakeholder trust in *waqf* institutions. *Islamic Economic Studies*, 25, 85–109.

Hasan, R, SA Siraj and MHS Mohamad (2017). Antecedents and outcome of *waqif*'s trust in *waqf* institution. *Journal of Economic Cooperation and Development*, 38(4).

Hashim, TS (2013). *Issues on Corporate Waqf*.

Hassan, A and MMA Shahid (2010). Management and development of the *awqaf* assets, in *Seventh International Conference — The Tawhidi Epistemology: Zakat and Waqf Economy*, pp. 309–328.

Hickson, R (2001). Financial services for the very poor, thinking outside the box. *Small Enterprise Development*, 12(2).

Ibrahim, SHM (2000). *The Need for Islamic Accounting: Perceptions of its Objectives and Characteristics by Malaysian Accountants and Academics*. University of Dundee.

Ihsan, H and S Ibrahim (2007). *Waqf* accounting and possible use of SORP 2005 to develop *waqf* accounting standards, in *Singapore International Waqf Conference*.

Ihsan, H and SHHM Ibrahim (2011). *Waqf* accounting and management in indonesian *waqf* institutions: The cases of two *waqf* foundations. *Humanomics*, 27(4), 252–269, doi: 10.1108/08288661111181305.

Iqbal, Z and MK Lewis (2009). *An Islamic Perspective on Governance*. Cheltenham: Edward Elgar Publishing Limited.

Iqbal, Z and A Mirakhor (2004). Stakeholders model of governance in Islamic economic system. *Islamic Economic Studies*, 11(2), 1–21.

Jensen, MC and WH Meckling (1976). Theory of the firm, managerial behavior, agency cost and ownership structure. *Journal of Financial Economics*, 3, 305–361.

Kahf, M (2007). Islamic *Waqf* origin and contribution. In *Singapore International Waqf Conference*.

Karim, M. (2009). *Problems and prospects of awqaf in Bangladesh: A legal perspective*. Accessed on 18 April, 2020 at: http://waqfacademy.org/wp-content/uploads/2013/02/PROBLEMS-AND-PROSPECTS-OF-AWQAF-IN-BANGLADESH-A-LEGAL-PERSPECTIVE-Muhammad-Fazlul-Karim.pdf.

Karim, N, M Tarazi and X Reille (2008). *Islamic Microfinance: An Emerging Market Niche*.

Kasim, N, SNN Htay and SA Salman (2016). Achieving effective *Waqf* management through compliance with Shari'ah governance practices. In *27th International Business Information Management Association Conference-Innovation Management and Education Excellence Vision 2020: From Regional Development Sustainability to Global Economic Growth, IBIMA 2016*.

Kearns, K, C Park and L Yankoski (2005). Comparing faith-based and secular community service corporations in Pittsburgh and Allegheny County, Pennsylvania. *Nonprofit and Voluntary Sector Quarterly*, 34(2), 206–231.

Kelton, ASA and Y Yang (2008). The impact of corporate governance on Internet financial reporting. *Journal of Accounting and Public Policy*, 27(1), 62–87. https://doi.org/10.1016/j.jaccpubpol.2007.11.001.

Khan, SR and SR Khan (2016). Microcredit in South Asia: Privileging women's perceptions and voices. *Progress in Development Studies*, 16(1), 65–80.

Khandker, SR, MB Khalily and HA Samad (2016). *Beyond Ending Poverty: The Dynamics of microfinance in Bangladesh.*

King Report (2002). *Executive Summary King Report on Corporate Governance, Summary King Report on Corporate Governance.* Parktown.

Lewis, M (2006). Accountability and Islam. In *Fourth International Conference on Accounting and Finance in Transition*, pp. 1–16. Adelaide.

Lokman, N, J Mula and J Cotter (2011). Corporate governance quality and voluntary disclosures of corporate governance information: Practices of listed Malaysian family controlled businesses. In *Proceedings of the Family Business*. Accessed on 18-04-2020 at http://www.fambiz.org.au/wp-content/uploads/Debating-the-Model-of-Relational-Governance-on-Family-Firm-Performance.pdf.

Magalhães, R and S Al-Saad (2013). Corporate governance in Islamic financial institutions: The issues surrounding unrestricted investment account holders. *Corporate Governance: The International Journal of Business in Society*, 13(1), 39–57.

Masruki, R and Z Shafii (2013). The development of *waqf* accounting in enhancing accountability'. *Middle-East Journal of Scientific Research 13 (Research in Contemporary Islamic Finance and Wealth Management)*, 13, 1–6.

Mayer, RC and JH Davis (1999). The effect of the performance appraisal system on trust for management: A field quasi-experimen. *Journal of Applied Psychology*, 84(1), 123–136.

Mayer, RC, JH Davis and FD Schoorman (1995). An integrative model of organizational trust. *Academy of Management Review*, 20(3), 709–734, doi: 10.2307/258792.

Mobin, MA and AUF Ahmad (2017). Achieving sustainable economic development through Islamic microfinance and potential of proposed two tier *mudārabah waqf* business model. In *Handbook of Empirical Research on Islam and Economic Life*, M Kabir Hassan (ed.), pp.193–212, doi: https://doi.org/10.4337/9781784710736.00016.

Morduch, J (1998). Does microfinance really help the poor?: New evidence from flagship programs in Bangladesh. Research Program in Development Studies, Woodrow School of Public and International Affairs.

Mustafa, MOA, MHS Mohamad and MA Adnan (2013). Antecedents of *zakat* payers' trust in an emerging *zakat* sector: An exploratory study. *Journal of Islamic Accounting and Business Research*, 4(1), 4–25.

Nahar, HS and H Yaacob (2011). Accountability in the sacred context: The case of management, accounting and reporting of a Malaysian cash awqaf institution. *Journal of Islamic Accounting and Business Research*, 2(2), 87–113. https://doi.org/10.1108/17590811111170520.

Noor, AHM, NAM Ali, A Abdullah and HH Tahir (2014). The *Waqf* governance framework in Malaysia. In *International Conference on Development of Social Enterprise and Social Business for Eradication of Extreme Poverty and Street Begging*, pp. 1–10. Chittagong: International Islamic University Chittagong.

Noordin, NH, SN Haron and S Kassim (2017). Developing a comprehensive performance measurement system for *waqf* institutions. *International Journal of Social Economics*, 44(7), 921–936.

Opawole, A and GO Jagboro (2017). Factors affecting the performance of private party in concession-based PPP projects in Nigeria. *Journal of Engineering, Design and Technology*, 15(1), 44–57, doi: 10.1108/JEDT-09-2015-0058.

Rahman, A (2019). *Women and microcredit in rural Bangladesh: an anthropological study of Grameen Bank lending*, doi: https://doi.org/10.4324/9780429503023.

Ramli, NM, NHM Salleha and NA Muhameda (2015). Discharging accountability through governance: cases from *waqf* institutions in Indonesia. *Research in Islamic Studies*, 2(1), 1–13, doi: 10.15364/ris15-0201-01.

Rani, MAM and AA Aziz (2010). *Waqf* management and administration in Malaysia: Its implementation from the perspective of islamic law. *Malaysian Accounting Review*, 9, 115–121.

Rosenberg, R, Gaul, S, W Ford and O Tomilova (2007). Access to Finance Forum – Reports by CGAP and Its Partners. Washington. Retrieved from https://www.cgap.org/sites/default/files/Forum-Microcredit-Interest-Rates-and-Their-Determinants-June-2013_1.pdf.

Rokyah, S (2005). *Determinants of Financial Reporting Practices on Waqf by Malaysian State Islamic Religgious Councils*. International Islamic University Malaysia.

Rotter, JB (1967). A new scale for the measurement of interpersonal trust. *Journal of Personality*, 35, 651–665.

Sadeq, AM (2002). *Waqf*, perpetual charity and poverty alleviation. *International Journal of Social Economics*, 29(1/2), 135–151.

Salganik, MJ and DD Heckathorn (2004). Sampling and estimation in hidden populations using respondent-driven sampling. *Sociological Methodology*, 34(1), 193–240.

Sargeant, A and S Lee (2004). Donor Trust and Relationship Commitment in the U.K. Charity Sector: The Impact on Behavior. Nonprofit and Voluntary Sector Quarterly, 33(June), 185–202. https://doi.org/10.1177/0899764004263321.

Saunders, M, P Lewis and Thornhill (2012). *Research Methods for Business Students*, 6th edition. Pearson Education Limited.

Seal, W and P Vincent-Jones (1997). Accounting and trust in the enabling of long-term relations. *Accounting, Auditing & Accountability Journal*, 406–431.

Shaikh, SA, AG Ismail and MHM Shafiai (2017). Application of waqf for social and development finance. *ISRA International Journal of Islamic Finance*, 9(1), 5–14.

Shirazi, NS (2006). Providing for the resource shortfall for poverty elimination through the instrument of *zakat* in low income muslim countries. *IIUM Journal of Economics and Management*, 1(1), 1–27. Accessed on 18 April, 2020 at: http://www.mendeley.com/research/providing-resource-shortfall-poverty-elimination-through-institution/.

Siraj, SSA (2012). *An Empirical Investigation into the Accounting, Accountability and Effectiveness of Waqf Management in the State Islamic Religious Councils (SIRCs) in Malaysia*. Cardiff University. Accessed on 18 April, 2020 at: http://orca.cf.ac.uk/46875/(Accessed: 27 May 2015).

Siswantoro, D, H Rosdiana and H Fathurahman (2018). Reconstructing accountability of the cash *waqf* (endowment) institution in Indonesia. *Managerial Finance*.

The World Bank (2015). *Worldwide Governance Indicators*. The World Bank Group.

Torres-Moraga, E, A Vásquez-Parraga and C Barra (2010). Antecedents of donor trust in an emerging charity sector: The role of reputation, familliarity, opportunism and communication. *Transylvanian Review of Administrative Sciences*, 29(3), 265–285. Accessed on 18 April, 2020 at: http://www.rtsa.ro/tras/index.php/tras/article/view/109.

Waal, A, R Goedegebuure and P Geradts (2011). The impact of performance management on the results of a non-profit organization. *International Journal of Productivity and Performance Management*, 60(8), 778–796.

Yaacob, HH (2006). *Waqf Accounting in Malaysian State Islamic Religious Institutions: The Case of Federal Territory SIRC*. International Islamic University Malaysia.

Zainon, S, R Atan and YB Wah (2014). An empirical study on the determinants of information disclosure of Malaysian non-profit organizations. *Asian Review of Accounting*, 25(1), 4–29, doi: 10.1108/ARA-04-2013-0026.

Zeni, NAM and NM Sapuan (2017). Revitalizing *waqf* governance: A theoretical perspectives. *International Journal of Advanced Biotechnology and Research*, 8(3), 305–311.

Chapter 2

Impact of Non-Intermediation Activities of Banks on Economic Growth and Volatility: An Evidence from OIC[#]

Mohsin Ali[‡]

School of Accounting and Finance
Faculty of Business and Law
Taylor's University, Malaysia
mohsin.ali@taylors.edu.my

Mansor H. Ibrahim[*] and Mohamed Eskandar Shah[†]

International Centre for Education in Islamic
Finance (INCEIF), Lorong Universiti A, Malaysia
[*]mansorhi@inceif.org
[†]eskandar@inceif.org

This paper investigates the impact of non-intermediation activities of banks on economic growth and volatility of OIC. For the purpose, we utilize LSDVC estimation approach using the sample of Organization of Islamic Countries (OIC) member countries for the period of 2001–2013. We find non-intermediation income to be insignificant for both economic growth and volatility of OIC member countries in general though it reduces volatility of Gulf Cooperation Council (GCC) economies. Intermediation activities are found to be insignificantly related with the growth of OIC member countries, but on the other hand, they are found to reduce volatility in OIC member countries. Our results are robust across different specifications and estimators.

Keywords: Non-interest/financing income (non-intermediation income); economic growth; economic volatility; OIC member countries.

1. Introduction

Long-term sustainable economic growth depends in large part on a well-functioning financial system. It is generally believed that financial intermediaries particularly the banking sector in a well-developed financial market affect economic growth positively by facilitating the allocation of capital to the real sector, enhancing allocation of resources and supporting firms to raise required investments. Empirical evidence suggests that development of the banking system is crucial for economic growth (King and Levine, 1993; Rajan and Zingales, 1998; Beck and Levine, 2004; Jalil *et al.*, 2010; Kendall, 2012; Law

---

[‡]Corresponding author.
[#]This Chapter first appeared in the *Singapore Economic Review*, Vol. 67, No. 1, doi: 10.1142/S0217590820420023. © 2022 World Scientific Publishing.

et al., 2013). Banks do this by mending the information problems between borrowers and lenders by monitoring the former and safeguarding a proper use of the depositors' funds.

Although literature has recognized the significance of an efficient banking sector for economic growth, an overleveraged and fragile banking system can also bring about major crises as witnessed during the global financial crisis (Beck *et al.*, 2009). Indeed, as a result of the crisis, bank performance and stability have been placed under close scrutiny. Particularly representatives of regulatory bodies in advanced countries have raised their concerns regarding the excessive size of the banking sector and have asked for restrictions (Turner, 2010; Trichet, 2010). An oversized financial sector could result in inefficient allocation of resources and can yield instability.

The perceived role of a bank has always been of an intermediary (Zhang, 2010), but in the wake of increasing competition the traditional intermediation activities, i.e., accepting deposits and providing financing, have been declining especially in the US and the UK (Allen and Santomero, 2001; Moshirian and Van der Laan, 1998; Rogers and Sinkey, 1999). In an era of financial deregulation, banks are left with no choice but to be more creative to survive in the market place. Banks, therefore, have tried to offset this reduction in profits with income derived from non-traditional banking activities.[1] Arguably, these traditional and non-traditional banking activities have their impact at both micro and macro level; at the micro level, they affect the profitability and performance of banks themselves, while at the macro level they contribute to economic growth and stability as a whole. In this paper, we will focus on the macro level impact of different banking activities.

The varying trends and enhanced competitiveness in the market place, the financial sector has started focusing on non-intermediation financial activities. These activities include issuance of guarantees, under writing arrangements and other auxiliary activities. The importance of these non-traditional activities in comparison to the traditional financial intermediation has increased over time since financial institutions have boosted their diversification efforts (Demirgüç-Kunt and Huizinga, 2010; Baele *et al.*, 2007). This increase can be seen in Figure 1. It shows averages of non-interest income to total income (in terms of percentage) for world in contrast to OIC countries.[2] For the last 15 years, the non-interest income for both World and OIC countries has been ranging from 37% to 43% of total income of the banks.

These percentages show an increasing trend of shifting towards non-intermediation activities with the exception of declining trend during the crisis period. Therefore, intermediation activities in themselves alone cannot be the representative of modern financial system. In addition, available studies do not reveal much about the effect of non-interest/financing income on growth and volatility (Beck *et al.*, 2014). Intuitively, intermediation and non-intermediation income may not exhibit the same effect on economic growth and volatility. Furthermore, they do not serve the same functions as well. Consequently,

---

[1] We have used "non-traditional activities", "non-intermediation activities" and "non-interest/financing income-based activities" alternatively in this study.
[2] Data Source: FRED (Federal Reserve Economic Data).

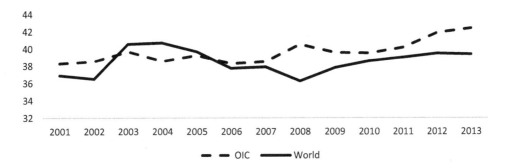

Figure 1. Comparison of Averages of Non-intrest Income to Total Income

non-intermediation activities are not expected to have the same effect on growth and volatility of an economy; an issue that is worth investigation.

Additionally, Basel 3 has put forward specific guidelines for non-intermediation activities. In almost all of the OIC countries (with the exception of Turkey and Malaysia) Basel 3 has not been implemented yet, which makes it important to the regulators who are considering to introduce Basel 3 regulation that while introducing they should deliberate on the differences in the non-intermediation activities in OIC countries as well as their impact on banks and economy, which makes this study more relevant.

2. Literature Review

Not much literature has addressed the macro economic impact of non-traditional activities. This macro-level impact of non-traditional activities can be related to micro-level (bank) evidence through the association between banks' performance and non-intermediation income. The bulk of research in this area focuses on the US banks only (e.g., Demsetz and Strahan, 1997; Stiroh, 2004; Stiroh and Rumble, 2006). However, international bank level evidence has emerged recently (e.g., Baele *et al.*, 2007; Laeven and Levine, 2007; Demirgüç-Kunt and Huizinga, 2010). As far as OIC countries are concerned, little literature exists on the impact of non-traditional activities on Islamic banks. There are country-level studies like Shahimi *et al.*, (2006) on Malaysian banks and Karakaya and Er (2013) on Turkish banks. Both studies found positive impact of non-interest/financing income on bank performance. Molyneux and Yip (2013) have studied the linkage between income diversification and performance of Islamic banks in six Muslim majority countries i.e., Malaysia, Saudi Arabia, Kuwait, United Arab Emirates, Bahrain and Qatar. They find Islamic banks to be less diversified as compared to their conventional counterparts and hence they are less vulnerable to earnings volatility. Generally, these studies conclude that diversification into non-intermediation activities comes at the cost of increased volatility. The indication on the outcome of increased exposure to non-intermediation activities on risk-adjusted performance measures is generally mixed. Beck *et al.* (2014) have shifted the focus towards macro-level impact of non-intermediation activities. They studied the impact of non-intermediation activities on the economic growth and volatility of economy by splitting the banking sector activities into intermediation (measured as credit to private sector by domestic banks) and non-intermediation activities. In addition to the non-interest income of banks, the authors also investigate the impact of important byproducts coming out from services provided by the banks, such as consulting, accounting and legal which also contribute to the activities of financial sector. Their results suggest that intermediation activities rise growth and decrease volatility in the long run, but they do not find any such impact for non-intermediation activities. Nonetheless, their findings suggest that intermediation activities stabilize the economy and non-intermediation activities increase the volatility in the short run.

In contrast to Beck et al. (2014), we specifically focus on the impact of non-interest/financing income of the banks (including trading, commission and fee income) on macroeconomic growth and volatility. We exclude the impact of income generated from other spin-offs (mentioned above) which are not a concern of our study. Our study concentrates on the non-interest/financing income of the banks so that we can evaluate the impact of income diversification strategies of banks on the economic growth and volatility. Considering lack of research in this area generally and in OIC countries particularly, we attempt to investigate this impact in OIC countries. OIC countries include a number of emerging economies some of which are striving to become global centers for Islamic finance which adds a new dimension to their financial sectors. Due to the significant role rendered by these emerging economies in the global financial markets, economic growth and volatility in OIC countries cannot be ignored and requires rigorous investigation.

3. Data, Model and Methodology

In this paper, we focus on the impact of non-intermediation income on the growth and volatility of OIC countries as a whole. Currently, OIC has 57 member countries. The issue of data availability remains a limitation in OIC member countries as most of them belong to developing countries and do not have proper reporting regulations in place. Thus, out of 57 countries our study could only focus on 48 countries for which considerable amount of data is available for each variable. We have only included the countries for which at least four years of data is available over the period of 2001–2013.

The empirical specification is designed to assess the impact of non-intermediation income of banks on economic growth and volatility of OIC member countries. Taking clues from Beck et al. (2014), we specify the basic growth and volatility dynamic equations as follows:

$$\text{growth}_{jt} = \beta_0 + \beta_1 \text{growth}_{jt-1} + \beta_2 \text{Intermediation}_{jt-1} + \beta_3 \text{non} - \text{Intermediation}_{jt-1}$$
$$+ \beta_4 GDPPC_{jt-1} + \beta_5 P_{jt-2} + \varepsilon_{jt} \quad (1)$$

$$\text{volatility}_{jt} = \varphi_0 + \varphi_1 \text{volatility}_{jt-1} + \varphi_2 \text{Intermediation}_{jt-2}$$
$$+ \varphi_3 \text{non} - \text{Intermediation}_{jt-2} + \varphi_4 GDPPC_{jt-2} + \varphi_5 P_{jt-2} + \varepsilon_{jt}. \quad (2)$$

The dependent variables are GDP per capita (GDPPC) growth as a proxy for economic growth and its standard deviation as a proxy for volatility. Growth has been calculated as the annual difference in the logarithm of real GDP per capita i.e. lnGDPPC$_t$ − lnGDPPC$_{t-1}$. Volatility is the standard deviation of the growth rate of three years rolling window for each country j. We adopt the average ratio of net non-interest/financing income to net operating income of banks in a country as proxy for non-interest/financing income which includes trading, fees and commission activities (NONINT). For control variables, we propose to include the variable intermediation, proxy by the log of the ratio of private credit to GDP (INTER). This variable has been used in the finance-growth literature to take care of the impact of financial intermediation on economic growth (Beck et al., 2000; Beck and Levine, 2004, among others). As policy variables (represented by P in the equations above) we include gross fixed capital formation (GFCF), inflation (INF), government expenditures to GDP (GOVEXP) and trade openness (OPEN) measured by the ratio of exports plus imports to GDP. Except inflation all these variables are used in logged form.

We estimate the impact of non-intermediation activities on the economic growth and volatility of OIC member countries. For the purpose, we use the bias-corrected least square dummy variable (LSDVC) model originally developed by Kiviet (1995, 1998), Judson and Owen (1999), Bun and Kiviet (2003), and, more recently enhanced by Bruno (2005) for unbalanced panels. We consider the following dynamic panel data model as Equation (1):

$$y_{it} = \alpha y_{i,t-1} + \beta f_{it} + \gamma_i + \delta_t + \varepsilon_{it} \quad i = 1,....,N \quad t = 1,....,T \qquad (3)$$

where y_{it} is the dependent variable that represents the growth rate of gross domestic product (GDP) per capita. The index i represents individual country, while t represents time period. The lagged dependent variable $y_{i,t-1}$ in Equation (3) shows the dependent variable as a dynamic process, allowing non-instantaneous adjustments.[3] In the equation, f_{it} represents a set of independent variables which include intermediation activities in a country, non-intermediation income of banks in a country, GFCF, inflation, government expenditure and trade openness. γ_i is the unobserved specific effects of the countries in the sample, δ_t is the time-specific effects and ε_{it} is the error term which is independent of all explanatory variables other than y_{it}. Equation (3) is a dynamic panel data model with individual effects theoretically linked to the regressors.

We estimate LSDVC (AH) and LSDVC (AB), which represents the bias corrected estimates initialized by Anderson and Hsiao (1982), and Arellano and Bond (1991), respectively. AH uses the second lag of dependent variable (in differenced or level form) as an instrument, whereas AB rely on a bigger numbers of internal instruments and that is why it is considered more efficient. Consistently with the Monte Carlo evidence in Bruno (2005), we found no substantial differences in LSDVC coefficients and standard errors among all initializations tried. The bootstrapped standard errors are generated using Monte Carlo simulations. Bootstrapped standard errors were computed through 50 replications.

For the purpose of robustness, we use LSDVC(AH), LSDVC(AB), System GMM and Difference GMM estimators to estimate our specifications [Equations (1) and (2)]. The number of instruments of the lagged explanatory variables have been less than the number

---

[3] In dynamic models, the lagged level of growth of GDP per capita is added to investigate persistence of effects.

of groups across the estimations. With regards to the post-estimation specification tests, as indicated across most of the specifications for the GMM-based estimation methods, the non-significance of the AR (2) statistics in Tables 2 and 3 indicate no second-order serial correlation in the first- differenced errors, which is a required condition for the consistency of the GMM estimates.[4] On applying the Hansen statistics of over-identifying restrictions to confirm the absence of correlation between the instruments and the error term, the null hypothesis is not rejected in the specifications using the GMM system estimator. This suggests that the over-identifying restrictions are valid, and hence the instruments are not correlated with the errors in the first-differenced equations.[5]

4. Results and Discussion

We present the descriptive statistics of the variables used in our study in Table 1. The average economic growth of the sample countries is positive, whereas standard deviations of their growth is found to be higher. On average, we found economic growth to be volatile. We can see that on average the proxy for aggregate non-intermediation activities are higher than the average for aggregate financial intermediation. Non-intermediation activities are also found to have lower variations as compared to intermediation activities.

We present our results in Tables 2 and 3. We estimate the results using a number of methodologies, namely LSDVC (AH), LSDVC (AB), DIFF-GMM and SYS-GMM.

Table 1. Descriptive Statistics

Variables	Mean	SD	Minimum	Maximum
INF	6.037321	7.185943	−35.83667	54.40018
Growth	2.323957	6.955044	−97.32408	71.61682
Volatility	2.966983	4.503076	0.01204	61.61793
NONINT	3.574099	0.464987	0.35429	4.56166
INTER	2.960236	0.915393	−0.22030	4.84601
GFCF	3.00481	0.42614	1.38809	4.14103
GDPPC	7.451916	1.438584	5.47938	11.03712
GOVEXP	2.593961	0.376528	1.42489	3.46194
IMPORT	26.15371	2.832751	21.15610	35.20448
OPEN	4.22964	0.477538	2.67445	5.66683

Note: In this table, INF refers to Inflation, Growth represents GDPPC growth, Volatility represents economic volatility, INTER represents aggregate intermediation income, GFCF represents Gross fixed capital formation. NONINT represents aggregate Non-intermediation income/activities, GDPPC represents gross domestic product per capita, GOVEXP represents government expenditure and OPEN represents openness to trade.

---

[4] The null of no first-order serial correlation was rejected across all specifications, which is also correct.

[5] Along these lines, it is also important to indicate symptoms of instrument proliferation include over-fitting bias, and whereby Windmeijer (2005) reports that reducing the instrument count cuts the average bias in the two-step estimate of the parameter of interest.

Table 2. Impact of Non-Intermediation Income on Economic Growth (Dependent Variable: lnGDPPC)

	(1) LSDVC AH	(2) LSDVC AH	(3) LSDVC AH	(4) LSDVC AB	(5) LSDVC AB	(6) LSDVC AB	(7) GMM DIFF	(8) GMM DIFF	(9) GMM DIFF	(10) GMM SYS	(11) GMM SYS	(12) GMM SYS
lnGDPPC$_{(t-1)}$	0.962***	0.947***	0.950***	0.951***	0.947***	0.950***	0.813***	0.807***	0.807***	0.989***	0.986***	1.004***
	(27.86)	(16.96)	(44.73)	(52.12)	(44.88)	(44.73)	(26.84)	(25.51)	(24.04)	(171.99)	(85.45)	(119.72)
lnINTER$_{(t-1)}$	−0.00941	−0.0101	−0.0113	−0.00730	−0.0102	−0.0113	0.0262**	0.0326**	0.0341**	−0.00216	−0.00135	−0.00909
	(−1.01)	(−0.85)	(−1.57)	(−1.14)	(−1.44)	(−1.57)	(2.28)	(2.13)	(2.26)	(−0.51)	(−0.17)	(−1.22)
lnNONINT$_{(t-1)}$	0.0000091	−0.000865	−0.000076	0.0000927	−0.0000773	−0.000076	0.00170	−0.000923	−0.000294	−0.00663	−0.00687	−0.000471
	(0.00)	(−0.17)	(−0.02)	(0.02)	(−0.15)	(−0.02)	(0.38)	(−0.20)	(−0.07)	(−1.38)	(−1.02)	(−0.11)
lnGFCF$_{(t-1)}$	0.0313***	0.0233**	0.0237**	0.0310***	0.0231**	0.0237**	0.0271*	0.0104	0.0128	0.0236**	0.0226*	0.0182
	(4.60)	(2.16)	(2.11)	(4.44)	(2.06)	(2.11)	(1.87)	(0.74)	(0.75)	(2.21)	(1.68)	(1.24)
lnGOVEXP$_{(t-1)}$	0.0262*	0.0197	0.0183	0.0252*	0.0198	0.0183	0.000823	0.00115	0.000718	0.00363	−0.00890	−0.00898
	(1.86)	(1.15)	(1.03)	(1.80)	(1.14)	(1.03)	(0.04)	(0.04)	(0.03)	(0.37)	(−0.85)	(−0.82)
INF$_{(t-1)}$	−0.000318	−0.000305	−0.000254	−0.000292	−0.000254	−0.000254	−0.000599	−0.000700*	−0.000710	0.0000370	0.0000235	0.0000920
	(−1.11)	(−0.72)	(−0.58)	(−0.98)	(−0.66)	(−0.58)	(−1.55)	(−1.73)	(−1.58)	(0.13)	(0.06)	(0.31)
lnOPEN$_{(t-1)}$		0.0277*	0.0262**		0.0270**	0.0262**		0.0675***	0.0658***		0.0153	0.00992
		(1.95)	(1.98)		(2.04)	(1.98)		(3.28)	(3.06)		(1.25)	(1.26)
GCC× NONINT$_{(t-1)}$			−0.0493			−0.0493			−0.00678			−0.0183***
			(−1.33)			(−1.33)			(−0.08)			(−3.11)
CRISIS			0.00332			0.00332			0.00232			−0.000604
			(0.59)			(0.59)			(0.45)			(−0.11)
_cons										0.0551	0.0432	−0.0464
										(1.35)	(0.69)	(−0.70)
N	521	431	431	521	431	431	472	389	389	521	431	431
N_g	48	41	41	48	41	41	48	41	41	48	41	41
ar1p							0.00501	0.0298	0.0304	0.000758	0.0109	0.0103
ar2p							0.588	0.283	0.257	0.641	0.285	0.302
Hansenp							0.970	0.998	0.998	0.999	0.999	1.000

Notes: t statistics in parentheses. *, ** and *** denote significance at 10%, 5% and 1%, respectively. In this table, GDPPC represents gross domestic product per capita, INTER refers to aggregate intermediation income, NONINT represents aggregate Non-intermediation income/activities, GFCF represents gross fixed capital formation, GOVEXP represents government expenditure, INF represents inflation, OPEN represents openness to trade and GCC× NONINT is an interaction term of GCC countries and non-intermediation income.

Table 3. Impact of Non-Intermediation Income on Economic Volatility (Dependent Variable: Volatility)

	(1) LSDVC AH	(2) LSDVC AH	(3) LSDVC AH	(4) LSDVC AB	(5) LSDVC AB	(6) LSDVC AB	(7) GMM DIFF	(8) GMM DIFF	(9) GMM DIFF	(10) GMM SYS	(11) GMM SYS	(12) GMM SYS
Volatility$_{(t-1)}$	0.567***	0.618***	0.605***	0.564***	0.613***	0.598***	0.504***	0.418***	0.447***	0.566***	0.718***	0.721***
	(15.20)	(8.73)	(9.12)	(15.96)	(9.79)	(10.21)	(13.13)	(3.75)	(4.71)	(10.50)	(13.96)	(12.26)
lnINTER$_{(t-2)}$	0.647	0.115	−0.0735	0.620	0.00878	−0.172	0.572	0.228	0.179	−0.218	−0.312**	−0.328**
	(1.58)	(0.26)	(−0.19)	(1.53)	(0.02)	(−0.46)	(1.06)	(0.45)	(0.27)	(−1.39)	(−2.26)	(−2.21)
lnNONINT$_{(t-2)}$	−0.0747	−0.0131	0.0331	−0.0706	−0.00382	0.0371	−0.0347	0.00940	0.108	0.286	0.258	0.134
	(−0.33)	(−0.06)	(0.14)	(−0.32)	(−0.02)	(0.16)	(−0.16)	(0.05)	(0.58)	(1.62)	(1.60)	(0.55)
GDPPC$_{(t-2)}$	−2.231***	−1.002	−0.500	−2.076***	−0.871	−0.368	−3.072*	−1.089	−0.891	0.252***	0.151	0.0954
	(−2.79)	(−1.05)	(−0.55)	(−2.69)	(−0.95)	(−0.47)	(−1.79)	(−0.59)	(−0.42)	(2.83)	(1.56)	(0.71)
lnGFCF$_{(t-2)}$	0.359	0.301	0.339	0.356	0.229	0.250	0.398	0.846	0.938	0.117	0.217	0.0380
	(0.83)	(0.65)	(0.60)	(0.84)	(0.52)	(0.46)	(0.56)	(1.14)	(1.17)	(0.22)	(0.43)	(0.07)
lnGOVEXP$_{(t-2)}$	−0.344	−0.491	−0.617	−0.248	−0.387	−0.468	1.020	1.155	0.653	−0.366	−0.192	−0.190
	(−0.42)	(−0.58)	(−0.75)	(−0.31)	(−0.47)	(−0.61)	(0.91)	(0.95)	(0.47)	(−1.07)	(−0.54)	(−0.58)
INF$_{(t-2)}$	−0.00557	0.0137	0.0166	−0.00481	0.0139	0.0168	−0.0240	0.00880	0.00172	−0.0104	0.0115	0.00828
	(−0.39)	(0.73)	(0.88)	(−0.34)	(0.76)	(0.92)	(−1.30)	(0.36)	(0.07)	(−0.56)	(0.50)	(0.35)
lnOPEN$_{(t-2)}$		−0.187	−0.302		−0.0735	−0.173		−1.547	−1.515		0.317	0.171
		(−0.26)	(−0.39)		(−0.10)	(−0.23)		(−1.12)	(−1.23)		(1.07)	(0.65)
GCCxNONINT$_{(t-2)}$			−0.458**			−0.441**			−6.811			0.107
			(−2.53)			(−2.54)			(−1.08)			(1.14)
Crisis			0.0907			0.101			0.189			−0.206
			(0.30)			(0.35)			(0.63)			(−0.60)
_cons										−0.577	−2.024	0.0619
										(−0.23)	(−0.93)	(0.02)
N	480	396	395	480	396	395	431	354	353	480	396	395
N_g	48	41	41	48	41	41	48	41	41	48	41	41
ar1p							0.000639	0.00959	0.00443	0.000927	0.00111	0.00104
ar2p							0.326	0.659	0.774	0.507	0.719	0.687
Hansenp							0.985	1.000	0.999	0.997	0.981	0.999

Notes: t statistics in parentheses: *, ** and *** denote significance at 10%, 5% and 1% respectively. In this table, GDPPC represents gross domestic product per capita, INTER refers to aggregate intermediation income, NONINT represents aggregate Non-intermediation income/activities, GFCF represents gross fixed capital formation, GOVEXP represents government expenditure, INF represents inflation, OPEN represents openness to trade and GCCxNONINT is an interaction term of GCC countries and non-intermediation income.

In case of each estimator, the first column presents the baseline estimation where the control variables include GFCF, Government expenditure and inflation, while the second column controls for the trade openness as well. The third estimation in case of each estimator include an interaction dummy (GCC and non-intermediation income) and a crisis dummy. The purpose of including GCC interaction dummy is to see whether the GDPPC growth of GCC countries behave differently to the changes in non-intermediation income as compared to other countries in the sample. In our sample, the GCC countries are the only countries classified as high-income countries and as per literature (Rioja and Valev, 2004; De Gregorio and Guidotti, 1995; Beck et al., 2014; Masten et al., 2008) the impact of finance (Intermediation and non-intermediation) differs for different countries with respect to their level of development and income. Since the time span of our study covers crisis period as well, we use Crisis dummy to see whether these countries have performed differently during the time of global financial crisis.

Table 2 presents results regarding the impact of non-intermediation activities and other control variables on the GDPPC growth of OIC member countries. The growth has been calculated as the annual difference in the logarithm of real GDP per capita i.e., $\ln\text{GDPPC}_t - \ln\text{GDPPC}_{t-1}$. Table 3 presents results about the impact of non-intermediation activities and other control variables on the volatility of GDPPC growth of OIC member countries. All variables are lagged to capture the possible past effects of these variables on the Countries' GDPPC growth and volatility. The results for most variables are fairly stable across regressions.

Following Beck et al. (2000), we consider following equation to measure the impact of non-intermediation on Growth.

$$\ln\text{GDPPC}_{jt} - \ln\text{GDPPC}_{jt-1}$$
$$= (\alpha - 1)\ln\text{GDPPC}_{jt-1} + \beta_1 \text{NONINT}_{jt-1} + \beta_2 \text{Inter}_{jt-1} + \beta_3 P_{jt-1} + \varepsilon_{jt}, \quad (4)$$

where GDPPC is GDP per capita, NON-INT represents non-intermediation income, Inter represents intermediation income, P shows policy variables used in the equation, ε is the error term. j and t in the subscripts represent country and time period, respectively. Equation (1) can be rewritten as

$$\ln\text{GDPPC}_{j,t} = \alpha\ln\text{GDPPC}_{j,t-1} + \beta_1 \text{NON-INT}_{j,t-1} + \beta_2 \text{Inter}_{j,t-1} + \beta_3 P_{j,t-1} + \varepsilon_{j,t}. \quad (5)$$

The results are reported in Table 2 and we start with discussing them. The estimated coefficient of the lagged dependent variable i.e., GDPPC_{t-1} variable remains significant across all the specifications. The coefficient remains around 0.9 or above in almost all the regressions suggesting a high level of persistence across the series. As far as our focus variable is concerned, the results show that the aggregate non-intermediation income is not significantly associated with the growth of OIC member countries. This finding remains consistent even after adding trade openness, and GCC× NONINT and Crisis dummies in the specification. Results from all the estimators further confirm non-significance of non-intermediation activities in explaining growth in OIC countries. Our findings are in line with the findings of Beck et al. (2014) where they also found non-intermediation activities to be insignificant for their total sample which consisted of both developed and developing countries. One possible reason of insignificance of the non-intermediation activities could be the weakening of overall finance-growth nexus over time, as Rousseau and Wachtel (2005, 2011), suggested that the nexus has become weaker in recent decades. They argued that in a number of developing economies financial liberalization is not escorted by the required expertise and regulatory skills. This as a result leads to booms in credit market and instability. Therefore, financial development (both intermediation and non-intermediation activities) may not be as effective in generating growth now as it used to generate in earlier decades. The insignificance of intermediation activities towards economic growth may also be attributed to the weakened finance-growth nexus. Another possible reason of insignificance of non-intermediation activities may be their low levels in the understudy countries.

Majority of the countries in our sample are developing low-income countries. In our sample, there are only six high-income countries which are all oil exporting and belong to the GCC.[6] Many studies have shown that the causes of growth vary in developing and high-income/developed countries due to the differences in their technological and regulatory advancements. For instance, Acemoglu *et al.* (2006) argue that developing countries which are quite far from the technological frontier may chase a capital accumulation-based growth strategy. On the other hand, developed and high-income countries those are near to the technological frontier are motivated to follow an innovation-based growth strategy. As per Allen and Gale (1999), traditional intermediation activities could be more appropriate in assisting accumulation of capital in developing countries whereas non-intermediation activities could be more advantageous to the financing of innovative activities. Moreover, it is more likely in developed countries which concentrate on professional services that due to the non-intermediation services, the spillover of technological advancement happens to the sectors other than the financial sector and as a result it increases the economic growth. Additionally, there is more wealth in high-income countries, more wealth management services are expected to be required and hence non-intermediation activities are expected to increase. To check whether the impact of non-intermediation income differs for the high-income countries (GCC) in our sample, we used an interaction dummy (GCC× NONINT) in our third specification. The GCC× NONINT dummy is found to be insignificant in across all estimators (except for SYS-GMM) showing that the impact of non-intermediation activities does not differ for the GCC countries in our sample. This finding is inconsistent with the discussion above and also with the findings of Beck *et al.* (2014). One possible reason of this contrast could be the high level of public investments by GCC countries in foreign assets which accumulate to 152% of GDP by the end of 2014.[7] Since most of the funds have been invested outside the GCC countries, the requirement of fund management services is not expected to grow and does not have an impact on the economic growth.

As mentioned above, intermediation activities (proxied by private credit to GDP) have no significant relation with the growth in OIC member countries as per both LSDVC

---

[6] As per Worldbank's World Development Indicators.
[7] MENA: Lower Oil Prices Present Challenges and Opportunities, Institute of International Finance report (2015).

estimators and SYS-GMM. Only in the regressions 7, 8 and 9, where we have used DIFF-GMM estimator, we find intermediation activities to be positively and significantly impacting the growth. Here, we follow what majority of the estimators suggest i.e., intermediation activities are not significantly associated with the economic growth. This finding is in line with those of Deidda and Fattouh (2002); Rousseau and Wachtel (2005, 2011) and Beck et al. (2014). One possible reason of the insignificance of intermediation activities can be attributed to the declining impact of financial sector on economic growth over the decades (which has been discussed in detail in previous paragraph). Gross fixed capital formation (GFCF) is found to be significant in most of the regressions. This finding is in line with the studies done by Solow (1962); Kim and Lau (1994) and Ozturk and Al-Mulali (2015). Inflation is found to be insignificant for economic growth in almost all the regressions. Government expenditure (proxy for infrastructure development) is found to have a significant and positive impact on the economic growth when we estimate our base model using LSDVC estimators. But in most of the regressions it is found to be insignificant and we follow the most consistent result. Our finding is in line with the findings of Kormendi and Meguire (1985) and Agell et al. (1999). In the second and third specifications under each estimator, we have added trade openness as another control variable. Openness has positive and significant relationship with growth across all the estimators (except for SYS-GMM). This finding is in line with Rajan and Zingales (1998), Baltagi et al. (2009) and Law and Singh (2014). As far as our crisis dummy is concerned, it remains insignificant across all the estimators indicating that the crisis does not affect economic growth of OIC member countries. This may be because most of the countries in our sample are developing countries and their banks did not play much role in causing the crisis. These banks from developing countries do not offer toxic products which were the main cause of the global financial crisis. Secondly, the markets in most of these countries are not as efficient in terms of their linkage with the financial markets of developed countries (Lin, 2008; Aizenman et al., 2015). So, these markets are not open to have any direct impact of financial shocks in developed countries. Thirdly, in most of these economies banks are more stringently regulated and are not allowed to indulge in the high-risk activities (Naudé, 2009; Barth et al., 2013).

Now we will shift our focus towards the impact of non-intermediation activities and other control variables on the volatility of economic growth. Table 3 has the volatility as the dependent variable for all its estimations. Volatility is the standard deviation of the growth rate of three years rolling window. The independent variables are the same as used in the estimations of Table 2. All variables are lagged by two years $(t-2)$ in order to cover the volatility period to capture the possible past effects.

As per results reported in Table 3, except for the DIFF-GMM results, the estimated coefficient of the lagged dependent variable remains significant and more than 0.5 in all the specifications. This suggests a high level of persistence across the series. As far as our focus variable is concerned, the results show that the aggregate country level non-intermediation income is not significantly associated with the volatility of economic growth of OIC member countries. This finding remains consistent even after adding trade openness in specification 2, and GCCxNon-Int and Crisis dummies in specification 3. The results from all the estimators (LSDVC (AH), LSDVC (AB), DIFF-GMM and SYS-GMM), confirm non-significance of non-intermediation income in explaining volatility of growth in OIC countries. Since most of our countries are low-income developing countries, our findings conform with the findings of Beck *et al.* (2014) where they also find non-intermediation activities to be insignificant for the volatility of economic growth in low-income countries. They however find non-intermediation activities to be significant in increasing volatility in high income countries. As stated by Beck *et al.* (2014) and Naudé (2009), one possible reason of insignificance of the non-intermediation activities can be that the type of non-intermediation activities being offered in developing countries are far less risky as compared to the non-intermediation activities offered in developed countries. The focus of the banks in developed countries has been on risky derivatives and trading mechanisms. On the other hand, in developing countries the focus has been on coming up with new banking products for unbanked segments of the society and developing distribution channels to spread the services to these segments. For instance, most of the OIC countries do not have derivative markets, suggesting minimal derivatives trading by banks barring the banks in Malaysia and Turkey.[8] The high-risk toxic assets like collateralized debt obligations and credit default swaps are literally non-existent in most of the low-income developing countries. So, the banks in most of the OIC countries do not indulge in high risk non-intermediation activities. Secondly, at least half of the OIC member countries have Islamic banks operating as important part of their financial system. Most of these high-risk non-intermediation activities are considered as non-Shariah compliant and Islamic banks are not allowed to participate in them. These are the reasons due to which the non-intermediation services being offered by the banks of OIC member countries do not impact their economic volatility.

As far as high-income countries (GCC countries) in our sample are concerned, we used GCCxNONINT dummy to see whether the impact of non-intermediation activities differ for the economic volatility in GCC countries. It is relevant to note that whilst the non-intermediation income variable is not significant across most of the specifications, on interacting the GCC dummy with the variable (GCCxNONINT), the estimated coefficient turns out to be negative and statistically significant in two (where LSDVC-based estimators are used) out of the four specifications. This suggests a significant difference between the impact of non-intermediation activities on economic volatility of the GCC and non-GCC countries (mostly low-income). In the case of the GCC countries, non-intermediation activities seem to decrease the economic volatility. Our results therefore seem to contradict with the findings of Beck *et al.* (2014), where they found non-intermediation to increase volatility in case of high-income countries. As discussed above, one possible reason of this contradiction could be the type of non-intermediation activities in GCC countries which requires further exploration. The non-intermediation activities seem to provide diversification benefits to the financial sector which promotes stability not only in the financial sector but also translates it into economic stability.

---

[8] http://stats.bis.org/statx/srs/table/a5.

Intermediation activities are found to be insignificant in all the regressions where we have used LSDVC and DIFF-GMM estimators. This suggests that these activities do not impact the economic volatility of OIC member countries. When we use SYS-GMM estimator, we find intermediation activities to be negative and significant at 5% (in estimations which include trade openness), suggesting that intermediation activities decrease volatility in OIC member countries. This is an expected finding as it is in line with the previous literature like Caballero and Krishnamurthy (2001), Aghion *et al.* (1999, 2010), Beck *et al.* (2014). As per the literature, possible reasons of the negative relationship between intermediation and volatility could be (1) intermediation activities help easing firms' cash constraints, (2) these activities reduce the dependence of financial contracts on borrowers' net worth and (3) these activities decrease volatility through its impact on the cyclical composition of investment. The presence of a steadying impact of intermediation in low-income countries may also be due to a comparatively more vital role of the financial sector as a shock absorber in low-income developing countries. On the other hand, fiscal and monetary policies are considered more effective in alleviating the economy in case of developed countries (Calderón *et al.*, 2016). As far as control variables are concerned, GDPPC is found to be negative and significant only in base model regressions. In all the other regressions, it is found to be insignificant. All the other control variables also remain insignificant in most of the specifications. The crisis dummy remains insignificant suggesting that there is no impact of crisis on the economic volatility of OIC member countries. As stated earlier as well, the reason of the insignificance of crisis could be that banks in our sample do not offer the toxic products which were the main cause of the global financial crisis because these products are still not common in developing economies. Secondly, the markets in most of these countries are not directly linked to the financial market in developed countries. Thirdly, in most of the economies of our sample, there are stringent regulations in place which do not allow the banks under their supervision to indulge in the high-risk activities.

5. Conclusion

To conclude, we find non-intermediation income to be insignificant for the economic growth of OIC member countries. This result remains consistent across different estimators. Non-intermediation activities do not impact the economic volatility of developing countries but for GCC countries it seemed to reduce volatility. Intermediation activities are found to be insignificantly related with the growth of OIC member countries, but on the other hand, they are found to reduce volatility in OIC member countries. Our results are generally robust across different specifications and estimators. Based on our findings, regulators may think to loosen up the control by decreasing the risk weights[9] applied to off-balance sheet items which are mostly related to non-intermediation activities. It is also pertinent to mention that the types of non-intermediation services being offered by the

---

[9] Risk-weights are recommended by the regulatory authorities to find the least amount of capital that banks must keep (based on the banks' risky portfolio which also include non-intermediation activities) in order to decrease the insolvency risk.

banks in OIC countries are not as risky as they are in developed countries. In almost all of the OIC countries (with the exception of Turkey and Malaysia), Basel 3 has not been implemented yet, which makes it important to the regulators who are considering to introduce Basel 3 regulation that while introducing they should deliberate on the differences in the non-intermediation activities in OIC countries as well as their impact on banks and economy. We recommend regulators to consider encouraging banks in OIC to expand their revenue sources as they increase bank profitability without impacting the economic volatility. As far as future research is concerned, it would be interesting to study the impact of different components of non-intermediation income on economy as different types of non-intermediation activities possess different characteristics.

References

Acemoglu, D, P Aghion and F Zilibotti (2006). Distance to frontier, selection, and economic growth. *Journal of the European Economic Association*, 4(1), 37–74.

Agell, J, T Lindh and H Ohlsson (1999). Growth and the public sector: A reply. *European Journal of Political Economy*, 15(2), 359–366.

Aghion, P, GM Angeletos, A Banerjee and K Manova (2010). Volatility and growth: Credit constraints and the composition of investment. *Journal of Monetary Economics*, 57(3), 246–265.

Aghion, P, E Caroli and C Garcia-Penalosa (1999). Inequality and economic growth: The perspective of the new growth theories. *Journal of Economic Literature*, 37(1), 1615–1660.

Aizenman, J, YW Cheung and H Ito (2015). International reserves before and after the global crisis: Is there no end to hoarding?. *Journal of International Money and Finance*, 52, 102–126.

Allen, F and D Gale (1999). Innovations in financial services, relationships, and risk sharing. *Management Science*, 45(9), 1239–1253.

Allen, F and AM Santomero (2001). What do financial intermediaries do?. *Journal of Banking & Finance*, 25(2), 271–294.

Anderson, TW and C Hsiao (1982). Formulation and estimation of dynamic models using panel data. *Journal of Econometrics*, 18(1), 47–82.

Arellano, M and S Bond (1991). Some tests of specification for panel data: Monte Carlo evidence and an application to employment equations. *The Review of Economic Studies*, 58(2), 277–297.

Baele, L, O De Jonghe and R Vander Vennet (2007). Does the stock market value bank diversification?. *Journal of Banking & Finance*, 31(7), 1999–2023.

Baltagi, BH, PO Demetriades and SH Law (2009). Financial development and openness: Evidence from panel data. *Journal of Development Economics*, 89(2), 285–296.

Barth, JR, C Lin, Y Ma, J Seade and FM Song (2013). Do bank regulation, supervision and monitoring enhance or impede bank efficiency?. *Journal of Banking & Finance*, 37(8), 2879–2892.

Beck, T and R Levine (2004). Stock markets, banks, and growth: Panel evidence. *Journal of Banking & Finance*, 28(3), 423–442.

Beck, T, A Demirgüc-Kunt and R Levine (2009). Financial Institutions and Markets across countries and over time, Policy Research Working Paper 4943, World Bank.

Beck, T, H Degryse and C Kneer (2014). Is more finance better? Disentangling intermediation and size effects of financial systems. *Journal of Financial Stability*, 10, 50–64.

Beck, T, R Levine and N Loayza (2000). Finance and the sources of growth. *Journal of Financial Economics*, 58(1), 261–300.

Bruno, GS (2005). Approximating the bias of the LSDV estimator for dynamic unbalanced panel data models. *Economics Letters*, 87(3), 361–366.

Bun, MJ and JF Kiviet (2003). On the diminishing returns of higher-order terms in asymptotic expansions of bias. *Economics Letters*, 79(2), 145–152.

Caballero, R and A Krishnamurthy (2001). A "vertical" analysis of crises and intervention: Fear of floating and ex-ante problems (No. w8428). National Bureau of Economic Research.

Calderón, C, R Duncan and K Schmidt-Hebbel (2016). Do good institutions promote countercyclical macroeconomic policies?. *Oxford Bulletin of Economics and Statistics*, 78(2), 650–670.

De Gregorio, J and PE Guidotti (1995). Financial development and economic growth. *World Development*, 23(3), 433–448.

Deidda, L and B Fattouh (2002). Non-linearity between finance and growth. *Economics Letters*, 74(3), 339–345.

Demirgüç-Kunt, A and H Huizinga (2010). Bank activity and funding strategies: The impact on risk and returns. *Journal of Financial Economics*, 98(3), 626–650.

Demsetz, RS and PE Strahan (1997). Diversification, size, and risk at bank holding companies. *Journal of Money, Credit, and Banking*, 29(3), 300–313.

Jalil, A, M Feridun and Y Ma (2010). Finance-growth nexus in China revisited: New evidence from principal components and ARDL bounds tests. *International Review of Economics & Finance*, 19(2), 189–195.

Judson, RA and AL Owen (1999). Estimating dynamic panel data models: A guide for macroeconomists. *Economics Letters*, 65(1), 9–15.

Karakaya, A and B Er (2013). Noninterest (nonprofit) income and financial performance at turkish commercial and participation banks. *International Business Research*, 6(1), 106.

Kendall, J (2012). Local financial development and growth. *Journal of Banking and Finance*, 36(2), 1548–1562.

Kim, JI and LJ Lau (1994). The sources of economic growth of the East Asian newly industrialized countries. *Journal of the Japanese and International Economies*, 8(3), 235–271.

King, RG and R Levine (1993). Financial intermediation and economic development. In *Financial Intermediation in the Construction of Europe*, Mayer, C and X Vives (Eds.), pp. 156–189. Centre for Economic Policy Research, London.

Kiviet, JF (1995). On bias, inconsistency, and efficiency of various estimators in dynamic panel data models. *Journal of Econometrics*, 68(1), 53–78.

Kiviet, JF (1998). Expectations of expansions for estimators in a dynamic panel data model: Some results for weakly-exogenous regressors (No. 98-027/4). Tinbergen Institute.

Kormendi, RC and PG Meguire (1985). Macroeconomic determinants of growth: Cross-country evidence. *Journal of Monetary Economics*, 16(2), 141–163.

Law, SH and N Singh (2014). Does too much finance harm economic growth?. *Journal of Banking & Finance*, 41, 36–44.

Laeven, L and R Levine (2007). Is there a diversification discount in financial conglomerates?. *Journal of Financial Economics*, 85(2), 331–367.

Law, SH, WNW Azman-Saini and MH Ibrahim (2013). Institutional quality thresholds and the finance–growth nexus. *Journal of Banking & Finance*, 37(12), 5373–5381.

Lin, JY (2008). The impact of the financial crisis on developing countries. Paper presented at the Korea Development Institute, 31 October. Seoul.

Masten, AB, F Coricelli and I Masten (2008). Non-linear growth effects of financial development: Does financial integration matter?. *Journal of International Money and Finance*, 27(2), 295–313.

Molyneux, P and J Yip (2013). Income diversification and performance of Islamic banks. *Journal of Financial Management, Markets and Institutions*, 1(1), 47–66.

Moshirian, F and A Van der Laan (1998). Trade in financial services and the determinants of banks' foreign assets. *Journal of Multinational Financial Management*, 8(1), 23–38.

Naudé, W (2009). The financial crisis of 2008 and the developing countries, WIDER Discussion Papers, World Institute for Development Economics (UNUWIDER), No. 2009/01, ISBN 978-92-9230-171-2.

Ozturk, I and U Al-Mulali (2015). Natural gas consumption and economic growth nexus: Panel data analysis for GCC countries. *Renewable and Sustainable Energy Reviews*, 51, 998–1003.

Rajan, RG and L Zingales (1998). Financial dependence and growth. *American Economic Review*, 88, 559–586.

Rioja, F and N Valev (2004). Finance and the sources of growth at various stages of economic development. *Economic Inquiry*, 42(1), 127–140.

Rogers, K and JF Sinkey (1999). An analysis of nontraditional activities at US commercial banks. *Review of Financial Economics*, 8(1), 25–39.

Rousseau, PL and P Wachtel (2011). What is happening to the impact of financial deepening on economic growth?. *Economic Inquiry*, 49(1), 276–288.

Rousseau, P and P Wachtel (2005). Economic growth and financial depth: Is the relationship extinct already? (No. DP2005/10). World Institute for Development Economic Research (UNU-WIDER).

Shahimi, S, AGB Ismail and SB Ahmad (2006). A panel data analysis of fee income activities in Islamic banks. *Journal of King Abdulaziz University: Islamic Economics*, 19(2), 22–36.

Solow, RM (1962). Technical progress, capital formation, and economic growth. *The American Economic Review*, 52(2), 76–86.

Stiroh, KJ (2004). Do community banks benefit from diversification?. *Journal of Financial Services Research*, 25(2–3), 135–160.

Stiroh, KJ and A Rumble (2006). The dark side of diversification: The case of US financial holding companies. *Journal of Banking & Finance*, 30(8), 2131–2161.

Trichet, J-C (2010). What role for finance? Lecture at Universidade Nova de Lisboa, Lisbon.

Turner, A (2010). What do banks do? Why do credit booms and busts occur and what can public policy do about it?. The Future of Finance: The LSE Report.

Windmeijer, F (2005). A finite sample correction for the variance of linear efficient two-step GMM estimators. *Journal of Econometrics*, 126(1), 25–51.

Zhang, Y (2010). Analysis of the systematic risk of financial institution in modern finance evolution. *International Journal of Economics and Finance*, 2(3), 234.

Chapter 3

Competition-Stability Relationship in Dual Banking Systems: Evidence from Efficiency-Adjusted Market Power[#]

Mudeer Ahmed Khattak[*]

Faculty of Business Administration, Iqra University Islamabad, Pakistan
mudeerkhattak@gmail.com

Omar Alaeddin

Universiti Kuala Lumpur
Business School, Universiti Kuala Lumpur, Malaysia
omar.alaeddin@unikl.edu.my

Moutaz Abojeib

Islamic Shariah Research Acadamy (ISRA), Malaysia
moutaz.aj@gmail.com

This research attempts to explore the impact of banking competition on financial stability employing a more precise measure of market power. It was found that Islamic banks are less stable and are enjoying lower market power. The analysis shows that higher market competition makes the banking sector vulnerable to defaults, supporting the "competition-fragility view". This research finds no difference in the relationship for Islamic banks indicates that Islamic banks might be involved in traditional banking activities as conventional banks. The results are consistent and robust to different estimation approaches and subsamples. This research carries regulatory and policy implications.

Keywords: Bank competition; efficiency-adjusted market power; stability; dual banking; Lerner index.

1. Introduction

Banking and especially Islamic Banking has observed a rapid growth in the past few decades, reaching over 60 countries, both in Islamic and non-Islamic. According to Islamic Financial Services Board (2019), the combined total worth of different Islamic financial services industry is estimated at USD 2.19 trillion as of 2Q18.[1] World Islamic banking assets growth has experienced an expansion of 7.2%, standing at approximately USD 1.56

---

[*] Corresponding author.
[#] This Chapter first appeared in the *Singapore Economic Review*, Vol. 67, No. 1, doi: 10.1142/S0217590820420096. © 2022 World Scientific Publishing.
[1] https://www.ifsb.org/download.php?id=5231&lang=English&pg=/index.php.

trillion at the end of 2018 (Islamic Financial Services Board, 2019). Looking at these figures it can be argued that the Islamic banking sector is growing which is making the banking sector more competitive. Therefore, it is not surprising to know that many countries have set an increase in Islamic Banking growth as one of the main plans to develop the banking industry in their countries. It is often believed that excessive competition could lead to instability in the banking sector. This competition might crumble the banks' franchise value. This erosion can lead the banks to take more risks to maintain the profits. Taking on riskier investments and policies will lead to more loan failures and instability (Keeley, 1990). On the flip side, competition might lead banks to take safer investment decisions and protection of the franchise value of the banks that would contribute to the banking stability (Boyd and Nicolo, 2005).

The global financial crisis and its aftermath restarted a debate revolving around the banking system. The effect of banking market competition on banks' risk-taking and hence, on banks' stability is one of the main dimensions of this debate. This debate has been the point of discussion since the 1990s (Keeley, 1990). However, the literature is still inconclusive. Therefore, it would be worth starting a new investigation to better understand the relationship between banking competition and banking system stability.

Islamic and conventional banks contest in most economies today and many of the conventional banks have recently opened Islamic banking "windows" that further increases the competition. however, the presence of Islamic banks in many countries is still very little. Having foreign banks in a country, who also opt the Islamic banking operations, also levers the banking competition. On the bright side, more innovation can be brought in Shariah-compatible financial products by the Islamic banks in the market. The Islamic banking industry is becoming more competitive globally. However, the impact of the competition on stability is still not clear. Very few studies investigate the association of competition and banking stability in dual banking economies. One of the main aims of this study is to address the shortcoming and to fill the gap in the literature.

Though the possible difference of the competition and stability relationship between conventional banks and Islamic banks is studied in few studies, however, these studies have either used concentration as a measure of market competition (Rizvi et al., 2019) or have used the traditional Lerner index (Abojeib, 2017; Kabir and Worthington, 2017) which assumes full efficiency of the banks and thus has gained criticism among the researchers. Clerides et al. (2015) and Koetter et al. (2012) argue that the conventional approach of computing the Lerner index assumes both profit efficiency (optimal choice of prices) and cost efficiency and fail to consider the possibility that banks may not exploit pricing opportunities resulting from market power. Controlling for inefficiency is particularly important because it can affect the difference between price and marginal cost, and consequently, the value of the Lerner index. Besides that, banks with greater market power might adopt a "Quiet life" and reduce their cost-efficiency. On the contrary, efficiency could also lead to a market concentrated in the hands of the most efficient banks. the Efficient Structure Hypothesis postulates that efficiency (and stability) may be driving market structure, and reverse causality is likely to prevail between the variables of interest. Therefore, we argue that the mentioned adjustments should be made before estimating the market power which enhances the literature on market power estimation in dual banking economies.

From a theoretical perspective, several factors may make the competition-stability relationship for Islamic banks different from the case of conventional banks (Kabir and Worthington, 2017). Therefore, it is worthwhile to study the relationship using extended measures of market competition in dual banking and explore any possible difference in the relationship for Islamic banks. Moreover, this study accounts for the effects of concentration, diversifications, and market share. As argued by the literature (IJtsma et al., 2017), concentration is one of the determinants of stability. Furthermore, an increase in diversification might increase/decrease banks' stability, therefore, diversification is argued as one of the main factors affecting banks' risk (Amidu and Wolfe, 2013; Rahim et al., 2013; Maharani and Setiyono, 2018).

Considering the above discussion regarding the competition-stability relationship, mixed results have been produced by using data from developed and developing countries for different periods. Previous studies also indicate that concentration and competition can exist at the same time and concentration does not necessarily mean that there is no competition in the market (Fu et al., 2014). The dual banking system, however, has been mostly neglected. It is worth exploring since this area of research is still rarely explored. If the competition is enhancing fragility in the banking industry, it can be fatal for the overall financial sector.

The reason behind opting to use specific countries among other Organization of Islamic Cooperation countries is the competition growth in the banking sectors in these countries with the expansion of the Islamic banking industry. Furthermore, while few pieces of research have focused on the comparative analysis in dual banking, most of these researches are in comparison to banking performance. Very few studies with a focus on the relationship of competition and stability are found in the literature, however, none of the studies are found using efficiency-adjusted Lerner indices (to the best of our knowledge). The main contributions of this research are sketched as; Firstly, the level of competition and stability is compared between conventional banks and Islamic banks. Secondly, this study explores the effects of banking competition on stability in dual banking using different measures of market power. Thirdly, it extends the literature on the possible difference (if any) of the relationship for Islamic banks.

The next section provides an explanation of the data and methodology which describes the data sources, econometric modeling and the specification of the variables. After this, the results are explained in the empirical analysis which is followed by the discussion on the results and the robustness checks. And lastly, the conclusion section provides the conclusion and policy implications of the research.

2. Data and Methodology

2.1. *Sample selection and data*

Data for this research is extracted from the FitchConnect database for the period of 2006–2017. This study considers only the commercial banks in the countries where Islamic Banks and conventional banks exist together. Countries in the sample are included because of these countries' significant share of Islamic banks' assets contributing to the country's overall banking assets. The final sample includes Malaysia, Brunei Darussalam, Saudi Arabia, United Arab Emirates, Qatar, Pakistan, Bahrain, Kuwait, Bangladesh, Turkey, and Indonesia are taken into consideration. These countries cover around 95%[2] of the global Islamic Banking asset. The study is restricted to the banks with at least four years of data (Beck et al., 2013). Few more filters are also taken into consideration providing the research objectives. This research uses unconsolidated financial statements to avoid any double-counting in estimations. Furthermore, the investment banks are excluded since they are not the focus of our research and the offshore banks are also excluded because they are not expected to be seen in competition with local banks in a country.

Besides the above, this research drops the observations with missing or negative values of any input or our factor prices, costs, equity, profits, and total assets. This is to ensure robustness in estimating the lerner indices (discussed in the next section). However, this filter was applied after the construction of the concentration measure and the market share (explained in Section 3.2). After this filter, gaps were removed in the data by considering the longest run within a panel. After applying these filters, the final sample size is 228 banks including 173 conventional banks and 55 Islamic banks.

2.2. Competition measures

2.2.1. Traditional lerner index

Instead of using measures of competition, studies usually use measures of market power. Reduction in market power implies a rise in the level of banking competition. This research uses the Lerner Index to explore the market power of each commercial bank in our sample. Lerner index is defined as the price above the cost a bank can set. It can be measured at each point in time and is discussed as not a long-run equilibrium measure, which gives it an advantage over H-statistic. Lerner Index ranges from 0 to 1. It swings towards 0 and the market is regarded as a pure-competitive market and where they have no power over pricing when P equals MC. On the contrary, When the Lerner is high, and it tends towards one, it reflects the high mark-up of P above the MC; indicating an increase in market power, giving banks the monopoly power. Following Forssbæck and Tanveer (2011), Weill (2011) and Beck et al. (2013), the Traditional Lerner index is given as follows:

$$\text{T\_Lerner}_{it} = (P_{it} - \text{MC}_{it})/P_{it}, \qquad (1)$$

P_{it} denotes the price (total operating income over total assets) whereas the MC_{it} denotes the marginal cost of bank i's output, in year t. To estimate the MC, a translog-cost-function is used employing a single output (total assets) and three different input prices (that are the price of the borrowed funds, price of labor, and the price of physical capital).[3]

2.2.2. Efficiency-adjusted lerner-index

Few studies of the recent past have argued that there are two problems with traditional Lerner Index estimation. Firstly, Efficient or stability might be driving the market structure

---
[2] IFSB, Stability Report, 2018/Iran and Sudan are excluded, as they are not dual banking countries.
[3] Detailed explanation is not reported to save space, however, it is available upon request.

of a banking sector, namely the Efficient Structure Hypothesis. Secondly, it is argued that the estimated profit-cost margin, estimated from the often used traditional Lerner-index, does not accurately reflect the true market power because it assumes both profit-efficiency and cost-efficiency (Clerides *et al.*, 2015; Koetter *et al.*, 2012). Thus, this study employs the efficiency-adjusted Lerner index as suggested by Koetter *et al.* (2012). Following Koetter *et al.* (2012), the efficiency-adjusted Lerner index can be stated as:

$$\text{Ad\_Lerner} = \frac{\pi_{it} + tc_{it} - mc_{it} * q_{it}}{\pi_{it} + tc_{it}}. \quad (2)$$

In the above equation, i and t signify a particular bank in a particular year; π denotes the bank profit, which is calculated as the net-income; tc is the total cost, adding the interest expenses and non-interest expenses; and q signifies the total output measured by the earning assets. To measure the earning assets, total loans, and total securities are used. The mc indicates the marginal cost. This research employs the Stochastic Frontier Analysis (hereafter: SFA) model of the Battese and Coelli (1995). Both SFA and the data envelopment analysis (DEA) have been widely used by the literature. The SFA has the advantage of dividing error into two components, while the DEA considers that all deviation is due to inefficiency, dismissing the effect of random errors. Following Koetter *et al.* (2012), while estimating the efficiency adjusted Lerner Index, equity (EQ) was also included in the model because it can be used to fund loans and reflects different risk attitudes of banks. To arrive at the estimation of the Cost-efficiency frontier, the model is modified as

$$\ln\text{TC}_{it} = \alpha_0 + \alpha_1 \ln Y_{\text{pit}} + \frac{1}{2}\alpha_2(\ln Y_{it}^2) + \sum_{j=1}^{3} \beta_j \ln w_{jit} + \lambda_1 \ln\text{EQ}_{it}$$

$$+ \frac{1}{2}\sum_{j=1}^{3}\sum_{k=1}^{3} \beta_{jk} \ln w_{jit} \ln w_{kit} + \sum_{j=1}^{3} \gamma_j \ln Y_{\text{pit}} \ln w_j + T_1 \text{Trend} \quad (3)$$

$$+ \frac{1}{2} T_2 \text{Trend}^2 + T_3 \text{Trend} \ln Y_{\text{pit}}^+ \sum_{j=1}^{3} \Psi_j \text{Trend} \ln w_{jit} + v_j + u_j.$$

Here, C indicates the bank's total cost; Y_p indicates the bank's outputs, and w denotes the three different input prices (that are the price of the borrowed funds, price of labor, and the price of physical capital) as in the traditional Lerner Index. Trend is a time trend to capture technical change. Unlike in the traditional Lerner Index, this research employs two outputs namely total securities and total loans. Here, it is assumed that ε is equal to $v_j + u_j$, where v is a two-sided random error that captures the impact of random noise and u, a non-negative inefficiency score, which captures the inefficiency relative to the frontier. Again, this research ensures the Linear homogeneity by standardizing all the factor prices and TC by ($w3$), as done for estimation of the traditional Lerner index. The MC can be estimated by taking the derivative of the Bank's total cost in the above equation in relation to the output, as expressed below

$$\text{MC}_{it} = \frac{\text{TC}_{it}}{Y_{it}} \left(\alpha_1 + \alpha_2 \ln y_{\text{pit}} + \sum_{j=1}^{3} \gamma_j \ln w_{jit} + T_3 \text{Trend} \right). \quad (4)$$

This research follows researches where p is defined as total revenues to total assets. However, the profit inefficiencies and inefficient allocation of resources should be considered while using the input factors. This could lead to an increase in the forgone profits. It is argued that profit inefficiencies are significantly larger than cost inefficiencies. Therefore, it is important to take care of profit inefficiencies. Besides this, since the interest here is to explore the banking competition level relative to the efficiency, it would be unrealistic to have a prior assumption that the banking sector is competitive. This research uses an alternative profit efficiency model as more appropriate to address this problem where the assumptions of perfect competition are not held. This alternative profit efficiency estimates how much profit a bank generates given its output factors. To overcome this issue, profit before tax (PBT) is used as a dependent variable and the equation is re-written as Equation (5).

Since the Profit variable can also take negative values, applying the natural logarithm of profits is a concern here. Dropping the observations with negative values does not seem a feasible approach as it will lead to a loss in the crucial observations. Bos and Koetter (2009) suggested a solution to censor the negative profits and make use of the available information at the same time. Therefore, an additional independent variable is employed, the negative profit indicator (NPI). NPI takes the value 1 if PBT is equal to or greater than 0, and it is equal to the absolute value of PBT if PBT is less than 0. Moreover, the value of PBT is also changed to 1 if PBT is negative. To estimate the profit efficiency frontier, the model is modified as

$$\ln \text{PBT}_{it} = \alpha_0 + \alpha_1 \ln Y_{\text{pit}} + \frac{1}{2} \alpha_2 (\ln Y_{it}^2) + \sum_{j=1}^{3} \beta_j \ln w_{jit}$$

$$+ \lambda_1 \ln \text{EQ}_{it} + \frac{1}{2} \sum_{j=1}^{3} \sum_{k=1}^{3} \beta_{jk} \ln w_{jit} \ln w_{kit} + \sum_{j=1}^{3} \gamma_j \ln Y_{\text{pit}} \ln w_j \quad (5)$$

$$+ T_1 \text{Trend} + \frac{1}{2} T_2 \text{Trend}^2 + T_3 \text{Trend} \ln Y_{\text{pit}}$$

$$+ \sum_{j=1}^{3} \Psi_j \text{Trend} \ln w_{jit} + \ln \text{NPI} + v_j + u_j.$$

2.3. Stability measure

Bank stability is measured with a z-score indicator following Demirgüç-Kunt and Detragiache (2009) and Azmi et al. (2019). The z-score can estimate an individual bank's risk. The Z-score calculates standard deviations, from which a bank is distant from losing its capital level. Z-score is a banks' risk proxy usually measured at the bank level.

It employs the accounting data to calculate the default probability of a bank. It compares the capital ratio to the change in returns to catch the volatility in returns. Z-Score can be written as

$$Z = (EQ/TA + ROAA)/sdROAA, \tag{6}$$

where ROAA is the Return on Average Assets, EQ/TA is Total equity over total assets, while *sd*ROAA is the standard deviation of ROAA. We use a three-year rolling window to estimate standard deviation, which is generally sufficient to allow for variation in the z-score. The high value of the z-score shows the higher stability of banks and vice versa, allowing to differentiate in the probability of insolvency in different groups.

2.4. Baseline Model and methodology

For exploring the impact of banking competition on banking stability, the following two dynamic empirical models are estimated:

$$\text{LnZscore}_{jt} = \beta_0 + \beta_1 \text{LnZscore}_{jt-1} + \beta_2 \text{Lerner}_{jt} + \beta_3 X_{jt} + \beta_4 \text{Macro}_{it} + \beta_5 \text{Crisis} + \varepsilon_{jt}. \tag{7}$$

Here, j, t, and i indicates the bank, year, and country, respectively. LnZscore$_{it}$ denotes a log of bank stability measure, the Zscore. A lagged dependent variable, LnZscore$_{it-1}$ is used in the models to capture the persistence in the banking level of stability. Lerner$_{it}$ indicates the traditional Lerner Index and Efficiency adjusted Lerner Index in the model, as the measures of market competition at the bank level. X_{it} is a vector of control variables at bank-level and industry level, such as the size of the bank, proxied by taking the log of total-assets (lnTA), Equity ratio *(EQTA)*, loans to total-assets *(GLTA)*, diversification *(Diversification)*, and Market share of deposits *(MS_dp)*. X_{it} further indicates, the industry-specific controls, such as the concentration measures, *HHI*, and *C3*. Lastly, Macro$_{jt}$ is a vector of country-level variables to control for country-specific characteristics such as GDP growth *(gdpgrowth)* and inflation *(inflation)*. The *Crisis* represents the crisis dummy to capture the impact of the financial crisis 2008–2009.

For the second objective of this research, the empirical models (Equation (7)) is extended to explore the difference in the impact of competition on stability for conventional banks and Islamic banks. The modified models are as follows:

$$\text{LnZscore}_{jt} = \beta_0 + \beta_1 \text{LnZscore}_{jt-1} + \beta_2 \text{Lerner}_{jt} + \beta_3 \text{Islamic} + \beta_4 \text{Lerner}_{jt} * \text{Islamic} \\ + \beta_5 X_{jt} + \beta_6 \text{Macro}_{it} + \beta_7 \text{Crisis} + \varepsilon_{it}. \tag{8}$$

The models are similar to Equation (7) except for a dummy variable and its interaction with Lerner Indices. Islamic is a dummy variable that takes the value of 1 for Islamic banks and 0 for conventional banks. With the introduction of the Islamic dummy, the model is enabled to test whether the average stability of Islamic banks significantly differs from the average stability of conventional banks. Besides the Islamic dummy, an interaction term is also incorporated to explore if there is any difference in the impact of competition on the stability of Islamic banks and conventional banks.

2.4.1. Independent variables

To control for bank-specific characteristics, this study employs equity ratio (EQTA). Turk Ariss (2010) suggested that banks with higher equity are more likely to engage in riskier activities. Banks' size is also controlled using a log of total assets (LnTA) (Čihák and Hesse, 2010; Moudud-Ul-Huq, 2019). It is also argued that size notably impacts a bank's stability since large banks, due to higher market powers, may take on more risk. The loan ratio (GLTA) is also controlled. Loan to asset ratio and asset size of banks have significant effects on the stability of banks (Rashid et al., 2017). This is derived by dividing the net loans by the total assets, to control the credit exposure effect of the bank. Income diversification (Diver) is included in the model to control for portfolio diversification which differs among different banks according to their investment strategies (Amidu and Wolfe, 2013; Deyoung and Roland, 2001). This is proxied by Non-interest/financing income/total income. Following Phan et al. (2019), this research also controls a market share of deposits. Banks having a greater share of deposits might enjoy higher earnings and having a higher share might make banks able to control for prices in a market in a specific country, and benefit from profit opportunities.

The research accounts for market concentration as a control for market structure using the Herfindahl-Hirschman Index (HHI). Boyd and Nicolo (2005) and Kasman and Kasman (2015) argue that concentration increases the lending rates. However, there also exists a concentration-stability view, where concentrated banking market is said to be better stable (IJtsma et al., 2017). C3 is an alternative concentration measure for the three biggest banks in a country. HHI is estimated by squaring the market share of each bank and then summing the squares, which equates as follows:

$$\text{HHI} = \sum_{j=1}^{n} (\text{MS}_n)^2. \quad (9)$$

A Crisis dummy is also included in the model to also control for any crisis effects while exploring the relationship, which may be altered due to the financial crisis. Crisis dummy takes a value of 1 for the year 2008–2009 and 0 otherwise. The model also includes the growth in Gross Domestic Product (gdpgrowth) to control for different levels of economic development across countries. The inflation rate is no doubt an important characteristic of a country. Here, it is controlled to consider the effects of uncertainty in macroeconomic factors on the stability of banks. Table 1 shows the Definition and sources of the variables used in this research.

2.4.2. Econometric approach

It should be noted that this research uses panel data, where time series (T) is fixed, and cross-sections (N) are large $(T<N)$. To control for the persistence of stability, a lagged dependent variable (LnZscore$_{jt-1}$) is included in the model, which might correlate with the error term. Besides this, some of the independent variables might be endogenous, for instance, the degree of market power (Berger et al., 2009) could be endogenous. The presence of the endogenous variables could lead to a correlation between the variable and error term which could make the estimation uncertain and biased. Therefore, the use of Pooled ordinary least squares (POLS), fixed effect (FE), and random effects (RE) might not

Table 1. Summary of the Variables and Their Sources

Variable	Definition	Source
Dependent Variables		
Z-scores	Sum of the equity ratio and total assets divided by the standard deviation of ROAA (sdROAA).	Fitch Connect Database Authors' calculation
Explanatory Variables		
Traditional Lerner Index (T_Lerner)	The traditional estimator of market power at the bank level.	Fitch Connect Database Authors' calculation
Efficiency-adjusted Lerner index (Ad_Lerner)	The efficiency-adjusted estimator of market power at the bank level.	Fitch Connect Database Authors' calculation
Control variables		
Equity ratio (EQTA)	The Ratio of Total Equity to Total Assets	Fitch Connect Database
Loan Ratio (GLTA)	control for extent of bank's lending (Net Loans/total assets).	Fitch Connect Database Authors' calculation
Diversification	Total Non-interest income/total income	Fitch Connect Database
Market Share of Deposits (MS_dp)	Total deposits of a bank/total deposits of all the banks	Fitch Connect Database
Concentration (HHI)	Banking Concentration in a country	Fitch Connect Database
Concentration of 3 largest banks (C3)	The concentration of 3 largest banks in a country.	Fitch Connect Database
Bank size (lnTA)	Logarithm of Total Assets; controls for bank's size	
Islamic	Dummy variable, takes value of 1 for Islamic banks and 0 otherwise	
Macroeconomic Variables		
Crisis	Dummy variable, takes value of 1 for the year 2008–2009 and 0 otherwise	
GDP (gdpgrowth)	Annual GDP growth rate	World Development Indicators
Inflation (inflation)	Annual Inflation rate	World Development Indicators

be most suitable here. This problem can be solved using instrumental variables in the model. However, finding instrumental variables that are highly related to the variable but uncorrelated with the error term is not simple. More importantly, the panel data like in this study, are more prone to heteroscedasticity. The issue with the use of instrumental variables is that it still does not consider the heteroscedastic nature of the data. One solution to address all the above issues is to use the Generalized Method of Moments approach.

Arellano and Bond (1991) came up with the original GMM estimator (also called first-differenced GMM), where instrument variables were introduced from the lagged levels of the explanatory variables and all the variables are modified by differencing and introduced instrument variables from the lagged values of the explanatory variables. Nonetheless, if there is a correlation in the error terms, the lagged values of the explanatory variables can turn out to be poor instruments. In our case, first-difference GMM might give us biased results. To estimate the baseline equations, that are Equations (7) and (8), this research uses the system GMM of Arellano and Bover (1995) and Blundell and Bond (1998) to get better and unambiguous estimators and better perceive the variable relationship of banking competition and stability. The system-GMM has smaller variances and it is thus more efficient, hence encouraging improvement in the precision in the estimator (Blundell and Bond, 1998). The system GMM is most suitable in conditions small T, Large N and when the dependent variable is dynamic (i.e., persistent); where control variables might correlate with the error term (i.e., control variables are not exogenous), where there is heteroscedasticity in data, which are more probable to be found in bank-level data. The two-step system GMM refines the quality of estimation while controlling for endogeneity, serial correlation, and heteroscedasticity issues.

3. Empirical Results and Discussion

3.1. *Descriptive statistics and correlation analysis*

Table 2 reports the full descriptive statistics of the variables. Starting with the stability measure, the mean zscore for the overall sample stands at 31.32. The average efficiency-adjusted Lerner index for the overall sample ranges from 0.01 to 0.94 with a mean value of 0.46. It is noted that on average, the efficiency-adjusted Lerner index is higher for conventional banks than the Islamic banks. The mean value of the traditional Lerner index stands at 0.32. The Traditional Lerner index also shows that conventional banks have higher market power in our sample. Furthermore, it is found that conventional banks (32.28) have a higher level of stability than Islamic banks (29.18). The descriptive statistic for total assets shows that conventional banks are on average bigger than the Islamic banks in our sample.

3.1.1. *Correlation analysis*

Table 3 shows the pairwise correlation of variables used in the analysis with their level of significance. The correlation coefficients range from −0.00317 to 0.83.7. The highest

Table 2. Descriptive Statistics

	z-score	Ad_Lerner	T_Lerner	lnTA	EQTA	GLTA	HHI	MS_dp	C3	Diver	Gdpgrowth	Inflation
Full Sample												
Obs	1,898	1,899	1,855	1,899	1,899	1,899	1,899	1,899	2,021	1,899	1,899	1,887
Mean	31.32	0.46	0.32	8.44	13.35	0.6	0.129	0.06	0.36	0.28	4.92	5.2
Std. Dev.	24.55	0.17	0.15	1.55	9.59	0.16	0.084	0.1	0.06	0.29	2.8	3.47
Min	−2.53	0.01	0	3.03	0.77	0	0.054	0	0.33	−0.59	−7.08	−4.86
Max	215.33	0.94	0.81	11.77	79.79	1.26	1	1	1	10.36	19.59	20.29
Conventional Banks												
Obs	1,489	1,490	1,477	1,490	1,490	1,490	1,490	1,490	1,582	1,490	1,490	1,481
Mean	32.28	0.46	0.33	8.47	13.05	0.6	0.128	0.06	0.36	0.28	4.93	5.41
Std. Dev.	25.06	0.17	0.15	1.62	8.41	0.15	0.08	0.1	0.05	0.3	2.72	3.35
Min	−2.53	0.01	0	4.28	0.77	0.01	0.054	0	0.33	−0.59	−7.08	−4.86
Max	215.33	0.94	0.8	11.77	78.97	0.93	1	1	1	10.36	19.59	20.29
Islamic Banks												
Obs	295	295	278	295	295	295	295	295	439	295	295	294
Mean	29.18	0.45	0.28	8.31	12.44	0.61	0.134	0.06	0.36	0.24	5	4.06
Std. Dev.	24.2	0.17	0.16	1.28	11.29	0.18	0.114	0.14	0.06	0.18	3.02	3.84
Min	1.43	0.02	0	3.03	2.93	0	0.054	0	0.33	−0.02	−5.24	−4.86
Max	169.12	0.91	0.81	10.63	79.79	1.26	1	1	1	1.32	19.59	20.29

Table 3. Correlation Matrix

	z-score	Ad_Lerner	T_Lerner	lnTA	EQTA	GLTA	HHI	MS_dp	C3	Diver	Gdpgrowth	Inflation
Z-score	1											
Ad_Lerner	0.139***	1										
Lerner	0.160***	0.301***	1									
lnTA	0.0925***	0.000867	0.380***	1								
EQTA	0.0743***	0.415***	0.181***	−0.315***	1							
GLTA	−0.0279	−0.0682**	0.0837***	0.180***	−0.383***	1						
HHI	0.0300	0.126***	0.305***	0.147***	0.0892***	−0.0681**	1					
MS_dp	0.0439	−0.0246	0.336***	0.460***	−0.116***	−0.0315	0.758***	1				
C3	−0.00516	−0.0575*	0.209***	0.0334	−0.0601**	0.00871	0.837***	0.702***	1			
Diver	−0.134***	0.0772***	−0.0806***	−0.0533***	0.134***	−0.249***	0.0150	−0.00317	0.0480*	1		
Gdpgrowth	0.0273	−0.0533*	−0.0734***	−0.0875***	−0.0318	0.0623***	−0.218***	−0.134***	−0.214***	−0.0238	1	
Inflation	−0.200***	−0.213***	−0.280***	−0.277***	−0.0232	0.0233	−0.177***	−0.123***	−0.122***	0.0131	0.0866***	1

Note: $^*p<0.05$, $^{**}p<0.01$, $^{***}p<0.001$.

correlation was observed among C3, the Market share of deposits (MS_dp), and the concentration (HHI). Therefore, C3, HHI, and MS_dp are put in separate model specifications while estimating the models in Tables 4 and 4. The relationship of the Z-score with the adjusted Lerner index and the traditional Lerner index turned out to be significant, suggesting the importance of competition in banking. Furthermore, it is observed that there is a weak correlation between the rest of the variables, and hence the existence of multicollinearity is rejected.

Table 4. Impact of Competition on Stability Using Traditional Lerner Index

	M1 lnzscore	M2 lnzscore	M3 lnzscore	M4 lnzscore
L.lnzscore	0.6499***	0.6635***	0.6692***	0.6689***
	[0.041]	[0.042]	[0.038]	[0.045]
T_Lerner	0.5551***	0.5141***	0.3611***	0.5590***
	[0.091]	[0.089]	[0.096]	[0.100]
lnTA	0.0747***	0.0711**	0.0400	0.1040***
	[0.028]	[0.028]	[0.025]	[0.031]
EQTA	0.0166***	0.0166***	0.0178***	0.0145***
	[0.003]	[0.003]	[0.002]	[0.003]
GLTA	0.6104***	0.7317***	0.8585***	0.4719***
	[0.107]	[0.099]	[0.095]	[0.118]
Diversification	0.2098***	0.2639***	0.2596***	0.2914***
	[0.072]	[0.075]	[0.069]	[0.088]
Gdpgrowth	0.0014	0.0026	0.0065**	−0.0021
	[0.003]	[0.003]	[0.003]	[0.003]
Inflation	−0.0012	0.0023	−0.0020	−0.0005
	[0.003]	[0.003]	[0.003]	[0.004]
Crisis	0.0173	0.0391	0.0419*	0.0320*
	[0.018]	[0.024]	[0.025]	[0.019]
HHI		0.5774*		
		[0.337]		
MS_dp			1.2977**	
			[0.538]	
C3				−1.5094**
				[0.608]
Constant	−0.3355	−0.5289*	−0.3301	0.0021
	[0.266]	[0.301]	[0.261]	[0.310]
Observations	1746	1746	1746	1746
Instruments	57.0000	65.0000	65.0000	57.0000
Groups	221.0000	221.0000	221.0000	221.0000
Arellano-Bond: AR(1)	0.0515	0.0512	0.0472	0.0520
Arellano-Bond: AR(2)	0.1497	0.1510	0.1389	0.1680
Sargan Test (p-Value)	0.5826	0.6318	0.4218	0.6275

Notes: Standard errors are in parentheses: *$p<0.1$, **$p<0.05$, ***$p<0.01$.

3.2. The impact of competition on stability

This research employs the system GMM technique. The absence of serial correlation is confirmed by the insignificant values of AR (1) and AR (2). The validity of the instruments is confirmed by an insignificant Sargan test, indicating the validation of overidentifying restrictions. This shows that the instruments used are uncorrelated with the error-term and have looked after the endogeneity and heteroscedasticity problem indicating the overall appropriateness of the model.

Estimating dynamic panel-data model in Equation (7), Tables 4 and 5 present five different model specifications showing the impact of banking Competition on stability (Zscore) using the Traditional Lerner index and Efficiency-adjusted Lerner index, respectively. The model specifications are as follows: (1) includes only banks specific variables, (2) includes Country-level characteristics in the model that are GDP growth and Inflation to the specification in the model (1). Model (3) adds the concentration measure, HHI to model (2). In Models (4) and (5), MS_dp and C3 are added to model (2), respectively.

The estimation results from Tables 4 and 5 give strong evidence that the Lerner indices are positive and are significant for all four model specifications. This shows strong evidence that competition impacts stability negatively. A higher degree of competition may result in a lower level of stability. These findings support the traditional competition-fragility view. The results are in line with the "competition-fragility" view and support the arguments of Dima et al. (2014), Forssbæck and Tanveer (2011), and Turk Ariss (2010). One of the possible explanations for this relationship can be that in high competition, banks compete to capture the market share of deposits by offering higher deposit rates. Banks also cut the lending rates to encourage lending. This can result in higher bank costs and lower bank revenues, thus resulting in a negative effect on banks' stability. Moreover, on the lending side banks also relax the lending conditions which impede the loan quality of the banks. Hence, banks further face bad debts and nonperforming loans which decreases the banks' stability through increased banks' risk.

It is important to discuss the significant control variables here. In Table 4, while using the Traditional Lerner Index, the total assets (lnTA) has a positive significant relationship in 4 out of 5 models' specifications. This indicates that with an increase in bank size, banks seem to become more resistant to risk which impacts the zscore positively. Moreover, it seems that big banks are benefiting from economies of scale. This argument is supported by the "too big to fail" argument of Mishkin (1999), where they do not easily fail even they take on more risks. LnTA shows consistent results in Table 5 in different model specifications while using the adjusted Lerner Index. With the expansion in bank size, banks enjoy economies of scale and hence better intermediation, better monitoring, and reduced rates. The capitalization ratio, EQTA, shows a positive relationship in all specifications. This implies that banks with a higher capitalization ratio tend to have relaxed conditions while extending loans or financings.[4] Banks with a higher capitalization ratio may be better

---

[4] Islamic Banks do not deal in loans, instead they finance on profit and loss sharing basis.

Table 5. Impact of Competition on Stability Using Adjusted Lerner Index

	M1 Lnzscore	M2 lnzscore	M3 lnzscore	M4 lnzscore
L.lnzscore	0.4111***	0.4006***	0.3357***	0.3220***
	[0.059]	[0.061]	[0.064]	[0.067]
Ad_Lerner	0.3371***	0.3150**	0.3952**	0.4307***
	[0.131]	[0.136]	[0.168]	[0.140]
lnTA	0.0591***	0.0557***	0.0662	0.0714***
	[0.016]	[0.017]	[0.046]	[0.018]
EQTA	0.0088***	0.0087***	0.0082***	0.0082***
	[0.003]	[0.003]	[0.003]	[0.003]
GLTA	0.1168	0.1278	0.0964	0.0786
	[0.130]	[0.131]	[0.180]	[0.141]
Diversification	−0.1725*	−0.1699*	−0.1449	−0.1455
	[0.091]	[0.091]	[0.092]	[0.100]
Gdpgrowth	0.0082**	0.0094**	0.0100**	0.0116**
	[0.004]	[0.004]	[0.004]	[0.005]
Inflation	−0.0131***	−0.0130***	−0.0109**	−0.0103**
	[0.004]	[0.004]	[0.004]	[0.004]
Crisis	0.0558**	0.0449	0.0510	0.0460
	[0.024]	[0.028]	[0.031]	[0.029]
HHI		0.5269		
		[0.754]		
MS_dp			0.1259	
			[1.459]	
C3				0.7950
				[1.573]
Constant	1.0971***	1.0955***	1.2307***	0.9370
	[0.235]	[0.236]	[0.346]	[0.604]
Observations	1782	1782	1782	1782
Instruments	18.0000	18.0000	16.0000	16.0000
Groups	227.0000	227.0000	227.0000	227.0000
AR(1)	0.0241	0.0241	0.0298	0.0281
AR(2)	0.2420	0.2512	0.2632	0.2792
Sargan (p-Value)	0.7003	0.6037	0.5670	0.6555

Note: Standard errors are in parentheses: *$p<0.1$, **$p<0.05$, ***$p<0.01$.

able to compensate for higher risks. Moreover, in Table 4, the Loan ratio (GLTA) is also seen positively significant in all regressions, which suggests that banks with higher lending operations have higher scores and are better stable. A possible reason for this relationship could be that banks with higher lending behaviors can accumulate profits, hence lending makes them more stable. HHI is positively significantly related to bank stability in Model (3). This suggests that the more concentrated the market, the more stable the banks.

This implies that concentrated banking markets are better stable (Azmi et al., 2019). Therefore, overall, it can be concluded that lower competition and high concentration levels simultaneously enhance bank stability. However, this coefficient for HHI is only significant in the case of the traditional Lerner index. For the market share of deposits (MS_dp), a positive significant relationship is found, suggesting that banks with higher deposits can use these deposits in lending and investing activities, where they can easily accumulate higher profits, enhancing stability. MS_dp does not show any significance in the case of the adjusted Lerner index. For C3, it is observed that it is not significant in the case of the adjusted Lerner index and is negatively significant in the case of the traditional Lerner index. This suggests that markets that are severely concentrated are less likely to be stable. The results for diversification are found to be contradicting in the Traditional Lerner Index and adjusted Lerner Index. Literature is also unclear about the relationship between diversification and stability. Interestingly, Crisis is found to positively significant which shows that banks in the sample managed to overcome the effects of the financial crisis and invest their equities effectively (based on a positive and significant coefficient) during the crisis period (2008–2009). This can be explained by the fact that the countries in the sample are developing countries and these countries were not much involved in causing the crisis. GDP growth is found to be positively significant as expected. For inflation, the coefficients show a consistently negative impact in most of the model specifications in Tables 4 and 5. This suggests that banks in high inflation countries are more likely to face higher risks and less stability.

3.2.1. Robustness checks

To add further credence to the main results, the baseline model is re-estimated using Pooled OLS, Random Effects, fixed effects, and Difference GMM estimators. Table 6 presents the robustness results.

The main results for the research objective are found to be strongly consistent in all estimations and are in line with the results of Tables 4 and 5. These results give strong support to the negative relationship between competition and stability regardless of Lerner indices, implying that higher competition may increase the risk of failure among banks. This is confirming the support of the traditional 'competition-fragility' view in the sample.

3.3. Impact of competition on stability for different bank types

Estimating the model in Equation (8), Table 7 confirms the overall results. It was found that the banks are experiencing a "competition-fragility" view regardless of the banking model. The interaction terms in Table 7 are observed as insignificant for both lerner indices. This indicates that the effect of competition on banking stability does not differ for both bank types.

It is evident from the results that the relationship is not different for Islamic banks. The results are in line with the findings of Nurul and Worthington (2015), who found no difference in the relationship between competition and stability for both types of banks. The study implies that more competition in the banking sector instigates the banks to take

Table 6. Robustness: Impact of Competition on Stability

	OLS lnzscore	OLS lnzscore	RE lnzscore	RE lnzscore	FE lnzscore	FE lnzscore	D-GMM lnzscore	D-GMM lnzscore
Ad_Lerner	0.1707*** (0.035)		0.1707*** (0.060)		0.1432*** (0.035)		0.1585*** (0.050)	
T_Lerner		0.4332*** (0.044)		0.4332*** (0.086)		0.4179*** (0.043)		0.4137*** (0.066)
lnTA	0.0046 (0.013)	-0.0334*** (0.012)	0.0046 (0.024)	-0.0334 (0.026)	-0.0232* (0.013)	-0.0559*** (0.012)	0.0422 (0.026)	-0.0518** (0.026)
EQTA	0.0408*** (0.001)	0.0427*** (0.001)	0.0408*** (0.004)	0.0427*** (0.005)	0.0416*** (0.001)	0.0431*** (0.001)	0.0474*** (0.004)	0.0381*** (0.006)
GLTA	0.2381*** (0.054)	0.2348*** (0.052)	0.2381*** (0.086)	0.2348*** (0.089)	0.2310*** (0.053)	0.2329*** (0.051)	0.1232 (0.079)	0.2500** (0.114)
Diversification	-0.0841*** (0.014)	-0.2097*** (0.023)	-0.0841 (0.068)	-0.2097 (0.130)	-0.0772*** (0.013)	-0.1966*** (0.023)	-0.0349 (0.025)	-0.1065 (0.107)
HHI	0.3034 (0.220)	0.2758 (0.210)	0.3034 (0.249)	0.2758 (0.245)	0.1577 (0.239)	0.1247 (0.226)	0.7696 (0.549)	-0.3524 (0.975)
Gdpgrowth	-0.0000 (0.002)	-0.0005 (0.002)	-0.0000 (0.002)	-0.0005 (0.002)	-0.0008 (0.002)	-0.0011 (0.002)	-0.0072** (0.003)	-0.0013 (0.006)
Inflation	0.0017 (0.002)	0.0009 (0.002)	0.0017 (0.002)	0.0009 (0.002)	0.0014 (0.002)	0.0008 (0.002)	0.0059*** (0.002)	-0.0040 (0.007)

Table 6. (Continued)

	OLS	OLS	RE	RE	FE	FE	D-GMM	D-GMM
	lnzscore	lnzscore	lnzscore	lnzscore	lnzscore	lnzscore	lnzscore	lnzscore
Crisis	-0.0304**	-0.0438***	-0.0304*	-0.0438***	-0.0406***	-0.0521***	-0.0515***	-0.0208
	(0.014)	(0.013)	(0.016)	(0.015)	(0.014)	(0.013)	(0.018)	(0.031)
L.lnzscore							0.1217***	0.2795**
							(0.041)	(0.136)
Constant	2.2730***	2.5997***	2.2730***	2.5997***	2.5865***	2.8527***		
	(0.136)	(0.125)	(0.257)	(0.285)	(0.138)	(0.123)		
Observations	2000	1955	2000	1955	2000	1955	1555	1525
Instruments							31.0000	14.0000
Groups	227.0000	221.0000	227.0000	221.0000	227.0000	221.0000	225.0000	219.0000
Arellano-Bond: AR(1)							0.0929	0.0567
Arellano-Bond: AR(2)							0.1369	0.1220
Sargan Test (p-Value)							0.1000	0.1581

Note: Standard errors are in parentheses: *$p<0.1$, **$p<0.05$, ***$p<0.01$.

Table 7. Impact of Competition on Stability for Different Bank Types

	M1 lnzscore	M2 lnzscore
L.lnzscore	0.4102***	0.4860***
	[0.053]	[0.074]
Ad_Lerner	0.4010**	
	[0.165]	
T_Lerner		0.9838***
		[0.179]
Islamic	0.1741	0.1083
	[0.128]	[0.173]
Islamic*Ad_Lerner	−0.2427	
	[0.195]	
Islamic *T_Lerner		−0.3106
		[0.331]
lnTA	0.0608***	0.0108
	[0.017]	[0.017]
Equity/Total Assets	0.0092***	0.0097***
	[0.003]	[0.003]
GLTA	0.0642	−0.0629
	[0.125]	[0.128]
Diversification	−0.2169**	−0.3818***
	[0.085]	[0.106]
HHI	−0.1861	−0.6373
	[0.422]	[0.397]
gdpgrowth	0.0091***	0.0049
	[0.003]	[0.003]
Inflation	−0.0135***	−0.0120***
	[0.004]	[0.003]
Crisis	0.0656***	0.0430*
	[0.025]	[0.025]
Constant	1.1074***	1.3732***
	[0.242]	[0.238]
Observations	1782	1746
Instruments	27.0000	27.0000
Groups	227.0000	221.0000
Arellano-Bond: AR(1)	0.0207	0.0371
Arellano-Bond: AR(2)	0.2656	0.1793
Sargan Test (p-Value)	0.7745	0.6993

Note: Standard errors are in parentheses: *$p<0.1$, **$p<0.05$, ***$p<0.01$.

Table 8. Robustness Check with Split Samples

	M1 Conventional Banks lnzscore	M2 Conventional Banks lnzscore	M3 Islamic Banks lnzscore	M4 Islamic Banks lnzscore	M5 Conventional Banks lnzscore	M6 Conventional Banks lnzscore	M7 Islamic Banks lnzscore	M8 Islamic Banks lnzscore
L.lnzscore	0.1559* (0.085)	0.0440 (0.053)	0.0924*** (0.018)	0.2512*** (0.022)	0.2892*** (0.067)	0.5598*** (0.111)	0.5055*** (0.085)	0.6937*** (0.116)
Ad_Lerner	0.2803** (0.116)		0.0756*** (0.015)		0.4321** (0.202)		0.1016* (0.056)	
T_Lerner		1.2519*** (0.330)		0.3791*** (0.062)		0.4832** (0.226)		0.5743** (0.272)
lnTA	0.0236 (0.039)	-0.0651 (0.048)	-0.0779*** (0.016)	0.0100 (0.011)	0.0672*** (0.020)	0.0158 (0.013)	0.1795*** (0.053)	0.0080 (0.025)
EQTA	0.0311*** (0.003)	0.0324*** (0.003)	0.0376*** (0.001)	0.0528*** (0.001)	0.0141*** (0.005)	0.0158*** (0.003)	0.0397*** (0.004)	-0.0003 (0.003)
GLTA	0.5849*** (0.170)	0.2479 (0.259)	0.1189*** (0.022)	0.1511*** (0.056)	0.0258 (0.174)	-0.0122 (0.114)	0.4232*** (0.151)	0.0270 (0.185)
Diversification	0.0426 (0.046)	-0.4785*** (0.176)	0.1155*** (0.014)	0.0048 (0.010)	-0.2416** (0.106)	-0.5190*** (0.148)	-0.2621*** (0.056)	0.0078 (0.051)
HHI	0.5020 (0.815)	10.0434*** (3.085)	1.4836*** (0.308)	0.1091 (0.205)	0.7393 (0.855)	0.4095 (0.841)	-4.5153*** (1.365)	-1.6500 (1.222)
gdpgrowth	-0.0029 (0.002)	-0.0100** (0.004)	-0.0021 (0.002)	-0.0030** (0.001)	0.0098* (0.006)	0.0060 (0.006)	-0.0018 (0.011)	-0.0045 (0.006)
Inflation	0.0020 (0.003)	0.0096** (0.004)	0.0018** (0.001)	0.0005 (0.002)	-0.0165*** (0.005)	-0.0068* (0.004)	-0.0005 (0.010)	-0.0080* (0.005)

Table 8. (Continued)

	M1	M2	M3	M4	M5	M6	M7	M8
	Conventional Banks lnzscore	Conventional Banks lnzscore	Islamic Banks lnzscore	Islamic Banks lnzscore	Conventional Banks lnzscore	Conventional Banks lnzscore	Islamic Banks lnzscore	Islamic Banks lnzscore
Crisis	−0.0388	−0.3956***	−0.1095***	−0.0461***	0.0304	0.0043	0.0047	−0.0936
	(0.024)	(0.099)	(0.042)	(0.012)	(0.037)	(0.046)	(0.354)	(0.081)
Constant					1.3333***	1.0281***	−0.2491	0.9493**
					(0.308)	(0.305)	(0.458)	(0.372)
	DGMM	D-GMM	D-GMM	D-GMM	S-GMM	S-GMM	S-GMM	S-GMM
Observations	1226	1211	329	313	1398	1381	384	365
Instruments	55.0000	14.0000	54.0000	36.0000	17.0000	24.0000	32.0000	24.0000
Groups	171.0000	169.0000	54.0000	49.0000	172.0000	170.0000	55.0000	51.0000
Arellano–Bond: AR(1)	0.0000	0.0000	0.0575	0.0250	0.0432	0.0592	0.0260	0.0009
Arellano–Bond: AR(2)	0.1767	0.2240	0.8575	0.2734	0.3533	0.1833	0.1340	0.1453
Sargan Test (p-Value)	0.5069	0.6947	0.9940	0.7225	0.9023	0.2039	0.9293	0.6108

Note: Standard errors are in parentheses: $^*p<0.1$, $^{**}p<0.05$, $^{***}p<0.01$.

on more risk, thus encouraging fragility, and banks might be investing in riskier portfolios to overcome the effects of the decline in margins, returns, and most importantly to maintain the market power. It further suggests that the business structure of Islamic and conventional banks might not be different much from each other.

3.3.1. Robustness check

To add credence to baseline results for the difference in the relationship between competition and stability for conventional banks and Islamic banks, a variety of robustness checks are performed. The sample is split into two subsamples, Islamic banks, and conventional banks, and the baseline model (model specification in M3 Tables 3 and 4) is re-estimated using differenced GMM and system GMM, estimator. In Table 8, models 1–4 are estimated using difference GMM, and models 5–8 are estimated using System GMM. The coefficients of Lerner indices are found to be positively significant in all estimations, suggesting that the impact of competition on stability is the same for both banking models. In other words, an increase in competition can lead to more risks in both banking models. Provided the main results for the relationship in different bank types and the robustness, it is evident that higher competition leads to higher risk-taking of banks which results in lower banking sector stability regardless of bank type.

4. Conclusion

This research attempts to explore the competition and level of stability within the dual banking system using an efficiency-adjusted Lerner Index, a more accurate measure of market power along with the traditional Lerner Index. The research investigates the relationship between competition and stability in 11 dual banking economies for the period of 2007–2017. Conventional banks are found to be more stable as compared to Islamic banks. In terms of market power (inverse of competition), it was found that Islamic banks have lower market power than conventional banks. The findings indicate that increased competition increases the probability of bank failure. This is found supporting the traditional 'competition-fragility' view in the literature. Addressing the possible difference in the relationship between competition and stability in different bank types, results suggest that competition in the market impacts both banks type the same way, making banks relax the lending conditions and lower the rates, thus jeopardizing banks' stability. The results are consistent regardless of estimation techniques, Lerner indices, or bank types, and 'competition-fragility view' is found to be prevailing in both bank types.

It is important to differentiate the measures of concentration and competition. Also, the results disapprove of the widespread understanding that Islamic banks are more stable and more resilient to adverse shocks in the financial crisis. These results also suggest to further enhance the stability implications of Islamic banks and policymakers should focus on improved regulation. These findings suggest that competition in the sampling countries should be well-regulated. Since the evidence from this research suggests no difference in the relationship between Islamic banks and conventional banks, a uniform competition strategy can be formed to govern both banking models within the sampling countries.

Based on these findings, regulators and policymakers can use different strategies to stabilize the market. One of the possibilities can be mergers. Regulators and policymakers are suggested to support and facilitate the mergers of S&M sized banks. Small banks merging with big banks can lead to a better stable and well-performing banking sector. However, to have controlled concentration in the market, the regulators need to be careful while endorsing the mergers.

References

Abojeib, MM (2017). *Competition–Stability Relationship in Dual Banking Systems Islamic vs. Conventional Banks* [INCEIF].

Amidu, M and S Wolfe (2013). Does bank competition and diversification lead to greater stability? Evidence from emerging markets. *Review of Development Finance*, 3(3), 152–166.

Arellano, M and S Bond (1991). Some tests of specification for panel data: Monte Carlo evidence and an application to employment equations. *The Review of Economic Studies*, 58(2), 277. https://doi.org/10.2307/2297968.

Arellano, M and O Bover (1995). Another look at the instrumental variable estimation of error-components models. *Journal of Econometrics*, 68(1), 29–51.

Azmi, W, M Ali, S Arshad and SAR Rizvi (2019). Intricacies of competition, stability, and diversification: Evidence from dual banking economies. *Economic Modelling*, 83, 111–126.

Battese, GE and TJ Coelli (1995). A model for technical inefficiency effects in a stochastic frontier production function for panel data. *Empirical Economics*, 20, 325–332.

Beck, T, O De Jonghe and G Schepens (2013). Bank competition and stability: Cross-country heterogeneity. *Journal of Financial Intermediation*, 22(2), 218–244.

Berger, AN, LF Klapper and R Turk-Ariss (2009). Bank competition and financial stability. *Journal of Financial Services Research*, 35(2), 99–118.

Blundell, R and S Bond (1998). Initial conditions and moment restrictions in dynamic panel data models. *Journal of Econometrics*, 87(1), 115–143.

Bos, JWB and M Koetter (2009). Handling losses in translog profit models. *Applied Economics*, 43(3), 307.

Boyd, JH and G De Nicolo (2005). The Theory of Bank Risk Taking and Competition Revisited. *The Journal of Finance*, LX(3), 1329–1343.

Čihák, M and H Hesse (2010). Islamic Banks and Financial Stability: An Empirical Analysis. *Journal of Financial Services Research*, 38, 95–113.

Clerides, S, MD Delis and S Kokas (2015). A new data set on competition in national banking markets. *Financial Markets, Institutions and Instruments*, 24(2–3), 267–311.

Demirgüç-Kunt, A and E Detragiache (2009). Basel core principles and bank soundness, does compliance matter? *Policy Research Working Paper*, November.

Deyoung, R and KP Roland (2001). Product mix and earnings volatility at commercial banks: Evidence from a degree of total leverage model. *Journal of Financial Intermediation*, 10(1), 54–84.

Dima, B, MS Dincă and C Spulbăr (2014). Financial nexus: Efficiency and soundness in banking and capital markets. *Journal of International Money and Finance*, 47, 100–124.

Forssbæck, J and C Tanveer (2011). Competition and bank risk-taking — an empirical study. Available at SSRN 1929112.

Fu, X (Maggie), Y Lin (Rebecca) and P Molyneux (2014). Bank competition and financial stability in Asia Pacific. *Journal of Banking and Finance*, 38(1), 64–77.

Islamic Financial Services Board. (2019). Islamic financial services industry stability report.

IJtsma, P, L Spierdijk and S Shaffer (2017). The concentration–stability controversy in banking: New evidence from the EU-25. *Journal of Financial Stability*, 33, 273–284.

Kabir, MN and AC Worthington (2017). The 'competition–stability/fragility' nexus: A comparative analysis of Islamic and conventional banks. *International Review of Financial Analysis*, 50, 111–128.

Kasman, S and A Kasman (2015). Bank competition, concentration and financial stability in the Turkish banking industry. *Economic Systems*, 39(3), 502–517.

Keeley, MC (1990). Deposit insurance, risk, and market power in banking. *American Economic Review*, 80(5), 1183–1200.

Koetter, M, JW Kolari and L Spierdijk (2012). Enjoying the quiet life under deregulation? Evidence from adjusted lerner indices for U.S. banks. *Review of Economics and Statistics*, 94(2), 462–480.

Maharani, NK and B Setiyono (2018). Do risk, business cycle, and competition affect capital buffer? An empirical study on islamic banking in ASEAN and MENA. *Journal of Islamic Monetary Economics and Finance*, 3(2), 181–200.

Mishkin, FS (1999). Financial consolidation: Dangers and opportunities. *Journal of Banking and Finance*, 23(2), 675–691.

Moudud-Ul-Huq, S (2019). Banks' capital buffers, risk, and efficiency in emerging economies: Are they counter-cyclical? *Eurasian Economic Review*, 9(4), 467–492.

Nurul, K and AC Worthington (2015). The 'competition–stability nexus': Is efficiency an appropriate channel? *Griffith Business School Discussion Papers Finance*, *1836*-(February 2016).

Phan, HT, S Anwar, WRJ Alexander and HTM Phan (2019). Competition, efficiency and stability: An empirical study of east Asian commercial banks. *North American Journal of Economics and Finance*, 50, 100990.

Rahim, A, A Rahman and R Rosman (2013). Efficiency of Islamic banks: A comparative analysis of MENA and Asian countries. *Journal of Economic Cooperation and Development*, 34(1).

Rashid, A, S Yousaf and M Khaleequzzaman (2017). Does Islamic banking really strengthen financial stability? Empirical evidence from Pakistan. *International Journal of Islamic and Middle Eastern Finance and Management*, 10(2), 130–148.

Rizvi, SAR, PK Narayan, A Sakti and F Syarifuddin (2019). Role of Islamic banks in Indonesian banking industry: An empirical exploration. *Pacific Basin Finance Journal*, 62, 101117.

Turk Ariss, R (2010). On the implications of market power in banking: Evidence from developing countries. *Journal of Banking and Finance*, 34(4), 765–775.

Weill, L (2011). Do Islamic banks have greater market power? *Comparative Economic Studies*, 53(2), 291–306.

Chapter 4

Shari'ah Oriented Precious Metal Backed Cryptocurrency: From *Shari'ah* Advisors' and Financial Experts' Perceptions[#]

Mousa Ajouz[*,§], Adam Abdullah[†,¶] and Salina Kassim[‡,||]

*College of Administrative Sciences and Informatics
Palestine Polytechnic University, Hebron, Palestine*

†*College of Economics and Management
Al-Qasimia University, Sharjah, UAE*

‡*Institute of Islamic Banking and Finance, IIUM, Malaysia*
§*mousa-ajouz@hotmail.com*
¶*aabdullah@alqasimia.ac.ae*
||*ksalina@iium.edu.my*

The suitability of assets-backed money has been the subject of considerable debate, although hampered in part by lack of theoretical and empirical evidence. Therefore, the motivation of this research is to investigate the perceptions of *Shari'ah* scholars and financial experts on the concepts and salient features of *Shari'ah*-compliant precious metal backed crypto-currency (PMC). To achieve this, this study adopted a qualitative method using semi-structured interview based on saturation technique. The results from *Shari'ah* advisors and financial experts indicated that the informants have differences of views on the assets-backed money, but they agreed that it ensures stability of money and adding the cryptocurrency technology is found to be desirable and recommendable. It is also found that PMC would be subjected to financial regulation challenges and using blockchain technology will increase the transparency. The informants agreed that PMC is closer to *Maqāsid al-Shari'ah* and there is some form of justice and equality compared to the current interest-based financial system. Therefore, the informants recommended the implementation of PMC.

Keywords: *Shari'ah* oriented; precious metal; cryptocurrency; perceptions.

1. Introduction

Money in whatever form is the common denominator to all modern economic transactions and undoubtedly remains a cardinal and common issue of discussion in Islamic economics and finance academic community discourses and beyond. However, how we define money has changed, and the issue of what money is, and what money should be, has become a controversial issue among scholars and economists. This discussion re-appears every time when a new concept of currency emerges. Much of the discussion focuses on the

---

§ Corresponding author.
# This Chapter first appeared in the *Singapore Economic Review*, Vol. 67, No. 1, doi: 10.1142/S0217590819420086. © 2022 World Scientific Publishing.

limitations of unbacked money or fiat money, which typically questions the viability of any new monetary system. For instance, Meera (2004:107) and Abdullah (2015:207, 2016b:14) argued that commodity money would ensure a long-term stability and justice in monetary system, eliminating monetary inflation, enhancing transparency and reducing some socio-economic problems, especially if the commodity is gold and silver (Meera, 2002:59; Meera and Larbani, 2006b; Bezemer, 2014). Nevertheless, Cizakca (2010:8) and Hasan (2008:12–13) claimed that the history of commodity money confirms its failure to curb inflation. But there is an inconsistency with this argument where the available empirical evidence reveals the exact opposite. (see Bordo, 2005:404; Abdullah, 2016b). However, several issues have arisen pertaining to the practice of fiat money to the extent that critiques have suggested to replicate precious metal electronically as an alternative to current interest-based monetary system, especially after the emergence of cryptocurrency.

Physical precious metal is argued to be an inefficient medium of exchange but an efficient store of value while cryptocurrency is found to be the efficient medium of exchange but inefficient store of value (Kiviat, 2015:582–585). Therefore, the advantages of cryptocurrency and precious metal are combined to introduce efficient medium of exchange and a store of value mechanism. However, there are issues which have not been capitalized or investigated from the perspective of *Shari'ah* advisors' and financial experts on concepts and salient features of precious metal backed cryptocurrency. Therefore, the aim of this research is to investigate *Shari'ah* advisors' and financial experts' perceptions on the concepts and salient features of precious metal backed cryptocurrency with regards to the usage of concepts, operation methods, *Shari'ah*-compliant, justice and equality and informants' preference.

2. Literature Review

2.1. *A primer on precious metal backed cryptocurrency*

Money today is no longer backed by any assets, on the contrary, it is backed by nothing, or even worse it is backed by debt obligation (Meera and Larbani, 2006b:18). The implication of such system is an excess of money supply as a result of aggregate deposit and loan interest in relation to demand. The effect is a decline in the value of money which leads to an exponential increase in prices over long term (Meera, 2002:57; Abdullah, 2015:205). These limitations have derived the development of alternative methods to transfer value that decentralized, trust less currency, not reliant on central authorities (Maurer *et al.*, 2013:265; Mullan, 2014:94). Therefore, Satoshi Nakamoto in 2009 introduced the world first cryptocurrency, Bitcoin (Nakamoto, 2008). However, even cryptocurrencies were not free from limitations, and were favorite targets for speculators, manipulators and illegal businesses, which led to significant fluctuations in its value (Janze, 2017; Corradi and Höfner, 2018:195–199). In addition, many *Shari'ah* issues also have been raised against cryptocurrencies and some countries have even prohibited them (Al-Qaradaghi, 2018:4; Islamic Economy Forum, 2018:25).

Meanwhile, the opposite of unbacked money is, of course, real money, money that has intrinsic value which cannot be created out of thin air like fiat money and cryptocurrencies (Meera and Larbani, 2006a:86). Precious metal has always preserved its value, as proven by history, which remained stable and trusted by economy (Abdullah, 2016b:40). Precious metal would be able to be a trustworthy store of value, which qualifies precious metal to reliably perform as a medium of exchange, a standard of deferred payment and a common measure of value. However, physical precious metal is argued to be the inefficient medium of exchange but the efficient store of value while cryptocurrency is found to be the efficient medium of exchange but inefficient store of value (Kiviat, 2015:582–585). Therefore, the advantages of cryptocurrency and precious metal were combined to introduce precious metal backed cryptocurrency (PMC). So far, there are more than 62 gold-backed cryptocurrency companies in operation (James, 2019). Interestingly, some of these companies are approved as *Shari'ah*-compliant such as HelloGold and OneGram Coin (HelloGold, 2018; OneGram, 2018). However, to the best of the author's knowledge there is no reliable resource that investigated in these cryptocurrencies.

The idea of PMC is simply an electronic representation of physical precious metal held offline in a secure vault, while users are circulating the encrypted electronic units. Fundamentally, it seeks to offer secure and efficient online methods to buy, sale, hold, earn, spend, send and redeem gold and silver (GoldMoney, 2017). The PMC value is always linked to the daily spot prices of gold and silver. Consequently, the value of PMC as expressed in terms of national currency will fluctuate on the basis of changing spot prices of gold and silver. However, users are always able to cash-out their PMC by converting it to national currency or redeem the physical gold and silver at the company itself or at any third-party exchange agent (Mullan, 2016:18,198).

It suffices to note here that in the crypto world, the blockchain ledger records every transaction from beginning to end, whether it is thousands of transactions or a single transaction, as each transaction occurs, it is recorded in blocks, and each block is linked to the previous and next block. The blockchain ledger keeps a record of every touchpoint along precious metal journey. It can track a precious metal path from mining till users or consumers hands with transparency and exceptional security. It holds certificate of authenticity, real-time records of every payment transaction as well as products details such as karat and serial numbers. That made blockchain ideal for recording the mining, refining and distribution of precious metal (Dorothal, 2017).

However, numerous theoretical studies have emerged to investigate some aspects with regard to gold and silver. In general, these studies aim in terms of their main approaches to argue for commodity moneys, like gold and silver (Meera and Larbani, 2006b; Shapiee and Zahid, 2010; Yaacob, 2012; Abdullah, 2016b). Meera (2002:92) for example proposed the usage of electronic gold at domestic transactions. Further, Meera (2004:95) suggested to implement gold in bilateral trade. Muhayiddin *et al.* (2015:125); Muhayiddin (2011:295) encouraged the usage of electronic gold dinar especially for traveling. Similarly, Omerčević (2013:17) recommended the introduction of monetary model which is built on a commodity-based information system. Although some studies have been carried out on commodity moneys, there have not been empirical investigations on *Shari'ah* advisors' and financial experts' perceptions on commodity moneys in general and on PMC in particular. Therefore, the main objective of this research is to fill up this gap.

2.2. Islamic monetary theory of value

The early Muslim Scholars emphasize that money is an instrument of transfer only (Including but not limited to Imam *Al-Gazali*, Al-Maqrīzī and *Ibn Khaldun*) (Abdullah, 2016b:244), while contemporary Islamic experts in economic and *Shari'ah* scholars appear to have implicitly accepted the current interest-based fiat monetary system although with some reservations (Jaffar *et al.*, 2017:247). On the other hand, conventional economists re-defined money as a commodity that come at a price (Abdullah, 2016b:244; Haneef and Barakat, 2006:22).

Over the years, the consequences of the absence of assets-backed money has risen which preoccupied the economists either by neoclassical or Keynesian theories. The contemporary monetary theories attempt to solve the consequences of the problem (inflation) instead of focusing on the problem itself which is the absence of assets-backed money. Thus, Keynesian focused on managing money supply by targeting interest rate, while, neoclassical focused on managing money supply by targeting quantity of money; however, both have failed in achieving economic security and stability in currency value (Abdullah, 2015:212).

Therefore, the Islamic Monetary Theory of Value (IMTV) developed by Abdullah (2016a:16, 2016b:237) will be adopted in this research. The IMTV highlighted the importance of restoring precious metal money or real money, to ensure a stable measure and store of value, a stable standard of deferred payment which would involve a stable medium of exchange that would be trusted at domestic and international level (Abdullah, 2016b:242). According to Abdullah (2015:207), in order to obtain a price stability, monetary authorities should pay attention to a stable value of money rather than focusing on the quantity of money, or interest rate, or even target prices. Abdullah empirically established that a high value currency (the cause) meant low prices (the effect) over the long term, or a low value currency (such as fiat money) would involve high prices. However, the IMTV appear to have ignored the practical means of restoring precious metal money or real money, but by one way or another this theory is supporting the philosophical framework that envisages the restoration of precious metal backed money.

2.2.1. Concept of precious metal backed cryptocurrency

Over the years, the monetary standards have diversified where the medium of exchange migrated from precious metal backed money *"as an assets of the public"* to fiat money backed by debt obligation *"as an assets of the banks"* which is *"debt organized into currency"* (Abdullah, 2016b:39; Carroll, 1964:100). In conventional theory of money, the intrinsic value matter is not a necessary attribute of money, where money can be anything. This position is supported by some modern *Shari'ah* scholars and financial experts (Jaffar *et al.*, 2017:247; Haneef and Barakat, 2006:31).

Meanwhile, asset-backed money is money backed by something tangible or valuable — generally a precious metal such as gold and silver. Imam Al-Gazali and Ibn Khaldun observed that only gold and silver as a reflection of the value of goods and services can play the role of medium of exchange (Abdullah, 2016b:240). As a result, the value and function of money in Islamic theory of money are different from conventional theory. The theory of money in Islam, rests upon the theory of value which asserts the intrinsic value of money. As stated in IMTV, the unit of account must have value or backed by real value such as precious metal to fulfill the role of money (Abdullah, 2016b:237). Accordingly, Muslim scholars were unanimous on the intrinsic value of money and several studies were carried out by Abdullah (2015, 2016); Cronin and Dowd (2001); Kiyotaki and Wright (1993) also emphasized on the intrinsic value.

However, a complete restoration of physical precious metal money once again may not be a feasible and viable course of action, but by benefiting from current technology, the concept of PMC would be much viable alternative than fiat money. Therefore, based on this reasoning, the following question is proposed:

Q1: How do *Shari'ah* advisors and financial experts perceive the concept of assets-backed money and PMC?

2.2.2. Operation methods

2.2.2.1. Financial regulations of precious metal backed cryptocurrency

Financial regulations in case of money stand for laws, rules or other orders implemented by relevant authorities, to supervise and regulate the financial institutions, payment mechanisms and other relevant entities. Nowadays, such regulations significantly affect the implementation of any monetary regime. In case of fiat money, central banks are the sole issuing authority of national currency (bank notes and coins). These central banks are responsible for declaring what type of money can be used and which one is legal tender (Hülsmann, 2004:33; Lietaer, 2013:69).

IMF in 1978 placed an embargo on the usage of gold as a currency; meanwhile, gold and silver became commodities that are traded freely in the market (Schwartz, 1987:370). However, there is no such embargo on silver (Yusuf *et al.*, 2013:101). This means the legal framework is not treating precious metal money as a currency, it is a commodity (Mullan, 2016:74). Therefore, most of the previous experiences in digital precious metal were operating through companies' framework, and the main functions they performed were facilitating payments and receiving deposit (Mullan, 2016:133). It is questionable if PMC can operate by following current financial regulations and what functions the operator should perform. Accordingly, the following question is proposed:

Q2: How do *Shari'ah* advisors and financial experts perceive effective financial regulations that govern PMC?

2.2.2.2. Payment and settlement in precious metal backed cryptocurrency

In some arrangements, payment in fiat money is done by transferring the value using fiat money which has no intrinsic value. If users have no money, the bank would create money for them using the loans means. For example, in credit card system when the card issuer verifies the information received, at this point if there is no sufficient fund in the cardholder account, the bank will create a matching deposit based on user credit efficiency; if the card holder has no credit efficiency, then the card issuer declines the transaction (Meera, 2002:15).

On the other hand, since PMC would be operated in a dual system, payment to other account holders in the system could be concluded using national currency or weight in metal at online platform. The user could pay in grams of precious metal (gold and/or silver) or same value in national currency which is similar to E-gold and GoldMoney experience (Mullan, 2016:28; GoldMoney, 2017). In addition, PMC would permit online micropayment as minor as 0.0001 g. This characteristic makes payment highly divisible and creates a practical micropayment system (Mullan, 2016:25). Thus, the system is built based on advance payment or debit concept, where the system confers the users the right to withdraw and circulate money up to the available amount in his account, this means the mechanism will not provide loans or credits for account holders (AAOIF, 2017:71). Thus, the payment and settlement in PMC and fiat money seem to be different in many ways. Accordingly, the following question is proposed:

Q3: How do *Shari'ah* advisors and financial experts perceive the payment and settlement method of PMC?

2.2.2.3. Transparency and auditing

Transparency in PMC is an essential factor since the system is built based on blockchain technology. The blockchain technology has created a network of different ledger systems, fortified to errors, misinterpretation and fraud that made blockchain ideal for recording the mining, refining and distribution of precious metal (Dorothal, 2017). In addition to the use of blockchain, a third-party financial auditing is also required. Financial auditing is the process of checking the accuracy of transactions and stocks of precious metal recorded; thus, monitors that all cryptocurrency issues are always equal or less than physical precious metal stored, and then provide this information in official reports. Since PMC is a *Shari'ah* — compliant mechanism, *Shari'ah* auditing also requires *Shari'ah* examination. This examination contains articles of association, policies, reports, financial statements, agreements, contracts, products, transactions, circulars, etc (AAOIF, 2015:1043).

In conclusion, the transparency of the current interest-based fiat monetary system is questioned. The interventions and manipulations in monetary system affect the value of money and the purchasing power of money, which led to eroding trust in the system (Abdullah, 2016b:252). Meanwhile, any monetary system should be more transparent and less vulnerable to interference in order to ensure a stable currency which in turn implies a stable purchasing power and thus a stable price as stated in the IMTV (Abdullah, 2016b:243). Hence, the following question is proposed:

Q4: How do *Shari'ah* advisors and financial experts perceive the transparency and auditing of PMC?

2.2.3. Is PMC a Shari'ah-compliant?

Shari'ah-compliant money is an instrument of transfer that completely satisfies the function of money in Islam, as a measure of value or unit of account (Abdullah, 2016b:76). The classical theory of money in Islam was solidly agreed by *Shari'ah* scholars as the coinage theory which rests upon the theory of value in the form of *Dinar* and *Dirham*. Such a theory has prevented any financial intermediation or government intervention, except to preserve the coinage quality, allowing the free adjustment of money value in terms of demand and supply (Abdullah, 2016b:72).

Islamic economic system is basically a "barter system", where the exchange would accrue when the value is exchanged; value for value. Money must have a counter-value (*'Iwad*) that inherently reflects intrinsic value to protect both exchange parties by protecting their wealth (*Māl*) as one of *Maqāsid al-Shari'ah* (Meera and Larbani, 2006a:84). Therefore, *Imam al-Ghazali* observed that "a counterfeit coin is one, which has got nothing of gold and silver (value). The coin in which there is something of gold and silver cannot be called counterfeit" (Al-Ghazali, 2004, 2:58). However, to safeguard *Maqāsid al-Shari'ah* and achieve the utility (*Maslahah*), value must be restored to money. Ibn Khaldun and his student *Al-Maqrizi*, clearly confirmed that the only Islamic currency in the form of gold and silver satisfies the *Maqāsid al-Shari'ah* in terms of wealth protection (*Māl*); meanwhile, interest-based fiat monetary system is not operating in the interest of public (*Maslahah*), but is clearly harmful to the public (*Mafsadah*) (Abdullah, 2016b:251).

In contrast to this, Hasan (2011:94) argues that fiat money derives its value from the general acceptability, not from the value of what it is made of, and it is recognized as a medium of exchange in *Shari'ah*. This view is supported by Haneef and Barakat (2006:22); Jaffar (2017:260) who found that the written literature of Islamic economic since the 1970s appears to have verifiably acknowledged the current fiat monetary system. Muslims scholars are aware that there would be ramifications for using something as medium of exchange other than what the *Shari'ah* intended (Abdullah, 2016b:77). However, commodity money was argued for being compatible with *Maqāsid al-Shari'ah* for its ability to protect wealth (*Māl*); meanwhile, fiat money for being counterproductive to *Maqāsid* (Meera and Larbani, 2006a:93, 2006b:30; Shapiee and Zahid, 2010:768). Hence, the following question is proposed:

Q5: How do *Shari'ah* advisors and financial experts perceive the *Shari'ah*-compliance of PMC?

2.2.4. Ensuring justice and equality

Islamic law tremendously emphasized various sources in Quran and Sunnah on justice, making it the corner stone of the *Shari'ah* (Abdul Razak, 2011:72). According to Kamali (2008:30) "achieving justice is one of the purposes of the *Shari'ah* which enables the establishment of equality by way of fulfilling rights and obligations through eliminating excess and disparity in all spheres of life". Hence, in order to achieve justice in contracts of exchange (*Uqud Al-Mu'awadat*), *Shari'ah* requires the transaction to be free from usury (*Riba*), uncertainty (*Gharar*), injustice and consuming wealth unjustly (CIBAFI, 2012:33–40).

According to the IMTV, injustice and transfer of wealth unjustly is deeply entrenched in the current interest-based financial system due to extensive, yet illusory expansion of currency issuance, which results in confiscation of wealth through inflation (Abdullah, 2016b:243). Alan Greenspan before he was appointed as a chairman of the Federal reserve asserted that: "There is no way to protect saving from confiscation through inflation. There is no safe store of value… Deficit spending is simply a scheme for the confiscation of wealth. Gold (or silver) stands in the way of this insidious process. It stands as protector of property rights" (Greenspan, 1966). In other words, in current interest-based fiat monetary system wealth is transferred and confiscated to the profit-and-loss statement of the private banking system (Abdullah, 2016b:243).

Other researchers, who have looked at fiat money from Islamic perspective, have found the incompliance of fiat money with *Shari'ah* law, Meera and Larbani, (2006b:17) for example, concluded that fiat money prevents the realization of *Maqāsid al-Shari'ah*. Shapiee and Zahid, (2010:768) argued that fiat money is inherently including usury (*Riba*) and *Gharar*, all of which bring about economic injustices. This view is also supported by Usmani (1999).

On the contrary, the alternative of fiat money is assets-backed money which has special qualities that cannot be created like fiat money (Meera and Larbani, 2006a:86). Restoring precious metal backed money is the main objective of PMC which ensures a long-term stability in monetary system, excellent medium of exchange, justice in monetary system, enhances transparency and reduces some socio-economic problems (Meera, 2002:57). In view of the foregoing, the following question is asked:

Q6: How do *Shari'ah* advisors and financial experts perceive the justice and equality of PMC?

2.2.5. Shari'ah advisors' and financial experts' preference

Based on the foregoing discussion, there are many features of precious metal over fiat money as stated in the IMTV (Abdullah, 2016b). PMC is money backed by real assets that has intrinsic value (Meera and Larbani, 2006a:86). PMC also deemed to be *Shari'ah* oriented money that is free from element of injustice. In addition, implementing PMC would ensure a long-run stability in monetary system, excellent medium of exchange, justice in monetary system, enhance transparency and reduce some socio-economic problems (Meera, 2002:57). Based on the features of the PMC over fiat money, there is a need to investigate *Shari'ah* advisors' and financial experts' (informants[1]) preference with regards to PMC by asking the last question:

Q7: Would *Shari'ah* advisors and financial experts support and recommend the implementation of PMC as a viable alternative payment mechanism?

---

[1] From here on the term informants will be used to express *Shari'ah* advisors and financial experts

3. Methodology

In this research, the *Shari'ah* advisors and financial experts from Malaysia have been identified as the primary target informants. The selection of the informants is based on judgement sampling where the selection criteria are based on their qualifications, area of specialization and working experience, this criterion is somehow similar to Abdul Razak (2011:132). Choosing the adequacy sample size in qualitative research is a controversial and important issue. However, since the objective of this study is only to gauge the opinions of the informants, saturation approach was adopted for determining the sample size (Charmaz, 2014:189).

A personal or face-to-face in-depth interview are employed, which has a variety of advantageous such as clarifying the questions, clear doubts, generating new questions and rich data can be obtained (Sekaran and Bougie, 2013:126). The research instrument for the informants is structured based on semi-structured theme. The interview consists of three sections. It begins with demographic information, followed by section (B) that explains and clarifies PMC. Lastly, section (C) contains questions concerning the concepts and salient features of PMC with regard to usage of concepts, operation methods, *Shari'ah*-compliance, justice and equality and informants' preference. The validity of interview questions was carried out by conducting face and content validity (Creswell, 2014:259).

4. Results and Discussions

As mentioned earlier, saturation approach is adopted for determining the sample size in this research (Charmaz, 2014:189). Out of the 251 codes developed in this study, 97 codes were developed from the first interviews, 54 and 45 codes were developed from the second and third interviews respectively, and only 55 codes were developed after the third interview till the sixth interview. Therefore, collecting data was stopped after the sixth interview because gathering more data no longer adds new codes (Guest *et al.*, 2006:78).

A total of six interviews sessions (three for *Shari'ah* advisors and three for financial experts) were conducted. Each interviewees quotation is numbered as (S1 to S3) for *Shari'ah* advisors, and as (F1 to F3) for financial experts for ease of reference to the informants' profile. Demographic profile of the informants showed that they are in different positions, four of them have Ph.D.'s degree while the rest have master's degree with various specializations such as *Usul Al-Fiqh*, Islamic transaction, Islamic finance and finance. They have working experience between 5 and 26 years. The following sections present the results of the interviews using the five common themes determined in this research.

4.1. *Concept of precious metal backed cryptocurrency*

The informants were asked about their opinion regarding the concept of assets-backed money and PMC. In analyzing their responses, it was found that there are differences in views whether money must be assets-backed or not, but all of them agreed that assets-backed ensures stability of money, especially, if that assets are precious metal; gold and silver. In addition, adding the cryptocurrency technology is found to have support from advisors and experts. However, the informants have different views on the condition of money, where *Shari'ah* advisors agreed that money can be non-assets-backed, one scholar (S3) clarified that: "At the first place *Shari'ah* did not provide any ruling about whether money must have assets-backed or not, and it is acceptable from *Shari'ah* point of view as long as it is guaranteed by government, but *Shari'ah* gives us some principle of money, which is the consistency of the value, recognized by government and people, and can store the value at least for the short-term."

However, this opinion gave the green light of fiat money to be circulated since it is legal tender (Lietaer and Dunne, 2013), and it can store the value for the short-term, but even in the short-term the Malaysian Ringgit lost 2.37^2 percent of its value in 2017, and these loses can grow in the long-term as proven by Abdullah (2015:205). Therefore, scholar (S3) took into consideration the long-term, where the non-assets-backed money displayed its inefficacy in storing the value of money for long-term. He further pointed out that: "Bimetallic money, gold and silver have a long-term store value, the value can be stored for long term and will retain just transaction for the long-term, but for the short-run it may be affected by demand and supply".

On the contrary, two of three financial experts opined that money must be assets-backed which will bring benefits to society. This is also supported by Meera and Larbani (2006a:86). One of the experts (F1) clarified that: "I strongly believe that money must be assets-backed and have actual intrinsic value to achieve three things: (1) Fair transaction, so there is no seigniorage, (2) Just exchange and (3) Sustainable economics and environments".

Despite the controversy whether money must be assets-backed or non-assets-backed, all advisors and experts agreed that with assets-backed money stability will be achieved (Abdullah, 2015:223). The stability of money will depend on whether the money is assets-backed, (S2) further elaborated that: "Assets-backed money is an ideal one, it can control the fluctuation of the value, because assets are deemed to be of fixed value and they are found because of their demand and supply. Therefore, anything that uses them as underlying would also have the same characteristic in terms of the stability and value".

On the other hand, the informants have a consensus (5 out of 6) on the concept of PMC. Obviously, there is general agreement on the concept of electronic representation of precious metal as long as the system is interconnected, which means the cryptocurrency issued are backed by 100% of assets, and these assets are *Shari'ah*-compliant, and there is proper auditing for the stocks and transactions (AAOIF, 2017:74–75; Kamali, 2007:2). In addition, adding the crypto concept to precious metal is found to be something desirable because the current way of transactions is all going to be fintech. (F1) supported the concept of PMC especially with current generation life style but he did not hide his concerns about the security and redeeming issues: "Definitely, I would support PMC because the current way of transaction is all going fintech and is using mobile payment system and all things like that. So, it is very appropriate for current generation. But the

---

[2] The change in Ringgit value from 2 Jan 2017 to 2 Jan 2018 $= \frac{5281.62 - 5158.90}{5158.90} = 2.37\%$

main issues are the security of transactions, the precious metal itself and the system... and redemption of precious metal should be easy and secure".

4.2. Operation methods

4.2.1. Financial regulations of precious metal backed cryptocurrency

The informants were asked about their opinion regarding to whether PMC can operate by following current financial regulations or not, and the functions the operator should perform. In analyzing their responses, it was found that it is difficult for PMC to operate in current regulatory environment. They also emphasized that any payment mechanism should only facilitate payments and receipt of deposits.

One of the experts (F3) further explained: "No, of course you will have some drastic changes in the financial regulation to accommodate PMC.... there will be so many legal and regularity issues on the precious metal as money not as commodities". (F2) further elaborated the role of International Monetary Fund in controlling central banks over the world, and the IMF regulation is forced to be abide by all central banks (Schwartz, 1987:370): "All countries are members in IMF, IMF does not allow the use of gold as a currency, even at domestic level, so it is an still international issue, it must have an alternative system, duel system".

On the other hand, (S1) assured that in Malaysia there is subsequent steps to provide a proper regulation for cryptocurrency industry, even though they are not recognizing cryptocurrency as money yet (BNM, 2018): "If we are talking about Malaysia they are yet to come up with such regulation, they have issued the guideline on the digital currency, is more or less on conceptual basic, but they did not recognize the cryptocurrency as money yet".

However, in the era of financial technology, people are going beyond regulations and central authorities. Blockchain allowed people to trust each other where they should not (Kiviat, 2015:577). For example, in cryptocurrency like Bitcoin people are exchanging value internationally with trust which never happened before. (S3) explained: "We can use PMC as money and make payments, but it is not recognized by government. Right now, we have a fintech, that sometimes needs not the regulations, the single regulation for blockchain is trust".

Majority of informants (5/6) agreed that SCPMC as a payment system should do normal operations such as facilitating payment and receiving deposit but not providing any loans in order to avoid the fractional reserve banking system, only *Al-Qard Al-Hasan* was acceptable for F3. *Shari'ah* scholar (S1) explained that: "Because of the regulation the functions should facilitate payment, receiving deposit, synchronizing the system, buying and selling precious metal, but not issuing loans because this is mainly payment and clearance system".

4.2.2. Payment and settlement in precious metal backed cryptocurrency

The informants were asked about their opinion regarding whether the grams or units of precious metal can be used in settling the payment, and whether the PMC system should be built based on debit concept. In analyzing their responses, it was found that it is possible to use grams or units of precious metal in settling the payment. They also highlighted that the system should be built based on debit concept where the users will be able to spend up to their account balance.

It is the ultimate objective of PMC to price things in grams or units of precious metal. (F1) assured that: "I strongly support this, because the moment you go and price things in grams or units of precious metal then the entire system will become completely stable. The payment system is not actually about minting the gold coin, it is pricing good and services in grams of precious metal, it is the game changer".

Pricing goods and services in grams of precious metal will depend on the acceptability of PMC, the more consumers use it the more merchant will accept, but all that depends on the believe that they will be able to use it as money in the future especially in an uncertain environment (Doorman, 2015:16). According to (S2): "I think that works at retail level. But when the seller accepts PMC, therefore, it depends on the regulations and the business environment. How far it can be accepted by the market?"

However, (F3) triggered an important issue related to the divisibility of PMC and the cost effectiveness of small transactions (Mullan, 2016:25; Rouse, 1994:8). (F3) pointed out that: "In electronic system you need to make sure that the unit system is divisible to the extent where people can buy something with 5 cents, 10 cents, and make sure these small transactions are basically costless". Thus, PMC would permit online micropayments as minor as 0.0001 g which is similar to previous experiences by E-gold. This characteristic made payment highly divisible and created a practical micropayment system (Mullan, 2016:25).

On the other hand, the informants generally agreed that the system should be built based on debit concept where the users will be able to spend if they own the cryptocurrency which is always linked to physical precious metal stored. No additional cryptocurrency will be issued out of thin air as assured by (F3) (AAOIF, 2017:71; Mullan, 2016:89).

4.2.3. Transparency and auditing

The informants were asked about their opinion regarding to whether PMC would be transparent, and whether it would be subjected to interventions and manipulations by authorities. In analyzing their responses, it was found that PMC system would be transparent since the system is built based on blockchain technology but that is linked to proper auditing. However, any monetary system is found to be subjected to interventions and manipulations by authorities, even if it is assets-backed system.

The informants generally agreed that PMC based on today's technology like blockchain is very secure and transparent (Dorothal, 2017). One of the experts (F1) explained that: "The transparency comes from how you build the system. Today, if we have a system based on blockchain, it would be said that transparency would be in very high level, the data is not in one place, it is fixed not adjustable. It is highly presiding, tracing the gold, so it is very difficult to counterfeit, very difficult to create out of nothing, and people will know the amount they circulate, and everybody can see".

In addition, transparency also requires appropriate auditing especially if we have precious metal involved in the system. In fact, people will exchange cryptocurrency which is only an electronic representation of the precious metal stored; therefore, auditing is always needed to ensure that the precious metal stored is equal to or more than cryptocurrency in circulation. This is in order to prevent any over issuance of the cryptocurrency more than the precious metal kept in the storage sites (Dorothal, 2017; Mullan, 2016:234). (F1) further elaborated that: "We need to add evaluation and auditing to the precious metal, the cryptocurrency must be tally with the precious metal in vault, and we need some financial audit to check this, and since it is using blockchain, data is published by default".

On the other hand, informants are found to have generally agreed that any monetary system would be subjected to interventions and manipulations by authorities even though it is backed by real assets. According to (F1), "if authorities want to intervene and manipulate, they need additional assets to do so but at times it will be there". However, *Shari'ah* advisors seem to have support on the role of government in money because according to Islamic principle of monetary policy, money must be controlled by government, it is governmental concern.

(S3) clarified that: "It is Islamic principle whether it is gold or silver, the money must be controlled by government, this is the Islamic principle of monetary policy. Even though we are in gold regime, the money itself must be regulated and controlled by government, must be supervised by government, the supervision of the money is more important than the money itself, let us say the money is fiat money, it is okay as long as the government supervises it. So, we need the government intervention, we need the authority". The intervention of authorities or central bank today is depending on the *Maslahah* of financial system and the society. (S2) stated that: "Whether central bank should or should not intervene depends on the *Maslahah*. It must be regulated by the *Maslahah* of the financial system".

4.3. Is PMC A Shari'ah-compliant?

The informants were asked about their opinion regarding whether PMC as "assets-backed money" is a *Shari'ah*-compliant medium of exchange, and to what extent it is satisfying *Maqāsid al-Shari'ah* in terms of protecting wealth (*Māl*). They also were asked about whether money must have a counter-value (*'Iwad*) in order to protect the exchange parties. In analyzing their responses, it was found that PMC is a *Shari'ah* oriented medium of exchange, but this is not exclusive, it is linked to the system design. It is also found that PMC is contributing to *Maqāsid al-Shari'ah* because it is protecting wealth (*Māl*). In addition, there was consensus on the necessity of having counter-value (*'Iwad*) in money, but there were differences of views on the source of the counter-value, which means the counter-value that should exist in money is not derived from the intrinsic value.

The result indicates that the informants agreed that PMC is a *Shari'ah* oriented medium of exchange because the precious metal itself is *Shari'ah*-compliant money and the cryptocurrency is only electronic representation of that money (AAOIF, 2017:74–75; Kamali, 2007:2). One of the experts (F1) further explained: "Defiantly yes, I find PMC as

Sharī'ah-compliant money because the physical precious metal remains somewhere, and electronic representative move as money, but it is redeemable, which is basically a *Sharī'ah*-compliant". (S3) further elaborated the system must be interconnected where the physical precious metal is linked to cryptocurrency and always there is balancing between them: "In term of *Sharī'ah*-compliance, of course PMC is *Sharī'ah*-compliant if the money (physical precious metal) and the system are embodied together one-for-one".

This is also supported by (F3) who pointed out that the assets-backed money cannot ensure the system to be *Sharī'ah*-compliant, it heavily depends on the system design even if it is not assets-backed it could be *Sharī'ah*-compliant and it can protect people wealth (Hasan, 2011:94). Accordingly, it is good to have assets-backed money, but it is not necessary. He further added: "If you have precious metal, and it is *Sharī'ah*-compliant, of course you can have it, there is no problem with it, but if you design your currency or monetary system in a manner which is also *Sharī'ah*-compliant, you might not need the assets. It is basically the system design".

On the other hand, informants agreed that PMC is contributing to *Maqāsid al-Sharī'ah* since it is backed by real value, it is protecting wealth (*Māl*) which was proven by history over long-term (Meera and Larbani, 2006a:93, 2006b:30; Shapiee and Zahid, 2010:768). (F1) expressed that: "PMC is contributing to *Maqāsid al-Sharī'ah* because it is protecting wealth, it does not allow seigniorage, and people cannot create value out of nothing, that is why inflation is very impossible under assets-backed money, it is so important to make sure that the monetary system contributes to *Maqāsid al-Sharī'ah*".

The above argument was supported by another scholar (S3), but he asserted on the governmental role in maintaining the value of precious metal to avoid speculators. He further explained: "If we use precious metal it is closer to *Maqāsid al-Sharī'ah*, it will protect people wealth, but we have to take into consideration short-term volatility for gold and silver, we must have government intervention to maintain the demand and supply, to maintain the value".

Although PMC satisfies *Maqāsid al-Sharī'ah* and it could contribute to solving the problems raised by fiat money, it cannot be considered as the only solution. (F3) expressed that: "I understand there is a problem with fiat money, and I do think from the aspect of *Maqāsid al-Sharī'ah*, our fiat money is not fulfilling *Maqāsid al-Sharī'ah*, inflation and injustice is basically part of the fiat money system. The only problem is that is the precious metal the solution or not? So, PMC can be one of the solutions but not the only solution".

Furthermore, the informants agreed on the necessity of having counter-value (*'Iwad*) in money (Meera and Larbani, 2006a:84), but there was a difference of views on the source of the counter-value (Hasan, 2008:2). In other words, non-assets-backed money like fiat money and Bitcoin have value, people are giving it its value, the only different between assets-backed money and non-assets-backed money in term of value is that they have different intrinsic usage, utility or benefits. (F3) further added: "I think that misconception among people, that when they say money or Bitcoin do not have value, and things have value, no, both things have value, it is only something that has different intrinsic usage, utility, or benefit".

In addition, the value of money nowadays is derived from different resources where precious metal derives its value from the metal itself and people demand. However, Bitcoin derives its value from people's trust, while fiat money derives its value from perception of the people, the government, the monetary and financial system, the political strength, the economic performance, balance of payment and trade, this is the overall backing fiat currency as stated by (F3).

4.4. *Ensuring justice and equality*

The informants were asked about their opinion regarding to whether PMC contains an element of injustice such as *Riba*, *Gharar* and consuming wealth unjustly, and to what extent it is preserving wealth and value of money. They also were asked about whether precious metal monetary system reduces some of the socio-economic problems that arise as a result of fiat money usage. In analyzing their responses, it was found that PMC is not free from *Riba*, *Gharar* because such elements depend on the system design. In terms of consuming wealth unjustly it was found that PMC can eliminate it. It also found that PMC at certain extent is preserving wealth and value of money for long-term. In addition, there was a general agreement that PMC can basically minimize some socio-economic problems, but it will not remove all the problems.

The results indicate that PMC in itself is free from *Riba*, *Gharar* and consuming wealth unjustly but that depends on the system design (CIBAF, 2012:33–40). One of the experts (F1) further explained: "If you use PMC properly that every movement of cryptocurrency is backed by precious metal most of the *Riba* will be eliminated except of *Riba al-Nasi'ah*. The *Gharar* in money itself is not there but in transaction. Consuming wealth unjustly also will be eliminated since there is no inflation. So, it helps in eliminating all these three, instead of contributing".

(S3) further elaborated that *Riba* and *Gharar* are depending on the government and the system used. It is related to the way we applied this money, but the currency itself does not have *Riba* and *Gharar*, this is much related to the system used, how we built the system: "If we use precious metal, I think we can eliminate some, but all that depends on the government and system they use, and how they use the monetary policy to control the demand and supply of money. *Gharar* and *Riba* are not related to money itself, they can be related to the system we use. Consumer wealth unjustly is affected by inflation I agreed can be eliminated".

However, this is different from Shapiee's and Zahid's (2010:768) conclusions where they argue that fiat money itself is inherently including usury (*Riba*) and suspicion in its value which contain *Gharar*, all of which bring about economic injustices and oppression. (S2) in response to that argued the relationships among people are different from the relationships between people and government. If we said the fiat money that people circulated is *Haram* this will spoil our lives.

In addition, the views of advisors and experts indicated that PMC is preserving wealth and value of money for long-term at certain extent. It has been proven by history that the value of precious metal increases over time because as time goes there is less gold under the ground. (F1) mentioned that: "Yes, it is preserving wealth and value of money because it has intrinsic value, so anything fulfills the criteria of money can be used as money, but some of them are better money than others such as gold and silver, and because its current nature their relative value to other things became constant and because of that they become a very good in preserving the value and wealth. Another Scholar (S3) further added that PMC can preserve the value of money, but that also needs the government intervention to protect the precious metal market.

However, (F3) argued that assets-backed money can preserve the value of money, but it is not necessary to have assets-backed to preserve the value (Hasan, 2011:94). It can have non-assets-backed, but the system is designed to preserve the value: "It can protect people wealth, yes it can be done. It is good to have an asset behind your money, but it is not necessary, and also you can have a system which is non-assets-backed, but it can protect people's wealth".

On the other hand, the informants agreed that PMC can reduce some socio-economic problems raised by fiat money (Meera, 2002:57), but it will not remove all the problems. One of the experts (F3) explained that: "Yes, it can basically minimize some socio-economic problems, but it will not remove all the problems. Because even real inflation can happen but of course it will not be rampant like today, yes, I think PMC will be more toward socio-economic justice". Another scholar (S2) further explained that precious monetary system can improve at least the value of money for the long-term (Abdullah, 2015:205; Meera, 2002:57). However, another scholar (S1) argued that even though PMC is a protector from inflation, some socio-economic problems will still be there: "In era of *Al-Khulafa' Al-Rasyidin* they used gold money but still some socio-economic problems existed, but for inflation, yes, it can be eliminated".

4.5. *Informants' preference*

In this section, the informants were asked about their preference regard to PMC. In analyzing their responses, it was found that there is a general acceptance and support for PMC. The overall results indicated their preference for PMC as a potential alternative to the current interest-based fiat monetary system. The main reason for their support is because PMC can create a just exchanging system, protecting and preserving the value for long-term, preserving the sovereignty of nation and preserving the sustainability of environmental system. This is because precious metal is by no means, perfect money not just as a store of value but they fit the function of money properly (Meera and Larbani, 2006a:88,93). (F1) showed that: "I strongly support the implementing of PMC because I think it can bring a lot of goodness into the present world, not only Muslim world, especially to financial system and global monetary system. It will create just exchange system, preserve the wealth and the sovereignty of nation and sustainability of environment system".

Similarly, the informants agreed that they will recommend other people as well to adopt PMC in their future transactions. That is because of the precious metal characteristics especially stability (Abdullah, 2015:223). (F1) further explained that: "Definitely, I will recommend others, I will ask government if they can do it, please do it, the only obstacles for government to do it is the international political structure".

However, majority of the informants (5 out of 6) found PMC a potential alternative of fiat money, but it requires the governmental support to implement the system which will protect the users. (S3) further elaborated: "If we have support from government maybe viable, that is why we need a support from government, and the government must have a political well to promote the electronic precious metal. We must find and work for an alternative of fiat money to the next future, but it must be backed by research".

In addition, PMC is still theoretical proposal of payment mechanism. It is a new currency with a new era of exchanging value, it must be carefully studied from all perspective such as information technology, system developer, data basis, accounting and financial perspective. (S1) stated that: "This is not a matter with *Shari'ah* expert works alone, *Shari'ah* has to work with IT system, data basis, accounting and finance experts, so that the system recognized this. We are talking about circulation".

Another *Shari'ah* advisor (S2) further pointed out that it is essential to investigate the effects of PMC on the financial and economical environments. He explained that: "So, Will BNM accept PMC as settle reserve? Will that affect the interest rate? Will that affect the lending limit? Will that affect the capital adequacy of the bank? If all these are viable plus is this PMC in line with the monetary policy of the country and it will not affect the financial stability then I will think BNM will allow to do that, otherwise it will affect the whole system".

5. Conclusion

The main objective of this research was to investigate in *Shari'ah* advisors' and financial experts' perceptions on the concepts and salient features of precious metal backed cryptocurrency with regards to the usage of concepts, operation methods, *Shari'ah*-compliant, justice and equality and informants' preference.

The investigation of the usage of concepts of precious metal backed cryptocurrency has shown that the informants have differences of views on the assets-backed money, but they agreed that it ensures stability of money. Adding the cryptocurrency technology is found to be desirable and recommendable.

The results of investigating on the method of operation showed that precious metal backed cryptocurrency would be subjected to financial regulation challenges which require modifications and improvements of the financial regulation. It is also found that pricing goods and services in grams or units of precious metal is the game changer. In addition, using blockchain technology in a regulatory industry such as precious metal will increase the transparency but that requires auditing.

In terms of *Shari'ah*-compliant, it is found that precious metal backed cryptocurrency is contributing to *Maqāsid al-Shari'ah* because it protects wealth (*Māl*). It can preserve wealth and value of money for long-term.

The informants generally feel that there is some form of justice and equality in precious metal backed cryptocurrency compared to current interest-based financial system. It was also found that the proposed model can reduce some socio-economic problems.

Finally, both *Shari'ah* advisors and financial experts recommend implementing precious metal backed cryptocurrency, but it is important to carefully investigate it from all perspectives.

The most important limitation lies in the fact that the current study was unable to investigate on the practical front of the precious metal backed cryptocurrency. Therefore, it is suggested to investigate on the practical terms and application of PMC in the future. In addition, in this research the targeted informants were limited to *Shari'ah* advisors and financial experts from Malaysia. Further studies, which include mixture of Middle Eastern, African and Asian Scholars, advisors and experts are therefore recommended.

References

AAOIFI. (2015). Governance standards. In *Accounting, Auditing and Governance Standards*, pp. 1043–1143. Kingdom of Bahrain: An-Nakheel Tower.

AAOIFI. (2017). Debit card, charge card and credit card. In *Shari'ah Standards for Islamic Financial Institutions*, pp. 67–81. Kingdom of Bahrain: An-Nakheel Tower.

Abdul Razak, D (2011). Diminishing partnership as an alternative Islamic home financing in Malaysia: Issues and perceptions. An Unpublished Doctoral Thesis Submitted to the University of Science, Malaysia.

Abdullah, A (2015). Economic security requires monetary and price stability: Analysis of Malaysian macroeconomic and credit data. *Al-Shajarah: Journal of the International Institute of Islamic Thought and Civilization (ISTAC)*, 205–247.

Abdullah, A (2016a). An Islamic monetary theory of value and equation of exchange: Evidence from Egypt (696–1517). *Humanomics*, 32(2), 1–28.

Abdullah, A (2016b). *The Islamic Currency*, 1st edn. International Council of Islamic Finance Educators.

Al-Ghazali, MAH (2004). *Ihya Ulum-ud-Din, translated by Al-Haj Maulana Fazlul Karim* Vol. 4, New Delhi: Islamic Book Service.

Al-Qaradaghi, A (2018). *Fatwa on the Islamic Ruling on Cryptocurrency*. Doha, Qatar: Private Office.

Bezemer, DJ (2014). Schumpeter might be right again: The functional differentiation of credit. *Journal of Evolutionary Economics*, 24(5), 935–950.

BNM (2018). Bank Negara Malaysia issues policy document for digital currencies. Available at www.bnm.gov.my (accessed on 15 September 2018).

Bordo, MD (2005). The Bretton Woods international monetary system: A historical overview. In *The Gold Standard and Related Regimes: Collected Essays*, pp. 395–500. Cambridge University Press.

Carroll, CH (1964). Organization of debt into currency and other papers. In *Originally Published in Hunt's Merchants' Magazine and Banker's Magazine between 1855 and 1897,* Republished by Edward C. Simons (Ed.), Princeton: D. Van Nostrand.

Charmaz, K (2014). *Constructing Grounded Theory*. Thousand Oaks, CA: Sage.

CIBAFI (2012). *The Certified Islamic Banker*. Manama, Kingdom of Bahrain.

Cizakca, M (2010). The case against the Islamic gold dinar. MPRA Paper 26645, University Library of Munich, Germany.

Corradi, F and P Höfner (2018). The disenchantment of Bitcoin: Unveiling the myth of a digital currency. *International Review of Sociology*, 28(1), 193–207.

Creswell, JW (2014). *Research Design: Qualitative, Quantitative, and Mixed Methods Approaches*, 4th edn. SAGE Publications, Inc.

Cronin, D and K Dowd (2001). Does monetary policy have a future. *Cato J.*, 21(2), 227–244.
Doorman, F (2015). *Our Money – Towards a New Monetary System*, 1st edn. Lulu Internet.
Dorothal, M (2017). The Power of Blockchain. *SOLARPLAZA*. Available at www.solarplaza.com.
GoldMoney. (2017). The goldmoney holding: Overview. Available at www.goldmoney.com (accessed on 25 August 2017).
Greenspan, A (1966). Gold and economic freedom. Published in Ayn Rand's "Objectivist" Newsletter in 1966, and Reprinted in Her Book, Capitalism: The Unknown Ideal, in 1967.
Guest, G, A Bunce and L Johnson (2006). How many interviews are enough? An experiment with data saturation and variability. *Field Methods*, 18(1), 59–82.
Haneef, MA and ER Barakat (2006). Must money be limited to only gold and silver: A survey of Fiqhi opinions and some implications. *JKAU: Islamic Economics*, 19(1), 21–34.
Hasan, Z (2008). Ensuring exchange rate stability: Is return to gold (Dinar) possible. *Islamic Economics*, 21(1), 3–25.
Hasan, Z (2011). Money creation and control from Islamic perspective. *Review of Islamic Economics*, 15(1), 93–111.
HelloGold. (2018). About Us. HelloGold, Available at www.hellogold.com (accessed on 31 July 2018).
Hülsmann, JG (2004). Legal tender laws and fractional-reserve banking. *Journal of Libertarian Studies*, 18(3), 33–55.
Islamic Economy Forum. (2018). Islamic Economic Forum's Declaration on Bitcoin. Islamic Economy Forum.
Jaffar, S, A Abdullah and AK Meera (2017). Fiat money: From the current Islamic finance scholars' perspective. *Humanomics*, 33(3), 274–299.
Jaffar, S (2017). *Viability of Implementing Direct Interest-Free Credit Clearance System: An Islamic Perspective*. International Islamic University Malaysia.
James. (2019). A guide to gold-backed cryptocurrency. GoldScape, Available at www.goldscape.net (accessed on 17 April 2019).
Janze, C (2017). Are cryptocurrencies criminals best friends? examining the co-evolution of bitcoin and darknet markets. In *Proc. Americas Conference on Information Systems (AMCIS)*, pp. 10. Boston, United States.
Kamali, MH (2007). *Qawa'id Al-Fiqh: The Legal Maxims in Islamic Law*. Association of Muslim Lawyers, U.K.
Kamali, MH (2008). *Shariah Law: An introduction*. Oxford, England: Oneworld Publications.
Kiviat, TI (2015). Beyond bitcoin: Issues in regulating blockchain tranactions. *Duke Law Journal*, 65(569), 569–608.
Kiyotaki, N and R Wright (1993). A search-theoretic approach to monetary economics. *The American Economic Review*, 83(1), 63–77.
Lietaer, B and J Dunne (2013). *Rethinking Money, How New Currencies Turn Scarcity into Prosperity*. Berrett-Koehler Publishers.
Lietaer, B (2013). *The Future of Money*. Random House.
Maurer, B, C Nelms and L Swartz (2013). When perhaps the real problem is money itself!: The practical materiality of Bitcoin. *Social Semiotics*, 23(2), 261–277.
Meera, AK and M Larbani (2006a). Seigniorage of Fiat Money and the Maqāsid al-Sharı'ah: The unattainableness of the Maqāsid. *Humanomics*, 22(1), 84–97.
Meera, AK and M Larbani (2006b). Seigniorage of fiat money and the Maqasid al-Shari'ah: The compatibility of the gold dinar with the Maqasid. *Humanomics*, 22(2), 17–33.
Meera, AK (2002). *The Islamic Gold Dinar*. Subang Jaya, Malaysia: Pelanduk Publications.
Meera, AK (2004). *The Theft of Nations: Returning to Gold*. Pelanduk Pubns Sdn Bhd.

Muhayiddin, M, R Abdullah and R Che-rahim (2015). Exploring intention to use electronic gold dinar as mechanism for travelling. *Int. Conf. Economics and Business Management (EBM-2015)*. pp. 125–131, Phuket, Thailand.

Muhayiddin, M-N (2011). Technology acceptance of a gold dinar based electronic payment system. *IBusiness*, 3(3), 295–301.

Mullan, P (2014). *The Digital Currency Challenge: Shaping Online Payment Systems Through US Financial Regulations*. Hampshire, England: Palgrave MacMillan.

Mullan, PC (2016). *A History of Digital Currency in the United States: New Technology in an Unregulated Market*. Virginia, USA: Palgrave.

Nakamoto, S (2008). Bitcoin: A peer-to-peer electronic cash system. White paper.

Omerčević, E (2013). Monetary systems, sustainable growth and inclusive economic development. *2nd Int. Conf. Islamic Economics and Economies of OIC Countries*. Kuala Lumpur, Malaysia.

OneGram. (2018). First OneGram Transaction Made. CCN. Available at www.ccn.com.

Rouse. (1994). Money: Its functions and characteristics. In *Money and Monetary Policy in Canada*, pp. 1–10. Toronto: Canadian Foundation for Economic Education.

Schwartz, AJ (1987). Alternative monetary regimes: The gold standard. In *Money in Historical Perspective*, pp. 364–390. Chicago, USA: University of Chicago Press.

Sekaran, U and RJ Bougie (2013). *Research Methods for Business: A Skill-Building Approach*, 6th edn. John Wiley & Sons.

Shapiee, R and A Zahid (2010). Addressing economic meltdown: An evaluation of fiat and credit money from Islamic Perspective. *US-China Law Review*, 11(2), 768–783.

Usmani, MT (1999). The text of the historic judgment on interest given by the supreme court of Pakistan. Available at www.albalagh.net (accessed on 5 October 2016).

Yaacob, SE (2012). The reality of Gold Dinar application in Malaysia. *Advances in Natural and Applied Sciences*, 6(3), 341–347.

Yusuf, MB, GM Ghani and AK Meera (2013). The challenges of implementing gold dinar in Kelantan: An empirical analysis. *International Journal of Institutions and Economics*, 5(3), 97–114.

Chapter 5

Individual's Behavior and Access to Finance: Evidence from Palestine[#]

Fadi Hassan Shihadeh
Palestine Technical University
Kadoorie, West Bank, Palestine
fadih20@gmail.com

Governments and global institutions are working to enhance economic development as a key for sustainability by including disadvantaged people (including the poor, women, youth, and illiterate) in the financial system. This paper uses the World Bank Global Findex Database (2014) for 1000 Palestinians to examine the influence of individual behavior on financial inclusion in Palestine. This study used empirical methods to determine whether individual socioeconomic characteristics influence financial inclusion in Palestine. The results indicated that females were less likely to be included in financial transactions, especially transactions involving borrowing and formal accounts. Further, we learned that borrowing behavior in Palestine leans toward informal sources. Formal institutions have made remarkable efforts to develop an inclusive financial infrastructure in Palestine. However, the country's unstable political climate continues to impede economic stability and individuals' motivation to use formal financial resources such as credit. More efforts to specifically encourage youth, the poor, and women to use formal banking could enhance their access to financial services. Adopting Islamic financial services, and online banking would also improve financial inclusion for all of Palestine's citizens and drive sustainable development. Further, theoretical and empirical studies of Palestine's economic development are recommended.

Keywords: Financial inclusion; Palestine; individual behavior; access to finance; Islamic services.

1. Introduction

Internationally, governments and organizations are working together to develop and implement rules, regulations, and procedures designed to help organizations achieve sustainable development in communities, economies, and countries. Development as a sustainability process requires commitment and active participation from all parties, both public and private, especially at the implementation stage. According to the Consultative Group to Assist the Poor (CGAP), comprehensive development goals include poverty reduction, gender equality, solid infrastructure, educational and employment opportunities, and access to quality healthcare (CGAP, 2016). As financial sources are considered the main drivers of these factors, the global agenda focuses on how individuals and small and medium enterprises (SME) can obtain access to adequate financing on reasonable terms.

[#]This Chapter first appeared in the *Singapore Economic Review*, Vol. 67, No. 1, doi: 10.1142/S0217590819420025. © 2022 World Scientific Publishing.

Financial inclusion can enhance the lives of the disadvantaged (i.e., the poor, women, youth, the illiterate) by enabling them to invest in businesses, gain access to health services, and acquire an education — all of which improve knowledge, skills, and employability. In 2010, the G20 determined that world development could be enhanced through financial inclusion, defined as making formal financial services available to all citizens in the community so they can cover their needs at an affordable price. Financial development focuses on measures at the country level, such as the performance of stock market indices and the percentage of bank loans to GDP, where financial inclusion is measured according to individuals' levels of access to and use of formal financial services (banks and other lending agencies). Thus, financial inclusion at the micro-level, which enhances financial development at the macro-level, is vital for the development of sustainability (CGAP, 2016).

Globally, among the disadvantaged, most youth have limited access to financial resources (United Nations, 2013). Financial resources can enable them to innovate and create their businesses, thereby alleviating poverty, reducing unemployment, and helping citizens cover their daily needs. It is understandable, then, that these factors improve the development process in any country, and as a philosophy, financial inclusion stands to improve the lives of the disadvantaged, in particular, thereby enhancing the sustainable development process in these economies. Having a good grasp of the individual socioeconomic characteristics that influence financial inclusion provides a better image of those who have little or no access to formal financial services and, therefore, those for whom this study should direct its attention regarding how to provide access to financial services. Consequently, formal institutions can develop regulations and procedures that would enhance both the access level and the infrastructure for comprehensive and sustainable development.

Previous studies found that most of the excluded individuals are poor, female, illiterate, and youth who mainly come from rural areas (Yuan and Xu, 2015; Shoji et al., 2012). Accordingly, this research focused on why these individuals are less likely to be included in the financial system, and what formal institutions could do to include them. Moreover, poor people, the illiterate, and youth are considered the world's majority. Thus, enhancing their financial inclusion will improve their lives through employment, education, and healthcare and reflect on the economy and its sustainable development.

This study examines the influence of individual's behavior on financial inclusion and whether the socioeconomic characteristics of individuals living in Palestine (age, gender, education, and income) influence this country's financial inclusion indicators. According to the Palestinian Central Bureau of Statistics (PCBS, 2015), Palestine suffers from high unemployment (around 26% in 2015) and unstable economic growth. Therefore, improving its financial system could enhance sustainable development (CGAP, 2010). The contribution of this study is to present new evidence from developing countries, which faces several issues could influence its financial inclusion level, therefore, recommending to the policymakers regarding the results and findings how they can develop the regulation according to the individual's behavior in Palestine.

2. Financial Inclusion Issues in Palestine

Government institutions in Palestine are working toward developing policies and regulations that aim to achieve economic stability and growth (Wang and Shihadeh, 2015). One of the central strategies is to enhance financial inclusion for disadvantaged members of Palestinian society; this is not an easy task, and a concerted effort is needed from all economic entities. Recently, the World Bank published its financial inclusion survey data, which indicated a slight evolution in national indicators. The results for the 2017 survey comes from the adults (+15:25%) who have a formal account. 6% have formal savings, and 7.2% participate in formal borrowing (World Bank, 2018). Table 1 presents developments in the main indicators of financial inclusion from the World Bank survey.

This section will present developments in financial inclusion in Palestine and other issues related to the country's aim to achieve sustainable financial inclusion as an overall development goal.

2.1. *National strategy for financial inclusion*

In 2013, the Palestine Monetary Authority (PMA) and the Palestine Capital Market Authority (PMCA) signed a Memorandum of Understanding to implement a national strategy for financial inclusion in Palestine. Recently, at the end of 2017, this Memorandum was authorized by the Palestinian government, thus supporting cooperation between the public and private sectors for enhancing financial inclusion in Palestine to achieve sustainable development. Of note, this formal Memorandum is essential for all parties in the country to implement a national strategy. Furthermore, the Alliance for Financial Inclusion (AFI) nominated PMA as one of the best central banks in the Middle East and North Africa (MENA) region for its adoption of financial inclusion. PMA follows best practices in enhancing the financial inclusion in Palestine, and instructions, rules, and regulations launched in the past, as well as updates, are being adopted to include more people in the financial system. Furthermore, this strategy draws primary lines to enhance financial inclusion as a factor for sustainable development.

2.2. *Developing the regulations and rules*

The process of developing regulations and rules is driven to keep pace with rapid developments in economic issues and problems. To enhance the economy, the participation is

Table 1. Financial Inclusion Indicators

Indicators	2011	2014	2017
Formal account	19.4	24.2	25
Formal Saving	5.5	5.1	6
Formal borrowing	4.1	4.7	7.2
Digital Payment	—	14.2	12.1

Source: Global Findex database. The numbers in %.

needed from all to attract deposits or use other sources such as direct and indirect credits (Shihadeh, 2018). Therefore, PMA, which represents the central banks in Palestine, is working to update banking regulations and rules in line with the global agenda; doing results in a high level of financial inclusion. Additionally, some of the regulations are related to the service price, to make financial products affordable and available for all, in keeping with the philosophy of financial inclusion. Thus, PMA requires banks to post service prices on their websites so any client can note and compare between banks to choose a suitable price. In furtherance of that, PMA posts indicative prices as high and low limits on its website. To cultivate relationships with its Palestinian clients, PMA established a complaints unit to receive feedback, complaints, and inquiries from clients. Moreover, PMA motivates banks to develop convenient services for all sectors, especially for females, youth, and SMEs, to achieve active participation from all in economic development as a sustainable process.

2.3. Digital channels

Although digital channels (i.e., mobile banking) are essential as a way to access financial resources and enhance financial inclusion, they are unavailable in Palestine. Notably, mobile banking as a digital channel leads to faster money turnover, reduces the cost of money, and is often more appropriate than other payment methods (Carlos and Tiago, 2017). The high cost of using mobile applications to access the internet for payments of service fees or buying is considered a barrier to implementation. On one hand, there is a data protection risk, which also delays activation of mobile payments. On the other hand, easy access and use of financial sources through digital channels could enhance innovation in business, especially among youth regarding creating their businesses (CGAP, 2016). Additionally, receiving or sending money through digital channels has many advantages such as low costs, time saved, security, where these advantages enhance sustainable development in Palestine.

Previous studies suppose that mobile banking can be a vital channel over traditional banking services (Donovan, 2012; Scharwatt *et al.*, 2015; ITU, 2013). Furthermore, through mobile banking, banks could easily promote their services and thus enhance financial inclusion (Aker and Mbiti, 2010; Ramada-Sarasola, 2012), and this could enhance sustainable development goals (CGAP, 2016). Mobile banking needs more research to examine factors which could influence both sides: demand and supply (Carlos and Tiago, 2017).

2.4. Banking penetration

Banks are considered the main driver of an economy's financial system; Palestine has achieved significant developments in banking penetration such as branch banking, ATMs, and POSs, which have spread to most cities and villages. The number of branches increased from 232 as of 2012 to 309 as of 2016, and the number of ATMs increased from 435 as of 2012 to 622 as of 2016. Further, the number of POSs went from 3,926 as of 2012 to 6,253 as of 2016 (Shihadeh *et al.*, 2017). Also, the number of individuals per branch is less than before; in 2014, there was one branch or office for every 16,000 individuals, but in 2015 there was one branch or office for every 15,600 individuals. Therefore, more branches serve fewer individuals, which leads to more effective banking services

(PCMA, 2013). By offering services near their customers, banks encourage more people to use financial services; these developments organize the financial inclusion infrastructure as a basis for sustainable development.

2.5. *Financial awareness*

Financial awareness activities geared toward women, youth, universities, and schools through the internet and other media channels have achieved notable developments in Palestine (Wang and Shihadeh, 2015). Moreover, there has been an increase in the number of courses and lectures organized by PMA and PCMA in cooperation with banks and other financial services providers. These courses aim to build a new generation of society members who have theoretical and practical experience in the financial system and sources. Recently, several conferences, workshops were held by PMA and PCMA to present financial inclusion to society members and outline the steps to implement the national strategy and agenda to enhance financial inclusion. Such awareness could enhance opportunities for disadvantaged people to participate in the development process by using formal sources to start a business, innovate, and thus decrease the unemployment rate to improve economic growth and sustainable development.

2.6. *Islamic finance*

The Palestinian banking system contains 15 banks: 3 Islamic banks, and 13 commercial banks. These banks are working to provide the financial services through branches, ATMs, and other channels to the citizens. Although the majority religion in Palestine is Islam, we can note that just three banks are offering financial services according to *Sharia'a* rules, and one of them was established in 2016. The *Sharia'a* rules mean that: "Islamic finance is the act of providing financial products or services that conform to Sharia, Islam's law and moral code. The defining characteristic of Islamic financial products is the avoidance of interest, known as "Riba", derived from the Quran's stipulation that only goods and services, and not money itself, are allowed to carry a price. Instead, Sharia-compliant finance promotes risk-sharing or profit-and-loss sharing principles in all forms of business transactions." (Demirgüç-Kunt *et al.*, 2013).

It is notable that the level of financial inclusion in Islamic countries is lower than in other countries (Kim *et al.*, 2018a). Therefore, developing appropriate services according to the Islamic rules required that banks can work in the promotion of the services through delivery channels, i.e., branches, ATMs, and Media. Further, banks through market research and surveys can find what kind of services people are looking for, thus, matching these needs with Islamic services, therefore, encouraging the citizens to access and use more financial sources (Shihadeh, 2018).

2.7. *Some barriers to financial inclusion in Palestine*

Understandably, the unstable political climate and conflict in Palestine are reflected in the country's economic growth, business, investment, and thus, on sustainable development.

Consequently, the issues in Palestine are considered a barrier to financial inclusion and sustainable development (Kabakova and Plaksenkov, 2018). Further, increases in deposit amounts are not matched by increases in loan amount. Request for credit for businesses or other kinds of firms comes in last of total loans (PMA, 2016). Therefore, this leads to decreased use of financial sources and increased cost of money, which lowers the number of new firms and limits new firms' growth. Accordingly, the unemployment rate, especially among youth and female, increases and has an adverse effect on economic growth and sustainable development.

Another barrier is related to collateral for loans. It is difficult to offer some forms of collateral, such as fixed assets. Palestine has a high unemployment rate and is classified as a low-income country with a small economy (World Bank, 2018). Thus, many people, especially youth, females, and the financially disadvantaged, do not have enough collateral or resources to use in seeking credit. These factors decrease the chances of reaching financial sources and may stall economic growth and sustainable development.

Moreover, there is no national currency in Palestine. People use three main currencies in daily life, and this lack of a national currency is considered another barrier to financial inclusion. Banks offer loans in different currencies and at different interest rates, although they prefer to lend currency in which they have the most liquidity. Therefore, borrowers carry more costs and risks in that they may borrow in one currency and deal with another one daily. Enhancing financial inclusion is difficult without solving the country's political issues and without a national currency. Moreover, efforts by the government and formal financial institutions could enhance the financial inclusion, but the political conflict in Palestine stymies the process.

The finance and mortgage sectors' contribution to achieving financial inclusion are weak. At the conclusion of the present research, no special laws exist to regulate the mortgage and finance sectors; instead, a set of instructions are intended to assist with their development (PCMA, 2013; Wang and Shihadeh, 2015). These sectors are made up of fewer companies due to a lack of law guaranteed protection. Only one company works in the mortgage business via a subsidiary. Furthermore, the lack of an integrated geographic correlation in the Palestinian territories weakens the process of achieving financial inclusion and hampers efforts to stabilize economic growth rates.

From the above, one can note that Palestine has made remarkable improvements in infrastructure (laws and regulations), banking penetration and financial awareness, but the political conflict and national currency issues stand as barriers to enhancing financial inclusion, and thus, economic growth and sustainable development suffer. Moreover, banks and other financial services such as microfinance, insurance, and financial leasing companies should direct their investments towards innovative new services that provide for all of society's modern needs, especially for disadvantaged people in Palestine.

The rest of this papers organized as follows: Section 3 presents the literature review; Section 4 presents the methodology; Section 5 presents the analyzed estimations, where, Section 6 presents the conclusion and policy implications.

3. Literature Review

Several studies examine financial inclusion levels among countries and comment on individual behavior regarding access to the financial services. Recently, Kim *et al.* (2018a) examined how religious and social inequality influence the financial inclusion among 152 countries which contains 48 countries from the Organization of Islamic Cooperation (OIC). They pointed out that the religions among countries are considered as significant determinants of financial inclusion. Further, the results indicated that education, and inequality between male and female, are considered as determinants of financial inclusion. The authors recommended conducting more research which cover more countries regarding the effect of religion on financial inclusion. Furthermore, Kim *et al.* (2018b) assessed how financial inclusion influence economic growth among Organization of Islamic Cooperation, OIC, countries. The study covered six regions with 55 countries which belongs to the Organization. The study used five indicators of financial inclusion such as, branches, ATMs, borrowers, and deposit accounts per 100,000 adults; also, the percentage of the life insurance premium volume to the economic growth is measured by GDP. The results indicated that financial inclusion has a significant effect on the economic growth in the OIC countries. Further, the researchers recommended that future research could use different factors related to the financial inclusion, i.e., education, income, gender.

Shihadeh (2018) studied the influence of individuals' socio-economic characteristics on their financial inclusion level in the Middle East, North Africa, Afghanistan, and Pakistan, MENAP region. The results of this study indicated that females and the poor have fewer opportunities to access financial resources. The results show that people in the region did not consider religion as an obstacle to access financial services. Further, the study recommended more studies about countries in the region regarding understanding how individual behavior influences the level of access. Furthermore, research focusing on whether religion among Islamic countries stands as a barrier to the use of financial services. Ben Naceur *et al.* (2015) and Demirguc-Kunt *et al.* (2014) in their studies examined the level of financial inclusion among Muslim countries. They pointed out that religion plays a negative role in lack of access to the financial services. The recommendations from their studies are: (i) developing Islamic banking services, (ii) improve the infrastructure of the financial system, (iii) restructure the regulation and rules regarding the enhancement access by individual and small firms in using financial services.

Korynski and Pytkowska (2016) used the Data Envelopment Analysis (DEA) approach to measure the financial inclusion among 27 countries from European Union countries. The financial infrastructure, demand conditions, and policies were used as input variables, where bank accounts, consumer credit, deposits, and insurance were used as output variables. They found that the European countries were using more inputs. Louis and Chartier (2017) recommended that achieving financial inclusion in South Africa could enhance banks' income, where providing financial services to the poor may reflect on the economy. Furthermore, enhancing financial inclusion requires an increase in organized teamwork for institutions such as banks, government, and other community organizations.

Jukan et al. (2017) analyzed the main indicators of financial inclusion in Balkan region (Albania, Bosnia and Herzegovina, Croatia, Kosovo, Montenegro, Macedonia, and Serbia). They found that Balkan countries achieved remarkable developments in the main indicators of financial inclusion. To achieve more developments, the Balkan governments should include national strategies to implement financial inclusion policies and cooperate with the private sector in each country. Furthermore, enhancing electronic tools such as ATMs, POSs, and mobile banking could improve the level of financial inclusion among countries in the region. Sajuyigbe (2017) pointed out that financial inclusion could be enhanced through social inclusion for all disadvantaged people, especially for women. Baza and Rao (2017) analyzed and measured the access and usage level of financial inclusion in Ethiopia. The study found that Ethiopia has notable improvements in the indicators of financial inclusion but still less than Sub-Saharan Africa. Distance, documentation issues, and lack of enough money stand as barriers to use of formal services, and disadvantaged people including females, youth, and the poor are more likely to be financially excluded.

Arun and Kamath (2015) addressed successful practices worldwide and focused on policies adopted by government institutions to enhance financial inclusion. Countries such as Peru, India, Kenya, and China have good scores in practicing and enhancing financial inclusion by developing rules and policies. Furthermore, some countries such as Kenya advanced payment methods; mobile banking has been adopted to increase bank market penetration and financial access. Allen et al. (2016) studied the character of 123 countries and over 124,000 individuals across the world, to examine and understand the factors which affect using the formal accounts as financial inclusion indicator across these countries and individuals. The study found that poor people and rural living where mostly financially excluded. Enhancing the financial inclusion was related with some government policies such as, lower cost for opening an account, less document needed to open an account, branching, government payments; all these factors affect the poor and rural living people to have a bank account. The study also addressed some factors that can be considered as barriers to financial inclusion like; lack of money, the financial services or opening an account is too expensive, the distance between living place and nearest branch is too far away, because someone else in the family already has an account. Iqbal and Sami (2017) testified to the influence of financial inclusion, measured by banking penetration and private credits on the economic growth measured by GDP. The data of the study covered seven years regarding India. The results of the study indicated that there is a significant relationship between banking penetration and credits ratio on the economic growth.

Most previous studies found that enhancing financial inclusion helps alleviate poverty and inequality and is significantly linked with social development and economic growth. However, previous studies focused on different countries and economies, and there are no studies focusing on Palestine as a developing nation. The importance of understanding financial inclusion for every country comes from recognizing individual behaviors that could influence financial inclusion; thus, implementation of sustainable development processes could be improved in the country. Therefore, formal institutions can develop regulations, policies, and rules that are consistent with factors that influence the financial inclusion. Doing so will lead to success in national agendas as a way for sustainable development.

4. Methodology

4.1. *Data*

The study used the World Bank's 2014 Global Findex Database, which covers 143 countries and includes responses from around 150,000 individuals, (Demirguc-Kunt *et al.*, 2015). *Gallup, Inc. surveyed in association with its annual Gallup World Poll. Using randomly selected, national representative samples, around 1,000 individuals in each economy were questioned. The target population is the civilian, non- institutionalized population for adults 15 and above.* To examine the individual socio-economic characteristics influencing the financial inclusion in Palestine, the selected data covered 1,000 individuals.

4.2. *Model*

The study analysis examined the following main financial inclusion indicators: formal account, formal saving, and formal borrowing. The individual characteristics used are related to age, gender, education, and income as independent variables. Furthermore, the study analyzes barriers to having a formal account, alternative borrowing sources, and online payment according to respondents' characteristics (Demirguc-Kunt *et al.*, 2014). As explained in the introduction, and based on previous studies and the global agenda, these individual characteristics are linked to lack of financial inclusion: female gender, age, education, and being poor. These characteristics influence financial inclusion indicators and are thus linked with sustainable development as a goal (Shihadeh, 2018; CGAP, 2016; Park and Mercado, 2015; Akudugu, 2013).

The main objective of the this study is to analyze the influence of individual behavior on financial inclusion indicators. Moreover, the respondent's answer is a binary variable (0, 1) for financial inclusion indicators and determinants (Zins and Weill, 2016; Fungacova and Weill, 2015; Allen *et al.*, 2016; Shihadeh, 2018). Thus, the logistic regression runs as follows:

$$Y_i = \alpha + \beta * \text{age}_i + \mu * \text{gender}_i + \sigma * \text{education}_i + \tau * \text{income}_i + \varepsilon_i,$$

where *Y* is financial inclusion indicators and other determinants for financial inclusion, and *i* represents the respondents. Age, gender, education, and income are the explanatory variables in the model.

This study used the Inverse Mills Ratio to determine whether the Heckman model can be robust in the estimation results. The results indicated that the coefficient of the Inverse Mills Ratio is insignificant. Therefore, the Heckman model does not fit the data. Also, Heckman indicates the same results as in the logistic regression (Allen *et al.*, 2016). For income, the study uses fifth income quintiles, but omit the fifth-richest income quintile from the analysis to avoid multicollinearity. For age, the study uses a number of years, and age squared to control the probability of a nonlinear relation of age with dependent variables.

5. Empirical Estimation

5.1. *The statistical descriptive*

Table 2 presents descriptive statistics of the independent variables of age, age^2, female-gender indicator, income quintiles, and education levels.

Continuing, Table 3 presents descriptive statistics for dependent variables: the main financial inclusion indicators, barriers to having a formal account, borrowing sources, and location in Palestine to compare indicators and factors which relate to the MENAP region.

In the table above, it is notable that Palestine achieved outstanding development regarding formal accounts. Thus, the mean for having a formal account was 32.3%, while the mean in MENAP^2 was 29.5%. Borrowing indicators in Palestine were higher than in MENAP^2, but other indicators were the same as the region. For barriers to having a formal account in Palestine, the results indicated that having no money and a family member having an account has the highest means, and these results are the same as the region. For borrowing sources, in Palestine and MENAP^2, the essential borrowing resources come from informal sources (i.e., store, friend, or family member). Further, medical purposes are considered the main reason to ask for credit in both Palestine and the region. In the next section, the study will examine and explain individual socioeconomic characteristics and the determinants of financial inclusion in Palestine.

Table 2. Descriptive Statistics for the Independent Variables

	Definition	Obs.	Mean	St. Dev.
Age	Age in number of years.	1000	37.32	16.864
Age2	Square age in a number of years	1000	1676.9	1485.46
Female	One if female, zero if else	1000	0.575	0.4946
Primary education	One if primary education, zero if else	1000	0.239	0.427
Secondary education	One if secondary education, zero if else	1000	0.614	0.4871
Tertiary education	One if tertiary education, zero if else	1000	0.146	0.3533
Income-poorest 20%	One if income is in the first income quintile, zero if else	1000	0.148	0.3553
Income-second 20%	One if income is in the second income quintile, zero if else	1000	0.186	0.3893
Income-third 20%	One if income is in the third income quintile, zero if else	1000	0.194	0.3956
Income-fourth 20%	One if income is in the fourth income quintile, zero if else	1000	0.188	0.3909
Income-fifth 20%	One if income is in the fifth income quintile, zero if else	1000	0.284	0.4511

Source: Global Findex database 2014.

Table 3. Descriptive Statistics for the Dependent Variables

Variables	Obs.	Mean	Std. Dev.	MENAP1 Mean	MENAP2 Mean
Financial Inclusion Indicators					
Formal account	1000	0.322	0.467	0.420	0.295
Formal Saving	1000	0.077	0.266	0.141	0.090
Formal Borrowing	1000	0.062	0.241	0.105	0.083
Reasons to not have a Formal Account					
Too far	1000	0.035	0.183	0.291	0.303
Too expensive	1000	0.135	0.341	0.316	0.338
Lack of documents	1000	0.064	0.244	0.291	0.305
Lack of trust	1000	0.072	0.258	0.284	0.294
Religious	1000	0.126	0.332	0.286	0.295
No money	1000	0.529	0.499	0.512	0.600
Family member have one	1000	0.158	0.364	0.123	0.122
Borrowing Sources					
Borrowed from formal	1000	0.062	0.241	0.105	0.083
Borrowed from store	1000	0.251	0.433	0.155	0.151
Borrowed from friend	1000	0.256	0.436	0.281	0.270
Borrowed from other private	1000	0.091	0.287	0.079	0.064
Online Payment	1000	0.023	0.151	0.109	0.048

MENAP[1:] all region countries, MENAP[2:] region without Gulf countries. *Source*: Global Findex database 2014.

5.2. The empirical estimations

5.2.1. Determinants of the main financial inclusion indicators

Table 4 shows the logistic estimation results for main financial inclusion indicators. The study used formal accounts, formal saving, and formal borrowing as dependent variables; age, gender, education, and income were used as explanatory variables. The global agenda focuses on formal access for general economic growth and to enhance lives because formal institutions have the most resources, are regulated, stable, and under government control, which directs resources to sectors in need. Consequently, the financial inclusion indicators are as follows: having an account means that the percentage of the adults 15+ have a formal account. Formal saving means that a percentage of adults 15+ have saved money at formal financial institutions during the past 12 months. Likewise, formal borrowing means that a percentage of adults 15+ have borrowed money from formal financial institutions during the past 12 months. Table 3 presents the logistic estimation results for individual characteristics as explanatory variables and financial inclusion indicators as a dependent variable.

Table 4 shows that age as an explanatory variable is positively significant with all financial inclusion indicators; it has a nonlinear relation with all indicators. For gender as a variable, the results indicated that female gender has a negative relationship with the formal account and formal borrowing, which means females are less likely to have formal

Table 4. The Main Financial Inclusion Indicators

Variables	Formal Account	Formal Saving	Formal Borrowing
Age	0.095***	0.063***	0.069***
	(0.014)	(0.023)	(0.023)
Age2	−0.001***	−0.000***	−0.001***
	(0.000)	(0.000)	(0.001)
Gender-Female	−0.376***	−0.110	−0.530***
	(0.094)	(0.128)	(0.138)
Secondary Education	0.240**	0.167	0.192
	(0.126)	(0.195)	(0.204)
Tertiary Education	1.334***	0.651***	0.803***
	(0.167)	(0.214)	(0.225)
Income-Poorest 20%	−1.193***	−1.063***	−0.545**
	(0.170)	(0.304)	(0.279)
Income-Poor 20%	−0.780***	−0.857***	−0.283
	(0.139)	(0.233)	(0.218)
Income-Middle 20%	−0.733***	−0.564***	−0.227
	(0.135)	(0.189)	(0.203)
Income-Rich 20%	−0.329***	−0.154	0.047
	(0.130)	(0.159)	(0.181)
Obs.	1000	1000	1000
LR chi2(9)	287.75	73.13	65.41
Prob > chi2	0.0000	0.0000	0.0000
Pseudo R2	0.229	0.1347	0.1407
Log likelihood	−484.49	−234.82	−199.73

Source: Global Findex database 2014. ***$p < 0.01$, **$p < 0.05$, *$p < 0.1$. Standard errors in parentheses.

accounts (37%) and less likely to borrow from formal sources (53%). Further, there is no relation between females and formal saving. As such, formal institutions should work harder to enhance females' opportunities to access and use formal financial services.

In Palestine, the PMA focused on financial awareness jointly with formal institutions such as PCMA and other banking and financial services companies. The PMA reported that around 31% of females have financial awareness, while the percentage of males is about 51% (PMA, 2017). Accordingly, financial services companies such as banks could offer services directed to females, especially for those who want to have small businesses, to enhance their use of financial sources. Notably, strengthening equality between males and females as a goal for comprehensive development does not come easily, especially regarding financial issues. In Palestine, a country in the Middle East, North Africa, Afghanistan, and Pakistan (MENAP) region, male citizens are responsible for working and providing money for the family, which requires opening a bank account, either savings or loan (World Bank, 2007). In Palestine, the unemployment rate for males was 22.5% and 39.2% for females in 2015 (PCBS, 2015). Enhancing social inclusion and equality regarding work opportunities for both males and females could improve financial inclusion (Zins and Weill, 2016), leading to sustainability in the development process.

Moreover, the study used two levels of education: secondary and tertiary education. The results indicated that secondary-educated people were positively associated with having a formal account, but there is no relationship between secondary education and formal saving and borrowing. Furthermore, the link becomes significantly positive when moved to higher-educated people, measured by tertiary education. Individuals with a tertiary-level education are more likely to have a formal account (coefficient more than 1.3) and formal saving with a coefficient factor of around 0.65, which is positively significant. Meanwhile, there is no relation between the "secondary education" and "formal borrowing" variables. This result means more-educated people are more likely to be financially included in Palestine.

Moreover, because the financial inclusion philosophy focuses on poor people to enhance their participation in the development process, the study used the first and fourth income quintiles to determine whether these quintiles influence financial inclusion indicators (CGAP, 2016; Park and Mercado, 2015; Zins and Weill, 2016). The results indicated that the poorest are less likely to have a formal account, with a negative coefficient around 1.2; the same is true for saving, with a coefficient around 1.06, where the official borrowing coefficient is around 0.54. That means being among the poorest could decrease one's opportunity to have an official account, formal saving, and formal borrowing (around 120%, 106% and 54%, respectively). Likewise, individuals in the second income quintile, which represents poor people, and the third income quintile, which represents middle-income people, are less likely to have a formal account and formal saving. Further, there is no relation between these income quintiles and formal borrowing. These quintiles, especially the poorest and neediest, require more services directed to them, not only to have an account but also to use financial services such as borrowing, which may lead to enhanced economic development.

Additionally, the fourth income quintile, which represents wealthy people, has a negatively significant relation with formal accounts, and there is no link between the fourth income quintile and formal saving and borrowing. Notably, that the negative coefficients became smaller when moving from the poorest to the wealthiest quintiles connected with a formal account. This finding means that the opportunity to have a formal account improved as income became better. Some of these results are consistent with those in Shihadeh's (2018) study, and others are inconsistent. In general, females and the poor do not have chances to access financial services.

5.2.2. *The barriers to having a formal account*

Table 5 presents obstacles to having a formal account in Palestine. The analysis used seven reasons for not having a formal account, based on the World Bank survey. Finding that age is significant with the six reasons displayed in Table 4 as a reason for not having a formal account, but in the negative direction, except the variables of "too expensive" and "lack of trust" are not significant. All reasons are in the negative direction and have small coefficients. Thus, barriers to having a formal account could decrease with age.

Table 5. Barriers to Having a Formal Account

Variables	Too Expensive	Lack of Doc.	Lack of Trust	Lack of Money	Religious Reasons	A Family Member has an Account
Age	−0.015	−0.088***	−0.011	−0.051***	−0.036***	−0.059***
	(0.015)	(0.017)	(0.017)	(0.012)	(0.014)	(0.015)
Age2	0.000	0.001***	0.000	0.001***	0.000**	0.0004***
	(0.000)	(0.001)	(0.000)	(0.000)	(0.000)	(0.0002)
Gender-Female	0.004	−0.080	−0.189	0.192**	0.055	0.432***
	(0.106)	(0.134)	(0.123)	(0.086)	(0.106)	(0.108)
Secondary Education	−0.374***	−0.407***	−0.240	−0.267**	−0.282**	−0.255*
	(0.134)	(0.184)	(0.161)	(0.118)	(0.139)	(0.148)
Tertiary Education	−1.659***	−0.989***	−1.248	−1.182***	−0.904***	−0.717***
	(0.388)	(0.333)	(0.387)	(0.168)	(0.236)	(0.205)
Income-Poorest 20%	0.485***	−0.069	0.066	0.918***	0.035	−0.775***
	(0.165)	(0.201)	(0.188)	(0.139)	(0.169)	(0.178)
Income-Poor 20%	0.259*	−0.399*	−0.143	0.810***	−0.063	−0.694***
	(0.162)	(0.215)	(0.191)	(0.128)	(0.163)	(0.163)
Income-Middle 20%	0.231	−0.395*	0.0163	0.772***	0.151	−0.317**
	(0.163)	(0.216)	(0.180)	(0.126)	(0.154)	(0.145)
Income-Rich 20%	0.1262	0.125	−0.183	0.457***	0.155	−0.160
	(0.171)	(0.185)	(0.199)	(0.127)	(0.157)	(0.143)
Observations	1000	1000	1000	1000	1000	1000
LR chi2(9)	58.6200	49.09	24.15	194.43	29.37	93.99
Prob > chi2	0.0000	0.0000	0.0041	0.0000	0.0006	0.0000
Pseudo R2	0.0741	0.103	0.0467	0.1406	0.0388	0.1077
Log likelihood	−366.4717	−213.292	−246.71	−594.25	−364.028	−389.34

Source: Global Findex database 2014. ***$p < 0.01$, **$p < 0.05$, *$p < 0.1$. Standard errors in parentheses.

In the analysis, no respondents indicated "too far" (distance) as a reason for not having a formal account, so excluded it from the analysis. PMA joined the AFI in 2010. Since then, there has been outstanding growth in banking penetration and financial inclusion in Palestine, including the development of branches and ATMs to reach rural areas and small villages, as discussed in Section 2.3. Further, females considered the lack of money and "family member has an account" as barriers to not having a formal account. These results may refer to the fact that females, in most cases, are not responsible for the family's financial issues, as males are responsible for providing for the family's needs.

The secondary and tertiary education variable was negatively associated with all barriers except lack of trust, which has no relation to education. Consequently, these reasons are not considered as a barrier to educated people having a formal account. For the poorest people, "too expensive" and lack of money are regarded as barriers to having a formal account. However, a family member with an account will not decrease this group's chances to have a formal account. Indeed, offering services at affordable prices will enhance their opportunities to have formal accounts and use formal financial services. Interestingly, poor people (second quintile) care less about financial issues than do the poorest. Furthermore, finding that the lack of money is positively associated with the third and fourth income quintiles; financial issues become less critical for middle-income and wealthy people. Meanwhile, female and the income quantiles are positively linked with lack of money as a barrier to not having a formal account, while age and education are negatively linked with this barrier. These results are inconsistent with Demirguc-Kunt et al. (2014), who indicated that in MENA, religion is considered a barrier to having a formal account. Further, these results are consistent with results from Shihadeh (2018), especially when related to religion.

5.2.3. Sources of alternative borrowing

Table 6 presents the logistic estimation results for borrowing sources linked with individuals' characteristics, thus, examines how the individuals' have to deal with alternative borrowing sources. Alternative borrowing sources addressed in the survey are as follows: formal and informal borrowing such as from stores, family or friend, and another private lender. As the financial inclusion agenda is concerned with formal borrowing sources, understanding alternative borrowing sources could enhance the national agenda and improve individuals' possibilities for accessing formal credit sources that offer convenient services with affordable prices.

The above table indicates that age, as a dummy variable, is positively correlated with all borrowing sources. Also, finding that females are less likely to borrow from formal sources; this return to the fact that females in MENA are less likely to borrow because of financial issues related to males (World Bank, 2007). There is no relation between females and other credit sources. For people with secondary-level educations, we did not find any relation with borrowing sources, while people with tertiary-level educations are more likely to borrow from both formal and informal sources, with a preference for

Table 6. Sources of Alternative Borrowing

Variables	From Formal Sources	From Store	From Family/Friend	From Another Private Lender
Age	0.069***	0.062***	0.054***	0.030*
	(0.023)	(0.014)	(0.014)	(0.018)
Age2	−0.0007***	−0.0007***	−0.0007***	−0.0004*
	(0.000)	(0.0002)	(0.0002)	(0.0002)
Gender-Female	−0.530***	−0.086	−0.065	−0.161
	(0.138)	(0.089)	(0.089)	(0.113)
Secondary Education	0.1920	−0.096	0.155	−0.070
	(0.204)	(0.119)	(0.125)	(0.155)
Tertiary Education	0.803***	0.069	0.364**	0.139
	(0.225)	(0.156)	(0.159)	(0.196)
Income-Poorest 20%	−0.545**	0.532***	0.554***	0.351**
	(0.279)	(0.147)	(0.140)	(0.182)
Income-Poor 20%	−0.283	0.426***	0.202	0.278*
	(0.218)	(0.135)	(0.135)	(0.172)
Income Middle 20%	−0.227	0.313**	0.048	0.216
	(0.203)	(0.134)	(0.135)	(0.171)
Income-Rich 20%	0.0465	0.293**	0.081	0.046
	(0.181)	(0.135)	(0.134)	(0.179)
Observations	1000	1000	1000	1000
LR chi2(9)	65.41	41.860	51.4500	12.580
Prob > chi2	0.0000	0.0000	0.0000	0.1824
Pseudo R2	0.1407	0.0372	0.045	0.021
Log likelihood	−199.73	−542.49	−543.11	−298.55

Source: Global Findex database 2014. ***$p < 0.01$, **$p < 0.05$, *$p < 0.1$. Standard errors in parentheses.

formal sources. However, they are more likely to borrow from a family member or friend, depending on the personal relationship, where there is no relationship with other informal sources.

Furthermore, the poorest people are more likely to borrow entirely from informal sources, which is addressed in the analysis, with a preference to borrowing from a family member or friend. They are less likely to borrow from formal sources because, as discussed, they are less likely to have a formal account. Poor people are more likely to borrow from informal sources especially from a store and other private sources with a preference for borrowing from a store, and no relation was found with formal sources. Unfortunately, there is no relationship between formal credit among middle-income and wealthy people; the expected results were that these groups would be more likely to borrow from formal sources than informal. Moreover, these two quintiles are positively linked with credit from a store as an informal source. These results reflect that individuals in the fourth quintile are less likely to have a formal account, as reflected in formal borrowing.

5.2.4. *Online payment*

As one of the most important instruments to enhance financial inclusion and make financial services more accessible, faster, and affordable, the global and national agenda must focus on online payments. Thus, internet services and the electronic payments tools have come far, especially regarding developments in using the internet globally as well as in Palestine. To keep up with online payments in Palestine, in 2016, PMA held a conference regarding the fundamental role of electronic payment services and to discuss tools necessary to start up this kind of payment system. Meanwhile, one of the main obstacles to using online payment is internet cost, which is high, especially when using a mobile phone. Table 7 presents how the individuals' socio-economic characteristics could influence online payments.

According to the Palestinian Central Bureau of Statistics (PCBS), in 2014, 48.3% of households had internet access. This percentage below the Middle East rate which is 56.3% as of May 2017 (Silva *et al.*, 2017). Furthermore, educated people are more likely to use the internet than are others (Demirguc-Kunt *et al.*, 2015). The results in Table 6 show that

Table 7. The Online Payment

Variables	Online Payment
Age	0.116***
	(0.044)
Age2	−0.001***
	(0.000)
Gender-Female	−0.276
	(0.192)
Secondary Education	0.684*
	(0.381)
Tertiary Education	1.108***
	(0.402)
Income-Poorest 20%	−0.072
	(0.305)
income-Poor 20%	−0.211
	(0.301)
income-Middle 20%	−0.233
	(0.289)
income-Rich 20%	−0.382
	(0.290
Observations	1000
LR chi2(9)	28.61
Prob > chi2	0.001
Pseudo R2	0.130
Log-likelihood	−95.19

Source: Global Findex database 2014. ***$p < 0.01$, **$p < 0.05$, *$p < 0.1$. Standard errors in parentheses.

people with secondary- and tertiary-level educations are more likely to use online payment systems. Further, there is no relation between online payment and the income quintiles and gender (female) used in this analysis. Therefore, enhancing access to digital payment could increase innovation, job creation, and thus support the national agenda to achieve sustainable development (Demirguc-Kunt et al., 2015).

6. Conclusions and Policy Implications

This paper addressed the individuals' behavior that influences financial inclusion as key for sustainable development in Palestine. The remarkable developments in the infrastructure of financial inclusion could enhance the agenda to achieve economic growth and equality, as factors for sustainable development. By understanding the characteristics of individuals who have little or no access to financial resources, policymakers can develop new rules and regulations and, ultimately, improve the economy. The development process focuses on the disadvantaged; including them in the financial system could improve their chances to work, innovate, operate a business, get an education, have access to health care, and save for the future, all leading to sustainable development as a continuous process.

For the main indicators of financial inclusion, the study finds that age has a positive influence on financial inclusion while being female reduces inclusion, especially for borrowing and having a formal bank account. The results indicate that females experience economic discrimination. For having a formal account, the analysis reveals that having less money is considered a primary reason for females not having formal accounts. Additionally, being in the low-income quintiles relates to not having formal accounts; this factor is also related to the high unemployment rate in Palestine and fewer chances of obtaining work. Borrowing behavior in Palestine tends toward informal sources, such as getting credit from stores and borrowing from family and other private sources. The results also show that many Palestinians are not interested in formal borrowing. The lack of interest leads to increased costs for banks and less money going into the economy, which could negatively influence economic growth.

Formal institutions, such as the PMA, the Palestine Capital Market Authority, and the Ministry of Higher Education have made exceptional progress toward developing a financial inclusion infrastructure in Palestine. However, the present unstable political climate continues to impede the country's economic stability and people's motivation to use formal financial resources such as credit. However, continued work toward the current goals, with more focus on online payment systems and offering innovative and affordable services, especially for adults, females, and the poor could enhance financial inclusion. Meanwhile, enhancing access will reflect on the country's economic growth and sustainable development process.

These findings point to the need for more research to understand why Palestinians do not use formal financial resources and whether social reasons factor into these economic decisions. Further, more research should be directed toward youth and females to test whether existing services cover their needs and whether they could start businesses if banks were to reduce collateral requirements and finance charges. These findings could help academics conduct more theoretical and empirical studies about Palestine. Moreover, as the majority religion in Palestine is Islam, is worth that banks and formal financial services developing their services according to the Islamic financial rules. Learning from successful stories among the world regarding adopting appropriate financial services for Muslims could enhance their accessing level to the financial services. Therefore, significant participation in the economic growth is indicated by previous studies.

Furthermore, policymakers could benefit from these findings regarding understanding the individual characteristics that will help them draw up government agendas for enhancing financial inclusion as a way toward economic growth and sustainable development. All entities in the country should work together to achieve better results for sustainable development in the long run. Some of these institutions and programs could work together to achieve financial inclusion and awareness in, for example, financial awareness programs in universities and schools, financing programs for SMEs and youth, and supporting innovative ideas through the provision of resources, technologies, and employment funds.

References

Aker, JC and IM Mbiti (2010). Mobile phones and economic development in Africa. *Journal of Economic Perspectives*, 24, 207–232.

Akudugu, MA (2013). The determinants of financial inclusion in Western Africa: Insights from Ghana. *Research Journal of Finance and Accounting*, 4(8), 1–9.

Allen, F, A Demirgüç-Kunt, L Klapper and MSM Peria (2016). The foundations of financial inclusion: Understanding ownership and use of formal accounts. *Journal of Financial Intermediation*, 27, 1–30, Available at: http://dx.doi.org/10.1016/j.jf.2015.12.003.

Arun, T and R Kamath (2015). Financial inclusion: Policies and practice. *IIMB Management Review*, 27, 267–287, https://doi.org/10.1016/j.iimb.2015.09.004

Ben Naceur, S, A Barajas and A Massara (2015). Can Islamic banking increase financial inclusion?. International Monetary Fund, Working Paper 15/31.

Baza, AU and KS Rao (2017). Financial Inclusion in Ethiopia. *International Journal of Economics and Finance*, 9(4), 191–201, https://doi.org/10.5539/ijef.v9n4p191.

Carlos, T and O Tiago (2017). Literature review of mobile banking and individual performance, *International Journal of Bank Marketing*, 35(7), 1044–1067, https://doi.org/10.1108/IJBM-09-2015-0143.

Consultative Group to Assist the Poor, CGAP (2016). Achieving the sustainable development goals, the role of financial inclusion. Retrieved from http://www.cgap.org/publications/achieving-sustainable-development-goals.

Demirgüç-Kunt, A, L Klapper (2013). Measuring financial inclusion: Explaining variation in use of financial services across and within countries. *Brookings Papers on Economic Activity*, 2013(1), 279–340.

Demirguc-Kunt, A, L Klapper and D Randall (2014). Islamic finance and financial inclusion: Measuring use of and demand for formal financial services among Muslim adults. *Review of Middle East Economics and Finance*, 10(2), 177–218, https://doi.org/10.1515/rmeef-2013-0062.

Donovan, K. (2012). Mobile money for financial inclusion. In *Information and Communications for Development 2012* (pp. 61–73). Washington, DC: The World Bank. doi:10.1596/978-0-8213-8991-1

Fungacova, Z and L Weill (2015). Understanding financial inclusion in China. *China Economic Review*, 34, 196–206, doi.org/10.1016/j.chieco.2014.12.004.

ITU. (2013). The Mobile Money Revolution - Part 2: Financial Inclusion Enabler, ITU-Technology Watch Report.

Iqbal, BA and S Sami (2017). Role of banks in financial inclusion in India. *Contaduríay Administración*, 62(2), 644–656, https://doi.org/10.1016/j.cya.2017.01.007.

Jukan, MK, A Babajić and A Softić (2017). Measuring financial inclusion in western Balkan countries – a comparative survey. International Conference on Economic and Social Studies (ICESoS), *At International Burch University.* 2017, http://dx doi.10.14706/icesos.1715.

Korynski, P and J Pytkowska (2016). Measuring Financial Inclusion in the EU: Financial Inclusion Score Approach.

Kim, DW, JS Yu and MK Hassan (2018a). The Influence of Religion and Social Inequality on Financial Inclusion. *The Singapore Economic Review*, https://doi.org/10.1142/S0217590817460031. Forthcoming

Kim, DW, JS Yu and MK Hassan (2018b). Financial inclusion and economic growth in OIC countries. *Research in International Business and Finance*, 43, 1–14, http://dx.doi.org/10.1016/j.ribaf.2017.07.178.

Kabakova, O and E Plaksenkov (2018). Analysis of factors affecting financial inclusion: Ecosystem view. *Journal of Business Research*, https://doi.org/10.1016/j.jbusres.2018.01.066.

Louis, L and Chartier F (2017). Financial Inclusion in South Africa: An Integrated Framework for Financial Inclusion of Vulnerable Communities in South Africa's Regulatory System Reform, *Journal of Comparative Urban Law and Policy.* 1(1), Article 13, http://readingroom.law.gsu.edu/jculp/vol1/iss1/13.

Palestinian Central Bureau of Statistics (2015). unemployment indicators in Palestine. http://www.pcbs.gov.ps/Portals/_Rainbow/Documents/unemployment-2015-02e.htm.

Consultative Group to assist the poor, CGAP. (2010). Financial access the World Bank Group.

Park, CY and Mercado Jr RV (2015). Financial inclusion, poverty, and income inequality in developing Asia. *Working Paper.* (426). Asian Development Bank. http://dx.doi.org/10.2139/ssrn.2558936.

Palestine Monetary Authority. (2016). *Annual Report 2015*. Ramallah–Palestine. Retrieved September, 2016. Retrieved from http://www.pma.ps.

Palestine Capital Market Authority. (2013). *Annual Report 2013: 2014*, Ramallah–Palestine. Retrieved from http://www.pcma.ps.

Palestine Monetary Authority. (2017). PMA Educational Brochures, 2017. http://www.pma.ps/Default.aspx?tabid=516&language=ar-EG. (In Arabic).

Ramada-Sarasola, M (2012). Can mobile money systems have a measurable impact on local development? Retrieved July 26, 2017, from http://papers.ssrn.com/sol3/papers.cfm?abstract_id=2061526.

Shihadeh, FH 2018. How individual characteristics influence financial inclusion: Evidence from MENAP. International Journal of Islamic and Middle Eastern Finance and Management. Forthcoming, doi: 10.1108/IMEFM-06-2017-0153.

Shihadeh, FH, A Hannon and XH Wang (2017),. The Financial Inclusion Development in Palestine. *Business and Economic Research*, 7(1), 189–198, https://doi.org/10.5296/ber.v7i1.11107.

Sajuyigbe, AS (2017). Influence of financial inclusion and social inclusion on the performance of women-owned businesses in Lagos state, Nigeria. *Scholedge International Journal of Management & Development*, 4(3), 18–27, http://dx.doi.10.19085/journal. sijmd040301.

Scharwatt, C, A Katakam, J Frydrych, A Murphy and N Naghavi (2015). State of the industry 2014: Mobile financial services for the unbanked. New York: GSMA. Retrieved from http://www.gsma.com/mobilefordevelopment/wpcontent/uploads/2015/03/SOTIR_2014.pdf.

Shoji, M, K Aoyagi, RJ Kasahara, Y Sawada and M Ueyama (2012). Social capital formation and credit access: Evidence from Sri Lanka. *World Development*, 40(12), 2522–2536.

Silva, P, Matos AD and Martinez-Pecino R (2017). E-inclusion: Beyond individual socio-demographic characteristics. *PLOS ONE*, 12(9): e0184545, https://doi.org/10.1371/journal.pone.0184545.

United Nations (2013). Youth financial inclusion http://www.uncdf.org/sites/default/files/Download/MB_CIFY_09MAY13.pdf.

World Bank. (2007). The status and progress of women in the Middle East & North Africa. Retrieved from http://siteresources.worldbank.org.

World Bank. (2018). The Little Data Book on Financial Inclusion 2018. World Bank, Washington, DC. © *World Bank*. https://openknowledge.worldbank.org/handle/10986/29654 License: CC BY 3.0 IGO." http://hdl.handle.net/10986/29654.

Wang, XH and FH Shihadeh (2015). Financial Inclusion: Policies, Status, and Challenges in Palestine. *International Journal of Economics and Finance*, 7(8), 196, doi: http://dx.doi.org/10.5539/ijef.v7n8p196.

Yuan, Y and L Xu. Are poor able to access the informal credit market? Evidence from rural households in China. *China Economic Review*, 2015, 33, 233–246, http://dx.doi.org/10.1016/j.chieco.2015.01.003.

Zins, A and L Weill (2016). The determinants of financial inclusion in Africa. *Review of Development Finance*, 6(1), 46–57, https://doi.org/10.1016/j.rdf.2016.05.001.

Chapter 6

Impact of Islamic Finance on Economic Growth: An Empirical Analysis of Muslim Countries[#]

Syeda Arooj Naz

Department of Management Sciences
COMSATS University Islamabad, Wah Campus, Pakistan
arooj.naz@live.com

Saqib Gulzar[*]

Department of Management Sciences
COMSATS University Islamabad, Wah Campus, Pakistan
saqibgulzar@ciitwah.edu.pk

Islamic finance is one of the most rapidly growing sectors of the global financial system. This paper empirically outlines the pure effect of Islamic finance including Islamic banking and Islamic bonds on economic growth in major Muslim countries. Current study has taken up Islamic banks' assets and Islamic banks' financing, total value of sukuk issued and real GDP as measuring proxies. For the analysis, PMG of ARDL framework has been utilized. The outcomes of the study revealed that in the long run, Islamic banks' assets, Islamic banks' financing and Islamic bonds are significantly correlated with real GDP in Muslim countries.

Keywords: Islamic banking; sukuk; GDP; PMG/ARDL.

1. Introduction

A financial setup that operates as per Shariah laws and principles is generally termed as Islamic finance. In Shariah, the receipt and payment of interest (riba), excessive uncertainty (gharar), gambling (maysir) and such financial activities which can be detrimental to society overall have sternly been barred (Benaissa *et al.*, 2005). Currently, Islamic finance incorporates Islamic banking, Islamic debt securities, takaful, Islamic equity markets, leasing and Islamic micro-finance. But the major share of Islamic finance assets about 95% comprises Islamic banking and Islamic bonds (International Monetary Fund, 2015). By 21st century, Islamic finance has reached a phase in which it has been expanding at a fast pace, globally opening investment and retail banks, asset management companies, financial and capital markets and broking houses. Consequently, it has become an important

---

[*]Corresponding author.
[#]This Chapter first appeared in the *Singapore Economic Review*, Vol. 67, No. 1, doi: 10.1142/S0217590819420062. © 2022 World Scientific Publishing.

area of global financial and economic system by capturing the interest of both Muslim and non-Muslim financiers. Islamic finance development influenced the global financial system in two ways. First, it has strengthened the global financial setup by providing new and novel veins. Secondly, it gave alternative financing resource opportunities to financiers and entrepreneurs having innovative business ideas and visions (Aksak and Asutay, 2012).

The key development in the Islamic finance sector has been undertaken in 2011, when the Thomson Reuters launched world's first Islamic finance benchmark rate, designed to provide an objective and dedicated indicator for the average expected return on Shariah compliant short-term interbank funding. The Islamic Development Bank (IDB), Statistical, Economic and Social Research and Training Centre for Islamic Countries (SESRIC) and Accounting and Auditing Organization for Islamic Financial Institutions (AAOIFI) are the real milestones of the Islamic financial system (Islamic Finance in OIC Member Countries, 2011). The World Islamic Banking Competitiveness Report (2016) revealed that in the last three decades, the global Shariah-compliant financial assets have grown at double-digit rates at an average of 15% per annum, starting from US$ 5 billion in the late 1980s to US$ 2.4 trillion in 2015.

The basic theory of Islamic banking declares that the interest is strictly prohibited; all the Islamic banks operate as per this firm belief. This basic principle has guided all the Muslim scholars and theoretical workers to develop a model of Islamic banking which differs from conventional banks. Such model holds that nobody can earn profit from others' loss. The modern birth of Islamic banking took place in the 1970s in Egypt. Islamic banking has appeared as a novel category of financial intermediators for global financial markets, investors, financiers and entrepreneurs (Kpodar and Imam, 2010). Since its inception, 500 Islamic financial institutions have been established so far, including more than 300 Islamic banks in 70 nations both Islamic and western nations worldwide (Jamaldeen, 2012). The countries such as Bahrain, Bangladesh, Jordan, United Kingdom, Iran, Malaysia, Sudan, Pakistan, Saudi Arabia, Singapore and the United Arab Emirates are successfully operating Islamic banking. In the last few years, especially after the global financial crises 2008, the world has been witnessed a prominent growth in Islamic banking and finance. It has been evidenced as most viable and sustainable banking system, in which most of the big conventional banks failed to endure their existence. The constant performance of Islamic financial institutions has shown the strength and significance to the world. As per facts of Ernst and Young report (2011–2012), Saudi Arabia has a major share of 35% in global Islamic banking assets, then Kuwait with 31%, Bahrain has 27% share, Qatar also showed its presence with 22% and UAE stands with 17%, respectively.

In parallel to Islamic banking, Islamic bond (sukuk) has also emerged as a novel and strong branch of Islamic finance. Sukuk is defined as: "Certificates of equal value representing undivided shares in ownership of tangible assets, usufructs and services or (in the ownership of) the real assets of particular projects or special investment activity" (AAOIFI, 2008). The structure of sukuk is designed in such a way to keep it in line with the teachings of Holy Quran. According to Shariah, the sukuk incorporates interest-free instrument features along with the unique characteristic which provides investor (sukuk holder) a fair ownership in that specific real asset or pool of assets (Vishwanath and Azmi, 2009). The history of modern Islamic bonds dates back in 1990s, when first domestic corporate sukuk was issued by a non-Muslim foreign-owned Malaysian corporation (Shell MDS), worth of MYR 125 million equal to 30 million US$ (Jawahra and Disooqi, 2010). Since 1999, numerous public and private institutions started issuing sukuk. From 2000 onwards, sukuk market hyped. According to IMF Report (2015), about 27 states around the globe have issued sukuk. Among them, Malaysia holds more than two-thirds of total gross value. Collectively, Saudi Arabia, Qatar, United Arab Emirates and Malaysia hold 90% of total sukuk issued.

In this study, we investigate the relationship between Islamic finance and economic growth, whether the growing trend of Islamic finance in Muslim countries leads to economic growth of that country or not. Numerous empirical studies have been conducted nationally and internationally on the correlation of financial development and economic growth. Majority studies are from Malaysia (Mun *et al.*, 2009), Germany (Antonios, 2010), Nigeria (Ovat, 2012), Sudan (Suliman and Dafaalla, 2011), Saudi Arabia (Alshamrani, 2014), Bahrain (Tabash and Dhankar, 2013), Bahrain (Asiri and Abdalla, 2015) and Kuwait (Trad and Bhuyan, 2015). All of them predicted strong relationship and notable contribution of financial development in economic growth. Apart from extensive research conducted on this topic, still meager amount of standings has been given to Islamic financial framework, particularly on relationship between Islamic bonds and economic growth. Therefore, current research is mainly concerned with the following research questions: (1) Does the Islamic finance show significant causal relationship with economic growth in the selected Muslim countries in the long run? (2) Is there any significant relationship between Islamic banking and economic growth in the selected Muslim countries in the long run? (3) Is there a significant relationship between Islamic bonds and economic growth in the selected Muslim countries in the long run?

In order to achieve the objectives, five Muslim states were selected, including Bahrain, Indonesia, Malaysia, Pakistan and Qatar, based on their notable contribution in Islamic finance through Islamic banking and Islamic bonds. These economies can provide better correlation results of Islamic finance and economic growth. According to IMF, the Islamic banking and Islamic bonds are the two main variables comprising almost 95% of the total Islamic finance assets. Therefore, this study has selected both Islamic banking and Islamic bonds. Further, Islamic banking has been measured through quarterly data of Islamic bank's assets and Islamic bank's financing, while Islamic bonds have been measured through the accumulated figure of Islamic bonds issued per quarter for all the selected Muslim countries over the period 2006–2015. The data are analyzed by pooled mean group/autoregressive distributed lag model, which is specially designed for panel data set to seek the cointegration among the selected variables.

The results of current study are evidences of Islamic finance and economic growth relationship. The study findings are in congruence with the results of Ansari (2012) which demonstrate that there is a relationship between Islamic bank's asset and real GDP, and both move together in the long run. However, at the emerging stage of development, the Islamic bank's assets quality suffers, which negatively affect the economic growth. The results of Islamic bank's financing have positive influence on economic growth (Abduh and Omar, 2012; Kassim, 2015; Farahani *et al.*, 2012; Elhachemi and Othman, 2016;

Yusof and Bahlous, 2013). This study has found that development of sukuk positively and significantly affected the economic growth, which is consistent with the results of Nayan *et al.* (2014), Khiyar and Galfy (2014) and Echchabi *et al.* (2016). Overall the results of the current study implied that in the long run, Islamic finance and economic growth hold bi-causality relationship which is theoretically supported by Patrick's hypothesis.

The remainder of this paper is organized as follows. The next section incorporates literature review which includes detailed theoretical and empirical discussion of published work on Islamic finance and economic growth; Section 3 discusses research methodology; Section 4 contains analysis of results; Section 5 presents discussion, conclusion, research implication, limitations and recommendations.

2. Literature Review

2.1. *Theoretical evidences on finance–growth nexus*

The relationship between finance and economic growth has been one of the intensely researched topics, particularly in the context of conventional finance, as early as seminal work of Bagehot who stated how real economy and financial systems are interrelated and financial system performs fundamental part in economic growth (Bagehot, 1873). Schumpeter's economic development theory (1911) proposed innovations *"new combinations"* that drive economic development. He concluded that financial system facilitates economic development in early stages of economic growth. Robinson (1952) asserted demand-following hypothesis as *"finance follows growth leads"*, it postulates that real economic growth leads to financial development. Gerschenkron (1962) studied the phenomena of causal relationships of financial sector and economic growth, by identifying two models *"demand following"* when economic growth generates a demand for financial services and *"supply leading"* when financial intermediation influences economic growth. Patrick (1966) further elaborated that supply-leading pattern can be seen during the initial stages of economic development, and afterwards it gradually swings to demand-following pattern. Thus, originally the causality shifts from finance to economic growth, such situation could be seen in developing countries while in highly developed economies, the demand-following pattern has been practiced. Cameron and Olga (1967) and Goldsmith and Raymond (1969) emphasized that financial intermediaries could have positive effect on economic growth because of its high efficiency and high volume of investment. King and Levine (1993b) stated *"Finance, entrepreneurship, and growth theory and evidence"* and concluded that well-organized financial systems stimulate economic growth through accelerating the rate of efficiency and productivity. Mckinnon (1973) and Shaw (1973) followed supply-leading hypothesis and proposed that *"financial repression theory"* states development of financial system drives growth of economy. Lucas (1988) believed in neutrality hypothesis, and he stated that correlation of finance and economic growth is unduly over valued because finance is an unnecessary component for the process of economic growth. Despite extensive literature on relation of finance and economic growth, the theoretical framework is somewhat unrefined and empirical evidence is rough. However, economists encouraged a surge of interest in the topic.

2.2. Empirical evidences on Islamic finance-economic growth

Islamic financial system is the appropriate system in boosting the economic development process, especially in Islamic countries (Elhachemi and Othman, 2015). The development of Islamic finance significantly related to economic growth in the long run. According to Islamic finance theory, economic development has a direct link with real economy and it also promotes social justice (Farahani *et al.*, 2012). Expansion in Islamic banks provokes the economic growth, and simultaneous expansion of real sector economy significantly arouses the expansion of Islamic banking (Abduh and Omar, 2012). The empirical studies of Tabash and Dhankar (2014) assessed the role of Islamic finance in economic growth by conducting a study in United Arab Emirates. They adopted IBF, GDP, GFCF and FDI as their variables. For data analysis unit root, cointegration and Granger causality tests were utilized. The outcome depicted positive association of Islamic bank's financing and economic growth in the UAE. However, their results further indicated unidirectional causal relationship, from Islamic bank's financing to economic growth; thus their results strengthen the Schumpeter's supply-leading concept. Their study indicated that Islamic bank's financing has positively contributed in UAE in long-term investments. Yusof and Bahlous (2013) examined the dynamics of Islamic banking and economic growth in GCC countries, Malaysia and Indonesia. For analysis, they utilized panel cointegration, impulse response functions and variance decompositions; they concluded that Islamic banking stimulates economic growth and Islamic financial institutions have triggered the GDP in short and long run.

Another study by Hassanudin *et al.* (2013) revealed the identical relationship in Bahrain. They witnessed a strong bi-directional causal relationship in long-run, and both Islamic finance and economic growth affect each other. Abduh *et al.* (2012) explored the correlation among the Islamic financial development and economic growth, along with the relation between conventional financial development and economic growth in Bahrain. The data were collected from Q1 (2000) to Q4 (2010) and utilized the Johanson cointegration and vector error correction model. The findings of the study confirmed a significant correlation among Islamic finance and economic growth in the long term. Whereas the short-term result is different. Overall, in their study, they found that Islamic financial development has a two-way relationship with economic growth. The conventional financial development has significant relationship with economic growth, both in long and in short term. Abusabha and Masoud (2014) studied the Islamic financial market role in economic development of Middle East and North African (MENA) countries. They utilized econometric models like unit root, co-integration and ARDL with Granger causality tests on quarterly data of MENA countries. Both Granger causality and co-integration test revealed that relationship does exist between Islamic bank's financing and economic growth both in long and short terms. Furthermore, bi-directional Granger causality exists between GDP and Islamic bank's financing in long run, which reflects Islamic bank's financing positively contributes to economic growth with long-term effect.

Shabri and Kassim (2015) concluded that Islamic finance and economic growth have significant relationships both in long and short run. The financial performance of Islamic banking sector has significant impact on the economic growth because Islamic banking is attracting majority of the banking consumers based on religion. Overall results showed that minor amendments in the financial structure of Islamic banking sector can escalate the industry's financial efficiency which ultimately can contribute a major part in the economic development of Pakistan (Ansari, 2012). Sassi and Goaied (2011) discussed the relationship between Islamic bank development and economic growth in the MENA countries. Unlike other studies, the outcome they got showed that in the MENA region the Islamic financial development has adversely affected economic growth.

Since the 1990s, research on sukuk has gained momentum and attracted many academicians, policy-makers and practitioners. However, the empirical side of literature is very little, in recent years innovative products of Islamic bonds brought a fresh blood to the Islamic capital and money market. Due to sukuk distinctive features and instrumental variety, it has not only captivated Muslims investors but the global markets as well. It is popular among investors and have significantly contributed to economic growth. It is appealing to Muslim investors due to their Shariah compliant characteristics. The popularity of sukuk as a long-term investment instrument might be attributed to their fixed return feature (Nayan et al., 2014). Well-developed sukuk markets would enhance access to financial services, deepen capital markets and create Shariah-compliant alternative for small and risk-averse investors (Khiyar and Galfy, 2014). There are various factors such as political commotion, regulatory quality, macroeconomic factors (economic size, GDP) and financial crisis which may control the development of sukuk in the Islamic finance industry. Therefore, the Islamic financial experts should focus on how to overcome these obstacles, mitigation of risk in these crucial times and make sukuk be more acceptable in the international market (Ahmad et al., 2015). Moreover, it has been found that Islamic bond is the most significant mechanism for collecting funds from the international capital markets. Today, local and multinational corporations and financial institutions are issuing sukuk and making sukuk as an essential subset of the international financial system (Salem et al., 2016).

In contrast to other studies, Talahma (2015) found different results as there is negative effect of Islamic bonds on the economic growth; the reason behind is that the Islamic instrument is not adding anything valued to the real economy but rather only increasing the level of debt. Echchabi et al. (2016) identified the potential effect of sukuk financing on economic growth in major sukuk-issuing countries including Gulf Cooperation Council (GCC) and Pakistan, Indonesia, Malaysia, Turkey, China, Germany, Kazakhstan, United Kingdom, Gambia, France, Singapore and Brunei. GDP, trade openness and GFCF were taken as economic growth proxies. They revealed that issuance of sukuk impacted the GDP and GFCF when all the countries were pulled together; no individual effect was recognized for GCC and Saudi Arabia.

The above examination of literature shows that the nexus of Islamic banking and economic growth has been well researched in individual as well as cross-country comparison. With respect to Islamic bonds and economic growth, few studies have been found in Malaysia (Nayan *et al.*, 2014; Khiyar and Galfy, 2014; Echchabi *et al.*, 2016). Therefore, to narrow down the gap in literature, the current research will empirically outline the pure effect of Islamic finance including collective role of both Islamic banking and Islamic bonds (sukuk) on economic growth in major Muslim countries, including Bahrain, Indonesia, Malaysia, Pakistan and Qatar. This is one of the pioneer studies which has an edge to other Islamic finance studies, unlike them, the accumulated figure of all Islamic banks and the whole Islamic bonds issued are being used. Real gross domestic product has been used as variable for economic growth. Little or no study has been found using pooled mean group as an econometric technique for this specific relationship. Therefore, to contribute to the existing literature by using different and innovative econometric techniques would be another edge.

Based on the above discussion this study proposes the following hypothesis:

H_1. *There is a positive long-run relationship between Islamic bank's assets and real GDP.*
H_2. *There is a positive long-run relationship between Islamic bank's financing and real GDP.*
H_3. *There is a positive long-run relationship between sukuk and real GDP.*

3. Research Methodology

3.1. *Research design*

Based on the theoretical framework, the hypothesis for the current study adopts the panel dataset (cross-sectional time series data) that runs across 10 years' time span from Q1:2006 to Q4:2015 The selected sample includes five major Muslim countries including Bahrain, Indonesia, Malaysia, Pakistan and Qatar. The study empirically analyze the relationship between Islamic finance and economic growth by considering total Islamic bank's assets, total Islamic bank's financing, total value of sukuk issued and real gross domestic product. These proxies are selected because they have captured whole Shariah-compliant financial instruments and give the picture of Islamic finance overall. The study also caters control variables to omit the possible effects of other growth-determining factors: Gross fixed

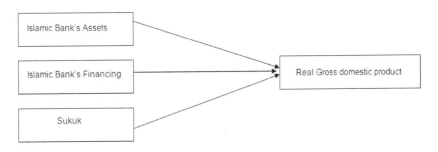

Figure 1. Proposed Conceptual Framework

capital formation, general government final expenditure and trade openness. The historical data set is extracted from the database of Department of Finance and Statistics of Pakistan, Islamic Banking Bulletin issued by State bank of Pakistan (SBP), Economic Survey of Pakistan, Security and Exchange Commission of Pakistan (SECP), International Financial Statistics (IFS), Central banks of (Bahrain, Indonesia, Malaysia, Pakistan and Qatar), International Monetary Fund (IMF), Federal Reserve Economic Database and World Bank database. The Figure 1 depicts the proposed conceptual framework.

3.2. Variables description

The variables of interest are explained in Table 1.

Table 1. Descriptive Information of Variables

Variable	Description	Measurement	Source
IBA	Islamic banking system development	Total Islamic bank's assets per quarter	State Bank of Pakistan, Bank Negara Malaysia, Qatar Central Bank, Bank Sentral Republik Indonesia, Indonesian Islamic bank outlook, Central Bank of Bahrain
IBF	Islamic banking system development	Total Islamic bank's financing per quarter	State Bank of Pakistan, Bank Negara Malaysia, Qatar Central Bank, Bank Sentral Republik Indonesia, Indonesian Islamic Bank Outlook, Central Bank of Bahrain
SUK	Islamic bond development	Net value of sukuk issued per quarter	International Islamic Financial Market Sukuk Report, Special Bulletin of Sukuk for Malaysia and Indonesia
GDP	Economic growth	Real GDP per quarter	World Bank Data
GFCF	Gross fixed capital formation	Gross fixed capital formation per quarter (control indicator)	World Bank Data
GGFE	General government final expenditure	Government expenditure on goods and services per quarter (control indicator)	World Bank Data
OPN	Trade openness	Total import plus export to GDP per quarter (control indicator)	World Bank Data

3.3. Diagnostic test

In this paper, the following diagnostic tests have been applied, since it is panel dataset, and ARDL/PMG allows following tests in software (E-views).

(1) First, normality of data has been checked via histogram. The result of Jarque Bera shows that residuals are normally distributed as P-value ≥ 0.05 (for details see Appendix A).
(2) Linearity assumption has already been via panel unit root test; test showed that the mean, variance, autocorrelation is all constant over time.

Along with diagnostic test, data have been checked for structural break for the year 2008 (Q1, Q2, Q3, Q4) since Global Financial Crisis hits the major financial markets in 2007–2008. According to Chow Test on regression of LnGDP, LnIBA, LnIBF, LnSUK, LnGFCF, LnGGFE, LnOPN (2008, Q1, Q2, Q3, Q4), no structural break has been found, since the p-value ≥ 0.05 (for details see Appendix B).

3.4. Data analysis procedure

3.4.1. Panel unit root test

The power panel unit root test is significantly greater in comparison to the low power standard time-series unit root test in finite samples. The recent literature (Levin *et al.*, 2002; Im and Pesaran, 2003; Breitung, 2000) advocates that panel unit root test gives much more reliable data stationarity results than individual unit root test. The panel unit root tests are of five types: Fisher tests including ADF and PP, Breitung (2000), Im and Pesaran (2003), Levin *et al.* (2002) and Hadri (2000). Časni *et al.* (2014), Doğan *et al.* (2014) and Simões (2011) applied panel unit root test for their panel data set. Therefore, current study also considers panel unit root test and would employ four types of tests: (i) ADF Fisher, (ii) Im and Pesaran (2003), (iii) Levin *et al.* (2002) (iv) PP Fisher, to verify the order of integration among all data-set series. Pesaran *et al.* (1999) upon importance of unit root discussed that although it is not obligatory to test order of integration of variables when ARDL model is applied as long as the concerned variables are integrating at level $I(0)$ and first difference $I(1)$, but to make sure that none of the variable exceeds $I(1)$ level, other reason is to avoid the invalidation of empirical results, non-stationary variables need to be treated before testing the co-integration and causality between the data variables.

3.4.2. Pooled mean group estimation of ARDL

The current study utilizes ARDL method; ARDL which stands for auto regressive distributed lag is a co-integration method. Pesaran *et al.* developed this method to analyze the lagged values. Number of recent studies (Časni *et al.*, 2014; Doğan *et al.*, 2014; Goswami and Junayed, 2006; Simões, 2011; Asghar *et al.*, 2015; Lee and Wang, 2015) utilized PMG/ARDL for long-run and short-run relationships that fluctuate across countries in panel data structure, Therefore, current study also considers same approach to measure the long-run impact. Pesaran et al. (1999) have developed the pooled mean group (PMG) and incorporated it within the ARDL framework to identify the existence of co-integration relation between the variables. The PMG is a blend of pooling and averaging of coefficients. It can be written as:

$$\Delta y_{i,t} = \phi_i EC + \sum_{j=0}^{q-1} \Delta X_{i,t-j}' \beta_{i,j} + \sum_{j=1}^{p-1} \lambda_{i,j} * \Delta y_{i,t-j} + \varepsilon_{i,t}, \quad (1)$$

where

$$EC_{i,t} = y_{i,t-1} - X_{i,t}'\theta, \quad (2)$$

where $\Delta y_{i,t}$ is the dependent variable, t represents the dimension of time period, $t = 1, 2, ..., T$ and "i" represents the dimension of cross-section, $i = 1, 2, ..., N$. p, q are optimal lag orders. $X_{i,t}$ is a vector of $K \times 1$ regressors that allowed area to be purely $I(0)$ or $I(I)$ or cointegrated, $\lambda_{i,j}$ is the coefficient of lagged dependent variable called scalars. The $\beta_{i,j}$ are $K \times 1$ coefficient vectors, where $\varepsilon_{i,t}$ is the error correction term and ϕ_i denotes the speed of adjustment. If $\phi_i = 0$, that indicates that there is no long run association between variables. If ϕ_i is negative and statistically significant that means in case of disturbance the variables converge to long-run equilibrium. Where in Equation (2) "θ" is group-specific speed of adjustment coefficient (expected that $\theta < 0$). $y_{i,t-1} - X_{i,t'}$ represents error correction term (ECT).

3.4.3. Panel causality test

The panel causality test is a specific type of Granger causality tests used in panel data set. The Granger causality is calculated by running bivariate regressions; there are numerous approaches to test Granger causality in panel data settings. Lee and Wang (2015) and Doğan et al. (2014) are among the recent studies who utilized panel causality test. This study also goes along with the panel causality to test the directional effect of variables upon each other.

3.5. Research model

Since this paper focuses on impact of Islamic finance on economic growth in the long run, in order to empirically capture this relationship; the model equation is estimated as follows:

$$LnGDP_{i,t} = \gamma_{0i} + \gamma_{1i}LnIBA_{i,t} + \gamma_{2i}LnIBF_{i,t} + \gamma_{3i}LnSUK_{i,t} + \gamma_{4i}LnGFCF_{i,t}$$
$$+ \gamma_{5i}LnGGFE_{i,t} + \gamma_{6i}LnOPN_{i,t} + \mu_i + \varepsilon_{i,t}$$

where $LnGDP$ represents logarithm of real gross domestic product, which is representation of economic growth, "$LnIBA$" is logarithm of total Islamic bank's assets and "$LnIBF$" is the logarithm of total Islamic bank's financing, which are the proxies for measuring Islamic banking. "$LnSUK$" is the logarithm of total value of sukuk issued for measuring Islamic bonds, "$LnGFCF$" is expressed as logarithm of gross fixed capital formation, "$LnGGFE$" is the logarithm of general government final expenditure and "$LnOPN$" represents the logarithm of trade openness (as a percentage of GDP), which are control variables. "μ_t" is the disturbance term. "$\varepsilon_{i,t}$" represents error term controlling the influence of unexpected shocks to real GDP. The γ_0 represents the intercept, and $\gamma_1,\ldots,\gamma_6$ represent the regression coefficients of six variables. The subscripts "i" and "t" symbolize for country cross-sections and time period, respectively.

4. Analysis of Results

4.1. Results of panel unit root tests

Before applying PMG/ARDL, there is need to check the statistical characteristics of the variables of interest, whether the data are stationary or not, therefore, the first step is to perform panel unit root tests. The unit root tests that usually employed are common unit root tests: Breitung (Breitung, 2000), LLC (Levin et al., 2002) and Hadri (Hadri, 2000) in addition to individual unit root tests: ADF Fisher test (Maddala and Wu, 1999; Choi, 2001) and IPS (Im and Pesaran, 2003). In order to determine the orders of integration, the following types of test are considered; ADF-Fisher, PP-Fisher, Levin, Lin and Chu (LLC), Im, Pesaran and Shin (IPS) unit root tests. Table 2 summarizes the results of panel unit root test.

The output presented in Table 2 revealed that according to Levin, Lin and Chu (LLC), the real gross domestic product (LnGDP), Islamic bank's assets (LnIBA), Islamic bank's financing (LnIBF), sukuk (LnSUK), gross fixed capital formation (LnGFCF), general government final expenditure (LnGGFE) and trade openness (LnOPN) have no unit root at their levels and hence integrated of order zero, $I(0)$ indicating that all the variables are stationary at level. The results of PP Fisher also showed that the real gross domestic product (LnGDP), Islamic bank's assets (LnIBA), Islamic bank's financing (LnIBF), sukuk (LnSUK), general government final expenditure (LnGGFE) have no unit root at their levels, hence integrated of order zero, $I(0)$ while gross fixed capital formation (LnGFCF) and trade openness (LnOPN) have unit root at their levels, therefore these variables are further checked at first difference, and they became stationary at $I(1)$. This study relied on

Table 2. Panel Unit Root Test

Variables	Individual Intercept @ $I(0)$				Individual Intercept @ $I(1)$			
	LLC	IPS	ADF Fisher	PP Fisher	LLC	IPS	ADF Fisher	PP Fisher
LnGDP	0.008**	0.085	0.137	0.000**	0.737	0.165	0.156	0.110
LnIBA	0.000**	0.094	0.098	0.000**	0.319	0.259	0.216	0.200
LnIBF	0.001**	0.102	0.137	0.000**	0.073	0.040**	0.052**	0.003**
LnSUK	0.052**	0.021**	0.040**	0.000**	0.046**	0.000**	0.000**	0.000**
LnGFCF	0.033**	0.540	0.518	0.085	0.356	0.026**	0.034**	0.032**
LnGGFE	0.010**	0.232	0.029**	0.001**	0.509	0.062	0.019**	0.000**
LnOPN	0.005**	0.094	0.111	0.108	0.950	0.133	0.028**	0.004**

Note: **Significant at 5% level.

Table 3. Pooled Mean Group Estimation of ARDL

Variable	Coefficient	Std. Error	t-Statistic	Prob*
Long-run equation				
Ln(IBA)	−0.044	0.014	−3.033	0.0039**
Ln(IBF)	0.041	0.006	6.582	0.0000**
Ln(SUK)	0.011	0.001	6.818	0.0000**
Ln(GFCF)	0.232	0.006	37.776	0.0000**
Ln(GGFE)	0.492	0.009	53.105	0.0000**
Ln(OPN)	0.149	0.020	7.160	0.0000**
Short-run equation				
COINTEQ01	−0.441	0.197	−2.240	0.029**
DLn(GDP(−3))	0.088	0.236	0.373	0.710
DLn(IBA(−3))	0.257	0.154	1.665	0.102
DLn(IBF(−3))	−0.070	0.030	−2.299	0.025**
DLn(SUK(−3))	0.005	0.006	0.795	0.430
DLn(GFCF(−3))	−0.026	0.059	−0.448	0.656
DLn(GGFE(−3))	−0.234	0.159	−1.468	0.148
DLn(OPN(−3))	0.103	0.091	1.124	0.266
C	3.385	1.526	2.218	0.031**
No. of countries	5			
No. of observations	180			
Log likelihood	1012.454			

Notes: Dependent variable: Gross domestic product (GDP); independent variable: Islamic bank's assets (IBA), Islamic bank's financing (IBF), Sukuk (SUK); control variable: Gross fixed capital formation (GFCF), General government final expenditure (GGFE), Trade openness (OPN).
**Significant at 5% level.

the results of Levin, Lin and Chu and PP Fisher, which showed that data are stationary at level $I(0)$ and at first difference $I(1)$, so the null hypothesis having unit root is rejected because there is no trend in the analyzed data so that is why alternative hypothesis has been accepted.

4.2. Results of PMG/ARDL

As discussed earlier, there are few assumptions that need to be fulfilled before applying PMG/ARDL approach, i.e., first and foremost when the variables are integrated at level $I(0)$ or at first difference $I(1)$, it is important just to confirm that no variables fall in second difference $I(2)$; secondly, when data are free from heteroscedasticity and autocorrelation and when it is normally distributed. This study caters the panel data setting with small number of cross-sections denoted by (N) and small number of observations denoted by (T), which requires PMG estimation form of ARDL. Table 3 explained the results of PMG/ARDL where specification chosen through the AIC criterion.

The result of pooled mean group estimation of ADRL shows the long-run and short-run coefficients between real gross domestic product (LnGDP) and institutions variables and the speed of adjustment. In the long run, as can be seen, the results show that there are five institutions variables namely, Islamic bank's financing (LnIBF), sukuk (LnSUK), gross fixed capital formation (LnGFCF), general government final expenditure (LnGGFE) and trade openness (LnOPN) are positively and statistically significant at 5% in influencing the real gross domestic product (LnGDP). Particularly, Islamic bank's financing (LnIBF) came up with positive coefficient value (0.041) where p-value is significant at (0.0000) ≤ 0.05, which shows that Islamic bank's financing (LnIBF) has significant and positive relationship with real gross domestic product (LnGDP) in the long run. Similarly, sukuk (LnSUK) shows positive coefficient value (0.011) where p-value is significant at (0.0000) ≤ 0.05, which shows that sukuk (LnSUK) has significant and positive relationship with real gross domestic product (LnGDP) in the long run.

On the other side, one variable Islamic bank's assets (LnIBA) came up with negative coefficient value (-0.044) where p-value is significant at (0.0039) ≤ 0.05, which means that Islamic bank's assets (LnIBA) have significant but negative relationship with real gross domestic product (LnGDP) in the long run, which means 1% improvement in Islamic bank assets (LnIBA) profile will reduce around 4.5% real gross domestic product (LnGDP) to Muslim countries and 1% increase in the Islamic bank financing (LnIBF) can increase 4.1% real gross domestic product (LnGDP) to Muslim countries. Besides that, 1% increase in the sukuk (LnSUK) issuance led to increase the real gross domestic product (LnGDP) of Muslim countries around 1.1%.

Thus, based on these findings, the policy-maker can promote the Islamic finance in Muslim countries by improving quality of Islamic financial institutions, which creates financing and investment profile in the long run. They should utilize the potential of Islamic instruments and focus on improving the regulatory and financial infrastructure to achieve this goal. The speed of the adjustment revealed by the coefficient of convergence is about -0.44 and it is always negative and significant, indicating that there is no omitted variable bias. However, in the short run, all explanatory variables are statistically insignificant in influencing the real gross domestic product (LnGDP). These findings signal that investors do consider the importance of Islamic financial institution variables to real gross domestic product (LnGDP) in the long run.

4.3. Results of panel causality test

Finally, panel causality test type introduced by Dumitrescu and Hurlin (2012) has been applied to find out whether a causal relationship exists between real gross domestic product (LnGDP) and institutions variables or not? Table 4 reports the statistical values and probabilities constructed under null hypothesis of non-causality.

Panel causality analysis indicates that two-way causality exists from Islamic bank's assets (LnIBA), Islamic bank's financing (LnIBF), issuance of sukuk (LnSUK) to real gross domestic product (LnGDP) and from real gross domestic product (LnGDP) toward Islamic bank's assets (LnIBA), Islamic bank's financing (LnIBF) and issuance of sukuk (LnSUK) in Muslim countries (Bahrain, Indonesia, Malaysia, Pakistan and Qatar), since all

Table 4. Panel Causality Test

Pairwise Dumitrescu Hurlin Panel Causality Tests			
Null Hypothesis	W-Stat.	Zbar-Stat.	Prob.
Ln_GFCF does not homogeneously cause Ln_GDP	4.115	4.363	1.E−05**
Ln_GDP does not homogeneously cause Ln_GFCF	7.228	8.809	0.0000**
Ln_GGFE does not homogeneously cause Ln_GDP	12.393	16.185	0.0000**
Ln_GDP does not homogeneously cause Ln_GGFE	6.241	7.400	1.E−13**
Ln_IBA does not homogeneously cause Ln_GDP	7.493	9.188	0.0000**
Ln_GDP does not homogeneously cause Ln_IBA	5.624	6.519	7.E−11**
Ln_IBF does not homogeneously cause Ln_GDP	4.805	5.348	9.E−08**
Ln_GDP does not homogeneously cause Ln_IBF	3.512	3.503	0.0005**
Ln_OPN does not homogeneously cause Ln_GDP	3.318	3.226	0.0013**
Ln_GDP does not homogeneously cause Ln_OPN	1.321	0.374	0.707
Ln_SUK does not homogeneously cause Ln_GDP	5.014	5.647	2.E−08**
Ln_GDP does not homogeneously cause Ln_SUK	3.213	3.075	0.002**

Note: **Significant at 5% level.

of probability values $p \leq 0.05$. Therefore, the null hypothesis is rejected, and it can be said that higher the flow of Islamic finance higher would be the economic growth. To this end, the causal relationship between Islamic finance and economic growth occurs in two-way direction, which supports the Patrick hypothesis of finance–growth causality.

5. Discussion and Conclusion

5.1. *Discussion*

Current research has been conducted to study the impact of Islamic finance on economic growth in Muslim countries (Bahrain, Indonesia, Malaysia, Pakistan and Qatar). The real gross domestic product (LnGDP) has been taken as dependent variable and the Islamic bank's asset (LnIBA) and Islamic bank's financing (LnIBF) and sukuk (LnSUK) are taken as independent variables, whereas the gross fixed capital formation (LnGFCF), general government final expenditure (LnGGFE) and trade openness (LnOPN) have been taken as control variables. As per findings of the study, the results of (H1), *There is a significant positive relationship between Islamic bank's asset and real gross domestic product (LnGDP) in long run*, are consistent with the results of Ansari (2012) who stated that the bank's assets can decline economic growth (GDP). Thus, the proposition is partly supported. It is suggested that there is relationship between Islamic bank's asset (LnIBA) and real gross domestic product (LnGDP); both can move together in long run, but the negativity in the relationship is because of emerging stage of Islamic bank's product due to which its total assets quality suffers, and it negatively affects the economic growth. The reason behind this could be that the Muslim countries including Bahrain, Indonesia, Malaysia, Pakistan and Qatar are not much developed in Islamic banking, globally these countries have negligible Islamic banking share and their economy is independent of Shariah complaint banking. However, once these Islamic institutions fully developed and show their presence globally, they would have positive effect on the economy.

Islamic bank's financing (LnIBF) has positive influence on economic growth (LnGDP); same has been proved through results. This study is in line with the studies of Abduh and Omar (2012), Kassim (2015); Farahani *et al.* (2012), Elhachemi and Othman (2016) and Yusof and Bahlous (2013) on same relationship, and their findings and reasons are fully supported that Islamic bank's financing (LnIBF) and economic growth (LnGDP) are positively and significantly interlinked. Thus (H2), *There is a significant positive relationship between Islamic bank's financing (LnIBF) and real gross domestic product (LnGDP) in long run* is fully supported. Thus, this implies that the economic development in Muslim countries (Bahrain, Indonesia, Malaysia, Pakistan and Qatar) can be promoted through Islamic bank's financing.

Similarly, it has been hypothesized that (H3) *sukuk has significant positive relationship with real gross domestic product (LnGDP) in long run*. Unlike Said and Grassa (2013) found that sukuk market and economic growth have negative and insignificant relationship. This study is consistent with the results of Nayan *et al.* (2014), Khiyar and Galfy (2014) and Echchabi *et al.* (2016); that development of sukuk has positive and noteworthy impact on economic growth.

5.2. Conclusion

In the wake of recent progress in financial system, Islamic finance has emerged globally as the dynamic branch of financial sector, due to its built-in qualities; e.g., interest-free, asset-based contracts, equity-based contracts, emphasizing risk sharing, entrepreneurship, prudence, economic growth and prosperity. Consequently, it can be assumed that Islamic financial system is resistant to financial speculations and immune to financial asset bubbles; therefore it is more risk-averse, safe and secure than the conventional financial system. This paper has empirically investigated the long run relationship of Islamic finance and economic growth in some major Muslim countries (Bahrain, Indonesia, Malaysia, Pakistan and Qatar) during the period of 2006–2015. The objectives of the study were mainly to identify the potential effect of Islamic banking and Islamic bonds on economic growth in major Muslim countries. The PMG/ARDL results indicated that Islamic bank's financing (LnIBF) and sukuk (LnSUK) have significant positive relationship with real gross domestic product (LnGDP), which means Islamic bank's financing and Islamic bonds (sukuk) move together with economic growth in the long run. On the contrary, Islamic bank's assets (LnIBA) have significant but rather negative relationship with real gross domestic product (LnGDP) in long run, which means both are inversely related. Panel causality test results demonstrated that bidirectional relationship exists between Islamic finance and economic growth, which supports Patrick finance–growth causality hypothesis.

The findings of this research would have significant contributions to the literature, researchers, and regulators; it will also provide insight into policy-makers and practitioners. Based on the results, it can be said that Islamic finance has effectively played its major role as financial intermediaries, which means developing countries can possibly handle their weak economies through expansion of Islamic finance, by utilizing Islamic financial engineering to derive novel Islamic financial products or services and marketing strategies; e.g., improvement of infrastructure as well as human capital to cater the growing demand of Islamic financial instruments in the future. Consider that Islamic banking system and Islamic capital markets as potential tools may lead to financial stability and eventually economic growth. Besides this, results show the contribution of Islamic banking system and Islamic bonds to the economic growth and in the long run to the economic welfare of Muslim countries. Since the relationship is bi-directional, both the Islamic finance and economic growth are interdependent and propel each other; for policy-makers it would be helpful to make such policies to ensure the stability of this sector. They should regularly monitor the implementation of Islamic financial policies and its implications on the macroeconomic conditions so that they can provide safeguard against any financial shocks or crisis. This study enriches the literature by its broad scope of Islamic finance and economic growth nexus of five Muslim countries over 10 years. Similarly, for researchers and analysts, it would be helpful to get the benefit of comparatively recent data set that imitates the latest scenario of Islamic finance–growth nexus in major issuing countries. More importantly, the study is one of the pioneer studies to outline the pure effect of Islamic finance including Islamic banking and Islamic bonds (*sukuk*) on economic growth in major Muslim countries.

Despite having contributions, this study holds some limitations, as the Islamic equity is an emerging sector of Islamic finance, due to unavailability of data it has been skipped in this study but strongly recommended for future research. Moreover, use of different control variables such as inflation, population and tax rates could give variation in results, because few Muslim states have given tax exemption to Islamic finance. Future researches should incorporate more dependent and independent variables which could enhance their results. They may also use other combinations of countries, comparison of developed and developing countries, Islamic and non-Islamic economies and countries having entire Islamic financial setup versus dual-financial setup, in link with economic indicators to get novelty in the results.

Appendix A. Normality Histogram (Jarque Bera)

Table A.1.

Null Hypothesis	Normal Distribution		
Skewness	Kutosis	Jarque Bera	Probability
0.231949	2.361760	4.669139	0.096852
No. of observations	180		

Dependent variable: Real gross domestic product (LnGDP).
Independent variable: Islamic bank's assets (LnIBA), Islamic bank's financing (LnIBF), sukuk (LnSUK).
Control variable: Gross fixed capital formation (LnGFCF), General government final expenditure (LnGGFE), Trade openness (LnOPN).
**Significant at 5% level.

Appendix B. Structural Breaks

Table B.1.

				Bahrain				
2008Q1	F-stats	1.370080	Prob	0.2594	Log likelihood	12.55935	Prob	0.0836
2008Q2	F-stats	1.481495	Prob	0.2174	Log likelihood	13.42642	Prob	0.0624
2008Q3	F-stats	1.918621	Prob	0.1072	Log likelihood	16.65757	Prob	0.0497
2008Q4	F-stats	0.083966	Prob	0.9974	Log likelihood	0.713315	Prob	0.9942
				Indonesia				
2008Q1	F-stats	0.967867	Prob	0.4531	Log likelihood	5.981985	Prob	0.3080
2008Q2	F-stats	1.016975	Prob	0.4251	Log likelihood	6.262908	Prob	0.2815
2008Q3	F-stats	1.146268	Prob	0.3581	Log likelihood	6.993230	Prob	0.2211
2008Q4	F-stats	1.529726	Prob	0.2104	Log likelihood	9.093969	Prob	0.1058
				Malaysia				
2008Q1	F-stats	0.921670	Prob	0.4944	Log likelihood	7.209463	Prob	0.3019
2008Q2	F-stats	1.034822	Prob	0.4240	Log likelihood	8.011292	Prob	0.2373
2008Q3	F-stats	1.368050	Prob	0.2617	Log likelihood	10.28335	Prob	0.1132
2008Q4	F-stats	1.918067	Prob	0.2140	Log likelihood	13.42770	Prob	0.0850
				Pakistan				
2008Q1	F-stats	1.182965	Prob	0.3758	Log likelihood	6.102584	Prob	0.2451
2008Q2	F-stats	1.301768	Prob	0.2563	Log likelihood	5.661663	Prob	0.2984
2008Q3	F-stats	1.484729	Prob	0.2094	Log likelihood	9.055516	Prob	0.1001
2008Q4	F-stats	1.288069	Prob	0.2234	Log likelihood	8.524581	Prob	0.2045
				Qatar				
2008Q1	F-stats	1.154941	Prob	0.3534	Log likelihood	7.853355	Prob	0.3129
2008Q2	F-stats	1.272758	Prob	0.2145	Log likelihood	8.369549	Prob	0.2128
2008Q3	F-stats	1.192354	Prob	0.1045	Log likelihood	8.549552	Prob	0.2087
2008Q4	F-stats	1.297183	Prob	0.2374	Log likelihood	8.519968	Prob	0.2063

Note: **Significant at 5% level.

References

Abduh, M, S Brahim and MA Omar (2012). A study on finance-growth nexus in dual financial system countries: Evidence from Bahrain. *World Applied Sciences Journal*, 20(8), 1166–1174.

Abduh, M and MA Omar (2012). Islamic banking and economic growth: The Indonesian experience. *International Journal of Islamic and Middle Eastern Finance and Management*, 5(1), 35–47.

Abusabha and Masoud (2014). Twinkle, twinkle, little star, how wonder Islamic finance: Up above the world so high, like a diamond in the sky. *Journal of Sustainable Development Studies*, 2(6), 294–332.

Accounting and Auditing Organization for Islamic Financial Institutions (AAOIFI) (2008). https://islamicbankers.files.wordpress.com/2008/09/aaoifi_sb_sukuk_feb2008_eng.pdf.

Ahmad, NW, N Ripain, NF Bahari and WS Shahar (2015). Growth and prospect of sukuk in Malaysian market: A review. In *Proc. 2nd Int. Conf. Management and Muamalah (2ndicomm)*, 16–17 November 2015.

Aksak, E and M Asutay (2012). Does Islamic finance make the world economically and financially safer? Islamic finance and its implications on sustainable economic growth. In *8th International Conference on Islamic Economics and Finance*, pp. 1–44.

Alshamrani, A (2014). Sukuk issuance and its regulatory framework in Saudi Arabia. *Journal of Islamic Banking and Finance*, 2(1), 305–333.

Ansari, S (2012). The role of Islamic banking industry in the economic growth of Pakistan, pp. 1–14.

Antonios, A (2010). Financial development and economic growth a comparative study between 15 European Union Member States. *International Research Journal of Finance and Economics*, 35, 143–149.

Asghar, N, S Qureshi and M Nadeem (2015). Institutional quality and economic growth: Panel ARDL analysis for selected developing economies of Asia. *Journal of South Asian Studies*, 30(2), 381–403.

Asiri, BK and MA Abdalla (2015). Economic growth and stock market development in Bahrain. *Journal of Applied Finance and Banking*, 5(2), 67–80.

Bagehot, W (1873). Bank Negara Malaysia, Homewood, IL. http://www.bnm.gov.my/index.php?.

Benaissa, NE, MP Parekh and M Wiegand (2005), A growth model for Islamic banking: As competition grows, incumbents must work harder to remain distinctive, *Mckinsey Quarterly* (October, 2005). https://www.mckinseyquarterly.com/A_growth_model_for_Islamic_banking_1694.

Breitung, J (2000). The local power of some unit root tests for panel data. In *Nonstationary Panels, Panel Cointegration, and Dynamic Panels. Advances in Econometrics*, B Baltagi (ed.), Vol. 15, pp. 161–178.

Cameron, R and C Olga (1967). *Banking in the Early Stage of Industrialization*, New York: Oxford University Press.

Časni, AC, AA Badurina and MB Sertić (2014). Public debt and growth: Evidence from Central Eastern and South-eastern European countries. *Zb. rad. Ekon. fak. Rij*, 32(1), 35–51.

Central Bank of Bahrain. http://www.cbb.gov.bh/page-p-statistical_bulletin.htm.

Choi, I (2001). Unit root tests for panel data. *Journal of International Money and Finance*, 20, 249–272.

Doğan, İ, NS Tülüce and A Doğan (2014). Dynamics of health expenditures in OECD countries: Panel ARDL approach. *Theoretical Economics Letters*, 4, 649–655. http://dx.doi.org/10.4236/tel.2014.48082.

Dumitrescu, EI and C Hurlin (2012). Testing for Granger non-causality in heterogeneous panels. *Economic Modelling*, 29(4), 1450–1460.

Echchabi, A, HA Aziz and U Idriss (2016). Dose Sukuk financing promote economic growth? An emphasis on the major issuing countries. *Turkish Journal of Islamic Economics*, 3(2), 63–73.

Elhachemi, HG and MA Othman (2015). Does the modern application of the islamic financial system is the new recommended architecture to promote growth and prevent the outbreak and spread of future crises? *International Journal of Scientific Research and Innovative Technology*, 2(6), 14–26.

Elhachemi, HG and MA Othman (2016). The impact of economic growth and financial crisis on Islamic financial development in terms of size in Iran. *International Journal of Economics and Financial Issues*, 6(S3), 116–124.

Ernst and Young (2011). *World Islamic Banking Competitiveness Report 2013–14: The Transition Begins*, London.

Farahani, G, Sadr Yazdan and SM Hossein (2012). Analysis of Islamic Bank's financing and economic growth: Case study Iran and Indonesia. *Journal of Economic Cooperation and Development*, 33(4), 1–24.

Gerschenkron, A (1962). *Economic Backwardness in Historical Perspective – A Book of Essays*. Cambridge, MA: Harvard University Press.

Goldsmith and W Raymond (1969). *Financial Structure and Development*. New Haven, CT: Yale University Press.

Goswami, GG and SH Junayed (2006). Pooled mean group estimation of the bilateral trade balance equation: USA vis-à-vis her trading partners. *International Review of Applied Economics*, 20(4), 515–526.

Granger, CWJ (1969). Investigating causal relations by econometric models and cross-spectral methods. *Econometrica*, 37(3), 424–438.

Hadri, K (2000). Testing for unit roots in heterogeneous panel data. *Econometrics Journal*, 3, 148–161.

Hassanudin, T, H Yousof, H Hanafi and Ebrahim (2013). Do Islamic banks contribute to the economic growth than conventional banks? The empirical investigations of Bahrain dual banking. *International Journal of Science Commerce and Humanities*, 1(3), 86–116.

Im, KS and MH Pesaran (2003). On the panel unit root tests using nonlinear instrumental variables, Mimeo, University of Southern California. International Islamic Financial Market (IIFM). www.iifm.net/news-updates?field_date_of_news…page=7.

International Monetary Fund (IMF) (2015). *Islamic Finance: Opportunities, Challenges, and Policy Options*, (April), International Capital Markets Department (ICMD), pp. 2–38.

Islamic Finance (2015). http://www.worldbank.org/en/topic/financialsector/brief/islamic-finance.

Islamic Finance in OIC Member Countries (2011). OIC report. www.sesrtcic.org/files/article/450.pdf.

Jamaldeen, F (2012). Islamic finance for dummies. http://www.dummies.com/store/product/Islamic-Finance-For-Dummies.productCd-0470430699.html.

Jawahra, S and A Disooqi (2010). Critical evaluation of legitimate issues concerning the ownership of the Bonds (sukuk) based on assets. In *Proceeds of the Symposium Islamic Sukuk, Presentation and Evaluation*, King Abd Al-Aziz University, Jeddah, Saudi Arabia, pp. 24–25.

Kassim, S (2015). Islamic finance and economic growth: The Malaysian experience. *Global Finance Journal*, 1–24.

Khiyar, KA and AA Galfy (2014). The role of Sukuk (Islamic Bonds) in economic development. *JFAMM*, 2, 31–35.

King, RG and R Levine (1993b). Finance, entrepreneurship, and growth: Theory and evidence. *Journal of Monetary Economics*, 32, 513–542.

Kpodar, K and PA Imam (2010). Islamic banking: How has it diffused? *IMF Working Papers*, 1–29.

Lee, YM and KM Wang (2015). Dynamic heterogeneous panel analysis of the correlation between stock prices and exchange rates. *Economic Research — Ekonomska Istraživanja*, 28(1), 749–772.

Levin, A, CF Lin and CSJ Chu (2002). Unit root test in panel data: Asymptotic and finite sample properties. *Journal of Econometrics*, 108, 1–24.

Lucas, RE (1988). On the mechanics of economic development. *Journal of Monetary Economics*, 22(1), 3–42. http://dx.doi.org/10.1016/0304-3932(88)90168-7.

Maddala, GS and S Wu (1999). A comparative study of unit root tests with panel data and a new simple test. *Oxford Bulletin of Economics and Statistics*, 631–652.

Mckinnon, RI (1973). *Money, Capital and Banking*. Washington, D.C.: Brooklyn Institution.

Mun, HW, TK Lin and YK Man (2009). FDI and economic growth relationship: An empirical study on Malaysia. *International Business Research*, 1(2), 11–18. https://www.researchgate.net/publication/42385846.

Nasr, BE, Parekh, P Mayank and M Wiegand (2005). A growth model for Islamic banking: As competition grows, incumbents must work harder to remain distinctive, *Mckinsey Quarterly* (2005). https://www.mckinseyquarterly.com/A_growth_model_for_Islamic_banking_1694.

Nayan, S, N Kadir, M Ahmad and FD Zakaria (2014). Supply of the Islamic bonds and GDP: Evidence from panel data. In *Proceedings of Islamic Business Management Conference (IBMC)*, pp. 38–42.

Ovat, OO (2012). Stock market development and economic growth in Nigeria: Market size versus liquidity. *Canadian Social Science*, 8(5), 71–76. http://www.cscanada.net/index.php/css/article/view/j.css.1923669720120805.549.

Patrick, HT (1966). Financial development and economic growth in underdeveloped countries. *Economic Development and Cultural Change*, 14(2), 174–189.

Pesaran, MH, H Shin and RP Smith (1999). Pooled mean group estimation of dynamic heterogeneous panels. *Journal of the American Statistical Association*, 94(446), 621–634.

Qarni, MO and S Gulzar (2019). Intra-EMU and non-EMU, EU stock markets' return spillover: Evidence from ESDC. *Empirica*, 1–35.

Robinson, JC (1952). *The Generalisation of the General Theory in the Rate of Interest and Other Essays*. London: Macmillan Press.

Said, A and R Grassa (2013). The determinants of Sukuk market development: Does macroeconomic factors influence the construction of certain structure of Sukuk? *Journal of Applied Finance and Banking*, 3(5), 251–267.

Salem, MB, M Fakhfekh and N Hachicha (2016). Sukuk Issuance and economic growth: The Malaysian case. *Journal of Islamic Economics, Banking and Finance*, 12(2), 202–214.

Sassi, S and M Goaied (2011). Financial development, Islamic banking and economic growth evidence from MENA region. *International Journal of Business and Management Science*, 4(2), 105–128.

Schumpeter, JA (1911). *Theory of Economic Development*. Cambridge: Harvard University Press.

Security and Exchange Commission of Pakistan/Sukuk Issuance Statistics. https://www.secp.gov.pk/data-and-statistics/capital-markets/.

Shabri, MA and SH Kassim (2015). Assessing the contribution of Islamic finance to economic growth: Empirical evidence from Malaysia. *Journal of Islamic Accounting and Business Research*, 6(2), 292–310.

Shaw, E (1973). *Financial Deepening in Economic Development*. New York: Oxford University Press.

Simões, MCN (2011). Education composition and growth: A pooled mean group analysis of OECD countries. *Panoeconomicus*, 4, 455–471.

Suliman, SZ and HA Dafaalla (2011). An econometric analysis of money demand function in Sudan: 1960–2010. *Journal of Economics and International Finance*, 3(16), 793–800.

State bank of Pakistan/Islamic Banking Bulletin (2016). http://www.sbp.org.pk/ibd/Bulletin/Bulletin-16.asp.

Tabash, MI and RS Dhankar (2013). An empirical analysis of the flow of Islamic banking and economic growth in Bahrain. *International Journal of Management Sciences and Business Research*, 3(1), 96–103.

Tabash, MI and RS Dhankar (2014). Islamic finance and economic growth: An empirical evidence from UAE. *Journal of Emerging Issues in Economics, Finance and Banking*, 3(2), 1069–1085.

Talahma, K (2015). Islamic bonds (Sukuk): Problems of reality and the requirements of development and competition, 1–28. http://www.law.uchicago.edu/files/file/talahmeh_islamic_bonds_6-22-2015-1.pdf.

Trad, SA and R Bhuyan (2015). Prospect of Sukuk in the fixed income market: A case study on Kuwait financial market. *International Journal of Financial Research*, 6(4), 175–186.

Vishwanath, SR and S Azmi (2009). An overview of Islamic ṣukūk bonds. *The Journal of Structured Finance*, 14(4), 58–67.

World Islamic Banking Competitiveness Report (2016). http://www.ey.com/…world-islamic-banking-competitiveness-report-2016/…/ey-world-isla.

Yusof, RM and M Bahlous (2013). Islamic banking and economic growth in GCC & East Asia countries: A panel co-integration analysis. *Journal of Islamic Accounting and Business Research*, 4(2), 151–172.

© 2025 World Scientific Publishing Company
https://doi.org/10.1142/9789819813735_0007

Chapter 7

Determinants of Credit Risk: A Comparative Analysis between Islamic and Conventional Banks in Bangladesh[#]

Md. Nurul Kabir

Department of Accounting and Finance
North South University
15, Block B, Bashundhara, Dhaka, Bangladesh
nurul.kabir@northsouth.edu

Mohammad Dulal Miah[*]

Department of Economics and Finance
University of Nizwa, Birkat Al Mawz
P. O. Box 33, PC 616 Nizwa, Oman
dulal@unizwa.edu.om

Rubaiya Nadia Huda

Department of Accounting and Finance
North South University
15, Block B, Bashundhara, Dhaka, Bangladesh
rubaiya.huda@northsouth.edu

The paper investigates the determinants of credit risk of Islamic and conventional banks in Bangladesh. In so doing, it collects data from 30 private commercial banks comprising of seven Islamic banks and 23 conventional banks for the period 2001–2018. Collected data are analyzed using GMM estimation technique. This method is perceived to be robust because it reduces the endogeneity problem that exists in the panel data set. Analysis of data shows that among the macro-economic variables, GDP growth decreases credit risk, whereas real interest rate and inflation increase credit risk. Bank-specific variables prove that both clusters of banks suffer from adverse selection and moral hazard problems. Results also indicate that competition has a risk-enhancing effect on banks, which supports the competition-fragility nexus. Further analysis shows that board size and board independence affect the credit risk of both clusters of banks. Findings of this study suggest some policy implications from macro, bank and governance perspectives. Specifically, banks should adopt 'speed limit' policy to reduce the poor quality loan. Also, competition in the banking industry should be regulated. Finally, central bank should maintain uniform capital adequacy ratio for both clusters of banks. Although this study is limited to private commercial banks in Bangladesh, the results can be generalized for other emerging economies.

Keywords: Credit risk; commercial banks; adverse selection; moral hazard; corporate governance.

---

[*]Corresponding author.
[#]This Chapter first appeared in the *Singapore Economic Review*, Vol. 67, No. 1, doi: 10.1142/S0217590820420011. © 2022 World Scientific Publishing.

1. Introduction

A stable and sound banking system is a critical prerequisite for the financial development and economic growth of a country. However, financial systems, in both developed and developing economies, are rarely stable owing to the fact that they are often rocked by local and international financial shocks. Frequent bubble-and-bust episodes in the financial markets — recent subprime meltdown, notorious Greek debt crisis and numerous other such banking disasters across the world — bear a clear manifestation that crises in the financial markets are systemic and recurrent. Calomiris and Haber (2015) analyze the history of the financial crisis for a sample of 117 countries from 1970 to 2010. It appears that only 34 countries (29%) were crisis-free from 1970 to 2010, whereas 62 experienced one, 19 suffered two, one underwent three and the other faced four crises. One of the root causes of these crises is the failure of adequately managing risk, particularly managing credit risk (Jorion, 2009).

Although Bangladesh did not face any explicit banking crisis in the past despite its banking system was in a state of distress for much of the period until the mid-1990s (Demirgüç-Kunt and Detragiache, 1998), credit risk has become a cause of great concern for policymakers and regulators alike very recently. As per the recent estimate by Bangladesh Bank, the Central Bank of Bangladesh, non-performing loans (NPLs) accounted for 10.4% (US$11 billion) of the total loan disbursed by commercial banks in 2018 (Bangladesh Bank, 2018). Massive accumulation of NPL resulted in liquidity crisis, which sometimes appeared so acute that the government was forced to inject fresh capital to keep the ailing banking system functional. Furthermore, two recent episodes — restructuring of Farmers Bank and liquidation of People's Leasing and Financial Services (PLFS) — raise further concern. The Farmers Bank, established in 2013, collapsed within four years of its inception due to a liquidity crisis fueled by its troubled loan. As of September 2017, the bank's NPL was 7.45% of the total outstanding loans, which skyrocketed to 58% as of September 2018, leading the bank to bankruptcy (the government later restructured the bank). Another financial institution, PLFS, is currently going through the liquidation process due to deterioration of its financial health triggered by the NPLs.

Despite its widespread importance, credit risk and its genesis are not studied coherently in the context of Bangladesh. However, some studies in the international context, which investigate the determinants of credit risk by considering both macro-economic and bank-specific factors, are available. These studies focus on different settings such as country-specific research (Ghosh, 2015; Louzis et al., 2012), cross-country analyses (Dimitrios et al., 2016; Kuzucu and Kuzucu, 2019; Makri et al., 2014) and emerging economies settings (Gulati et al., 2019; Mpofu and Nikolaidou, 2018). Very few studies exist in the context of Bangladesh (Zheng and Moudud-Ul-Huq, 2017; Miah and Sharmeen, 2015) that focus on identifying the factors that influence the credit risks.

The paucity of existing studies that examine the determinants of credit risk in the banking sector of Bangladesh provides the primary motivation for this research. Also, the existing studies suffer from several limitations with regard to methodological issues. Three such issues are notable and worth to mention. First, Zheng and Moudud-Ul-Huq (2017) and Miah and Sharmeen (2015) consider only bank-specific variables ignoring macro-economic and governance variables, which are also relevant, as shown in the literature. Secondly, the existing studies use accounting-based credit risk measurements, such as the NPL ratio and the Z-score. These indicators are based on the past information, hence may not be informative in assessing future outcomes. Further, management can manipulate accounting figures (Altman and Saunders, 1997). Thus, alternative market-based measurement is essential to measure the credit risk of banks. Thirdly, prior studies did not consider the persistence of credit risk and endogeneity problem, two fundamental issues common to most panel datasets; hence the findings of these studies could be biased. These critical limitations are addressed in this paper to provide robust evidence on the significant determinants of credit risk in Bangladesh.

Finally, there is a continuing debate as to whether separate regulatory requirements for Islamic banks are to be put in place since Islamic banks operate based on Shariah guidelines, which prohibit interest and urge to comply with social justice (Alam et al., 2019). However, existing literature in the context of Bangladesh does not offer any guidelines regarding this issue. This study aims to identify the determinants of credit risk for both Islamic and conventional banks separately that would provide essential policy guidelines.

To achieve the above-stated objectives, we use both macro-economic and bank-specific variables. Based on the prior literature, three macro-economic determinants, GDP growth rate, real interest rate and inflation, and six bank-specific hypotheses — adverse selection, moral hazard, management efficiency, competition, size and regulation — are selected as independent variables. As a proxy of credit risk, two accounting-based measures, NPL ratio and Z-score, and one market-based measure, Merton's distance-to-default (DD), are used. The study applies the generalized method of moments (GMM) estimation technique to 30 private commercial banks over the period 2001–2018. It further investigates the impact of corporate governance attributes and ownership structure on credit risk to broaden the understanding of the determinants of credit risk from a governance perspective.

The contribution of this paper is four-fold. First, unlike the existing studies which mostly adopt traditional measures of credit risk, this study applies market-based measure such as Merton's DD as a proxy for credit risk along with accounting-based measures such as NPL ratio and the Z-score. Secondly, this study uses dynamic panel data estimation techniques such as system GMM to find the determinants of credit risk in Bangladesh. According to the literature, this estimation technique is more robust and could solve the endogeneity problem that exists in the panel data set. Thirdly, based on contemporary studies, this research includes macro-economic, bank-specific and governance-specific determinants of credit risk in Bangladesh. Finally, this is the first study that also provides a comparative analysis of the determinants of credit risk between Islamic and conventional banks in the context of Bangladesh.

The paper is structured as follows. Section 2 describes some stylized facts about NPLs in the Bangladesh banking sector; Section 3 reviews the literature on the determinants of credit risk for both Islamic and conventional banks. Section 4 presents the variable measurement, sample, data sources and the estimation technique, and Section 5 provides a baseline result proceeding to further analysis of the impact of governance on credit risk. In Section 6, the paper concludes with a summary of our findings and the contribution of the study.

2. Stylized Facts of Credit Risk in the Banking Sector of Bangladesh

The rise of NPL in Bangladesh stemmed basically from the government's initiatives during the initial stage of liberation (1972–1981). The government introduced 'expansion of credit' policies, which directed banks to provide loans on relatively more accessible terms. A substantial amount of loan was disbursed by the state-owned commercial banks (SCBs) and state-owned development financial institutions (DFIs) on lowered credit granting criteria. They also provided loans to support unprofitable state-owned enterprises. All these resulted in the accumulation of huge NPL, especially in SCBs and DFIs. To reduce the level of NPL, the government adopted various financial measures. In the late 1990, the Financial Sector Reform Project (FSRP) was introduced, which enacted new laws, regulations and instruments to restore fiscal discipline. Besides, a Banking Reform Committee was formed to speed up the process of recovery of default loans of state-owned banks. In 2000, the Structural Adjustment Performance Review Initiative (SAPRI) was enacted to improve the monitoring and screening standards of the banking industry.

The government also enacted the Bank Company (Amendment) Act 2003 and the Money Loan Court Act 2003, to facilitate the settlement of default loan cases. Also, the central bank directed all commercial banks to maintain a 9% capital adequacy ratio (CAR) of risk-weighted assets (RWAs), with a core capital of at least 4.5% of RWA. As a result of all these steps, the amount of NPLs declined to a large extent during the early 2000s. This is evident from Table 1, which shows that gross NPL and net NPL as a percentage of total loan in Bangladesh banking industry decreased from 34.9% and 28.8% in 2000 to 13.6% and 7.2% in 2005, respectively.

The declining trend of NPL was further accelerated by the introduction of the credit risk grading system in 2006, which made it mandatory for banks to analyze the borrowers' credit risk and also helped prevent fresh NPLs. As a result, both gross NPL and net NPL to total loan declined to 6.1% and 0.7%, respectively, by the year 2011. Among bank groups, DFIs have the highest percentage of gross NPL and net NPL to total loans. Foreign commercial banks (FCBs) have the lowest percentage in those categories (Table 1). The reason for higher NPLs for DFIs and SCBs compared with other types of banks can be attributed to directive and policy lending issued by the central bank. Inefficient assessment of loan application and inadequate follow-up and supervision of disbursed loans resulted in low quality assets that still dominate the banks' portfolio. On the contrary, private commercial banks (PCBs) and FCBs did not have to follow directive and policy lending instructions from the government, which resulted in a lower percentage of gross NPL and net NPL to total loans for these banks (Ahmed *et al.*, 2006).

In 2012, the gross NPL and net NPL to total loan suddenly increased to 10% and 4.4%, respectively. It was mainly because of the issuance of new guidelines with regard to classification scheme and rescheduling of loans (Bangladesh Bank, 2013). A few

Table 1. Gross NPL and Net NPL by Year and Types of Banks

Year	Gross Non-Performing Loans as a Percent of Total Loans					Net Non-Performing Loans as a Percent of Total Loans				
	SCBs	DFIs	PCBs	FCBs	Total	SCBs	DFIs	PCBs	FCBs	Total
2000	38.6	62.6	22	3.4	34.9	34.1	54.6	15.5	−0.1	28.8
2001	37	61.8	17	3.3	31.5	32.8	54.5	10.5	−0.3	25.6
2002	33.7	56.1	16.4	2.6	28	30.1	48	10.5	−0.4	22.6
2003	29	47.4	12.4	2.7	22.1	28.3	38.3	8.3	0.1	18.8
2004	25.3	42.9	8.5	1.5	17.6	17.6	23	3.4	−1.5	9.8
2005	21.4	34.9	5.6	1.3	13.6	13.2	22.6	1.8	−2.2	7.2
2006	22.9	33.7	5.5	0.8	13.2	14.5	23.6	1.8	−2.6	7.1
2007	29.9	28.6	5	1.4	13.2	12.9	19	1.4	−1.9	5.1
2008	25.4	25.5	4.4	1.9	10.8	5.9	17	0.9	−2	2.8
2009	21.4	25.9	3.9	2.3	9.2	1.9	18.3	0.5	−2.3	1.7
2010	15.7	24.2	3.2	3	7.3	1.9	16	0	−1.7	1.3
2011	11.3	24.6	2.9	3	6.1	−0.3	17	0.2	−1.8	0.7
2012	23.9	26.8	4.6	3.5	10	12.8	20.4	0.9	−0.9	4.4
2013	19.8	26.8	4.5	5.5	8.9	1.7	19.7	0.6	−0.4	2
2014	22.23	32.81	4.98	7.3	9.7	6.1	25.5	0.8	−0.9	2.7
2015	21.5	23.2	4.9	7.8	8.8	9.2	6.9	0.6	−0.2	2.3
2016	25.1	26	4.6	9.6	9.2	11.1	10.5	0.1	1.9	2.3
2017	26.5	23.4	4.9	7	9.3	11.2	9.7	0.2	0.7	2.2
2018	28.2	21.7	6	6.7	10.4	11.7	7.4	0.8	0.8	2.7

Source: Compilation from the annual report of Bangladesh Bank.
Notes: This table presents gross NPL and net NPL as a percentage of total loans by year and by types of Banks. SCB, state-owned commercial banks; DFI, state-owned development financial institutions; PCB, private commercial banks; FCB, foreign commercial banks.

high-profile fraudulent loans also jarred the banking industry. The DFIs and SCBs continued to have higher NPL levels due to their previous accumulated bad loans, which they were reluctant to write off because of the potential impact on the bottom line of the banks. Although the NPL level decreased in 2013, there was a slight spike in 2014 due to the political unrest experienced by the country, which caused hardship for some borrowers to honor their loan repayment commitments. From 2016 onwards, there is a slight increasing trend for both gross NPL and net NPL to total loans. At the end of June 2018, the gross NPL to the total loan accounted for 10.4%, and net NPL to the total loan stood at 2.4%. This increasing trend naturally alarms the stakeholders and policymakers as it raises concern about the stability of the financial system.

3. Literature Review

Credit risk is a major source of financial instability in the banking sector. Extant literature has examined the determinants of credit risk in the banking system, particularly after the global financial crisis. These studies can roughly be divided into two strands in terms of elements they have considered to examine banks' credit risk. The first strand considers only macro-economic determinants of credit risk such as GDP, inflation, real interest rate, exchange rate, etc. (Ali and Daly, 2010; Castro, 2013; Festić *et al.*, 2011; Rinaldi and Sanchis-Arellano, 2006). The other strand of literature combines both macro-economic and bank-specific variables. Sample countries included in the extant literature also vary. Most studies of the literature are country-specific, whereas limited evidence on multi-country setting is also available. The following subsections provide macro-economic and bank-specific determinants of credit risk followed by a literature review on the determinants of credit risk in the context of Islamic banks.

3.1. Macro-economic determinants of credit risk

Of the various macro-economic factors considered in the literature, real GDP growth is the most dominant factor that influences the credit risk in the banking system. A higher GDP growth of an economy is expected to increase the ability of repayment of a debt by an individual or corporation. Hence, during economic upturn of a country, credit risk is expected to decline. Khemraj and Pasha (2009) find a significant negative relationship between NPL and GDP growth rates for the Guyanese banking sector. Similarly, Mpofu and Nikolaidou (2018), in the context of Sub-Saharan African banks, and Das and Ghosh (2007), for state-owned Indian banks, show a negative relationship between GDP growth and credit risk.

Besides GDP growth, literature also considers other macro-economic factors to explain the credit risk of banks. Among them, real interest rate (Chaibi and Ftiti, 2015; Das and Ghosh, 2007; Khemraj and Pasha, 2009), inflation (Alhassan *et al.*, 2014; Klein, 2013), effective exchange rate (Khemraj and Pasha, 2009; Nkusu, 2011), unemployment rate (Louzis *et al.*, 2012; Nkusu, 2011), market capitalization (Beck *et al.*, 2013a,b,c; Das and Ghosh, 2007), lending rate (Beck *et al.*, 2013a,b,c; Louzis *et al.*, 2012) and stock market index (Nkusu, 2011) are widely considered.

3.2. Bank-specific determinants of credit risk

Researchers also have investigated the effect of bank-specific determinants along with macro-economic factors on credit risk. Studies included both single- and multi-country settings. In their paper, Berger and DeYoung (1997) examined the existence of causality among loan quality, cost efficiency and bank capital. They formulated three testable hypotheses and examined them applying Granger Causality test on the U.S. data. They found that cost inefficiency increases problem loans, especially for thinly capitalized banks, which confirms the bad management hypothesis. In a subsequent study, Louzis *et al.* (2012) extended these hypotheses and introduced diversification, too-big-to-fail (TBTF) and bad management II hypotheses as determinants of credit risk. Using GMM estimation techniques, they found that bad management and TBTF hypotheses can explain the rise of NPL in the Greece banking sector.

There are other bank-specific variables which are also believed to be correlated with credit risk. For instance, Salas and Saurina (2002) show that credit growth, bank size, capital ratio and market power explain the variations of credit risk in the Spanish banking sector. Apart from these, literature also used profitability ratio (Chaibi and Ftiti, 2015; Klein, 2013; Louzis *et al.*, 2012), solvency ratio (Louzis *et al.*, 2012), capital adequacy ratio (Ahmad and Ariff, 2007a,b; Espinoza and Prasad, 2010), credit growth (Espinoza and Prasad, 2010; Khemraj and Pasha, 2009), liquidity (Ahmad and Ariff, 2007a,b) and Herfindahl–Hirschman index (HHI) (Alhassan *et al.*, 2014), as bank-specific determinants of credit risk.

3.3. Credit risk of Islamic banks vis-à-vis the conventional banks

As noted in the previous discussion, most studies focus on identifying the determinants of credit risk of conventional banks. However, literature examining the determinants of credit risk of Islamic banks is limited, especially in the case of comparative study between Islamic and conventional banks in developing countries. Moreover, scholars focusing on the credit risk of Islamic banks tend to assess only the risk involved with certain financial products (Haron and Hock, 2007; Hasan, 2002; Khalil *et al.*, 2002; Warninda *et al.*, 2019). Abedifar *et al.* (2013), however, investigate the determinants of credit risk and insolvency risk of Islamic and conventional banks of OIC (Organization of Islamic Cooperation) countries. They find that size is positively related to the credit risk of Islamic banks.

Similarly, Čihák and Hesse (2010) study the financial stability of Islamic banks in 20 countries. They find that banks with higher loan to asset ratio are financially less stable because of the leverage effect. In addition, size, income diversity and governance (efficiency) have a positive influence on stability, whereas competition has a negative influence on stability. They further show that large Islamic banks are more exposed to liquidity risk than large conventional banks. Other studies (Rosly *et al.*, 2005; Sarker, 1999; Siddiqui, 2008) find similar factors that influence credit risk of Islamic banks. Saeed and Izzeldin (2016) demonstrate that profit efficiency is inversely related to default risk for both Islamic and conventional banks in GCC countries.

Few observations can be drawn from the literature review. First, the extant literature is confined to developed nations or in a multi-country setting. Hence, findings from these studies are inconclusive and may not be applicable to a particular country, especially to an emerging economy like Bangladesh. Secondly, factors affecting credit risk could be different between Islamic and conventional banks. Thirdly, most of the studies used NPL ratio, an accounting-based measurement of credit risk, which may not be robust. Our study aims to fill this gap by incorporating both market-based and accounting-based measurement of credit risk, a longer time period, and by considering both macro-economic and bank-specific determinants that could affect the credit risk.

4. Methodology

4.1. *Data*

Data for this study are drawn from 30 private commercial banks comprising of seven Islamic banks and 23 conventional banks for the period 2001–2018. Our balanced panel consists of 638 bank-year observations (114 observations for Islamic banks and 524 observations for conventional banks). Bank-specific data are collected from the Fitchconnect database whereas macro-economic variables are collected from the World Development Indicator database of the World Bank.

4.2. *Variables and testable hypothesis*

4.2.1. *Dependent variables*

This study applies NPL ratio, Z-score and Merton's DD as proxies for credit risk. Over the years, a number of credit risk measurement techniques have been developed. These techniques include external ratings, accounting-based techniques and market-based techniques. Accounting-based techniques include credit risk Z-score, Altman's Z-score and NPL analysis, whereas market-based techniques include Merton's probability of default, value at risk (VaR) and CreditMetrics™ (Allen *et al.*, 2012; Altman and Saunders, 1997; Colquitt, 2007). Following Kabir *et al.* (2015), we use a combination of both accounting-based and market-based measures as our dependent variables. NPL ratio and the Z-score are taken as accounting-based measures and Merton's DD as the market-based measure for credit risk.

(i) *NPL ratio*: NPL ratio is measured by dividing the total amount of impaired loans held by a bank by the net amount of loans (Beck *et al.*, 2013a,b,c; Louzis *et al.*, 2012). A higher NPL ratio indicates a higher probability of bank insolvency.

(ii) *Z-score*: Z-score is the most commonly used measure to evaluate bank soundness or stability. The Z-score uses profit, capital and the standard deviation of profit, to calculate the theoretical riskiness of banks (Beck *et al.*, 2013a,b,c; Čihák and Hesse, 2010). It measures how many standard deviations a bank is from exhausting its capital base. To calculate the Z-score, we use the following:

$$Z = (\text{ROA} + E/A)/\sigma\text{ROA}, \qquad (1)$$

where ROA = return on assets, which is net profit divided by total assets; E/A = total equity divided by total assets and σROA = standard deviation of ROA over a three-year period. Generally, a three-year window for the standard deviation of ROA is sufficient to allow for variation in the Z-score. A higher value of Z indicates increased solvency of banks and *vice versa*.

(iii) *Merton's DD*: Recent literature has adopted the DD model as a proxy for stability because it overcomes many problems associated with accounting-based stability measures (Anginer *et al.*, 2014; Chava and Purnanandam, 2010; Hillegeist *et al.*, 2004; Jokipii and Monnin, 2013; Koutsomanoli-Filippaki and Mamatzakis, 2009). The DD model is calculated using market information following the theory of Merton (1974) and Black and Scholes (1973). The Merton (1974) model assumes that the equity of a firm is equivalent to a call option on the firm's assets, given that equity holders are the residual claimants on the firm's assets after all liabilities have been met. In this model, the strike price of the call option is the book value of the firm's liabilities. If the value of the firm's assets is lower than the strike price, the value of equity is zero. The Merton model has two important assumptions. First, the total market value of the firm's underlying assets follows a geometric Brownian motion:

$$dV_A = \mu V_A dt + \sigma_A V_A dW, \tag{2}$$

where V_A is a firm's assets value, μ is the expected instantaneous periodic rate of return on assets, σ_A is the instantaneous standard deviation of the rate of return on assets or asset volatility and dW is a standard Weiner process. The second assumption is that the firm has issued a single discount bond maturing in T periods. Under this assumption, the equity of the firm is a call option on the underlying value of the firm's asset with a strike price, denoted by V_A, equal to the face value of firm's debt X at a time-to-maturity of T. The current market value of equity, V_E, can be expressed by using Black and Scholes (1973) option pricing formula for call options:

$$V_E = V_A N(d_1) - X e^{-rT} N(d_2), \tag{3}$$

where

$$d_1 = \frac{\ln\left(\frac{V_A}{X}\right) + (r + 0.5\sigma_A^2)T}{\sigma_A \sqrt{T}}. \tag{4}$$

$d_2 = d_1 - \sigma_A \sqrt{T}$, where r is the risk-free rate, σ_A is the instantaneous standard deviation of the rate of return on the value of assets of banks (asset volatility) and N is the cumulative density function of the standard normal distribution.

Two equations are required to calculate DD. The first is Equation (2), which states that the value of the firm's equity is a function of the value of the firm. The second is related to the volatility of its equity:

$$\sigma_E = \left(\frac{V_A}{E}\right) \frac{\partial E}{\partial V} \sigma_v. \tag{5}$$

In the Black–Scholes–Merton model, we can show that $\frac{\partial E}{\partial V} = N(d_1)$, such that under the assumption of Merton's model, the relation between the volatilities of the firm and its equity is

$$\sigma_E = \left(\frac{V_A}{E}\right) N(d_1) \sigma_A, \qquad (6)$$

and the DD and probability of default are:

$$DD_t = \frac{\ln\left(\frac{V_{A,t}}{X_t}\right) + \left(\mu - \frac{1}{2}\sigma_A^2\right)T}{\sigma_A \sqrt{T}}, \qquad (7)$$

$$PD = N(-DD), \qquad (8)$$

where DD = distance-to-default, PD = probability of default, V_A = value of assets, σ_A = volatility of assets, X_t = total liabilities, μ = expected asset return, T = time period and N = cumulative probability distribution. The higher the DD (PD), the lower (higher) the default risk.

4.2.2. Independent variables

Based on past literature, three macro-economic determinants, GDP growth rate (Louzis et al., 2012), real interest rate (Altunbas et al., 2010; Delis and Kouretas, 2011) and inflation (Alhassan et al., 2014), are selected as independent variables. Along with macroeconomic factors, some hypotheses based on bank-specific variables are also examined. The five bank-specific hypotheses are adverse selection (Salas and Saurina, 2002), moral hazard (Louzis et al., 2012; Salas and Saurina, 2002), management efficiency (Berger and DeYoung, 1997), competition (Beck et al., 2013a,b,c; Das and Ghosh, 2007), scale effect (Chaibi and Ftiti, 2015) and effectiveness of regulation (Ahmad and Ariff, 2007a,b). A detailed description of the independent variables along with the direction of their effect on banks' credit risk, as observed from the present literature, is given in Table 2.

4.2.2.1. Macroeconomic variables

(i) *GDP growth rate*: A common definition of GDP is adopted. As seen in past studies (Das and Ghosh, 2007; Khemraj and Pasha, 2009; Louzis et al., 2012), banks' credit risk decreases when GDP growth rate increases. In line with this justification of the extant literature, a significant negative relationship between GDP growth rate and NPL is expected.
(ii) *Real interest rate*: Real interest rate is calculated by subtracting the inflation rate from the nominal interest rate. An increase in the real interest rate in an economy may also lead to an increase in the cost of borrowing that reduces borrower's repaying ability and thus expected to have a positive impact on credit risk (Chaibi and Ftiti, 2015).
(iii) *Inflation*: The impact of inflation on credit risk is inconclusive in the literature. For example, Alhassan et al. (2014) and Klein (2013) report that there is a negative relationship between inflation and credit risk. They argue that an increase in inflation

Table 2. Definition of Variables

Variable	Symbol	Definition	Expected Sign	Source
Dependent variable				
Non-performing loans	NPL	Ratio of net non-performing loans to total loans		Fitchconnect/Annual report
Z-score	ZSCORE	(ROA+ Equity to Asset)/standard deviation of ROA		Fitchconnect/Annual report
Distance-to-default	DD	Risk neutral distance-to-default based on Merton (1974)		Authors' calculation
Independent variable				
GDP growth rate	GDP	Real GDP growth rate	−	World Bank Database
Inflation	INF	Year on year of CPI index	+	World Bank Database
Real interest rate	RIR	Nominal interest rate-inflation	+	World Bank Database
Bank-specific variables				
Growth of gross loans	GGL	Year on year change of total loan	+	Fitchconnect/Annual report
Loan to deposit ratio	LDR	Total gross loan/total customer deposit	+	Fitchconnect/Annual report
Equity to asset ratio	ETA	Total equity/total asset	+	Fitchconnect/Annual report
Return on equity	ROE	Net income/total equity	−	Fitchconnect/Annual report
Cost inefficiency	INEFF	Ratio of non-operating expense and total asset	+	Fitchconnect/Annual report
Lerner	LERNER	Price-marginal cost/price	+/−	Authors' calculation
Total asset	SIZE	Logarithm of total asset	+/−	Authors' calculation
Total capital ratio	TCR	Capital adequacy ratio defined by Basel II	−	Fitchconnect/Annual report
Crisis	CRISIS	1 for the period 2007–2009, otherwise 0		Authors' calculation
Other variables included in additional analysis				
Board size	BSIZE	Natural logarithm of total number of directors	−	Annual report
Board independence	BRDIND	Number of independent directors/total number of directors	+	Annual report
Insider ownership	INSIDER	Percentage of shareholding by bank's CEO, directors and employees	−	Annual report
Institutional ownership	INST	Percentage of shareholding by institutions	+	Annual report

Note: Table 1 defines the variables included in Equation (11) and in additional analysis section.

reduces the real income, resulting in an increased risk of non-payment of loans. On the contrary, Khemraj and Pasha (2009) show a positive relationship between inflation and credit risk.

4.2.2.2. Bank-specific variables

(i) *Adverse selection hypothesis*: Adverse selection is measured by the growth of credit (GGL). Higher credit growth shows the bank's aggressive lending behavior that can lead to an adverse selection of borrowers. Adverse selection problem will be worse if credit expansion takes place in a new geographic area or sector where the bank has no adequate or previous experience (Salas and Saurina, 2002). This adverse selection can, in turn, increase credit risk. Jimenez and Saurina (2006), for the Spanish banking sector, and Das and Ghosh (2007), for Indian SOCBs, find that credit growth is positively associated with credit risk. Based on this argument, we develop the following hypothesis.

H1: There is a positive relationship between credit growth and credit risk.

(ii) *Moral hazards hypothesis*: Following Louzis *et al.* (2012), we use equity to asset ratio (ETA) and loan to deposit ratio (LDR) as proxies for moral hazard. Banks tend to assume more risk in their pursuit of materializing higher profit when their own stake on the firm is insignificant. This behavior of agents is termed in the literature as 'moral hazard'. Altunbas *et al.* (2007) argue that thinly capitalized banks tend to accept higher risk, which in most cases leads to higher NPLs. Based on this argument, we develop the following hypothesis.

$H2_a$: There is a positive relationship between capital to asset ratio and credit risk.

Similarly, loans to deposit ratio are expected to capture the extent to which a particular bank is willing to advance loan against its deposits. Although banks have to adhere to the rules set by the government to maintain a minimum LDR, they may undertake riskier projects within the boundary of the prescribed ratio. Laeven *et al.* (2016) find that systemic risk is positively related to the size and negatively associated with banks' capital. This means that where the owner's own stake on the bank is not significant, banks tend to choose riskier projects expecting to realize a higher profit from risky ventures. Therefore, we can expect a positive relationship between the LDR and credit risk.

$H2_b$: There is a positive relationship between LDR and credit risk.

(iii) *Management efficiency*: Prior studies on credit risk determinants show a significant relationship between efficiency and credit risk. Berger and DeYoung (1997) argue that lower efficiency raises costs as banks do not monitor borrowers adequately, which, in turn, increases the probability of credit risk. Efficient managers are likely to accumulate fewer amounts of bad loans compared with their inefficient counterparts. We use two efficiency measures: profit efficiency and cost-efficiency. Profit efficiency is captured by ROE, which is expected to have a negative relationship with NPL.

Ghosh (2015) argues that banks with higher profitability have lower incentives to engage in riskier projects. In contrast, cost inefficiency (INEFF) is expressed by the ratio of non-interest expense to total assets. Cost inefficiency is expected to have a positive relationship with NPL.

$H3_a$: Profit efficiency is expected to have a negative association with credit risk.
$H3_b$: Cost inefficiency is expected to have a positive association with credit risk.

(iv) *Competition*: Competition-stability/fragility hypothesis is one of the most widely investigated topics in the area of banking. Competition, on the one hand, can erode the franchise value of the banks leading to financial fragility (Ariss, 2010). On the other hand, competition in the banking sector can enhance banks' stability through bringing about efficiency, new technologies and loan diversification (Fiordelisi and Mare, 2014; Kabir and Worthington, 2017). Thus, the relationship between competition and credit risk cannot be known *a priori*. We measure competition by using the Lerner index[1].

H4: The relationship between competition and credit risk is not known a priori.

(v) *Size*: Size has been used extensively as one of the significant determinants of credit risk. Size is measured by the logarithm of the total assets of each bank for a particular year. In general, large banks have better risk management procedures, more diversification opportunities that help them to lower the credit risk (Salas and Saurina, 2002). Moreover, larger-scale (size) provides them economic benefits for using sophisticated screening and monitoring technologies. In contrast, because of 'too-big-to-fail' perception, bigger banks engage in excessive risk-taking activities or relax their criteria for loan sanctioning that may eventually lead to higher credit risk (Louzis *et al.*, 2012).

H5: The relationship between size and credit risk is not known a priori.

(vi) *Regulatory requirement*: Regulatory capital requirement is measured by the total capital adequacy ratio (TCR). Bank for International Settlement (BIS) urges banks to follow the Basel accord in regard to their capital requirement. One of the key elements of Basel accord is capital adequacy ratio (CAR), where banks are asked to maintain a minimum amount of capital based on the degree of risk they are exposed. Although some of the past researchers, for example, Rime (2001), found no relationship between regulatory pressure and the level of credit risk, recent studies show that there is a negative relationship between bank regulatory capital and credit risk (Maji and De, 2015). Ahmad and Ariff (2007a,b) find that regulatory capital is crucial for those banks in emerging economies that offer multi-products.

H6: There is a negative relationship between CAR and credit risk.

---

[1] It has been used extensively in the field of banking literature as a measurement of competition. The value of the Lerner index lies between 0 and 1. The higher the Lerner index value, the lower the competition is. Lerner index = (Price − Marginal cost)/Price. Our calculation of the Lerner index mainly draws on the stochastic frontier estimation approach proposed by Kumbhakar *et al.* (2012) and Coccorese (2014).

(vii) *Crisis dummy*: In addition to these macro-economic and bank-specific variables, we also control the crisis period in the regression model to see whether the recent global crisis of 2007–2009 has an adverse impact on the credit risk of Bangladeshi banks. We use a dummy variable CRISIS with a value of 1 for the year 2007–2009 and 0 otherwise.

4.3. *Estimation techniques*

Since the dataset is a panel and equation model is static at this stage, we begin our primary analysis by estimating the regression equation using panel estimation technique. Of the various available panel estimation techniques for the static model, both random effect (RE) and fixed effect (FE) models are frequently used in the literature (Sufian, 2011). Hence, we estimate the regression equation by using both RE and FE models. The result of the Hausman test indicates that the FE model is better than the RE model (results not reported here).

As argued in the literature, panel data models such as RE, FE or pooled OLS may be biased and yield inconsistent results due to possible correlations between the unobserved cross and time-specific effects and the regressors (Baltagi, 2008). Furthermore, the literature suggests that credit risk proxies such as NPL ratio, Z-score or DD are endogenous variables. Finally, like other bank-specific variables, credit risk proxies also show a tendency to persist over time (Jiménez and Saurina, 2004; Louzis *et al.*, 2012). Therefore, we adopt a dynamic specification of the models by including a lagged dependent variable among the regressors. The inclusion of lagged dependent variables would also result in a correlation between the regressors and error term. To overcome both auto-correlation and endogeneity problems, we employ dynamic panel data estimation techniques, namely, GMM estimator proposed by Arellano and Bond (1991). Recent literature on banking that investigates the determinants of credit risk also uses the GMM estimation technique (Castro, 2013; Ghosh, 2015; Louzis *et al.*, 2012).

A general dynamic model specification is as follows:

$$Y_{it} = c + \delta Y_{it-1} + \beta(L)X_{it} + \varepsilon_{it} \quad I = 1,\ldots,N; \quad t = 1,\ldots,T \quad \varepsilon_{it} = v_i + v_{it}, \tag{9}$$

where subscript *i* denotes the number of cross-sections and *t* denotes time dimension of the panel sample, Y is the dependent variable (Z-score, NPL or DD), Y_{it-1} is the lagged dependent variable, X_{it} is the $k \times 1$ vector of explanatory variables including the variable of interest other than the y_{it-1}, ε_{it} is the disturbance with v_i, the observed bank-specific effect and v_{it}, the idiosyncratic error. Here the assumption is ε_{it} follows a one-way error component model where $v_i \sim \text{IID}(0, \sigma^2 v)$ and independent of $v_{it} \sim \text{IID}(0, \sigma^2 v)$. δ indicates the speed of adjustment to equilibrium. Athanasoglou *et al.* (2008) argue that a value of δ between 0 and 1 indicates that credit risk persists, and they will return to their level. A value of δ close to 0 means that the industry is highly competitive, and the value of δ close to 1 indicates less competitive.

The equation is estimated based on the two-step system GMM since it provides more reliable results when the variables are close to a random walk (Roodman, 2009).

The system GMM estimator uses the levels equation to obtain a system of two equations: one differenced and one in levels. This allows the introduction of more instruments and can improve efficiency. We apply the Windmeijer (2005) finite-sample correction to the reported standard errors in system GMM since standard errors obtained from standard two-step system GMM are severely downward biased. Specifying Windmeijer corrected standard errors also produces variance-covariance estimates that are robust to heteroscedasticity.

Consistency of GMM estimation heavily depends on two important conditions: validity of instruments used in the moment condition and the assumption of serial independence of the residuals condition. In order to check the over-identification of valid instruments used in the regression, Hansen specification test proposed by Arellano and Bond (1991) and Blundell and Bond (1998) are used. Under the null hypothesis of valid moment conditions, the Hansen test statistics are asymptotically distributed as chi-square. Furthermore, no second-order autocorrelation is checked using the method proposed by Arellano and Bond (1991).

Based on the foregoing discussion, the baseline model for the determinants of credit risk takes the following form:

$$\Delta CR_{it}^h = \alpha \Delta CR_{it-1}^h + \sum_{j=1}^{2} \beta_{1j}^h \Delta GDP_{t-j} + \sum_{j=1}^{2} \beta_{2j}^h \Delta \text{Real Interest Rate}_{t-j}$$
$$+ \sum_{j=1}^{2} \beta_{3j}^h \Delta \text{Inflation}_{t-j} + \acute{\eta}_i^h + \varepsilon_i^h. \qquad (10)$$

Adding the bank-specific variables and crisis dummy with the above regression based on the hypothesis derived in the previous section

$$\Delta CR_{it}^h = \alpha \Delta CR_{it-1}^h + \sum_{j=1}^{2} \beta_{1j}^h \Delta GDP_{t-j} + \sum_{j=1}^{2} \beta_{2j}^h \Delta RIR_{t-j} + \sum_{j=1}^{2} \beta_{3j}^h \Delta \text{Inflation}_{t-j}$$
$$+ \sum_{j=1}^{2} \beta_{4j}^h X_{it-j}^h + \sum_{j=1}^{2} \beta_{5j}^h \text{Crisis}_{it-j}^h + \acute{\eta}_i^h + \varepsilon_i^h, \qquad (11)$$

where X_{it-j}^h denotes the bank-specific variables, and Crisis_{it-j}^h is a dummy variable that takes 1 if the years are between 2007 and 2009, zero otherwise.

In this equation, all macro-variables are treated as exogenous and instrumented, as suggested by the literature. Here, bank-characteristic variables are considered as weakly endogenous and use their second lag to instrument for them. In addition, crisis dummy to control the impact of the crisis on financial stability in the Bangladesh banking sector is applied.

5. Empirical Results and Discussion

5.1. *Summary statistics*

Table 3 exhibits the summary statistics of credit risk proxies as well as other variables used in the regression model. Proxies of credit risk such as NPL ratio, Z-score and the DD show

Table 3. Summary Statistics

	N	Mean	Median	STDEV	MIN	MAX	N	Mean	Median	STDEV	MIN	MAX	t-Test
			Islamic Bank						Conventional Bank				
Credit risk proxies													
NPL (%)	114	14.72	4.76	24.16	0.2	82	524	8.7	4.69	11.72	0	98.17	−3.71***
ZSCORE	114	12.45	10.25	36.77	−47.01	85.36	524	19.25	15.98	62.14	−9.52	30.13	−8.62***
DD	84	1.41	1.71	2.7	−13.12	6.44	524	1.63	1.63	2.68	−27.06	8.48	−0.67
Bank-specific variable													
GGL (%)	114	46.65	20.54	159.95	0.03	1286.49	524	47.81	19.33	148.18	2	123.52	−0.07
LDR (%)	114	95.35	89.8	22.25	5.68	138.9	524	84.94	83.25	48.59	9.91	230	−0.47
ETA (%)	114	1.77	6.21	14.77	−47.4	14.35	524	10.11	7.37	11.55	12.94	65.79	−7.89***
ROE (%)	114	9.52	1	23.2	−57.47	92.22	524	13.22	1.09	25.99	−82.08	124	−4.02***
INEFF (%)	114	2.03	1.98	0.7	0.94	4.73	524	2.47	2.22	1	0	10.05	−0.67
LERNER	114	0.17	0.17	0.05	0.04	0.32	524	0.16	0.16	0.07	0.03	0.66	−0.07
SIZE (US$' 000)	114	1520.83	577.2	2260.83	28.51	11480.71	524	1567.84	801.72	1757.17	12.44	14998.35	−0.56
TRC (%)	114	3.9	11.4	26.25	−70.24	16.65	524	14.96	11.73	15.47	−29.08	96.94	−6.49***
Macro-economic variables			Full sample										
GDP (%)	638	6.17	6.46	0.97	3.83	7.86							
INF (%)	638	6.4	6.22	2.08	2.01	11.4							
RIR (%)	638	5.61	5.51	1.63	3.07	9.26							

Notes: This table presents the summary statistics of credit risk proxies, bank-specific variables and macro-economic variables used in the baseline regression analysis. t-test indicates mean difference in bank-specific variables between Islamic and conventional banks. Definitions of variables are reported in Table 2.

that Islamic banks have significantly higher credit risk than their conventional counterparts. The mean values of NPL ratios are 14.72% and 8.70% for Islamic and conventional banks, respectively, and the difference between the means of these two clusters of banks is significant at 1% level. Similarly, Z-score has a mean value of 12.45 multiples for Islamic banks and 19.25 multiples for conventional banks. The market measurement of credit risk, DD, also shows a similar result between these two banking systems. Our findings are consistent with the findings of Čihák and Hesse (2010) and Kabir *et al.* (2015).

Among the bank-specific variables, we find that the rate of credit growth (GGL) does not differ significantly between these two banking systems. LDR has a mean value of 95.35% for Islamic banks and 84.94% for conventional banks. This shows that Islamic banks are expanding their businesses more rapidly compared to conventional banks. Bank profitability, measured by ROE, averages 9.52% for Islamic banks and 13.22% for conventional banks. This result indicates that conventional banks in Bangladesh enjoy higher profits than their Islamic counterparts. Inefficiency (INEFF), measured by non-interest expense to total assets, exhibits a higher ratio for conventional banks than their Islamic counterparts. Market power (LERNER) between these two banking systems does not differ significantly as both have similar Lerner index score. As expected, Islamic banks are smaller in size than conventional banks as the total asset (SIZE) is much lower for Islamic banks than conventional banks. The total regulatory capital (TCR) ratio is lower for Islamic banks than for conventional banks, and the difference between these two clusters is statistically significant.

The average GDP growth rate is 6.17% over the sample period, with a standard deviation of 0.97. The average (median) inflation (INF) rate is 6.40% (6.22%) and ranges between 2% to approximately 12% during the sample period. The real interest rate (RIR) has a mean value of 5.61%.

5.2. Correlation matrix

The pair-wise correlation matrix is reported in Table 4. The correlations between the NPL ratio and the Z-score, NPL ratio and DD are negative and significant. The higher correlation suggests that most of the banks with a high NPL ratio have low Z-score and DD, suggesting that Z-score and DD are the alternative proxies of credit risk. The result also reveals several significant relationships ($p < 0.05$) among independent variables. Bank-specific variables such as ETA, ROA, INEFF, LERNER show a significant relationship with both NPL and the Z-score. The highest correlation is observed between ROA and NPL ratio (0.56); therefore, multicollinearity is not a problem in the estimation. Additionally, we compute and examine the variance inflation factor (VIF) for each independent variable. In all cases, the VIFs are below 3 (not reported here), which are far below the critical value of 10, suggesting that multicollinearity is not an issue in the model.

5.3. Baseline regression results

Table 5 reports the empirical results of the baseline regression model. The results show a stable coefficient for each variable considered in this model. Sargan's over-identification

Table 4. Correlation Matrix

	NPL	ZSCORE	DD	GGL	LDR	ETA	ROA	INEFF	LERNER	SIZE	TRC	GDP	RIR	INF
NPL	1													
ZSCORE	−0.4563*	1												
DD	−0.1847*	0.0762	1											
GGL	−0.0537	0.0427	0.064	1										
LDR	−0.0106	0.0298	0.0245	−0.0125	1									
ETA	−0.3283*	0.3975*	0.1264	0.0785	0.1367*	1								
ROA	−0.5573*	0.4866*	0.2071*	0.0181	0.0531	0.4311*	1							
INEFF	0.1872*	−0.1528*	0.0584	−0.0004	−0.0092	−0.0576	−0.3036*	1						
LERNER	−0.1826*	0.2482*	0.0825	−0.0686	0.1775*	0.2019*	0.5565*	−0.1478*	1					
SIZE	0.0787	−0.0559	0.0528	−0.0753	−0.0326	−0.1172	−0.1235	−0.0506	−0.0997	1				
TRC	−0.4933*	0.3611*	0.0356	0.2442*	−0.0882	0.2936*	0.4173*	−0.2697*	−0.0723	−0.0908	1			
GDP	0.0187	0.0695	0.1519	−0.0668	0.0103	0.104	−0.0249	0.0804	0.1084	0.3246*	0.0267	1		
RIR	0.0009	−0.0872	−0.3301*	0.1119	0.0296	−0.0749	−0.0195	−0.0983	−0.0963	−0.3011*	0.0099	−0.3328	1	
INF	−0.0925	0.0371	0.3143*	−0.0557	−0.0472	0.0106	0.0666	0.0775	0.0531	0.0553	−0.0068	0.3158*	−0.4620*	1

Notes: This table presents correlations between dependent variable, firm-level control variables and macro-economic variables. *Indicates two-tailed significance at the 0.05 level or less. Definitions of variables are reported in Table 2.

test confirms the validity of the instruments used for endogenous variables, and the instruments are properly identified. First-order negative autocorrelation is present in all three estimation results; however, inconsistency could have been considered if second-order autocorrelation was present. In our estimation results, the presence of the second-order autocorrelation hypothesis is rejected, indicating estimation is consistent. It is worth mentioning that lagged dependent variables for all three models are highly significant, which indicates that the credit risk in the banking system of Bangladesh is persistent.

Table 5. Regression Result Based on Two-Step GMM Estimation Techniques

	NPL	ZSCORE	DD	NPL	ZSCORE	DD
	Islamic Bank			Conventional Bank		
Dependent Variable	(1)	(2)	(3)	(4)	(5)	(6)
NPL_{t-1}	0.436***			0.624***		
	(5.35)			(20.01)		
$ZSCORE_{t-1}$		0.306***			0.346***	
		(2.72)			(6.01)	
DD_{t-1}			0.120**			0.054***
			(2.44)			(2.89)
GGL	0.022**	−0.007	−0.001	0.020*	0.041**	0.000
	(2.39)	(−0.76)	(−0.74)	(1.83)	(−2.38)	(0.45)
LDR	0.060***	0.008	−0.039*	0.016**	−0.013*	−0.056**
	(4.17)	(0.70)	(−1.73)	(2.62)	(−1.69)	(−2.55)
ETA	−0.402**	−0.118	0.510*	0.084	−0.003	−0.072
	(−2.07)	(−1.28)	(1.81)	(0.97)	(−0.08)	(−0.65)
ROE	−0.977**	0.390*	1.293**	−1.485***	0.277***	1.596***
	(−2.20)	(1.96)	(2.09)	(−5.64)	(3.04)	(5.97)
INEFF	44.143	−14.261	11.012	113.468**	−19.394	−70.326*
	(0.56)	(−0.27)	(0.10)	(2.24)	(−1.20)	(−1.83)
LERNER	−0.401**	−1.996	−0.868	−17.147***	−1.141	10.021**
	(−2.08)	(−0.83)	(−0.13)	(−3.07)	(−0.69)	(2.45)
SIZE	−0.255***	0.089	0.199**	−0.628**	0.010	0.456*
	(−2.77)	(0.50)	(2.48)	(−2.38)	(0.10)	(1.84)
TRC	−0.271**	0.182***	0.215	−0.137***	0.016*	0.038*
	(−2.18)	(2.69)	(1.27)	(−4.95)	(1.76)	(1.82)
CRISIS	−0.865	−0.247	0.335	0.330	−0.344	−0.633
	(−0.93)	(−1.06)	(0.53)	(0.56)	(-0.21)	(−0.82)
GDP	−0.896***	0.224	0.876*	−0.216	0.206**	0.230
	(−3.90)	(1.57)	(1.95)	(−0.71)	(2.55)	(1.18)
INF	0.161	−0.055	−0.030	−0.473***	−0.000	−0.049
	(1.43)	(−0.91)	(−0.20)	(−4.20)	(−0.01)	(−0.64)
RIR	−0.260	0.097	−0.217	0.402**	0.065	−0.409***
	(−1.47)	(1.02)	(−0.86)	(2.15)	(1.30)	(−3.03)

Table 5. (Continued)

Dependent Variable	NPL	ZSCORE	DD	NPL	ZSCORE	DD
	Islamic Bank			Conventional Bank		
	(1)	(2)	(3)	(4)	(5)	(6)
Constant	16.370***	−1.367	6.013	19.388***	−0.438	−1.065
	(4.12)	(−0.54)	(1.09)	(3.51)	(−0.32)	(−0.30)
AR(1)	−3.89	−1.72	−1.96	−3.51	−1.57	−2.01
	(0.000)	(0.086)	(0.050)	(0.002)	(0.116)	(0.046)
AR(2)	0.14	1.04	−1.14	0.07	1.05	−1.4
	(0.892)	(0.299)	(0.253)	(0.943)	(0.293)	(0.162)
Hansen	36.399	34.839	18.224	28.400	26.675	10.868
Sargan	0.210	0.320	0.270	0.190	0.300	0.250

Notes: The table presents the result of estimating Equation (11) using two-step GMM estimation technique. The dependent variables are NPL ratio in columns (1) and (4), Z-score in columns (2) and (5) and DD in columns (3) and (6). In the interests of brevity time dummies are unreported. Standard errors are corrected for heteroscedasticity and autocorrelation and are clustered at the bank level. AR is a serial correlation test of order I using residuals in first differences, asymptotically distributed as $N(0,1)$ under the null of no serial correlation. Hansen is the test of the over-identifying restrictions, asymptotically distributed as X^2 under the null of no correlation between the instruments and the error term. Sargan *p*-value reports the *p*-value of the test of over identifying restrictions, which test the null that instruments in the GMM estimation are uncorrelated with error term. Definitions of variables are reported in Table 2. *t*-statistics are in parentheses. Superscripts ***, **, * indicate statistical significance at 1%, 5% and 10% level, respectively.

These results also confirm the validity of model specification as well as the estimation technique used for this analysis.

Bank-specific effects

Analysis of bank-specific variables shows that growth of credit (GGL) — a proxy of adverse selection problem — has a significant positive correlation with NPL ratio for both clusters of banks and significant negative correlation with the Z-score for conventional banking, implying that both banking clusters face adverse selection problem. This result is compatible with the theoretical argument mentioned earlier (see, for example, Alessi and Detken, 2018; Jimenez and Saurina, 2006). This relationship can be explained by the fact that both types of banks expand their loan products to new geographic areas about which they do not have adequate prior experience. Particularly Islamic banks have more incentive to expand their business as most of the Islamic banks in Bangladesh are relatively new compared to their conventional counterparts.

LDR shows a positive and significant relationship with the NPL ratio and significant negative relation with the Z-score and DD for conventional banks. These results indicate that conventional banks suffer from a moral hazard problem. A positive relationship between LDR and NPL indicates that the higher the LDR for a bank, the more it relies on depositors' funds, which leads to higher credit risk. A major portion of the funds that a bank lends is supplied by the deposit accounts. Bank knows that depositors are secured, to a certain extent, by the national deposit insurance scheme. Thus, a bank's tendency to invest in risky projects proves the moral hazard hypothesis. This finding is also applicable to Islamic banks, as LDR has a positive and significant influence on credit risk.

In contrast, ETA shows a significant negative relation with NPL for Islamic banks, which further provides support to the moral hazard hypothesis. This finding conforms to those of Salas and Saurina (2002) and Hancock and Wilcox (1994). No significant relation between ETA and credit risk is evident for conventional banks. The coefficient of ETA ratio for conventional banks is higher than that for Islamic banks, which is consistent with the above findings.

ROE, a measure of management efficiency, shows a significant negative impact on the credit risk of both Islamic and conventional banks. This implies that the efficiency of bank managers in screening and monitoring can substantially contribute to reducing credit risk. Moreover, profitability provides banks with an increased capacity to spend sufficient resources for screening and monitoring, which results in lower credit risk. The result is consistent with the findings of Saeed and Izzeldin (2016). Cost inefficiency (INEFF) has a significant positive influence on increasing credit risk for conventional banks but shows no significant effect on Islamic banks.

Lerner index (LERNER) is used to measure the competition in the banking sector. Lerner index appears to have a negative impact on credit risk for both Islamic and conventional banks. In line with the competition-fragility nexus, our results support that higher market power increases the stability for both Islamic and conventional banks. The result is consistent with the findings of Kabir and Worthington (2017). The competition-fragility view can be further supported by the 'scale' hypothesis. Size appears to be positively (negatively) related to DD (NPL) for both Islamic and conventional banks indicating that the larger the size, the greater is the stability which proves an old adage 'too big to fail'. Moreover, larger banks possess higher financial capacity to institutionalize screening and monitoring technologies, which, in turn, helps reduce credit risk. This result, in the context of Bangladesh, can be explained by the fact that the number of banks is comparatively more than the country can practically and profitably support. The financial market is not matured enough to absorb the pressure of excess competition. Thus, size appears to have a risk-reducing impact on banks, which extends support to the banks 'franchise value hypothesis' proposed by Hellmann *et al.* (1997) for developing and emerging economies.

The regulatory capital requirement, which is measured by the total capital adequacy ratio (TRC), shows a significant negative relationship with credit risk for Islamic and conventional banks. It implies that banks that have higher capital adequacy ratio have lower credit risk, which supports the effectiveness of a bank's regulation. Thus, it can be proposed that the Basel requirement is successfully fulfilling its objective for both types of banks.

As expected, the crisis dummy does not show any significant relationship with the proxies of credit risk in the context of Bangladesh because the economy did not face any adverse impact from the global financial crisis. The economy of Bangladesh is still domestic market-oriented. Financial institutions are not highly involved with foreign transactions. Hence, the economy did not face any significant impact from the financial crisis.

Macro-economic effects

As for macro-economic variables, the GDP growth rate has a negative influence on credit risk. The effect of the real interest rate (RIR) on credit risk is positive and significant as expected. A higher real interest rate decreases DD and increases the NPL ratio for conventional banks (not significant for Islamic banks as this cluster of banks presumably does not deal with interest). An increase in the real interest rate in an economy may lead to an increase in the cost of borrowing, which makes it difficult for borrowers to repay their principal and interest. This eventually leads to the higher credit risk of banks. This result supports the finding of Beck *et al.* (2006) and Castro (2013). Inflation (INF) negatively affects the credit risk of conventional banks only. Although this finding seems to be a little counterintuitive, the result, however, implies that the central bank tightens monetary policy when the inflation of the economy is high. Contractionary monetary policy is associated with lower loan expansion which leads to lower credit risk.

5.4. Additional analysis

5.4.1. Impact of corporate governance attributes on credit risk

Like macro-economic and bank-specific variables, governance variables can also affect bank's risk-taking and hence default risk. Recent literature in the banking has investigated the impact of different governance attributes on credit risk (Srivastav and Hagendorff, 2016; Switzer *et al.*, 2018; Switzer and Wang, 2013). The separation of ownership and control in large corporations leads to a potential conflict between the stockholders and the bondholders, on the one hand, and between management and shareholders, on the other (Jensen and Meckling, 1976). This conflict of interest calls for establishing effective corporate governance so that the objectives of managers are aligned to those of shareholders. Following Switzer *et al.* (2018) and Switzer and Wang (2013), we further investigate the impact of corporate governance attributes and ownership structure on credit risk in the Bangladeshi banking sector. Particularly, in this additional analysis, we are interested to examine the impact of two governance attributes — board size and board independence — and two attributes of ownership structure — insider ownership and institutional ownership — on credit risk. In this additional analysis section, due to data unavailability on corporate governance, our sample covers the period 2009–2018.

Board size is one of the important governance attributes that has a significant impact on performance and also risk-taking behavior of firms. Board of directors acts as a mediator between shareholders and managers. According to the resource dependency theory, a board's primary function is to effectively monitor managers to ensure that the executives are not gorging excessive risk. Based on this theory, a large board can effectively monitor the activities of managers. In contrast, large board size may give rise to internal conflicts that restrict the efficiency of monitoring (Lipton and Lorsch, 1992). Furthermore, a large board incurs higher agency costs and lowers performance, leading eventually to a higher probability of default. Jensen (1993) argues that large boards are not efficient due to potential free ride problems and internal conflicts among directors. Empirical evidence on the impact of board size on default risk is also inconclusive. We measure the board size (BSIZE) as the logarithm of the total number of directors on the board in a particular year.

Prior literature also suggests that board independence plays a significant role in reducing the credit risk of firms. Independent directors are in a better position to protect the interest of general shareholders and can limit managers' excessive risk-taking behavior. Switzer and Wang (2013) show a significant negative relationship between board independence and credit risk. Board independence (BRDIND) is measured by the fraction of outside directors on the board.

We depict the results of the board structure on banks' credit risk in Table 6. The results show that board size (BSIZE) is positively related to credit risk for conventional banks

Table 6. Impact of Board Attributes on Credit Risk in Islamic and Conventional Banks

	Distance-to-Default (DD)			
	Islamic Bank		Conventional Bank	
Dependent Variable	(1)	(2)	(3)	(4)
BSIZE	1.945***		−0.617***	
	(2.94)		(−2.79)	
BRDIND		1.053**		0.781**
		(2.40)		(2.63)
ROE	0.063	0.549	0.848***	0.669
	(0.74)	(0.81)	(5.64)	(0.95)
ETA	0.056***	−0.501	0.027	0.441*
	(3.09)	(−0.70)	(0.62)	(1.68)
SIZE	0.148	0.042	0.748***	−1.349*
	(0.71)	(0.03)	(3.11)	(−1.88)
CRISIS	1.230**	0.107	0.244	−1.560
	(2.04)	(0.06)	(0.57)	(−1.20)
GDP	−1.478***	−0.190	−0.451**	−0.734
	(−5.37)	(−0.23)	(−2.06)	(−1.33)
INF	0.022	0.312	0.018	0.180
	(0.23)	(0.64)	(0.32)	(0.71)
RIR	−0.776***	−0.623	−0.415***	−1.227***
	(−5.96)	(−0.84)	(−4.17)	(−2.87)
Constant	8.719***	10.812	1.202	16.874**
	(2.83)	(0.82)	(0.50)	(2.16)
R-square	0.340	0.359	0.422	0.457
Adjusted R-square	0.255	0.240	0.410	0.441

Notes: The table presents the impact of board attributes on credit risk in Islamic and conventional banks using RE model. The dependent variable is DD. Columns (1) and (2) report regression results for Islamic banks and columns (3) and (4) report regression results for conventional banks. Definitions of variables are reported in Table 2. *t*-statistics are in parentheses. Superscripts ***, **, * indicate statistical significance at 1%, 5%, and 10% levels, respectively.

(Column 3) at 1% level of significance, whereas larger boards reduce credit risk for Islamic banks (Column 1). The long history of conventional banks may have created a sort of standard risk-appetite as well as a management technique, which leaves the larger board not only redundant but also detrimental. However, Islamic banks benefit from larger boards as they are still in the learning stage.

Unlike board size, we find a negative relationship between board independence and banks' credit risk for both Islamic and conventional banks at 5% level of significance. Independent boards in Bangladesh act as whistle blowers during the firm's distress period. Outside directors on the board create pressure on corporate decision-makers to focus on protecting the interest of stakeholders. They do so by implementing objective monitoring of managers, which, in turn, limits self-interested managerial behavior. This eventually results in lower risk-taking by managers and dominant shareholders.

5.4.2. Impact of ownership structure on credit risk

The implication of corporate ownership on firms' default risk can be viewed from the typical principal–agent relation. In the presence of separation between ownership and control, there will be '… some divergence between the agent's decisions and those decisions which would maximize the welfare of the principal' (Jensen and Meckling, 1976, p. 482). The two dominant types of shareholders in a bank are managerial (insider) ownership and institutional ownership. Insiders tend to utilize corporate resources to pursue their self-interest, including diverting corporate resources for personal benefits, at the expense of other shareholders and bondholders. Furthermore, higher insider ownership may also give more power that might increase the managerial moral hazard problem. However, empirical findings on the relationship between inside-ownership and firm's risk are mixed, which can be attributed to differences in sample countries and periods.

In contrast, institutional investors can monitor managerial opportunistic behavior and agency costs to the benefit of both stockholders and bondholders. Since institutional investors are generally long-term value-oriented investors, they limit the level of risk a firm can take. Similar to insider ownership, empirical evidence on the relationship between institutional ownership and banks' default risk is inconclusive. For example, Switzer *et al.* (2016) find that institutional shareholdings reduce default risk for Canadian financial firms. On the contrary, Switzer and Wang (2013) document that higher institutional shareholdings increase default risk for US commercial banks.

By using a data set collected manually for the period 2009–2018 on 30 listed Bangladeshi banks, we investigate the impact of insider and institutional ownership on credit risk. Insider ownership (INSIDE) is defined as the percentage of outstanding shares held by corporate insiders. Institutional stock-holding (INST), as representative of institutional ownership, is defined as the percentage of a firm's total outstanding shares held by various institutions. Following Switzer *et al.* (2016), we control bank-specific variables such as ROE, ETA, SIZE and macro-economic variables such as GDP, INF and RIR, and crisis dummy in the regression model. Regression results are reported in Table 7.

Table 7. Impact of Ownership Structure on Credit Risk in Islamic and Conventional Banks

	Distance-to-Default (DD)			
	Islamic		Conventional	
Dependent Variable	(1)	(2)	(3)	(4)
INSIDER	−1.564**		−0.118**	
	(−2.53)		(−2.26)	
INST		1.956**		0.574***
		(2.26)		(2.98)
ROE	0.181**	0.211***	0.940***	0.867***
	(2.42)	(2.70)	(5.71)	(4.77)
ETA	−0.028	−0.048**	−0.020	−0.008
	(−1.52)	(−2.45)	(−0.38)	(−0.18)
SIZE	0.006	0.353	0.830***	0.553*
	(0.02)	(1.49)	(2.62)	(1.94)
CRISIS	1.928***	1.503**	0.247	0.472
	(2.99)	(2.32)	(0.53)	(1.00)
GDP	−1.088***	−1.413***	−0.496**	−0.416*
	(−3.59)	(−4.45)	(−2.02)	(−1.69)
INF	0.190*	0.136	0.009	−0.007
	(1.76)	(1.32)	(0.14)	(−0.11)
RIR	−0.782***	−0.798***	−0.408***	−0.416***
	(−5.71)	(−5.64)	(−3.76)	(−3.67)
Constant	11.883***	10.913***	−0.268	1.272
	(3.65)	(3.48)	(−0.10)	(0.48)
R-square	0.46	0.73	0.33	0.34
Adjusted R-square	0.38	0.57	0.29	0.27

Notes: This table presents the impact of ownership structure on credit risk in Islamic and conventional banks using RE model. The dependent variable is DD. Columns (1) and (2) report regression results for Islamic banks and columns (3) and (4) report regression result for conventional banks. Definitions of variables are reported in Table 2. *t*-statistics are in parentheses. Superscripts ***, **, * indicate statistical significance at 1%, 5% and 10% levels, respectively.

Columns (1) and (3) report the result of the effect of insider ownership on credit risk. As expected, we find that insider ownership is negatively related to distance to default of both Islamic and conventional banks at 5% level of significance. This result is expected in the context of Bangladesh, where most banks are family-controlled. Family dominant insider ownerships tend to expropriate outside shareholders and bondholders. Founding members of private commercial banks borrowed more than six times their capital in 2016. Directors, mainly founding members, borrowed about approximately US$8.25 billion, more than 14% of the total loan disbursed on that year (Sharmeen *et al.*, 2019).

Columns (2) and (4) of Table 7 exhibit the impact of institutional ownership on credit risk. We find that institutional ownership reduces default risk for both Islamic and conventional banks at 5% and 1% level of significance, respectively. Institutional investors in Bangladesh, mostly non-bank financial institutions, are active investors who insist on a high standard of corporate governance. We further note that the coefficient of INST is much higher for Islamic banks (1.956) than for conventional banks (0.574), implying that institutional investors of Islamic banks are more active in limiting the riskier projects than conventional banks' investors. Hence, their presence in the banks is associated with lower default risk.

6. Conclusion

The findings of this research offer several important implications in terms of policy and regulations. First, the macro-economic finding suggests that inflation increases the credit risk of banks which has an important implication for monetary policy of the country. In particular, care should be taken in designing monetary policy so that expansionary policy does not spark inflation which is likely to pose a threat to the banking sector by increasing credit risk. Also, it is observed that credit expansion is accompanied by higher credit risk which indicates asymmetry of information. An increase in lending by banks often gives rise to poor loan quality as the increase in number deters the lender's capacity to assess and monitor borrowers properly. In such a circumstance, as Honohan (1997) suggested, 'speed limit' can be applied to lending activities that possess a significant risk to banks' loan portfolio and create problem loans. This stricter regulation for loans will help minimize poor loan quality. Furthermore, to mitigate information asymmetry, credit rating agencies, which are currently unable to produce required information and deliver optimal services due to various obstacles including lack of proper infrastructure, can be strengthened and utilized.

Thirdly, competition-fragility nexus indicates that regulatory authority should restrict competition in the Bangladeshi banking sector. This prescription conforms to the broader theoretical model of financial restraint policy. Excessive competition is quite harmful for the productivity and resilience of financial intermediaries, especially when they are immature owing to the short-history or smaller firm size. Regulating competition in such a banking system may create 'rent' as franchise value for banks and provides incentive for increasing firms' efficiency and productivity. The first step of easing competitive pressure in the Bangladeshi banking sector can start by imposing a restriction on new entrants as it is already alleged that the economy has more banks than it can profitably support. Fourth, we suggest that at this stage, there is no need to have separate regulatory requirements with regard to capital adequacy for Islamic banks. Finally, board independence works as a safeguard against credit risk. Thus, board independence should be enhanced by including more independent members in the board. As per the revised corporate governance guidelines of Bangladesh, independent directors should constitute at least 20% of the total number of board members. Although this number may perceive to be low in terms of international standard, firms most often fail to meet this requirement. Hence, regulatory authority can apply soft coercion instead of sheer encouragement to induce firms to comply with this regulatory policy at least for the sake of reducing credit risk.

Our research is currently limited to private commercial banks only in Bangladesh. Further research could incorporate the state-owned commercial banks, foreign banks and other specialized banks to illustrate a comprehensive scenario on the determinants of credit risk in the banking industry. Our research also could be extended to non-bank financial institutions to be able to compare with the banking industry.

Acknowledgments

We are grateful for the comments and guidance from the editor and two anonymous referees. The paper has also benefited from comments and discussion with Parmendra Sharma and Sharif Nurul Ahkam.

References

Abedifar, P, P Molyneux and A Tarazi (2013). Risk in Islamic banking. *Review of Finance*, 17(6), 2035–2096.

Ahmad, NH and M Ariff (2007a). Multi-country study of bank credit risk determinants. *International Journal of Banking and Finance*, 5(1), 135–152.

Ahmad, NH and M Ariff (2007b). Multi-country study of bank credit risk determinants. *International Journal of Banking and Finance*, 5(1), 6.

Ahmed, E, Z Rahman and RI Ahmed (2006). Comperative analysis of loan recovery among nationalized, private and Islamic commercial banks of Bangladesh.

Alam, N, SS Binti Zainuddin and SAR Rizvi (2019). Ramifications of varying banking regulations on performance of Islamic banks. *Borsa Istanbul Review*, 19(1), 49–64. doi:https://doi.org/10.1016/j.bir.2018.05.005.

Alessi, L and C Detken (2018). Identifying excessive credit growth and leverage. *Journal of Financial Stability*, 35, 215–225.

Alhassan, AL, A Kyereboah-Coleman and C Andoh (2014). Asset quality in a crisis period: An empirical examination of Ghanaian banks. *Review of Development Finance*, 4(1), 50–62.

Ali, A and K Daly (2010). Macroeconomic determinants of credit risk: Recent evidence from a cross country study. *International Review of Financial Analysis*, 19(3), 165–171.

Allen, DE, RJ Powell and AK Singh (2012). Beyond reasonable doubt: Multiple tail risk measures applied to European industries. *Applied Economics Letters*, 19(7), 671–676.

Altman, EI and A Saunders (1997). Credit risk measurement: Developments over the last 20 years. *Journal of Banking and Finance*, 21(11–12), 1721–1742.

Altunbas, Y, S Carbo, EP Gardener and P Molyneux (2007). Examining the relationships between capital, risk and efficiency in European banking. *European Financial Management*, 13(1), 49–70.

Altunbas, Y, L Gambacorta and D Marques-Ibanez (2010). Bank risk and monetary policy. *Journal of Financial Stability*, 6(3), 121–129.

Anginer, D, A Demirguc-Kunt and M Zhu (2014). How does competition affect bank systemic risk? *Journal of Financial Intermediation*, 23(1), 1–26.

Arellano, M and S Bond (1991). Some tests of specification for panel data: Monte Carlo evidence and an application to employment equations. *The Review of Economic Studies*, 58(2), 277–297.

Ariss, RT (2010). On the implications of market power in banking: Evidence from developing countries. *Journal of Banking and Finance*, 34(4), 765–775.

Athanasoglou, PP, SN Brissimis and MD Delis (2008). Bank-specific, industry-specific and macroeconomic determinants of bank profitability. *Journal of International Financial Markets, Institutions and Money*, 18(2), 121–136.

Baltagi, B (2008). *Econometric Analysis of Panel Data* (Vol. 1): John Wiley & Sons.

Bangladesh Bank. (2013). Annual Report 2013.

Bangladesh Bank. (2018). Annual Report 2018.

Beck, R, P Jakubik and A Piloiu (2013a). Non-performing loans: What matters in addition to the economic cycle? ECB Working Paper No. 1515. Available at SSRN: https://ssrn.com/abstract=2214971, lst accessed on Febryary 2, 2020.

Beck, T, O De Jonghe and G Schepens (2013b). Bank competition and stability: Cross-country heterogeneity. *Journal of Financial Intermediation*, 22(2), 218–244.

Beck, T, A Demirgüç-Kunt and O Merrouche (2013c). Islamic vs. conventional banking: Business model, efficiency and stability. *Journal of Banking and Finance*, 37(2), 433–447. doi:https://doi.org/10.1016/j.jbankfin.2012.09.016

Beck, T, A Demirgüç-Kunt and R Levine (2006). Bank concentration, competition, and crises: First results. *Journal of Banking and Finance*, 30(5), 1581–1603.

Berger, AN and R DeYoung (1997). Problem loans and cost efficiency in commercial banks. *Journal of Banking and Finance*, 21(6), 849–870.

Black, F and M Scholes (1973). The pricing of options and corporate liabilities. *The Journal of Political Economy*, 637–654.

Blundell, R and S Bond (1998). Initial conditions and moment restrictions in dynamic panel data models. *Journal of Econometrics*, 87(1), 115–143.

Calomiris, CW and SH Haber (2015). *Fragile by Design: The Political Origins of Banking Crises and Scarce Credit*, Vol. 48. Princeton University Press.

Castro, V (2013). Macroeconomic determinants of the credit risk in the banking system: The case of the GIPSI. *Economic Modelling*, 31, 672–683.

Chaibi, H and Z Ftiti (2015). Credit risk determinants: Evidence from a cross-country study. *Research in International Business and Finance*, 33, 1–16.

Chava, S and A Purnanandam (2010). Is default risk negatively related to stock returns? *Review of Financial Studies*, 23(6), 2523–2559.

Čihák, M, and H Hesse (2010). Islamic banks and financial stability: An empirical analysis. *Journal of Financial Services Research*, 38(2–3), 95–113.

Coccorese, P (2014). Estimating the Lerner index for the banking industry: A stochastic frontier approach. *Applied Financial Economics*, 24(2), 73–88.

Colquitt, J (2007). *Credit Risk Management: How to Avoid Lending Disasters and Maximize Earnings*. McGraw Hill Professional.

Das, A and S Ghosh (2007). Determinants of credit risk in Indian state-owned banks: An empirical investigation.

Delis, MD and GP Kouretas (2011). Interest rates and bank risk-taking. *Journal of Banking and Finance*, 35(4), 840–855.

Demirgüç-Kunt, A and E Detragiache (1998). The determinants of banking crises-evidence from developing and developed countries. *IMF Staff Papers*, 45(1), 81–109.

Dimitrios, A, L Helen and T Mike (2016). Determinants of non-performing loans: Evidence from Euro-area countries. *Finance Research Letters*, 18, 116–119. doi: https://doi.org/10.1016/j.frl.2016.04.008

Espinoza, RA and A Prasad (2010). *Nonperforming Loans in the GCC Banking System and their Macroeconomic Effects*. International Monetary Fund.

Festić, M, A Kavkler and S Repina (2011). The macroeconomic sources of systemic risk in the banking sectors of five new EU member states. *Journal of Banking and Finance*, 35(2), 310–322.

Fiordelisi, F and DS Mare (2014). Competition and financial stability in European cooperative banks. *Journal of International Money and Finance*, 45, 1–16.

Ghosh, A (2015). Banking-industry specific and regional economic determinants of non-performing loans: Evidence from US states. *Journal of Financial Stability*, 20, 93–104.

Gulati, R, A Goswami and S Kumar (2019). What drives credit risk in the Indian banking industry? An empirical investigation. *Economic Systems*, 43(1), 42–62.

Hancock, D and JA Wilcox (1994). Bank capital and the credit crunch: The roles of risk-weighted and unweighted capital regulations. *Real Estate Economics*, 22(1), 59–94.

Haron, A and JLH Hock (2007). Inherent risk: Credit and market risks. *Islamic Finance: The Regulatory Challenge*, 2.

Hasan, Z (2002). Mudaraba as a mode of finance in Islamic banking: Theory, practice and problems.

Hellmann, T, K Murdock and J Stiglitz (1997). Financial restraint: Toward a new paradigm. In *The Role of Government in East Asian Economic Development: Comparative Institutional Analysis*, M Aoki, H Kim and M Okuno-Fujiwara (eds.), pp. 163–207. Oxford: Clarendon Press.

Hillegeist, SA, EK Keating, DP Cram and KG Lundstedt (2004). Assessing the probability of bankruptcy. *Review of Accounting Studies*, 9(1), 5–34.

Honohan, P (1997). Banking system failures in developing and transition countries: Diagnosis and predictions.

Jensen, MC (1993). The modern industrial revolution, exit, and the failure of internal control systems. *The Journal of Finance*, 48(3), 831–880.

Jensen, MC and WH Meckling (1976). Theory of the firm: Managerial behavior, agency costs and ownership structure. *Journal of Financial Economics*, 3(4), 305–360.

Jimenez, G and J Saurina (2006). Credit cycles, credit risk, and prudential regulation. *International Journal of Central Banking*.

Jiménez, G and J Saurina (2004). Collateral, type of lender and relationship banking as determinants of credit risk. *Journal of Banking and Finance*, 28(9), 2191–2212.

Jokipii, T and P Monnin (2013). The impact of banking sector stability on the real economy. *Journal of International Money and Finance*, 32, 1–16.

Jorion, P (2009). Risk management lessons from the credit crisis. *European Financial Management*, 15(5), 923–933.

Kabir, MN, A Worthington and R Gupta (2015). Comparative credit risk in Islamic and conventional bank. *Pacific-Basin Finance Journal*, 34, 327–353.

Kabir, MN and AC Worthington (2017). The 'competition–stability/fragility' nexus: A comparative analysis of Islamic and conventional banks. *International Review of Financial Analysis*, 50, 111–128.

Khalil, AF, C Rickwood and V Murinde (2002). Evidence on agency contractual problems in Mudarabah financing operations by Islamic banks. *Published in Iqbal and Llewellyn*, 57–94.

Khemraj, T and S Pasha (2009). The determinants of non-performing loans: An econometric case study of Guyana.

Klein, N (2013). *Non-performing Loans in CESEE: Determinants and Impact on Macroeconomic Performance*. International Monetary Fund.

Koutsomanoli-Filippaki, A and E Mamatzakis (2009). Performance and Merton-type default risk of listed banks in the EU: A panel VAR approach. *Journal of Banking and Finance*, 33(11), 2050–2061.

Kumbhakar, SC, S Baardsen and G Lien (2012). A new method for estimating market power with an application to Norwegian sawmilling. *Review of Industrial Organization*, 40(2), 109–129.

Kuzucu, N and S Kuzucu (2019). What drives non-performing loans? Evidence from emerging and advanced economies during pre- and post-global financial crisis. *Emerging Markets Finance and Trade*, 55(8), 1694–1708. doi:10.1080/1540496X.2018.1547877

Laeven, L, L Ratnovski and H Tong (2016). Bank size, capital, and systemic risk: Some international evidence. *Journal of Banking and Finance*, 69, S25–S34.

Lipton, M and JW Lorsch (1992). A modest proposal for improved corporate governance. *The Business Lawyer*, 59–77.

Louzis, DP, AT Vouldis and VL Metaxas (2012). Macroeconomic and bank-specific determinants of non-performing loans in Greece: A comparative study of mortgage, business and consumer loan portfolios. *Journal of Banking and Finance*, 36(4), 1012–1027.

Maji, SG and UK De (2015). Regulatory capital and risk of Indian banks: A simultaneous equation approach. *Journal of Financial Economic Policy*, 7(2), 140–156.

Makri, V, A Tsagkanos and A Bellas (2014). Determinants of non-performing loans: The case of Eurozone. *Panoeconomicus*, 61(2), 193–206.

Merton, RC (1974). On the pricing of corporate debt: The risk structure of interest rates. *The Journal of Finance*, 29(2), 449–470.

Miah MD and K Sharmeen (2015). Relationship between capital, risk and efficiency. *International Journal of Islamic and Middle Eastern Finance and Management*, 8(2), 203–221.

Mpofu, TR and E Nikolaidou (2018). Determinants of credit risk in the banking system in Sub-Saharan Africa. *Review of Development Finance*, 8(2), 141–153.

Nkusu, MM (2011). *Nonperforming Loans and Macrofinancial Vulnerabilities in Advanced Economies*. International Monetary Fund.

Rime, B (2001). Capital requirements and bank behaviour: Empirical evidence for Switzerland. *Journal of Banking and Finance*, 25(4), 789–805.

Rinaldi, L and A Sanchis-Arellano (2006). Household debt sustainability: What explains household non-performing loans? An empirical analysis.

Roodman, D (2009). A note on the theme of too many instruments. *Oxford Bulletin of Economics and Statistics*, 71(1), 135–158.

Rosly, SA, M Ayub, I Toutounchian, Z Hasan and W Al-Zuhayli (2005). Critical issues on Islamic banking and financial.

Saeed, M and M Izzeldin (2016). Examining the relationship between default risk and efficiency in Islamic and conventional banks. *Journal of Economic Behavior and Organization*, 132, 127–154.

Salas, V and J Saurina (2002). Credit risk in two institutional regimes: Spanish commercial and savings banks. *Journal of Financial Services Research*, 22(3), 203–224.

Sarker, MAA (1999). Islamic banking in Bangladesh: Performance, problems, and prospects. *International Journal of Islamic Financial Services*, 1(3), 15–36.

Sharmeen, K, R Hasan and MD Miah (2019). Underpinning the benefits of green banking: A comparative study between Islamic and conventional banks in Bangladesh. *Thunderbird International Business Review*, 61(5), 735–744.

Siddiqui, A (2008). Financial contracts, risk and performance of Islamic banking. *Managerial Finance*, 34(10), 680–694.

Srivastav, A and J Hagendorff (2016). Corporate governance and bank risk-taking. *Corporate Governance: An International Review*, 24(3), 334–345.

Sufian, F (2011). Profitability of the Korean banking sector: Panel evidence on bank-specific and macroeconomic determinants. *Journal of Economics and Management*, 7(1), 43–72.

Switzer, LN, Q Tu and J Wang (2018). Corporate governance and default risk in financial firms over the post-financial crisis period: International evidence. *Journal of International Financial Markets, Institutions and Money*, 52, 196–210.

Switzer, LN and J Wang (2013). Default risk estimation, bank credit risk, and corporate governance. *Financial Markets, Institutions and Instruments*, 22(2), 91–112.

Switzer, LN, J Wang and Q Tu (2016). Corporate governance and default risk in financial firms over the post financial crisis period: International evidence. *Melbourne Business School*.

Warninda, TD, IA Ekaputra and R Rokhim (2019). Do Mudarabah and Musharakah financing impact Islamic Bank credit risk differently? *Research in International Business and Finance*, 49, 166–175.

Windmeijer, F (2005). A finite sample correction for the variance of linear efficient two-step GMM estimators. *Journal of Econometrics*, 126(1), 25–51.

Zheng, C and S Moudud-Ul-Huq (2017). Banks' capital regulation and risk: Does bank vary is size? Empirical evidence from Bangladesh. *International Journal of Financial Engineering*, 4(2&3), Article ID 1750025, 1–27.

Chapter 8

Comparative TFP Growth between GCC Conventional and Islamic Banks Before and After the 2008 Financial Crisis[#]

Azzeddine Azzam[*,‡] and Belaid Rettab[†]

[*]*Department of Agricultural Economics*
University of Nebraska-Lincoln
103E Filley Hall, Lincoln, Nebraska, USA

[†]*Dubai Chamber*
Dubai, UAE
[‡]*azzam1@unl.edu*

This paper measures and compares the performance of GCC conventional and Islamic banks in terms of total factor productivity growth (TFPG) before and after the 2008 financial crisis. The sources of TFPG are technical change, size economies, and observed asset growth. Technical change and size economies are measured by estimating a translog cost function and factor share equations. Results show that Islamic banks outperformed conventional banks overall and across different sizes. To the extent that product and process innovation improves TFPG, Islamic banks have weathered the 2008 financial crisis by being more innovative than conventional banks.

Keywords: Conventional versus Islamic banking; GCC; total factor productivity growth; 2008 financial crisis.

1. Introduction

By exposing the pitfalls of conventional finance, the 2008 financial crisis (hereafter the crisis) brought Islamic finance into the limelight as a serious alternative (Chapra, 2009), so much so that even the Vatican called on conventional banks to "look at the rules of Islamic finance to restore confidence amongst their clients at a time of global economic crisis" (Totaro, 2009). What particularly stood out in the aftermath of the crisis was that while 123 conventional banks failed in the United States alone (Hidayat and Abdu, 2012), not a single Islamic bank failed in 2008 (Wilson, 2009).

In theory, Islamic banks are expected to be more resilient to financial crises than conventional banks for several reasons (Amba and Almukharreq, 2013). One is prudent lending. Because Islamic finance is asset-based and stipulates risk-sharing between lender and borrower, rather than charge a fixed rate of interest and tie lending to borrowers' collateral, Islamic banks are more cautious about what projects to finance than

---

[‡] Corresponding author.
[#] This Chapter first appeared in the *Singapore Economic Review*, Vol. 67, No. 1, doi: 10.1142/S0217590820420047. © 2022 World Scientific Publishing.

conventional banks. Another reason is that Islamic finance prohibits the use of the very risk-hedging techniques and financial instruments used by conventional banks (Kettel, 2010), such as collateralized debt obligations and credit default swaps, which many believe led to the crisis. Yet another reason is the funding structure of Islamic banks (Wilson, 2009; Bourkis and Nabi, 2013). In contrast to conventional finance, where the source of funding is largely from wholesale markets, such as other banks, money market funds, and treasuries; the source of funding for Islamic finance is mostly from deposits. So when credit from the wholesale credit market dried up in 2008, Islamic banks were not exposed.

Whether and how Islamic banks have outperformed conventional banks during the crisis in practice is an empirical question that has progressively been receiving more scholarly interest as the crisis recedes into the past. In a comprehensive survey of contemporary Islamic banking literature, Hassan and Aliyu (2018) identified 18 articles that were published between 2010 and 2017 about the differential effect of the crisis on Islamic banks versus conventional banks, covering different geographical locations, periods, and using different methodologies. The empirical evidence from this literature suggests that Islamic banks have not overwhelmingly outperformed conventional banks from 2008 and onwards. While some authors believe the reason is that Islamic banks mimic conventional banks and, therefore, are not true to their theoretical business model (Bourkis and Nabi, 2013), others believe that Islamic banks cannot be true to their theoretical business model because many of the assumptions of the model are not met in practice (Mirakhor and Krichene, 2009).

Upon reflection, however, conclusions from the previous empirical literature are drawn largely from the disparate ratios used as indicators of cost, revenue, and profit performance. A shortcoming of such ratios is that, although they are simple to compute, and each individually offers information about one dimension of the financial health of banks, they are partial performance indicators and there is no clear-cut procedure for using them together to draw an overall picture of the financial health of a bank or its relative financial performance to other banks (Alexakis *et al.*, 2019). More importantly, other indicators like asset growth, for example, which were at high levels until 2007, now seem inadequate as indicators of the health of the banking sector in light of the crisis in 2008. This suggests that, in retrospect, the phenomenal pre-crisis growth in Islamic bank assets may have largely been driven by accumulation rather than productivity and efficiency with which banks convert *all* factors of production into output. The appropriate measure in the latter case is total factor productivity growth (TFPG), where factor productivity total is the ratio of output to *all* factors of production.

In light of the preceding, this paper aims to contribute to the toolkit for examining the comparative effect of the crisis on total factor productivity growth of Islamic and conventional banking using GCC as a case study. Like Alexakis *et al.* (2019, pp. 1–2), we limit our study to GCC banks to avoid the sample selection bias deficiencies inherent in studies that, to enlarge the sample size, mix several countries with disparate banking regulations and economic conditions.

For methodology, we follow Nadiri and Schankerman (1981) who extended the growth accounting framework (Solow, 1957) to include returns to scale from a parametrically estimated cost function. As will be shown in the model section of this paper, the decomposition is simple to implement, requiring three elements: technical change, growth of assets, and cost elasticities. Growth in assets is observable from the data. Technical change and cost elasticities are estimated using a dual industry cost function, which requires data that is readily available in sources like Bankscope. As far as we know, the decomposition we implement in this paper has yet to be applied to comparative TFPG analysis of conventional versus Islamic finance.

As will be detailed in the literature review section, comparative efficiency and productivity analysis of Islamic and conventional banks is dominated by Data Envelopment Analysis (DEA) and Stochastic Frontier Analysis (SFA), two methods that focus on measuring technical efficiency at the decision-making unit (DMU), where deviations from the frontier, or best practice, are translated into efficiency scores for each DMU. Use of the respective methods is best illustrated by two recent studies: Al-Jarrah *et al.* (2017) and Alexakis *et al.* (2019). Al-Jarrah *et al.* (2017) implement SFA to estimate cost-efficiency scores for GCC and non-GCC banks in the Middle East and North Africa and examines the changes in the scores pre- and post-crisis. Alexakis *et al.* (2019) use DEA to decompose TFPG into efficiency and productivity changes up to the crisis and following the crisis, assuming constant and variable returns to scale.

While there are different methods for measuring efficiency and productivity, and, as shall be shown later, each has its advantages and disadvantages, we implement ours for the following reasons. First, as discussed earlier, it is simple to implement and, in light of the dominance of DEA and SFA in examining the comparative performance of Islamic versus conventional banks, our paper adds to the toolkit by demonstrating how to decompose TFPG into its sources using parametric rather than non-parametric measures of returns to scale. Second, to the extent that TFPG can be driven by product and process innovation, which can translate into lower costs of financial intermediation, we posit that comparing pre- and post-crisis TFPG between conventional and Islamic banks using information from a cost function is tantamount to comparing how the two types of banks have responded to the crisis by innovating to enhance productivity (Alexakis *et al.*, 2019).

The link between TFPG and innovation is well established in the endogenous economic growth literature (Romer, 1990; Aghion and Howitt, 1992). As a corollary, since by definition TFPG measures the growth of output not attributed to the growth of inputs, it follows that differences in TFPG between conventional and Islamic banks are attributable to their respective business models. Moreover, to the extent that the costs of intermediation have implications for the competitiveness and economic growth of the overall economy, a banking sector with positive (negative) TFPG enhances (diminishes) the competitiveness and overall economic growth in the sector's host country.

The rest of the paper is organized as follows. The next section briefly highlights the concepts of productivity and efficiency. Section 3 reviews the literature on pre- and post-crisis comparative performance of Islamic and conventional in terms of productivity and efficiency. Section 4 defines TFPG algebraically and lays out the cost function approach to measuring and decomposing TFPG and its sources in a general form. Section 5 translates the approach into a specific form using the translog cost function. Estimates of the translog cost function are shown in Section 6. Section 7 provides pre- and post-crisis estimates of TFPG by type of bank. The final section summarizes and concludes.

2. Efficiency and Productivity Concepts and Methods

In this section, we briefly highlight the difference between productivity and efficiency, the principal methods employed for their measurement, and weaknesses and strengths of each method.[1]

Efficiency analysis is essentially a benchmarking technique where the benchmark is a production frontier which traces the maximum output(s) a firm can obtain from inputs given the current state of technology. A firm is said to be technically efficient (inefficient) if it operates at (below) the frontier. However, a technically efficient firm does not necessarily have the highest total factor productivity (TFP). To achieve the highest TFP possible, a firm must operate at the optimal scale at the production frontier. This is easy to visualize in the single output single input case as shown in Figure 1. While firms B and C are technically efficient, and A is technically inefficient, firm B has higher productivity than firm A but lower productivity than C. Point C defines the optimal scale where average product, measured by the ray emanating from the origin, is tangent to the marginal product of the production frontier.

The preceding model can be extended to account for technical change and objectives of firms, such as profit maximization or cost minimization. Technical change, which adds a time dimension to efficiency and productivity analysis, would in the simple case illustrated in Figure 1, shift the production frontier F' upwards, altering the optimal scale and position of the firms relative to the new frontier. When accounting for firm objectives, performance is measured by the degree of economic efficiency which encompasses technically

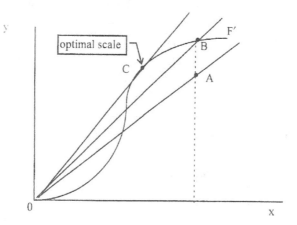

Source: Coelli et al. (2005).

Figure 1. Productivity, Technical Efficiency and Scale Economies

---

[1] The discussion draws from Coelli et al. (2005) who provide extensive detail about the underlying theory and practice of productivity and efficiency measurement. Applications to banking are discussed in Bauer et al. (1993).

efficiency (operating relative to the production frontier) and allocative efficiency (choice of the input or output relative to their optimal combination at given prices of inputs and outputs), and scale efficiency (scale of operation relative to the optimal). Hence, the sources of TFPG are technical change, technical efficiency change, scale efficiency change, and allocative efficiency change. In the realistic case of multiple output and multiple inputs, outputs and inputs need to be aggregated into indices for TFP measurement.

As described by Coelli *et al.* (2005), there are four methods for measuring efficiency and/or productivity: Production models, index numbers, DEA and SFA. The four methods can be grouped in two ways: parametric (production models and SFA) versus non-parametric (TFP indices and DEA), or whether they assume firms are technically efficient (production models and index numbers) or inefficient (DEA and SFA). Production models and TFP indices can be applied to time series at the industry level or cross-sections of firms at each point in time to measure technical change and/or TFP growth at the aggregate level. The most widely used index for measuring productivity change is the DEA-based Malmquist total factor productivity index (MTFPI). DEA and SFA are used to either compare the relative efficiency of firms using cross-section data at a point in time or measure technical change and efficiency changes using panel data. Multiple regression models are often used to correlate efficiency scores with other variables such as financial ratios, bank size, concentration ratio, geographical region, and so forth.

Each method has advantages and shortcomings. The advantage of parametric methods (Production models and SFA) over non-parametric methods (index numbers and DEA) is hypothesis testing, particularly with regards to scale economies. Within parametric methods, while the production function is purely technical, the cost function is behavioral in the sense that the objective of the firm is to choose the cost-minimizing level of factors of production given exogenous factor prices for a given level of output or outputs, similar to the cost function used in SFA (Chambers, 1988). As we show below, the major driver of TFPG besides technical change is the cost elasticity, i.e., the proportionate response of cost to a proportionate response in output. The assumption of constant returns scale, often invoked in DEA studies, eliminates the role of the cost elasticity in the determination of TFPG. However, results from parametric methods are very much influenced by the choice of functional form, assumptions about the behavior of firms (profit maximizers or cost minimizers), and assumptions about the distribution of errors. Production models, unlike SFA, constrain firms or industries to be technically efficient, which may not be the case and, in the case of production functions, do not accommodate more than one output. Nonparametric methods can easily accommodate multiple outputs/inputs and do not require any particular functional form. Index numbers are simple to calculate, needing only two observations, compared to DEA which uses linear programming and large sample sizes for robust estimates. Unlike parametric methods, DEA does not account for data noise, making non-parametric estimates of returns to scale less reliable that the parametric ones.

The method we use in this paper is largely used in the economic growth accounting literature pioneered by Solow (1957). That literature is concerned with TFPG in the whole economy or aggregate sectors thereof, like manufacturing (Nadiri and Schankerman, 1981) and agriculture (Avila and Evanson, 2010). The idea behind growth accounting is captured

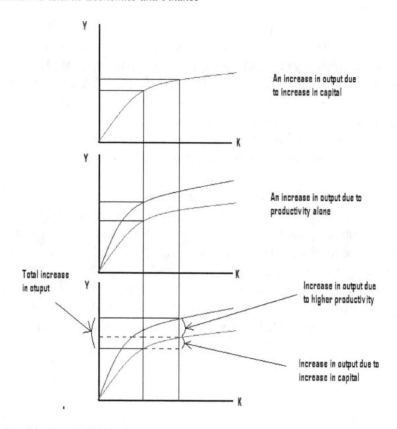

Source: https://en.wikipedia.org/wiki/Growth_accounting.

Figure 2. Graphical Growth Accounting Model

in Figure 2 for the simple case of a single output (Y) and a single capital input (K) model. The top panel shows the total increase in output Y due to an increase in K. The middle panel shows the increase in output due to higher productivity alone, due to technical change, as depicted by the shift in the production frontier. The bottom panel shows the two drivers of growth in Y, higher productivity and increased capital. Clearly, the curvature of the production frontier affects the magnitude of each of the two drivers. If the production function is linear, returns to scale are constant and, therefore, productivity is driven solely by technical change. This demonstrates the importance of careful characterization and estimation of the production structure or its dual, the cost structure, to obtain reliable estimates of scale economies. The formal theoretical and empirical framework of the model are discussed in the model section after the literature review.

3. Literature Review

An Econlit and Google Scholar search of studies using the efficiency and productivity measurement methods to examine the effect of the 2008 financial crisis on the performance of Islamic and Conventional banks revealed 13 studies. Eight used DEA (Zeitun and Benjelloun, 2012; Abu-Alkheil *et al.*, 2013; Said, 2013; Sufian *et al.*, 2014; Rosman *et al.*,

Table 1. Studies of Efficiency and Productivity during the 2008 Global Financial Crisis

Author(s)	Period	Geographic Region/Bank Type	Methodology	Main Findings
Al-Jarrah et al. (2017)	2007–2013	GCC and ENA countries/IBs and CBs	SFA	GFC affected efficiency negatively. Large banks are more cost-efficient than small banks.
Alexakis et al. (2019)	2006–2012	GCC/IBs and CBs	MPI	TFP of IBs and CBs increased up the financial crisis than declines. Both banks are more aligned following GFC.
Alqahtani et al. (2017)	2008/2009 and 2011/2012	GCC/IBs and CBs	DEA and SFA	IBs more cost-efficient in 2008/2009 but less profit efficient in 2011/2012.
Nurul and Abd Wahab (2016)	2008–2013	12 IBs in Malaysia	DEA	IBs more resilient to GFC than conventional banks.
Sufian et al. (2014)	2004–2010	India and Pakistan	DEA	Indian banking sector more efficient than Pakistani banking sector during GFC.
Bahrini (2015)	2006–2011	33 IBs in 10 MENA countries	MPI	TFP declined during the GFC period.
Belanès et al. (2015)	2005–2011	GCC/IBs	DEA	Most IBs remained technically efficient during GFC. The largest drop in overall efficiency occurred two years after the financial crisis.
Makni et al. (2015)	1993–2013	Different world regions/Islamic funds	DEA	Islamic funds weathered GFC.

Table 1. (Continued)

Author(s)	Period	Geographic Region/Bank Type	Methodology	Main Findings
Mobarek and Kalonov (2014)	2004–2006 and 2007–2009	OIC countries/IBs and CBs	DEA and SFA	Both DEA and SFA indicate CBs are more efficient than their Islamic counterparts. Bank size influences overall efficiency. Larger CBs have higher efficiency than larger IBs.
Rosman et al. (2014)	2007–2010	Several countries/IBs	DEA	IBs technically efficient during GFC although scale inefficient.
Abu-Alkheil et al. (2013)	2008–2009	UK and Switzerland/IBs and CBs	DEA	CBs are more cost-efficient than IBs During GFC.
Said (2013)	2006–2009	Middle Eastern and non-Middle Eastern countries/IBs	DEA	The efficiency of large IBs declines during 2009. All banks increased efficiency during GFC. GCC IBs are most efficient.
Zeitun and Benjelloun (2012)	2005–2010	Jordan/IBs and CBs	DEA	GFC has a significant impact on efficiency.

Notes: DEA = Data Envelopment Analysis. SFA = Stochastic Frontier Analysis. MPI = Malmquist Productivity Index.

2014; Belanès et al., 2015; Makni et al., 2015; Nurul and Abd Wahab, 2016), 2 use a combination of DEA and SFA (Mobarek and Kalanov, 2014; Alqahtani et al., 2017; Al-Jarrah et al., 2017), and 2 use MPI (Bahrini, 2015; Alexakis et al., 2019). Table 1 lists the studies in the descending order of their publication date. Reported for each study are the author(s), the sample period, the geographic region/bank type, methodology, and main findings.

Studies that focus on the GCC region, as we do in this paper, report lower performance for both Islamic banks (IBs) and conventional banks (CBs) following the crisis. Alexakis et al. (2019) find that TFP increased for both IBs and CBs then declined, Alqahtani et al. (2017) report lower profit efficiency for IBs after the crisis, and Belanès et al. (2015) report lower overall efficiency two years after the crisis. In sum, there seems to have been a productivity and efficiency slowdown among GCC banks after the crisis. The slowdown is also reported by studies that combine GCC countries with MENA countries (Bahrini, 2015; Al-Jarrah et al., 2017).

Studies that consider only IBs across several counties including MENA, find that the banks weathered the crisis (Rosman et al., 2014; Makni et al., 2015). CBs seem to outperform IBs only when the sample countries is expanded to countries outside GCC and MENA to include other OIC countries (Mobarek and Kalanov, 2014), or narrowed to include only European countries (Abu-Alkheil et al., 2013). Finally, studies that correlate bank size with efficiency consistently find that the larger the bank the higher the technical efficiency.

The take-away is that the evidence from the literature is as mixed as the methods used, geographical boundaries chosen, and periods covered. However, it seems that the negative effect of the crisis is largely found in studies that considered more or less homogeneous regions. To the extent, as we mentioned earlier, that there may be sample selection deficiencies in studies that mix banks from several countries with heterogeneous banking regulations and economic conditions, such studies may not be as reliable as those focusing on homogenous regions.

4. *TFPG* and its Decomposition: Model Definition

Consider a firm producing output Y using r inputs x_r for $r = 1, 2, \ldots, R$. Then the firm's TFP is given by the ratio

$$\text{TFP} = \frac{Y}{F},$$

where F is an aggregate of all the r inputs. TFPG is the difference between the growth rate (hereafter indicated by a "dot") in output and the growth rate in the aggregate input

$$\text{TFPG} = \dot{Y} - \dot{F} = \dot{Y} - \sum_{r=1}^{R} s_r \dot{x}_r, \quad (1)$$

where s_r is the share of the rth input in total revenue. Alternatively, TFPG is the growth in output not accounted for by the growth in conventional inputs, such as labor and capital.

Also known as the Solow residual, TFPG is thought of as technology-driven output growth after accounting for the input-driven component.

The input-driven component can be measured using either a production function or a cost function. Since a production function considers only factors of production as explanatory variables, and not their prices, the estimates of the elasticities of production, which measure the responsiveness of output to changes in the level of the factors of production, are biased because input prices affect the level of factor employment (Chambers, 1988). Biased elasticities of production result in biased estimates of scale elasticities. The latter is essential in sorting out the portion of TFPG caused by a movement along the production function due to scale economies from the portion caused by a shift in the production function due to technical change.

For our intended application, we adopt the intermediation approach to measuring a bank's production structure (Heffernan, 1996). Banks are considered as intermediaries who produce assets using labor, capital, and borrowed funds as inputs using a technology represented by the cost function

$$C = h(Y, w_1, w_2, w_3, T), \tag{2}$$

where Y is assets, w_1 is the price of labor, w_2 is the price of capital, w_3 is the price of borrowed funds and T is an index of the state of technology. Unlike the cost function used in SFA (Al-Jarrah et al., 2017), the cost function given by (2) assumes banks operate at the cost frontier, i.e., technically efficient.

Differentiation of (2) with respect to T gives the rate of growth of cost

$$\dot{C} = \epsilon \dot{Y} + \sum_{r=1}^{3} s_r \dot{w}_r + \dot{T}. \tag{3}$$

In words, the rate of growth in costs, $\dot{C}$, consists of three components: the rate of growth rate in assets $\dot{Y} = \frac{\partial \ln Y}{\partial T}$ weighted by the cost elasticity, $\frac{\partial \ln C}{\partial \ln Y}$; the growth rate in inputs expressed as the growth rate in factor prices $\dot{w}_r$ weighted by their respective shares in total cost s_r for $r = 1, 2, 3$ as shown in Equation (1); and $\dot{T} = \frac{\partial \ln C}{\partial T}$ is the shift in the cost function caused by a change in the state of technology. The first component of (3) represents a movement along the cost function. The second and third represent shifts in the cost function.

Solving for $\dot{T}$ from (3) yields and using the expression for $\dot{F}$ from (1) yields

$$\dot{T} = \dot{C} - \epsilon \dot{Y} - \sum_{r=1}^{3} s_r \dot{w}_r = -\epsilon \dot{Y} + \sum_{r=1}^{3} s_r \dot{x}_r = -\epsilon \dot{Y} + \dot{F}. \tag{4}$$

Solving for $\dot{F}$ from (1) and substituting the result in (4) yields the formula for TFPG

$$\text{TFPG} = -\dot{T} + \dot{Y}(1 - \epsilon) = -\frac{\partial \ln C}{\partial T} + \frac{\partial \ln Y}{\partial T}\left(1 - \frac{\partial \ln C}{\partial \ln Y}\right). \tag{5}$$

The term $\frac{\partial \ln C}{\partial T}$ is the technical change effect. It measures the component of the growth attributed to the shift in the cost function due to technical change. The term $\frac{\partial \ln Y}{\partial T}\left(1 - \frac{\partial \ln C}{\partial \ln Y}\right)$

is the scale effect. It measures the component of the growth attributed to the movement along the cost function weighted by the one minus the cost elasticity. If the cost elasticity $\frac{\partial \ln C}{\partial \ln Y} = 1$, banks are said to operate with neither economies nor diseconomies of scale. In this case, TFPG is driven solely by technical change. Asset growth raises up (reduces) TFPG when economies (diseconomies) of scale $\frac{\partial \ln C}{\partial \ln Y} < 1 (>1)$. While asset growth, $\frac{\partial \ln Y}{\partial T}$, can be measured directly from observed data, measurement of $\frac{\partial \ln C}{\partial T}$ and $\frac{\partial \ln C}{\partial \ln Y}$ require estimation of a cost function (2) jointly with factor shares. This is discussed in the next section.

5. *TFPG* and its Decomposition: Model Specification

For estimation, we assume the cost function given by (2) to be of the translog form:

$$\ln C = \alpha_0 + \alpha_y \ln Y + \beta_1 lw_1 + \beta_2 lw_2 + \beta_3 lw_3 + \gamma_{1y} \ln y \ln w_1 + \gamma_{1y} \ln y \ln w_2$$
$$+ \gamma_{1y} \ln y \ln w_3 + 0.5\{\beta_{11}(\ln w_1)^2 + \beta_{22}(\ln w_2)^2 + \beta_{33}(\ln w_3)^2$$
$$+ 2\beta_{12} \ln w_1 \ln w_2 + 2\beta_{13} \ln w_1 \ln w_3 + 2\beta_{23} \ln w_2 \ln w_3\}$$
$$+ \theta_{yT} \ln yT + \delta_{1T} lw_1 T + \delta_{2T} lw_2 T + \delta_{3T} lw_3 T + \theta_T T + 0.5\theta_{TT} T^2. \tag{2'}$$

The associated factor share equations are given by

$$S_1 = \beta_1 + \gamma_{1y} \ln Y + \beta_{11} lw_1 + \beta_{12} lw_2 + \beta_{13} lw_3 + \delta_{1T} T,$$
$$S_2 = \beta_2 + \gamma_{2y} \ln Y + \beta_{12} lw_1 + \beta_{22} lw_2 + \beta_{23} lw_3 + \delta_{2T} T,$$
$$S_3 = \beta_3 + \gamma_{3y} \ln Y + \beta_{13} lw_1 + \beta_{23} lw_2 + \beta_{33} lw_3 + \delta_{3T} T,$$

where cost (C), output (Y) and factor prices (w_1, w_2 and w_3) are defined as in Weill (2011).

C is the total cost (personnel expenses + non-interest expenses + interest expenses) in million USD, Y is the total assets in million USD, w_1 is the price of labor (personnel expenses/total assets), w_2 is the price of physical capital (non-interest expenses/fixed assets), w_3 is the price of borrowed funds (interest expenses/all funding).

The other variables are T is the time index, S_1 is the share of labor expenses in total cost, S_2 is the share of capital expenses in total cost and S_3 is the share of borrowed funds in total cost.

Obtaining $\frac{\partial \ln C}{\partial T}$ and $\frac{\partial \ln C}{\partial \ln Y}$ from (2') and substituting the expressions into (5) allows us to write TFPG in terms of the cost function parameters estimates as follows:

$$\dot{\text{TFP}} = -(\theta_T + \theta_{TT} T + \theta_{yT} \ln y + \delta_{1T} lw_1 + \delta_{2T} lw_2 + \delta_{3T} lw_3)$$
$$+ \frac{\partial \ln Y}{\partial T}(1 - (\gamma_{1y} \ln w_1 + \gamma_{1y} \ln w_2 + \gamma_{1y} \ln w_3 + \theta_{yT} T)). \tag{5'}$$

The estimates are presented in the next section.

6. Data and Estimation of the Translog Cost Function

Data for the variables defined in the preceding section were obtained for GCC (Bahrain, Kuwait, Qatar, Saudi Arabia, United Arab Emirates) conventional and Islamic banks from

Table 2. Observations by Country and Type of Bank

Country	Conventional Banks	Islamic Banks
Bahrain	190	56
Kuwait	77	13
Qatar	74	32
Saudi Arabia	142	15
United Arab Emirates	199	45
Total	682	161

the Bankscope database from 1998 until 2012.[2] In total, there are 682 observations for conventional banks and 161 for Islamic banks. Table 2 shows the breakdown of observation by country and type of bank. Descriptive statistics are in Table 3.

Other variables appended to the cost function are GCC member country fixed effects, and asset quintile dummy variables to allow for size effects. Table 4 shows the quintiles and associated asset descriptive statistics. The parameter estimates of the respective cost functions of conventional and Islamic banks, standard errors, and adjusted R-squares are in Table 5. Noting that the parameter estimates that are statistically significant at least at 5% level are shaded in gray, it is clear that most the estimates are statistically significant and, judging by the adjusted R-squares, the fit is very good.

6.1. Computed TFPG and its sources type of bank

Estimates of TFPG by type of bank are in Table 6. Column-wise, we present for each type of bank TFPG and its two sources: technical change and scale effects. Technical change represents the shift in the cost function for a given level of assets. Scale effects represent a movement along the cost function as assets change given technical change. Row-wise, the first row shows the pre-crisis overall average of TFPG and its components, the post-crisis overall average of TFPG and its components, and the difference between the two. After that, we provide TFPG and its sources by quintile. The pre-crisis period covers the 5 years preceding the crisis (2003–2007). The post-crisis period covers the 5 years including 2008 (2008–2012).

Starting with the pre-crisis average TFPG, conventional banks had negative TFPG (−1.9%) and Islamic banks had positive TFPG (3.9%). This means that, before the crisis, while input growth outpaced output growth by 1.9% in conventional banking, output growth outpaced factor growth by 3.9% in Islamic banking. So, pre-crisis, Islamic banks demonstrated superior performance in terms of the productive efficiency of the factors of production they employed to generate assets. This is in sharp contrast to the finding by Alexakis et al. (2019) who find positive total factor productivity growth among conventional banks in years leading to the financial crisis.

---

[2] The most recent study on GCC banks (Alexakis et al., 2019) covers the 2006–2012 period.

Table 3. Descriptive Statistics (1998–2012)

Variables	Description	Conventional Banks (682 Observations)				Islamic Banks (161 Observations)			
		Mean	SD	MIN	MAX	Mean	SD	MIN	MAX
C	Total cost (US$ million)	484	548	7	333	338	495	8	2441
Y	Total Assets (US$ million)	12108	15821	55	100784	8128	13219	69	71302
w_1	Price of labor (personnel expenses/total assets)	0.010	0.009	0.003	0.077	0.017	0.015	0.004	0.084
w_2	Price of capital (non-interest expenses/fixed assets)	2.597	4.990	0.092	47.5	3.200	4.187	0.240	31.235
w_3	Price of borrowed funds (interest expenses/all funding)	0.031	0.017	0.003	0.102	0.107	0.546	0.00009	5.773
s_1	Share of labor expenses in total cost	0.469	0.176	0.130	0.851	0.336	0.198	0.0006	0.847
s_2	Share of non-interest expenses share in total cost	0.338	0.113	0.090	0.704	0.426	0.134	0.1001	0.771
s_3	Share of interest expenses share in total costs	0.194	0.068	0.040	0.423	0.239	0.079	0.050	0.429

Table 4. Quintiles and Associated Asset Descriptive Statistics (US$ Million)

Quintile	Conventional Banks (682 Observations)					Islamic Banks (161 Observations)				
	N	Mean	SD	MIN	MAX	N	Mean	SD	MIN	MAX
1	136	524	256	55	1111	32	265	118	69	483
2	137	2441	829	1122	3783	32	997	263	505	1442
3	136	6072	1410	3790	8804	33	2303	655	1474	4090
4	137	13781	3039	8930	19931	32	6533	2442	4175	11991
5	136	37783	17804	20390	100784	32	30721	14607	13944	71302

Table 5. Cost Function Parameter Estimates for Conventional and Islamic Banks

Variable	Parameter	Conventional		Islamic	
		Estimate	Standard Error	Estimate	Standard Error
Intercept	α_0	0.462	0.268	1.709	0.781
$\ln y$	α_y	0.915	0.024	0.749	0.079
$\ln y \ln w_1$	γ_{1y}	0.011	0.002	0.008	0.007
$\ln y \ln w_2$	γ_{2y}	0.012	0.002	−0.016	0.006
$\ln y \ln w_2$	γ_{3y}	−0.024	0.003	0.008	0.005
$\ln y T$	θ_{yT}	0.005	0.001	0.030	0.005
lw_1	β_1	−0.199	0.027	−0.073	0.077
lw_2	β_2	0.144	0.042	0.648	0.067
lw_3	β_3	1.054	0.042	0.424	0.047
$(\ln w_1)^2$	β_{11}	−0.232	0.004	−0.149	0.014
$(\ln w_2)^2$	β_{22}	0.019	0.005	−0.014	0.010
$(\ln w_3)^2$	β_{33}	−0.082	0.006	−0.032	0.005
$\ln w_1 \ln w_2$	β_{12}	0.065	0.003	0.065	0.010
$\ln w_1 \ln w_3$	β_{13}	0.166	0.004	0.083	0.007
$\ln w_2 \ln w_3$	β_{23}	−0.084	0.005	−0.051	0.005
$lw_1 T$	δ_{1T}	0.005	0.001	0.001	0.003
$lw_2 T$	δ_{2T}	0.001	0.001	−0.002	0.002
$lw_3 T$	δ_{3T}	−0.007	0.001	0.001	0.002
T	θ_T	−0.063	0.017	−0.360	0.057
T^2	θ_{TT}	0.004	0.001	0.015	0.003
Q_1	σ_1	−0.085	0.086	0.077	0.327
Q_2	σ_2	−0.073	0.056	−0.215	0.240
Q_3	σ_3	−0.024	0.040	−0.366	0.189
Q_4	σ_4	−0.054	0.028	−0.244	0.128
	Adj R^2	0.97		0.96	

Table 6. TFPG and Its Sources by Type of Bank and by Quintile

	Conventional					Islamic				
	TFPG	Technical Change	Scale Effects	Asset Growth	Cost Elasticity	TFPG	Technical Change	Scale Effects	Asset Growth	Cost Elasticity
All banks										
Pre-crisis average:	−0.019	−0.020	0.001	0.223	0.999	0.039	0.010	0.029	0.287	0.903
Post-crisis average:	0.0001	−0.001	0.001	0.056	0.978	0.092	0.073	0.019	0.076	0.766
Change	0.019	0.019	0.000	−0.167	−0.021	0.053	0.063	−0.010	−0.211	−0.137
1st quintile										
Pre-crisis average	−0.019	−0.016	−0.003	0.167	1.015	0.095	0.088	0.007	0.061	0.894
Post-crisis average	0.009	0.011	−0.002	−0.171	0.996	0.123	0.152	−0.029	−0.147	0.794
Change	0.028	0.027	0.002	−0.338	−0.018	0.028	0.064	−0.035	−0.209	−0.100
2nd quintile										
Pre-crisis average	−0.016	−0.017	0.000	0.306	1.001	0.078	0.029	0.049	0.468	0.927
Post-crisis average	0.006	0.007	−0.001	−0.016	0.974	0.111	0.109	0.002	0.005	0.770
Change	0.023	0.024	−0.001	−0.322	−0.027	0.033	0.080	−0.047	−0.463	−0.157
3rd quintile										
Pre-crisis average	−0.019	−0.021	0.002	0.195	0.996	0.044	0.018	0.026	0.260	0.901
Post-crisis average	0.005	0.001	0.004	0.151	0.974	0.142	0.094	0.048	0.200	0.742
Change	0.025	0.022	0.002	−0.045	−0.022	0.098	0.076	0.022	−0.060	−0.158
4th quintile										
Pre-crisis average	−0.022	−0.025	0.002	0.194	0.996	0.012	−0.022	0.034	0.341	0.904
Post-crisis average	−0.001	−0.002	0.004	0.048	0.975	0.098	0.060	0.038	0.167	0.765
Change	0.022	0.023	0.002	−0.146	−0.021	0.086	0.083	0.004	−0.175	−0.139
5th quintile										
Pre-crisis average	−0.019	−0.023	0.988	0.232	0.988	−0.015	−0.044	0.029	0.270	0.891
Post-crisis average	−0.007	−0.009	0.981	0.085	0.981	0.041	0.013	0.028	0.115	0.756
Change	0.012	0.014	−0.007	−0.147	−0.007	0.056	0.057	−0.001	−0.154	−0.135

The negative TFPG in conventional banking is due largely to negative technical progress (−2.0%). The scale effects are negligible because the cost elasticity of 0.999 indicates neither economies of diseconomies of scale, meaning that TFPG among conventional banks is driven mostly by technical change. On the other hand, the positive TFPG in Islamic banking is driven by technical progress (1.0%) and growth in scale effects (2.9%). The latter is driven by asset growth (28.7%) and scale economies (0.903).

It is worth noting that had one only used asset growth as a measure of performance before the crisis, we would conclude that Islamic banks enjoyed 6.4% (0.287–0.223) more asset growth than conventional banks, not realizing that Islamic banks also utilized their resources considerably more efficiently than conventional banks because of scale economies.

Not surprisingly, asset growth dipped from a pre-crisis average (2003–2007) of 22.3 to a post-crisis (2008–2012) 5.6 for conventional banks, and from 28.7% to 7.6% for Islamic banks. Still post-crisis TFPG among Islamic banks was 9.2%, which is multiple times higher than 0.01% TFPG among conventional banks. This time, however, Islamic banks not only experienced a noticeable improvement in technical change relative to conventional banks, but they also saw their declining scale effects offset by technical change. This is an indication of a combination of a downward shift in the cost of doing business that is considerably larger for Islamic banks because of the relatively higher improvement in their scale economies. While the cost elasticity of Islamic banks declined from 0.903 to 0.766, that of conventional banks declined from 0.999 to 0.978.

Looking at the change in TFPG between the pre- to the post-crisis period, Islamic banks registered a 5.3% improvement compared to 1.9% improvement by conventional banks, implying that, overall, Islamic banks outperformed conventional banks by improving TFPG during the onset and in the aftermath of the crisis. Again, this in sharp contrast to the findings to the study by Alexakis *et al.* (2019) who report that "the two banking systems become more aligned after the global financial crisis".

Next we examine the comparative patterns of TFPG by asset quintile before and after the crisis. Before the crisis, while conventional banks' TFPG was negative and relatively similar across bank sizes, Islamic banks' TFPG was positive except for the largest banks and, interestingly, the smaller the bank the higher the *TFPG*. In the case of conventional banks, the driver of negative TFPG was negative technical change even though asset growth ranged from 17% to 23%. In the case of Islamic banks, the drivers of positive TFPG were technical change and scale effects. The latter were driven by asset growth that was higher than conventional banks' assets growth across all quintiles except the first, and scale economies.

After the crisis, conventional banks' TFPG was positive for banks in the first three quintiles and negative for banks in the last 2 quintiles. Interestingly, the smaller the bank the higher is TFPG. This occurred even though the smallest banks suffered the largest decline in asset growth. Islamic banks' TFPG was positive and higher than conventional banks' TFPG across all quintiles, with the smaller Islamic banks outperforming the larger ones. Again, this took place despite the larger decline in asset growth among the smaller Islamic banks.

The inter-period change in performance by quintile reveals the following with regards to performance and bank size. First, Islamic banks outperformed conventional banks across all quintiles, except the first, representing the smallest banks in terms of assets, where the inter-period difference is in the order of 2.8% for both banks. Second, the gap between the performance of Islamic banks and conventional banks increases with bank size. In other words, as Islamic banks become larger, they gain more ground in terms of total factor productivity change than their conventional counterparts. Third, while there is hardly any variation in TFPG across all size categories of conventional banks, the opposite is true for Islamic banks. For the latter, TFPG peaks at the third quintile and declines afterwards.

In sharp contrast with the GCC results obtained by studies listed in Table 1, ours show strong performance of IBs relative to CBs pre- and post-financial crisis. However, except for the study by Alexakis *et al.* (2019), who focus on GCC, use a sample period that overlaps with ours, and estimate TFPG using DEA, our results are not comparable with results from other studies because of the country composition of their samples, sample period, and sole focus on efficiency scores without TFPG. In this sense, we may conclude the following with regards to our findings compared to those by Alexakis *et al.* (2019). Using a parametric method like ours that accounts for (parametrically estimated) returns to scale, but does not consider technical inefficiency, yields results that confirm the superior performance of Islamic over conventional banking pre- and post-crisis. Using a non-parametric technique like Alexakis *et al.*'s (2019), which also accounts for (non-parametrically measured) returns to scale but considers technical inefficiency, yields results that favor conventional banks pre-crisis and show the alignment between the two types of banks post-crisis. Whether the difference is driven by the assumption that banks operate on the frontier (technically efficient), or by non-parametric measures of returns to scale by Alexakis *et al.*'s (2019), is an issue worth investigating future research. One suggestion is to extend our model to account for technical inefficiency in the measurement of TFPG.

7. Summary and Conclusions

The purpose of this paper is to measure and compare the pre- and post-crisis performance of conventional and Islamic banks in GCC. Performance is measured by TFPG, defined as the growth in the ratio of all inputs to output. By considering all inputs, their substitutability and complementary, TFPG has more information content about performance than disparate financial ratios. Financial ratios are partial productivity measures that do not account for interdependence between inputs and there is no clear-cut method for aggregating the ratios into a single measure of performance.

Designating the 2003–2007 period as pre-crisis and the 2008–2012 period as post-crisis, we compute the period averages of TFPG and its two sources (technical change and scale effects) and the difference between period averages by bank type for the whole sample and subsamples based on asset quintiles. Results show that although both Islamic and conventional banks experienced a decline in asset growth post-crisis, Islamic banks outperformed conventional banks overall as well as across asset quintiles. The superior performance of Islamic banks is driven by higher technical change and improved scale economies relative to the pre-crisis period. To the extent that product and process innovation improve TFPG, we conclude that Islamic banks have weathered the crisis by being more innovative than conventional banks with the onset of the financial crisis.

This begs the question of why conventional banks have not been at least as innovative as Islamic banks in our sample. There are several possibilities. One is "lack of a learning-by-doing effect" (Sun, 2007). Conventional banks in the GCC could have adopted the most advanced technology but have not realized the full benefit of the technology during the pre- and post-crisis period. Another possibility is that their underperformance is not associated with technology at all but with low-quality management, market power and consequent barriers to entry (National Research Council, 2007). Recent evidence suggests that both conventional and Islamic banks in GCC do exert some degree of market power (Azzam and Rettab, 2013). Yet another possibility is that even both Islamic and conventional banks exert market power, the latter may be more prone to the "quiet life" behavior, foregoing efficiency for market power rents. Since all GCC countries have competition laws already in place (Casoria, 2017), enforcing such laws could lead to more innovation by checking market power.

We close with a caveat and a suggestion for future research. Our finding of the superior performance of Islamic banks pre- and post-financial crisis should be interpreted with caution because it is in sharp contrast with a semi-comparable recent study (Alexakis *et al.*, 2019) which also measure *TFPG* and its sources among GCC banks using DEA results. Whether the difference is driven by the assumption technically efficiency underlying our model, or by non-parametric measures of returns to scale by Alexakis *et al.*'s (2019), is an issue worthy of further investigation. One suggestion is to extend the model in our paper to account for technical inefficiency.

References

Abu-Alkheil, AM, B Hans-Peter and WA Khan (2013). Comparative performance of Islamic and conventional banks in Europe. *American Journal of Finance and Accounting*, 3, 1–23.

Aghion, P and P Howitt (1992). A model of growth through creative destruction. *Econometrica*, 60, 323–351.

Alexakis, C, M Izzeldin, J Johnes and V Pappas (2019). Performance and productivity in Islamic and conventional banks: Evidence from the global financial crisis. *Economic Modelling*, 79, 1–14.

Al-Jarrah, IM, KSA Abdulqader and S Hammoudeh (2017). Cost-efficiency and financial and geographical characteristics of banking sectors in the MENA countries. *Applied Economics*, 49, 3523–3537.

Alqahtani, F, DG Mayes and K Brown (2017). Islamic bank efficiency compared to conventional banks during the global crisis in the GCC region. *Journal of International Financial Markets, Institutions and Money*, 51, 58–74.

Amba, MS and F Almukharreq (2013). Impact of the financial crisis on the Islamic banks vs conventional banks — evidence from GCC. *International Journal of Financial Research*, 4, 83–93.

Avila, AFD and RE Evanson (2010). Total factor productivity growth in agriculture: The role of technological capital. In *Handbook of Agricultural Economics*, Vol. 4, pp. 3769–3822. Burlington: Academic Press.

Azzam, A and B Rettab (2013). Market power versus cost-efficiency under uncertainty: Conventional versus Islamic banking in the GCC. *Applied Economics*, 15, 2011–2022.

Bahrini, R (2015). Productivity of MENA Islamic banks: A bootstrapped malmquist index approach. *International Journal of Islamic and Middle Eastern Finance and Management*, 8, 508–528.

Bauer, PW, AN Berger and DB Humphrey (1993). Efficiency and productivity growth in U.S. banking. In *The Measurement of Productive Efficiency: Techniques and Applications*, HO Fried, CAK Lovell and SS Schmidt (eds.), pp. 386–423. New York: Oxford University Press.

Belanès, A, Z Ftiti and R Regaïeg (2015). What can we learn about Islamic banks efficiency under the subprime crisis? Evidence from GCC region. *Finance Pacific-Basin Journal*, 33, 81–92.

Bourkis, K and MS Nabi (2013). Islamic and conventional banks' soundness during the 2007-2008 financial crisis. *Review of Financial Economics*, 22, 68–77.

Casoria, M (2017). Competition law in the GCC countries: The tale of a blurry enforcement. *Chinese Business Review*, 16, 141–149.

Chambers, RG (1988). *Applied Production Analysis: A Dual Approach*. Cambridge: Cambridge University Press.

Chapra, U (2009). The global financial crisis: Can Islamic finance help? *New Horizon*, (170), 20–23.

Coelli, TJ, DSP Rao, CJ O'Donnell and GE Battese (2005). *An Introduction to Efficiency and Productivity Analysis*. New York: Springer Science & Business Media.

Hassan, MK and S Aliyu (2018). A contemporary survey of Islamic banking literature. *Journal of Financial Stability*, 34, 12–43.

Heffernan, S (1996). *Modern Banking in Theory and Practice*. UK: John Wiley and Sons Ltd.

Hidayat, SE and M Abdu (2012). Does financial crisis give impact on Bahrain Islamic banking? A panel regression analysis. *International Journal of Economics and Finance*, 7, 79–87.

Kettel, B (2010). *Islamic Finance in a Nutshell*. UK: John Wiley and Sons.

Makni, R, O Benouda and E Delhoumi (2015). Large scale analysis of Islamic equity funds using a meta-frontier approach with data envelopment analysis. *Research in International Business and Finance*, 34, 324–337.

Mirakhor, A and N Krichene (2009). Recent crisis: Lessons for Islamic finance. *Journal of Islamic Economics, Banking and Finance*, 5, 10–58.

Mobarek, A and A Kalonov (2014). Comparative performance analysis between conventional and Islamic banks: Empirical evidence from OIC countries. *Applied Economics*, 46, 253–270.

Nadiri, MI and MA Schankerman (1981). Technical change, returns to scale, and the productivity slowdown. *The American Economic Review*, 71, 314–319.

National Research Council (2007). Enhancing productivity growth inthe information age: Measuring and sustaning the new econom, Jorgensen, DW and CW Wessner (editors). Washington, D.C.: The National Academies Press.

Nurul, MM and N Abd Wahab (2016). Examining the relationship between risks and efficiency of Islamic banks in Malaysia. *International Journal of Islamic Business*, 1, 90–116.

Romer, P (1990). Endogenous technological change. *The Journal of Political Economy*, 98 (Part 2), S71–S102.

Rosman, R, N Abd Wahab and Z Zainol (2014). Efficiency of Islamic banks during the financial crisis: An analysis of Middle Eastern and Asian countries. *Pacific-Basin Finance Journal*, 28, 76–90.

Said, A (2013). Evaluating the overall technical efficiency of Islamic banks operating in the mena region during the financial crisis. *International Journal of Economics and Financial Issues*, 3, 26–434.

Solow, RM (1957). Technical change and the aggregate production function. *The Review of Economics and Statistics*, 39, 312–320.

Sufian, F, SMA Ashif and F Kamarudin (2014). Technical efficiency of single versus dual banking sectors: A comparative analysis of India and Pakistan. *International Journal of Financial Services Management*, 7, 219–245.

Sun, C-H (2007). The conundrum of economic miracle: Manufacturing growth with TFPG. *The Journal of Developing Areas*, 40, 157–172.

Totaro, L (2009). Vatican says Islamic finance may help western banks in crisis. Available at https://www.cimer.org.au/wp-content/uploads/documents/vatican.pdf (accessed May 2, 2020).

Weill, L (2011). Do Islamic banks have greater market power? *Comparative Economic Studies*, 53, 291–306.

Wilson, R (2009). Why Islamic finance is successful? Islamic banks are unscathed despite of financial crisis. Available at http://www.kantakji.com/fiqh/files/markets/b214.pdf (accessed August 18, 2013).

Zeitun, R and H Benjelloun (2012). The efficiency of banks and financial crisis in a developing economy: The case of Jordan. *International Review of Accounting, Banking & Finance*, 4, 1–20.

Chapter 9

Does Foreign Aid Help or Hinder the Institutional Quality of the Recipient Country? New Evidence from the OIC Countries[#]

Mohammad Ashraful Ferdous Chowdhury[*], Mohamed Ariff[†], Mansur Masih[‡,¶] and Izlin Ismail[§]

[*]*INCEIF, Kuala Lumpur, Malaysia and Department of Business Administration*
Shahjalal University of Science & Technology, Sylhet, Bangladesh

[†]*Emeritus Professor, INCEIF, Kuala Lumpur, Malaysia*

[‡]*Senior Professor, Finance/Islamic Finance*
UniKL Business School, Kampung Baru
50300 Kuala Lumpur, Malaysia

[§]*Senior Lecturer, Department of Finance & Banking*
University of Malaya, Malaysia
[¶]*mansurmasih@gmail.com*

This study examines the impact of foreign aid on the institutional quality (IQ) of the OIC countries. Using the data of OIC countries for the three-year average period from 1991 to 2016, the system GMM finds that aid in general deteriorates the IQ for the aid recipient countries. However, quantile regression suggests that the negative impact of foreign aid on institutional quality (IQ) is relatively greater in the countries where the existing quality of institution is poor. The findings of the study suggest that improving the existing capacity is essential for reaping the optimum benefit of foreign aid on institutional development.

Keywords: Foreign aid; institutional quality; OIC countries; system GMM; quantile regression.

1. Introduction

Foreign aid is a key ingredient of the foreign capital flows and plays a significant contribution in the developing countries. Tierney *et al.* (2011) reports that the donors from various countries donated more than $7 trillion US dollar to developing nations since the World War II. With the higher aid flows, the recipient countries can develop immensely through the knowledge, expertise and financial support (see Arndt *et al.*, 2015; Juselius *et al.*, 2014; Hansen and Tarp, 2001). A few nations are constantly reliant on external aid. For example ODA represented 40% of the government budget and 6.2% of GDP in Burkina Faso amid 1960–1999 and in Mauritania, for 37% and 12%, respectively (see Dijankov *et al.*, 2008). Despite a significant flow of foreign aid is coming to

---

[¶]Corresponding author.
[#]This Chapter first appeared in the *Singapore Economic Review*, Vol. 67, No. 1, doi: 10.1142/S0217590819420037. © 2022 World Scientific Publishing.

developing countries, still a number of countries are not been able to grow out of poverty. Collier and Hoeffler (2004) identified poor good governance structure is one of the major traps of why so many millions are still trapped in extreme poverty. Various investigations have demonstrated that the radical anti-aid view holds that foreign aid supplants domestic resources, worsens domestic income inequality and trade balance, an in general aid makes governments in developing nations inefficient and corrupt (Quazi and Alam, 2015).

Along with the macroeconomic effect, a fascinating area of research has emerged that investigates the connection between foreign aid and the institutional quality (IQ) in developing countries (Jones and Tarp, 2016; Asongu and Nwachukwu, 2016; Busse *et al.*, 2017). Some scholars (Goldsmith, 2001; Dunning, 2004; Ear, 2007; Charron, 2011; Okada and Samreth, 2012) believe that foreign aid can play a vital role for the institutional development through the quality of civil administration, boost policy and planning capacity, and strengthen central institutions, while other scholars consider that the aid weakens the quality of political institutions (see Deaton, 2013; Booth, 2011; Rajan and Subramanian, 2007). The opponents of foreign aid propose that the aid can hinder the host government's internal revenue collection process. As the host government are no longer dependent on the consent of the parliament or of the population at large, foreign aid are often said to weaken the accountability of the country (Moyo, 2009; Moss *et al.*, 2008). Likewise, Djankov *et al.* (2008) remarked aid as "curse" as too much aid dependence can undermine the IQ, weaken the accountability, and encourage rent seeking and corruption. A number of studies such as Kangoye (2013) confirmed that aid volatility[1] is also associated with more corruptions and more rent seeking activities in the aid recipient countries, while others have the opposite conclusions (Tavares, 2003). However, Askarov and Doucouliagos (2015) finds that total aid has no effect on overall quality of governance. Recent studies such as Feeny *et al.* (2019) and Fielding (2014) argued that the positive or negative outcome of foreign aid rather depends on the absorptive capacity of the recipient countries.

Like many developing nations, a large number of OIC member countries are precariously dependent on foreign aid or Official Development Assistance (ODA) inflows. SESRIC (2018) reports based on UNCTAD estimation, developing countries including OIC countries face an annual gap of $2.5 trillion out of $3.3 trillion to $4.5 trillion every year for the infrastructural development, food security, climate change mitigation and adaptation, health, and education. The report also claimed that the OIC countries were affected more so than any other parts of the world by large-scale humanitarian crises and natural disasters and it causes a huge budget deficit every year in majority Muslim countries. So, foreign aid is inherently important to all Muslim-majority countries for balancing their budgets. The recent statistics show that Muslim countries figure prominently in the ranking of funds received for humanitarian assistance. For the five-year period 2006 to 2010, Muslim-majority countries comprise half of the top 10 recipient nations in terms of ODA (Clarke and Tittensor, 2016). According to International Humanitarian Report (2016), Afghanistan, Indonesia and Pakistan were among the top 10 recipient

---

[1] Aid volatility refers the deviation between the aid commitments and disbursement approval or the gap between what is committed and what is disbursed.

countries of humanitarian aid in 2013. In a similar vein, the recent data from 2012–2017 show that Muslim countries are among the top recipients of ODA (International Humanitarian Aid Report, 2017). Ishnazarov and Cevik (2017) in their recent studies found that the OIC countries are the largest aid beneficiary and receiving 50% of the total ODA from 2002 to 2013.

On the other hand, the IQ structures of Muslim countries are significantly in poor status (Mirakhor and Askari, 2017). Ideally, Muslim countries should have high IQ as Islam promotes freedom of choice, property rights, the rule of law, good governance and a fair economic system. For any country, rule of law is the fundamental pillar of the sustainable development and poverty reduction (Anjinappa, 2015). But along with the poor rule of law, the overall existing IQ of majority Muslim countries is unsatisfactory. Alaabed *et al.* (2016) found that the Muslim countries are lagging behind in terms of the principles of *Maqasid Al Shari'ah* (Objective of Shari'ah). Islamicity Rankings (2017)[2] reports that only three countries Malaysia (41) and United Arab Emirates (40) and Qatar (45) are within the first 50 of overall Islamicity index. Having population of 1.79 billion people (23.8% of the total world population), OIC countries constitute a considerable part of the developing world and reflect high levels of heterogeneity and divergence in terms of socio-economic development (SESRIC, 2018). Ishnazarov and Cevik (2017) in their recent studies argued that the OIC countries represent a variety of geographical locations, politically and culturally heterogeneous. Amir-ud-Din (2014) and Anto (2011) found the IQ of the OIC differs significantly across each other as 23 countries out of 57 are ranked outside 100.

Too much aid dependency of the Muslim countries on the one hand and the weak institutional infrastructure and the intriguing features of social and economic indicators of Muslim countries on the other hand make this study more interesting. So, the objective of this study is to investigate whether foreign aid contributes to the institutional development of the OIC countries. This study examines the impact of foreign aid on IQ from three angles: (a) the aggregate effect of aid on IQ, (b) aid volatility and its effect on governance, and finally (c) the marginal effect and nonlinearity of aid and IQ of the recipient countries.[3] In detail, the study boils down to the following three objectives:

(1) The first objective of this study is to investigate whether aid flows contribute to the IQ of the OIC countries or not.
(2) The second objective of the study is to find out the impact of aid volatility or aid unpredictability on the IQ of the aid-recipient countries.
(3) The third and final objective of the study is to investigate how foreign aid affects the IQ when different countries have different institutional infrastructure. Alternatively, the aim of this research objective is to find out how aid impacts the low institutionally developed and the high institutionally developed countries.

---

[2] *Islamicity Rankings* is an index developed for measuring the IQ of the Muslim countries with four key dimensions: economic islamicity, legal and governance, human and political rights, international relations Islamicity. The detail is available in this link: http://islamicity-index.org/wp/links-downloads/index-elements/.
[3] Details are available in Section 2.4.

This study is novel in number of ways: Firstly, a voluminous number of studies considered the different countries from different regions. However, as we discussed earlier, the OIC countries are the highest recipients of foreign aid but no comprehensive study has yet been conducted to find out its impact on their institutional development. Focusing exclusively on the OIC countries, this study makes a unique contribution and enhances our deeper understanding of aid and IQ nexus in the aid literature. Secondly, unlike the previous studies, our study considered two governance databases i.e., International Country Risk Guide (ICRG) and World Governance Index (WGI), for testing the robustness of the empirical findings. Thirdly, our study integrates three disparate strands of literature in one single study by putting a coherent empirical structure on them. Finally, this study also contributes to the existing literature regarding the effectiveness of aid on the IQ by focusing on the distribution of institutional dynamics.

The remainder of the paper is structured as follows. Section 2 addresses the literature review and hypotheses of the study, Section 3 provides the data and methodology of the study and Section 4 summarizes the model estimations and main findings of the study and finally Section 5 outlines the conclusion and policy implications for the decision makers.

2. Foreign Aid and Institutional Quality — Prior Studies and Hypotheses Development

With the higher aid inflows, beneficiary nations gain advantage from the money related assets as well as from learning, expertise and technical assistance. However, there is no evidence of any aid allocation set aside for institutional improvement. Looking into the vast majority of the investigations of the most recent two decades, this study distinguishes four unique strands of evidence in this context: (i) aid improves IQ; (ii) aid erodes IQ; and (iii) unpredictability/volatility of aid flows can affect the IQ; and (iv) the relationship between aid and IQ is nonlinear. Table 1 summarizes prior literature into four strands.

2.1. Aid literature on Muslim-majority OIC countries

Although majority Muslim countries are the top recipients of foreign aid but aid literature relating to Muslim-majority countries is extremely scarce. A few studies such as Alterman and von Hippel (2007), Harrigan and El-Said (2009) examined the political economy of foreign aid and found that aid allocations are substantially influenced by the donors' domestic political considerations, including commercial advantage and foreign policy objectives such as migration and terrorism. An earlier work by Harrigan and El-Said (2009) found that the allocations of US aid to Israel and Jordan are much higher than the aid allocation to Iran, Sudan and Yemen. Bellers (1993) examined the financial development assistance practices of Saudi Arabia and found that the aid practice of Saudi Arabia to be highly politicized and lacking transparency. Neumayer (2003) found that poor Arab, Sub-Saharan African and Muslim countries and nations that support Saudi Arabia in the UN general assembly were more likely to get aid. Likewise, Villanger (2007) who showed that Muslim aid tends to be very generous and at the same time very volatile as it is driven

Table 1. Review of Literature

Researchers	Main Findings
First-Strand: Aid Improves IQ	
Jones and Tarp (2016)	Positive but very small effect is found between foreign aid on political institution in the sampled 104 countries for the period 1983–2010.
Kersting and Kilby (2014)	Long run positive but short run impact of aid on democracy uncovers positive relationship for bilateral aid but not from multilateral in the sampled 122 countries for the period 1972–2011.
Dadasov (2017)	Based on the data of 103 developing nations, authors found aid can improve IQ.
Dutta and Williamson (2015)	Using a panel of 108 countries over the period 1971 to 2010, Aid can develop economic freedom of the recipient country when it is democratic rather than autocratic.
Quazi and Alam (2015)	Aid has positive association with the IQ of aid-dependent countries in the sampled south and east Asian countries.
Gibson et al. (2015)	Technical assistance improves the democratization in the African countries.
Asongu (2012)	Using a panel data of 52 African countries over the period 1996 to 2010, the author found that aid mitigates corruption in the African continent.
Busse et al. (2017)	Foreign aid can improve the regulatory quality when the aid is allocated for business drives in the developing nations.
Asongu (2015a)	Foreign aid has positive effect on corruption in African region.
Mohamed et al. (2015)	Foreign aid has reduction effect on the corruption level of sub-Saharan countries (SSA)
Carnegie and Marinov (2017)	Based on the Cingranelli–Richards (CIRI) Human Rights Dataset, authors concluded that aid has short term positive effects on human rights and democracy.
de Croix and Delavallade (2013)	Aid is not negatively correlated with corruption across countries.
Second-strand: Aid deteriorates IQ	
Rajan and Subramanian (2007)	Using the data over the period 1980 to 2010 of developing nations, authors concluded that aid dependence can erode the tax structure and finally it deteriorates the IQ of the host country.
Asongu (2012)	Aid is detrimental to government effectiveness in African sampled countries.
Asongu (2013)	Foreign aid is detrimental to IQ in all aspects.
Kalyvitis and Vlachaki (2012)	Based on the data from 64 aid-dependent countries in the period 1967–2002, the study found a negative relationship existing between aid and IQ. Furthermore, the study found the effect was larger in low democratic status to begin with.
Booth (2011)	Negative and it might offset the exchange rate through Dutch disease.
Busse and Gröning (2009)	Using the three years average data from 1984 to 2004 for 106 countries, authors found aid has a negative impact on governance.
Young and Sheehan (2014)	Aid flows are associated with deterioration in political and economic institutions, legal system and property rights.

Table 1. (*Continued*)

Researchers	Main Findings
Wako (2017)	Aid affects negatively the growth and IQ in the sub-Saharan African countries.
Fielding (2014)	Negative relationship between the variation in political rights over time and variation in governance aid.
Djankov *et al.* (2008)	For a sample of 108 countries over the period 1960–1999, authors found aid has negative impact on democracy.
Isopi (2015)	(1) donors do not tend to discriminate between corrupt and non- corrupt recipients; and (2) foreign aid can fuel corruption without reducing poverty
Moyo (2009)	Foreign aid increases the dependency, poverty and corruption
Third Strand: Mixed/No effect of Aid on IQ	
Asongu and Nwachukwu (2016)	Foreign aid does not have any significant impact on political rights
Dunning (2004)	Aid has no impact on the democratic development in African region before the 1987 but relation becomes positive and significant afterwards.
Menard and Weill (2016)	No significant causality exists between aid and corruption in either direction.
Ear (2007)	Other than VA, aid has no significant impact on other governance indicators.
Fourth Strand: Aid Volatility and IQ	
Kangoye (2013)	Higher aid volatility leads to higher corruption in the sampled 80 recipient countries.
Kalyvitis and Mallik (2012)	Based on the data of 78 countries over the period 1984 to 2004, the study found the nexus between aid and growth is negative but it depends on the initial institutional capacity of the recipient country.
Iulai (2014)	Aid volatility shows adverse impacts on the recipient countries.
Afawubo and Mathey (2017)	Aid is positively associated with savings and investment, its volatility is harmful to savings and investment. However, when higher quality institutions exist, the volatility of aid has a less negative impact on savings and investment.
Fifth Strand: Nonlinearity of Aid and IQ	
Brazys (2016)	Aid may simultaneously improve and hinder governance. So, relationship between aid and governance could be positive and negative.
Asongu (2015b)	The effects of foreign aid on corruption and institution are positive; constitutionally positive, conditionally positive with magnitude dependent on the initial institutional capacity level of the recipient countries in the African region.
Okada and Samreth (2012)	Using quantile regression, the study found aid reduces the corruption level at different percentiles in 120 developing countries.
Asongu (2015)	Using panel quantile, foreign-aid is more negatively correlated with countries of higher IQ than with those of lower quality in African region.

Table 1. (*Continued*)

Researchers	Main Findings
Mohamed *et al.* (2015)	Based on the data from sub-Saharan countries over the period 2000 to 2010, the study found that the impact of foreign aid on corruption is likely to be more noteworthy in countries that experience a higher level of corruption.

by political, commercial and religious interests. Ahmed (2006) in his doctoral thesis found that local NGOs are often used by a political party to preach their political ideals in Bangladesh. By using time series data from 1972 to 2010, Nasir *et al.* (2012) found a positive association between foreign aid and terrorism in Pakistan.

Based on the literature review in the previous section, this study clearly found that the relationship between aid and IQ of the recipient country is vague and inconclusive. Some researchers are proponent of aid on institutional development, some are completely opposite. There are a few studies which found the relationship between aid and IQ is conditional and it is subject to the existing capacity of the recipient countries. The following subsections explain the theoretical underpinnings and hypotheses development of aid and IQ nexus.

2.2. *Positive effects of ODA*

Beginning with the mid-1990s, researchers, for example, Brautigam (1992) and Lancaster (2000) started to conjecture on the potential of using foreign aid to foster better governance which in turn would facilitate economic development. Degnbol and Martinussen (2002) argued aid can be utilized to encourage better administration in three ways: first, "enhancing state capacity" to increase the efficiency of utilizing the public resources and the quality of public administration; second, "strengthening state–society linkage institutions and procedures" to incorporate judicial reform and strengthening the rule of law; and third, "empowerment of civil society organizations" to engage with the decision-making process with their government with lower cost. Each of these channels can play a positive role of foreign aid on the IQ of the aid recipient countries.

There are a few channels through which aid can influence decidedly specific properties of institutions and can play an impetus role for change. For instance, Knack (2001) and Freytag and Heckelman (2012) contend that aid flows may make an imperative commitment to change by serving to finance improvements in institutions. Knack (2004) contends again that aid can add to the democratization of a nation through technical assistance in the electoral process and fortifying legislature and judiciaries. Aid can also work indirectly thorough income, training and education. By enhancing education level and training, aid may expand the beneficiary's capacity for open and transparent government and educated citizens' cooperation. High levels of aid can possibly enhance the quality of governance through improving the legal system, improving the quality of civil administration, strengthening policy and planning capacity and accountability. Furthermore, aid conditionality from the donors to recipient countries triggers to initiate specific reforms to improve the quality of governance prior to receiving aid packages. It may also enhance the accountability of recipient governments. A good example can be South Korea, Taiwan and Botswana which have utilized foreign aid for socio-economic development (Bräutigam and Knack, 2004).

2.3. Adverse effects of ODA

While there are solid reasons behind the positive impact of aid on IQ, there are also some reasons that aid can undermine IQ. Busse and Gröning (2009) note that the "moral hazard" and rent seeking associated with high levels of aid could prompt a negative effect of aid on governance. Likewise, Moss et al. (2008) claim that aid can erode the quality of institution through rent seeking and corruption. Too much aid reliance can undermine the IQ, hinder the responsibility and encourage rent seeking and corruption. Thus, over time, the institutions of recipient countries are likely to become geared toward unproductive activities.

Svensson (2000) finds foreign aid is associated with increased corruption and this impact is more prominent in ethnically heterogeneous nations. There are conceivable reasons why aid flows may be adverse to a beneficiary's IQ. For instance, aid beneficiary government might not have the motivation or inclination to or undertake tax reforms or to be responsive and responsible to its nationals. Baumol (1990) and Djankov et al. (2008) consider aid to be a "curse" for the beneficiary nation as it applies and exerts a corrupting influence on its institutions. Rajan and Subramanian (2007), Kalyvitis and Vlachaki (2012), Heckelman and Knack (2008) find aid can hinder (rather than encourage) market-oriented reforms.

Prasad and Nickow (2016) remarked the aid as a curse for the developing countries as it destroys the economies in the following three ways: Firstly, a large inflow of aid can disrupt the growth due to the corruption and temptation. Secondly, aid may weaken bureaucratic institutions by placing heavy external demands on them, and by poaching staff away from the state. Thirdly, aid may undermine advancement by debilitating the force for setting up strong tax administration. In the event that aid is given as credits which increment the nation's obligation load, absence of reliable tax administration will prompt an ever bigger part of the budget setting off to the overhauling of obligation, which thus may obstruct improvement (Bräutigam and Knack, 2004; Moore, 2004). Foreign aid can disrupt the political stability of the non-democratic regime of the naturally resourceful countries. For example, Ravetti et al. (2018) found that the foreign aid and natural resources can act as a double curse on autocratic regime. It reduces the accountability and increases the returns to corruption and moral hazard, engendering looting and sudden departures of political leaders.

H1: *Foreign aid can help improve the IQ of the recipient.*

2.4. Aid volatility and institutional quality

The volatility of aid flows is measured as the deviation of actual aid flows from the expected aid flows. The aid volatility arises either because of the policy changes by the donor or external shocks in the global economy. In either case, aid vulnerability may adversely affect government expenditure, and specifically investment. A diminishment of public investment may thus prompt lower private speculation, and eventually additionally to bring down development. Bulíř and Hamann (2008) identified that the effect of aid volatility is particularly severe when the shortfall of aid and domestic revenue deficit coincidentally happens simultaneously in the aid-dependent country. Lensink and Morrissey (2000) investigate the impact of volatile aid flows and found that aid in itself contributes to higher growth, but that the effectiveness of aid is diminished when aid flows are more volatile.

In addition to the economic consequences of the aid volatility, there are some studies which found that the aid volatility can affect the political environment of the recipient country. For example, Kangoye (2013) explored the political economy of 80 developing countries over the period 1984 to 2004 and compared the political power and rent seeking behavior of the corrupted leaders with the aid volatility. The author argued that the politicians aim to increase the rent they capture and where they have inter temporal smoothing considerations, greater volatility of aid can lead them to engage more than proportionally (compared with the optimal path) in rent seeking since they face a shortfall risk of aid. Likewise, Robinson *et al.* (2006) used the resource curse theory for explaining the aid volatility and its impact on the political institution of the recipient countries. Ventelou (2001) found that the greater the aid volatility, the greater the incentives for kleptocrat leaders to engage in rent seeking in countries where IQ is poor. Likewise, Arellano *et al.* (2009) examined the aid volatility and its effect on welfare. They found that lower aid volatility is beneficial for consumption (welfare enhancing), whereas higher aid volatility leads to consumption volatility (welfare impeding). However, a recent study of Asongu and Nnanna (2019) found that aid unpredictability or instability improves government standards especially political and general governance.

H2: *Foreign aid volatility has adverse effect on the IQ of the recipient.*

2.5. Marginal effect and nonlinearity of foreign aid on institutional quality

Following the comparative thinking, another branch of research has contended that a vital piece of the story is disregarded by not considering the absorptive limit of the aid-getting nations. Brayzs (2015) first introduced the Laffer curve to find the relationship between aid and governance structure of the aid recipient countries. They argued that aid and governance need not be linear always and they found too much of foreign aid can lead to counterproductive result in the governance. This branch of research infers that the aid and development relationship may demonstrate diminishing returns (Feeny and McGillivray, 2011). Some studies applied quadratic functions to examine the nonlinearity between aid and growth relationship (e.g., Hansen and Tarp, 2001; Dalgaard and Hansen, 2001; Lensink and White, 2001). These studies argue that aid is effective in increasing growth with diminishing returns and many aid recipient countries may have limited capacity to absorb foreign resources and, hence, aid beyond a certain threshold may actually harm the economic growth.

In a similar vein, recent studies such as Mohamed *et al.* (2015), Okada and Samreth (2012), Askarov and Doucouliagos (2015) found that aid–institution relationship is heterogeneous and it is contingent on the initial level or absorption capacity of the aid recipient country. Brazys (2016) asserted that aid-governance relationship need not be linear, but rather aid may simultaneously improve and hinder governance. So, relationship between aid and governance could be positive or negative. By using quantile regression, they investigated the effect of aid at different levels of IQ and they found that the aid-institution nexus is not symmetric; rather it has a marginal effect. Mohamed *et al.* (2015) results suggest that generally aid has a mitigating effect on corruption. The effect is bigger in countries with low corruption perception index (CPI) scores (i.e., in more corrupt countries). Okada and Samreth (2012) found that aid reduces the corruption level but the reduction effect is greater in less corrupt countries. So, this study will test the nonlinearity or marginal effect of the OIC countries with the following hypothesis:

H3: *The relationship between increased aid and IQ is nonlinear and depends on the "initial level" of IQ.*

3. Data and Methodology

3.1. *Data*

This study employs the panel data consisting of annual observations of the OIC countries with the average of every three years aggregated from 1991 to 2016. However, a few countries, including Saudi Arabia, Qatar, Bahrain, and Kuwait, are dropped from the list as they are not aid recipients, rather they are aid donors. Finally, this study considered annual data of 38 countries from OIC region. This study uses the ODA data as a measure of the amount of foreign aid a country receives. The data of ODA along with the following variables are collected from the OECD and DataStream database. Since an increase in dollar per capita may not be a good measure of aid dependency (because of the changes in dollar value itself), a look at the foreign aid as a percentage of the GNI is likely to provide a better picture of the phenomenon (see Moniruzzaman, 2012). For representing the dependent variable, this study applies two types of dataset of IQ: first, the ICRG dataset and second, the WGI, as suggested by Kaufmann *et al.* (2010). Both datasets have similarities for explaining political and governance structure of the countries. For example, key indicators like political stability, corruption, regulatory quality, bureaucratic quality, etc. are considered in both datasets. In our study, the ICRG dataset is used as a base in the empirical section, while the second dataset is applied for testing the robustness of the study. Askarov and Doucouliagos (2015) made a meta-analysis of aid and its effect on governance and they found that nearly two-thirds (64%) of researchers used these two dataset separately. However, in this study both of these datasets are used simultaneously to identify the impact of aid on institutions.

In WGI, the IQ variables include: the rule of law, regulation quality, corruption-control, government effectiveness, VA, and political stability. Kaufmann *et al.* (2010) illustrated that these six aggregate indicators can be reported in two ways: (1) in their standard normal units, ranging from approximately −2.5 to 2.5, and (2) in percentile rank terms from 0 to 100, with higher values corresponding to better outcomes. For the ease of interpretation, this study adopts the latter option in all empirical models. The ICRG index is composed of five components: government stability, corruption, law and order, democratic accountability and bureaucratic quality. Control variables such as inflation, unemployment, trade openness, economic growth, population growth are applied in this study. These control variables are broadly consistent with the causes of IQ (Goel and Nelson, 2005; Lambsdorff, 2006). Javed (2016) found Trade openness and economic growth are the significant determinants of the IQ.

3.2. Methodologies

3.2.1. Static model (fixed and random effects)

Following the prior studies (Asongu, 2015; Dadasov, 2016; Askarov and Doucouliagos, 2015), this study adopts following equation using the static panel model to examine the relationship between the foreign aid and the IQ of the host country:

$$\text{IQ(ICRG)} = \alpha + \beta_1 \text{ODA to GNI} + \beta_2 \text{POP} + \beta_3 \text{TRDO} + \beta_4 \text{INF} + \beta_5 \text{UEM} + \beta_6 \text{EG} + \varepsilon. \quad (1)$$

Here, the dependent variable is the IQ measured by ICRG index.
Independent variables:

ODA to GNI (%)	=	Official development assistance to Gross National Income (%),
POP	=	Population growth,
TRDO	=	Trade openness,
INF	=	Inflation rate,
UEM	=	Unemployment rate,
EG	=	Economic growth,
ε	=	Error term.

Since the sample considers all countries over a particular time period, the fixed effects model is adopted in the analysis. Furthermore, the opportunity to use a fixed effects rather than a random effects model has been tested with the Hausman test.

3.2.2. Dynamic model — system GMM

Like recent studies, our study also believes that there should be dynamic relationship between aid and IQ. That's why, after the static models, this study considered the dynamic panel models with the following justifications: (i) The dependent variable — IQ is very likely to be dependent on the past one (Dadasov, 2017). (ii) As mentioned earlier aid flow, the main variable of our research interest is endogenous by nature (see Dutta and Williamson, 2016). The reason of the endogeneity is that the allocation of aid flow is dependent on many factors including the IQ of the recipient countries. The same idea is applicable to some of our control variables. (iii) Unobserved time invariant factor may affect both IQ and other independent variables. (iv) In cross country macro data, the error terms are subject to heteroskedasticity and serial correlation.

As static panel models suffer from above-mentioned problems, "difference" GMM suggested by Arellano and Bond (1991) can eliminate the fixed effects. However, it fails to remove the problem of correlation between the lagged dependent variable and the error term which requires the use of "instruments". One possible solution is the use of appropriate lags of the dependent and independent variables as instruments. However, one potential problem with the "differenced" equation is that the lagged "levels" of regressors may be weak instruments for the "differenced" variables (see Yalta and Yalta, 2012).

In order to address the above-mentioned problems, this study applied dynamic system GMM proposed by Arellano and Bond (1991) and Blundell and Bond (1998). Some recent studies such as Busse *et al.* (2017) strongly recommend system GMM as it deals effectively with reverse causality by using lagged levels and differences as a set of instruments for the endogenous variables. Based on this context, the system GMM is used based on the following two equations for addressing our first research objective:

$$IQ_{it} = a_i + b_t + \beta_1 IQ_{t-1} + \beta_2 AID + \beta'_3 X_{it} + \varepsilon_{it}, \qquad (2)$$

$$\Delta IQ_{it} = b_t + \beta_1 \Delta IQ_{t-1} + \beta_2 \Delta AID_i + \beta'_3 \Delta X_{it} + \Delta \varepsilon_{it}, \qquad (3)$$

where i indicates the country $(i = 1,...,N)$ and t indicates the time period $(t = 1,...,T_i)$ IQ indicates Institutional Quality, the dependent variable of our study. AID refers to the ODA to GNI (%) form. X_{it} is the set of control variables. a_i and b_t denote country and time effects, respectively. Finally, ε_{it} is the unobservable error term. Using system GMM methodology, Equation (2) is first transformed into Equation (3) using first-differences (Δ) that eliminates the country fixed effects. Then both equations are estimated simultaneously whereby lagged first-differences of all potential endogenous variables are used as their own instruments in the level Equation (2), and lagged levels of the respective variables are used as instruments in the first-difference Equation (3). (see Dadasov, 2017). However, system GMM suffers from the two following problems: (a) To make the estimates asymptotically more efficient, the system GMM uses two-step procedure but standard errors of the estimates tend to be critically biased. (b) Another problem with the two-step GMM is the "instrument proliferation" which results in biases in the coefficient and their standard errors (Roodman, 2009).

For addressing the second research objective of the study as to how aid volatility affects the IQ, we need to measure the aid volatility first. Like some prior studies (Fielding and Mavrotas, 2008; Kangoye, 2013), our study applied 4-year rolling standard deviation of the change in the foreign aid expressed in logarithmic terms. Finally, after finding the aid volatility, the following formula for the system GMM will be used to conduct the empirical analysis:

$$IQ_{it} = a_i + b_t + \beta_1 IQ_{t-1} + \beta_2 AIDV + \beta'_3 X_{it} + \varepsilon_{it}, \quad (4)$$

$$\Delta IQ_{it} = b_t + \beta_1 \Delta IQ_{t-1} + \beta_2 \Delta AIDV_i + \beta'_3 \Delta X_{it} + \Delta \varepsilon_{it}, \quad (5)$$

where i indicates the country ($i = 1,\ldots,N$) and t indicates the time period ($t = 1,\ldots,T_i$) IQ indicates Institutional Quality, the dependent variable of our study. AIDV refers to the aid volatility (standard deviation) of the ODA to GNI (%) form. The AIDV variable is measured before taking the average of every three years aggregated from 1991 to 2016. X_{it} is the set of control variables. a_i and b_t denote country and time effects, respectively. Finally, ε_{it} is the unobservable error term.

3.2.3. Quantile regression

Due to the diversity of the income level, political structure and IQ of the sampled OIC countries in our study, the dataset of our study is highly skewed (heavy tailed distribution). So, OLS estimation is inappropriate in such a situation because of the normality problem of the distribution. This is why, this study adopts the quantile regression suggested by Koenker and Bassett (1978) for examining the third research question. While OLS regression focuses on mean, quantile regressions are able to describe the entire conditional distribution of the dependent variable (Coad and Rao, 2006). Unlike OLS, the error term and dependent variable in quantile regression need not be distributed normally. So, quantile regression technique allows us to examine if the relationship among institutional dynamics and foreign-aid differs throughout the distributions of the institutional dynamics (Asongu, 2015). Like Mohamed et al. (2015), Asongu (2013), this study would be able to carefully assess the incidence of development assistance throughout the conditional distribution with particular emphasis on countries with strong and worst weak institutions by using the following quantile formula:

$$y_{it} = \acute{x}_{it} \beta_0 + \varepsilon \theta_{it} \quad \text{with Quant}_\theta(y_{it}|x_{it}) = \acute{x}_{it} \beta_0, \quad (6)$$

where i denotes country, t denotes time, y_{it} denotes IQ, $\acute{x}_{it}$ is a vector of regressors, β is the vector of parameters to be estimated, ε is vector of residuals. $\text{Quant}_\theta(y_{it}|x_{it})$ denotes θth conditional quantile of y_{it} given x_{it}. θth regression quantile, $0 < \theta < 1$, solves the following problem:

$$\min_\beta \frac{1}{n} \left\{ \sum_{i,t: y_{it} \geq \acute{x}_{it}\beta} \theta |y_{it} - \acute{x}_{it}\beta| + \sum_{i,t: y_{it} < \acute{x}_{it}\beta} (1-\theta)|y_{it} - \acute{x}_{it}\beta| \right\} = \min_\beta \frac{1}{n} \sum_{i=1}^n \rho_\theta \varepsilon_{\theta it}, \quad (7)$$

where $\rho_\theta(\cdot)$ which is known as the "check function", is defined as

$$\rho_\theta(\varepsilon_{\theta it}) = \begin{cases} \theta \varepsilon_{\theta it} & \text{if } \theta \varepsilon_{\theta it} \geq 0, \\ (\theta - 1)\varepsilon_{\theta it} & \text{if } \theta \varepsilon_{\theta it} \leq 0. \end{cases} \quad (8)$$

According to Buchinsky (1998), as one increases θ continuously from 0 to 1, one traces the entire conditional distribution of y_{it}, conditional on x_{it}. Since the quantile regression is more appropriate than the OLS and other static models for testing our hypothesis, this study considered the 20th, 40th, 60th, 80th and 90th quantiles as shown here:

$$Q_{0.20}(IQ) = \alpha_{0.20} + \beta_{0.20,1}X + \beta_{0.20,2} \text{ ODA to GNI} + \varepsilon_{0.20it}, \quad (9)$$

$$Q_{0.40}(IQ) = \alpha_{0.40} + \beta_{0.40,1}X + \beta_{0.40,2} \text{ ODA to GNI} + \varepsilon_{0.40it}, \quad (10)$$

$$Q_{0.60}(IQ) = \alpha_{0.60} + \beta_{0.60,1}X + \beta_{0.60,2} \text{ ODA to GNI} + \varepsilon_{0.60it}, \quad (11)$$

$$Q_{0.80}(IQ) = \alpha_{0.80} + \beta_{0.80,1}X + \beta_{0.80,2} \text{ ODA to GNI} + \varepsilon_{0.80it}, \quad (12)$$

$$Q_{0.90}(IQ) = \alpha_{0.90} + \beta_{0.90,1}X + \beta_{0.90,2} \text{ ODA to GNI} + \varepsilon_{0.90it}, \quad (13)$$

Here, IQ denotes Institutional Quality, X is set of control variables and ODA to GNI (%) refers to foreign aid flows.

4. Models Estimation and Discussions

4.1. Descriptive statistics

Table 2 which presents some basic descriptive statistics for the main variables used in the empirical analyses (data are averaged over 1991–2016), shows that the values of aid as a percentage to GNI is around 7%. Based on the ICRG dataset, the IQ of the sampled country is only 52 out of 100, which is relatively lower, compared to that of the developed countries. WGI, another dataset of governance, shows the score is even less than one-third of the total score. These results are consistent with the findings of Askari *et al.* (2017) that made an index called Islamicity Index where he found that none of the Muslim countries are in the top 40 and the score ranges between 40% and 44%.

Table 2. Descriptive Statistics

	ICRG	WGI	ODA to GNI	POP	TRDO	INF	UEM	EG
Mean	52.407	29.29	7.040	2.1760	70.062	22.954	9.730	4.171
Median	53.962	24.454	3.500	2.2666	63.056	5.283	8.250	4.350
Max.	74.428	40.030	66.780	6.690	255.850	1000.00	27.66	24.560
Min.	0.0000	11.713	0.003	−1.570	15.410	−7.166	1.63	−19.283
Std. Dev.	11.618	5.699	9.176	1.173	36.099	91.34	5.59	4.147
Skewness	−1.5563	0.108	2.589	−0.039	2.041	7.956	0.90	−0.514
Kurtosis	7.697	2.594	12.620	4.565	8.718	71.493	3.324	11.899
Obs.	304	248	304	304	304	304	304	304

Notes: The dependent variable is IQ and is measured by the ICRG and WGI index. ODA to GNI (%): official development assistance to Gross National Income (%); POP refers to the population growth, TRDO indicates trade openness; INF is the inflation rate, UEM refers unemployment rate and finally EG is the economic growth.
Source: Author's estimation.

From the macroeconomic perspectives, the average annual economic growth of the sampled countries is 4.17%. The unemployment rate and inflation rate of the sampled countries are 9% and 22%, respectively. This study also reveals that the considerable variation exists in the inflation rate of the sample countries, as few countries like Syria and Yemen are in under the war crisis. The standard deviation of ICRG and WGI is found 11.61 and 5.69 respectively and these figures indicate that the existing level of IQ is varied among the OIC countries.

4.2. Correlation matrix

For understanding the basic relationship between our dependent and independent variables, a correlation matrix is constructed in Table 3. The results show that the impact of aid and aid volatility are negatively correlated with the IQ of the aid-dependent countries. For example, the ratio of ODA to GNI and aid volatility is negatively and statistically significant to ICRG by 0.22 and −0.15, respectively.

In addition to the aid variable, there are some macroeconomic factors, such as inflation and unemployment which are negatively related with the IQ. However, as expected, the trade openness, economic growth are positively and significantly related with the IQ of the aid-dependent countries. This result can be a primary source of evidence that the aid and institutions are negatively correlated. Another purpose of making correlation matrix is to see issues resulting from over parametrization and multicollinearity. Since the pair correlation of variables is less than 0.80, there does not appear to be any serious concerns in terms of mulitcollinearity (see Gujarati *et al.*, 2009).

Table 3. Correlation Matrix

	ICRG	LAIDV	ODA to GNI (%)	POP	TRDO	INF	UEM	EG
ICRG	1							
LAIDV	−0.1557*	1						
ODA to GNI	−0.2267*	0.0783	1					
POP	0.0408	0.1782*	0.2083*	1				
TRDO	0.1469*	−0.1168	−0.0212	−0.2046*	1			
INF	−0.5779*	0.0623	−0.0349	−0.1962*	0.0347	1		
UEM	0.0343	−0.0692	−0.0268	−0.1391	0.1525	0.0232	1	
EG	0.2826*	−0.0102	0.0400	0.1739*	−0.0166	−0.3900	0.0209	1

Notes: The dependent variable IQ is measured by the ICRG and WGI index; ODA to GNI (%): official development assistance to Gross National Income (%); POP refers to the population growth, TRDO indicates trade openness; INF is the inflation rate, UEM refers to unemployment rate and finally EG is the economic growth.
*, ** and *** indicate significance at the 10%, 5% and 1% levels, respectively.
Source: Author's estimation.

4.3. Results of static panel models

The descriptive statistics in the earlier section found the negative correlation between the changes in foreign aid and IQ of the host country. For better understand of the nexus between foreign aid and IQ, the basic empirical models have been estimated using the fixed effects method and the random effects method, results are shown in Table 4. To check which method is more appropriate, Hausman test is applied and found that the fixed effects method is more acceptable compared to the random effects.

The first and foremost important variable of interest of our study is the coefficient of aid flows and the impact on the IQ of the aid-dependent countries. It is found that the ratio of ODA to GNI has a negative and statistically significant impact on the ICRG index at 1% level of significance. This study employed static panel methods such as fixed effects and random effects for hypothesis testing. However, the study accepted the fixed effects model

Table 4. Static Models Estimations

	(1)	(2)	(3)	(4)
	\multicolumn{4}{c}{Dependent Variable: ICRG}			
Variables	Fixed	Fixed Effects-Lag	Random Effects	Random Effect-Lag
L.ICRG	—	−0.00784**	—	−0.00759***
		(0.00288)		(0.0028)
ODAGNI	−0.0303***	−0.0254***	−0.0273***	−0.0235***
	(0.00844)	(0.00801)	(0.00754)	(0.00722)
EG	−0.00565	0.187	−0.0182	0.172
	(0.0959)	(0.124)	(0.0939)	(0.122)
INF	−0.0637***	−0.0584***	−0.0662***	−0.0601***
	(0.00616)	(0.00615)	(0.00596)	(0.00596)
UEM	−0.280	−0.362	−0.0345	−0.0771
	(0.276)	(0.254)	(0.160)	(0.156)
TRDO	−0.0443	−0.0376	0.0155	0.0160
	(0.0316)	(0.0306)	(0.0223)	(0.0222)
POP	−0.00018	−0.000249	0.0000647	0.000016
	(0.00029)	(0.0002853)	(0.0002456)	(0.0002394)
Constant	55.13***	58.31***	56.09***	61.50***
	(14.02)	(13.28)	(11.78)	(11.31)
Observations	294	287	294	287
R-squared	0.406	0.422		
Number of idc	38	38	38	38

Notes: The dependent variable IQ is measured by the ICRG and WGI index; ODA to GNI (%): official development assistance to Gross National Income (%); POP refers to the population growth, TRDO indicates trade openness; INF is the inflation rate, UEM refers to unemployment rate and finally EG is the economic growth.

This study tested the Hausman test and found p-value 0.017 meaning fixed effects model is more valid.

*, ** and *** indicate significance at the 10%, 5% and 1% levels, respectively.

as the *p*-value found is 0.017 in the Hausman test. By using the fixed effects method, it is found that a 1% increase in the ODA to GNI ratio decreases the ICRG index −0.030%. The similar result exists when we use the random effects method.

Theoretically, foreign aid flows should discharge governments from restricting income requirements and empower them to focus enforcing good governance. The financial and technical support enables developing countries to ensure proper IQ (see Busse *et al.*, 2017; Sachs, 2005). However, our results reveal that aid flows erode the governance quality of the recipient countries. One possible explanation could be: due to moral hazard problems and rent seeking, high levels of aid could delay or block necessary domestic reforms to improve regulations (Bräutigam and Knack, 2004; Heckelman and Knack, 2008). The other possible reason could be the presence of weak institutions and rent seeking practices of the corrupt government of the aid recipient countries.

Among the macroeconomic variables, inflation has an adverse effect on the IQ of the aid-dependent countries. In a similar vein, the other financial liberalization variables, such as the trade openness has negative but statistically insignificant relationship with the IQ of the OIC countries. This study also examined whether there is any dynamic relationship existing or not in the model. The results found that the dynamic relationship exists in the model since the lag-dependent variables are statistically significant.

4.4. Results of dynamic models — system GMM

Although this study relied on the results of the "system" GMM result but for the robustness and consistency of the findings, this study also applied "difference" GMM. Columns 2 and 4 are for the "difference" GMM estimation. The result of the difference GMM is also consistent with system GMM. The system GMM tries to deal with weak instrument problem by augmenting these instruments. System GMM does not require the panel data to be normally distributed. However, system GMM of any assumption on the panel distribution is only consistent when there is no second-order autocorrelation within the error term and second, when the model is not over-identified (i.e., when the instruments are valid). Therefore, Table 5 reports two tests: the Arrelano and Bond test of first- and second-order autocorrelation in the residuals and the Hansen test of over-identification. The *p*-value of AR(2) suggests that there is no second-order autocorrelation in the residual within all models in Table 5. Furthermore, the number of instruments is less than the number of groups (i.e., countries).

On the whole, the validity of the instruments used as a necessity for system GMM is confirmed, as indicated by the *p*-values of the Hansen J test. In all the models in Table 4, the *p*-value of Hansen's J test for over identification restrictions is higher than the critical level of 0.05 and even 0.10 meaning that the joint validating of instruments is not rejected. Like Dadasov (2017), this study also follows another "rule of thumb" and assuring that the number of instruments is not exceeding the number of countries. So, considering all test statistics of these models we can conclude that the estimated models are adequately specified.

Table 5. Dynamic Model Estimation — System GMM

Variables	Dynamic Models		Dynamic Models		Dynamic Models with Aid Volatility	
	(2) D-GMM	(3) S-GMM	(4) D-GMM	(5) S-GMM	(6) S-GMM	(7) S-GMM
	\multicolumn{6}{c}{Dependent Variable: IQ measured by ICRG}					
	ICRG	ICRG	WGI	WGI	ICRG	WGI
L.ICRG	0.488***	0.484***	1.252***	1.116***	0.568***	1.050***
	(0.0778)	(0.0905)	(0.281)	(0.102)	(0.0872)	(0.0585)
Aid volatility	—	—	—	—	−0.0257**	−0.0725**
	—	—	—	—	(0.013)	(0.033)
ODA to GNI	−0.175**	−0.134**	−0.4367*	−0.377	−0.114**	−0.0205**
	(0.0824)	(0.0601)	(2.350)	(0.369)	(0.0557)	(0.00874)
INF	−0.029***	−0.0367***	0.00851	0.0120	−0.0290***	0.00156
	(0.00463)	(0.00569)	(0.00888)	(0.0183)	(0.00379)	(0.0131)
UEM	−0.292	−0.117	0.00733	−0.0109	−0.0201	−0.0285***
	(0.598)	(0.120)	(0.148)	(0.0164)	(0.0890)	(0.0107)
EG	0.0424	0.0841	0.0364	0.0302*	0.101	0.121
	(0.145)	(0.109)	(0.0267)	(0.0174)	(0.138)	(0.118)
TRDO	−0.0135	0.0390*	−0.0124	−0.00366	0.0232*	−0.00501
	(0.0592)	(0.0230)	(0.00990)	(0.00692)	(0.0140)	(0.00482)
POP	0.780**	−0.106	−0.354	−0.260*	0.0637	−0.231***
	(0.391)	(0.396)	(0.528)	(0.156)	(0.338)	(0.0857)
Obs.	213	251	229	223	254	213
No. of instr.	18	24	12	23	19	13
No. of Groups	38	38	31	31	38	31
AR(1)	0.018	0.032	0.006	0.002	0.018	0.024
AR(2)	0.404	0.716	0.972	0.488	0.138	0.098
Hansen J test (p-value)	0.334	0.301	0.345	0.349	0.351	0.254

Notes: The dependent variable is IQ and is measured by the ICRG and WGI index. ODA to GNI (%): official development assistance to Gross National Income (%); POP refers to the population growth; TRDO indicates trade openness; INF is the inflation rate, UEM refers to unemployment rate and finally EG is the economic growth.

Two-step system GMM results by using robust standard errors corrected for finite samples (by using Windmeijer's, 2005, correction) and Hansen J tests never reject the validity of the over-identifying restrictions.

If p-value > 0.05, we confirm the validity of instruments. AR(2) is a test for the second-order serial correlation and is asymptotically distributed as $N(0,1)$ under the null of no serial correlation. If p-value > 0.05, we confirm no serial correlation at order 2 in the first-differenced errors and the model is well specified.

*, ** and *** indicate significance at the 10%, 5% and 1% levels, respectively.

Furthermore, in the light of Table 5, we explore our main conjecture about the aid impact on the IQ of the sample countries. First we explore the role of aid on the IQ (columns 2–4) and then we examine the dynamic effects of aid volatility on the IQ. The coefficient of system GMM indicates that there is a negative and statistically significant association between aid and IQ — for both WGI and ICRG — at 5% level of significance. This result is consistent with our earlier static model results. By using the differenced and system GMM for the ICRG dataset, it is found that if there is 1% increase in the ODA to GNI ratio; the IQ will be decreased by −0.17% and −0.13%, respectively. A similar result has been found in our second dataset of IQ i.e., world governance index (WGI). Both differenced GMM and system GMM found a negative impact of aid on the institutional infrastructure of the sampled OIC countries.

Among all the control variables, inflation, population growth and the unemployment rates are negatively associated with the IQ. Like the static models, trade openness (TO), another proxy variable of financial liberalization (the ratio of exports and imports to GDP), has a negative but insignificant association with the IQ of the sampled OIC countries. However, the effect of inflation rate and IQ is relatively higher and statistically significant. Based on the ICRG dataset in differenced GMM and system GMM, it is found that 1% increase in inflation will erode IQ by −0.029% and −0.036%. These results are consistent with prior studies such as Busse and Gröning (2009), Djankov et al. (2008), Wako (2017) who argued that the aid can impact negatively on the IQ. With regards to the population growth, our results found a negative association with the IQ. Like Busse and Gröning (2009), we also believe that the higher population growth can pose information asymmetry problems and higher transaction costs which financially impede institutional developments. Finally, as expected our study also reveal that the unemployment problem can also erode the IQ.

Aid volatility, another research question of this study, concludes with similar findings. By using the system GMM the coefficient between aid volatility and IQ is negative. For instance, by using the ICRG and WGI index, if there is 1% increase in aid volatility, the IQ will decrease by 0.025% and 0.0725%, respectively. The ODA to GNI ratio is also negatively associated with IQ of the recipient countries in all models. Our result is consistent with Kangoye (2013) who found 1% increase in the aid volatility leads to 0.32% corruption in the aid recipient countries. A possible reason advanced by the author is that the greater the aid volatility the greater the incentive of kleptocrat leaders to be involved in rent seeking practices especially in the countries where IQ is weak. Likewise, Afawubo and Mathey (2017) found when higher quality institutions exist, the volatility of aid has a less negative impact on savings and investment. Other than the direct institutional impact of aid volatility on the aid recipient countries, few studies such as Hudson and Mosley (2008), Iulai (2014) found that aid can negatively impact initially on the macroeconomic performance of the aid recipient countries which indirectly hamper the different components of the IQ of the host country.

4.5. Results of quantile regression

From our earlier static and GMM results, we found that IQ in the recipient countries is negatively associated with aid inflows and aid volatility. However, it is yet to explore the heterogeneous effect of aid effects on our IQ meaning that we are not sure yet how does the aid impact on the country where existing IQ is good or bad. For this purpose, this study employs quantile regression to investigate the relationship among institutional dynamics and foreign-aid flows throughout the distributions of institutional dynamics (Koenker and Hallock, 2001). For the purpose of our result interpretation, it is important to note that the lower quantiles (in conditional distributions) of the dependent variable denote less IQ index of the recipient countries. Alternatively, the upper quantile indicates the high IQ of the aid recipient countries (see Asongu, 2015).

As shown in the quantile regression in Table 6, the aid-IQ nexus is negative in terms of magnitude across distributions and specifications. However, the marginal negative effect of aid on IQ decreases in the upper quantile of the distribution. This implies the low-IQ countries are more affected than the high-IQ countries. Alternatively, the high-IQ countries are more likely to benefit from development assistance (in terms of general economic growth) than their low-IQ counterparts. Foreign aid is more negatively correlated with countries of lower quantiles than those of higher quantiles, meaning that aid impacts the IQ badly when the country has poor IQ at the initial stage.

From the summary in Table 6, it is noticeable that the negative nexuses are not significantly different across specifications and distributions. However, the magnitude of negative incidence of ODA on IQ statistically significantly decreases from the bottom

Table 6. Quantile Regression at Different Percentiles when ICRG is Dependent Variable

Variables	(1) OLS	(2) Q_{25}	(3) Q_{40}	(4) Q_{60}	(5) Q_{80}	(6) Q_{90}
			Dependent Variable: ICRG			
ODAGNI	−0.0257***	−0.0329***	−0.0196***	−0.0147	−0.0107	−0.0132*
	(0.00729)	(0.00906)	(0.00675)	(0.00914)	(0.0125)	(0.00783)
EG	−0.118	−0.0994	−0.0852	−0.0142	−0.201	−0.144
	(0.108)	(0.203)	(0.219)	(0.252)	(0.297)	(0.398)
INF	−0.0754***	−0.0993***	−0.0848***	−0.0803***	−0.0698***	−0.0742***
	(0.00658)	(0.0164)	(0.0196)	(0.0144)	(0.0162)	(0.0165)
UEM	0.0109	−0.0200	−0.00868	−0.0440	−0.0524	−0.0219
	(0.103)	(0.172)	(0.125)	(0.132)	(0.112)	(0.195)
TRDO	0.0515***	0.0758	0.0582**	0.0588**	0.0460***	0.0167
	(0.0172)	(0.0494)	(0.0279)	(0.0254)	(0.0151)	(0.0174)
POP	−0.0628	−0.751	−1.045	−0.563	−0.687	−1.332
	(0.508)	(1.394)	(0.739)	(0.517)	(0.467)	(0.860)
Const.	43.80***	42.56*	39.63**	52.51***	59.54***	78.28***
	(10.40)	(25.01)	(19.29)	(17.35)	(16.93)	(20.57)

Notes: The dependent variable is IQ and is measured by the ICRG and WGI index. ODA to GNI (%): official development assistance to Gross National Income (%); POP refers to the population growth, TRDO indicates trade openness; INF is the inflation rate, UEM refers to unemployment rate and finally EG is the economic growth.

*Denotes significance at 10% level; ** Denotes significance at 5%; *** Denotes significance at 1%.

(0.25 and 0.40 quantiles) to the top distributions (0.80 and 0.90 quantiles). This suggests the positive aid correlations are more present in top quantiles of the IQ distribution. Alternatively, the negative impact of aid is more evident in the low-IQ countries. This finding is consistent across specifications with the slight exception of the 0.90 quantile in Table 6.

For robustness, WGI data is used to examine the effect of aid on IQ at different distributions. The results of WGI are in line with the findings of ICRG data. In Table 7, it can be seen that the aid is negatively related with the IQ at different percentiles. For example, aid is negatively related at the Q_{20}, Q_{40}, Q_{60}, Q_{80}, Q_{90}; however, the lower quantile is more statistically significant than the upper quantile. So, it can be said that aid is more challenging to the low-IQ countries in comparison with the high-IQ countries. This finding of marginal effect of aid on IQ is consistent with Okada and Samreth (2012) and Mohamed et al. (2015) who concluded that the marginal effect is bigger in countries with low IQ.

Among all control variables, most of them are significant with the right signs since inflation and population growth seriously infringe on IQ, while investment (public, domestic and private) improves it. Estimates of fixed effects, controlling for the unobserved heterogeneity in legal origins, trade openness and income-levels, also have the expected signs. Based on WGI data, income indicated by GDP per capita is positively related to the IQ of the sampled countries at various distributions. The results imply that higher income

Table 7. Quantile Regression at Different Percentiles When WGI is Dependent Variable

	OLS_res	Q_{20}_res	Q_{40}_res	Q_{60}_res	Q_{80}_res	Q_{90}_res
			Dependent Variable: WGI			
ODA to GNI	−0.078950* (0.0316714)	−0.0898*** (0.02705)	−0.109503** (0.03648)	−0.1188524** (0.04471)	−0.000276 (0.02981)	−0.0214 (0.01513)
EG	0.25681*** (0.037653)	0.3238*** (0.067831)	0.33382*** (0.04337)	0.220120*** (0.05315)	0.172518*** (0.03544)	0.146925*** (0.01799)
UEP	−0.0018626 (0.0020251)	−0.0035513 (0.003648)	−0.00371 (0.00233)	−0.00129 (0.00286)	−0.00085 (0.00191)	0.000694 (0.00097)
INF	−0.00866*** (0.001848)	−0.00985** (0.003330)	−0.00942*** (0.00213)	−0.011417*** (0.00261)	−0.0048667** (0.00174)	−0.003362*** (0.00088)
POP	0.0219193 (0.0141169)	0.0096396 (0.025431)	0.0353835* (0.01626)	0.020941 (0.01993)	0.0273662* (0.01329)	0.033202*** (0.00675)
TRDO	0.00155*** (0.0004128)	0.00231** (0.000743)	0.001489** −0.00048	0.0014842* −0.00058	0.000301 −0.00039	0.000159 −0.0002
Constant	−1.75332	−1.159911	−0.8922958*	−0.63051	1.036787**	1.34847***

Notes: The dependent variable is IQ and is measured by the ICRG and WGI index. ODA to GNI (%) official development assistance to Gross National Income (%); POP refers to the population growth, TRDO indicates trade openness; INF is the inflation rate, UEM refers to unemployment rate and finally EG is the economic growth.
*Denotes significance at 10% level; ** Denotes significance at 5%; *** Denotes significance at 1%.

can improve the IQ of all countries irrespective of its initial level of IQ. Similar to earlier findings, inflation is negatively correlated with IQ of the OIC countries. These findings are consistent with the OLS results.

This study conjectures a comparative nonlinear connection for the impact of aid on institutions. Aid may positively affect IQ up to a certain level, beyond which aid's marginal contributions would decline and may even turn negative. This would happen when excessive amount of aid flow inject into the economy and exceed the 'abosrption' limit, it is relatively easier that the aid flow could divert into the non-productive channel. Without improving the existing absorption capacity of the aid recepient country, the excessive amount of foreign aid cannot be consumed legitimately and in this manner ends up having a negative impact. Similar to our findings, Fielding (2014) concluded that the outcome of aid depends on the existing institutional characteristics of the recipient countries.

For the validity of the findings of the quantile regressions, the bootstrap procedure is employed to construct a joint distribution allowing us to devise F-statistics to test for the equality of the estimated coefficients across various pairs of quantiles. Table 8 reports the F-tests and the related p-values for the uniformity of quantile slope coefficients over the different sets of quantiles. This test is based on the bootstrapped standard errors utilizing 1000 replications. The F-tests reject the null hypothesis of homogeneous coefficients at the 1% significance level for all pairs of quantiles meaning that the effect of the explanatory variables is different across the different parts of the distribution.

Furthermore, this study employs the graphical evidence of nonlinearity and marginal effect between aid and IQ by applying ICRG data and WGI data in Figures 1 and 2, respectively. Both figures depict the quantile regression estimates and the OLS estimates and found that the quantile regression estimates vary widely when the level of IQ increases.

Table 8. F-Test Results of Quantile Regression

$H_0 = Q_{20} = Q_{40}$	$H_0 = Q_{40} = Q_{60}$	$H_0 = Q_{60} = Q_{80}$	$H_0 = Q_{80} = Q_{90}$
Quantile Regression Results Based on ICRG			
Test whether coefficient are equal between Q_{20} and Q_{40}	Test whether coefficient are equal between Q_{40} and Q_{60}	Test whether coefficient are equal between Q_{60} and Q_{80}	Test whether coefficient are equal between Q_{80} and Q_{90}
$F(1913) = 0.12$	$F(1,283) = 1.78$	$F(1,283) = 0.14$	$F(1,283) = 1.34$
Probability $> F = 0.000$	Probability $> F = 0.000$	Probability $> F = 0.000$	Probability $> F = 0.000$
Quantile regression results based on WGI			
Test whether coefficient are equal between Q_{20} and Q_{40}	Test whether coefficient are equal between Q_{40} and Q_{60}	Test whether coefficient are equal between Q_{60} and Q_{80}	Test whether coefficient are equal between Q_{80} and Q_{90}
$F(1,477) = 1.50$	$F(1,477) = 0.12$	$F(1,477) = 8.14$	$F(1,477) = 3.10$
Probability $> F = 0.000$	Probability $> F = 0.000$	Probability $> F = 0.000$	Probability $> F = 0.000$

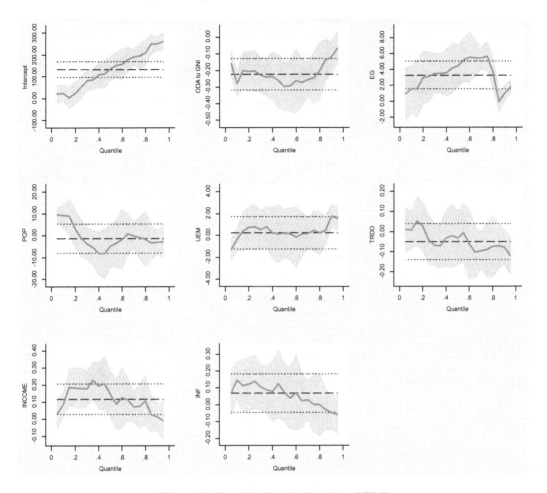

Figure 1. Quantile Graphs Based on ICRG

Furthermore, both figures ratify that the OLS estimates fail to estimate the nexus between aid flows and IQ for the institutionally developed countries and poor institutionally developed countries separately.

Figure 1 presents the regression lines derived by the quantile regression against the OLS methods. According to the ICRG dataset in Figure 1, there is marked variability between IQ across quantiles (0.20 to 0.90), suggesting that previous research on IQ, which is based on the approximation of the mean function of the conditional distribution, delivers an incomplete picture of the efficiency dispersion across countries. In particular, the nexus between aid and IQ is clearly different from conditional mean (OLS) critical level at the lower quantile (before 0.20) and upper quintile (after 0.80).

In Figure 2, the same trend is depicted where the nonlinearity is found before 0.20 quantile and after 0.80 quantile. This suggests that the quantile regression analysis clearly provides a more comprehensive picture of the underlying range of disparities in IQ that the classical estimation would have missed out.

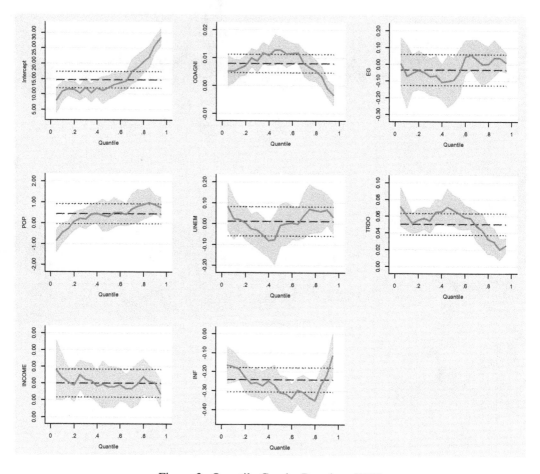

Figure 2. Quantile Graphs Based on WGI

5. Conclusions and Policy Implications

The nexus between aid and IQ is multifaced (Dijkstra, 2018). This study reviews the aid practices and IQ of Muslim countries. This study analyzes the nexus between the aid and IQ from three perspectives: firstly, the aggregate impact of foreign aid on IQ, secondly, the aid volatility and its effect on governance, and finally the nonlinearity of aid and IQ of the recipient countries. For the aggregate effect of aid on IQ, this study with help of system GMM tends to find that the overall impact of aid flows on IQ is negative. Specifically, aid flows appear to be associated with a deterioration in the political stability, corruption, government stability and other governance indicators. Aid volatility, the second focal point of this study has adverse effect on the IQ of the aid-dependent countries. The negative effect of aid volatility on institutions may increase through rent seeking and corruption. Finally, this study examines the nonlinear or heterogeneous relationship between aid and IQ by using quantile regression. The results tend to indicate that the nexus of aid and institutional development is contingent on the existing institutional capacity of the aid-dependent countries. The findings of this hypothesis suggest that a heterogeneous relationship exists between the strong and weak countries in terms of IQ. In most of the cases, the results suggest that the effect or magnitude of the negative impact of aid on IQ is manifested especially in countries with weak institutions rather than in countries with strong institutions. Most precisely, the findings broadly tend to indicate that the best and worst countries in terms of institutions respond differently to development assistance. The findings of this study contribute to the following policy implications: firstly, since the institutional impact of aid is not homogenous to all aid recipient countries and also, the nexus between the aid and IQ depends on the absorptive capacity of the countries, taking too much aid without improving the existing IQ may not be useful. Secondly, the donor and aid-receiving government or authority should try to maintain that aid flows are fairly steady so that the aid volatility is reduced. Government and policy makers should make sure a proper coordination and harmonization between the donor and the recipient parties for the aid distribution and management. Finally, as low institutionally developed countries are too weak or unscrupulous to judicially handle large aid flows, the donors and the governments should devote a high amount of support and resource to oversight and controls.

Although the findings of the study have a significant contribution to the literature of foreign aid and policy making but still this study is subject to some limitations. For example, this study concludes with the policies based on an overall impact of the foreign aid on the institutional structure of the recipient countries. As foreign aid is not evenly distributed across all parts of a recipient country, the clear-cut conclusion of its impact on institutional development may not be always accurate. In regard to this limitation, the reasoning, however, could be better established if the field survey data could be adopted. The future research could further explore and shed lights on it.

Acknowledgment

We would like to acknowledge the financial support kindly provided by MOHE-UM-INCEIF Islamic Finance Research Grant RPIF10-17INCEIF.

This paper is part of the first author's successfully completed Ph.D. dissertation. The authors are grateful to reviewers for their valuable comments which improved the quality of the paper immensely.

References

Afawubo, K and S Mathey (2017). The effectiveness of aid on savings and investment in Sub-Saharan Africa: Do volatility and institutional quality matter? *Applied Economics*, 49(51), 5212–5230.

Ahmed, SI (2006). Resurgence of Islam in Bangladesh politics. *South Asian Journal*, 11(1), 161.

Alaabed, A, H Askari, Z Iqbal and A Ng (2016). Benchmarking objectives of Shari'ah (Islamic law): Index and its performance in select OIC countries. *International Journal of Pluralism and Economics Education*, 7(3), 218–253.

Alterman, JB and K von Hippel (2007). Preface. In *Understanding Islamic Charities*. JB Alterman and K von Hippel (eds.), Washington: Center for Strategic and International Studies.

Amir-ud-Din, R (2014). 'Maqasid al-Shari'ah: Are we measuring the immeasurable?', *Islamic Economic Studies*, 22(2), 1–32.

Anjinappa, G (2015). Rule of law: A fundamental pillar enabling sustainable development and reduction of poverty in India. *International Journal of Asian Business and Information Management (IJABIM)*, 6(1), 38–50.

Arellano, C, A Bulíř, T Lane and L Lipschitz (2009). The dynamic implications of foreign aid and its variability. *Journal of Development Economics*, 88(1), 87–102.

Arellano, M and S Bond (1991). Some tests of specification for panel data: Monte Carlo evidence and an application to employment equations. *The Review of Economic Studies*, 58(2), 277–297.

Arndt, C, S Jones and F Tarp (2015). Assessing foreign aid's long-run contribution to growth and development. *World Development*, 69, 6–18.

Askari, H, H Mohammadkhan and L Mydin (2017). *Reformation and Development in the Muslim World: Islamicity Indices as Benchmark*. Berlin: Springer.

Askarov, Z and H Doucouliagos (2015). Aid and institutions in transition economies. *European Journal of Political Economy*, 38, 55–70.

Asongu, SA (2013). On the effectiveness of foreign aid in institutional quality. *European Economics Letters*, 2(1), 12–19.

Asongu, SA (2015a). On the dynamic effects of foreign aid on corruption. *European Economics Letters*, 4(1), 5–10.

Asongu, SA (2015b). Institutional benchmarking of foreign aid effectiveness in Africa. *International Journal of Social Economics*, 42(6), 543–565.

Asongu, SA (2012). On the effect of foreign aid on corruption. *Economics Bulletin*, 32(3), 2174–2180.

Asongu, SA and JC Nwachukwu (2016). Foreign aid and governance in Africa. *International Review of Applied Economics*, 30(1), 69–88.

Asongu, S and J Nnanna (2019). Foreign aid, instability and governance in Africa (No. 19/022). African Governance and Development Institute.

Baumol, WJ (1990). Entrepreneurship: Productive, unproductive, and destructive, *Journal of Political Economy*, 98(5), Part 1, 893–921.

Bellers, J (1993). Aiding their Moslim friends: Saudi Arabia's development policy. *Development and Cooperation*, 4, 28–29.

Booth, D (2011). Aid, institutions and governance: What have we learned? *Development Policy Review*, 29(s1), s5–s26.

Brautigam, D (1992). Governance, economy, and foreign aid. *Studies in Comparative International Development*, 27, 3.

Bräutigam, D (2000). *Aid Dependence and Governance*, (Vol. 1). Stockholm: Almqvist and Wiksell International.

Bräutigam, DA and S Knack (2004). Foreign aid, institutions, and governance in sub-Saharan Africa. *Economic Development and Cultural Change*, 52(2), 255–285.

Brazys, S (2016). Aid and governance: Negative returns? *The European Journal of Development Research*, 28(2), 294–313.

Bulíř, A and AJ Hamann (2008). Volatility of development aid: From the frying pan into the fire? *World Development*, 36(10), 2048–2066.

Busse, M and S Gröning (2009). Does foreign aid improve governance? *Economics Letters*, 104(2), 76–78.

Busse, M, R Hoekstra and RD Osei (2017). The effectiveness of aid in improving regulations: An empirical assessment. *South African Journal of Economics*, 85(3), 368–385.

Carnegie, A and N Marinov (2017). Foreign aid, human rights, and democracy promotion: Evidence from a natural experiment. *American Journal of Political Science*, 61(3), 671–683.

Charron, N (2011). Exploring the impact of foreign aid on corruption: Has the "anti-corruption movement" been effective? *The Developing Economies*, 49(1), 66–88.

Clarke, M and D Tittensor (2016). *Islam and Development: Exploring the Invisible Aid Economy.* UK: Routledge.

Coad, A and R Rao (2006). Innovation and market value: A quantile regression analysis. *Economics Bulletin*, 15(13).

Collier, P and A Hoeffler (2004). Aid, policy and growth in post-conflict societies. *European Economic Review*, 48(5), 1125–1145.

Dadasov, R (2017). European aid and governance: Does the source matter? *The European Journal of Development Research*, 29(2), 269–288.

Dalgaard, CJ and H Hansen (2001). On aid, growth and good policies. *Journal of development Studies*, 37(6), 17–41.

Degnbol-Martinussen, J (2002). Development goals, governance and capacity building: Aid as a catalyst. *Development and Change*, 33(2), 269–279.

De la Croix, D and C Delavallade (2013). Why corrupt governments may receive more foreign aid. *Oxford Economic Papers*, 66(1), 51–66.

Dijkstra, G (2018). Aid and good governance: Examining aggregate unintended effects of aid. *Evaluation and Program Planning*, 68, 225–232.

Djankov, S, JG Montalvo and M Reynal-Querol (2008). The curse of aid. *Journal of Economic Growth*, 13(3), 169–194.

Dunning, T (2004). Conditioning the effects of aid: Cold War politics, donor credibility, and democracy in Africa. *International Organization*, 58(2), 409–423.

Dutta, N and CR Williamson (2016). Aiding economic freedom: Exploring the role of political institutions. *European Journal of Political Economy*, 45, 24–38.

Ear, S (2007). Does aid dependence worsen governance? *International Public Management Journal*, 10(3), 259–286.

Feeny, S and M McGillivray (2011). Scaling-up foreign aid: Will the "Big Push" work? *The World Economy*, 34(1), 54–73.

Feeny, S, P Hansen, S Knowles, M McGillivray and F Ombler (2019). Donor motives, public preferences and the allocation of UK foreign aid: A discrete choice experiment approach. *Review of World Economics*, 155(3), 511–537.

Fielding, D (2014). The Dynamics of Aid and Political Rights. *The World Economy*, 37(9), 1197–1218.

Fielding, D and G Mavrotas (2008). Aid volatility and donor–recipient characteristics in "Difficult Partnership Countries". *Economica*, 75(299), 481–494.

Freytag, A and JC Heckelman (2012). Has assistance from USAID been successful for democratization? Evidence from the transition economies of Eastern Europe and Eurasia. *Journal of Institutional and Theoretical Economics JITE*, 168(4), 636–657.

Gibson, CC, BD Hoffman and RS Jablonski (2015). Did aid promote democracy in Africa? The role of technical assistance in Africa's transitions. *World Development*, 68, 323–335.

Goel, RK and MA Nelson (2005). Economic freedom versus political freedom: Cross-country influences on corruption. *Australian Economic Papers*, 44(2), 121–133.

Goldsmith, AA (2001). Foreign aid and statehood in Africa. *International Organization*, 55(1), 123–148.

Gujarati, D, DC Porter and S Gunasekar (2005), *Basic Econometrics*, 5th edn., Chennai: McGraw Hill Education (India) Private Limited.

Hansen, H and F Tarp (2001). Aid and growth regressions. *Journal of Development Economics*, 64(2), 547–570.

Harrigan, J and H El-Said (2009). *Aid and Power in the Arab World: IMF and World Bank Policy-Based Lending in the Middle East and North Africa.* Berlin: Springer.

Heckelman, JC and S Knack (2009). Aid, economic freedom, and growth. *Contemporary Economic Policy*, 27(1), 46–53.

Hudson, J and P Mosley (2008). Aid volatility, policy and development. *World Development*, 36(10), 2082–2102.

International Humanitarian Aid Report (2016). Available at: http://devinit.org/post/global-humanitarian-assistance-report-2016/.

International Humanitarian Aid Report (2017). Available at: http://devinit.org/wp-content/uploads/2017/06/GHA-Report-2017-Full-report.pdf.

Ishnazarov, D and N Cevik (2017). Aid effectiveness in OIC member countries: Beyond economics indicators. *International Journal of Economics, Management and Accounting*, 25(2), 315–336.

Islamicity Rankings (2017). Available at: http://www.heritage.org/index/].http://islamicity-index.org/wp/islamicity-rankings/, accessed March 31, 2017.

Isopi, A (2015). 18 Aid and corruption: An incentive problem. *Handbook on the Economics of Foreign Aid*, Edward Elgar Publishing Limited, p. 305.

Iulai, L (2014). Aid volatility: Is it a problem in Tuvalu? *Asia and the Pacific Policy Studies*, 1(2), 379–394.

Javed, O (2016). Determinants of institutional quality: A case study of IMF programme countries. In *The Economic Impact of International Monetary Fund Programmes*, pp. 7–35. Cham: Springer.

Jones, S and F Tarp (2016). Does foreign aid harm political institutions? *Journal of Development Economics*, 118, 266–281.

Juselius, K, NF Møller and F Tarp (2014). The long-run impact of foreign aid in 36 African countries: Insights from multivariate time series analysis. *Oxford Bulletin of Economics and Statistics*, 76(2), 153–184.

Kalyvitis, S and I Vlachaki (2012). When does more aid imply less democracy? An empirical examination. *European Journal of Political Economy*, 28(1), 132–146.

Kangoye, T (2013). Does aid unpredictability weaken governance? Evidence from developing countries. *The Developing Economies*, 51(2), 121–144.

Kathavate, J and G Mallik (2012). The impact of the Interaction between institutional quality and aid volatility on growth: theory and evidence. *Economic Modelling*, 29(3), 716–724.

Kaufmann, D, A Kraay and M Mastruzzi (2010). The worldwide governance indicators: A summary of methodology, data and analytical issues. World Bank Policy Research (No. 5430). Working paper.

Kersting, E and C Kilby (2014). Aid and democracy redux. *European Economic Review*, 67, 125–143.

Knack, S (2004). Does foreign aid promote democracy? *International Studies Quarterly*, 48(1), 251–266.

Knack, S (2001). Aid dependence and the quality of governance: Cross-country empirical tests. *Southern Economic Journal*, 68(2), 310–329.

Koenker, R and G Bassett (1978). Regression quantiles. *Econometrica*, 46(1), 33–50.

Koenker, R and KF Hallock (2001). Quantile regression. *Journal of Economic Perspectives*, 15(4), 143–156.

Lambsdorff, JG (2006). Measuring corruption — the validity and precision of subjective indicators (CPI). In *Measuring Corruption*, C Sampford, A Shacklock, C Connors and F Galtun (Eds.), pp. 81–100. Aldershot, UK: Ashgate.

Lancaster, C (2000). *Transforming Foreign Aid: United States Assistance in the 21st Century*. USA: Peterson Institute.

Lensink, R and O Morrissey (2000). Aid instability as a measure of uncertainty and the positive impact of aid on growth. *The Journal of Development Studies*, 36(3), 31–49.

Lensink, R and H White (2001). Are there negative returns to aid? *Journal of Development Studies*, 37(6), 42–65.

Menard, AR and L Weill (2016). Understanding the link between aid and corruption: A causality analysis. *Economic Systems*, 40(2), 260–272.

Mirakhor, A and H Askari (2017). Institutional structure of a sound economy. In *Ideal Islamic Economy*, pp. 119–137. Palgrave Macmillan, New York.

Mohamed, MR, SR Kaliappan, NW Ismail and WNW Azman-Saini (2015). Effect of foreign aid on corruption: Evidence from Sub-Saharan African countries. *International Journal of Social Economics*, 42(1), 47–63.

Moniruzzaman, M (2012). Foreign aid, foreign debt, and development: The muslim world scenario. In *The Muslim World in the 21st Century*, pp. 173–193. Netherlands: Springer.

Moore, M (2004). Revenues, state formation, and the quality of governance in developing countries. *International Political Science Review*, 25(3), 297–319.

Moss, T, G Petterson and N Van de Walle (2008). An aid-institutions paradox? A review essay on aid dependency and state building in Sub-Saharan Africa. In *Reinventing Foreign Aid*, W Easterly (ed.)., pp. 255–281. Cambridge, MA: MIT Press.

Moyo, D (2009). *Dead Aid: Why Aid is Not Working and How There is Another Way for Africa*. New York: Farrar, Straus and Giroux.

Nasir, M, FU Rehman and M Orakzai (2012). The nexus: Foreign aid, war on terror, and conflict in Pakistan. *Economic Modelling*, 29(4), 1137–1145.

Neumayer, E (2003). What factors determine the allocation of aid by Arab countries and multi-lateral agencies? *Journal of Development Studies*, 39(4), 134–147.

Okada, K and S Samreth (2012). The effect of foreign aid on corruption: A quantile regression approach. *Economics Letters*, 115(2), 240–243.

Prasad, M and A Nickow (2016). Mechanisms of the "Aid Curse": Lessons from South Korea and Pakistan. *The Journal of Development Studies*, 52(11), 1612–1627.

Quazi, RM and A Alam (2015). Foreign aid and quality of governance in developing countries: An econometric case study of South Asia and East Asia. *International Business Research*, 8(9), 16.

Rajan, R and A Subramanian (2007). Does aid affect governance? *The American Economic Review*, 97(2), 322–327.

Ravetti, C, M Sarr and T Swanson (2018). Foreign aid and political instability in resource-rich countries. *Resources Policy*, 58, 277–294.

Robinson, JA, R Torvik and T Verdier (2006). Political foundations of the resource curse. *Journal of Development Economics*, 79(2), 447–468.

Roodman, D (2009). A note on the theme of too many instruments. *Oxford Bulletin of Economics and Statistics*, 71(1), 135–158.

Sachs, J (2005). *The End of Poverty: How We Can Make It Happen in Our Lifetime*. UK: Penguin.

SESRIC Economic Outlook (2018). Available at: http://www.sesric.org/oicstat.php.

Svensson, J (2000). Foreign aid and rent-seeking. *Journal of International Economics*, 51(2), 437–461.

Tavares, J (2003). Does foreign aid corrupt? *Economics Letters*, 79(1), 99–106.

Tierney, MJ, DL Nielson, DG Hawkins, JT Roberts and MG Findley (2011). More dollars than sense: refining our knowledge of development finance using AidData. *World Development*, 39(11), 1891–906.

Ventelou, B (2001). Équilibres et stabilité de la corruption dans un modèle de croissance: l'effet de la rémunération des politiciens. *L'Actualit Économique*, 77(3), 339–356.

Villanger, E (2007). Arab foreign aid: Disbursement patterns, aid policies and motives. In *Forum for Development Studies*, Vol. 34, No. 2, pp. 223–256. Taylor & Francis Group.

Wako, HA (2018). Aid, institutions and economic growth in sub-Saharan Africa: Heterogeneous donors and heterogeneous responses. *Review of Development Economics*, 22(1), 23–44.

Yalta, AY and AT Yalta (2012). Does financial liberalization decrease capital flight? A panel causality analysis. *International Review of Economics and Finance*, 22(1), 92–100.

Young, AT and KM Sheehan (2014). Foreign aid, institutional quality, and growth. *European Journal of Political Economy*, 36, 195–208.

Chapter 10

The Investment Account Holders Disclosure Level in the Annual Reports of Islamic Banks: Construction of IAHs Disclosure Index[#]

Raoudha Saidani[*,‡], Neila Boulila Taktak[*,§] and Khaled Hussainey[†,¶]

[*]Institute of Advanced Business Studies (IHEC Carthage)
University of Carthage, Tunisia

[†]Faculty of Business and Law, University of Portsmouth, UK
[‡]saidaniraoudha@hotmail.fr
[§]neila_boulila@yahoo.fr
[¶]khaled.hussainey@port.ac.uk

This paper aims to measure the IAHs disclosure level in the annual reports of Islamic banks. To do this, we develop a specific IAHs disclosure index based on Accounting and Auditing Organization for Islamic Financial Institutions (AAOIFI) standards. We use manual content analysis of 49 full-fledged Islamic banks' annual reports over the period 2011–2015 across 10 countries. The findings of this study show that the overall level of IAHs disclosure is 28%. Indeed, the sampled Islamic banks provide fewer disclosures related to IAHs. This study contributes to enrich the knowledge of Islamic accounting literature by exploring directly the IAHs disclosure level in the annual reports of Islamic banks via self-constructed IAHs disclosure index based on AAOIFI accounting standards. It can help regulators in different countries to understand and strengthen the IAHs disclosure practices in Islamic banks by imposing AAOIFI disclosure requirements in terms of IAHs reporting.

Keywords: Investment account holders; Islamic banks; IAHs disclosure index; AAOIFI accounting standards; manual content analysis.

1. Introduction

The global financial crisis has led to a crisis in investors' confidence towards the conventional banking system and increased interest to the Islamic finance industry, in particular Islamic banks as they are recognized by their resilience during the financial crisis. Thus, transparent disclosures and relevant information stimulate the interests of investors in achieving better allocation of their funds and eventually to a better decision making. According to the IMF Working Paper of November (2002, p. 12) "Information disclosure is more important in an Islamic environment than it is in a conventional system because of the profit and loss sharing principle and the implied lack of protection for investment depositors which are at the core of Islamic banking". Investment Account Holders (IAHs)

[‡]Corresponding author.
[#]This Chapter first appeared in the *Singapore Economic Review*, Vol. 67, No. 1, doi: 10.1142/S0217590820420035. © 2022 World Scientific Publishing.

represent the main source of financing for Islamic banks and yet, they are not allowed to interfere in the management of their funds. Indeed, IAHs are not authorized neither to designate the board of directors, nor the members of Sharia Board and the external auditors (Al-Baluchi, 2006). Thus, disclosure of relevant information for IAHs in the annual reports of Islamic banks is very important, because it contributes to reducing information asymmetry and to protect the IAHs' rights.

It is in this sense that Islamic banks are expected to provide more relevant disclosures in their annual reports that the IAHs find useful. Previous studies have mainly focused on CSR disclosure, corporate governance disclosure, Sharia governance and compliance with Accounting and Auditing Organization for Islamic Financial Institutions (AAOIFI) Standards levels in Islamic banks (e.g., Maali et al., 2006; Haniffa and Hudaib, 2007; Hassan and Harahap, 2010; Farook et al., 2011; Ullah, 2013; Farag et al., 2014; Abdullah et al., 2015; El-Halaby and Hussainey, 2015; El-Halaby et al., 2017).

There are very few studies that include IAHs as one of the categories of their disclosure indices, such as corporate governance disclosure indices in Islamic banks (e.g., Abdullah et al, 2015; Srairi, 2015; Sulaiman et al., 2015). However, to the best of our knowledge, there have been no prior studies which investigate directly the level of IAHs disclosure in Islamic banks' annual reports through the development of a specific IAHs disclosure index. Therefore, this study contributes to fill this gap in existing Islamic accounting literature. According to Sarea and Hanefah (2013), the AAOIFI accounting standards may reflect the unique characteristics of Islamic banks. Since the IAHs are considered unique to Islamic banks, we developed a specific IAHs disclosure index based mainly on AAOIFI IAHs reporting standards to measure the IAHs disclosure level in the annual reports of a sample of 49 full-fledged Islamic banks over the period 2011–2015. This is the first study which investigates directly the extent of IAHs disclosure practices in the annual reports of Islamic banks using a self-constructed IAHs disclosure index based on AAOIFI accounting standards. Using manual content analysis, the findings indicate that the sampled Islamic banks provide poor disclosures in relation to IAHs (28%) as they disclose below 50% of the AAOIFI IAHs disclosure requirements. This study could enrich the existing literature on corporate disclosure and transparency in Islamic banks. It can also help regulators bodies in different countries to improve IAHs disclosure practices in Islamic banks by imposing the application of AAOIFI accounting standards.

The remainder of this paper is organized as follows. Section 2 presents the role of IAHs in Islamic banks. Section 3 provides the relevant literature review. Section 4 describes the research methodology. Section 5 presents and discusses the results. The robustness test is covered in Section 6 and finally Section 7 concludes the study.

2. The Role of IAHs in Islamic Banks

Islamic banks, like other financial institutions, need deposits to ensure their survival and functioning. According to AAOIFI Conceptual Framework (AAOIFI, 2010, p. 15) "an asset is a resource controlled by an IFI,[1] whether financed by owners or its investment

---

[1] Islamic Financial Institution (IFI).

account holders, as a result of a past transactions, event or condition which provides the IFI an enforceable right over the resource and gives it an economic benefit, present or future". This means that Islamic banks hold capital mainly from two categories of stakeholders, namely Shareholders and Investment Account Holders.

The investment accounts[2] are unique to Islamic financial institutions and defined as "funds received for the purpose of investment on a profit sharing or participation basis under Mudaraba arrangements" (AAOIFI, 2010, p. 15). The deposits are mostly collected from the IAHs which represent the main source of funds for Islamic banks compared to shareholders' funds (Al-Deehani et al., 1999; Al-Baluchi, 2006; Archer and Karim, 2009; Archer et al., 2010; Alshattarat and Atmeh, 2016). The investment account holders provide economic resources, usually cash, to the IFI for investment purposes with the expectation of receiving profits attributable after paying the IFI a share of the profit and a fee where relevant (AAOIFI, 2010, p. 15).

Furthermore, there are two types of investment accounts, namely unrestricted investment accounts and restricted investment accounts. The unrestricted investment account is considered by AAOIFI as on-balance sheet account where the investor fully authorizes the bank to invest the funds without restrictions as to where, how and what purpose the funds should be invested, given that funds in unrestricted investment accounts are commingled with the bank's own funds, whereas restricted investment account represent an off balance sheet account where the investor restricts the manner as to where, how and for what purpose the funds are to be invested (Abdul Rahman, 2010). Unrestricted investment accounts are often the most common accounts in Islamic banks. According to Van Greuning and Iqbal (2008, p. 195), "Unrestricted IAHs are the third and the most important category of Islamic bank accounts. They constitute the majority of deposits and are a characteristic feature of Islamic finance, posing distinctive challenges..." The authors added that "Unrestricted account holders usually enter into a Mudarabah contract with the Islamic bank, in which the Islamic bank manages their funds and pays a share of returns according to a predetermined profit- and loss-sharing ratio".

Accordingly, IAHs funds can be classified neither as liability nor as equity. Thus, they are presented as a separate item between liabilities and owners' equity in the statement of financial position of Islamic banks that adopt AAOIFI standards, whereas Islamic banks that adopt IAS/IFRS standards classified these funds as liabilities (Alshattarat and Atmeh, 2016; Sori, 2017).

Despite the status of IAHs as major stakeholders, they are not allowed to interfere in the management of their funds. Unlike the shareholders, IAHs have no voting rights and have not even the right of equal access to relevant information. Indeed, IAHs are allowed to designate neither the board members, nor the members of Sharia Board and the external auditors. In the last resort, they can withdraw their funds (Archer et al., 1998; Karim, 2001; Al-Baluchi, 2006). However, IAHs withdrawals are not beneficial to Islamic banks (i.e., Shareholders). Hence, the latter has an incentive to maintain a higher level of IAH

---

[2] Investment Accounts are also known under other names including Profit Sharing Investment Accounts (PSIAs), Profit Loss Sharing deposits, Mudaraba Investment Accounts or Mudaraba funds.

investment as a source of profits via the mudarib share. Nevertheless, IAHs should be protected from the risk of volatility in their returns at the expense of shareholders. Thus, the latter should sacrifice a part or his entire mudarib share of profits to smooth the returns paid to IAHs. This is known as displaced commercial risk and Islamic banks do their best to mitigate this risk through the use of two types of reserves, namely profit equalization reserve and investment risk reserve (Archer *et al.*, 1998; Archer *et al.*, 2010).

On the whole, IAHs have no representation on the board of directors, although they are of great importance as providers of funds to Islamic banks. Therefore, this category of stakeholders needs relevant information about the management of their funds in order to protect their rights and to reach better decision-making. This is why Islamic banks have to be transparent to their IAHs by disclosing essential information for them in their annual reports.

3. Literature Review

Despite the importance of the IAHs, there are very few disclosure studies in the Islamic banking industry that include IAHs as one of the categories of their disclosure indices and not as the overall disclosure index (e.g., Abdullah *et al.*, 2015; Srairi, 2015; Sulaiman *et al.*, 2015).

Al-Baluchi (2006) examined in his thesis a sample of 34 Islamic banks located in Bahrain, Qatar, Jordan and Sudan for the year 1997 (before implementation of AAOIFI Standards) and 2002 (after implementation of AAOIFI Standards) to explore the level of voluntary disclosure in the annual reports of Islamic banks. To measure the overall level of disclosure, he developed a voluntary disclosure index for the year 2002 based on AAOIFI standards, which mainly involves FAS1 and FAS5, FAS6 and FAS 11, and consisting of 104 items classified into four groups, being "Disclosure of general corporate information", "Disclosure of Reports", "Disclosure of financial information in the financial statements" and "Disclosure of information in the notes to the financial statements". The findings showed that the average voluntary disclosure level was 44%. In all, Al-Baluchi (2006) revealed that the level of voluntary disclosure increased after the implementation of AAOIFI Standards.

Abdullah *et al.* (2015) explored the extent of voluntary corporate governance disclosure of 67 Islamic banks in the SEA and GCC regions for the year 2009. Thus, they constructed a disclosure index based on the OECD Principles of Corporate Governance (2004), the Basel Committee on Bank Supervision (2006) Report, the AAOIFI Standards (2010), the IFSB guidelines, other standards and previous studies on corporate governance disclosures. Then, the index included a total of 81 items classified into 13 disclosure categories. The findings revealed that the average level of voluntary corporate governance disclosure is 37.01% with a low level of 35.86% related to disclosure on "Equitable treatment of fund providers and other significant stakeholders".

Moreover, Sulaiman *et al.* (2015) examined a sample of 16 Islamic Financial Institutions (IFIs) in Malaysia to determine the disclosure quality of corporate governance in their annual reports for the year 2009. For this purpose, they developed a corporate governance disclosure index, as a proxy for disclosure quality, based on the BNM guidelines (2007), Governance standards issued by AAOIFI (2008) and IFSB guidelines (2006) and consisting of 123 items grouped into 14 dimensions. Using content analysis, they found a corporate governance disclosure level of 51.42%. Their results also revealed that risk management committee disclosure is the most disclosed dimension of the disclosure index with a mean score of 85.16%, whereas, customers/IAHs information is the least disclosed dimension with a mean score of 2.68%.

Sraïri (2015) focused on 27 Islamic banks located in 5 Arab Gulf countries to investigate the impact of corporate governance disclosure level on bank performance. To measure the corporate governance disclosure level, he developed a disclosure index that contains 63 items classified into six major governance categories, namely board structure, risk management, transparency and disclosure, audit committee, Sharia supervisory board and investment account holders. Indeed, these disclosure items and categories were selected based on prior studies and international benchmarks such as the OECD guidelines (2004), corporate governance codes in the GCC countries, corporate governance standards promulgated by AAOIFI and the IFSB framework. Subsequently, he analyzed the content of the annual reports over the period 2011–2013 and he revealed a corporate governance disclosure level of 54% with Sharia governance information being the highest mean disclosure category (71%) and disclosures on IAHs being the lowest mean disclosure category (37%) of corporate governance disclosure.

In the light of the above, it seems obvious that the disclosures on IAHs represented low levels of corporate governance disclosure. In addition, Sulaiman *et al.* (2015) and Sraïri (2015) revealed that IAHs, as governance disclosure category, were the less disclosed category of their corporate governance disclosure indices.

In reviewing the literature, it seems that previous studies were mainly focused on CSR disclosure, corporate governance disclosure, Sharia governance and compliance with AAOIFI Standards levels in Islamic banks. The findings of most of these studies indicated low levels of disclosures and they were far below authors' expectations. However, to the best of our knowledge, no studies have investigated directly the level of IAHs disclosure in the annual reports of Islamic banks via the construction of a specific IAHs disclosure index using AAOIFI standards. Therefore, this study contributes to fill this gap in existing Islamic Accounting literature.

4. Research Methodology

4.1. Sample selection

The aim of this study is to measure the IAHs disclosure level in the annual reports of Islamic banks. Thus, we focused on secondary data which are the annual reports of Islamic banks. Indeed, the annual reports are considered as the only source in which essential IAHs information should be disclosed.

The sample consists of 49 full-fledged Islamic banks over the period 2011–2015 which involves 245 observations across 10 countries. Furthermore, the sampled Islamic banks were selected using the list of banks, which is presented in Islamic Banks and Financial

Institution Information database called "IBISONLINE" (www.ibisonline.net). It should be noted that the selection of our sample was based primarily on the Islamic banks' annual reports which are available on their official websites for the period 2011–2015. However, to ensure the homogeneity of our sample, we excluded Islamic banks that publish only interim or financial statements. Further, we excluded a number of Islamic banks that are not found in the Internet Site because they are closed or merged.

The AAOIFI standards 2010 edition is used in the current study. It is considered as the most recent available edition of AAOIFI standards. Therefore, it covered the sample period of the five most recent years (2011–2015) during the conduction of this study. This means that the year of beginning of the study is 2011 which is the year of application of the 2010 edition of the AAOIFI standards, while the year of 2015 is the year in which the last available annual report is found in the Islamic banks' websites during the conduction of the study.

4.2. Construction of the IAHs disclosure index

Self-constructed disclosure index as a measure of either level or quality of corporate disclosures has been well acknowledged in the accounting disclosure literature. It is used in a variety of corporate disclosure studies in general (for example, Cerf, 1961; Barrett, 1976; Cooke, 1989a; Botosan, 1997; Hassan, 2012) and disclosure studies in the Islamic banking industry in particular. Indeed, there are a number of studies that developed disclosure index through content analysis to evaluate the extent of disclosure within the annual reports of Islamic banks (e.g., Maali et al., 2006; Haniffa and Hudaib, 2007; Hassan and Harahap, 2010; Abdullah et al, 2015; Sulaiman et al., 2015; Srairi, 2015; El-Halaby and Hussainey, 2016). In this study, the level of IAHs disclosure corresponds to the level of disclosure of essential information oriented for IAHs in the annual reports of Islamic banks. Referring to these previous studies, it is also measured through the construction of a specific disclosure index. Thus, by following Hussainey (2004), the construction of our disclosure index involves the following steps.

4.2.1. Selecting the initial list of disclosure items

As aforementioned, there is no prior study relating directly to the extent of IAHs disclosure in the annual reports of Islamic banks through the construction of a disclosure index based on AAOIFI Accounting standards. However, there are a number of studies that include IAHs as one of the disclosure categories of their disclosure indices (Abdullah et al, 2015; Srairi, 2015; Sulaiman et al., 2015). Then, the first list of disclosure items was developed based on reviewing the relevant disclosure literature, AAOIFI accounting standards (FAS 1, FAS2, FAS 3, FAS 4, FAS 5, FAS 6, FAS 11 and GSIFI 6)[3] and based on the current practice in Islamic banks (pilot study). Indeed, we carried out a pilot study, to refine the list of items, by scoring 35 annual reports of 7 Islamic banks across 7 different countries for a period of five years (2011–2015). We used manual content analysis to extract relevant

---

[3] See Appendix B.

items related to IAHs issues from the selected annual reports. Then, five disclosure categories and 61 items in the IAHs disclosure index, which could be observed in the annual reports of Islamic banks, were initially selected.

4.2.2. Selecting the final list of disclosure items

As noted by Hussainey (2004, p. 49), "Different methodologies are applied in the literature to select the final list of disclosure topics. These methodologies include: (1) sending out questionnaires to the users of financial reports, (2) conducting interviews or (3) relating to recommendations provided by the accounting profession and accounting standards". In this study, the initial list of disclosure items was reviewed by two professors in Accounting having knowledge in Islamic finance and two accounting professionals, who are working in the Islamic banking industry. Then, after discussing with them and as a result of their recommendations, we made some amendments to the disclosure index to enhance its validity. Overall, a disclosure item was retained in the disclosure index if it was disclosed by at least one Islamic bank (Al-Baluchi, 2006). Accordingly, the final list of disclosure items consists of 53 items classified into three disclosure categories namely: (1) Investment Account Holders (27 items), (2) Products (Murabaha, Mudaraba and Musharaka) (23 items) and (3) IAHs Risk Management (3 items) (see Appendix A).

4.2.3. Scoring of the IAHs disclosure index

After developing the IAHs disclosure index and ensuring its validity, we proceeded to the weighting of the disclosure index. Indeed, an unweighted scoring approach is employed to examine the presence or absence of the IAHs disclosure items in the annual reports of Islamic banks. This method has been previously used by many researchers (e.g., Cooke, 1989b; Gray et al., 1995b; Al-Baluchi, 2006; Haniffa and Hudaib, 2007; Abdullah et al., 2013). According to them, the main reasons for not giving weights to disclosure items are that each item of disclosure is equally important and to avoid subjectivity. Indeed, weighted approach reflects the perception rather than actual information needs of the users of financial information (Al-Baluchi, 2006). In addition, since our disclosure index was developed using the AAOIFI accounting standards, the latter does not mention in its regulation if there are more important items than others. Thus, the unweighted scoring approach is more suitable for this study. In any case, it has been shown previously that regardless of the approach adopted (weighted or unweighted), the results of the two approaches are similar (Inchausti, 1997).

The measure of IAHs disclosure level is obtained by analyzing the content of the annual reports of each Islamic bank and for each year. Then, by using a dichotomous approach, each item is given a score 1 if it is disclosed in the annual report and 0 if it is not disclosed and the disclosure index score of each bank was then calculated as follows:

$$\mathrm{D\_IAHs}_{it} = \sum_{i=1}^{N} X_{ji}/N,$$

where D_IAHs_{it} is the Total IAHs disclosure score of Islamic bank i and for the year t, N is the Total number of items in the IAHs disclosure index (53 items),

X_{ji} is the equal to 1 if the item j is disclosed in the annual report of the Islamic bank i and 0 if it is not disclosed.

Subsequently, to determine the total index of the whole sample, individual scores were added together and that total was then divided by the total number of items, which summarizes the overall extent of IAHs disclosure in a single number (Hussainey, 2004).

4.3. Reliability of IAHs disclosure measure

Once the scoring method is assigned, we used manual content analysis to determine the extent of IAHs disclosure in the annual reports of all the sampled Islamic banks. According to Hussainey (2004, p. 53), "Traditional content analysis via manual reading is generally more effective than the computerized analysis in identifying certain themes in the texts". Indeed, it permits the quantitative assessment of achieved reliability (Beattie et al., 2004). However, this approach is not without criticism. Thus, it is extremely time-consuming process, specifically with the presence of large volumes of textual data. Furthermore, human coders could make mistakes during their analyses. They could overlook some text of relevant content, potentially affecting the validity of the measure (Hussainey, 2004). Weber (1990, p. 12) states that "To make valid inferences from the text, it is important that the classification procedure be reliable in the sense of being consistent: Different people should code the same text in the same way". It is then necessary to assess the reliability of the IAHs Disclosure measure. Reliability is defined by Neuendorf (2002, p. 112) as "the extent to which a measuring procedure yields the same results on repeated trials".

According to Krippendorff (2004a), there are three types of reliability for content analysis, which are stability, reproducibility and accuracy. He pointed out that reproducibility, which is defined as the extent to which different coders produce the same results when coding the same content, is the strongest measure of reliability.

Therefore, after completing the content analysis process, we designated an independent coder to review a sample of four Islamic banks for a period of 3 years (2013–2015), which represent a total of 12 randomly selected annual reports. First, we explained to the independent coder the purpose of our research and the disclosure categories and items included in the IAHs disclosure index. Second, we provided him some decision rules to replicate the coding process of the selected annual reports. Then, we compared the results obtained from the two coders (i.e., we compared both the total scores from the two coders) to ensure that the discrepancies between the coders are few, or that the discrepancies have been re-analyzed and the differences resolved (Milne and Adler, 1999).

In doing so, we used Krippendorff's alpha test, which is considered as the most appropriate measure of reliability in content analysis. Krippendorff (2004b) required an alpha ≥ 0.800 for acceptable level of inter-coder reliability with a minimum of 0.667 (Krippendorff, 2004b). In this research, Krippendorff's alpha coefficient is 0.836, which is widely acceptable since it exceeds the required minimum threshold of 0.667 and also above 0.800. We can say then that we have achieved a satisfactory level of reliability of the IAHs Disclosure measure.

Table 1. Correlation Among the Components of IAHs Disclosure Index

	IAHs Disc Level	IAHS	PRODUCTS	RISKMGT
IAHs Disc Level	1.0000			
IAHS	0.8888*	1.0000		
PRODUCTS	0.8379*	0.4992*	1.0000	
RISKMGT	0.5533*	0.5569*	0.3013*	1.0000

Notes: IAHs disc level: the level of IAHs Disclosure; IAHS: IAHs category; PRODUCTS: Products category; RISKMGT: IAHs risk management category.
* Correlation is significant at the 5% level.

On the other hand, Botosan (1997) highlighted the importance to assess the validity of the disclosure index. For that, he suggested four analyses, which are the correlation among the components of disclosure index, Cronbach's coefficient alpha, the correlation between disclosure scores and firm characteristics identified in prior studies to be associated with the level of corporate disclosures, and the correlation between the disclosure scores and the AIMR-FAF disclosure scores (Hussainey, 2004).

Thus, to check the validity of our IAHs disclosure index, we perform the correlation analysis between the IAHs disclosure level and the different categories of IAHs disclosure index (IAHs, Products, and IAHs risk management). (Botosan, 1997) supposed that the components of the disclosure index have to be positively and significantly correlated with one another to ensure the validity of the disclosure index.

Table 1 shows that all the categories of IAHs disclosure index are positively and significantly correlated with the IAHs disclosure level. Thus, the IAHs disclosure index is validated.

5. Results and Discussion

In this section, we analyze and interpret the results of IAHs disclosure index of the sampled Islamic banks during the period between 2011 and 2015. Table 2 presents the descriptive statistics. It indicates that the average of overall IAHs disclosure level is 28%. It means that the sample Islamic banks disclosed only 28% of the IAHs disclosure index, which is very low as they disclosed below 50% of the AAOIFI IAHs disclosure requirements. Then, it is evident that a very few number of the sample Islamic banks comply with AAOIFI accounting standards related to IAHs reporting.

Furthermore, it is observed that IAHs disclosure level varies from 4% to 74%. Thus, Al Baraka Islamic Bank (Bahrain) has the highest IAHs disclosure level (74% in 2011, 2012 and 2013) followed by Khaleeji Commercial Bank (Bahrain) (68% in 2014 and 2015), while both Alinma Bank (Saudi Arabia) and Boubyan Bank (Kuwait) have the lowest IAHs disclosure level (4%). The very wide range between the lowest and the highest IAHs disclosure level can be explained by the variety of standards adopted by those Islamic banks. Thus, both Alinma Bank and Boubyan Bank adopt IAS/IFRS standards, whilst Al Baraka Islamic Bank adopts AAOIFI accounting standards. Moreover, the table shows that

Table 2. Descriptive Statistics

Variable	N	Mean	Std. Dev.	Min	Max
IAHS category	245	0.264	0.211	0.000	0.778
PRODUCTS category	245	0.314	0.220	0.000	0.870
RISKMGT category	245	0.144	0.216	0.000	0.667
IAHs Disc level	245	0.280	0.182	0.038	0.736
Level of IAHs funds	245	0.416	0.251	0.000	0.794
AAOIFI	245	0.367	0.483	0	1
ROA	245	0.007	0.047	−0.303	0.246
SIZE	245	14.978	1.641	10.416	18.248
GDP growth rate	245	4.836	2.294	0.500	13.400
Inflation rate	245	4.038	2.844	−0.900	11.900

Note: N: number of observations; RISK MGT: Risk management; IAHs Disc level: Total IAHs disclosure level.

the standard deviation value is 0.182 which indicates that there are a large dispersion in IAHs disclosure level between the sample banks and the overall IAHs disclosure level deviate from the expected disclosure level (i.e., more than 50%).

In all, this result is far below our expectations given that IAHs, as the main source of funds for Islamic banks, have no way of knowing about the management of their funds except the annual report in which relevant IAHs information should be disclosed.

Regarding the disclosure categories included in our disclosure index, Table 2 reports that among the three disclosure categories, Products category has the highest disclosure level which is 31%, whereas IAHs Risk Management has the lowest disclosure level of 14%. This means that IAHs are more interested in products disclosure than other disclosures. This makes sense as IAHs may seek above all to maximize profit through investing in profitable products offered by the Islamic bank. As to IAHs Risk Management, the low level of disclosure is explained by the fact that Islamic banks do not disclose in their annual reports the risks or losses related to IAHs, especially to Unrestricted IAHs, which makes their investments very risky. Finally, as for IAHs category, the mean disclosure level is 26% which is very low. It means that the majority of the sample Islamic banks do not disclose enough information about IAHs disclosure practices.

Our results are similar to those of Srairi (2015) and Sulaiman *et al.* (2015) who found very low levels of IAHs index (as category of their governance disclosure index) (37% and 2.68%, respectively). Srairi (2015) noted that the sample banks do not disclose information about the risks and rights of IAHs, investment and asset allocation. Also, he noticed that there was a lack of information on the bases for profits allocation between shareholders and IAHs in the most of the GCC Islamic banks' annual reports. Sulaiman *et al.* (2015) also found the same results as Srairi (2015) regarding the lack of information on risk management issues in Malaysian Islamic banks' annual reports.

Table 2 also presents some descriptive statistics of our sample. It indicates that the average ratio of total IAHs funds to total assets for the whole sample is around 42% with standard deviation of 0.251. Furthermore, it is observed that IAHs funds level varies from a minimum value of 0 to maximum of 0.794. In addition, the descriptive analysis shows that only 37% of the sampled Islamic banks adopt AAOIFI standards. The majority of the sampled Islamic banks adopt IAS/IFRS and local standards (63%).

The average profitability measured by ROA is 0.007. The average size for the sampled banks measured by log total assets is 14.978. The values of bank size ranges from 10.416 to 18.248 with standard deviation of 1.641 which indicates poor dispersion within the sample. The average GDP growth rate in the sampled countries is 4.836% with standard deviation of 2.294%. There is a notable disparity in GDP growth rate from one country to the other, with a minimum rate of 0.5% and a maximum rate of 13.4%. Similarly, the average inflation rate of the sampled countries which measured by Consumer price index over the period from 2011 to 2015 is 4.038% with standard deviation of 2.844%. There is also a huge disparity in the inflation rate with the values ranging from −0.9% to 11.9%.

Table 3 presents the average IAHs disclosure level for each country. It can be observed that Qatar has the highest IAHs disclosure level of 55% followed by Jordan (51%), while Turkey, Saudi Arabia and Kuwait have the lowest IAHs disclosure level of 9%, 12% and 14%, respectively. This is consistent with the results of Srairi (2015) who found that Qatar achieved the first rank in IAHs disclosure category (40%), whilst Kuwait and Saudi Arabia had the lowest IAHs index scores of 34% and 36%, respectively.

Figure 1 shows the average IAHs disclosure levels over the period 2011–2015 and for each country for the whole sample. The results show insignificant differences between the five years. This means that there is no change in IAHs disclosure levels over the five years. This can be explained by the standard form (i.e., the same form of publication) of the annual reports published between 2011 and 2015. The change in IAHs disclosure levels is only observed between different countries. It can be explained by the variety of standards (AAOIFI standards, IAS/IFRS standards and Local standards) adopting by the sampled Islamic banks. This finding is consistent with El Halaby and Hussainey (2015) who suggested that the change in disclosure levels was based on adopted accounting standards.

Table 3. The IAHs Disclosure Level by Country

Country	N	Mean	Min	Max
Bahrain	13	0.366	0.109	0.709
Qatar	3	**0.555**	0.540	0.574
Jordan	2	0.506	0.408	0.604
UAE	4	0.353	0.264	0.426
Saudi Arabia	4	0.120	0.038	0.215
Kuwait	5	0.137	0.042	0.196
Turkey	4	**0.090**	0.075	0.094
Pakistan	3	0.260	0.208	0.313
Bangladesh	7	0.246	0.226	0.291
Malaysia	4	0.198	0.075	0.257

Note: N: number of banks.

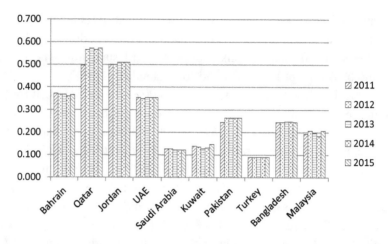

Figure 1. The IAHs Disclosure Levels by Year and Country for the Whole Sample

Table 4 shows that Jordan has the highest disclosure score related to IAHs category (64%) followed by Qatar and Bahrain (40% and 33%, respectively), while Saudi Arabia has the lowest disclosure score (7%). As for Products category, the highest disclosure score is achieved by Qatar (76%) followed by UAE (50%) and Bahrain (42%), whilst Malaysia scores the lowest (17%). Turkey does not disclose any information about products since the level of disclosure is 0%. Later, Qatar reaches the highest IAHs disclosure level relating to Risk management category (33%) followed by Bangladesh (29%) and Bahrain (25%), whereas Malaysia and Kuwait have the lowest disclosure score (8% and 1%, respectively). For the other countries, the table shows that there is no disclosure of IAHs risk management issues as the disclosure scores are 0%.

Table 4. The IAHs Disclosure Level by Country and Disclosure Category

Country	N	IAHS (%)	PRODUCTS (%)	RISK MGT (%)	Total IAH disc (%)
Bahrain	13	33	42	25	37
Qatar	3	40	**76**	**33**	**55**
Jordan	2	**64**	41	0	51
UAE	4	27	50	0	35
Saudi Arabia	4	7	20	0	12
Kuwait	5	11	19	1	14
Turkey	4	18	0	0	9
Pakistan	3	20	36	0	26
Bangladesh	7	28	20	29	25
Malaysia	4	24	17	8	20

Notes: *N*: number of banks; RISK MGT: Risk management; IAHs Disc level: Total IAHs disclosure level.

In all, although Bahrain is the country where AAOIFI accounting standards have been developed for Islamic financial institutions, it does not rank first in terms of all disclosure categories of the IAHs disclosure index.

Table 5 summarizes our main findings in terms of IAHs disclosure level by more details on the categories of the IAHs index (i.e., sub-categories). As indicated in the table, for IAHs category, General disclosure on IAHs has the highest disclosure score, which is around 39%. On the other hand, disclosures on Restricted IAHs have the lowest disclosure score of 10%. As to disclosures on Unrestricted IAHs, the overall disclosure score is around 30%. Regarding Products category, we find that Murabaha has the highest disclosure score of 53%, whilst Musharaka scores the lowest (21%).

As shown in Table 6, the IAHs Risk Management disclosure category is classified into three risk management practices that may attract IAHs interest, such as Restricted and Unrestricted IAHs risk management and Displaced Commercial Risk (DCR). Then, it appears that Unrestricted IAHs risk management practices are the most disclosed

Table 5. The IAHs Disclosure Level by Disclosure Subcategory

Categories	Sub-Categories	IAH Disclosure Level (%)
IAHs	General	**39**
	UIAHs	30
	RIAHs	**10**
	Total	**26**
Products	Murabaha	**53**
	Mudaraba	23
	Musharaka	**21**
	Total	**31**
RISK MGT*		14
Total IAH Disc		**28**

Notes: UIAHs: Unrestricted IAHs; RIAHs: Restricted IAHs; RISK MGT*: Risk management (see more details in Table 6); Total IAHs Disc: Total IAHs disclosure level.

Table 6. IAHs Risk Management Disclosure Index

Risk Management Disclosure	Total IAHs Disclosure (%)
RIAHs RISK Management	3
UIAHs RISK Management	24
DCR Management	16

information of the IAHs risk management index with a mean score of 24%, whilst Restricted IAHs risk management practices are the least disclosed information with a mean score of 3%. As for the DCR, it scores only 16% across the whole sample which indicates a considerable lack of disclosure on whether Islamic banks face the DCR. Further, we find only nine Islamic banks that disclose about the DCR. This is consistent with the results of Abdul Rahman et al. (2013) who found poor disclosure on the DCR by Islamic banks in the MENA region with a mean score of 3%. They noted that only 3 out of 20 Islamic banks disclosed the DCR as one of the risks they face.

Table 7 classifies the IAHs disclosure index into two main groups of Islamic banks namely banks that adopt AAOIFI accounting standards and those that adopt other standards (IAS/IFRS and local standards). Thus, it is evident that Islamic banks adopting AAOIFI standards achieve high IAHs disclosure levels (41%) compared to those adopting other standards (20%). This means that Islamic banks applying AAOIFI accounting standards disclose more information about IAHs practices issues than those applying other standards. This result is in line with that of Suandi (2017) who argued that applying accounting standards that do not take into account the specificities of Islamic banks leads to poor disclosures pertaining to Profit Sharing Investment Accounts (PSIAs) and noted that Islamic banks applying AAOIFI accounting standards present more comparable and transparent practices of accounting for PSIAs. This is also due to the fact that, unlike IAS/IFRS standards, the AAOIFI accounting standards may reflect the unique characteristics of Islamic banks (Sarea and Hanefah, 2013).

As the IAHs are considered unique to Islamic banks, those who adopt AAOIFI accounting standards should achieve greater levels of IAHs disclosure. Nevertheless, the IAHs disclosure level is still very low (41%) as the banks disclosed less than 50% of the disclosure items required by AAOIFI accounting standards. Then, it is observed that even Islamic banks applying AAOIFI accounting standards are not fully complied with these standards. This result is consistent with that of Al-Baluchi (2006) who found that some Islamic banks in Bahrain were not in full compliance with AAOIFI standards and with low voluntary disclosure levels. Similarly, this result is in line with that of Ajili and Bouri (2017) who found that Islamic banks in the GCC had not fully complied with all the IFRS and AAOIFI disclosure requirements. This can be explained by the fact that AAOIFI has no power to enforce the application of its standards on Islamic banks globally (Karim, 2001; Sarea and Hanefah, 2013). On the other hand, the results show that Islamic banks

Table 7. The IAHs Disclosure Level by Standards

Standards	N	Mean	Min	Max
AAOIFI	18	**0.413**	0.075	0.736
Others	31	**0.201**	0.038	0.434

Note: N: number of banks; Others: Local and IAS/IFRS Standards.

adopting other standards (i.e., Local and IAS/IFRS Standards) disclose 20% of the AAOIFI IAHs disclosure requirements. This indicates that there is a convergence movement towards the AAOIFI standards in these Islamic banks.

To sum up, as a result of our findings mentioned above, it seems obvious that the sampled Islamic banks have poor disclosures for IAHs. Thus, particular attention needs to be paid to IAHs reporting to boost IAHs confidence and avoid massive withdrawal of their funds.

6. Robustness Test

In order to check the robustness of the results of the IAHs disclosure index, we exclude the category of IAHs Risk Management as it consists only of 3 items, compared to IAHs and products categories (27 and 23 items, respectively), which may leads to biased results. Then, we compare the new IAHs disclosure index (without IAHs risk management category) with the previous one. The new IAHs index consists of 50 items classified into two categories which are IAHs and Products. The results indicate that the new IAHs disclosure index is 0.287 (around 29%) which is almost the same in comparison with the previous IAHs disclosure index (28%). Thus, we conclude that there is no significant difference between the two indices, which proves the robustness of our results.

7. Conclusion

Disclosure of relevant information for IAHs in Islamic banks' annual reports is very important since IAHs, despite their status as the main source of funding for Islamic banks, are not allowed to monitor or interfere in the management of their funds. Thus, they need transparent disclosures to protect their rights and to achieve better decision-making.

In this study, we investigate the extent of IAHs disclosure in the annual reports of 49 full-fledged Islamic banks over the period 2011–2015 and across 10 countries. For this purpose, we developed a specific IAHs disclosure index with three main disclosure categories and 53 items based on AAOIFI accounting standards.

Using manual content analysis, the results revealed that the overall IAHs disclosure level is 28% which is very low. Indeed, Qatar has the highest IAHs index score of 55% while Turkey scores the lowest (9%). It should be noted as well that Products disclosures are the most disclosed category of the IAHs index across the whole sample with a mean score of 31%, whereas the least attention is given to IAHs risk management disclosures which achieved a mean score of 14%. Interestingly, IAHs disclosure category and more especially, disclosures on Unrestricted IAHs have very low levels which are 26% and 30%, respectively. Therefore, we can say that Islamic banks give less attention to IAHs disclosure practices despite their great importance as providers of funds to Islamic banks.

Moreover, it can be observed that even Islamic banks that adopt AAOIFI accounting standards have not fully complied with AAOIFI disclosure requirements in terms of IAHs reporting. Hence, it is obvious that there are still great gaps between IAHs disclosure requirements and current practices. AAOIFI accounting standards should have been applied by all Islamic banks around the world with special regard to IAHs reporting. Thus, both AAOIFI and IASB should increase its efforts to harmonize the accounting practices of Islamic banks in order to achieve higher levels of IAHs disclosure in Islamic banks. Alternatively, regulators bodies in different countries around the world should impose the adoption of AAOIFI accounting standards for all Islamic banks to strengthen disclosure practices for IAHs. In other words, Islamic banks have unique characteristics that differ from their conventional counterparts, especially in the case of investment account holders. In addition, it has been shown that the latter is not treated by IFRS standards but it is taken into account by AAOIFI standards (Grais and Pellegrini, 2006; Hassan et al., 2019a). Thus, regulators should consider the uniqueness of IAHs in Islamic banks and their importance as major stakeholders. As a consequence, they should protect their interest by imposing the application of AAOIFI standards.

Moreover, as suggested in a number of the previous studies (e.g., Archer et al., 1998; Chapra and Ahmed, 2002; Grais and Pellegrini, 2006; Ghayad, 2008; Safieddine, 2009; Hamza, 2016), IAHs should be represented in the board of an Islamic bank to control the behavior of managers and protect their rights.

The unavailability of annual reports in the websites of several Islamic banks across different countries around the world is the main limitation of our study. As a consequence, our study covered only 10 countries and this makes the sample size very small in each country. Thus, the findings reported in the current study cannot be generalized. In spite of that, this study provides new insights on IAHs disclosure practices in Islamic banks. In addition to the content analysis of annual reports, future research may use a questionnaire survey administered to IAHs in measuring the extent of IAHs disclosure in order to better understand the information needs of IAHs. Also, future researchers could examine the new accounting standard FAS 27 "Investment Accounts" (AAOIFI, edition 2015) and replicate our IAHs disclosure index. The latter will be useful in future research on the determinants and consequences of IAHs disclosure in Islamic banks. Finally, to extend the sample size, future studies could cover other countries outside the GCC region, MENA, and Southeast Asia as highlighted by Hassan et al. (2019b).

Acknowledgments

We would like to thank the editor and the anonymous reviewers for their valuable comments and suggestions on this research.

Appendix A. IAHs Disclosure Index

Table A.1.

Categories	No	Disclosure Items	D	References
Investment Account Holders (IAHs)		*General Disclosures on Investment Account Holders*		
	1	Disclosure of the share of unrestricted investments in the profits (losses) of the period and the returns of each type of investment accounts and their rate of return.		Para 27, FAS 1, AAOIFI (2010)
	2	Bases of allocation of assets, expenses and profit in relationto IAH funds.		Annual reports and IFSB 4 (2007)
	3	Disclosure of the assets jointly financed by the Islamic bank and unrestricted investment account holders and those exclusively financed by the Islamic bank.		Para 37, FAS 1, AAOIFI (2010)
	4	The share of unrestricted investment account holders in the profit equalization reserve shall be presented under the equity of unrestricted investment account holders, and the share of the Islamic bank (in respect of the bank's profit sharing as mudarib) in this reserve shall be presented as part of reserve under owner's equity in the statement of financial position.		Para 22, FAS 11, AAOIFI (2010)
	5	The bases applied to determine Profit Equalization Reserve (PER) and Investment Risk Reserve (IRR).		Para 25, FAS 11, AAOIFI (2010)
	6	The changes occurred during the financial period in the PER and the IRR. The disclosure shall include the balance of each type of reserve at the beginning of financial period, additions, uses and recoveries during the financial period, and the balance at the end of the financial period.		Para 26, FAS 11, AAOIFI (2010)
	7	Off-balance sheet exposures arising from investment decisions, such as commitments and contingencies.		Annual reports and IFSB 4 (2007)
		Disclosures on Unrestricted Investment Account Holders		
	8	Magnitude of balances of all unrestricted investment accounts and their equivalent and other accounts by type in foreign countries.		Para 17, FAS 1, AAOIFI (2010)
	9	Distribution of unrestricted investment accounts and their equivalent by type in accordance with their respective periods to maturity.		Para 18, FAS 1, AAOIFI (2010)

Table A.1. (*Continued*)

Categories	No	Disclosure Items	D	References
	10	A disclosure of bases for profit allocation between owners' equity and unrestricted investment account holders.		Para 2, FAS 5, AAOIFI (2010)
	11	A disclosure of bases for charging expenses to unrestricted investment accounts.		Para 3, FAS 5, AAOIFI (2010)
	12	A disclosure of bases for charging provisions, and the parties to whom they revert once they are no longer required.		Para 4, FAS 5, AAOIFI (2010)
	13	Disclosure of the total administrative expenses charged to unrestricted investment accounts.		Para 5, FAS 5, AAOIFI (2010)
	14	Disclosure of the percentages for profit allocation between owner's equity and various unrestricted investment account holders.		Para 6, FAS 5, AAOIFI (2010)
	15	Disclosure if the Islamic bank has increased its percentage of profits as a mudarib, after fulfilling the necessary Shari'a requirements, during the financial period.		Para 7, FAS 5, AAOIFI (2010)
	16	At the end of a financial period, equity of unrestricted investment account holders shall be measured at their book value.		Para 5, FAS 6, AAOIFI (2010)
	17	Profits of an investment jointly financed by the Islamic bank and unrestricted investment account holders shall be allocated between them according to the contribution of each of the two parties in the jointly financed investment.		Para 6, FAS 6, AAOIFI (2010)
	18	Disclosure of the percentage of the funds of unrestricted investment account holders which the Islamic bank has agreed with them to invest in order to produce returns for them.		Para 15, FAS 6, AAOIFI (2010)
	19	Equity of unrestricted investment account holders shall be presented as an independent category in the statement of financial position of the Islamic bank between liabilities and owners' equity.		Para 16, FAS 6, AAOIFI (2010)
Disclosures on Restricted Investment Account Holders				
	20	Information on equity of restricted investment account holders shall be presented in the statement of changes in restricted investments and their equivalent or at the foot of the statement of financial position.		Para 17, FAS 6, AAOIFI (2010)
	21	A disclosure of bases for profit allocation between owners' equity and restricted investment account holders.		Para 11, FAS 5, AAOIFI (2010)

Table A.1. (*Continued*)

Categories	No	Disclosure Items	D	References
	22	A disclosure of bases for charging provisions, and the parties to whom they revert once they are no longer required.		Para 12, FAS 5, AAOIFI (2010)
	23	Disclosure of the percentages of profit allocation between owners' equity and restricted investment account holders.		Para 13, FAS 5, AAOIFI (2010)
	24	Assets and liabilities relating to equity of restricted investment account holders and their equivalent shall be treated separately from the Islamic bank's assets and liabilities.		Para 9, FAS 6, AAOIFI (2010)
	25	In the case of more than one type of restricted investment accounts in the form of investment funds or portfolios, the amount of each type shall be recognized separately.		Para 11, FAS 6, AAOIFI (2010)
	26	At the end of a financial period, equity of restricted investment account holders shall be measured at its book value (balance recorded in the books of the Islamic bank).		Para 13, FAS 6, AAOIFI (2010)
	27	In case the Islamic bank has funds invested in restricted investment accounts whether from its own equity or from other funds at its disposal, the Islamic bank shall share in the profits earned on such funds in its capacity as provider of funds.		Para 14, FAS 6, AAOIFI (2010)
Products (Murabaha, Mudaraba and Musharaka)		*Murabaha*		
	28	The assets possessed by the Islamic bank for the purpose of selling them on the basis of Murabaha or Murabaha to the purchase orderer shall be measured at the time of their acquisition on an historical cost basis.		Para 2, FAS 2, AAOIFI (2010)
	29	If the Islamic bank finds that there is an indication of possible non-recovery of the costs of goods available for sale on the basis of Murabaha or Murabaha to the purchase orderer who is not obliged to fulfill his promise, the asset shall be measured at the cash equivalent (i.e., net realizable) value.		Para 4, FAS 2, AAOIFI (2010)
	30	Short-term or long-term Murabaha receivables shall be recorded at the time of occurrence at their face value. Murabaha receivables are measured at the end of the financial period at their cash equivalent value i.e., the amount of debt due from the		Para 7, FAS 2, AAOIFI (2010)

Table A.1. (*Continued*)

Categories	No	Disclosure Items	D	References
		customers at the end of the financial period less any provision for doubtful debts.		
	31	Revenues and costs of goods sold shall be recognized at the time of concluding the sale contract, subject to the deferral of profits in 2/4/2.		Para 8, FAS 2, AAOIFI (2010)
	32	Deferred profits shall be offset against Murabaha receivables in the statement of financial position.		Para 9, FAS 2, AAOIFI (2010)
	33	The bank should disclose in the notes accompanying the financial statements whether it considers the promise made in the Murabaha to purchase orderer as obligatory or not.		Para 16, FAS 2, AAOIFI (2010)
	34	The disclosure requirements stated in Financial Accounting Standard No. 1: General Presentation and Disclosure in the Financial Statements of Islamic Banks and Financial Institutions should be observed.		Para 17, FAS 2, AAOIFI (2010)
		Mudaraba		
	35	Mudaraba financing capital shall be recognized when it is paid to the mudarib or placed under his disposition.		Para 3, FAS 3, AAOIFI (2010)
	36	Mudaraba financing transactions shall be presented in the Islamic bank's financial statements under the heading of "Mudaraba financing". Mudaraba capital provided in the form of non-monetary assets shall be reported as "non-monetary Mudaraba assets".		Para 6, FAS 3, AAOIFI (2010)
	37	Mudaraba capital provided in kind by the Islamic bank shall be measured at the fair value of the assets and if the valuation of the assets results in a difference between fair value and book value, such difference shall be recognized as profit or loss to the Islamic bank itself.		Para 8, FAS 3, AAOIFI (2010)
	38	Expenses of the contracting procedures incurred by one or both parties shall not be considered as part of the Mudaraba capital unless otherwise agreed by both parties.		Para 9, FAS 3, AAOIFI (2010)
	39	If the whole Mudaraba capital is lost without any misconduct or negligence on the part of the mudarib, the Mudaraba shall be terminated and the account thereof shall be settled and the loss shall be treated as a loss to the Islamic bank.		Para 12, FAS 3, AAOIFI (2010)
	40	Profits or losses in respect of the Islamic bank's share in Mudaraba financing transactions that commence and end during a single financial period shall be recognized at the time of liquidation.		Para 14, FAS 3, AAOIFI (2010)

Table A.1. (*Continued*)

Categories	No	Disclosure Items	D	References
	41	Disclosure in the notes to the financial statements for a financial reporting period if the Islamic bank has made during that period a provision for decline in the value of Mudaraba assets.		Para 19, FAS 3, AAOIFI (2010)
	42	Disclosure separately the assets jointly financed by the IFI and those exclusively financed by the bank.		Para 20, FAS 3, AAOIFI (2010)
		Musharaka		
	43	The Islamic bank's share in Musharaka capital shall be recognized when it is paid to the partner or made available to him on account of the Musharaka and shall be presented under "Musharaka Financing".		Para 3, FAS 4, AAOIFI (2010)
	44	Musharaka capital provided in kind by the Islamic bank shall be measured at the fair value of the assets and if the valuation of the assets results in a difference between fair value and book value, such difference shall be recognized as profit or loss to the Islamic bank itself.		Para 5, FAS 4, AAOIFI (2010)
	45	Expenses of the contracting procedures incurred by one or both parties shall not be considered as part of the Musharaka capital unless otherwise agreed by both parties.		Para 6, FAS 4, AAOIFI (2010)
	46	The Islamic bank's share in the constant Musharaka capital shall be measured at the end of the financial period at historical cost.		Para 7, FAS 4, AAOIFI (2010)
	47	The Islamic bank's share in the diminishing Musharaka shall be measured at the end of a financial period at historical cost after deducting the historical cost of any share transferred to the partner (such transfer being by means of a sale at fair value). The difference between historical cost and fair value shall be recognized as profit or loss in the Islamic bank's income statement.		Para 8, FAS 4, AAOIFI (2010)
	48	The Islamic bank's share of profits for any period, resulting from partial or final settlement between the Islamic bank and the partner, shall be recognized in its accounts for that period of the extent that the profits are being distributed; the Islamic bank's share of losses for any period shall be recognized in its accounts for that period to the extent that such losses are being deducted from its share of the Musharaka capital.		Para 12, FAS 4, AAOIFI (2010)
	49	Disclosure in the notes to the financial statements for a financial reporting period if the Islamic bank has made during that period a provision		Para 17, FAS 4, AAOIFI (2010)

Table A.1. (*Continued*)

Categories	No	Disclosure Items	D	References
		for a loss of its capital in Musharaka financing transactions.		
	50	Disclosure separately the assets jointly financed by the IFI and those exclusively financed by the bank.		Para 18, FAS 4, AAOIFI (2010)
IAHs Risk management	51	Risk management practices in relation to investments of restricted investments account holders' funds.		App. GSIFI No 6, AAOIFI (2010)
	52	Appropriate risk management measures in relation to fiduciary obligations of Mudarib (Unrestricted investments account holders).		App. GSIFI No 6, AAOIFI (2010)
	53	Displaced commercial Risk Management.		Annual reports
		Total score		

Note: **D**: 1 if the item is disclosed in the annual report and 0 if it is not disclosed.

Appendix B. List of AAOIFI Standards using in the construction of the IAHs disclosure index

Table B.1.

AAOIFI Standards	Description
FAS 1	General Presentation and Disclosure in the Financial Statements of Islamic Banks and Financial Institutions
FAS 2	Murabaha and Murabaha to the Purchase Orderer
FAS 3	Mudaraba Financing
FAS 4	Musharaka Financing
FAS 5	Disclosure of Bases for Profit Allocation between Owners' Equity and Investment Account Holders
FAS 6	Equity of Investment Account Holders and Their Equivalent
FAS 11	Provisions and Reserves
GSIFI 6	Statement on Governance Principles for Islamic Financial Institutions

Source: AAOIFI standards 2010 edition.

References

Abdul Rahman, AR (2010). *An Introduction to Islamic Accounting Theory and Practice*. Kuala Lumpur: CERT Publications.

Abdul Rahman, R, A Kighir, L Oyefeso and O Abdel Salam (2013). Risk management disclosure practices of Islamic banks in the Mena region: An empirical analysis. *Middle East Journal of Scientific Research*, 15(1), 152–160.

Abdullah, A, M Percy and J Stewart (2013). Shari'ah disclosures in Malaysian and Indonesian Islamic banks: The Shari'ah governance system. *Journal of Islamic Accounting and Business Research*, 4(2), 100–131.

Abdullah, A, M Percy and J Stewart (2015). Determinants of voluntary corporate governance disclosure: Evidence from Islamic banks in the Southeast Asian and the Gulf cooperation council regions. *Journal of Contemporary Accounting & Economics*, 11(3), 262–279.

Accounting and Auditing Organization of Islamic Financial Institutions(AAOIFI). (2008). Accounting, Auditing and Governance Standards for Islamic Financial Institutions No. 1 to 6. Bahrain: Accounting and Auditing Standards for Islamic Financial Institutions.

Accounting and Auditing Organisation for Islamic Financial Institutions (AAOIFI) (2010). Accounting, auditing and governance standards for Islamic financial institutions. AAOIFI, Manama, Bahrain.

Ajili, H and A Bouri (2017). Comparative study between IFRS and AAOIFI disclosure compliance: Evidence from Islamic banks in Gulf Co-operation Council countries. *Journal of Financial Reporting and Accounting*, 15(3), 269–292.

Al-Baluchi, AEA (2006). The impact of AAOIFI standards and other bank characteristics on the level of voluntary disclosure in the annual reports of Islamic Banks. Ph.D. Thesis, School of Management, University of Surrey.

Al-Deehani, T, R Karim and V Murinde (1999). The capital structure of Islamic banks under the contractual obligations of profit sharing. *International Journal of Theoretical and Applied Finance*, 2(3), 243–283.

Alshattarat, W and M Atmeh (2016). Profit-sharing investment accounts in Islamic banks or mutualization, accounting perspective. *Journal of Financial Reporting and Accounting*, 14(1), 1–31.

Archer, S and RA Karim (2009). Profit-sharing investment accounts in Islamic banks: Regulatory problems and possible solutions. *Journal of Banking Regulation*, 10(4), 300–306.

Archer, S, R Karim and T Al Deehani (1998). Financial contracting, governance structure and the accounting regulation of Islamic banks: An analysis of agency theory and transaction cost of economics. *Journal of Management and Governance*, 2(2), 149–170.

Archer, S, RA Karim and V Sundararajan (2010). Supervisory, regulation, and capital adequacy implications of profit-sharing investment accounts in Islamic finance. *Journal of Islamic Accounting and Business Research*, 1(1), 10–31.

Bank Negara Malaysia (BNM). (2007). Guidelines on Corporate Governance for Licensed Islamic Banks (GP1-i). Kuala Lumpur: Bank Negara Malaysia.

Barrett, ME (1976). Financial reporting practices: Disclosure and comprehensiveness in an international setting. *Journal of Accounting Research*, 14(1), 10–26.

Basel Committee on Banking Supervision (BCBS), (2006). Enhancing corporate governance for banking organisations. Paper, BCBS, Basel, Switzerland.

Beattie, V, B McInnes and S Fearnley (2004). A methodology for analyzing and evaluating narratives in annual reports: A comprehensive descriptive profile and metrics for disclosure quality attributes. *Accounting Forum*, 28(3), 205–236.

Berelson, B (1952). *Content Analysis in Communication Research*. New York: Free Press.

Botosan, CA (1997). Disclosure level and the cost of equity capital. *The Accounting Review*, 72(3), 323–349.

Cerf, AR (1961). *Corporate Reporting and Investment Decisions*. Berkeley: The University of California Press.

Chapra, MU and H Ahmed (2002). Corporate governance in Islamic financial institutions. Islamic Development Bank, Islamic Research and Training Institute, Periodical Document No. 6.

Cooke, TE (1989a). Voluntary corporate disclosure by Swedish companies. *Journal of International Financial Management and Accounting*, 1(2), 171–195.

Cooke, TE (1989b). Disclosure in the corporate annual reports of Swedish companies. *Accounting & Business Research*, 19(74), 113–224.

El-Halaby, S, K Hussainey and A Al-Maghzom (2017). Multi-disclosures in the context of national cultures: Evidence from Islamic banks. *Advances in Accounting Behavioral Research*, 20, 117–157.

El-Halaby, S and K Hussainey (2016). Determinants of compliance with AAOIFI standards by Islamic banks. *International Journal of Islamic and Middle Eastern Finance and Management*, 9(1), 1–21.

El-Halaby, S (2015). Accountability practices of Islamic banks: A stakeholders' perspective. Doctoral Thesis, United Kingdom, Plymouth University.

El Halaby, S and K Hussainey (2015). The determinants of social accountability disclosure: Evidence from Islamic banks around the world, *International Journal of Business*, 20(3), 202–223

Farag, H, C Mallin and K Ow-Yong (2014). Corporate social responsibility and financial performance in Islamic banks. *Journal of Economic Behavior & Organization*, 103, S21–S38.

Farook, S, MK Hassan and R Lanis (2011). Determinants of corporate social responsibility disclosure: The case of Islamic banks. *Journal of Islamic Accounting and Business Research*, 2(2), 114–141.

Ghayad, R (2008). Corporate governance and the global performance of Islamic banks. *Humanomics*, 24(3), 207–216.

Grais, W and M Pellegrini (2006). Corporate governance and stakeholders' financial interests in institutions offering Islamic financial services. World Bank Policy Research Working Paper 4053.

Gray, R, R Kouhy and S Lavers (1995b). Methodological themes: constructing a research database of social and environmental reporting by UK companies. *Accounting, Auditing and Accountability Journal*, 8(2), 78–101.

Hamza, H (2016). Does investment deposit return in Islamic banks reflect PLS principle? *Borsa Istanbul Review*, 16(1), 32–42.

Haniffa, R and M Hudaib (2007). Exploring the ethical identity of Islamic banks via communication in annual reports. *Journal of Business Ethics*, 76, 97–116.

Hassan, A and SS Harahap (2010). Exploring corporate social responsibility disclosure: The case of Islamic banks. *International Journal of Islamic and Middle Eastern Finance and Management*, 3(3), 203–227.

Hassan, MK (2012). A disclosure index to measure the extent of corporate governance reporting by UAE listed corporations. *Journal of Financial Reporting and Accounting*, 10(1), 4–33.

Hassan, MK, S Aliyu, M Huda and M Rashid (2019a). A survey on Islamic Finance and accounting standards. *Borsa Istanbul Review*, 19(Suppl 1), S1–S13.

Hassan, MK, S Aliyu and M Hussain (2019b). A contemporary review of Islamic finance and accounting literature. *The Singapore Economic Review*, S0217590819420013, http://doi.org/10.1142/S0217590819420013.

Hussainey, K (2004). A study of the ability of (partially) automated disclosure scores to explain the information content of annual report narratives for future earnings. Doctoral Thesis in Accounting, Manchester, University of Manchester.

IFSB 4 (2007). Disclosures to promote transparency and market discipline for institutions offering Islamic financial services (Excluding Islamic Insurance (Takaful) Institutions And Islamic Mutual Funds). Islamic Financial Services Board, Kuala Lumpur.

IMF Working Paper No. WP/02/192 (2002). Islamic financial institutions and products in the global financial system. International Monetary Fund.

Inchausti, BG (1997). The Influence of Company Characteristics and Accounting Regulation on Information Disclosed by Spanish Firms, *The European Accounting Review*, 6(1), 45–68.

Islamic Financial Services Board (IFSB) (2006). Guiding Principles on Corporate Governance for Institutions Offering Only Islamic Financial Services (Excluding Islamic Insurance (Takaful) Insitutions and Islamic Mutual Funds). Kuala Lumpur: Islamic Financial Services Board.

Karim, RAA (2001). International accounting harmonization, banking regulation, and Islamic banks. *The International Journal of Accounting*, 36, 169–193.

Krippendorff, K (2004a). *Content Analysis: An Introduction to Its Methodology*, 2nd edition. Thousand Oaks, CA: Sage.

Krippendorff, K (2004b). Reliability in content analysis: Some common misconceptions and recommendations. *Human Communication Research*, 30(3), 411–433.

Maali, B, P Casson and C Napier (2006). Social reporting by Islamic banks. *Abacus*, 42(2), 266–289.

Milne, M and R Adler (1999). Exploring the reliability of social and environmental disclosures content analysis. *Accounting, Auditing and Accountability Journal*, 12(2), 237–256.

Neuendorf, KA (2002). *The Content Analysis Guidebook*. Thousand Oaks, CA: Sage.

Organisation for Economic Co-operation and Development (OECD), (2004). OECD Principles of Corporate Governance, France.

Safieddine, A (2009). Islamic financial institutions and corporate governance: New insights for agency theory. *Corporate Governance: An International Review*, 17(2), 142–158.

Sarea, AM and MM Hanefah (2013). The need of accounting standards for Islamic financial institutions: Evidence from AAOIFI. *Journal of Islamic Accounting and Business Research*, 4(1), 64–76.

Sori, ZM (2017). Accounting conceptual frameworks: MASB vs. AAOIFI. Available at SSRN: http://dx.doi.org/10.2139/ssrn.2900666.

Srairi, S (2015). Corporate governance disclosure practices and performance of Islamic banks in GCC countries. *Journal of Islamic Finance*, 4(2), 1–17.

Suandi, AB (2017). Classification of profit-sharing investment accounts: A survey of financial statements of Islamic banks in Asia. *International Journal of Islamic and Middle Eastern Finance and Management*, 10(3), 351–370.

Sulaiman, M, NA Majid and NM Arifin (2015). Corporate governance of Islamic financial institutions in Malaysia. *Asian Journal of Business and Accounting*, 8(1), 65–93.

Ullah, H (2013). Compliance of AAOIFI guidelines in general presentation and disclosure in the financial statements of Islamic banks in Bangladesh. *International Journal of Social Science Research*, 1(2), 111–123.

Van Greuning, H and Z Iqbal (2008). *Risk Analysis for Islamic Banks*. Washington, DC: The World Bank.

Weber, RP (1990). *Basic Content Analysis*, 2nd edition. Newbury Park, CA: Sage.

© 2025 World Scientific Publishing Company
https://doi.org/10.1142/9789819813735_0011

Chapter 11

AAOIFI Accounting Standards and a Theory of Interest-Free Banking[#]

Assyad Al-Wreiket

Department of Accounting
Frostburg State University, USA

Ali Ashraf[*]

Department of Marketing and Finance
Frostburg State University, USA
aashraf@frostburg.edu

Ola Al-Sheyab

Department of Management
Frostburg State University, USA

M. Kabir Hassan

Department of Finance
University of New Orleans, USA

Ivan Julio

Boston University, USA

Based on the Accounting and Auditing Organization for Islamic Financial Institutions (AAOIFI) issued six new Financial Accounting Standards (FAS) in 2017, we derive the cost of financing formulas for various Islamic financing contracts. Later, we present a simple theoretical framework for interest-free Islamic banking based on the *Basic Limited-Participation Model* seminal approach developed by Lucas (Lucas, RE Jr. (1990). Liquidity and interest rates. *Journal of Economic Theory*, 50(2), 237–264.) and Fuerst's (Fuerst, TS (1992). Liquidity, loanable funds, and real activity. *Journal of Monetary Economics*, 29(1), 3–24.), and later followed by Walsh (Walsh, C (1998). Money in the short run: Informational and portfolio rigidities. In *Monetary Theory and Policy*, pp. 211–223. Cambridge, Mass.: MIT Press.). We compare the competing theoretical models for conventional banks and for interest-free Islamic banks and formulate testable hypothesis. To complement our models, we provide empirical evidence by using a unique sample of 15 banks from Bangladesh that provide both conventional banking and Islamic banking services. Results suggest that Islamic bank profit rates and conventional bank interest rates are correlated in an economic environment where conventional and Islamic banks dwell under same regulatory framework.

Keywords: Interest rates; financial institutions; banks; depository institutions.

---

[*]Corresponding author.
[#]This Chapter first appeared in the *Singapore Economic Review*, Vol. 67, No. 1, doi: 10.1142/S0217590819420074. © 2022 World Scientific Publishing.

1. Introduction

Over the last four decades, Islamic finance has evolved as a competent alternative and competitor to the traditional interest-based financial system. It has seen a phenomenal growth in predominantly Muslim countries and has expanded to western economies. Several factors contribute to the growth of Islamic finance. *First*, the discovery of oil and energy along with higher economic growth in emerging Muslim economies; *second*, due to religious preference, a segment of Muslim population remained unbanked and underserved, making this sector of the population an untapped source of funding; and *third*, research and innovation in Islamic finance as a response to an ever-increasing demand from customers.

Although the first traditional commercial bank is the Bank of England, established in 1694 A.D, the history of modern Islamic bank is rather recent, and it goes back to the first Islamic bank named Mit Ghamr bank in Egypt established in 1963, and the establishment of the Islamic Development Bank in 1975 (Asutay *et al.*, 2013). Since then, Islamic finance has evolved in terms of both size and scope over the last four decades, and expanded Shariah compliant products in different alternative investment classes: Shariah compliant mutual fund, equity vehicles, venture capital investments, Sukuks, and Takaful firms. Innovation in Islamic finance has played an important role in expanding its operations (Al Rahahleh *et al.*, 2019). The total size of Islamic finance industry increased from 150 billion USD in 1990s to over 1 trillion USD during the global financial crisis of 2007, and around $1.5 trillion dollar by 2013. In 2016, the total size becomes 2.2 trillion USD that includes: Islamic banks for 73%, Takaful for 2%, other IFIs for 6%, Sukuk for 16%, and Islamic funds for 4% of the total assets. Overall, average projected growth of Islamic finance assets is around 9.5% (ICD-Thomson Reuters, 2017). The number of operating Islamic financial institutions (IFIs) has also grown significantly from 270 in 2007 to 1407 in 2016. Besides, 44 countries have at least one type of Islamic finance regulations and 1075 scholars representing IFIs (IFSB, 2018).

The exuberant growth in Islamic finance over the last four decades has led to evolution of accounting rules, Shariah' standards and regulatory coherence in Islamic finance. In 1991, the Accounting and Auditing Organization for Islamic Financial Institutions (AAOIFI) started its journey in Bahrain based on the Agreement of Association signed by the leading IFIs. Currently, AAOIFI has members from more than 45 countries that include IFIs, and financial regulators. Since its initiation, AAOIFI has formulated and promoted Shariah standards, accounting rules for Shariah compliant contracts to ensure compliance of industry best practice in Islamic financial industry.

Three trends of academic research in Islamic finance literature are relevant to our research. *First*, early Islamic finance literature focus on the Shariah compliance financial contracts, the need for Islamic finance to help the economy growth process in general, and theoretical premises. *Second*, as Islamic finance matures over the last four decades, researches become more data-driven and focus on comparative performance of conventional and Islamic finance across the world. Although these two trends of research on Islamic finance are very rich, few papers present economic theory and mathematical models on Islamic banking. Bashir (1983) is a pioneer study on modeling Islamic banking; he identifies components of balance sheet components of Islamic bank and solve for optimal capital structure. Later, Khan (1986) extends from macro-economic model by Metzler (1951) to explain interest free banking system. A few other studies, like: Khan (1986) and Ahmed (2002), studies also focus on developing theoretical models on Islamic banks. Third set of literature in Islamic finance focuses on formulations of legal framework, AAOIFI standards and regulations.

We contribute to the existing literature of theoretical models and empirical research on Islamic finance in several unique ways. First, we derive the cost of financing for various Shariah compliant contracts based on the AAOIFI accounting standards. Second, this paper presents one of the early comprehensive theoretical models for Islamic banking. Third, we compare two alternate cases for Islamic banking and compare them with a model for conventional interest-based banking and derive testable hypothesis. Finally, we relate the theoretical models to existing empirical research on Islamic banking by analyzing a unique dataset of 15 banks from Bangladesh that provide both conventional banking and Islamic banking services. This dataset is unique for several reasons. First, Islamic windows deposit rates are not analyzed in the existing literature yet. Second, analyzing Islamic deposit rates and conventional deposit rates of the same banks allows us to control for the bank specific unique characteristics.

2. A Primer on Shariah Permissible Banking

2.1. *Prohibition of interest in Islam*

In traditional economic system, interest rate is considered as one of the fundamental tools that binds through the financial and economic ecosystem. Often defined as cost of fund, interest rates are used by the monetary authorities as tools to manage monetary policy by increasing or decreasing the monetary supply and demand. The idea of interest-free financial and economic system is not much appreciated in the conventional financial system, and many perceive that such an economic system may not work without interest rates.

On the contrary, Islam, as a religion, strictly prohibits dealing with interest rates. Islamic Shariah laws not only prohibits any use of Interest or *Riba*, it also prohibits use of *Gharar* (excess risk-taking) and *Maisir* (gambling), and any trade or dealing in non-permissible or Haram act or products, like: alcohol, drugs, pork, and other prohibited acts and products. This delineation of permissible (*Halal*) and non-permissible (*Haram*) acts and financial activities separates Islamic finance from the conventional finance.

2.2. *Shariah permissible financial contracts*

Islamic finance literature identifies three major types of Islamic financial contracts: (a) *Debt instruments*, (b) *Quasi-debt instruments, and* (c) *Profit-and-Loss (PLS) instruments* (Zaher and Kabir Hassan, 2001).

Debt Instruments comprise of *Murabaha* contract that is a purchase and resale contract where the Islamic bank purchase a physical asset on behalf of a customer and agrees into a predetermined price for reselling the asset to the customer. Another form of popularly used debt instrument is *Salam* that is a purchase contract with deferred delivery of goods, and in essence opposite to *Murabaha* contract; Islamic banks use *Salam* in agricultural financing. Besides *Murabaha* and *Salam*, other forms of debt contracts include: *Istisna* (a pre-delivery leasing instruments for long-term project financing), and *Qard-al-Hasan* (benevolent loan with no interest).

Quasi-debt Instruments include *Ijara contracts* that are similar to lease contracts in conventional secular financing and can be structured in several ways. In an *Ijara* contract, the Islamic bank buys and owns the physical asset and then leases the asset to the client during this process, Islamic bank bears the risks associate with ownership.

PLS Sharing Instruments capture the true essence and core values of an Islamic finance. *Musharaka* contracts are equity participation contract in which Islamic bank and the customer contribute to the project jointly and share the ownership of the project. Profits and loss are shared by both the parties as per pre-agreed terms and conditions, and usually at the pro-rata of ownership stakes. *Mudaraba*, on the other hand, is a financial contract set up in a trustee structure in which profits are shared by both parties at pre-agreed terms and conditions. However, the financing entity bears the losses except in the case of misconduct, negligence, or violation of the conditions agreed upon by the bank (Zaher and Hassan, 2001).

3. Literature Review

3.1. *Theoretical models on banking and Islamic finance*

Santomero (1984) is one of the early survey papers to summarize the literature on banking theory and identifies several seminal papers. Klein (1971) is the pioneer in presenting theoretical models for the banking firms; Klein model considers deposits as inputs and loans and investments as outputs for the banking firm, and analyzes the impact of regulations, controlling interest rates as a monetary policy tool, and others in the credit disbursement process. Later, Sealey and Lindley (1977) presents a representative agent model for financial institutions and solves for general equilibrium conditions for markets for deposit and securities. Much later, Walsh (1998) presents a model for banking based on a Basic Limited-Participation Model based on earlier works by Lucas (1990) and Fuerst's (1992).

Early literature on Islamic finance focused on the Shariah compliance issues, the theoretical and jurisprudential analysis of financial contracts. Khan and Mirakhor (1992) survey theoretical models in the Islamic banking literature until 1990 and find that only a few papers present theoretical models for Islamic banking. Bashir (1983) is one of the early papers to present a theoretical model for Islamic banks from the portfolio management perspective; he identifies balance sheet components of Islamic banks and their relevant costs and solves for the optimal debt-equity mix that maximizes stockholders' return using financial information of an Islamic bank in Sudan to calibrate the model.

Khan (1986) employs a modified canonical principle-agent model to explain interest free banking system based on Metzler (1951) *macro-economic model*. A contemporaneous work by Mirakhor (1987) analyzes the Tobin-Markowitz portfolio choices in an Islamic financial system. Later, Ahmed (2002) formulates a theoretical model for Islamic banks that considers: (a) an Islamic bank as a liquidity provider, and (b) an Islamic bank as an investment intermediary. Ahmed (2002)'s model integrates Islamic banking with broader macroeconomic structure where Islamic banks take part in a liquidity market and market forces determine demand and supply for liquidity and cost of funds.

In this paper, we use the Basic Limited-Participation Model proposed by Lucas (1990) and Fuerst's (1992), and later followed by Walsh (1998), and derive two competing models: one model for conventional banks, and another model for Islamic banks, and then analyze the implications of these theoretical models.

3.2. Empirical literature on Islamic banking

A large body of empirical literature investigates performance of Islamic banking across different cultural and geographic regions. Recent studies, Parashar (2010), Bourkhis and Nabi (2013), and Mollah *et al.* (2017) focus on comparative performances of Islamic banks and conventional banks. More recently, a trend of empirical studies focuses on Islamic bank risk taking and efficiency. Kabir and Worthington (2017) find evidence supporting the competition-stability/fragility nexus hypothesis by using both Islamic and conventional banks in 16 developing economies from 2000 to 2012 period. They find the effect of market power on stability is greater for conventional banks than Islamic banks. Later, Abuzayed *et al.* (2018) investigate diversification strategies for listed and unlisted conventional banks and Islamic banks in the Gulf Cooperation Council (GCC) countries from 2001 to 2014 sample period; they find that both types of banks can reduce risk through increasing levels of diversification. However, conventional banks are more adversely impacted by risks compared to their peer Islamic banks.

Hassan *et al.* (2019) present comparative analysis of liquidity risks of 52 conventional and Islamic banks from the OIC (Organization of Islamic Cooperation) countries for the period of 2007 to 2015. They identify a negative relation between credit risk and liquidity risk for both types of banks and find supporting evidence that Islamic banks generally manage risks better than conventional banks. An earlier study by Yanikkaya *et al.* (2018) uses dynamic panel data for a large cross-country dataset of conventional and Islamic banks between 2007 and 2013 and find that although Islamic banks prefer to use Murabah products, the use of PLS sharing products like: Mudaraba and Mushraraka products may reduce risk significantly. Several recent studies investigate relation between Shariah Supervisory Board (SSB) and corporate governance in Islamic banks. Safiullah and Shamsuddin (2018) study the composition of SSB and risk taking in Islamic banks in 28 countries. They find that Islamic banks generally have higher liquidity risk, lower credit risk, lower insolvency risk, and similar operational risk compared to conventional banks, and increase in SSB size and members' academic qualifications reduces operational and insolvency risks in Islamic banks. A contemporaneous study by Safiullah and Shamsuddin (2019) employs stochastic meta-frontier model to compare efficiency for conventional and Islamic banks and finds that Islamic banks are 4% more cost efficient but otherwise

17% less profit efficient; besides, stronger SSB generally improve Islamic banks' profit efficiency.

Other than Iran, Islamic banks and conventional banks co-exist under same regulatory and economic structure; Islamic banks compete with conventional banks in offering their products and services to their customers. Several recent studies find relation between Islamic banks profit and deposit rates with conventional interest rates. Chong and Liu (2009) find only a smaller segment of Islamic financing based on PLS contracts, and Islamic deposits are closely pegged with conventional deposit rates. Later, Ergeç and Arslan (2013) finds that, under a dual economic system, Islamic bank profit rates and conventional bank interest rates are correlated with each other. More recently, Cevik and Charap (2015) use time series data and Granger causality technique and identifies long-term cointegration between conventional bank deposit rates and Islamic banks' PLS Sharing investment account returns.

Our economic model provides a theoretical framework that shows the linkage and difference between interest-based conventional financial system and interest-free Islamic financial system.

3.3. AAOIFI standards and Islamic banking

The AAOIFI is a non-profit organization formed in 1990 to promote financial reporting according to the principles and rules of Shariah's rules across the globe. AAOIFI has released over 100 standards in the fields of Shariah jurisprudence, accounting, auditing, ethics, and corporate governance for Islamic finance. More recently, the AAOIFI (2017) releases new six Financial Accounting Standards (FAS) which provide guidelines for accounting and reporting principles for Islamic financing. For example:

1. FAS 28 for "Murabaha" & any deferred payment sales,
2. FAS 30 for Impairment and Credit Losses,
3. For investment AAOIFI created 2 standards:
   a. FAS 31 Agency Investment
   b. FAS 33 Investment in Sukuk Shares and Similar Instruments
4. FAS 34 Financial Reporting for Sukuk-holders
5. FAS 35 for Risk Reserves.

These standards are considered the best practice guidelines for accounting, reporting, and disclosures that IFIs may follow.

1. FAS 28 for "Murabaha" & any deferred payment sales

FAS 28 specifically deals with application and interpretations of definitions of Commodity Murabaha, control, deferred payment sales, inventory, fair value, Musawama, etc. Objective of FAS 28 is to report the principles for recognition, disclosures, and measurements of deferred payment transactions (Baydoun et al., 2018). It explains that an inventory is recognized at cost only when it is acquired i.e., the buyer has the complete possession of that inventory. Besides, the receivable is recognized on the face value and after the inventory is sold to the buyer according to the agreement between them (Sharairi, 2016).

2. FAS 30 for Impairment and Credit Losses

The main objective of the FAS 30 is to bring different impairment models under a single standard; it covers the topic of impairment, credit losses, and onerous commitment that were undefined before the introduction of this standard (Hassan and Mollah, 2018). This standard covers forward-looking impairment for different credit losses. It resolves the basic issues that financial analysts face due to the difference in accounting principles of IFRS and AAOIFI.

3. Two standards by AAOIFI for Investment

a. FAS 31 Investment Agency

FAS 31 explains the definitions and scope of the terms "Wakala", "Wakeel", and "Muwakkil" that are used for an agent. FAS 31 defines the concept of investment agency, obligations and related assets, and responsibilities and rights of the principle and the agent. Investments are managed through a pass-through investment vehicle or a Wakala venture (Hassan and Rashid, 2018).

b. FAS 33 Investment in Sukuk Shares and Similar Instruments

FAS 33 is another new standard introduced by AAOIFI. It provides the principles for the classification of different types of investments and covers the topics of Sukuk shares and related investments made by financial institutions. FAS 33 also identifies and defines different types of investments and their measurement, presentation, and disclosure rules that the IFIs should follow (Bhatti, 2018). FAS also elaborates on accounting treatment and disclosure of various investments to ensure a true and fair view of financial reporting for users.

4. FAS 34 Financial Reporting for Sukuk-holders

FAS 34 presents principles of financial reporting standards and accounting for Sukuk-holders in the financial statements of financial institutions (Habib, 2018). FAS 34 covers the definitions and standards for fair value, control and payoff structure of Sukuk, and special purpose vehicle; it makes accounting and financial reporting easier for auditors and financial analysts to determine the performance of an IFI. Under FAS 34, a Sukuk transaction is recorded if the consideration is paid or agreed to pay in the future; revenues and expenses related to Sukuk are recognized at cost when the contract between the parties takes place. Besides, presentation and reporting need to be done systematically to ensure transparency and fair view (Bhatti and Azmat, 2018).

5. FAS 35 for Risk Reserves

FAS 35 presents the standards related to the reporting and recording of various risks reserves. The primary objective of FAS 35 is to mitigate various risks that may affect the decision of its stakeholders located in different regions. It does not apply on statutory, regulatory, or other country risks that have no direct link with the financial reporting

(Baydoun et al., 2018). The beneficiaries of FAS 35 standard are participatory investors of IFIs, as it enhances the knowledge of stakeholders so that they can easily review the performance of an IFI (Sharairi, 2016). Commonly used measurement tools are: Internal Rate of Return (IRR), Profit Equalization Reserve (PER), and risk reserves. IFRS and GAAP also provide assessment and identification of various risks; AAOIFI FAS 35 clarifies risk reserve standards across countries are harmonized.

4. The Interest Free Banking Model

In this section, *first*, we formulate the cost of financing for most commonly used Sharaiah compliant Islamic financing contracts based on AAOIFI accounting and Shariah standard; *later*, based on these costs of financing formula, we build the theoretical economic model and derive equilibrium conditions.

4.1. *Cost of financing in Shariah compliant contracts*

1. Cost of financing of debt-based instruments

a. Cost of Murabaha financing:

The cost of Murabaha financing is the difference between the purchase price of the asset (or good) and the sales price; this represents the amount of profit that the Islamic Bank makes. The average cost of Murabaha financing is calculated using the following formula:

$$\text{ACM} = \frac{G_{SB} - C_m}{G_{SB} \times n},$$

where G_{SB} is the value of goods sold to customer by the bank; C_m is the cost of goods purchased by the bank and n is the number of periods. If we assume that $\mathcal{M}$: is the profit $= G_{SB} - A$; C_m: cost of financing by Murabaha $= \mathcal{M}$; n: the time for financing by *Murabaha*.

$$\begin{cases} A = C_m \times \text{ACM} \times n. \\ A = \mathcal{M}. \\ G_{SB} = C_m + \mathcal{M}. \end{cases}$$

In this transaction, the cost of *Murabaha* financing for the customer is the profit margin that the Islamic Bank (IB) receives. There are significant differences in terms of calculating the cost of *Murabaha* financing in IBs and the cost of financing loans in conventional banks. First, IBs provide financing against the commodity specified in the contract and this creates a link between the commodity and the cash. Second, Islamic finance does not allow a modification in the profit margin agreement under any circumstance. Third, in the case of default, while conventional banks still charge and accrue interests, IBs do not.

b. Cost of Salam financing

The cost of financing for the Salam contract is the difference between the present and the future item price; in other words, is the amount of difference between the price of the commodity at time t or spot, and the forward price of the commodity in $t + 1$. Then, cost of financing Salam contract becomes:

$$\text{ACS} = \frac{F - D}{D \times n},$$

where F: price of the goods, future; D: price of the goods, today; C_s: The cost of Salam $= (F) - (D)$; and ACs: Average cost of funding of the Salam.

c. Cost of Istsnaa financing

Recently, Islamic Banks (IB) and IFIs are using Istsnaa contracts frequently to finance different types of projects: housing, construction of buildings, plants, roads, etc., manufacturing of aircrafts, ships, machines, equipment, etc. Istsnaa is contract to purchase now, for a definite price, something that may be manufactured or constructed later according to agreed specifications (Zarqa, 1997). Cost of Istisna' is the difference between the price of the goods produced today and the price of the goods produced later, and average nominal cost (AC) can be written as:

$$\text{ACM} = \frac{F_{PM} - L}{L \times n},$$

where, F_{PM}: Futures price for "Musnna" manufactured products; L: the price of Musnna manufactured products; n: Istisnaa for years; C_i: The cost of Istsna'a. $= (F_{PM}) - (L)$; and AC_i: the average cost of funding Istsnaa.

d. Cost of lease financing (ending with ownership option)

Average cost of lease (ending with ownership) is based on the difference between the total rental value of the asset and the asset purchased in cash and can be written as follows:

$$AC_i = \frac{\sum_{i=1}^{n} L_i - A}{A \times n},$$

where, L_i: premium rent; A: Original purchase price in cash; n: the average duration of the lease; C_i: the cost of lease ownership; AC_i: average cost of lease ownership.

2. Cost of financing by participation in Profit and Loss sharing contracts

a. Cost of financing by participating in permanent capital project:

Islamic Banks (IBs) may take part in equity investments in the companies by buying ordinary shares in these companies. The cost of participation for the firms is the cost of the issuance of common stock owned by the IB. Here, the calculation of the cost of ordinary shares is similar as in the traditional banks and can be illustrated in the following relationship:

$$\text{COS}_p = \frac{R_i}{P_i - D} + g,$$

where, R_i: dividends in the year i; P_i: the share price in the year i; D: issue expenses and the distribution of profits; g: the expected growth rate; COS_p: cost of issued ordinary share. It also measures the cost of capital at the lowest rate of return to maintain the amount invested; it is also the cost of capital that is required to maintain the amount of capital in monetary units and the same purchasing power. Besides, this cost of participating capital also includes elements that may lead to a reduction and decrease the amount or value funds invested as follows:

- *Zakat*: The price varies according to the nature of money. Zakat deductions from funds to decrease the quantity. So, zakat is a cost for the IB.
- *Inflation*: Inflation is another component included in this cost of capital.

Then, the cost of capital at its minimal needs to include the rate of Zakat by the nature of the activity, and the inflation rate; hence, we have the following relationship:

$$M_r = Z + I,$$

where, M_r: minimum acceptable return; Z: percentage of Zakat funds by the nature of the activity; I: the rate of inflation. As, IB does not aim at just preserving the capital (original investment), we may add a premium to the Minimum acceptable to compute the cost of capital. Then, the cost of capital for the IB is given by:

$$C_p = M_r + X,$$

where, X: is the risk premium as measured by the standard deviation of return activity.

b. *Cost of financing to participate in any transaction*

In the financial contracts, Islamic Bank contributes up to a certain percentage of the value of the deal and the customer contributes the remaining value. When Islamic banks and customers enter the contracts, they also agree to what percentage the bank would receive from this deal; this represents the cost of financing for the customer. Average annual cost of which can be determined according to the following relationship:

$$\text{AAC}_i = \frac{D * P\%}{M \times n},$$

where, D: deal; $P\%$: percentage of participation in the bank as a result of the deal; M: the amount of the contribution of the bank in the transaction; n: duration in years; AAC_p: average annual cost to participate.

c. *Cost of financing for partnership ended Bittamleek*:

Islamic banks to participate in some of the projects ended Bittamleek gradually over time by paying a partner of the bank as part of its risk to turn ownership of the entire project for the benefit of the client. Thus, it is determined by the cost of participating ended Bittamleek by average annual cost of participation according to the relationship of the following:

$$\text{AAC}_B = \frac{\sum_{i=1}^{n} R_i}{M \times n},$$

where, R_i: the Bank's share of the profits in the year (i); M: the amount of the Bank's participation; n: duration in years.

d. Cost of Mudarabah financing:

The money provided by the employer as a capital project Mudarabah, and the required return is the same as the return to the capital of participation, they must not be less than the return of Mudarabah. To calculate the cost of Mudarabah, according to the relationship of the following:

$$C_k = M + X,$$

where, C_k: the cost of Mudarabah funds; M: minimum acceptable return; X: the risk premium.

4.2. Customer and banker relationships in conventional versus Islamic bank

There are several differences between customer and bank relationship in a conventional bank and in an Islamic bank; we recognize these differences as we build the models in latter sections.

4.2.1. Differences and similarities

The major difference between the conventional banks and Islamic banks is the way they deal with risk. While both conventional banks and Islamic Banks perform the role of intermediary and "trustee" of money of public, Islamic Banking prohibits the use of Riba, and rather depends on profit and loss and risk sharing.

Hasan *et al.* (2010) analyze the case of Kuwait Finance House (KFH) and show that Islamic banks are more stable compared to peer conventional banks. Beck *et al.* (2010) analyze bank risk taking during the global financial crisis of 2007, and find that during financial crisis, the Islamic banks keep more liquidity compared to the conventional banks, and the IBs performance is much better than conventional bank. Jaffar and Manarvi (2011) use CAMEL risk ranking for five Islamic Banks and five conventional banks of Pakistan over a period of five years sample period and find that the Islamic banking system is more efficient in sustaining Asset quality and Capital Adequacy as compared to conventional banking system. IBs profitability is positively related with their loans and equity. But there is significant no difference between the two types of banks when it comes to liquidity (Jaffar and Manarvi, 2011).

The global financial crisis has adversely affected conventional banking systems. Johnes *et al.* (2014) find that the Islamic Banks remain insulated from the financial crisis mostly due to the Shariaah's prohibitions on participations of conventional interest-based derivatives. However, recently, the practitioners and scholars of Islamic banking have introduced commodities that resemble conventional banking products yet involves the replacement of interest rate payments and contingent pay structures.

Islamic banking system faces various challenges due to the entrenchment of conventional banks and their popularity with the majority public (Ahmad and Saif, 2010). Unlike the conventional banking system, IFIs lack a supportive legal and supervisory framework. Besides, IFIs face additional challenges in: (a) working capital management, (b) capital budgeting, and (c) financing (Islam and Sultana, 2019).

Both types of banking systems play similar role in reducing informational asymmetric problems by producing information for clients and businesses; they aim at minimizing the transactional expenses by facilitating the diversification process for investors and savers.

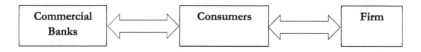

Note: (Authors, 2020)

Figure 1. Commercial Banking Model

The significant difference is that Islamic Banks strictly operate under the Shariah rules and regulations. Another key difference is how Conventional banks creates credit where they use money as commodity to create additional credits, and in the process liked with inflation. The IBs create credits by creating and holding underlying real assets; in the process, money is linked with the real assets leading to the contribution towards economic progress (Hasan *et al.*, 2010).

Before we progress towards our theoretical models, below we talk about the difference in customer-and-banker relationship in the two banking systems.

A. In commercial banks

In a commercial banking model, as shown in Figure 1, a customer contacts the bank and finds the goods that he or she likes to buy from the firms. The customer deals with the bank and the firm they purchase their good from; at the end of the day the bank will decide to finance the goods or not. The customer will be owning the goods after the bank finance that goods. The bank adds the interest in the top of the principle for the goods and the customer will make the payments to the bank. Thus, we can say that the customer will deal with two parties at the end.

B. In Islamic bank

For the Islamic banks, the story is different (see Figure 2). The customer goes to the Islamic bank and asks to finance the goods; the Islamic bank purchases that goods from the firm and then resales it to the customer for a profit higher than the purchasing price. The goods are now owned by the Islamic bank, not by the firm, when it is financed to the customer (Mervyn and Latifa, 2001). So, customer deals only with Islamic bank after purchasing the product.

4.3. *A basic model for conventional commercial bank*

First, we re-produce the *Basic Limited-Participation Model* seminal approach developed by Lucas (1990) and Fuerst's (1992), and later followed by Walsh (1998) for conventional banks. We assume that each household has number of members and all households remain identical in equilibrium, and define:

a. P_t: Price of the goods.
b. C_t: purchased consumption goods.

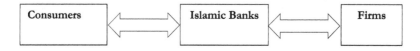

Note: (Authors, 2020)

Figure 2. Islamic Banking Model

c. M_t: household has money in the beginning of the period.
d. D_t: deposited in the bank (in nominal terms).

$$P_t C_t \leq M_t - D_t$$

N_t^s Labor work for the firms. To pay workers, firms must take out bank loans. N_t^d And, the purchase of goods is subject to cash-in-advance constraint:

$$P_t w_t N_t^d \leq L_t,$$

where, L_t: nominal bank loans; w_t: real wage. Firm profits, in nominal terms, is:

$$\pi_t^f = P_t Y(N_t^d) - P_t w_t N_t^d - R_t^L L_t,$$

where, $Y(N_t^d)$: Firm's production knowledge; R_t^L is interest rate on loans that bank charges; R^D is the rate banks agreement to take deposits from households and pay interest; R^L is the interest rate at Banks that create loans to firms. Also, the central bank makes transfers to banks. Then balance sheet of the bank is:

$$L_t = H_t + D_t,$$

H: central bank transfers. Now, the Bank Profits become:

$$\pi_t^b = R_t^L L_t + H_t - R_t^D D_t = (R_t^L - R_t^D) D_t + (1 + R_t^L) H_t.$$

As the bank maximizes profit, equilibrium suggests:

$$R_t^L = R_t^D \equiv R.$$

Thus, $\pi_t^b = (1 + R_t^L) H_t$.

Households (HH) choose D_t to make their financial portfolio, as central bank transfer H_t. In reaction to the monetarist injection, the households have no power to adjust their portfolio. After H_t Banks and firms are able to respond, the HH's budget constraint is:

$$P_t w_t N_t^s + M_t - D_t + (1 + R_t) D_t + [\pi_t^f] + [\pi_t^b] - P_t C_t = M_{t+1}.$$

As M_{t+1}: is household has money in the next period. After adding $[\pi_t^f]$, $[\pi_t^b]$, we have:

$$P_t w_t N_t^s + M_t - D_t + (1 + R_t) D_t + [P_t Y(N_t^d) - P_t w_t N_t^d - R_t^L L_t]$$
$$+ [(1 + R_t^L) H_t] - P_t C_t = M_{t+1}.$$

Then, divide all nominal variables by P_t.

$$w_t N_t^s + m_t - R_t d_t + Y(N_t^d) - w_t N_t^d + h_t + R_t l_t - C_t = \left(\frac{P_{t+1}}{P_t}\right) m_{t+1}.$$

m_t: real money holdings of the typical household. Then, the cash-in advance constraint turn out to be $C_t \leq m_t - d_t$ and the wage-in-advance constraint $w_t N_t^d \leq l_t$. Divided by P_t

In equilibrium, $d_t = \frac{D_t^s}{P_t}$; $m_t = \frac{M_t^s}{P_t}$; $h_t = \frac{H_t^s}{P_t}$; $N_t^s = N_t^d = N_t$; $l_t = h_t + d_t$.

Household's first choice over consumption and hours of work:

$$u(C_t) - v(N_t^s),$$
$$u_c, v_N \geq 0, \quad u_{cc} \leq 0, \quad v_{NN} \geq 0.$$

Then, the Household function can be written as:

$$V(m_t) = \max_d E\{[u(C_t) - v(N_t^s) + \beta V(m_{t+1})]\}.$$

And maximization subject to:

$$m_t - d_t \geq C_t,$$

$$w_t N_t^s + m_t - R_t d_t + Y(N_t^d) - w_t N_t^d + h_t + R_t l_t - C_t - \left(\frac{P_{t+1}}{P_t}\right) m_{t+1} = 0,$$

$$\omega_t N_t^s + m_t + R_t^D d_t + (1 + R_t^L) h_t + [Y(N_t^d) - \omega_t N_t^d - R_t^L l_t] - C_t - m_{t+1}\frac{P_{t+1}}{P_t} = 0$$

$$\text{and} \quad l_t \geq w_t N_t^d.$$

We assume λ_1, λ_2 and λ_3 as the Lagrangian multipliers related to the above three constraints. We identify that d_t is selected before the household knows the existing level of transfers. Later, it is chosen in the best or most favorable way. The first-order conditions for the most favorable way is selected of $d_t, C_t, N_t^d, N_t^s, l_t$ and m_{t+1} include:

$$[d]: E_h[-\lambda_{2t} + R_t^D \lambda_{1t}] = 0, \tag{1}$$

$$[c]: u'(C_t) = \lambda_{1t} + \lambda_{2t}, \tag{2}$$

$$[N_t^s]: -v'(N_t^s) + w_t \lambda_{2t} = 0, \tag{3}$$

$$[N_t^d]: \lambda_{2t} Y'(N_t^d) - w_t(\lambda_{3t} + \lambda_{2t}) = 0, \tag{4}$$

$$[l_t]: \lambda_{3t} - \lambda_{2t} R_t^L = 0, \tag{5}$$

$$[m]: -\lambda_{2t}\left(\frac{P_{t+1}}{P_t}\right) + \beta V_m(m_{t+1}) = 0, \tag{6}$$

$$[V_m]: V_m(m_t) = E_h[\lambda_{2t} + \lambda_{1t}]. \tag{7}$$

E_h prospects with detail to the distribution of h_t and is used to (1) and the envelope condition (7), as d is selected before knowing h_t. Then, λ_{2t} represents the marginal utility of income and can differ from marginal utility of consumption, and the value of liquidity in the goods and the loan market can be measured as multipliers λ_{1t} and λ_{3t}. Then, Subtracting Equation (2)–(5), we get:

$$\lambda_{3t} - \lambda_{1t} = [1 + R_t]\lambda_{2t} - u'(C_t). \tag{8}$$

Subtracting Equation (2)-(6)-(7)

$$\lambda_{2t} = \beta\left(\frac{P_t}{P_{t+1}}\right) V_m(m_{t+1}) = \beta\left(\frac{P_t}{P_{t+1}}\right) E_h u'(C_{t+1}). \tag{9}$$

Using (9), these last two equations can be readjusted as

$$u'(C_t) = \beta \left(\frac{1+R_t}{1+\gamma_{t+1}} \right) E_h u'(C_{t+1}) - (\lambda_{3t} - \lambda_{1t}), \qquad (10)$$

where $1 + \gamma_{t+1} = \left(\frac{P_{t+1}}{P_t} \right)$.

Now we know that $R_t^L = R_t^D$, this equation can be re-written as from (1) and (5):

$$E_h \lambda_{1t} = E_h[\lambda_{3t}].$$

After the household chooses its portfolio, it must be equal, λ_{1t} and λ_{3t} are the value of money transfer to the merchandises and the value of transfer to the loan by depositing it in a bank, respectively. As households cannot move funds between the periods, the two multipliers can vary. The labor market from (4) and (5) Labor demand condition:

$$Y'(N_t^d) = (1 + R_t^L) w_t.$$

The cost of borrowing funds to finance the firm's wage is greater than the real wage; the firm equates the marginal product of labor (MPL) to the marginal cost of labor. This creates obstacles between MPL and the real wage because of the nominal interest rate. Households cannot purchase consumption goods until period $t+1$ of wages earned in period t, from labor suppliers, wages earned in period t. From (3)

$$\frac{v'(N_t^s)}{\lambda_{2t}} = w_t.$$

Then, in equilibrium, $N_t^s = N_t^d = N_t$, and equal the two equations together from:

$$\frac{v'(N_t^s)}{\lambda_{2t}} = \frac{Y'(N_t^d)}{(1+R_t)}.$$

From this equilibrium, we find an interesting information, especially about how the nominal interest rate can be derived from the relation between the marginal rate of substitution and the MPL.

4.4. Model for Islamic bank

We extend the *Basic Limited-Participation Model* seminal approach developed by Lucas (1990) and Fuerst's (1992), and later followed by Walsh (1998) for Islamic banks by removing the interest rate from the model. In the following sections, we introduce two alternate cases for Islamic Banks.

Islamic Banking: CASE 1:

In this case, the Islamic bank gets a return on the loans based on a predetermined profit-&-loss sharing rate of α_t where $0 \leq \alpha_t < 1$. So, overall profits for the firm would be for example:

$$\Pi_t^f = (1 - \alpha_t) \tilde{\Pi}_t^f,$$

where

$$\tilde{\Pi}_t^f = P_t Y(N_t^d) - P_t \omega_t N_t^d$$

As firms take out bank loans to pay workers from an Islamic bank, banks nominal profit is:

$$\Pi_t^f = (1 - \alpha_t)[P_t Y(N_t^d) - P_t \omega_t N_t^d],$$

where: $Y(N_t^d)$ is the production function, L_t^i equals nominal bank loans, α_t is a predetermined profit/loss sharing rate by Islamic banks.

Another way to think about the profit/loss sharing rate is to realize that the $(1 - \alpha_t)$ is equivalent the amount of equity (profit share) given to the firm's manager and α_t is the fraction of "equity" retained by the bank (*see Proof 01 and Proof 02 in Appendix B for more*). Then, profits for the representative "Islamic" bank becomes:

$$\Pi_t^{ib} = \alpha_t[P_t Y(N_t^d) - P_t \omega_t N_t^d - L_t^i] - D_t^i + \alpha_t L_t^i.$$

Under the household's budget constraint:

$$\underbrace{P_t \omega_t N_t^s}_{\substack{\text{Income} \\ \text{from work}}} + \underbrace{(M_t - D_t^i)}_{\substack{\text{Money holding – deposits:} \\ \text{Money available to purchase} \\ \text{consumption goods}}} + \underbrace{(1 + R_t^D) D_t^i}_{\substack{\text{Income} \\ \text{from Deposits}}} + \underbrace{\Pi_t^{fi} + \Pi_t^i}_{\substack{\text{Household own} \\ \text{firm and banks,} \\ \text{so they get profits}}} = P_t C_t + M_{t+1}.$$

Now, within an Islamic banking setting we have no interest rate. So:

$$R_t^D = 0.$$

Thus,

$$P_t \omega_t N_t^s + (M_t - D_t^i) + D_t^i + \Pi_t^{fi} + \Pi_t^i - P_t C_t = M_{t+1},$$
$$P_t \omega_t N_t^s + M_t + \Pi_t^f + \Pi_t^i - P_t C_t = M_{t+1}.$$

From the profit function, we derive:

$$\Pi_t^{ib} = \alpha_t[P_t Y(N_t^d) - P_t \omega_t N_t^d - L_t^i] - (1 - \alpha_t) D_t^i + \alpha_t H_t^i,$$
$$\Pi_t^f = (1 - \alpha_t)[P_t Y(N_t^d) - P_t \omega_t N_t^d].$$

Substituting Π_t^{ib} and Π_t^f into the household's budget constraint, we get:

$$P_t \omega_t N_t^s + M_t + (1 - \alpha_t)[P_t Y(N_t^d) - P_t \omega_t N_t^d] + \alpha_t[P_t Y(N_t^d) - P_t \omega_t N_t^d - L_t^i]$$
$$- (1 - \alpha_t) D_t^i + \alpha_t H_t^i - P_t C_t = M_{t+1}.$$

Then, by Dividing by P_t, we get (*see Proof 03 in Appendix B for more details*).

$$\omega_t N_t^s + m_t - (1 - \alpha_t) d_t^i + \alpha_t h_t^i + [Y(N_t^d) - \omega_t N_t^d - \alpha_t l_t^i] - C_t = m_{t+1} \frac{P_{t+1}}{P_t}.$$

Under equilibrium:

$$m_t = \frac{M_t^s}{P_t} = \frac{M_t}{P_t},$$

where M_t^s is the nominal supply of money:

$$N_t^s = N_t^d = N_t.$$

Household's preferences over consumption and hours of work is given by:

$$u(C_t) - v(N_t^s),$$

where:

$$u_c, v_N \geq 0, \quad u_{cc} \leq 0, \quad v_{NN} \geq 0.$$

The value function for the household can be written as:

$$V(m_t) = \max_{d_t} E \left\{ \max_{\{C_t\}, \{N_t^s\}, \{N_t^d\}, \{l_t^i\}, \{m_{t+1}\}} [u(C_t) - v(N_t^s) + \beta V(m_{t+1})] \right\} \quad (1)$$

subject to:

$$C_t \leq m_t - d_t^i \quad (2)$$

$$\omega_t N_t^s + m_t - (1-\alpha_t)d_t^i + \alpha_t h_t^i + [Y(N_t^d) - \omega_t N_t^d - \alpha_t l_t^i] - C_t - m_{t+1}\frac{P_{t+1}}{P_t} = 0 \quad (3)$$

$$\omega_t N_t^d \leq l_t^i. \quad (4)$$

λ_1, λ_2, and λ_3 are the Lagrangian multipliers associated with these three constraints. Note that d_t is chosen before the household knows the current level of transfers.

$$h_t = l_t - d_t \rightarrow \underbrace{h_t}_{\text{transfer by central bank}} + \underbrace{d_t}_{\text{deposit}} = l_t.$$

E_h denotes expectations with respect to the distribution of h_t and is applied to envelope condition:

$$L(\cdot) = E_h \Big\{ [u(C_t) - v(N_t^s) + \beta V(m_{t+1})] + \lambda_{1,t}[m_t - d_t^i - C_t]$$

$$+ \lambda_{2,t}\Big[\omega_t N_t^s + m_t - (1-\alpha_t)d_t^i + \alpha_t h_t^i + [Y(N_t^d) - \omega_t N_t^d - \alpha_t l_t^i]$$

$$- C_t - m_{t+1}\frac{P_{t+1}}{P_t}\Big] + \lambda_{3,t}[l_t^i - \omega_t N_t^d] \Big\}.$$

Then, First Order Conditions (FOC) are:

$$d_t: E_h[-\lambda_{1,t} + \lambda_{2,t}\alpha_t] = 0 \quad (5)$$

$$C_t: u'(C_t) - \lambda_{1,t} - \lambda_{2,t} = 0 \quad (6)$$

$$C_{t+1}: u'(C_{t+1}) - \lambda_{1,t+1} - \lambda_{2,t+1} = 0 \quad (6')$$

$$N_t^s: -v'(N_t^s) + \lambda_{2,t}\omega_t = 0 \quad (7)$$

$$N_t^d: \lambda_{2,t}(Y'(N_t^d) - \omega_t) - \lambda_{3,t}\omega_t = 0 \quad (8)$$

$$l_t: -\lambda_{2,t}\alpha_t + \lambda_{3,t} = 0 \tag{9}$$

$$\beta V_m(m_{t+1}) - \lambda_{2,t}\frac{P_{t+1}}{P_t} = 0, \quad (10) \tag{10}$$

Envelope condition:

$$V_m(m_t) = E_h(\lambda_{1,t} + \lambda_{2,t}), \quad (11) \tag{11}$$

Now, one step ahead:

$$V_m(m_{t+1}) = E_h(\lambda_{1,t+1} + \lambda_{2,t+1}), \quad (11') \tag{12}$$

From Equation (5):

$$E_h[-\lambda_{1,t} + \lambda_{2,t}\alpha_t] = 0, \quad (5) \to E_h[\lambda_{1,t}] = E_h[\lambda_{2,t}\alpha_t].$$

From (9):

$$l_t: -\lambda_{2,t}\alpha_t + \lambda_{3,t} = 0, \quad (9) \to \lambda_{2,t}\alpha_t = \lambda_{3,t}$$

Then,

$$(5) \to E_h[\lambda_{1,t}] = E_h[\lambda_{2,t}\alpha_t] \to (5)$$
$$\to E_h[\lambda_{1,t}] = E_h[\lambda_{3,t}]$$

Using the earlier result that $R_t^D = R_t^L = R$ Equation (5), we can write:

$$E_h[\lambda_{1,t}] = E_h[\lambda_{3,t}].$$

Combining (6), and (9), we get:

$$(9) \to \lambda_{2,t}\alpha_t = \lambda_{3,t}$$
$$u'(C_t) - \lambda_{2,t} = \lambda_{1,t}, \quad (6)$$

Then, subtracting (6) from (9):

$$\lambda_{2,t}\alpha_t - u'(C_t) + \lambda_{2,t} = \lambda_{3,t} - \lambda_{1,t}$$
$$(1+\alpha_t)\lambda_{2,t} - u'(C_t) = \lambda_{3,t} - \lambda_{1,t}$$
$$u'(C_t) = \lambda_{1,t} + \lambda_{2,t}, \quad (6)$$

From equation (10) and envelope condition equation (11):

$$(10) \to \lambda_{2,t} = \beta\left(\frac{P_t}{P_{t+1}}\right)V_m(m_{t+1})$$

$$V_m(m_{t+1}) = E_h(\lambda_{1,t+1} + \lambda_{2,t+1}), \quad (11')$$

$$(10) \to \lambda_{2,t} = \beta\left(\frac{P_t}{P_{t+1}}\right)E_h(\lambda_{1,t+1} + \lambda_{2,t+1})$$

$$(10) \to \lambda_{2,t} = \beta\left(\frac{P_t}{P_{t+1}}\right)E_h(u'(C_{t+1}))$$

Now, introducing above expression into: $(1+\alpha_t)\lambda_{2,t} - u'(C_t) = \lambda_{3,t} - \lambda_{1,t}$

$$(1+\alpha_t)\lambda_{2,t} - u'(C_t) = \lambda_{3,t} - \lambda_{1,t}$$

$$(1+\alpha_t)\beta\left(\frac{P_t}{P_{t+1}}\right)E_h(u'(C_{t+1})) - u'(C_t) = \lambda_{3,t} - \lambda_{1,t}$$

$$\frac{(1+\alpha_t)}{\frac{P_{t+1}}{P_t}}\beta E_h(u'(C_{t+1})) - (\lambda_{3,t} - \lambda_{1,t}) = u'(C_t).$$

We define $\frac{P_{t+1}}{P_t} = (1+\pi_{t+1})$, where π_{t+1} is the increase in price level,

$$\frac{(1+\alpha_t)}{(1+\pi_{t+1})}\beta E_h(u'(C_{t+1})) - (\lambda_{3,t} - \lambda_{1,t}) = u'(C_t),$$

$$u'(C_t) = \frac{(1+\alpha_t)}{(1+\pi_{t+1})}\beta E_h(u'(C_{t+1})) - (\lambda_{3,t} - \lambda_{1,t}).$$

As household makes its portfolio choice, the value of sending money to the goods market (as measured by $\lambda_{1,t}$) and of sending it to the loan market by depositing it in a bank (as measured by $\lambda_{3,t}$) must be equal. Ex post, the two multipliers can differ, $\lambda_{1,t} \neq \lambda_{3,t}$, because households cannot reallocate funds between the two markets during the period.

$$u'(C_t) = \beta\frac{(1+\alpha_t)}{(1+\pi_{t+1})}E_h(u'(C_{t+1})) - (\lambda_{3,t} - \lambda_{1,t})$$

$$\frac{u'(C_t) + (\lambda_{3,t} - \lambda_{1,t})}{\beta E_h(u'(C_{t+1}))} = \frac{(1+\alpha_t)}{(1+\pi_{t+1})}$$

If $\lambda_{3,t} - \lambda_{1,t} = 0 \rightarrow \lambda_{3,t} = \lambda_{1,t}$

$$\frac{u'(C_t)}{\beta E_h(u'(C_{t+1}))} = \frac{(1+\alpha_t)}{(1+\pi_{t+1})}.$$

Now, turning to the labor market. Combining (17) (18) and (19) we get:

$$Y'(N_t^d) = \omega_t(1+\alpha_t)$$

$$\rightarrow Y'(N_t^d) = \underbrace{\overbrace{\omega_t}^{\text{real wage}} + \omega_t\alpha_t}_{\text{Marginal cost of labor}}.$$

Firm equates the MPL to the marginal cost of labor, but this is greater than the real wage because of the cost of borrowing funds to finance the firm's wage bill (*see Proof 04 in Appendix B for more*).

$$N_t^s: -v'(N_t^s) + \lambda_{2,t}\omega_t = 0,$$

$$N_t^d: \lambda_{2,t}(Y'(N_t^d) - \omega_t) - \lambda_{3,t}\omega_t = 0,$$

$$N_t^s: -v'(N_t^s) + \lambda_{2,t}\omega_t = 0, \quad (7) \rightarrow v'(N_t^s) = \lambda_{2,t}\omega_t$$

$$N_t^s = N_t^d = N_t$$

$$(7) \rightarrow v'(N_t) = \lambda_{2,t}\omega_t \rightarrow \frac{v'(N_t)}{\lambda_{2,t}} = \omega_t$$

$$Y'(N_t^d) = \omega_t(1+\alpha_t)$$

Intro (7):

$$\rightarrow Y'(N_t) = \frac{v'(N_t)}{\lambda_{2,t}}(1+\alpha_t)$$

$$\frac{v'(N_t)}{\lambda_{2,t}} = \frac{Y'(N_t)}{(1+\alpha_t)}$$

Here, α_t is a predetermined fraction of the firm's net revenue (revenue from selling output minus the original loan). Let us call it the **profit sharing percentage** required by banks to lend the money,

$$\frac{v'(N_t)}{\lambda_{2,t}} = \frac{Y'(N_t)}{(1+\alpha_t)}.$$

This reveals how "the profit-sharing rule" drives a wedge between the marginal rate of substitution and the MPL. Since the injection is received initially by banks, it increases the supply of loans $D_t + H_t$ because D_t is predetermined by the household's portfolio choice. Equilibrium requires a rise in loan demand, and this is induced by a fall in the **profit-sharing percentage** required by banks to lend the money.

$$Y'(N_t^d) = \omega_t(1+\alpha_t)$$

the fall in α_t increases the demand for labor at each real wage (decreases the marginal productivity of labor).

Islamic Banking: CASE 2:

In this case, before output is realized the firm borrows money from the Islamic bank to pay workers and agree to payback a fixed amount, x, which is the result of a markup applied by the Islamic bank.

$$x = (1+\theta_t)L_t.$$

Firm profits (if firms must take out bank loans to pay workers from an Islamic bank) expressed in nominal terms, are (*see Proof 05 in Appendix B for more*):

$$\Pi_t^f = P_t Y(N_t^d) - P_t \omega_t N_t^d - \theta_t L_t,$$

where:
$Y(N_t^d)$ is the production function.
L_t^i equals nominal bank loans.
θ_t is the markup applied by the Islamic bank.

Profits for the representative "Islamic" bank are:

$$\Pi_t^b = (1+\theta_t)H_t^i + \theta_t D_t^i,$$

where θ_t is a predetermined markup charged by the Islamic bank (*see Proof 06 in Appendix B for more details*). The household's budget constraint

$$\underbrace{P_t\omega_t N_t^s}_{\substack{\text{Income}\\\text{from work}}} + \underbrace{(M_t - D_t^i)}_{\substack{\text{Money holding – deposits:}\\\text{Money available to purchase}\\\text{consumption goods}}} + \underbrace{(1+R_t^D)D_t^i}_{\substack{\text{Income}\\\text{from Deposits}}} + \underbrace{\Pi_t^{fi} + \Pi_t^i}_{\substack{\text{Household own}\\\text{firm and banks,}\\\text{so they get profits}}} = P_t C_t + M_{t+1}$$

within an Islamic banking setting we have:

$$R_t^D = 0,$$
$$\Pi_t^b = (1+\theta_t)H_t^i + \theta_t D_t^i,$$
$$\Pi_t^f = P_t Y(N_t^d) - P_t\omega_t N_t^d - \theta_t L_t.$$

Substituting Π_t^{ib} and Π_t^f into the household's budget constraint, we have (*Refer to Proof 07 in Appendix for more details*):

$$\omega_t N_t^s + m_t + \theta_t d_t^i + (1+\theta_t)h_t^i + [Y(N_t^d) - \omega_t N_t^d - \theta_t l_t^i] - C_t = m_{t+1}\frac{P_{t+1}}{P_t}.$$

Equilibrium:

$$m_t = \frac{M_t^s}{P_t} = \frac{M_t}{P_t},$$

where M_t^s is the nominal supply of money:

$$N_t^s = N_t^d = N_t.$$

Household's preferences over consumption and hours of work be given by:

$$u(C_t) - v(N_t^s),$$

where:

$$u_c, v_N \geq 0, \quad u_{cc} \leq 0, \quad v_{NN} \geq 0.$$

The value function for the household can be written as

$$V(m_t) = \max_{d_t} E\left\{\max_{\{C_t\},\{N_t^s\},\{N_t^d\},\{l_t^i\},\{m_{t+1}\}} [u(C_t) - v(N_t^s) + \beta V(m_{t+1})]\right\} \qquad (1)$$

subject to:

$$C_t \leq m_t - d_t^i \qquad (2)$$

$$\omega_t N_t^s + m_t + \theta_t d_t^i + (1+\theta_t)h_t^i + [Y(N_t^d) - \omega_t N_t^d - \theta_t l_t^i] - C_t - m_{t+1}\frac{P_{t+1}}{P_t} = 0 \qquad (3)$$

$$\omega_t N_t^d \leq l_t^i \qquad (4)$$

Let λ_1, λ_2 and λ_3 be the Lagrangian multipliers associated with these three constraints. Note that d_t is chosen before the household knows the current level of transfers and so must be picked based on expectations but knowing the other variables will subsequently be chosen optimally

$$h_t = l_t - d_t \rightarrow \underbrace{h_t}_{\text{transfer by central bank}} + \underbrace{d_t}_{\text{deposit}} = l_t.$$

E_h denotes expectations with respect to the distribution of h_t and is applied to envelope condition:

$$L(\cdot) = E_h \Big\{ [u(C_t) - v(N_t^s) + \beta V(m_{t+1})] + \lambda_{1,t}[m_t - d_t^i - C_t]$$

$$+ \lambda_{2,t} \Big[\omega_t N_t^s + m_t + \theta_t d_t^i + (1+\theta_t) h_t^i + [Y(N_t^d) - \omega_t N_t^d - \theta_t l_t^i]$$

$$- C_t - m_{t+1} \frac{P_{t+1}}{P_t} \Big] + \lambda_{3,t}[l_t^i - \omega_t N_t^d] \Big\}$$

FOC:

$$d_t: E_h[-\lambda_{1,t} + \lambda_{2,t}\theta_t] = 0, \tag{5}$$

$$C_t: u'(C_t) - \lambda_{1,t} - \lambda_{2,t} = 0, \tag{6}$$

$$C_{t+1}: u'(C_{t+1}) - \lambda_{1,t+1} - \lambda_{2,t+1} = 0, \tag{6'}$$

$$N_t^s: -v'(N_t^s) + \lambda_{2,t}\omega_t = 0, \tag{7}$$

$$N_t^d: \lambda_{2,t}(Y'(N_t^d) - \omega_t) - \lambda_{3,t}\omega_t = 0, \tag{8}$$

$$l_t: -\lambda_{2,t}\theta_t + \lambda_{3,t} = 0, \tag{9}$$

$$\beta V_m(m_{t+1}) - \lambda_{2,t}\frac{P_{t+1}}{P_t} = 0. \tag{10}$$

Envelope condition:

$$V_m(m_t) = E_h(\lambda_{1,t} + \lambda_{2,t}) \tag{11}$$

one step ahead Envelop condition:

$$V_m(m_{t+1}) = E_h(\lambda_{1,t+1} + \lambda_{2,t+1}). \tag{11'}$$

From Equation (5)

$$E_h[-\lambda_{1,t} + \lambda_{2,t}\theta_t] = 0, \quad (5) \rightarrow E_h[\lambda_{1,t}] = E_h[\lambda_{2,t}\theta_t]$$

From (9):

$$l_t: -\lambda_{2,t}\theta_t + \lambda_{3,t} = 0, \quad (9) \rightarrow \lambda_{2,t}\theta_t = \lambda_{3,t}$$

$$(5) \rightarrow E_h[\lambda_{1,t}] = E_h[\lambda_{2,t}\theta_t] \rightarrow (5)$$

$$\rightarrow E_h[\lambda_{1,t}] = E_h[\lambda_{3,t}]$$

When the household makes its portfolio choice, the value of sending money to the goods market (as measured by $\lambda_{1,t}$ and of sending it to the loan market by depositing it in a bank (as measured by $\lambda_{3,t}$) must be equal. Ex post, the two multipliers can differ, $\lambda_{1,t} \neq \lambda_{3,t}$, because households cannot reallocate funds between the two markets during the period. Combining (6) and (9)

$$(9) \rightarrow \lambda_{2,t}\theta_t = \lambda_{3,t}$$
$$u'(C_t) - \lambda_{2,t} = \lambda_{1,t}, \quad (6)$$

Subtracting (6) from (9):

$$\lambda_{2,t}\theta_t - u'(C_t) + \lambda_{2,t} = \lambda_{3,t} - \lambda_{1,t}$$
$$(1+\theta_t)\lambda_{2,t} - u'(C_t) = \lambda_{3,t} - \lambda_{1,t}$$
$$u'(C_t) = \lambda_{1,t} + \lambda_{2,t}, \quad (6)$$
$$\rightarrow \beta V_m(m_{t+1}) = \lambda_{2,t}\frac{P_{t+1}}{P_t}, \quad (10) \rightarrow \lambda_{2,t} = \beta\left(\frac{P_t}{P_{t+1}}\right)V_m(m_{t+1})$$

From (10) plus Envelope condition:

$$(10) \rightarrow \lambda_{2,t} = \beta\left(\frac{P_t}{P_{t+1}}\right)V_m(m_{t+1})$$
$$V_m(m_{t+1}) = E_h(\lambda_{1,t+1} + \lambda_{2,t+1}), \quad (11')$$
$$(10) \rightarrow \lambda_{2,t} = \beta\left(\frac{P_t}{P_{t+1}}\right)E_h(\lambda_{1,t+1} + \lambda_{2,t+1})$$
$$(10) \rightarrow \lambda_{2,t} = \beta\left(\frac{P_t}{P_{t+1}}\right)E_h(u'(C_{t+1})).$$

Now, introducing above expression into $(1+\theta_t)\lambda_{2,t} - u'(C_t) = \lambda_{3,t} - \lambda_{1,t}$

$$(1+\theta_t)\lambda_{2,t} - u'(C_t) = \lambda_{3,t} - \lambda_{1,t},$$
$$(1+\theta_t)\beta\left(\frac{P_t}{P_{t+1}}\right)E_h(u'(C_{t+1})) - u'(C_t) = \lambda_{3,t} - \lambda_{1,t},$$
$$\frac{(1+\theta_t)}{\frac{P_{t+1}}{P_t}}\beta E_h(u'(C_{t+1})) - (\lambda_{3,t} - \lambda_{1,t}) = u'(C_t).$$

Define $\frac{P_{t+1}}{P_t} = (1+\pi_{t+1})$

$$\frac{(1+\theta_t)}{(1+\pi_{t+1})}\beta E_h(u'(C_{t+1})) - (\lambda_{3,t} - \lambda_{1,t}) = u'(C_t),$$
$$u'(C_t) = \frac{(1+\theta_t)}{(1+\pi_{t+1})}\beta E_h(u'(C_{t+1})) - (\lambda_{3,t} - \lambda_{1,t}).$$

When the household makes its portfolio choice, the value of sending money to the goods market (as measured by $\lambda_{1,t}$ and of sending it to the loan market by depositing it in a bank (as measured by $\lambda_{3,t}$) must be equal. Ex post, the two multipliers can differ, $\lambda_{1,t} \neq \lambda_{3,t}$, because households cannot reallocate funds between the two markets during the period.

$$u'(C_t) = \beta \frac{(1+\theta_t)}{(1+\pi_{t+1})} E_h(u'(C_{t+1})) - (\lambda_{3,t} - \lambda_{1,t}),$$

$$u'(C_t) + (\lambda_{3,t} - \lambda_{1,t}) = \beta \frac{(1+\theta_t)}{(1+\pi_{t+1})} E_h(u'(C_{t+1})),$$

$$\frac{u'(C_t) + (\lambda_{3,t} - \lambda_{1,t})}{\beta E_h(u'(C_{t+1}))} = \frac{(1+\theta_t)}{(1+\pi_{t+1})}.$$

If $\lambda_{3,t} - \lambda_{1,t} = 0 \rightarrow \lambda_{3,t} = \lambda_{1,t}$

$$\frac{u'(C_t)}{\beta E_h(u'(C_{t+1}))} = \frac{(1+\theta_t)}{(1+\pi_{t+1})}.$$

Turning to the labor market, Combining (7) (8) and (9) we get:

$$Y'(N_t^d) = \omega_t(1+\theta_t),$$

$$\rightarrow Y'(N_t^d) = \underbrace{\overbrace{\omega_t}^{\text{real wage}} + \omega_t \theta_t}_{\text{Marginal cost of labor}}.$$

Firm equates the MPL to the marginal cost of labor, but this is greater than the real wage because of the cost of borrowing funds to finance the firm's wage bill (see *Proof 08 in Appendix B for more*).

$$N_t^s: -v'(N_t^s) + \lambda_{2,t}\omega_t = 0, \quad (7)$$

$$N_t^d: \lambda_{2,t}(Y'(N_t^d) - \omega_t) - \lambda_{3,t}\omega_t = 0, \quad (8)$$

$$N_t^s: -v'(N_t^s) + \lambda_{2,t}\omega_t = 0, \quad (7) \rightarrow v'(N_t^s) = \lambda_{2,t}\omega_t$$

$$N_t^s = N_t^d = N_t$$

$$(7) \rightarrow v'(N_t) = \lambda_{2,t}\omega_t \rightarrow \frac{v'(N_t)}{\lambda_{2,t}} = \omega_t$$

$$Y'(N_t^d) = \omega_t(1+\theta_t).$$

Intro (7):

$$\rightarrow Y'(N_t) = \frac{v'(N_t)}{\lambda_{2,t}}(1+\theta_t),$$

$$\frac{Y'(N_t)}{(1+\theta_t)} = \frac{v'(N_t)}{\lambda_{2,t}},$$

$$\frac{v'(N_t)}{\lambda_{2,t}} = \frac{Y'(N_t)}{(1+\theta_t)}.$$

Here, θ_t is a predetermined markup applied by the bank

$$\frac{v'(N_t)}{\lambda_{2,t}} = \frac{Y'(N_t)}{(1+\theta_t)}.$$

This reveals how "the markup" drives a wedge between the marginal rate of substitution and the MPL. Now we consider what happens if there is a monetary injection H_t. Since the injection is received initially by banks, it increases the supply of loans $D_t + H_t$ because D_t is predetermined by the household's portfolio choice. Equilibrium requires a rise in loan demand, and this is induced by a fall in the markup required by banks to lend the money.

$$Y'(N_t^d) = \omega_t(1+\theta_t),$$

the fall in θ_t increases the demand for labor at each real wage (decreases the marginal productivity of labor).

4.5. *Comparison between equilibriums for conventional and Islamic banking model*

From the MPL for the three models, we find:

Comparison of Labor Market Equilibrium

Commercial Bank Model	Islamic Bank: Case 01	Islamic Bank: Case 02
$Y'(N_t^d) = (1+R_t^L)\omega_t$	$Y'(N_t^d) = \omega_t(1+\alpha_t)$	$Y'(N_t^d) = \omega_t(1+\theta_t)$
where:	*where*:	*where*:
• $Y'(N_t^d)$ is MPL	• $Y'(N_t^d)$ is MPL	• $Y'(N_t^d)$ is MPL
• R_t^L is interest rates on loan	• α_t is profit-loss-rates	• θ_t is mark-up
• ω_t is real wage	• ω_t is real wage	• ω_t is real wage

In a dual economy, conventional banking and Islamic banking co-exist under same economic and regulatory environment. Conventional banks and Islamic banks compete for customer outreach and market shares; both types of banks hire employees and compete in the same labor market. Since conventional banking and Islamic banking co-exist under same regulatory and economic environment, we argue that the labor market equilibrium for Conventional Banking and Islamic Banking shall be equal. If MPL and real wages are exactly same for conventional banks and Islamic banks, then R_t^L (interest rates on loan for conventional banks), α_t (profit-loss-rates for Islamic banks), and θ_t (mark-ups for Islamic banks) should be same.

However, under imperfect market condition when MPL and real wages are not same, lending rates for conventional banks and profit-loss rates and mark-ups charged by Islamic banks should be proportional or correlated. In the empirical analysis of the following segment of the paper, we analyze this argument from the models whether conventional bank interest rates and Islamic bank profits rates are correlated or not.

5. Empirical Evidence

The banking industry in Bangladesh is an example of co-existence of dual banking system within one economy; the central bank of Bangladesh serves as the regulatory authority for both conventional and Islamic banks. More recently, more and more conventional banks are providing Islamic banking windows, as a separate subsidiary. Bangladesh Bank website discloses the deposit rates for 15 conventional banks that also provides Islamic banking services through their Islamic Banking windows. We consider this dataset for two reasons. *First*, this is a unique dataset as no empirical studies are done based on this dataset yet. *Second*, this data allows us to control for bank specific risk as we are comparing the relation between the Islamic banking deposit rates and conventional banking deposit rates, of the same banks and their respective windows.

5.1. Data

Special Notice Deposits (SND) are short-term deposits; and banks provide higher rate of returns to attract more deposits from prospective depositors. Bangladesh Bank discloses monthly data on five different deposit sizes of SND and their respective deposit rates: (a) less than 10 million Bangladesh Taka, (b) between 10 to 250 million Taka, (c) 250 to 500 million Taka, (d) 500 million to 1 billion Taka, and (e) more than 1 billion Taka. Our sample consist of cross-sectional data for deposit rates as of on March 2019 for these five different SND deposits, and deposit rates for five fixed deposit sizes for the Islamic windows, and for their conventional counterpart principals.

This sample is unique in a sense that the sample provides opportunity to use conventional banking and Islamic banking window as control group for each other. We identify the deposit rates corresponding to the SND deposits, and then we pool the deposit rates, and then conduct several alternative empirical specifications to find out the relation between the conventional deposit rates and the Islamic banking window profit rates.

Table 1. Cost of Financing for Different Islamic Contracts

Name of the Contracts	Equation
Murabaha financing	$ACM = \frac{G_{SB} - C_m}{G_{SB} \times n} \times 100$
Funding by Salam:	$ACS = \frac{F-D}{D \times n} \times 100$
Funding Istsna'a:	$AC_i = \frac{F_{PM} - L}{L \times n} \times 100$
Financing Rent To Own	$AC_l = \frac{\sum_{i=1}^{n} L_i - A}{A \times n} \times 100$
To participate in the permanent capital	$COS_p = \frac{R_i}{P_i - D} + g$
To participate in a particular Transaction	$AAC_T = \frac{R \times P\%}{M \times n} \times 100$
Participation ended Bi-ttamleek	$AAC_B = \frac{\sum_{i=1}^{n} R_i}{M \times n} \times 100$
Mudarabah	$C_K = M + X$

5.2. Sample statistics

Table 2 presents the descriptive statistics for five Special Note Deposits rates and five different maturities of Fixed Deposit rates for the 15 banks with both conventional operations and Islamic banking windows. Table 2 also includes Welch t-statistics of differences of mean for the respective categories of rates between the conventional banks and Islamic banks.

Average conventional bank savings deposit rate is 2.883% compared to the average Islamic bank window's deposit rate of 2.858%, which is not statistically different. Out of 11 classes of deposit rates, for eight occasions, we find deposit rates for conventional banks are not significantly different from Islamic banking window's deposit rates. On two occasions, for SND for 500 million to 1 billion taka, and 1 billion taka and above, conventional bank deposit rates are significantly higher that Islamic bank deposit rates. On the contrary, for long-term deposits, for 3 years and more maturity, we find that Islamic bank window's average deposit rate is 5.742% that is significantly higher than respective conventional bank deposit rate of 3.695%.

To summarize, the descriptive statistics show that conventional bank deposit rates are generally higher than Islamic windows' deposit rates on nine occasions although they are significant in two occasions; on two occasions, Islamic banking rates are higher than conventional banking rates. There is no monotonic consistent pattern in the cross-sectional deposit rates.

5.3. Empirical specifications

In the earlier section, we present and compare the conventional banking model, and two alternative cases for Islamic banking models, and we argue that if both types of banks co-exist under one economic and regulatory environment, lending rates for conventional banks and profit-loss rates and mark-ups charged by Islamic banks should be proportional or correlated. We extend this argument and hypothesize that:

H_0: Conventional bank interest rates and *Islamic bank profit rates are not correlated.*
H_a: Conventional bank interest rates and *Islamic bank profit rates are not correlated.*

Descriptive statistics for 15 banks in Bangladesh with both Islamic banking window's rate and conventional banking rate does not show any monotonic relationship. Hence, a regression analysis may provide more insight about the relations between conventional deposit rate and Islamic deposit rates.

We identify 10 million taka SND deposit rate as base rate, and analyze whether the banks provide higher deposit rates to attract additional deposits. We identify the banks and their corresponding deposit rates, and the additional taka value of deposits that banks want to attract over the base deposit amount. Then we pool the deposit rates and deposit sizes and include a dummy for Islamic banking window.

We use several alternate specifications. First, we consider a nested model with pooled OLS and we include Islamic Dummy as a dummy variable that takes 1 for Islamic Banking

Table 2. Descriptive Statistics of Conventional Deposit Rates & Islamic Banking Window Profit Rate

	Savings Deposit	SND Deposit					Fixed Deposit				
		<10 mill. Taka	10 mill. but <250 mill.	250 mill. but <500 mill.	500 mill. but <1 billion Taka	1 billion Taka and above	3 months but <6 months	6 months but <1 year	1 year but <2 years	2 years but <3 years	3 years and above
Conventional banking											
Mean	2.883	2.250	2.760	3.333	3.793	4.233	4.967	6.223	6.617	6.067	3.695
Std. Deviation	0.944	0.911	0.892	1.249	1.542	1.811	1.509	1.431	1.436	2.915	3.263
No. of Obs.	15	15	15	15	15	15	15	15	15	15	15
Islamic Banking Window											
Mean	2.858	2.383	2.593	2.799	2.959	3.166	4.907	6.149	6.480	6.613	5.742
Std. Deviation	1.123	0.996	0.937	0.947	0.939	1.176	1.547	1.721	1.781	1.904	1.546
No. of Obs.	15	15	15	15	15	15	15	15	15	15	15
Welch t-statistics of differences											
	0.067	−0.381	0.501	1.320	**1.790**	**1.914**	0.108	0.128	0.231	−0.608	**−2.196**

Window deposit rates, and zero for conventional banking deposit rates. We consider two forms of this specification; *first*, we only consider the Islamic Dummy as constant intercept as a fixed effect for Islamic deposit rates. *Second*, we allow Islamic Dummy to interact with Base Rate and Log(Add Deposit).

$$\text{Rate} = C + \text{BaseRate} + \text{Log(AddDeposit)} \tag{1}$$

$$\text{Rate} = C + \text{BaseRate} + \text{Log(AddDeposit)} + \text{IslamicDummy} \tag{2}$$

$$\text{Rate} = C + \text{BaseRate} + \text{Log(AddDeposit)} + \text{IslamicDummy} + \text{BaseRate} * \text{IslamicDummy} + \text{Log(AddDeposit)} * \text{IslamicDummy} \tag{3}$$

Table 3 presents regression results for model (1), (2), and (3). We also consider a set of alternate specifications; we regress Islamic Banking Window's profit rate over base interest

Table 3. Pooled OLS Estimates of Profit Rate: Nested Model

$$\text{Rate} = C + \text{BaseRate} + \text{Log(AddDeposit)} \tag{1}$$
$$\text{Rate} = C + \text{BaseRate} + \text{Log(AddDeposit)} + \text{IslamicDummy} \tag{2}$$
$$\text{Rate} = C + \text{BaseRate} + \text{Log(AddDeposit)} + \text{IslamicDummy} + \text{BaseRate} * \text{IslamicDummy} + \text{Log(AddDeposit)} * \text{IslamicDummy} \tag{3}$$

Dependent Variable: RATE

Method: Least Squares

Variable	Model (1) Coefficient	Model (2) Coefficient	Model (3) Coefficient
C	−11.497*	−7.421*	−11.497*
	(0.006)	(0.001)	(0.000)
BaseRate	0.745*	0.775*	0.745*
	(0.000)	(0.000)	(0.000)
Log(AddDeposit)	0.672*	0.463*	0.672*
	(0.001)	(0.000)	(0.000)
IslamicDummy	—	−0.754*	7.405*
	—	(0.000)	(0.099)
BaseRate*IslamicDummy	—	—	0.056*
	—	—	(0.774)
LOG(AddDeposit)*IslamicDummy	—	—	−0.417*
	—	—	(0.064)
R-squared	0.331	0.448	0.465
Adjusted R-squared	0.308	0.434	0.441
No. of observations	120	120	120

Note: *1%, **5%, ***10%.

Table 4. Alternate OLS Estimates of Profit Rate

$$\text{ProfitRate} = C + \text{BaseProfit} + \text{Rate} + \text{Log(AddDeposit)} \quad (4)$$
$$\text{ProfitRate} = C + \text{BaseProfit} + \text{Log(AddDeposit)} \quad (5)$$
$$\text{ProfitRate} = C + \text{BaseRate} + \text{Log(AddDeposit)} \quad (6)$$

Dependent Variable: Profit

Variable	Model (4) Coefficient	Model (5) Coefficient	Variable	Model (6) Coefficient
C	−3.548*	−4.092*	C	−3.343*
	(0.089)	(0.042)		(0.246)
BaseProfit	0.797*	0.801*	BaseRate	0.515*
	(0.000)	(0.000)		(0.000)
Rate	0.054*	—		
	(0.347)	—		
Log(AddDeposit)	0.218*	0.255*	Log(AddDeposit)	0.255*
	(0.044)	(0.012)		(0.079)
R-squared	0.649	0.643		0.250
Adj. R-squared	0.630	0.631		0.224
No. of Obs.	60	60		60

Note: *1%, **5%, ***10%.

rate of conventional banks, and base profit rates separately. Table 4 presents regression results for model (4), (5), and (6).

$$\text{ProfitRate} = C + \text{BaseProfit} + \text{Rate} + \text{Log(AddDeposit)} \quad (4)$$
$$\text{ProfitRate} = C + \text{BaseProfit} + \text{Log(AddDeposit)} \quad (5)$$
$$\text{ProfitRate} = C + \text{BaseRate} + \text{Log(AddDeposit)} \quad (6)$$

5.4. Regression results

Table 2 presents the results on pooled Ordinary Least Squared (OLS) with dummy variable regression. We consider deposit rates for 10 million Taka SND as the base rate. *Model* (1) does not identify the deposit rates for Islamic banking windows separately; results suggest that deposit rates are positively related with *BaseRate*, and log of additional liquidity; this suggests that banks provide higher deposits to attract larger deposits.

Model (2) considers *Islamic Dummy* as additional variable; *Islamic Dummy* is 1 for Islamic Banking Deposit rates and zero for conventional bank deposit rates. We find *Islamic Dummy* coefficient as negative and statistically significant suggesting that Islamic bank deposits are generally lower compared to conventional deposits rates. In *Model* (3), we allow *Islamic Dummy* interact with other explanatory variable, and we find that slope for interactions of *Islamic Dummy* are not significantly different.

Table 4 presents regression results for Model (4), (5), and (6), where the Islamic Banking Window's deposit rates are dependent variable. We find that Islamic Banking deposit rates are positively related with Islamic bank base rate; but, they are not related with conventional bank interest rates. However, Model (6) shows that Islamic banking profit rates are positively related with conventional bank base rates.

To summarize, from Tables 3 and 4 results, we conclude that Islamic banking deposit rates are generally lower than conventional bank deposit rates, and they are positively related with conventional bank deposit rates. Our sample 11 banks, generally provides higher deposit rates to attract higher deposits through both conventional banking services and Islamic banking windows.

6. Conclusion

We formulate cost of funding for different financial contracts based on the AAOIFI guidelines, and use these formula into our theoretical model based on the *Basic Limited-Participation Model* seminal approach developed by Lucas (1990) and Fuerst's (1992), and later followed by Walsh (1998). Our model shows us how much the interest rate or no interest rate effect a wedge between the marginal rate of substitution and the MPL. In conclusion, on cost of funding for the banks, we find that the cost of funding from traditional banks determined based on the *interest rate* charged by a traditional bank. Cost of funding from Islamic banks determined based on the *profit rate*, in the case of sharing funding formulas margin is determined based on the proportion of the Bank's participation in the outcome of the project in the state funding formulas to participate in the profit or loss.

When we compare the cost of funding from traditional banks and Islamic banks, we find that the *profit/loss sharing rate* and the *interest rate* charged are not equal. Fixed and predetermined interest rate charged by traditional commercial banks create a fixed financial burden for the participating firm or the business, as the business is obliged to make interest payments no matter what the business situation is. On the other hand, a client of Islamic bank in a profit/loss sharing arrangement has less financial burden, as Islamic bank shares the risk of loss and the firm is not obliged to pay a fixed profit rate.

To complement our theoretical model, we use a unique sample of 15 banks from Bangladesh that provides both conventional banking and Islamic banking services, and we show that deposit rates of two banking systems are interrelated. We find that Islamic banking deposit rates are generally lower than conventional bank deposit rates, and they are positively related with conventional bank deposit rates. These results are consistent with Cevik and Charap (2015) that find long-term relationship between conventional interest rates and Islamic banking profit rates. Our findings are also similar to Chong and Liu (2009) who find that although Islamic banking is not based on interest, the profit rates are essentially interrelated with conventional deposit rates.

Appendix A. Recursive Methods, Value Function

$$\max_{\{c_t, k_t\}} \sum_{t=0}^{\infty} \beta^t u(c_t), \quad s.t.$$
$$c_t = f(k_t) + (1-\delta)k_t - k_{t+1}, \quad (i')$$
$$c_t \geq 0, \quad k_t \geq 0$$
$$k_0 \text{ given}$$

Substituting (i') into the objective function our problem can be reduced further to:

$$\max_{\{k_t\}} \sum_{t=0}^{\infty} \beta^t u(f(k_t) + (1-\delta)k_t - k_{t+1}), \quad s.t.$$
$$f(k_t) + (1-\delta)k_t - k_{t+1} \geq 0$$
$$k_t \geq 0$$
$$k_0 \text{ given}.$$

Solving for $\{k_t\}$ we can recover $\{y_t, c_t, i_t, h_t\}$. The First-Order Condition is:

$$k_t : \beta^t u'(f(k_t^*) + (1-\delta)k_t^* - k_{t+1}^*)[f'(k_t^*) + (1-\delta)]$$
$$- \beta^{t-1} u'(f(k_{t-1}^*) + (1-\delta)k_{t-1}^* - k_t^*) = 0.$$

Two Boundary Conditions

$$TVC$$
$$k_0 \text{ given}$$

Bellman equation

$$V(k) = \max_{c, k'} \{u(c) + \beta V(k')\}.$$

subject to:

$$k' = f(k) + (1-\delta)k - c$$
$$c \geq 0, \quad k' \geq 0, \quad k \text{ given}$$

Bellman equation

$$V(k) = \max_c \{u(c) + \beta V(f(k) + (1-\delta)k - c)\}.$$

subject to:

$$c \geq 0, \quad k \text{ given}$$

FOC:

$$c: u'(c) - \beta V'(k') = 0.$$

Envelope condition, at the optimum:

$$V(k) = u(c) + \beta V(f(k) + (1-\delta)k - c),$$

$$V'(k) = \underbrace{\frac{\partial u(c)}{\partial k}}_{=0} + \beta V'(k')(f'(k) + (1-\delta)),$$

$$V'(k) = \beta V'(k')(f'(k) + (1-\delta)),$$

combining with FOC

$$u'(c) = \beta V'(k')$$
$$V'(k) = \beta V'(k')(f'(k) + (1-\delta)).$$

Other way: Choose k' as a control variable

Bellman equation

$$V(k) = \max_{c,k'} \{u(c) + \beta V(k')\}.$$

subject to:

$$c = f(k) + (1-\delta)k - k'$$
$$c \geq 0, \quad k' \geq 0, \quad k \text{ given}.$$

Bellman equation

$$V(k) = \max_{k'} \{u(f(k) + (1-\delta)k - k') + \beta V(k')\}.$$

subject to:

$$f(k) + (1-\delta)k - k' \geq 0$$
$$k' \geq 0, \quad k \text{ given}.$$

FOC:

$$k': -u'(c) + \beta V'(k') = 0 \rightarrow u'(c) = \beta V'(k').$$

Envelope condition, at the optimum:

$$V(k) = u(c) + \beta V(f(k) + (1-\delta)k - c),$$
$$V'(k) = u'(c)[f'(k) + (1-\delta)]$$

one period ahead

$$V'(k') = u'(c')[f'(k') + (1-\delta)]$$

combining envelope with FOC

$$u'(c) = \beta V'(k'), \qquad (i)$$
$$V'(k') = u'(c')[f'(k') + (1-\delta)], \qquad (ii)$$

combining (i) and (ii) we get:

$$V'(k') = u'(c')[f'(k') + (1-\delta)],$$

$$\frac{u'(c)}{\beta} = u'(c')[f'(k') + (1-\delta)],$$

$$\frac{u'(c)}{\beta u'(c')} = [f'(k') + (1-\delta)].$$

Now that we have this Euler equation as a description of the solution,

$$\max_{\{c_t, k_t\}} \sum_{t=0}^{\infty} \beta^t u(c_t), \quad s.t.$$

$$c_t = f(k_t) + (1-\delta)k_t - k_{t+1}, \tag{i'}$$

$$c_t \geq 0, \quad k_t \geq 0$$

$$k_0 \text{ given}$$

Appendix B. Islamic Banking: Case 01

Proof 01:

Suppose period t is divided in two subperiods, t_0 (the beginning of period t) and t_1 (the end of period t). At t_0 firms gets a loan L_t from the bank and pays the worker $P_t \omega_t N_t^d$. So, partial profits at t_0 are

$$\Pi_{t_0}^f = L_t - P_t \omega_t N_t^d.$$

In the case of an Islamic financial system, at t_1 the firm's output is realized and the firm pays back the loan L_t to the islamic bank. So, partial profits at t_1 are

$$\Pi_{t_1}^f = P_t Y(N_t^d) - L_t.$$

Thus, if there is no discounting, total profits at the end of period t are:

$$\tilde{\Pi}_t^f = \Pi_{t_0}^f + \Pi_{t_1}^f = [L_t - P_t \omega_t N_t^d] + [P_t Y(N_t^d) - L_t],$$

$$\tilde{\Pi}_t^f = P_t Y(N_t^d) - P_t \omega_t N_t^d,$$

where $\tilde{\Pi}_t^f$ is the net revenue before paying off the loan to the bank.

Notice that in an Islamic financial system, the Islamic bank will get a return on the loans based on a predetermined profit \ loss sharing rate α_t where $0 \leq \alpha_t < 1$. So, overall profits for the firm would be:

$$\Pi_t^f = (1 - \alpha_t)\tilde{\Pi}_t^f,$$

$$\Pi_t^f = (1 - \alpha_t)[P_t Y(N_t^d) - P_t \omega_t N_t^d].$$

Given, P_t, ω_t and α_t, the firm chooses N_t^d that maximizes:

$$\Pi_t^f = (1 - \alpha_t)[P_t Y(N_t^d) - P_t \omega_t N_t^d].$$

Proof 02:

Suppose period t is divided in two subperiods: t_0, which is the beginning of period t and t_1, the end of period t. At t_0, the bank gets deposits D_t^i and lends L_t^i to the firm. The bank also receives transfers, H_t^i from the central bank. So, partial profits at t_0 are:

$$\Pi_{t_0}^b = D_t^i - L_t^i + H_t^i.$$

At t_1 firm's output is realized and firm pays back the loan L_t^i. The bank returns D_t^i to the depositors. The prohibition of riba, i.e., the ban on interest makes $R_t^D = 0$ and $R_t^L = 0$. The Islamic bank gets paid based on a predetermined profit \ loss sharing rate α_t. Thus, partial profits at t_1 are

$$\Pi_{t_1}^b = \alpha_t[P_t Y(N_t^d) - P_t \omega_t N_t^d] - D_t^i.$$

Thus, if there is no discounting, total profits for the representative Islamic bank at the end of period t are:

$$\Pi_t^b = \Pi_{t_0}^b + \Pi_{t_1}^b = [D_t^i - L_t^i + H_t^i] + \alpha_t[P_t Y(N_t^d) - P_t \omega_t N_t^d] - D_t^i, \quad s.t.$$
$$L_t^i = D_t^i + H_t^i$$
$$\Pi_t^b = \alpha_t[P_t Y(N_t^d) - P_t \omega_t N_t^d] - L_t^i + H_t^i, \quad s.t.$$
$$L_t^i = D_t^i + H_t^i.$$

Introducing the bank's balance sheet constraint into the objective function, we have:

$$\Pi_t^b = \alpha_t[P_t Y(N_t^d) - P_t \omega_t N_t^d] - D_t^i.$$

Adding and subtracting $\alpha_t L_t^i$, we get:

$$\Pi_t^{ib} = \alpha_t[P_t Y(N_t^d) - P_t \omega_t N_t^d - L_t^i] - D_t^i + \alpha_t L_t^i,$$
$$\Pi_t^{ib} = \alpha_t[P_t Y(N_t^d) - P_t \omega_t N_t^d - L_t^i] - D_t^i + \alpha_t(D_t^i + H_t^i),$$
$$\Pi_t^{ib} = \alpha_t[P_t Y(N_t^d) - P_t \omega_t N_t^d - L_t^i] - (1 - \alpha_t)D_t^i + \alpha_t H_t^i.$$

Proof 03:

The household's budget constraint

$$\underbrace{P_t \omega_t N_t^s}_{\substack{\text{Income} \\ \text{from work}}} + \underbrace{(M_t - D_t^i)}_{\substack{\text{Money holding - deposits:} \\ \text{Money available to purchase} \\ \text{consumption goods}}} + \underbrace{(1 + R_t^D) D_t^i}_{\substack{\text{Income} \\ \text{from Deposits}}} + \underbrace{\Pi_t^{fi} + \Pi_t^i}_{\substack{\text{Household own} \\ \text{firm and banks,} \\ \text{so they get profits}}} = P_t C_t + M_{t+1}$$

within an Islamic banking setting we have:

$$R_t^D = 0.$$

Thus,

$$P_t \omega_t N_t^s + (M_t - D_t^i) + D_t^i + \Pi_t^{fi} + \Pi_t^i - P_t C_t = M_{t+1},$$
$$P_t \omega_t N_t^s + M_t + \Pi_t^f + \Pi_t^i - P_t C_t = M_{t+1}.$$

Also, recall that:

$$\Pi_t^{ib} = \alpha_t[P_tY(N_t^d) - P_t\omega_tN_t^d - L_t^i] - (1-\alpha_t)D_t^i + \alpha_tH_t^i$$
$$\Pi_t^f = (1-\alpha_t)[P_tY(N_t^d) - P_t\omega_tN_t^d].$$

- Substituting Π_t^{ib} and Π_t^f into the household's budget constraint, we have:

$$P_t\omega_tN_t^s + M_t + (1-\alpha_t)[P_tY(N_t^d) - P_t\omega_tN_t^d] + \alpha_t[P_tY(N_t^d) - P_t\omega_tN_t^d - L_t^i]$$
$$- (1-\alpha_t)D_t^i + \alpha_tH_t^i - P_tC_t = M_{t+1},$$
$$P_t\omega_tN_t^s + M_t + [P_tY(N_t^d) - P_t\omega_t - \alpha_tL_t^i] - (1-\alpha_t)D_t^i + \alpha_tH_t^i - P_tC_t = M_{t+1},$$
$$P_t\omega_tN_t^s + M_t - (1-\alpha_t)D_t^i + \alpha_tH_t^i + [P_tY(N_t^d) - P_t\omega_t - \alpha_tL_t^i] - P_tC_t = M_{t+1}.$$

- Dividing by P_t we get

$$\omega_tN_t^s + \frac{M_t}{P_t} - (1-\alpha_t)\frac{D_t^i}{P_t} + \alpha_t\frac{H_t^i}{P_t} + \left[Y(N_t^d) - \omega_tN_t^d - \alpha_t\frac{L_t^i}{P_t}\right] - C_t = \frac{M_{t+1}}{P_t},$$

$$\omega_tN_t^s + m_t - (1-\alpha_t)d_t^i + \alpha_th_t^i + [Y(N_t^d) - \omega_tN_t^d - \alpha_tl_t^i] - C_t = \frac{M_{t+1}}{P_{t+1}}\frac{P_{t+1}}{P_t},$$

$$\omega_tN_t^s + m_t - (1-\alpha_t)d_t^i + \alpha_th_t^i + [Y(N_t^d) - \omega_tN_t^d - \alpha_tl_t^i] - C_t = m_{t+1}\frac{P_{t+1}}{P_t}.$$

Proof 04:

$$N_t^s: -v'(N_t^s) + \lambda_{2,t}\omega_t = 0, \quad (7)$$

$$N_t^d: \lambda_{2,t}(Y'(N_t^d) - \omega_t) - \lambda_{3,t}\omega_t = 0, \quad (8)$$

$$l_t: -\lambda_{2,t}\alpha_t + \lambda_{3,t} = 0, \quad (9)$$

$$N_t^s: -v'(N_t^s) + \lambda_{2,t}\omega_t = 0, \quad (7)$$

$$N_t^d: \lambda_{2,t}(Y'(N_t^d) - \omega_t) = \lambda_{3,t}\omega_t,$$

$$(8) \rightarrow Y'(N_t^d) - \omega_t = \frac{\lambda_{3,t}}{\lambda_{2,t}}\omega_t \rightarrow Y'(N_t^d) = \left(1 + \frac{\lambda_{3,t}}{\lambda_{2,t}}\right)\omega_t$$

$$l_t: -\lambda_{2,t}\alpha_t + \lambda_{3,t} = 0, \quad (9) \rightarrow \alpha_t = \frac{\lambda_{3,t}}{\lambda_{2,t}}$$

Intro (9) into (8) we get

$$Y'(N_t^d) = \left(1 + \frac{\lambda_{3,t}}{\lambda_{2,t}}\right)\omega_t \rightarrow Y'(N_t^d) = (1+\alpha_t)\omega_t.$$

Appendix C. Islamic Banking: Case 02

Proof 05:

Suppose period t is divided in two subperiods, t_0 (the beginning of period t) and t_1 (the end of period t). At t_0 firms gets a loan L_t from the bank and pays the worker $P_t\omega_tN_t^d$. So, partial profits at t_0 are

$$\Pi^f_{t_0} = L_t - P_t \omega_t N^d_t.$$

Recall that before output is realized the firm borrowed money from the Islamic bank to pay workers and agree to payback a fixed amount, x, which is the result of a markup applied by the Islamic bank.

$$x = (1+\theta_t)L_t.$$

Thus, the firm's profits after paying the agreed markup over the inputs used in the production process to the Islamic bank is:

$$\Pi^f_{t_1} = P_t Y(N^d_t) - (1+\theta_t)L_t,$$

where $0 \leq \theta_t < 1$.

Thus, if there is no discounting, total profits at the end of period t are:

$$\Pi^f_t = \Pi^f_{t_0} + \Pi^f_{t_1} = L_t - P_t \omega_t N^d_t + P_t Y(N^d_t) - (1+\theta_t)L_t,$$
$$\Pi^f_t = -P_t \omega_t N^d_t + P_t Y(N^d_t) - \theta_t L_t,$$
$$\Pi^f_t = P_t Y(N^d_t) - P_t \omega_t N^d_t - \theta_t L_t.$$

Given, P_t, ω_t, and α_t, the firm chooses N^d_t that maximizes:

$$\Pi^f_t = P_t Y(N^d_t) - P_t \omega_t N^d_t - \theta_t L_t.$$

Proof 06:
Suppose period t is divided in two subperiods: t_0, which is the beginning of period t and t_1, the end of period t. At t_0 the bank gets deposits D^i_t and lends L^i_t to the firm. The bank also receives transfers, H^i_t from the central bank. So, partial profits at t_0 are

$$\Pi^b_{t_0} = D^i_t - L^i_t + H^i_t.$$

At t_1 firm's output is realized and firm pays back the loan L^i_t. The bank returns D^i_t to the depositors. The prohibition of riba, i.e., the ban on interest makes $R^D_t = 0$ and $R^L_t = 0$. The Islamic bank gets paid based on a predetermined markup θ_t applied by the bank. Thus, partial profits at t_1 are

$$\Pi^b_{t_1} = (1+\theta_t)L_t - D^i_t.$$

Thus, if there is no discounting, total profits for the representative Islamic bank at the end of period t are:

$$\Pi^b_t = \Pi^b_{t_0} + \Pi^b_{t_1} = [D^i_t - L^i_t + H^i_t] + (1+\theta_t)L_t - D^i_t, \quad s.t.$$
$$L^i_t = D^i_t + H^i_t$$
$$\Pi^b_t = [-L^i_t + H^i_t] + (1+\theta_t)L_t, \quad s.t.$$
$$L^i_t = D^i_t + H^i_t.$$

268 Introduction to Islamic Economics and Finance

Introducing the bank's balance sheet constraint into the objective function, we have:

$$\Pi_t^b = (1+\theta_t)L_t - D_t^i.$$

Adding and subtracting $\theta_t D_t^i$, we get:

$$\Pi_t^b = (1+\theta_t)L_t - D_t^i + \theta_t D_t^i - \theta_t D_t^i,$$
$$\Pi_t^b = (1+\theta_t)L_t - (1+\theta_t)D_t^i + \theta_t D_t^i,$$
$$\Pi_t^b = (1+\theta_t)(L_t - D_t^i) + \theta_t D_t^i,$$
$$\Pi_t^b = (1+\theta_t)H_t^i + \theta_t D_t^i.$$

Proof 07:

The household's budget constraint

$$\underbrace{P_t \omega_t N_t^s}_{\substack{\text{Income} \\ \text{from work}}} + \underbrace{(M_t - D_t^i)}_{\substack{\text{Money holding - deposits:} \\ \text{Money available to purchase} \\ \text{consumption goods}}} + \underbrace{(1+R_t^D)D_t^i}_{\substack{\text{Income} \\ \text{from Deposits}}} + \underbrace{\Pi_t^{fi} + \Pi_t^i}_{\substack{\text{Household own} \\ \text{firm and banks,} \\ \text{so they get profits}}} = P_t C_t + M_{t+1}$$

within an Islamic banking setting we have:

$$R_t^D = 0,$$
$$\Pi_t^b = (1+\theta_t)H_t^i + \theta_t D_t^i,$$
$$\Pi_t^f = P_t Y(N_t^d) - P_t \omega_t N_t^d - \theta_t L_t.$$

Substituting Π_t^{ib} and Π_t^f into the household's budget constraint, we have:

$$P_t \omega_t N_t^s + (M_t - D_t^i) + D_t^i + \Pi_t^{fi} + \Pi_t^i - P_t C_t = M_{t+1},$$
$$P_t \omega_t N_t^s + M_t + \Pi_t^f + \Pi_t^i - P_t C_t = M_{t+1},$$
$$P_t \omega_t N_t^s + M_t + P_t Y(N_t^d) - P_t \omega_t N_t^d - \theta_t L_t + (1+\theta_t)H_t^i + \theta_t D_t^i - P_t C_t = M_{t+1},$$
$$P_t \omega_t N_t^s + M_t + \theta_t D_t^i + (1+\theta_t)H_t^i + [P_t Y(N_t^d) - P_t \omega_t N_t^d - \theta_t L_t] - P_t C_t = M_{t+1}.$$

Dividing by P_t we get

$$\omega_t N_t^s + \frac{M_t}{P_t} + \theta_t \frac{D_t^i}{P_t} + (1+\theta_t)\frac{H_t^i}{P_t} + \left[Y(N_t^d) - \omega_t N_t^d - \theta_t \frac{L_t^i}{P_t}\right] - C_t = \frac{M_{t+1}}{P_t},$$
$$\omega_t N_t^s + m_t + \theta_t d_t^i + (1+\theta_t)h_t^i + [Y(N_t^d) - \omega_t N_t^d - \theta_t l_t^i] - C_t = m_{t+1}\frac{P_{t+1}}{P_t}.$$

Proof 08:

$$N_t^s: -v'(N_t^s) + \lambda_{2,t}\omega_t = 0, \quad (7)$$
$$N_t^d: \lambda_{2,t}(Y'(N_t^d) - \omega_t) - \lambda_{3,t}\omega_t = 0, \quad (8)$$
$$l_t: -\lambda_{2,t}\theta_t + \lambda_{3,t} = 0, \quad (9)$$

$$N_t^s: -v'(N_t^s) + \lambda_{2,t}\omega_t = 0, \quad (7)$$

$$N_t^d: \lambda_{2,t}(Y'(N_t^d) - \omega_t) = \lambda_{3,t}\omega_t, \quad (8) \rightarrow Y'(N_t^d) - \omega_t = \frac{\lambda_{3,t}}{\lambda_{2,t}}\omega_t \rightarrow Y'(N_t^d) = \left(1 + \frac{\lambda_{3,t}}{\lambda_{2,t}}\right)\omega_t$$

$$l_t: -\lambda_{2,t}\theta_t + \lambda_{3,t} = 0, \quad (9) \rightarrow \theta_t = \frac{\lambda_{3,t}}{\lambda_{2,t}}$$

Intro (9) into (8) we get

$$Y'(N_t^d) = \left(1 + \frac{\lambda_{3,t}}{\lambda_{2,t}}\right)\omega_t \rightarrow Y'(N_t^d) = (1 + \theta_t)\omega_t$$

References

AAOIFI (2017). Newly Issued Standards. Retrieved from Accounting and Auditing Organization for Islamic Financial Institutions http://aaoifi.com/newly-issued-standards/?lang=en.

Abuzayed, B, N Al-Fayoumi and P Molyneux (2018). Diversification and bank stability in the GCC. *Journal of International Financial Markets, Institutions and Money*, 57, 17–43.

Ahmad, A and MI Saif (2010). Islamic banking experience of Pakistan: Comparison between Islamic and conventional banks. *International Journal of Business and Management*, 5(2), 137.

Ahmed, H (2002). A microeconomic model of an Islamic bank. The Islamic Research and Teaching Institute (IRTI).

Al Rahahleh, N, M Ishaq Bhatti and F Najuna Misman (2019). Developments in risk management in Islamic Finance: A review. *Journal of Risk and Financial Management*, 12(1), 37.

Asutay, M, AF Aysan and CC Karahan (2013). Reflecting on the trajectory of Islamic Finance: From Mit Ghamr to the globalisation of Islamic Finance. *Afro Eurasian Studies*, 2, 5–14.

Bashir, BA (1983). Portfolio management of Islamic banks: 'Certainty model'. *Journal of Banking & Finance*, 7(3), 339–354.

Baydoun, N, M Sulaiman, RJ Willett and S Ibrahim (2018). *Principles of Islamic Accounting*. Hoboken, NJ: John Wiley & Sons.

Beck, T, A Demirgüç-Kunt and O Merrouche (2010). Islamic vs. conventional banking: Business model, efficiency and stability. World Bank Policy Research Working Paper Series No. 5446, Washington, DC, the World Bank.

Bhatti, A and S Azmat (2018). *Rethinking Islamic Finance: Markets, Regulations and Islamic Law*. New York, NY: Taylor & Francis.

Bhatti, M (2018). *Islamic Law and International Commercial Arbitration*. London, UK: Routledge.

Bourkhis, K and MS Nabi (2013). Islamic and conventional banks' soundness during the 2007–2008 financial crisis. *Review of Financial Economics*, 22(2), 68–77.

Cevik, S and J Charap (2015). The behavior of conventional and Islamic bank deposit returns in Malaysia and Turkey. *International Journal of Economics and Financial Issues*, 5(1), 111–124.

Chong, BS and MH Liu (2009). Islamic banking: Interest-free or interest-based? *Pacific-Basin Finance Journal*, 17(1), 125–144.

Ergeç, EH and BG Arslan (2013). Impact of interest rates on Islamic and conventional banks: The case of Turkey. *Applied Economics*, 45(17), 2381–2388.

Fuerst, TS (1992). Liquidity, loanable funds, and real activity. *Journal of Monetary Economics*, 29(1), 3–24.

Habib, SF (2018). *Fundamentals of Islamic Finance and Banking*. Hoboken, NJ: John Wiley & Sons.

Hasan, M, M Maher and J Dridi (2010). The effects of the global crisis on Islamic and conventional banks: A comparative study. IMF Working Papers, Vol., pp. 1–46, 2010. Available at SSRN: https://ssrn.com/abstract=1750689.

Hassan, A and S Mollah (2018). *Islamic Finance: Ethical Underpinnings, Products, and Institutions*. New York, NY: Springer.

Hassan, K and M Rashid (2018). *Management of Islamic Finance: Principle, Practice, and Performance*. London, UK: Emerald Group Publishing.

Hassan, MK, A Khan and A Paltrinieri (2019). Liquidity risk, credit risk and stability in Islamic and conventional banks. *Research in International Business and Finance*, 48, 17–31.

ICD-Thomson Reuters. (2017). ICD-. Thomson Reuters Islamic Finance Development Report 2017. THOMSON REUTERS. Retrieved June 10, 2019, from https://www.zawya.com/mena/en/ifg-publications/231017094152F/.

IFSB. (2018). Islamic Financial Services Industry Stability Report 2018.

Islam, S and T Sultana (2019). Practice of Islamic financial management in Bangladesh: Evidence from Islamic banks. *International Journal of Islamic Banking and Finance Research*, 3(1), 1–12.

Jaffar, M and I Manarvi (2011). Performance comparison of Islamic and Conventional banks in Pakistan. *Global Journal of Management and Business Research*, 11(1), 60–66.

Johnes, J, M Izzeldin and V Pappas (2014). A comparison of performance of Islamic and conventional banks 2004–2009. *Journal of Economic Behavior & Organization*, 103, S93–S107.

Kabir, MN and AC Worthington (2017). The 'competition–stability/fragility' nexus: A comparative analysis of Islamic and conventional banks. *International Review of Financial Analysis*, 50, 111–128.

Khan, SM (1986). Islamic Interest-Free Banking: A Theoretical Analysis. Staff Papers-International Monetary Fund, Vol. 33, 1, pp. 1–27.

Khan, MS and A Mirakhor (1992). Theoretical studies in Islamic Banking and Finance, The Institute for Research and Islamic Studies. *JKAU: Islamic Economics*, 4, 51–79.

Klein, MA (1971). A theory of the banking firm. *Journal of Money, Credit and Banking*, 3(2), 205–218.

Lucas, RE Jr. (1990). Liquidity and interest rates. *Journal of Economic Theory*, 50(2), 237–264.

Mervyn, KL and MA Latifa (2001). *Islamic Banking*. Edward Elgar Publishing.

Metzler, LA (1951). Wealth, saving, and the rate of interest. *Journal of Political Economy*, 59(2), 93–116.

Mirakhor, A (1987). Analysis of short-term asset concentration in Islamic banking. IMF Working Paper. 87/67.

Mollah, S, MK Hassan, O Al Farooque and A Mobarek (2017). The governance, risk-taking, and performance of Islamic banks. *Journal of Financial Services Research*, 51(2), 195–219.

Parashar, SP (2010). How did Islamic banks do during global financial crisis? *Banks and Bank Systems*, 5(4), 54–62.

Safiullah, M and A Shamsuddin (2018). Risk in Islamic banking and corporate governance. *Pacific-Basin Finance Journal*, 47, 129–149.

Safiullah, M and A Shamsuddin (2019). Risk-adjusted efficiency and corporate governance: Evidence from Islamic and conventional banks. *Journal of Corporate Finance*, 55, 105–140.

Santomero, AM (1984). Modeling the banking firm: A survey. *Journal of Money, Credit and Banking*, 16(4), 576–602.

Sealey Jr, CW and JT Lindley (1977). Inputs, outputs, and a theory of production and cost at depository financial institutions. *The Journal of Finance*, 32(4), 1251–1266.

Sharairi, MH (2016). *The Potential Adoption of Islamic Accounting Standards Developed by the Accounting and Auditing Organization for Islamic Financial Institutions (AAOIFI) by Islamic Banks in the United Arab Emirates*. Canberra, ACT: University of Canberra.

Walsh, C (1998). Money in the short run: Informational and portfolio rigidities. In *Monetary Theory and Policy*, pp. 211–223. Cambridge, Mass.: MIT Press.

Yanikkaya, H, N Gumus and YU Pabuccu (2018). How profitability differs between conventional and Islamic banks: A dynamic panel data approach. *Pacific-Basin Finance Journal*, 48, 99–111.

Zarqa, MA (1997). Istisna' financing of infrastructure projects. *Islamic Economic Studies*, 4(2), 67–74.

Zaher, TS and M Kabir Hassan (2001). A comparative literature survey of Islamic finance and banking. *Financial Markets, Institutions & Instruments*, 10(4), 155–199.

Chapter 12

Domains and Motives of *Musharakah* Spur in the Islamic Banking Industry of Pakistan[#]

Muhammad Nouman[*,‡], Karim Ullah[†,§] and Shafiullah Jan[†,¶]

[*]*Institute of Business and Management Sciences (IBMS)*
The University of Agriculture Peshawar, Pakistan

[†]*Institute of Management Sciences Peshawar, Pakistan*
[‡]*mnouman@aup.edu.pk*
[§]*karim.Ullah@imsciences.edu.pk*
[¶]*shafiullah.jan@imsciences.edu.pk*

Participatory financing schemes, including *Musharakah* and *Mudarabah*, are theoretically claimed to be the ideal modes of Islamic financing, but their practice is restrained by several factors. That is why Islamic banks have a consistent tendency to avoid participatory financing on the assets side throughout the world. However, recently this trend has started changing in Pakistan and Indonesia where the share of participatory finance has raised significantly in the financing portfolio of Islamic banks. The present paper explores this recent spur of participatory finance in Pakistan in terms of its domains of applications and the responsible factors. The findings lead to a novel posteriori framework which shows that the shift toward participatory financing is primarily characterized by increase in working capital financing and commodity operations financing through *Musharakah* mode Islamic banks. Moreover, five factors contribute to the spur of participatory financing including: (i) introducing varieties in *Musharakah*, (ii) enhanced applicability, (iii) high volume projects, (iv) government interventions, and (v) regulator's role. The framework can significantly advance understanding with respect to the implementation theory of participation financing within Islamic banking and related *Shariah* compliance and regulation.

Keywords: Diminishing *Musharakah*; Islamic banking; *Musharakah*; qualitative content analysis; Pakistan; participatory financing; running *Musharakah*.

1. Introduction

The modes of Islamic finance are usually based on two principles, namely (i) participation and (ii) non-participation (ElGindi *et al.*, 2009; Sundararajan and Errico, 2002; Jan and Asutay, 2019). Participatory financing schemes, including *Musharakah* and *Mudarabah*, are the essence of Islamic financial products (Aggarwal and Yousef, 2000; Hearn *et al.*, 2012) and represent the true spirit of the Islamic banking (Algaoud and Lewis, 2007; Ariff, 1988; Lewis, 2008; Zaher and K Hassan, 2001). Therefore, the advocates of Islamic

---

[¶]Corresponding author.
[#]This Chapter first appeared in the *Singapore Economic Review*, Vol. 67, No. 1, doi: 10.1142/S0217590819500620. © 2022 World Scientific Publishing.

Table 1. Financing Mix of Islamic Banks in Pakistan (Percentage Share)

Modes	Dec 2012	Dec 2013	Dec 2014	Dec 2015	Dec 2016	Dec 2017	Dec 2018
Murabahah	39.7	40.6	30.1	24.5	15.8	13.2	13.6
Ijarah	9.3	7.7	7.7	6.6	6.8	6.4	6.2
Musharakah	0.8	6.7	11.0	14.0	15.6	22.0	19.9
Mudarabah	0.2	0.2	0.1	0	0	0	0
Diminishing *Musharakah*	36.2	30.8	32.6	31.7	34.7	30.7	33.3
Salam	3.0	4.0	4.5	5.3	4.4	2.8	2.4
Istisna	6.5	5.6	8.3	8.6	8.4	8.2	9.1
Others	4.3	4.4	5.6	9.3	14.3	16.7	15.5
Total	100	100	100	100	100	100	100

Source: State Bank of Pakistan (2012–18).

banking claim that Islamic banks ought to apply and promote participatory financing (Khan, 2010; Usmani, 2007).

In practice, the Islamic banks prefer to adopt participatory modes for the deposits. However, they traditionally tend to avoid participatory financing as the main financing scheme (Abdul-Rahman *et al.*, 2014; Abedifar *et al.*, 2015; Marizah and Nazam, 2016; Shahid *et al.*, 2015). By far, the non-participatory arrangements are the most dominant modes of financing globally (Nouman, 2019). However, over the past few years, efforts have been made to increase reliance on the participatory financing particularly in Pakistan and Indonesia. Consequently, the makeup of financing portfolio of Islamic banks has started changing in Pakistan and Indonesia with the growing use of *Musharakah* and *Istisna*, and a shift away from *Murabahah* and *Ijarah* (Vizcaino, 2015).

The recent statistics published by State Bank of Pakistan indicate that the assets side of the balance sheet of Islamic banks operating in Pakistan has transformed swiftly in the recent years. The share of *Murabahah* financing in the overall financing mix of Islamic banks has dropped from the 39.7% in December 2012 to 13.6% by the December 2018 (see Table 1). On the other hand, the share of *Musharakah* financing has grown from 0.8% to 19.9% within less than a decade (December 2012 to December 2018). However, compared to Pakistan this transformation is more gradual in Indonesia as *Murabahah* still represents more than a half of the financing mix of Islamic banks (Vizcaino, 2015). This transformation indicates a persistent adaptation of the Islamic financial system, as a whole, to new requirements of the market and society (Ullah and Al-Karaghouli, 2017; Ullah and Patel, 2011).

The shift in the financing portfolio of Islamic banks poses direct challenge to the extant literature. It was frequently argued that participatory financing has serious practical limitations (See for example Bacha, 1995; Karim, 2002; Sumarti *et al.*, 2014). Therefore, Islamic banks cannot apply these arrangements unless the constraints are properly dealt with (Nouman and Ullah, 2014; Nouman *et al.*, 2018). Hence, the recent spur of participatory financing being a contemporary development provides a well-timed research opportunity, in terms of two focal questions: (i) how Islamic banks apply participatory financing? and (ii) what factors underpin their growth? To answer these questions, an exploratory qualitative study undertaken whereby evidence from multiple sources including in-depth narrative interviews, related documents, and websites is analyzed using the Qualitative Content Analysis (QCA) to conceptualize posteriori framework of domains and motives of *Musharakah* Spur in Pakistan.

The rest of the paper is structured as follows: Section 2 presents perspectives form the extant literature to provide insight into the overall context of this research. Section 3 presents the methodological stance of the study. The analysis and findings are presented in Section 4. Section 5 presents policy implications and agenda for future research while Section 5 concludes the paper.

2. Literature Review

The earliest writings on the subject of Islamic finance can be traced back to the forties of the 20th century (Siddiqi, 1981). According to Nienhaus (1983) and Siddiqi (2006) the early literature till the end of nineteen-seventies, which can be characterized as the theory of Islamic banking, was largely a supplication for the replacement of interest with profit and loss sharing in banks (See for example, Ahmad, 1972; Ghanameh, 1973; Maududi, 1969; Qureshi, 1946; Siddiqi, 1969). The main emphasis of the early literature was on highlighting the evils of interest and emphasizing the underlying benefits of the participatory financing (Nienhaus, 1983; Siddiqi, 2006). Moreover, it placed the religious obligation and greater social welfare responsibility upon Islamic banks to strive for achieving the broader goals of *Shari'ah* that could be realized by synthesizing their operations on partnership basis (Dusuki and Abozaid, 2007). However, no attention was paid to developing theoretical arguments or mechanism to assure the capital protection in the system based on partnership (Hasan, 2005; Ismail, 2002). That is why soon after the advent and proliferation of *Murabahah* financing during the late nineteen-seventies and early eighties,[1] it conquered the operations of Islamic banks and pushed participatory financing to a corner accounting for less than 10% in the operations of Islamic banks (Siddiqi, 2006).

In the late 1980s, when the prevailing divergence in the theory and practice of the Islamic banks became evident, the researchers and Islamic economists started paying attention to its possible explanations and solutions. The study by Nienhaus (1983) was amongst the pioneering studies in terms of describing the problems of the newly born Islamic banking, particularly the constraints to the application of participatory financing. Similarly, Khan (1983) created the moral hazard hypothesis as an explanation of the constraints to participatory financing (Khan, 1995). Similarly, the study by Haque and Mirakhor (1986) was the first attempt towards modeling the Islamic participatory financing arrangements and analyzing their implications. Moreover, they used the lens of agency theory, for the first time, to explain constraints to these arrangements. Their study aimed at formulating investment behavior in a participatory financing arrangement as a

---

[1] *Murabahah* was first modified by Humud (1976) as a tool for extending credit without violating the *Shari'ah* rules (El-Gamal, 2006).

principle-agent problem and analyzed the relevant issues under the moral hazard and uncertainty conditions.

These studies were followed by a stream of literature, providing divergent explanations for the tendency of Islamic banks to avoid participatory financing. For example (Ascarya, 2010), and Sadique (2012) claim that upper management of Islamic financial institutions is not committed and sincere in adopting participatory financing. On the other hand, Akacem and Gilliam (2002); Khan (1995); and Samad *et al.* (2005) argue that projects and clients to be financed through participatory financing require to be evaluated very carefully for which managerial skills, and expertise is required; however, IFIs lack skillful human resource. Similarly, Amrani (2012) and Kayed (2012) claimed that there is a low demand for participatory financing. On the contrary, according to Bacha (1997); Chong and Liu (2009) agency problems are the most dominant hurdles in the application of participatory financing. Table 2 summarizes the key constraints to participatory financing suggested by the studies published till 2014.

Due to the divergence in the literature, there was no unified understanding of the constraints to participatory financing. To bridge this gap, Nouman and Ullah (2014) attempted to integrate the divergent literature. They came up with a list of 24 different constraints to participatory finance; however, they did not develop the typology of the constraints. Building upon the study of Nouman and Ullah (2014), Nouman *et al.* (2018) developed a holistic typology for better conceptualization of the underlying constraints to participatory financing. They conducted a systematic review of the literature to identify all those factors that contribute to the lower preference for *Musharakah* and *Mudarabah* based financing. Moreover, a coherent constraints framework was developed, using the qualitative evidence synthesis method, which categorizes the constraints into three distinct categories namely uncertainty, low demand, and regulatory hurdles.

The constraints framework indicates that three major constraints contribute to the lower preference of Islamic banks for participatory financing: *First*, there are several factors that induce uncertainty in the participatory financing arrangements. These factors include: lack of reliability and trustworthiness in the society, lack of skilled HR, higher costs associated to the project appraisal and monitoring, risk-averse depositors, and agency problems including the asymmetric information, adverse selection and moral hazard problems. *Second*, the entrepreneurs have lower demand for participatory financing due to few inherent characteristics of *Musharakah* and *Mudarabah* and external factors including: the less applicability of participatory financing, complications in structuring and dealing with such arrangements, higher cost, lack of secrecy and independence, external interference in the business affairs, unfair treatment in taxation, severe competition, and lack of understanding and familiarity in the society. *Third*, the current regulatory structure restrains the viability of participatory financing in several ways. The major regulatory constraints include: non-supportive regulatory framework, restrictive prudential regulations, weak property rights, weak judicial systems, inefficient auditing and accounting systems, lack of liquid and deep secondary markets, and lack of government support.

In the nutshell, the extant literature suggests that the contemporary regulatory, economic, and social settings are not conducive to the participatory financing and put the

Table 2. Constraints to Participatory Financing Highlighted in the Extant Literature

Contributor	Explicitly Mentioned Hurdles
Nienhaus (1983)	Severe competition, higher cost, lack of skilled HR
Haque and Mirakhor (1986)	Principal-agent problems, moral hazards, higher project appraisal monitoring costs, asymmetric information, unsupportive regulatory and legal framework
Roy (1991)	Lack of skilled HR, inability to generate quick returns, unsupportive state policies, unsupportive regulatory and legal framework, severe competition, lack of applicability
Khan (1995)	Moral hazards, asymmetric information, adverse selection, less applicability, disclosure of business secrets, complicated to structure and deal with, unsupportive regulatory and legal framework, higher risk, lack of applicability
Bashir (1996)	Principal-agent problems, moral hazards, asymmetric information, adverse selection
Abdalla (1999)	Higher risk, lower demand, restrictive banking laws, lack of skilled HR, higher project appraisal and monitoring costs, lack of trustworthiness
Dar et al. (1999)	Unprotected property rights, principal-agent problems, less applicability, moral hazards, unfair tax treatment, Illiquid and shallow secondary market, risk averse depositors, lower demand, severe competition
Sadr (1999)	Asymmetric information, adverse selection, moral hazards, higher project appraisal, and monitoring costs
Warde (2000)	Asymmetric information, moral hazards, complicated to structure and deal with, lack of skilled HR
Abalkhail and Presley (2002)	Asymmetric information, adverse selection, moral hazards, principal-agent problems, higher project appraisal, and monitoring costs
Hasan (2002)	Higher risk, lack of skilled HR, unsupportive regulatory and legal framework, principal-agent problems
Iqbal and Llewellyn (2002a)	Principal-agent problems, asymmetric information, adverse selection, moral hazards, higher project appraisal, and monitoring costs
Khalil et al. (2002)	Principal-agent problems, asymmetric information, higher risk, adverse selection, moral hazards, higher project appraisal, and monitoring costs
Sadr and Iqbal (2002)	Asymmetric information, adverse selection, moral hazards, higher risk, higher project appraisal, and monitoring costs
Sundararajan and Errico (2002)	Higher risk, complicated to structure and deal with, unsupportive regulatory and legal framework, principal-agent problems, asymmetric information, moral hazards
Yousef (2004)	Unsupportive regulatory and legal framework, principal-agent problems
Iqbal and Molyneux (2005)	Unsupportive regulatory and legal framework, lack of skilled HR, asymmetric information, adverse selection, moral hazards, principal-agent problems, higher costs
Siddiqi (2006)	Adverse selection, moral hazards, higher project appraisal and monitoring costs, lack of trustworthiness, unsupportive regulatory and legal framework, inability to generate quick returns, shallow secondary markets

Table 2. (*Continued*)

Contributor	Explicitly Mentioned Hurdles
Ayub (2007)	Less applicability, higher risk, bound to invest in less risky avenues, principal-agent problems, moral hazards
Greuning and Iqbal (2007)	Higher risk, higher project appraisal and monitoring costs, lack of trustworthiness, risk averse depositors, asymmetric information
Mirakhor and Zaidi (2007)	Higher project appraisal and monitoring costs, lack of skilled HR, higher risk, principal-agent problems, moral hazards
Ahmed (2008)	Lack of skilled HR, higher risk, external interference, moral hazards, higher project appraisal, and monitoring costs
Chong and Liu (2009)	Severe competition, risk averse depositors, principal-agent problems, asymmetric information, moral hazards, higher project appraisal and monitoring costs, higher risk
Khan (2010)	Asymmetric information, adverse selection, moral hazards, lack of trustworthiness, restrictive banking laws, unprotected property rights, higher risk, severe competition, lack of skilled HR, unfair tax treatment
Mansoori (2011)	Bound to invest in less risky avenues, higher risk, lack of trustworthiness, adverse selection, moral hazards, poor auditing and accounting systems, lack of skilled HR
Shaikh (2011)	Higher risk, moral hazards, poor auditing and accounting systems, lack of trustworthiness, disclosure of business secrets, less applicability, unfair tax treatment, lower demand, unsupportive regulatory and legal framework
Huda (2012)	Asymmetric information, adverse selection, moral hazards, higher project appraisal and monitoring costs, higher risk, unsupportive regulatory and legal framework
Kayed (2012)	Uncommitted upper management, lack of skilled HR, lack of trustworthiness, poor auditing and accounting systems, unsupportive regulatory and legal framework, higher risk, unsupportive state policies, lack of understanding in the society
Sadique (2012)	Uncommitted upper management, complicated to structure and deal with, principal-agent problems
Al-Muharrami and Hardy (2013)	Asymmetric information, moral hazards, higher project appraisal and monitoring costs, risk averse depositors, higher risk
El-Komi and Croson (2013)	Asymmetric information, adverse selection, moral hazards, higher project appraisal and monitoring costs, higher risk
Abdul-Rahman *et al.* (2014)	Principal-agent problems, asymmetric information, adverse selection, moral hazards, higher project appraisal and monitoring costs, unsupportive regulatory and legal framework, unprotected property rights, unfair tax treatment

non-participatory and interest-based financing at an advantageous position. Therefore, the non-participatory financing is expected to dominate the Islamic banking operations unless serious reforms are made by regulatory bodies and Islamic banks (Nouman and Ullah, 2014; Nouman *et al.*, 2018).

Consistent with the view of Nouman *et al.* (2018), serious efforts have been made over the past few years to resolve the constraints to participatory financing, particularly in Pakistan and Indonesia (Vizcaino, 2015). Consequently, the makeup of financing portfolio of Islamic banks has started changing in Pakistan and Indonesia with the growing use of *Musharakah* and a shift away from *Murabahah* (Vizcaino, 2015). However, being a contemporary development, there is lack of evidence on what factors have contributed to the recent shift in the financing behavior of Islamic banks operating in Pakistan. Thus, the present study contributes to the Islamic banking and finance literature by providing insights into the recent spur of participatory financing in the Islamic banking industry of Pakistan in terms of its domains and the contributing factors.

3. Research Methodology

The present study is exploratory in nature and uses the qualitative research approach to develop the posteriori framework of factors inducing the growth of participatory financing in Pakistan. It is based on an interpretation of qualitative data primarily generated through 20 in-depth interviews, which is an approach consistent with procedure recommended for theory development. Moreover, multiple sources of data are used to establish triangulation as suggested by Yin (2003). Data from the multiple sources (including in-depth interviews, related documents, and official websites) is converged in the analysis process rather than being handled individually. Each data source acts as one piece of the "puzzle," with each piece contributing to the researcher's understanding of the whole phenomenon. According to Baxter and Jack (2008), "this convergence adds strength to the findings as the various strands of data are braided together to promote a greater understanding of the case" (p. 554).

3.1. *Data and sample*

In-depth interviews have been used as a primary source of evidence. However, the interview schedule was pre-tested using the pilot focus group discussions following Baker (1994); Peat *et al.* (2002); Polit *et al.* (2001). The purpose of these pilot studies was to arrive at a clear definition of the study focus and refine the data collection technique as suggested by Frankland and Bloor (1999).

Pilot study is "a trial study carried out, before a research design is finalized, to assist in defining the research question or to test the feasibility, reliability and validity of the proposed study design" (Thabane *et al.*, 2010, p. 2). Pilot study is a commonly used procedure intended to test the quality of the interview protocol (Chenail, 2011). It helps in identifying whether the proposed instruments or methods are too complicated or inappropriate (Van Teijlingen and Hundley, 2001). Moreover, it helps in identifying potential researcher biases (Chenail, 2011). According to Peat *et al.* (2002), a pilot study if conducted properly can allow the investigator to address the researcher bias and the instrumentation issues.

Following Chenail (2011), focus group participants were selected using the selection criteria employed in the main study. The purposive selections were made to choose the

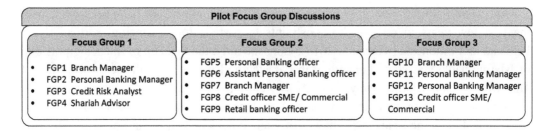

Figure 1. Structure of Focus Group Discussions

experienced and on-the-job personnel from the selected banks. In literature, there is no clear guidance on the ideal duration and number of participants in a focus group discussion (Ullah, 2014). However, four to five participants were selected for each focus group discussion following Ullah (2014). In total, 13 respondents participated in the focus group discussions, where two focus groups consisted of four respondents while one focus group had five respondents. The participants included those employees of Islamic banks who were directly involved in dealing the financing cases of different sectors e.g., SME, corporate, consumer, and export financing. Figure 1 illustrates the structure of focus groups discussions (FGP represents focus group participant).

Focus group discussions helped in identifying the key areas where Islamic banks are currently applying *Musharakah* financing in Pakistan. Moreover, the interview questions were refined and new questions were added using the insight gained from piloting. The following open-ended questions were put forward for the discussions:

(a) Which financing products of your bank are based on Musharakah?
(b) How your organization design and practice *Musharakah* based financing products?
(c) What factors do you think have contributed to the rapid increase of *Musharakah* financing in Islamic banks?
(d) Did government and regulatory bodies play any role in the *Musharakah* spur?

The data collected and results generated during the pilot study are typically for pre-testing purpose and are usually not mixed with the data and results generated in the main study (Chenail, 2011). However, Van Teijlingen and Hundley (2001) argue that in qualitative research studies some or all part of the data generated in the pilot study is often used as a part of the main study. Contamination of the results is a matter of less concern in qualitative research studies since data collection in such studies is progressive in nature and a subsequent interview in a series would be often better compared to the previous one. This is because the interviewers usually gain insights from the preceding interviews and use these to improve the interview schedules and question. However, the present study uses the findings of the focus group discussions for the pre-testing purpose only following Chenail (2011) approach and does not mix these findings with the results generated in the study.

After piloting, in-depth interviews were conducted to identify the factors that underpin the shift towards participatory financing in the Islamic banking industry of Pakistan.

A total of 20 in-depth interviews are conducted with the Islamic banking personnel who are directly involved in either designing financial services or executing the cases of commodity operations financing, working capital financing, or consumer financing. The appropriateness of an employee for interview was determined keeping in view his/her role in the dealing with and/or evaluation of the project or client for *Musharakah* financing arrangements. Those employees were selected for interview that are either:

(a) involved in dealing the cases of working capital financing, consumer financing, or commodity operations financing.
(b) responsible for the assessment of the clients, assets or projects particularly in the risk management division, or
(c) design financial services.

The potential participants were identified through snowball sampling technique. Moreover, the number of interviews was determined through saturation principle (following Brown, 2008) and convention within service literature (following Ullah, 2014). For example: Han (2010) used 10 in-depth interviews; Segelström (2010) used 17 interviews; Stickley *et al.* (2010) used 7 interviews; and Sangiorgi (2008) used 14 interviews to conceptualize service design practices in different contexts. Interviews were conducted at four different Islamic banks because the contextual differences enhance the validity of findings by establishing a repeated chain of evidence within different contexts (Yin, 2003). Therefore, interviews were conducted at four different Islamic banks. Moreover, multiple branches of each bank operating in four major cities of Pakistan (including Islamabad, Karachi, Lahore, and Peshawar) were considered during the data collection.

Related documents are considered as a source of evidence for triangulation, including (i) Islamic banking bulletins issued by the State Bank of Pakistan, (ii) annual reports, announcements, minutes of the meetings and other written reports issued by the Islamic banks, and (iii) articles and information appearing on the relevant websites. During the in-depth interviews, the participants were requested to provide any documents that may be of value to the present study. Moreover, the official websites of each Islamic bank and the regulatory authority (i.e., State Bank of Pakistan) were explored. Similarly, the annual reports of each bank were explored to find any relevant piece of information.

3.2. Data analysis

Qualitative Content Analysis (QCA) is used for the analysis of the collected data. QCA is a method that is used to describe the meaning of qualitative data systematically (Mayring, 2000; Schreier, 2012). According to Hsieh and Shannon (2005), QCA is "a research method for subjective interpretation of the content of text data through the systematic classification process of coding and identifying themes or patterns" (p. 1278). In this technique, the discussion material is classified into effective number of categories representing similar meanings. Researcher can ensure the validity of the inference by complying with the process of systematic coding. Thus, this approach helps in interpreting the qualitative data in a scientific manner (Moretti *et al.*, 2011).

When applying QCA for the analysis of data, researchers choose between the inductive and the deductive approach to QCA (Elo and Kyngas, 2008; Mayring, 2000). The choice of these two approaches depends upon the objectives of the research (Elo and Kyngas, 2008) and the nature of the problem under consideration (Moretti *et al.*, 2011). The major differences between these two approaches are based on the way the categories are being derived from the data (Kohlbacher, 2006; Moretti *et al.*, 2011).

Inductive approach allows researchers to derive coding categories inductively from the collected data (Mayring, 2000). This approach is usually appropriate in the situations where the existing literature or theory is limited (Hsieh and Shannon, 2005). Instead of relying on the preconceived categories, researchers allow new insights to emerge by immersing themselves in the data (Kondracki and Wellman, 2002), that results in a posteriori framework (Ullah, 2014). Mayring (2000) describes this approach as "inductive category development" while Hsieh and Shannon (2005) describe it as "conventional content analysis".

Compared to the inductive approach, the QCA using a deductive approach follows a more structured process (Hickey and Kipping, 1996). In the deductive approach, the codes are being derived from the exiting theory, framework, or literature (Cavanagh, 1997; Kondracki and Wellman, 2002), and is usually called a priori framework. Researchers start with identifying key variables or concepts as initial coding categories from the prior research or existing theory (Potter and Levine-Donnerstein, 1999). In this approach, the goal is to extend or validate an existing theory or theoretical framework (Hsieh and Shannon, 2005). Mayring (2000) describes this approach as "deductive category development" while Hsieh and Shannon (2005) describe it as "directed content analysis".

The inductive approach has been applied in the present study, as the two focal questions are looking to explore and identify domains and factors of the recent spur in participatory financing. The actual analysis is conducted using the Nvivo software. For this purpose, the researcher focused on the two main functions of Nvivo including data management and nodes making.

3.3. *Justification for selecting qualitative content analysis*

The present study justifies QCA on the following grounds:

First, in QCA the object of analysis can be written documents, video tapes, observation protocols, transcripts of interviews or discourses, or any other type of recorded communication. Thus, in a comprehensive study where different types of data have to be used, the QCA can be applied for the analysis of multiple sources of evidence.

Second, QCA attempts to synthesize openness besides being a strictly controlled methodology characterized by a step-by-step procedure of data analysis. This unique dual nature strengthens its strong ability to deal with complexity. QCA successfully covers and grasps the complexity underlying a social setting under consideration and the resulting social data by applying a comprehensive and holistic data analysis approach. Moreover, the procedures of summary, explication, and structuring reduce complexity step-by-step and bring key themes to the surface in an iterative process.

Finally, QCA has the ability to cover both the manifest and latent content meaning (Cho and Lee, 2014). Thus, unlike classical quantitative content analysis, context is also central to the analysis and interpretation in the QCA. This helps in analyzing a complex social phenomenon in a comprehensive and holistic way.

4. Analysis and Findings

4.1. *The key areas of participatory financing in practice*

Analysis of the data indicates that Islamic banks are currently offering participatory financing (i.e., *Musharakah* financing) in almost all major areas of financing except export financing. Several financing products of the leading Islamic banks are based on the principle of *Musharakah*:

First, Islamic banks currently allow *Musharakah* financing to the SMEs and Corporations for working capital financing and financing of fixed assets like land, building, machinery, vehicles, etc. In a working capital, financing arrangement bank invests funds in the business on profit and loss sharing basis. These funds are utilized to meet the operational needs of a business. Bank in return gets share in the profit and loss of the business in the ratio of capital contribution.

> "We are providing financing on Musharakah basis to the corporate sector and SMEs for financing their day to day working capital requirements. Our major focus is on corporate sector however we are also considering the top performing SMEs for working capital financing."
>
> *Participant 3, Credit officer SME/Commercial Sector*

On the other hand, in case of fixed assets bank and business become joint owners of an asset. Business utilizes the asset and in return pays a certain rent to the bank for the bank's share of asset.

> "We finance fixed assets on Musharakah basis where a portion of capital say 30% is invested by the business while the rest is paid by the bank. Thus the bank and the business become joint owners of the asset. It can be applied for any type of fixed asset including land, building, machinery, equipment, fixtures, and vehicles etc."
>
> *Participant 7, Personal Banking Officer*

Second, the consumer financing products particularly house and car financing schemes of various Islamic banks are based on *Musharakah*. In a consumer financing arrangement, Islamic bank and the customer become joint owner of a durable consumer product (e.g., house or car) by contributing a certain amount of financing. Customer uses the asset and in return agrees to a periodic rent (usually monthly) to the bank for the use of the asset.

> "We are applying Musharakah for house financing and car financing only. Previously car financing was practiced through Ijarah, but now we are applying Musharakah mode of financing for this purpose."
>
> *Participant 8, Personal Banking Officer*

In house financing arrangement, Islamic bank and the customer contribute a certain amount of financing which is utilized for purchasing, construction, or renovation of the property. Customer participates with the Islamic bank in the joint ownership of property under consideration. The bank's share in the property is divided into ownership units and the price of each unit is determined. Customer promises (through undertaking to purchase) to buy the bank's share in the property gradually over a certain period of time. Customer uses the property and in return pays a periodic rent (usually monthly) to the bank. Moreover, bank sells a certain number of units to the customer every month. Consequently, the bank ownership decreases in the property while the customer's ownership increases every month. The rent is adjusted every month on the basis of bank's remaining ownership (units) in the property. Eventually, title to the property is completely transferred to the customer. Thus, the customer becomes sole owner of the property while the bank's ownership diminishes.

On the other hand, the car financing product of most of the major Islamic banks is based on the principle of *Ijarah*. However, two Islamic banks have based their car financing based on the principle of diminishing *Musharakah*. The mechanism of the car financing is similar to the house financing. However, unlike house financing, the ownership of the car is not divided into distinct units. Moreover, the monthly rent is adjusted in a way that it remains constant throughout a year and does not decrease with decrease in the bank's ownership. This is done to distribute the rent equality throughout a year.

Third, Islamic banks are offering participatory financing to government departments for the commodity operations financing. Commodity operation financing refers to the financing provided either to government, public sector corporations or private sector for procurement of either soft or hard commodities. Hard commodities include the natural resources that need to be extracted or mined like oil, coil, gold, etc. On the other hand, soft commodities include the agricultural products and livestock such as wheat, cotton, corn, sugar, coffee, milk, beef, etc. In Pakistan, the government's commodity operations aims at supporting the prices of domestic agricultural products, particularly wheat.

> "The commodity operations of government are also financed by Islamic banks on Musharakah basis. For example our bank has recently provided Rs. 9.5 billion to Punjab food department for commodity operations."
>
> *Participant 2, Financial Service Designer & Shari'ah Advisor*

Finally, Islamic banks are providing participatory financing through *Musharakah Sukuk* to government and private sectors.

> "In addition to the above, short term Musharakah Sukuk were developed by the Bank for the power producer LALPIR Power in addition to the

previously developed Sukuk for the power generation sector for KAPCO and HUBCO."

Shariah Advisor Report,[2] 2013, p. 12.

"During the year the structuring and documentation of more than 15 syndicated transactions were reviewed under my supervision most prominent of them were Engro Rupiyah Retail Sukuk, Engro Fertilizers Sukuk, LalPir Short term Shirkat ul Aqad Sukuk, and project financing transactions for power sector"

Shariah Advisor Report,[3] 2014, p. 92

In a nutshell, Islamic banks are currently offering participatory financing through *Musharakah*-based products for the financing needs of SME, corporate, consumer, and government sectors.

4.2. Factors inducing the growth of participatory financing

Analysis of the data shows that many factors have induce the spur of participatory financing in Pakistan. These factors have been derived inductively from the interviews and have been classified into five distant categories.

The findings of the study suggest that five major factors contribute to the growth of participatory financing in Pakistan including the introduction of new products, increased applicability, financing huge projects, government interventions, and role of the State Bank of Pakistan. The proceeding subsections provide a brief discussion of these factors.

(i) *Development of new Variants of Musharakah*

The major reason behind the shift in the financing portfolio of the Islamic banking industry of Pakistan can be attributed to the recent adaptations in the service design of *Musharakah* financing (Nouman, 2019) through enactment of varieties in the product structures to enable the product sustainability in new contexts (Ullah and Al-Karaghouli, 2017). Adaptation refers to the process of altering the contents or structure of a service product into context (Ullah, 2015). It can be defined as "the ability to make incremental adjustments as a result of environmental changes, goal structure changes, or other changes." (Fiol and Lyles, 1985, p. 811).

Islamic banks have adapted the standard *Musharakah* mode to create a variety of financial services in different contexts (Ayub, 2016; Nouman, 2019) by developing two variants of *Musharakah* including diminishing *Musharakah* and running *Musharakah*.

> "Musharakah is not practiced in our bank. Islamic banks are reluctant to go towards pure Musharakah based financing. However, banks do apply

---

[2] Usmani (2013).
[3] Usmani (2014).

different variants of Musharakah including diminishing Musharakah and running Musharakah."

Participant 6, Credit Hub Manager

The diminishing *Musharakah* was introduced several years ago and is used for the financing of fixed assets. It has emerged from *Musharakah* (*Shirkat-al-Milk*). It is in fact a *Musharakah* cum *Ijarah* arrangement where bank and client become joint owners of an asset. The client uses the asset on *Ijarah* basis and in return pays a predetermined rent to the bank. The bank share in the property is divided into units and the price of each unit is determined. Customer has to pay rent for the bank's outstanding units and has to purchase a certain number of units every month. Consequently, the share of customer increases while the share of bank decreases every month.

> "Our house financing product is based on diminishing Musharakah whereby customer contributes 30% of the required capital, while 70% capital is contributed by the bank. Thus, the bank and customer becomes joint owner of the property".

Participant 4, Personal Banking Officer

Diminishing *Musharakah* can be applied for the financing of any fixed asset including land, building, plant, machinery, equipment, fixtures, vehicles, etc. Currently, Islamic banks are offering diminishing *Musharakah*-based products to businesses and consumers. The house financing product of all Islamic banks is based on diminishing *Musharakah*. On the other hand, the car financing product of few Islamic banks is based on diminishing *Musharakah*.

Recently, Islamic banks have introduced a new variant of *Musharakah* called the running *Musharakah* to meet the daily operational needs of businesses (Ayub, 2016; Nouman, 2019; Tahir and Khan, 2016). This is consistent with the view of Ullah and Al-Karaghouli (2017) who suggest that due to various varieties, Islamic banking adjust to various requirements through enabled varieties in its parameters, which ultimately results in the product sustainability.

> "We are applying Musharakah on the financing side in two forms including diminishing Musharakah and running Musharakah. Diminishing Musharakah was practiced from the beginning however running Musharakah has been introduced recently as a product."

Participant 15, Credit Risk Analyst

Running *Musharakah* is based on the principle of *Shirat ul Aqad* and basically involves the joint ownership of a business venture (Ahmed *et al.*, 2016). In the running *Musharakah* arrangement, bank provides capital to the business usually for short term and shares the profit and losses of the business in the ratio of capital contribution. Unlike pure *Musharakah*, where actual profit and loss of the business is shared among all partners, a ceiling rate is decided in the running *Musharakah* arrangement for the distribution of profit. If the actual profit of the business is below the ceiling rate, the actual profit is shared with the bank in the ratio of capital contribution. However, if the profit exceeds the ceiling rate, bank's share of profit is calculated on the basis of the ceiling rate (Ayub, 2016; Tahir and Khan, 2016). The profit above the ceiling rate goes to the client and bank has no or a negligible claim on the additional profit.

> "In running Musharakah client has to share their profit up to a pre-determined ceiling rate because profitable businesses are never ready to share their actual profit with the bank because their actual profit is usually very high compared to the interest rate at which they can raise capital from the market."
>
> *Participant 17, Credit officer Corporate Sector*

Running *Musharakah* is currently used for working capital financing (Ahmed et al., 2016; Tahir and Khan, 2016) in the SME and corporate sectors, and for commodity operations financing in the government sector. It is currently offered to only reliable clients including blue chip corporations, top performing SMEs, and government.

> "Pure Musharakah is not applied on the financing side because it is not suitable for financing purposes. We are applying Musharakah on the financing side in the form of running Musharakah. It is currently offered to stable businesses particularly the blue chip corporations and government departments."
>
> *Participant 14, Manager Credit Assessment Department*

Islamic banks claimed that pure *Musharakah* cannot be applied in the current business environment because it lacks flexibility and does not meet the needs of the modern industry (Nouman and Ullah, 2014, 2016). Our findings suggest that Islamic banks have adapted *Musharakah* keeping in view the needs of the industry to increase its viability and meet the growing demands of the industry. For example, one of the most dominant factors contributing to the lower demand for pure *Musharakah* is its higher cost of financing. One of the basic reasons for this problem is the requirement of *Musharakah* to share the actual profit of the business. Clients do not want to share their actual profits with the bank, because they may end up paying a very high cost of financing compared to the prevalent market rate. Therefore, if Islamic banks ask entrepreneur to share their actual profit with the bank, they will never do so, because they may get financing from conventional banks at a comparatively lower rate since conventional banks offer financing on a pre-determined rate without having any concern with the actual profit.

To resolve this issue, in running Musharakah (RM) arrangement the profit distribution ratio is linked to Karachi Inter Bank Offered Rate (KIBOR) contrary to the pure Musharakah arrangement, where actual profit of the business is shared among the partners. Thus, in a RM arrangement financier gets capital at the prevalent market rate. Furthermore, the cost of financing in RM arrangement is not only competitive but also offers additional benefits. RM offers an additional risk sharing feature which is not present in non-participatory based or conventional financing schemes. In RM, if the actual profit is higher than the ceiling (KIBOR) rate, bank gets share up to the ceiling rate, and profit above the ceiling rate goes to the entrepreneur. However, bank gets share on the actual profit ratio, if actual profit is lower than the ceiling rate. Furthermore, if business incurs losses, bank is responsible to share losses of the business in the ratio of capital contribution. This adaptation has provided a competitive edge to RM over the non-participatory modes of Islamic finance, and conventional financing. Moreover, it has led to resolve the demand issue.

In a nutshell, the constraints to the *Musharakah* financing have reduced significantly as an outcome of the adaptations in *Musharakah*. Hence, the introduction of the new variant of *Musharakah* is the major factor inducing the spur of *Musharakah* financing in Pakistan.

> "Musharakah has increased obviously due to introduction of running Musharakah because as I told you pure Musharakah is not practiced in any bank."
>
> *Participant 6, Credit Hub Manager*

This is consistent with the view of Comfort (2009) who claims that constraints can trigger the process of adaptation resulting in the restructuring of the components or operations of the system or organization in a new form. This adaptation eventually leads to the resolution of constraints and increase in the effectiveness of the organization (Comfort, 2009), and sustainability of its products (Ullah and Al-Karaghouli, 2017). Similarly, Huber (1991) suggests organizations to be "self-designing" or "experimenting" organizations, i.e., they should adapt their goals, domains, processes, products, and structures to ensure their survival in the changing environments. The experimentation helps organizations in remaining flexible and learning about a variety of design features.

(ii) *Increased Applicability*

Pure *Musharakah* is acclaimed to have limited applicability in the modern world due to lack of flexibility (Ayub, 2007). However, the applicability of *Musharakah* financing has increased significantly with the introduction of running *Musharakah* (Ahmed et al., 2016; Ayub, 2016) because it has been tailored to the needs of the Islamic banks and clients and is therefore more viable and flexible than the pure *Musharakah* and other modes.

Other modes like *Salam, Ististna,* and *Murabahah* involve several documentation requirements and other formalities e.g., conditions of transfer of ownership, taking/giving delivery, issue of invoices and multiple deliveries in different consignments, etc. On the other hand, in running *Musharakah* a certain amount is sanctioned to the business for a certain time period which can be used to support their daily operational needs. The business can withdraw or deposit any amount just like a current account. At the maturity of *Musharakah*, the actual profit of business keeping in view their inventory turnover, cost of goods sold and indirect expenses.[4] Similarly, the share of bank in the profit/loss is

---

[4] For detailed discussion on the structuring of running *Musharakah* and estimation of profit and investment, see Ayub (2016) and Ahmed et al. (2016).

calculated on the outstanding capital basis which represents the actual amount of bank's funds being used by the business (Ayub, 2016). Business does not need to maintain separate records for the running *Musharakah*. Rather, the financial statements are used for the estimation of profit or losses incurred during a period. Therefore, the documentation requirements and other juristic requirements are negligible in running *Musharakah*.

Due to its inherent flexibility and ease of management, Islamic banks have developed several new products based on running *Musharakah*. As a result, Islamic banks have got access to several new areas including working capital financing, commodity operations financing, and *Sukuk*. The introduction of running *Musharakah* has increased the viability of *Musharakah* financing in the modern world and has opened new avenues of investment for Islamic banks in several ways. For example,

First, previously Islamic banks used to apply *Murabahah* or *Istisna*' mode for working capital financing. Due to limited applicability of these modes, Islamic banks were capable of offering inventory financing only and could not finance the day-to-day operational needs of the businesses. With the introduction of running *Musharakah*, Islamic banks are now capable of financing the day-to=day operational needs of businesses.

> "We have recently introduced running Musharakah for financing the daily operational needs of the businesses e.g., the payment of utility bills, wages to labor and other miscellaneous payments, etc. We cannot apply other modes like Murabahah, Salam, and Istisna' etc for this purpose because these are basically the asset based financing modes."
>
> *Participant 11, Credit officer SME/Commercial Sector*

Second, Islamic banks are used to finance the commodity operations using *Murabahah* mode of finance. However, government departments were not comfortable with *Murabahah* due to high documentation requirements and other formalities, and its lack of flexibility. Islamic banks have overcome these issues by applying running *Musharakah* for commodity operations financing. That is why the share of *Musharakah* financing in the overall financing portfolio of Islamic banking industry has raised significantly.

> "We faced two problems in Murabahah. First the documentation requirement was very high… Secondly, there was lack of flexibility in case of Murabahah. Government department has a very high priority for the flexibility… Therefore, government departments were demanding us to develop a structure in which first, the documentation requirement is low and secondly they get advantage in case of early repayment. Both of these issues got resolved in running Musharakah."
>
> *Participant 13, Financial Service Designer*

Finally, Islamic banks are developing new financing solutions based on the running *Musharakah*.

> "During the year the bank remained focus on increasing the ratio of Shirkat ul Aqd based financing which is commendable while bank launched foreign currency (FCY) based Running Musharakah to increase the scope of Shirkat ul Aqd."
>
> Shariah Advisor Report[5], 2014, p. 92

In a nutshell, the applicability and demand of *Musharakah* financing has increased significantly with the introduction of running *Musharakah*. Islamic banks have got access to new areas including working capital financing, and commodity operations financing. Furthermore, Islamic banks have converted various products from non-participative modes of financing to *Musharakah*. Therefore, the share of *Musharakah* financing has increased significantly while the share of *Ijarah* and *Murabahah* has dropped in the financing portfolio of Islamic banking industry.

(iii) *Financing High Volume Projects*

Running *Musharakah* is usually offered to large corporations for working capital financing, and government departments for commodity operations financing. The size of each contract of working capital financing is usually more than a hundred million while the size of each commodity operations financing is usually in billions.

> "Actually, we have done very few financing deals based on running Musharakah but the amount of financing in each deal is very large. This is because running Musharakah is usually offered to large industries only."
>
> Participant 1, Credit Officer Corporate Sector

> "Presently PKR 37 billion worth of financing has been done by *** bank on running Musharakah bases in the commodity operations while our bank has done 20 billion worth of financing. Similarly, *** bank has also invested a huge sum of money in the same department. Thus, if you combine these few large investments with this single government department, it will cover more than 70% or 80% of whole financing done on Musharakah basis."
>
> Participant 14, Manager Credit Assessment Department

Hence, though the number of financing deals and clients are very small in case of running *Musharakah*, the size of each financing arrangement is very large.

> It is encouraging to mention that several Government Institutions like Pakistan Agricultural Storage & Services Corporation Ltd. (PASSCO), Trading Corporation of Pakistan (Pvt.) Ltd (TCP), Punjab Food Department, etc., have used Shariah-compliant financing products and services

---

[5] Usmani (2014).

of our bank to meet their financing needs which also include the biggest Running Musharakah disbursement of Rs 9.5bn to Punjab Food Department.

Shariah Advisor Report,[6] 2015, p. 98

Because of the several huge financing contracts signed during the last few years, the share of *Musharakah* financing has increased very rapidly from 0.2% to 19% in a very short span of time.

(iv) *Role of SBP*

State Bank of Pakistan (SBP) has played a vital role in the promotion of participatory financing in Pakistan (Vizcaino, 2015). For example:

First, SBP is assisting government in creating investment opportunities for Islamic banks to solve the excess liquidity problem. A steering committee has been formed called the Islamic Banking Promotion Committee that is chaired by the federal finance minister and the deputy governor State bank of Pakistan is its member. The major focus of this committee is to persuade the government to take steps for the promotion of Islamic banking and finance. These efforts are playing an important role in the growth of Islamic banking and Musharakah financing.

> "State bank creates demand for Islamic financing from the government. For example if you consider Sukuk or other similar products, they are always created by government due to the demand by the State bank of Pakistan. State bank does so because they want to help Islamic banks in liquidity management."

Participant 13, Financial Service Designer

Second, SBP is also trying to strengthen the system to increase the viability of participatory financing. For this purpose, SBP is striving to impose different restrictions on defaulters.

> "In case of default the report is forwarded to the State Bank of Pakistan where his status is updated as defaulter in the CIB database. In such cases the client would not be allowed to use any type of banking and financial services in future. Even he is not allowed to open an account in any bank."

Participant 16, Credit Portfolio Analyst

Third, the SBP regulations have also played role in the introduction of running *Musharakah*. For example, SBP issued instructions to Islamic banks vide BPD Circular No. 1 dated January 21, 2004 that binds the banks in Pakistan to benchmark all corporate

---

[6](Usmani, 2015).

lending, including the "Overdraft and Running Finance" with the KIBOR with spread as the parties may mutually decide (Ayub, 2016). This circular was amended in 2016 vide IBD Circular No. 01 dated September 08, 2016 to allow exemption from KIBOR as benchmark rate for participatory and *Wakalah* modes based products. However, these instructions have provided grounds for introduction of running *Musharakah*.

Finally, SBP developed the strategic plan for five years (2014–2018) to boost the growth and development of Islamic banking industry in Pakistan. This plan focuses on strengthening the mechanism of consultation with different stakeholders, increase efforts for awareness creation, broadening and deepening the product base of Islamic banks, removing inconsistencies and confusions in regulatory, legal, and taxation environment, doubling the outreach of Islamic banks and increasing their market share to 15% of banking system during the next five years (Islamic Banking Department, 2014). The SBP targeted to enable policy environment and develop incentive mechanisms to stimulate the participative financing. For this purpose, State bank of Pakistan is committed to work closely with other stakeholders to develop products based on *Mudarabah* and *Musharakah* (Islamic Banking Department, 2014).

(v) *Government interventions*

Government has also played an important role in the growth of overall Islamic banking in general and participatory financing in particular. Federal government advises its subsidiaries to finance a portion of funds for commodity operations from Islamic banks to solve the excess liquidity problem being faced by Islamic banking industry in Pakistan. The assets creation of Islamic banking industry is very weak due to which Islamic banks are facing the liquidity management problems particularly in short run. Therefore, in those areas where Islamic banking structure can be adopted easily, government orders various departments to take financing from Islamic banks to safeguard them from failure.

> "Punjab food department is getting order from the government to get a certain portion of financing from the Islamic banking sector. Thus they are bound to come towards Musharakah due to government order. A committee has been formed by the federal government that pushes them time and again to create opportunities for Islamic banks."

Participant 2, Financial Service Designer & Shari'ah Advisor

Furthermore, the government institutions including the NAB, FIA, NADRA, etc. are also trying to strengthen the system to reduce the chances of fraud and increase the viability of participatory financing.

> "All the default cases are shared with the State Bank of Pakistan (SBP), NAB, FIA, and FBR. They do investigation on their own ends and take certain actions as well. For example the CNIC of defaulters may get blocked. This whole team is lead by the SBP. When SBP gets the default

case they instruct the other departments through circulars to start investigation or take certain actions."

Participant 14, Manager Credit Assessment Department

Thus, government is playing its role by creating financing opportunities for Islamic banks especially in the commodity operations. Moreover, government institutions are playing their role in strengthening the system to develop an environment that is conducive to the growth and success of participatory financing arrangements.

5. Implications for Policy and Future Research

Findings of the study suggest, besides other factors, that the recent spur of participatory financing in Pakistan is driven by the increase in the commodity operations financing using running *Musharakah*. This shift is induced by the Government of Pakistan's tendency to increase the commodity financing swiftly to support the domestic wheat price in the wake of boosting its production and discouraging its smuggling.[7] However, the SME sector is affected severely due to the rapid growth in the commodity financing in Pakistan (Dawn, 2010) because financing extended to government departments for commodity operations has risen drastically during the past few years, while the financing extended to SME sector has declined significantly during the same period. Thus the drastic decrease in the SME credit is due to the hefty increase in the banks' lending for commodity operations (Dawn, 2010).

Thus, contrary to the expectations, the increase in *Musharakah* based financing is restraining financing to SME sector. It is usually argued that the promotion of participatory financing in Islamic banks will reduce the financial constraints faced by SMEs (Huda, 2012; Wilson, 2002). However, paradoxically, the share of SME financing in the financing portfolio of the Islamic banking industry is decreasing gradually due to increase in the *Musharakah* financing (see Table 3). This is because the commodity financing constitute the major portion of (running) *Musharakah*-based financing while its application is very limited in the SME sector. Therefore, Islamic banks ought to promote its application in the SME sector. Moreover, there is a need for serious policy reforms by government and regulatory authorities to ensure sufficient flow of formal credit to SME sector.

The present study also implies agenda for future research:

First, the participatory finance constraints framework proposed by Nouman *et al.* (2018) suggests that the viability of both *Musharakah* and *Mudarabah* based financing arrangements is restrained by the same factors. The present study suggests that adaptation has enhanced the viability of *Musharakah* financing and enabled Islamic banks to allow it in several areas including working capital financing, commodity operations financing, and

---

[7] See Chapra (1985); Ebrahim and Safadi (1995); ElGindi *et al.* (2009); Iqbal and Llewellyn (2002b); Iqbal and Molyneux (2005); Karsten (1982); Kayed (2012); Khan and Mirakhor (1990); Said and Elangkovan (2014); Usmani (2002); Warde (2000); Zaher and Hassan (2001) for detailed discussion on the inherent benefits of the financing based on *Musharakah* and *Mudarabah*.

Table 3. Sector Wise Financing Portfolio of Islamic Banking Industry of Pakistan

Sector	Sep-11 (%)	Sep-12 (%)	Sep-13 (%)	Sep-14 (%)	Sep-15 (%)	Sep-16 (%)	Sep-17 (%)	Sep-18 (%)
Corporate Sector	70.1	70.7	69.4	74.8	73.5	79.8	71.3	72.7
SMEs	5.4	4.8	4.1	3.8	2.8	3.2	3.1	3.0
Agriculture	0.0	0.0	0.1	0.3	0.8	0.7	0.5	0.3
Consumer Finance	15.6	14.9	13.2	13.0	11.3	11.8	10.8	10.5
Commodity Financing	7.1	7.4	11.3	6.2	7.9	2.8	12.3	11.6
Others	1.8	2.2	1.9	2.0	3.7	1.7	1.9	3.1
Total	100.0	100.0	100.0	100.0	100.0	100.0	100.0	100.0

Source: State Bank of Pakistan (2012–2018).

Sukuk. However, Islamic banks still avoid *Mudarabah*-based financing (see Table 1). Future studies ought to investigate whether adaptation can help Islamic banks in reducing constraints to *Mudarabah*-based financing.

Second, this study suggests that service systems, particularly Islamic banks develop new products through adaptation to cope with the constraints posed by the environment. The leading academics in service-system design research also view the service systems as similar to natural ecosystems, that adapt and self-adjust (Maglio *et al.*, 2009; Pareigis *et al.*, 2012). Therefore, our findings are consistent with the service-system design literature (e.g., Cabiddu *et al.*, 2013; Patrício *et al.*, 2011; Ullah, 2014; Vargo and Lusch, 2011; Vargo *et al.*, 2008) and organizational learning literature (e.g., Comfort, 2009; Crossan *et al.*, 1999; Cyert and March, 1963; Fiol and Lyles, 1985; Gomes and Wojahn, 2017; Huber, 1991; Levitt and March, 1988) which also suggests that organizations adapt to solve challenges posed by the environment. However, the current theories of service-system design and organizational learning are inadequate in terms of conceptualizing the potential structural variations inherent in the organizational adaptation (Safavi, 2014; Ullah, 2014). Therefore, future studies should consider the adaptation in *Musharakah* as a case study to enhance the knowledge about the way service-systems adapt their products to cope with the restraining factors in the environment. Future studies ought to develop a conceptual model of adaptation in *Musharakah* to conceptualize the typology of service adaptation and its underlying outcomes.

Third, the present study investigates the revival of *Musharakah* financing in Pakistan. However, the share of *Musharakah* financing is also increasing in Indonesia (Vizcaino, 2015). Therefore, a similar study in the Indonesian context could reveal interesting insights.

Fourth, *Musharakah* and *Mudarabah* are considered as the ideal financing modes due to their several inherent benefits. However, the present study suggests that the basic structure of *Musharakah* has been adapted. Therefore, future studies should investigate whether the variants of *Musharakah* also offer the inherent benefits of pure *Musharakah*. Finally, further insights are required to reflect upon the *Shariah* position about the adaptations in the *Shariah*-based contracts and synchronize these with the *Shariah* juridical principles. Therefore, there is a need for further research in this line of thinking.

6. Conclusion

The findings of the study are consistent with the view that Islamic finance, particularly the participatory finance, is a dependent system for which an economic setting based on Islamic principles is requisite. The viability of participatory financing depends upon the presence of a true Islamic state where the legal, economic, political, social, religious, and educational institutions function as a whole complimenting each other.

Though findings suggest that the regulatory authorities, particularly the State Bank of Pakistan (SBP), have played their role in promoting participatory environment. However, the overall economic, political, social, and legal environment has not changed at all. There are still several factors in the social and regulatory settings of developing countries, including Pakistan, that restraint the application of participatory financing in its true spirit. For example, the present regulatory environment of most developing countries including Pakistan is characterized by weak regulatory framework, inefficient judicial system, and weak property rights. Furthermore, the trustworthiness in the society has not improved whatsoever and the participatory financing arrangements are still prone to the agency problems including asymmetric information, adverse selection, and moral hazards.

Building upon the above notion, it can be concluded that the most dominant motive of the *Musharakah* spur in Pakistan can be attributed to the recent adaptation in *Musharakah*. The *Musharakah* adaptation has allowed the Islamic banks to cope with the constraints to participatory financing and reduce their reliance on the current regulatory and legal framework for disputes resolution and protection of their property rights. This is consistent with the view of Comfort (2009) who suggests that adaptation may enable an organization to operate within its environment with more purpose and persistence, thereby temporarily resolving the paradox of excessive environmental influence that hinders the achievement of specific goals. This adaptation process is the evidence of organizational learning that enable the organizations to understand and interpret their environments and develop viable strategies to cope with the constraints (Daft and Weick, 1984; Fiol and Lyles, 1985; Starbuck *et al.*, 1978). Therefore, the shift away from *Murabahah* towards *Musharakah* is not simply a matter of reform or a minor change in the financing style, but a change in the role of Islamic banks in society and the relationship between Islamic banks and entrepreneurs.

References

Abalkhail, M and JR Presley (2002). How informal risk capital investors manage asymmetric information in profit/loss-sharing contracts. In *Islamic Banking and Finance: New Perspectives on Profit-Sharing and Risk*, M Iqbal and DT Llewellyn (eds.), pp. 111–134. Cheltenham, UK. Northampton, MA, USA: Edward Elgar.

Abdalla, MG-E (1999). Partnership (Musharakah): A new option for financing small enterprises? *Arab Law Quarterly*, 14(3), 257–267.

Abdul-Rahman, A, RA Latif, R Muda and MA Abdullah (2014). Failure and potential of profit-loss sharing contracts: A perspective of New Institutional, Economic (NIE) Theory. *Pacific-Basin Finance Journal*, 28, 136–151.

Abedifar, P, SM Ebrahim, P Molyneux and A Tarazi (2015). Islamic banking and finance: Recent empirical literature and directions for future research. *Journal of Economic Surveys*, 29(4), 637–670.

Aggarwal, RK and T Yousef (2000). Islamic banks and investment financing. *Journal of Money, Credit and Banking*, 32(1), 93–120.

Ahmad, SM (1972). *Economics of Islam: A Comparative Study*. Lahore: Mohammad Ashraf.

Ahmed, GA (2008). The implication of using profit and loss sharing modes of finance in the banking system, with a particular reference to equity participation (partnership) method in Sudan. *Humanomics*, 24(3), 182–206.

Ahmed, MM, M Farooq and M Arsalan (2016). Running musharakah product of Islamic banks: An alternative of running finance. *Al-Idah*, 33, 8–17.

Akacem, M and L Gilliam (2002). Principles of Islamic banking: Debt versus equity financing. *Middle East Policy*, 9(1), 124–138.

Al-Muharrami, S and DC Hardy (2013). Cooperative and Islamic Banks; What can they learn from each other? International Monetary Fund Working Paper, WP/13/184.

Algaoud, LM and MK Lewis (2007). Islamic critique of conventional financing. In *Handbook of Islamic Banking*, MK Hassan and MK Lewis (eds.), Cheltenham, UK: Edward Elgar.

Amrani, F (2012). Financing cost and risk sharing in Islamic finance: A new endogenous approach. *Paper Presented at the 29th International Symposium on Money, Banking and Finance*, Nantes-France.

Andrews, KR (1971). *The Concept of Corporate Strategy*. Homewood: Dow Jones-Irwin.

Ariff, M (1988). Islamic banking. *Asian-Pacijlc Economic Literature*, 2(2), 48–64.

Ascarya (2010). The lack of profit-and-loss sharing financing in Indonesia's islamic banks revisited. *Review of Indonesian Economic and Business Studies*, 1(1), 57–80.

Ayub, M (2007). *Understanding Islamic Finance*. England: John Wiley & Sons Ltd.

Ayub, M (2016). Running Mushārakah by Islamic banks in Pakistan: Running from Mushārakah or moving back to square one (Editorial). *Journal of Islamic Business and Management*, 6(1), 7–18.

Bacha, OI (1995). Conventional versus Mudarabah financing: An agency cost perspective. *Journal of Islamic Economics*, 4(1&2), 33–49.

Bacha, OI (1997). Adapting mudarabah financing to contemporary realities: A proposed financing structure. *The Journal of Accounting, Commerce & Finance*, 1(1), 26–54.

Baker, TL (1994). *Doing Social Research*, 2nd edn. New York: McGraw-Hill Inc.

Bashir, AHM (1996). Investment under profit-sharing contracts: The adverse selection case. *Managerial Finance*, 22(5/6), 48–58.

Baxter, P and S Jack (2008). Qualitative case study methodology: Study design and implementation for novice researchers. *The Qualitative Report*, 13(4), 544–559.

Brown, T (2008). Design thinking. *Harvard Business Review*, 86(6), 1–10.

Cabiddu, F, TW Lui and G Piccoli (2013). Managing value co-creation in the tourism industry. *Annals of Tourism Research*, 42(1), 86–107.

Cavanagh, S (1997). Content analysis: Concepts, methods and applications. *Nurse Researcher*, 4, 5–16.

Chapra, MU (1985). *Towards a Just Monetary System*. Leicester, UK: The Islamic Foundation.

Chenail, RJ (2011). Interviewing the investigator: Strategies for addressing instrumentation and researcher bias concerns in qualitative research. *The Qualitative Report*, 16(1), 255–262.

Cho, JY and E-H Lee (2014). Reducing confusion about grounded theory and qualitative content analysis: Similarities and differences. *The Qualitative Report*, 19(32), 1–20.

Chong, BS and M-H Liu (2009). Islamic banking: Interest-free or interest-based? *Pacific-Basin Finance Journal*, 17, 125–144.

Comfort, LK (2009). Organizational learning and change: Evolving systems in a global community. In *Knowledge Management, Organizational Intelligence and Learning, and Complexity*, LD Kiel (ed.), Vol. III, pp. 1–22. Oxford, UK: EOLSS Publishers Co. Ltd.

Crossan, MM, HW Lane and RE White (1999). An organizational learning framework: From intuition to institution. *The Academy of Management Review*, 24(3), 522–537.

Cyert, RM and JG March (1963). *A Behavioral Theory of the Firm*. Englewood Cliffs, NJ: Prentice-Hall.

Daft, RL and KE Weick (1984). Toward a model of organizations as interpretation systems. *Academy of Management Review*, 9, 284–295.

Dar, HA, DI Harvey and JR Presley (1999). Size, profitability, and agency in profit and loss sharing in Islamic banking and finance. *Paper Presented at the Second Harvard University Forum on Islamic Finance: Islamic Finance into the 21st Century*. Cambridge, Massachusetts.

Dawn (2010). Commodity finaning and credit squeeze. *Dawan*.

Dusuki, AW and A Abozaid (2007). A critical appraisal on the challenges of realizing Maqasid Al-Shariaah in Islamic banking and finance. *International Journal of Economics, Management and Accounting*, 15(2), 143–165.

Ebrahim, MS and A Safadi (1995). Behavioral norms in the Islamic doctrine of economics: A comment *Journal of Economic Behavior and Organization*, 27, 151–157.

El-Gamal, MA (2006). *Islamic Finance: Law, Economics, and Practice*. New York, USA: Cambridge University Press.

El-Komi, M and R Croson (2013). Experiments in Islamic microfinance. *Journal of Economic Behavior & Organization*, 95, 252–269.

ElGindi, T, M Said and JW Salevurakis (2009). Islamic alternatives to purely capitalist modes of finance: A study of Malaysian banks from 1999 to 2006. *Review of Radical Political Economics*, 41(4), 516–538.

Elo, S and H Kyngas (2008). The qualitative content analysis process. *Journal of Advanced Nursing*, 62(1), 107–115, doi: 10.1111/j.1365-2648.2007.04569.x.

Fiol, CM and MA Lyles (1985). Organizational learning. *The Academy of Management Review*, 10(4), 803–813.

Frankland, J and M Bloor (1999). Some issues arising in the systematic analysis of focus group material. In *Developing Focus Group Research: Politics, Theory & Practice*, R Barbour and J Kitzinger (eds.). London: Sage.

Ghanameh, AH (1973). *The Interest Less Economy in Contemporary Aspects of Economic and Social Thinking in Islam*. Gary, Indiana: Muslim Students Association of US and Canada.

Gomes, G and RM Wojahn (2017). Organizational learning capability, innovation and performance: Study in small and medium-sized enterprises (SMES). *Revista de Administração*, 52, 163–175.

Greuning, HV and Z Iqbal (2007). Banking and the risk environment. In *Islamic Finance: Regulatory Challenge*, S Archer and RAA Karim (eds.) pp. 16–23, 11–36. Singapore: John Wiley and Sons.

Han, Q (2010). *Practices and Principles in Service Design: Stakeholders, Knowledge and Community of Service*, PhD thesis, University of Dundee, Scotland.

Haque, NU and A Mirakhor (1986). Optimal profit-sharing contracts and investment in an interest-free Islamic economy. International Monetary Fund Working Paper, WP/86/12.

Hasan, Z (2002). Mudaraba as a mode of finance in Islamic banking: Theory, practice and problems. *The Middle East Business and Economic Review*, 14(2), 41–53.

Hasan, Z (2005). Islamic banking at the cross roads: Theory versus practice. In *Islamic Wealth Creation*, M Iqbal and R Wilson (eds.). UK: Edinburgh University Press.

Hearn, B, J Piesse and R Strange (2012). Islamic finance and market segmentation: Implications for the cost of capital. *International Business Review*, 21, 102–113.

Hickey, G and C Kipping (1996). Issues in research. A multi-stage approach to the coding of data from open-ended questions. *Nurse Researcher*, 4, 81–91.

Hsieh, H-F and SE Shannon (2005). Three approaches to qualitative content analysis. *Qualitative Health Research*, 15(9), 1277–1288.

Huber, GP (1991). Organizational learning: The contributing processes and the literatures. *Organization Science*, 2, 88–115.

Huda, AN (2012). The development of islamic financing scheme for SMEs in a developing country: The Indonesian case. *Procedia-Social and Behavioral Sciences*, 52, 179–186.

Humud, S (1976). *Tatwir Al-A'mal Al-Masrifiyya bima Yattafiqu wa Al-Shari'ah Al-Islamiyya (Arabic)*. Cairo: Dar Al-Ittihad Al-'Arabi lil-Tiba'a.

Iqbal, M and DT Llewellyn (2002a). Introduction. In *Islamic Banking and Finance: New Perspectives on Profit-Sharing and Risk*, M Iqbal and DT Llewellyn (eds.). Cheltenham, UK. Northampton, MA, USA: Edward Elgar.

Iqbal, M and DT Llewellyn (eds.). (2002b). *Islamic Banking and Finance: New Perspectives on Profit-Sharing and Risk*. Cheltenham, UK. Northampton, MA, USA: Edward Elgar.

Iqbal, M and P Molyneux (2005). *Thirty Years of Islamic Banking: History, Performance and Prospects*. New York: Palgrave Macmillan.

Islamic Banking Department (2014). Strategic Plan: Islamic Banking Industry of Pakistan 2014–2018 Pakistan: State Bank of Pakistan.

Ismail, AH (2002). *The Deferred Contracts of Exchange: Al Qur'an in Contrast with Islamic Economists: Theory of Banking and Finance*. Malaysia: Institute of Islamic Understanding (IKIM).

Jan, S and M Asutay (2019). *A Model of Islamic Development: An Approach in Islamic Moral Economy*. Cheltenham: Edward Elgar.

Jan, S, Z Khan and K Ullah (2018). Reflecting on Islamic development process and Sen's capabilities approach. *Abasyn Journal of Scoial Sciences*, 11(1), 37–48.

Jan, S (2013). *A Critique of Islamic Finance in Conceptualising a Development Model of Islam: An Attempt in Islamic Moral Economy*. Doctoral thesis, Durham University, UK.

Karim, AA (2002). Incentive-compatible constraints for Islamic banking: Some lessons from Bank Muamalat. In *Islamic Banking and Finance: New Perspectives on Profit-Sharing and Risk*, M Iqbal and DT Llewellyn (eds.), pp. 95–108. Cheltenham, UK. Northampton, MA, USA: Edward Elgar.

Karsten, I (1982). Islam and Financial Intermediation. *Staff Papers (International Monetary Fund)*, 29(1), 108–142.

Kayed, RN (2012). The entrepreneurial role of profit-and-loss sharing modes of finance: Theory and practice. *International Journal of Islamic and Middle Eastern Finance and Management*, 5(3), 203–228.

Khalil, AFAA, C Rickwood and V Murinde (2002). Evidence on agency-contractual problems in mudarabah financing operations by Islamic banks. In *Islamic Banking and Finance: New Perspectives on Profit-Sharing and Risk*, M Iqbal and DT Llewellyn (eds.), pp. 57–92. Cheltenham, UK. Northampton, MA, USA: Edward Elgar.

Khan, F (2010). How 'Islamic' is Islamic Banking? *Journal of Economic Behavior & Organization*, 76, 805–820.

Khan, MS and A Mirakhor (1990). Islamic Banking: Experiences in the Islamic Republic of Iran and in Pakistan. *Economic Development and Cultural Change*, 38(2), 353–375.

Khan, T (1995). Demand for and supply of PLS and mark-up funds of Islamic banks: Some alternative explanations. *Islamic Economic Studies*, 3(1), 1–46.

Khan, WM (1983). Towards an interest free Islamic economic system: A theoretical analysis of prohibiting debt financing, Ph.D, Boston University.

Kohlbacher, F (2006). The use of qualitative content analysis in case study research. *Forum Qualitative Sozialforschung/Forum: Qualitative Social Research*, 7(1), 1–30.

Kondracki, NL and NS Wellman (2002). Content analysis: Review of methods and their applications in nutrition education. *Journal of Nutrition Education and Behavior*, 34, 224–230.

Levitt, B and JG March (1988). Organizational learning. *Annual Review of Sociology*, 14(1), 319–338.

Lewis, MK (2008). In what ways does Islamic banking differ from conventional finance? *Journal of Islamic Economics, Banking and Finance*, 4(3), 9–24.

Maglio, PP, SL Vargo, N Caswell and J Spohrer (2009). The service system is the basic abstraction of service science. *Information Systems and e-Business Management*, 7(4), 395–406.

Mansoori, MT (2011). Is "Islamic Banking" Islamic? Analysis of current debate on Sharı'ah legitimacy of Islamic banking and finance. *Islamic Studies*, 50(3/4), 383–411.

Marizah, M and D Nazam (2016). Islamic corporate financing: Does it promote profit and loss sharing? *Business Ethics: A European Review*, 25(4), 482–497.

Maududi, SAA (1969). *Ma'ashiyat e Islam (Urdu)*. Lahore: Islamic Publications.

Mayring, P (2000). Qualitative content analysis. *Forum: Qualitative Social Research*, 1(2), 1–10.

Ministry of Finance (2018). *Debt Policy Statement 2018–19*. Debt Policy Coordination Office, Ministry of Finance.

Mirakhor, A and I Zaidi (2007). Profit-and-loss sharing contracts in Islamic finance. In *Handbook of Islamic Banking*, K Hassan and M Lewis (eds.), pp. 49–63. Edward Elgar Publishing.

Moretti, F, L Van Vliet, J Bensing, G Deledda, M Mazzi, M Rimondini and I Fletcher (2011). A standardized approach to qualitative content analysis of focus group discussions from different countries. *Patient Education and Counseling*, 82(3), 420–428.

Nienhaus, V (1983). Profitability of Islamic PLS banks competing with interest banks: Problems and prospects. *Journal of Research in Islamic Economics*, 1(1), 37–47.

Nouman, M (2019). Constraints, adaptation, and outcomes framework of particpatory financing in Islamic banking. PhD, Institute of Management Sciences, Peshawar, Pakistan.

Nouman, M and K Ullah (2014). Constraints in the application of partnerships in Islamic banks: The present contributions and future directions. *Business & Economic Reivew*, 6(2), 47–62.

Nouman, M and K Ullah (2016). New perspectives on partnership contracts in Islamic banks. *1st CEIF International Conference on Towards Financial Inclusion: Developments in Islamic Economics, Banking and Finance*, Peshawar, Pakistan.

Nouman, M, K Ullah and S Gul (2018). Why Islamic banks tend to avoid participatory financing? A demand, regulation, and uncertainty framework. *Business & Economic Review*, 10(1), 1–32.

Pareigis, J, P Echeverri and B Edvardsson (2012). Exploring internal mechanisms forming customer servicescape experiences. *Journal of Service Management Learning*, 23(5), 677–695.

Patrício, L, RP Fisk, JF Cunha and L Constantine (2011). Multilevel service design: From customer value constellation to service experience blueprinting. *Journal of Service Research*, 14(2), 180–200.

Peat, J, C Mellis, K Williams and W Xuan (2002). *Health Science Research: A Handbook of Quantitative Methods*. London: Sage.

Polit, DF, CT Beck and BP Hungler (2001). *Essentials of Nursing Research: Methods, Appraisal and Utilization*, 5th edn. Philadelphia: Lippincott Williams & Wilkins.

Potter, WJ and D Levine-Donnerstein (1999). Rethinking validity and reliability in content analysis. *Journal of Applied Communication Research*, 27(3), 258–284.

Qureshi, AI (1946). *Islam and the Theory of Interest*, 1st edn. Lahore, Pakistan: Muhammad Ashraf Publishers.

Roy, DA (1991). Islamic banking. *Middle Eastern Studies*, 27(3), 427–456.

Sadique, MA (2012). *Capital and Profit Sharing in Islamic Equity Financing: Issues and Prospects*. Kuala Lumpur: The Other Press.

Sadr, K (1999). The role of Musharakah financing in the agricultural bank of Iran. *Arab Law Quarterly*, 14(3), 245–256.

Sadr, K and Z Iqbal (2002). Choice between debt and equity contracts and asymmetrical information: Some empirical evidence. In *Islamic Banking and Finance: New Perspectives on Profit-sharing and Risk*, M Iqbal and DT Llewellyn (eds.), pp. 139–154. Cheltenham, UK. Northampton, MA, USA: Edward Elgar.

Safavi, SM (2014). A performative view of knowledge exploitation and exploration: A case study of a higher education merger, PhD Thesis, University of Edinburgh.

Said, MM and K Elangkovan (2014). Prosperity and social justice consequences of applying ethical norms of Islamic finance: Literature review. *Journal of Economics and Sustainable Development*, 5(2), 99–107.

Samad, A, ND Gardner and BJ Cook (2005). Islamic banking and finance in theory and practice: The experience of Malaysia and Bahrain. *The American Journal of Islamic Social Sciences*, 22(2), 69–86.

Sangiorgi, D (2008). *Service Design as Design of Activity System. Intenrational Service Design Northumbria (ISDN3)*, Northumbria, United Kingdom.

Schreier, M (2012). *Qualitative Content Analysis in Practice*. London: Sage.

Segelström, F (2010). Visualizations in service design. Licentiate of PHILOSOPHY Thesis, Linköpings Universite, Sweden.

Shahid, A, Shagufta, N Ahmad, H Ahmad and MN Shafique (2015). An exploratory study of SHARI'AH compliance in Islamic banking: Evidences from Bangladesh. *Arabian Journal of Business and Management Review (Nigerian Chapter)*, 3(9), 37–43.

Shaikh, MA (2011). Contemporary Islamic banking: The issue of Murābahah. *Islamic Studies*, 50(3/4), 435–448.

Siddiqi, MN (1969). *Ghair Soodi Bank kari (Urdu)*. Lahore: Islamic Publications.

Siddiqi, MN (1981). *Muslim Economic Thinking*. Leicester: Islamic Foundation.

Siddiqi, MN (2006). Islamic banking and finance in theory and practice: A survey of state of the art. *Islamic Economic Studies*, 13(2), 1–48.

Starbuck, WH, A Greve and B Hedberg (1978). Responding to crisis. *Journal of Business Administration*, 9(2), 112–137.

State Bank of Pakistan. (2012–18). *Islamic Banking Bulletin*. Islamic Banking Department, State Bank of Pakistan.

Stickley, T, G Stacey, K Pollock, A Smith, J Betinis and S Fairbank (2010). The practice assessment of student nurses by people who use mental health services. *Nurse Education Today*, 30(1), 20–25.

Sumarti, N, V Fitriyani and M Damayanti (2014). A mathematical model of the profit-loss sharing (PLS) scheme. *Procedia — Social and Behavioral Sciences*, 115, 131–137.

Sundararajan, V and L Errico (2002). Islamic financial institutions and products in the global financial system: Key issues in risk management and challenges ahead. International Monetary Fund Working Paper Working Paper, WP/02/192.

Tahir, S and A Khan (2016). Islamic banking: Why not Mushārakah financing? *Journal of Islamic Business and Management*, 6(1), 61–76.

Thabane, L, J Ma, R Chu, J Cheng, A Ismaila, LP Rios and CH Goldsmith (2010). A tutorial on pilot studies: The what, why and how. *BMC Medical Research Methodology*, 10(1), 1–10.

Ullah, K (2014). Adaptable service-system design: An analysis of Shariah finance in Pakistan. PhD Thesis, Brunel University, London.

Ullah, K (2015). Evolutionary Islamic Banking service. *Journal of Islamic Banking and Finance*, 3(2), 91–96.

Ullah, K and W Al-Karaghouli (2017). *Understanding Islamic Financial Services: Theory and Practice*. Kogan Page Publishers.

Ullah, K and NV Patel (2011). Addressing emergent context of Shariah compliant financial services: A service designing construct. *International Review of Business Research Papers*, 7(3), 81–93.

Usmani, MT (2002). *An Introduction to Islamic Finance*. The Hague: Kluwer Law International.

Usmani, MT (2007). *An Introduction to Islamic Finance*. Karachi, Pakistan: Maktaba Ma'ariful Qur'an.

Usmani, MI (2013). *Shariah Advisor's Report — 2013*. Pakistan: Meezan Bank Limited.

Usmani, MI (2014). *Shariah Advisor's Report — 2014*. Pakistan: Meezan Bank Limited.

Usmani, MI (2015). *Shariah Advisor's Report — 2015*. Pakistan: Meezan Bank Limited.

Van Teijlingen, E and V Hundley (2001). The importance of pilot studies. *Social Research UPDATE*(35).

Vargo, SL and RF Lusch (2011). It's all B2B… and beyond: Toward a systems perspective of the market. *Industrial Marketing Management*, 40(2), 181–187.

Vargo, SL, PP Maglio and MA Akaka (2008). On value and value co-creation: A service systems and service logic perspective. *European Management Journal*, 26(3), 145–152.

Vizcaino, B (2015). Islamic loan books shift towards profit-sharing in Indonesia, Pakistan. *Banking and Financial News*. Available at http://uk.reuters.com/article/islam-financing-loans-idUKL5N0XJ07K20150430.

Warde, I (2000). *Islamic Finance in the Global Economy*. Edinburgh: Edinburgh University Press.

Wilson, R (2002). The interface between Islamic and conventional banking. In *Islamic Banking and Finance: New Perspectives on Profit-Sharing and Risk*, M Iqbal and DT Llewellyn (eds.), pp. 196–218. Cheltenham, UK. Northampton, MA, USA: Edward Elgar.

Yin, RK (2003). *Case Study Research: Designs and Methods*, 3rd edn. Thousand Oaks, CA: Sage Publications.

Yousef, TM (2004). The murabaha syndrome in Islamic finance: Laws, institutions and politics. In *The Politics of Islamic Finance*, C Henry and R Wilson (eds.). Edinburgh: Edinburgh University Press.

Zaher, TS and MK Hassan (2001). A comparative literature survey of Islamic finance and banking. *Financial Markets, Institutions & Instruments*, 10(4), 155–199.

Chapter 13

Financial Inclusion, Institutional Quality, and Financial Development: Empirical Evidence from OIC Countries[#]

Minhaj Ali

School of Economics
Zhongnan University of
Economics and Law, P. R. China
Minhajali556@gmail.com

Muhammad Imran Nazir

School of Finance
Zhongnan University of
Economics and Law, P. R. China

Shujahat Haider Hashmi[*]

School of Economics
Huazhong University of
Science and Technology, P. R. China
shujahat_hashmi@hotmail.com

Wajeeh Ullah

School of Economics
Zhongnan University of
Economics and Law, P. R. China

This unique study examines the moderation effect of institutional quality (IQ) on the relationship between financial inclusion (FI) and financial development (FD) of 45 Organization of Islamic Cooperation (OIC) countries. For empirical analysis, panel data are used for the period 2000–2016. We use the Arellano–Bond generalized method of moments (GMM) and two-stage least-squares (2SLS) method in our estimations to draw multidimensional results. The empirical results confirm the significant positive relationship between FI, IQ and FD. Interestingly, we find that IQ moderates FI and has a significant positive impact on FD. Our findings are robust to alternative econometric specifications of FI, IQ and FD. Therefore, policymakers must sensibly understand the pivotal role of FI and IQ in establishing sustainable future development of OIC countries.

Keywords: Financial inclusion; institutional quality; financial development; GMM; 2SLS; OIC.

---

[*]Corresponding author.
[#]This Chapter first appeared in the *Singapore Economic Review*, Vol. 67, No. 1, doi: 10.1142/S0217590820420084. © 2022 World Scientific Publishing.

1. Introduction

Over the past years, there has been an increased interest in exploring the finance-growth nexus. Those studies have shown that financial development (FD) contributes to economic growth through both direct and indirect channels (Le *et al.*, 2016). In recent years, numerous studies have shown that institutions positively and significantly influence economic growth and development (Khan *et al.*, 2019). FD is an integral part of economic development, and a well-organized financial system leads to economic prosperity. During the last decade, many researchers were set to investigate the role of institutions' quality in the relationship between FD and economic growth, like Hasan *et al.* (2009), Minea and Villieu (2010), Aggarwal and Goodell (2010) and Rachdi and Mensi (2012). These studies conclude that the financial system, set into a well-organized institutional structure, has a positive effect on economic growth.

The financial sector plays a vital role in the distribution of scarce economic resources, and the financial activities engaged in this process support economic growth (Graff, 2003). It is worth noting that few studies have focused on the direct impact of institutional quality (IQ) on FD (e.g., Girma and Shortland, 2008; Law *et al.*, 2013). Most of these researchers established a strong correlation between IQ and FD and concluded that IQ increases FD.

Hartmann *et al.* (2007) describe FD as a process of achieving financial innovation and institutional and organizational developments in a financial system to decrease the amount of asymmetric information, improve the inclusiveness of markets, reduce transaction costs and promote competition. Therefore, the scope of FD comprises improvements in products, organizations and institutions in the banking sector, non-banking financial organizations and capital markets. Han and Shen (2015) claim that the prompt rapidity of FD results in a total factor productivity growth by improving the inconsistency in resource allocation. Similarly, Yu *et al.* (2017) describe two financial functions, namely, financial access and financial efficiency, as essential factors of FD that produce a spillover effect through economic development. FD also performs as a poverty reduction instrument and an economic promoter when the liquid liabilities and credit to the private sector are used as measures (Rashid and Intartaglia, 2017).

Andrianova *et al.* (2011) highlight the crucial role of the government as a political institution that increases large trading monopolies, thereby empowering the development of financial systems globally. Anwar and Cooray (2012) argue that progress in political rights and civil liberties increases the benefits of FD in South Asia by positively contributing to the economic growth. Ro *et al.* (2017) argue that the measures of financial market productivity and effectiveness are more important than the size of the financial market in promoting economic growth.

In contrast, an increasing number of studies have shown that financial inclusion (FI) positively and significantly influences economic growth and development. FI received much attention from scholars, government administrators and other financial stakeholders. The evidence from worldwide research efforts has shown that there is a relationship between levels of financial exclusion and economic growth. FI means the ease and availability of formal financial services, such as bank deposits, credits, insurance, etc., for all members of an economy (Anand and Chhikara, 2013). According to Kim *et al.* (2018), a high level of inclusivity in a financial society means that the conditions in which most of an economy's stakeholders are using formal financial framework agree them to benefit from financial services and strive for their stable position in the economy.

In the existing literature, the relationship between FI and economic growth has not been sufficiently studied. There is an on-going discussion on the nexus between a financial system (in terms of financial deepening) and growth. Schumpeter (1912) underscores the vital role of the banking system in economic growth. McKinnon (1973) and Shaw (1973) studied that an efficient and effective flow of funds from banks through their public network leads to innovation and FD. The banking system is a robust financial intermediation system that leads to long-run economic growth and improved productivity (King and Levine, 1993). Therefore, these arguments support the finance–growth association. According to Beck and De La Torre (2006), access to financial services that are delivered responsibly and conveniently or outreach of the financial system has become an essential concern for several policymakers in developing countries. Therefore, over the past decade, FI has made its impact on the mind of policymakers of several developed and emerging countries (Zuleika, 2010). In that context, Chakravarty and Pal (2013) argue that FI is quite critical in the framework of achieving inclusive growth and encroachment of an economy. Since the well-being of a population depends on various characteristics such as income, health, housing, etc., access to financial services can also be considered as a necessary component for the well-being of humanity.

On the other side, Muslims, who are nearly one-fourth of the world's population, make themselves separate from the present financial system. The cause behind this is that the existing financial system goes against the values of Islamic religious called Shari'ah. In recent years, however, thanks to the beginning of Shari'ah-complaint financial products and insurances, which allow for financial exceptions by a flexible understanding of Shari'ah, which plays a crucial role in enhancing the level of FI of Islamic states, there are a lot of growing concerns (Mohieldin *et al.*, 2011).

There is a lack of studies in the literature associating FI as part of FD (Sharma, 2016). The different economic views might perceive FI as an objective that will experience an extra cost or treat it as something that will lead to an incompetent division of resources and eventually to the decline of economic development (Sharma, 2016). However, under no circumstance can one disagree with the dynamic role of FI in terms of financial persistence of the society and the general development of all demographic limitations (Mani, 2016).

We contribute to the FD literature in several ways. First, this is one of only a few cross-country studies that underline FI and its role in the progress of the financial sector. FI is known as a part of the economic development process, which expands the growth by making healthy and suitable environments either through a supply-leading or a demand-following channel (Sharma, 2016). Moreover, instability of institutions tends to cause instability in macroeconomic policy, which ultimately affect FD. Levine (1998) confirms that institutions play an essential role in the performance of financial markets. Secondly, based on the arguments mentioned above, this study also examines the moderation effect of IQ on the relationship between FI and FD. To the best of our knowledge, no previous study has presented a comparison between OIC countries. Thus, we use cross-country data to fill this research gap.

Thirdly, this study employs both FI index (FII) and IQ index (IQI) for empirical analysis. FII is based on four indicators (i.e., automated teller machines per 100,000 adults, commercial bank branches per 100,000 adults, depositors with commercial banks per 1000 adults and life insurance premium volume to GDP). IQI is based on six dimensions of governance (i.e., control of corruption, government effectiveness, political stability and absence of violence, regulatory quality, the rule of law and voice and accountability).

Fourth, the empirical findings will enrich the existing literature by providing reliable outcomes and understanding the nexus among finance and IQ literature in general and concerning the Organization of Islamic Cooperation (OIC) countries in particular. In doing so, we have applied the latest econometric methodologies such as the generalized method of moments (GMM) and two-stage least-squares (2SLS) approaches to address the issue of endogeneity, heteroscedasticity, autocorrelation and omitted variable bias. Lastly, the research outcome is beneficial for the policymakers of the OIC countries to implement suitable policies about FI and IQ and provide scope for policy debate.

The remainder of this study is organized as follows: Section 2 provides the literature review. Section 3 highlights the data and the methodology for this study. The empirical results and discussion will be presented in Section 4. Finally, Section 5 concludes the paper and highlights some policy implications.

2. Literature Review

A large number of previous studies imperatively focused on explaining the role of FD in growth patterns, in which each study has a different feature to improve the understanding of the subject. The distinguished works, e.g., Schumpeter (1912), Gurley and Shaw (1955), McKinnon (1973) and Shaw (1973), are essential to study the nexus between FD and growth. The theory states that the development of the banking sector is one of the essential elements of economic growth. Ge and Qiu (2007), Tsoukas (2011), Kendall (2012), Han and Shen (2015) and Mimir (2016) highlight a positive association between FD and economic growth or its drivers such as investment or openness. The literature on the influence of IQ on FD is abundant (Baltagi *et al.*, 2009; Law *et al.*, 2013; Hafer, 2013). However, many studies have focused on the relationship among FD, FI and economic growth (Adeniyi *et al.*, 2015; Dabos and Gantman, 2012; Gokmenoglu *et al.*, 2015; Sharma, 2016; Kim *et al.*, 2018).

Several recent studies provide empirical evidence on the link between IQ and FD (Rodrik *et al.*, 2002; Klomp and de Haan, 2014; Bonnal and Yaya, 2015; Le *et al.*, 2016). Levine (1997) claims that institutions play a vital role in the execution of financial markets. Arestis and Demetriades (1997) and Demetriades and Andrianova (2004) suggested that the possible outcome from FD is generally determined by the quality of financial regulation and the rule of law. According to Aghion *et al.* (2009), financial institutions and markets help in attaining a reasonably safe rate of return. Active financial institutions help in reducing agency problems through monitoring.

Girma and Shortland (2008) studied the influence of democracy characteristics and the change of political rule on FD. The study used the data of advanced and emerging economies over the period 1975–2000 by employing the GMM as an estimation technique. The authors revealed that the degree of democracy and political stability are essential elements for FD. Baltagi *et al.* (2009) confirmed the effect of IQ and financial/trade openness on FD for advanced and developing nations from 1980 to 2003. They found no significant relationship between IQ and FD. Huang (2010) emphasized the short-term benefits of improving institutions on FD for low-income countries. The study used the data of 90 developed and emerging countries from 1960 to 1999. Law *et al.* (2013) found that the impact of finance on economic growth was positive and significant only after a certain level of institutional development had been achieved by using a sample of 85 countries over the period 1980–2008 and utilized the threshold estimation technique. Notably, the qualities of formal institutions like the rule of law, bureaucratic quality, control of corruption or government effectiveness and the overall comprehensive institution had a vibrant role in the finance–growth link. As per their findings, the influence of finance on economic growth was non-existent until the optimal level of the institution was reached. Hafer (2013) investigated the influence of economic freedom on FD by using the data of 81 countries from 1980 to 2009. The outcomes show that economies with higher levels of economic freedom have higher levels of FD. Le *et al.* (2016) examined the factors of financial sector development in Asia from 1995 to 2011. They applied the GMM approach to a panel data set of 26 countries in the region. The analysis was done for the whole panel along with subpanels of advanced and developing nations. They found that enhanced governance and IQ raise financial sector progress in emerging nations, whereas economic growth and trade openness are critical elements of financial depth in developed countries. Kutan *et al.* (2017) studied the role of IQ in the association of FD and economic growth in the Middle East and North African countries and find that FD contributes to economic growth only in the existence of IQ.

A pioneer research work on FD and economic growth by Beck *et al.* (2000) established that there is a significant association between financial intermediary development and both real per capita GDP development and total factor productivity development. They employed the averaged data of cross-country over the period 1960–1995. Employing the GMM method to account for the issue of likely endogeneity of the regressors, they found that enhanced active financial intermediaries increase resource distribution and increase total factor productivity progress with positive outcomes for long-run economic growth. Similarly, using the same approach of data examination, Levine *et al.* (2000) revealed that the exogenous factor of financial intermediary growth is positively related to economic development. They also established that cross-country dissimilarities in legal and accounting structures help account for differences in the financial progress. Christopoulos and Tsionas (2004) examined the long-run association between financial depth and economic growth, taking the data from 10 emerging nations. They examined data by panel unit root and panel cointegration methods. They found a long-run association between FD and economic growth in 10 developing economies. Recently, Farooq and Yasmin (2017) explored the association between fiscal policy uncertainty and economic growth by incorporating the critical role of FD in Pakistan over the period 1970–2011. They employed the auto-regressive distributed lag (ARDL) method for analysis. The outcomes of the study revealed that FD increases economic growth by decreasing the adverse effect of fiscal policy uncertainties. Similarly, Bojanic (2012), Uddin *et al.* (2013), Jedidia *et al.* (2014) and Samargandi *et al.* (2014) using time-series approaches for data investigation have also found a positive influence of FD on economic growth.

In contrast, in the late 1990s, FI has received much attention from policymakers to discuss the issue of generally excluded people and research studies about the financial exclusion of society (Collard, 2007). Aduda and Kalunda (2012) and Ravikumar (2012) define the term "financial inclusion" as the process to integrate all segments of society under the umbrella of the recognized financial system. Bhaskar (2013) argues that the financial stability of an economy entails access to financial services at a cheaper cost. Inclusive development and enhancement lead to economic growth and healthy FD (Rillo, 2014). Similarly, Chibba (2009) highlights that FI helps to manage poverty and enhance the inclusive growth of the economy.

Sarma (2008) and Arora (2010) constructed a multidimensional index of FI to measure "financial inclusion" in terms of the banking institutions and the role of the banking institutions. Moreover, Demirguc-Kunt and Klapper (2012) conducted an initial survey on the basis of the Global Findex Database indicators developed by the World Bank in 2012 to understand the dissimilarity in the usage of financial services across and within 148 countries. Sarma (2008), Arora (2010) and Demirguc-Kunt and Klapper (2012) concluded their model work by analyzing their robust FI index across countries.

There are a few studies on the nexus between FI and economic growth. Onaolapo (2015) investigates the impact of FI on the economic growth in Nigeria. The study showed that overall financial activities significantly increase economic growth through the decrease in poverty. Sharma (2016) examined the nexus between FI and economic growth in India. The regression results confirm the positive and significant correlation between the several dimensions of FI and GDP. The results of Granger causality analysis reveal a bi-directional link between geographical outreach and economic growth and a unidirectional connection between the number of deposit/loan accounts and GDP. However, no relationship was found between the usage of banking services and economic growth. Similarly, Kim *et al.* (2018) studied the association between FI and economic growth in the OIC countries by employing several econometric techniques such as the GMM, panel VAR and panel Granger causality. The panel dynamic regression results show the positive association between FI and economic growth in OIC countries. The results of Granger causality analysis show that variables of FI Granger cause economic growth, but economic growth does not Granger cause these variables of FI. Also, the impulse response function (IRF) results derived from the panel VAR technique suggest that the overall impact of FI on the economic growth of the OIC countries is positive.

Recently, several studies explored the role of FI in increasing Islamic banking and individual's characteristics. Shihadeh (2018) analyzed how individuals' characteristic impacts FI in the Middle East, North African, Afghanistan and Pakistan (MENAP) by using the World Bank Global Findex Database 2014 for 16 countries in the region. A probit estimation approach was employed to analyze the marginal impact of FI on the characteristics of individuals existing in the MENAP region. These characteristics contain age, gender, education and income. The outcomes revealed that women and the poor are less likely to be involved in financial systems; however, the level of education improves FI. As underprivileged individuals consider that access to the loan is essential to enhance their living standards, the study found that the poor are more likely to borrow for health problems than for other essentials. Besides, individuals in various income quintiles are more likely to utilize informal financial services, but educated people are more likely to utilize proper services. Asyatun (2019) examined the regional variables (income level, educational level, income inequality, population size and banking accessibility) that are important in promoting FI in Indonesia. The period of the study is from 2012 to 2015. By employing the panel data estimation technique, the findings indicated that income level, educational level and banking accessibility have a significant influence on FI in Indonesia. Khmous and Besim (2020) examined the Islamic banking share and individual characteristics that affect FI in 14 Middle Eastern and North African (MENA) economies with different income levels. This study used the data from the 2014 World Bank Global Findex database by employing the probit estimation method. The outcomes revealed that FI, mainly in middle-income MENA economies, is lower than the worldwide average. However, being male, wealthy and older positively influence FI in these economies; education does not. Islamic banking practices also promote FI, particularly for persons with strong religious associations. The influence of Islamic banking on FI is found to be more generous in middle-income MENA economies. Banna and Alam (2020) investigated the efficiency scores of 153 Islamic banks of 32 economies from 2011 to 2017 by utilizing data envelopment analysis and Simar–Wilson double bootstrapping regression methods to conclude how FI and its interaction effect with economic growth affect Islamic banking efficiency to stimulate inclusive, sustainable growth. The results revealed that to increase the efficiency of Islamic banks, FI must play a vital role. Besides, the impact of the interaction between FI and economic growth proposes that FI plays a vital role in sustainable growth, which makes a positive association between inclusive, sustainable progress and the proficiency of Islamic banks. The summary of the selected works is presented in Table 1.

The above comprehensive review of the empirical literature provides a strong theoretical foundation for investigating the significant roles of FI, IQ and FD in promoting economic growth. Also, these studies covered numerous economies and regions worldwide; however, there are no related studies that focusded on the OIC countries. Due to this scarcity, the present study has its motivation to concentrate and examine the impact of FI and IQ on FD in OIC countries.

2.1. *Hypothesis development*

Since the pioneering work of North (1981) on institutional economics, researchers have consistently supported the idea that IQ is one of the crucial elements in the progress of the

Table 1. Summary of the Studies Incorporated in the Literature Review

Author	Sample/Region	Period	Method	Findings
Girma and Shortland (2008)	110 countries	1975–2000	GMM	IQ is essential for FD
Baltagi et al. (2009)	42 developing countries and 32 developed and developing countries	1980–2003	GMM	Insignificant relationship between IQ and FD
Huang (2010)	90 developed and emerging countries	1960–1999	LSDVC and GMM	The study highlighted the short-term benefits of improving institutions on FD for low-income countries
Law et al. (2013)	85 countries	1980–2008	Threshold estimation technique	This study found that the impact of finance on economic growth was positive and significant only after a certain level of institutional development had been achieved
Hafer (2013)	81 countries	1980–2009	OLS	The results show that countries with higher levels of economic freedom have higher levels of FD
Le et al. (2016)	Asia	1995–2011	GMM	This study concluded that improved governance and IQ raise financial sector development in emerging economies
Kutan et al. (2017)	21 MENA countries	1980–2012	CCEP	FD contributes to economic growth only in the presence of IQ
Beck et al. (2000)	77 countries	1960–1995	GMM	This study found that better financial intermediaries rise in total factor productivity growth with positive effects for long-run economic growth
Levine et al. (2000)	74 countries	1961–1995	GMM	FD is positively linked to economic growth
Christopoulos and Tsionas (2004)	10 developing countries	1970–2000	Panel co-integration technique	They found a long-run relationship between FD and economic growth
Farooq and Yasmin (2017)	Pakistan	1970–2011	ARDL	FD promotes economic development
Bojanic (2012)	Bolivia	1940–2010	Cointegration and causality method	FD increases economic growth
Uddin et al. (2013)	Kenya	1971–2011	ARDL	FD increases economic growth
Jedidia et al. (2014)	Tunisia	1973–2008	ARDL	FD increases economic growth

Table 1. (*Continued*)

Author	Sample/Region	Period	Method	Findings
Samargandi et al. (2014)	Saudi Arabia	1968–2010	ARDL	FD increases the economic growth of the Saudi non-oil region in the long run
Onaolapo (2015)	Nigeria	1982–2012	OLS	Financial activities significantly increase economic growth through the reduction in poverty
Sharma (2016)	India	2004–2013	VAR	The study found a positive relationship between economic growth and many dimensions of FI
Kim et al. (2018)	OIC countries	1990–2013	GMM	The regression outcomes indicate the positive relationship between FI and economic growth in OIC countries
Shihadeh (2018)	MENAP	2014	Probit estimation technique	The level of education improves FI. Besides, individuals in various income quintiles are more likely to utilize informal financial services
Asyatun (2019)	Indonesia	2012–2015	Panel data estimation	The outcomes revealed that income level, educational level and banking accessibility have a significant influence on FI in Indonesia
Khmous and Besim (2020)	14 MENA countries	2014	Probit estimation technique	The outcomes revealed that FI, mainly in middle-income MENA economies, is minor than the worldwide average. Islamic banking practices also promote FI, particularly for persons with strong religious associations
Banna and Alam (2020)	153 Islamic banks of 32 economies	2011–2017	Data envelopment analysis and Simar–Wilson double bootstrapping regression	The outcomes suggested that to enhance the proficiency of Islamic banks, FI must play a dynamic role

Notes: LSDVC is the bias-corrected least-squares dummy variable estimator, OLS denotes ordinary least squares, CCEP indicates common correlated effect mean pooled, GMM signifies the generalized method of moments, ARDL is autoregressive-distributed lag, VAR represents vector auto-regression, FD is financial development, IQ is institutional quality, OIC is Organization of Islamic Cooperation, MENAP stands for the Middle East, North African, Afghanistan and Pakistan and MENA is Middle Eastern and North African.

economy (Acemoglu and Verdier, 1998). Al-Yousif (2002) stated that the association between FD and economic progress could not be generalized across nations because economic plans are country-specific, and their accomplishment is contingent on the effectiveness of the institutions executing them. Mardan (2017) reports the restrictions to outward fundraising, comprising tax policies and interest immunities, that control the optimal utilization of funding opportunities and thus resulting in FD; these strict guidelines are more evident in less financially advanced countries compared with financially advanced economies. Singh and Delios (2017) discussed the role of governance in stimulating board independence and instigating expanding plans with different national and international projects, of which the latter be contingent on the interconnection of board corporations with the central networks of other corporations. In nations where the legal system is comparatively developed, financiers have higher degrees of safety. When such a societal system guards the legitimate interests and rights of its stakeholders, they become keener to finance and thus enhance the development of the country. Furthermore, under robust institutions and systems, a country's consumer market is more vigorous and effective.

FI becomes an essential program at the domestic and global levels as there are 2.6 billion individuals, or more than 50% of the world population, not having access to loans, savings and insurance (CGAP, 2013). A high level of FI will go along with a robust financial system, and individuals with lower income levels would have a better influence of FI on FD than individuals with higher income (CGAP, 2013). This is due to FI induced by better insinuations for the development of the financial sector. Thus, FD is prominently contingent on the degree of FI and vice versa. An increase in FI can encourage financial sector development because the progress of the financial sector in an economy is determined by the number of persons that have access to funds, and the level of FI can also be contingent on the level of FD (Anarfo *et al.*, 2019). The FI is likely to raise inclusive growth in various nations. Improving FI increases bank-based deposit as a source of credit. The credit can increase real sector performance. These deposits would decrease poverty, enhance income distribution and increase the stability of the financial system in order to attain the inclusive growth of the country (Khan, 2011).

Researchers also examine the impact of financial sector development on economic development and base their arguments on the crucial roles of an effective financial system in an economy. Creane *et al.* (2003) classified these roles as generally covering the mobilization of funds, elevation of investment through documentation and funding of favorable business opportunities, checking organizational operations, allowing for dealing, risk divergence, equivocation and enabling goods and services exchanged. By executing these roles, Seetanah *et al.* (2008) discussed that financial systems eventually result in the immediate increase of human capital and physical capital, distribution of resources proficiently and faster technological progression, all of which increase economic progress and development. The argument on the impact of economic progress on the development of the financial sector is extensively examined. Most empirical studies have found confirmation of a positive association between economic progress and financial sector development, and this shows that there exists a reverse causality between economic development and financial sector progress (Odhiambo, 2011).

Moreover, Giné and Townsend (2004) used empirical evidence from Thailand to show increasing access to financial services results in better growth. The term economic progress has been devised to describe growth that contains the poor and marginalized people in the economy. This fact is likely to arise due to the rise in the usage of financial services and products, which tends to increase FD, poverty alleviation and income equality (Beck *et al.*, 2008). Therefore, FI may contribute to the development of the country through the channel of FD or might directly affect poverty and income inequality, hence leading to economic progress.

According to Saydaliyev *et al.* (2020), IQ is an essential element that influences the decision-making process of people to increase access to financial facilities offered by specific financial organizations. In contrast, Hafer (2013) argued that IQ increases the development of the financial sector. Therefore, considering these assumptions, this is essential and innovative to check the moderation effect of IQ on the relationship between FI and FD.

In summary, all of the above arguments recommend that FI and IQ could be an essential element for financial sector development. Thus, given the profound nature of FI, IQ and FD in OIC countries, this study proposes the following hypothesis:

H_1: FI is positively associated with FD.
H_2: IQ is positively related to FD in economies with higher quality institutions.
H_3: IQ positively moderates the relationship between FI and FD.

3. Methodology

3.1. Variables and data source

This study examines a sample of 45 OIC countries that are used as the data sample to examine the effect of the financial inclusion index (FII) and institutional quality index (IQI) on FD. In this research, dynamic panel data are used for the period 2000–2016, taken from the Global Financial Development Database (GFDD), World Governance Indicators (WGI), World Development Indicators (WDI) of the World Bank, International Monetary Fund Database (IMF) and Heritage Foundation Database (HFD). The sample has been selected for this analysis based on the availability of reliable data. Our sample consists of OIC countries that are expected to lead the global economic growth in the future and provides potential opportunities to investors across the globe. The names of the countries are listed in Table A.1 (see Appendix A).

3.1.1. Dependent variable

FD is our dependent variable measured by a comprehensive index constructed by Svirydzenka (2016) and obtained from the IMF. As explained in Figure 1, this index summarizes the depth, access and efficiency of the financial institutions and financial markets.

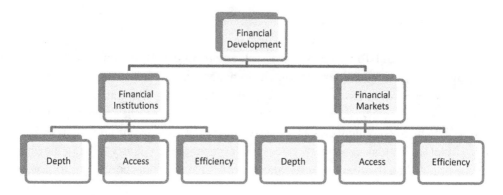

Source: The dataset is maintained by the IMF Strategy, Policy and Review Department.

Figure 1. Overview of the FD Index

3.1.2. Independent variables

The IQI: The data of IQ are taken from the WGI for all countries over the period 2000–2016. The WGI measures have six dimensions of governance which are as follows: control of corruption (COC), government effectiveness (GOE), political stability and absence of violence (POS), regulatory quality (REQ), the rule of law (ROL) and voice and accountability (VOA) (Dwumfour and Ntow-Gyamfi, 2018). To make an index of IQ, we employ PCA on these six dimensions.

The FII: The data of FI are taken from WDI of the World Bank. Due to the unavailability of the data, we only choose the following measurements: automated teller machines per 100,000 adults, commercial bank branches per 100,000 adults, depositors with commercial banks per 1000 adults, life insurance premium volume to gross domestic product (GDP) of FI to make a composite FI index by using PCA. Prior studies indicate that few variables can control FD. Therefore, control variables are as follows: we control FD along with economic growth as measured by real GDP per capita (Pradhan *et al.*, 2014). We use GDP as a proxy for economic growth. For trade openness (TOP), the ratio of imports and exports to GDP is incorporated because this proxy is a simple and common indicator of trade openness as recommended by Harrison (1996), and population growth rate per year (POG) by Kutan *et al.* (2017), to construct a robust and possibly realistic analysis. The definitions of the variables and their data source are reported in Table A.2 (see Appendix A).

The theoretical association between the variables is shown in a general functional form as:

$$FD = f(\text{FII}, \text{IQI}, \text{IQI} * \text{FII}, \text{GDP}, \text{TOP}, \text{POG}), \tag{1}$$

where FD is the financial development, FII is the financial inclusion index, IQI is the institutional quality index, IQI*FII shows the moderation effect of IQI and FII, GDP represents the economic growth, TOP shows trade openness and POG is the population growth rate.

3.2. Regression model

We first use PCA to generate a composite index of FD, FI and IQ. According to Batuo *et al.* (2018) and Le *et al.* (2016), PCA allows the orthogonal linear transformation of FI and IQ measurements (high dimension) into composite indexes (low dimension) to functionalize the research objective. The PCA of the FII is reported in Table A.3 (see Appendix A). Table A.3 indicates that the highest eigenvalue is 2.43327, followed by 0.970439, 0.34013 and 0.256165 for second, third and fourth components, respectively. The first principal component denotes 60.83% of the standard deviation in all variables, whereas the second, third and fourth explain 24.26%, 8.5% and 6.4% of the overall standard deviation, respectively. Figure A.1 in Appendix A shows the scree plot of the eigenvalues, specifying the numbers of the factors that have to signify FI. We select comp1 to generate FI index because comp2, comp3 and comp4 carry small or negative values. Similarly, the results of PCA of the IQI in Table A.4 (see Appendix A) specify that the maximum eigenvalue is 4.26458, followed by 0.878614, 0.466406, 0.201672, 0.108266 and 0.0804605 for second, third, fourth, fifth and sixth factors, respectively. The first principal component indicates 71.08% of the standard deviation in all variables, whereas the second, third, fourth, fifth and sixth show 14.64%, 7.7%, 3.3%, 1.8% and 1.3% of the overall standard deviation respectively. Figure A.2 in Appendix A explains the scree plot of the eigenvalues, stating the statistics of the components that represent IQ. In this case, we also choose comp1 to generate FI index because comp2, comp3, comp4, comp5 and comp6 have small or negative values:

$$FII_{it} = 0.5649 ATM_{it} + 0.5650 BRC_{it} + 0.5762 DCB_{it} + 0.1720 LIN_{it}, \quad (2)$$

$$IQI_{it} = 0.4523 COC_{it} + 0.4506 GOE_{it} + 0.3783 POS_{it} + 0.4428 REQ_{it}$$
$$+ 0.4641 ROL_{it} + 0.1943 VOA_{it}, \quad (3)$$

where the index of FI and IQ is an aggregate value of FI and IQ measures and the coefficient score of every factor.

We then employ the OLS, GMM and 2SLS regressions to measure the association among FII, IQI and FD and also the moderating role of FII*IQI. The regression model is described as follows:

$$Y_{it} = \alpha_0 + \alpha_1 X_{it} + \alpha_2 P_{it} + \mu_{it}, \quad (4)$$

where Y is the dependent variable, FD, X is the explanatory variable, FII and IQI, P is the matrix of the controls over Y (i.e., trade openness, population growth rate and economic growth), i denotes the countries, t denotes the time and μ is an error term.

4. Empirical Results and Discussion

In this section, we explain the empirical results and examine the impact of FII and IQI on FD in OIC countries.

Tables 2 and 3, respectively, describe the descriptive statistics and the correlation coefficients of the variables used in our model. The descriptive statistics of the variables were in terms of mean, standard deviation, minimum and maximum values for the variables. The first column presents the variable proxy, the second column shows the mean values, the third column presents the standard deviation values (std. dev.) and the fourth

Table 2. Descriptive Statistics

Variables	Mean	Std. Dev.	Min	Max
FD	−1.6992	0.6298	−2.9402	−0.4341
FII	−0.1442	0.9956	−3.9717	1.3617
IQI	−0.4702	1.2621	−6.8275	0.7998
GDP	7.8798	1.4681	5.7879	12.1999
TOP	4.2389	0.4083	3.1497	5.1747
POG	0.7769	0.5617	−2.5669	2.5708

Notes: FD indicates financial development, FII represents financial inclusion index, IQI shows the index for institutional quality, GDP is a measure of economic growth, TOP captures the trade openness and POG denotes population growth rate.

Table 3. Correlation Coefficients Matrix

Variables	FD	FII	IQI	GDP	TOP	POG
FD	1					
FII	0.3993*	1				
IQI	0.3901*	0.5149*	1			
GDP	0.3849*	0.6515*	0.6329*	1		
TOP	0.0872*	0.2746*	0.3589*	0.3536*	1	
POG	0.0979*	0.0027	0.3090*	0.2415*	0.1486*	1

Note: * shows the significance level at 1%.

and fifth columns show the minimum and maximum values, respectively. The FD is significantly correlated with all the regressors (i.e., FII, IQI, GDP, TOP and POG).

4.1. *Baseline results*

We examine the primary OLS results reported in Table 4. Model 1 shows the impact of FII on FD, whereas model 2 reports the effect of IQI on the FD of OIC countries, and model 3 shows the result of IQI*FII on FD with FII, IQI and other control variables. These findings explain the association between variables. Model 1 explains that FII will increase FD by 0.32 unit and significant at the statistical 1% level. Model 2 shows that IQI will also increase FD by 0.32 unit and significant at the statistical 1% level. In model 3, the interactive term IQI*FII shows a 0.30 unit increase in FD and is significant at the statistical 1% level. Besides, GDP is also significantly and positively related to FD in model 1 and 2, whereas POG shows no effect on FD. Only TOP shows a negative and significant impact on FD. The adjusted R^2 shows that using a simple OLS regression with controls, FD is positively driven by around 48.9% with FII and other controls variables in model 1, and 48.8% with IQI and other control variables in model 2 and 46.2% with the FII, IQI, IQI*FII and other control variables.

Table 4. IQ, FI and FD

Variables	Model 1	Model 2	Model 3
FII	0.328***		0.366***
	(0.0518)		(0.0525)
IQI		0.322***	0.223***
		(0.0511)	(0.0503)
IQI*FII			0.308***
			(0.0436)
GDP	0.171***	0.200***	0.0414
	(0.0366)	(0.0339)	(0.0383)
TOP	−0.0029**	−0.0037***	−0.0063***
	(0.0014)	(0.0014)	(0.0014)
POG	0.0361	−0.0219	−0.0205
	(0.0222)	(0.0221)	(0.0222)
Constant	−1.220***	−1.244***	0.0418
	(0.275)	(0.274)	(0.305)
F-statistics	45.58	45.43	46.38
Prob. value	0.0000	0.0000	0.0000
Adj. R^2	0.4892	0.4887	0.4628

Notes: *** and ** denote the significance level at 1% and 5%, respectively. The values of standard errors are presented in parentheses.

4.2. *2SLS estimation*

This study applies 2SLS estimation. To address the issue of endogeneity in the panel data, we analyze the impact of FII and IQI on FD of the OIC countries using 2SLS. We use three instrument variables, such as property rights, financial freedom and monetary freedom (Maruta, 2019). Instrumental variables are used when the dependent variable's error terms are correlated with the independent variables. As can be seen in Table 5, financial freedom (FIF), monetary freedom (MOF) and property rights (PRO) have a significant effect on FII, IQI and IQI*FII as an instrument variable (IV). This finding explains the significance of including IV in the analysis to obtain reliable estimates. The FII translates into a 1.36 unit increase in FD with IV and significant at the statistical 5% level. IQI shows a 0.44 unit increase in FD with IV and significant at the statistical 1% level, and the interactive term IQI*FII shows a 1.08 unit increase in FD with IV and significant at the statistical 1% level.

The OLS estimation in Table 4 helps to explain the behavior of FII, IQI and IQI*FII, and other control variables and the subsequent magnitude with which they affect FD. This econometrical association provides a substructure for thoroughly understanding the medium through which these variables strive for FD. Table 5 plots such association comprehensively when the FII, IQI and IQI*FII are instrumented with FIF, MOF and PRO. All variables (FII, IQI and IQI*FII) positively and significantly contribute to describing the FD of OIC countries.

Table 5. IQ, FI and FD (2SLS)

Variables	Model 1	Model 2	Model 3
FII	1.362**		0.610***
	(0.216)		(0.0814)
IQI		0.443***	0.130*
		(0.0707)	(0.0713)
IQI*FII			1.088***
			(0.216)
GDP	−0.295	0.126***	−0.103*
	(0.286)	(0.0375)	(0.0585)
TOP	−0.0050**	−0.0033*	−0.0119***
	(0.0024)	(0.0018)	(0.0024)
POG	0.132**	−0.0068	−0.0984***
	(0.0605)	(0.0195)	(0.0343)
Constant	2.376	−0.798***	1.407***
	(2.211)	(0.307)	(0.514)
Wald Chi^2	92.35	127.70	156.24
Prob. value	0.0000	0.0000	0.0000
Wu–Hausman test	3.7878	7.9006	20.9062
Prob. value	0.0516	0.0049	0.0000
Hansen test	2.9082	3.8269	1.2271
Prob. value	0.1109	0.0694	0.2680

Notes: ***, ** and * represent the statistically significant level at the 1%, 5% and 10%, respectively; the values of standard errors are presented in parentheses.

4.3. *Arellano–Bond GMM estimation method*

We employ Arellano and Bond (1991)'s GMM because the results of GMM are more robust and reliable than the 2SLS approach. Through GMM, we can remove the autocorrelation of the error term and decrease the correlation between endogenous variables and the error term. Therefore, to address the endogeneity issues in our models, we use two-step system GMM recommended by Blundell and Bond (1998). Thus, to address the issues of endogeneity between variables, individual-specific heteroscedasticity, autocorrelation and omitted variable bias, this paper utilized the two-step system GMM estimation technique. Table 6 shows the result of the two-step system GMM. Model 1 indicates that FII will increase FD by 0.08 unit and significant at statistical 5% level. This finding supports the argument of Rajan (2015) that universal access to financial services would lead to an increase in the FD of a country. The positive relationship between FII and FD recommends that an increase in financial services, availability of more bank branches and ATMs can promote OIC countries' FD in the long run. It is easy to understand these results because of the structure of the OIC countries' financial system. Therefore, the inclusion of the whole society inside the financial system through successful banking penetration and access leads to the ultimate FD of a country. Model 2 explains that IQI will also increase FD by 0.08

Table 6. IQ, FI and FD (Two-Step System GMM)

Variables	Model 1	Model 2	Model 3
L.FD	0.774***	0.810***	0.788***
	(0.0596)	(0.0501)	(0.0627)
FII	0.0896**		0.0879**
	(0.0402)		(0.0342)
IQI		0.0824**	0.0554**
		(0.0314)	(0.0222)
IQI*FII			0.0684**
			(0.0263)
GDP	0.0591*	0.0661**	0.0225
	(0.0326)	(0.0269)	(0.0180)
TOP	−0.0016	−0.0023**	−0.0023***
	(0.0010)	(0.0009)	(0.0008)
POG	0.0132	−0.0077	−0.0006
	(0.0140)	(0.0149)	(0.0139)
Constant	0.1277	−0.1660	−0.2289
	(0.1010)	(0.1640)	(0.1490)
AR(2)	0.85	0.86	0.84
Hansen test	23.18	19.13	15.67
Prob. value	0.240	0.119	0.268

Notes: Hansen test overid value is insignificant, indicating the validity of instruments and are not over-identified. Overall, the Hansen test shows that the two-step system GMM is correctly specified with no identification issues. ***, ** and * indicate statistical significance at the 1%, 5% and 10% levels, respectively. The values of standard errors are presented in parentheses.

unit and significant at a statistical 5% level. These results support the findings of Khan et al. (2019). A delicate and confident treatment of IQI can form robust institutional frameworks (Islam et al., 2002). The essential role of the financial sector's ineffective distribution of limited economic resources and total factor productivity growth of Han and Shen (2015) depend upon the established institutional framework (Jain et al., 2017). This finding supports the arguments of Law and Azman-Saini (2012) that a quality institutional environment is essential in describing FD. Therefore, the institutional elements play a vital role in economic and FD and create pressure on policymakers to initiate stabilized developments to address the uncertainty (Cherif and Gazdar, 2010). In model 3, the interactive term IQI*FII shows a 0.06 unit increase in FD and also significant at a statistical 5% level.

Although GDP is significantly and positively related to FD in model 1 at a statistical 10% level and model 2 at a statistical 5% level, POG shows no effect on FD. Only TOP shows a negative and significant impact on FD with a statistical 5% level in model 2 and at a statistical 1% significance level in model 3, respectively. The relationship between FII, IQI and IQI*FII on FD is empirically tested using a generalized two-step method of moments (GMM). The results are presented in Table 6. Following the settings used by Aggarwal *et al.* (2011), the lagged term for FD was incorporated into the analysis. The lagged items of the endogenous variables were chosen as instrumental variables. These findings are in line with the findings of Kim *et al.* (2018).

The Hansen test overid value is insignificant, indicating the validity of instruments is not over-identified. Overall, the Hansen test prob. value shows that a two-step system GMM estimator is correctly specified with no identification issues. Access to funds and their effective allocation create capital buildup and productivity improvements, which ultimately lead to better financial prospects (Levine and Zervos, 1998). The convenient availability of financial services improves the movements of cash and credit and helps society with the flow of currency (Burgess and Pande, 2005). This finding is consistent with current literature that the association between finance and growth might be dependent on IQ and financial depth (Demetriades and Andrianova, 2004; Rioja and Valev, 2004). This result indicates that FI has a positive influence on FD as well as the moderation effect of IQ. The IQ has strengthened the combined effect on FD because the good practices of different institutions play a leading role in FD and also in economic growth. The findings indicate that IQI increases the financial sector development of OIC countries. Most developing countries have low values for IQ, which suggest that policies to establish governance and institutions would significantly promote the financial depth in the region (Le *et al.*, 2016).

Table 7. IQ, FI and FD (Robustness)

Variables	Model 1	Model 2	Model 3
FII	0.328***		0.366***
	(0.0494)		(0.0534)
IQI		0.322***	0.223***
		(0.0287)	(0.0290)
IQI*FII			0.308***
			(0.0370)
GDP	0.171***	0.200***	0.0414
	(0.0346)	(0.0263)	(0.0296)
TOP	−0.0029***	−0.0037***	−0.0063***
	(0.0009)	(0.0012)	(0.0011)
POG	0.0361*	−0.0219	−0.0205
	(0.0189)	(0.0198)	(0.0216)
Constant	−1.220***	−1.244***	0.0418
	(0.287)	(0.197)	(0.271)
R-squared	0.193	0.193	0.269
Wald test	203.16	172.85	272.56
Prob. value	0.0000	0.0000	0.0000

Notes: *** and * show statistically significant levels at 1% and 10% levels, respectively. The values of standard errors are presented in parentheses.

4.4. Robustness checks

In this section, we examine a robustness analysis to ensure the reliability of the study's empirical results. Tables 4–6 show that FII, IQI and IQI*FII have a positive and significant impact on FD in all the results. We noted that their impact is positive and significant at statistical 1% and 5% levels in all regressions, respectively. We report the results of panel-corrected standard error (PCSE) robustness checks in Table 7.

This result supports our findings in the main analysis. In Table 7, we check the effect of FII, IQI and IQI*FII on FD with other macroeconomic variables (GDP, TOP, POG) as these variables have significant contributions to FD. Therefore, we find that the FII, IQI and IQI*FII have significant positive effects on FD at a statistical 1% level. The GDP also shows a significant positive impact on FD in model 1 and 2 at a statistical 1% level, and in model 1, POG also indicates a positive impact on FD at a statistical 10% level. In contrast, TOP shows significant negative relation toward FD in all models at the statistical 1% level. This finding is in line with the main analysis results. Therefore, the overall impact of FII, IQI and IQI*FII has a significant and positive effect on FD.

5. Conclusion

In this study, we empirically examine the impact of FII, IQI and IQI*FII on FD with control variables (GDP, TOP and POG) from a panel of 45 OIC countries over the period 2000–2016. FI and IQ have received much attention in recent years. This study used principal component analysis for making a composite index of FII and IQI. Moreover, this study employs the recently developed macro-econometrics panel data estimation techniques. For this, we set up the panel data for the 45 OIC countries and performed dynamic panel data analysis using OLS, 2SLS and GMM estimation techniques to reveal the association between FII, IQI, and IQI*FII on FD with other control variables.

Our empirical results confirm the significant positive effect of FII, IQI and IQI*FII on FD. The control variable, such as GDP, also shows a substantial positive effect on FD; TOP indicates a significant negative impact on FD in all the regression models, whereas POG shows, only in model 1 of Table 5 and model 1 of Table 7, positive effect on FD. These findings demonstrate the significant positive association between FII, IQI, IQI*FII and FD in OIC countries. This outcome proposes that an increase in financial services and the quality of the institutions leads to FD both in the short and in the long run.

The empirical findings present some specific policy recommendations. First, the key implication of this study is that it could encourage remarkable devotion of the policymakers in OIC countries to carry out strategies and approaches to create a more empowering atmosphere for FI, which eventually would stimulate the inclusive progress of their economies. Secondly, developing economies have entered into a tough phase in the development of their institutional and financial structures, and not all developing economies are equal in terms of their institutional and financial abilities. Therefore, policymakers must sensibly understand the pivotal role of FI and IQ in establishing sustainable future development. Thirdly, administrations are therefore required to form strong institutions that investigate corruption, ensure the rule of law and make government executives more answerable to the general public. Lastly, the administrations of OIC countries must have robust legitimate and institutional structures to create an atmosphere in which the financial sector prompts and accelerates economic growth.

This study focused on banking institutions; however, better outcomes may emerge if microfinance institutions are incorporated because these institutes have better penetration in rural regions. Future research work must confirm these outcomes in light of the role played by microfinance institutions. This paper focuses on the OIC economies, and thus, the outcomes are limited only to the OIC and emerging countries. However, future work may include developed countries to generalize these outcomes in a broader perspective.

Acknowledgment

We would like to show our sincere gratitude to the editors and two anonymous reviewers whose comments and suggestions significantly enhanced the quality of this paper.

Appendix A

Table A.1. The OIC Countries and World Bank Classification Based on Geographic Regions and Income Level

Geographic Region	Name of Country	Income Level
East Asia and Pacific	Brunei Darussalam	High income
	Indonesia	Lower middle income
	Malaysia	Upper middle income
Europe and Central Asia	Albania	Upper middle income
	Azerbaijan	Upper middle income
	Kazakhstan	Upper middle income
	Kyrgyz Republic	Low income
	Tajikistan	Low income
	Turkey	Upper middle income
Latin America and Caribbean	Suriname	Upper middle income
Middle East and North Africa	Algeria	Upper middle income
	Djibouti	Lower middle income
	Egypt	Lower middle income
	Iran	Upper middle income
	Jordan	Upper middle income
	Kuwait	High income
	Lebanon	Upper middle income
	Libya	Upper middle income
	Morocco	Lower middle income

Table A.1. (*Continued*)

Geographic Region	Name of Country	Income Level
	Oman	High income
	Qatar	High income
	Saudi Arabia	High income
	Syria	Lower middle income
	Tunisia	Upper middle income
	United Arab Emirates	High income
	Yemen	Lower middle income
South Asia	Bangladesh	Low income
	Pakistan	Lower middle income
Sub-Saharan Africa	Benin	Low income
	Burkina Faso	Low income
	Cameroon	Lower middle income
	Chad	Low income
	Cote d'Ivoire	Lower middle income
	Gabon	Upper middle income
	Guinea	Low income
	Mali	Low income
	Mauritania	Lower middle income
	Mozambique	Low income
	Niger	Low income
	Nigeria	Lower middle income
	Senegal	Lower middle income
	Sierra Leone	Low income
	Sudan	Lower middle income
	Togo	Low income
	Uganda	Low income

Source: World Bank.

Table A.2. Description of Variable

Variable	Acronyms	Description
FD	Financial development	This index summarizes the depth, access and efficiency of the financial institutions and financial markets established by Svirydzenka (2016) and obtained from the IMF
FII	Financial inclusion index	This index consists of four variables, which are as follows: automated teller machines per 100,000 adults, commercial bank branches per 100,000 adults, depositors with commercial banks per 1000 adults and life insurance premium volume to GDP, data obtained from WDI and GFDD

Table A.2. (*Continued*)

Variable	Acronyms	Description
IQI	Institutional quality index	This index consists of six dimensions of governance, which are as follows: control of corruption, government effectiveness, political stability and absence of violence, regulatory quality, the rule of law and voice and accountability (Dwumfour and Ntow-Gyamfi, 2018). The data of IQ are taken from the WGI
GDP	Gross domestic product	GDP is a proxy of economic growth, and data are taken from WDI
TOP	Trade openness	The ratio of imports and exports to GDP, data are taken from WDI
POG	Population growth rate	Population growth rate per year, data are taken from WDI
FIF	Financial freedom	The data of this instrument variable are taken from HFD
MOF	Monetary freedom	The data of this instrument variable are taken from HFD
PRO	Property rights	The data of this instrument variable are taken from HFD

Notes: GFDD is Global Financial Development Database, WGI is World Governance Indicators, WDI is World Development Indicators, IMF is the International Monetary Fund Database and HFD is Heritage Foundation Database.

Table A.3. Principal Component Analysis for Composite FII

Eigenvalues of Matrix				
Component	Eigenvalue	Difference	Proportion	Cumulative
1	2.43327	1.46283	0.6083	0.6083
2	0.970439	0.630308	0.2426	0.8509
3	0.34013	0.0839653	0.0850	0.9360
4	0.256165	—	0.0640	1.0000
Eigenvectors (loadings)				
Variables	Comp1	Comp2	Comp3	Comp4
ATM	0.5649	−0.1473	0.6324	−0.5091
BRC	0.5650	0.0228	−0.7591	−0.3225
DCB	0.5762	−0.1688	0.0860	0.7950
LIN	0.1720	0.9743	0.1283	0.0684

Note: ATM is automated teller machine per 100,000 adults, BRC shows commercial bank branches per 100,000 adults, DCB indicates commercial banks per 1000 adults and LIN denotes life insurance premium volume to GDP.

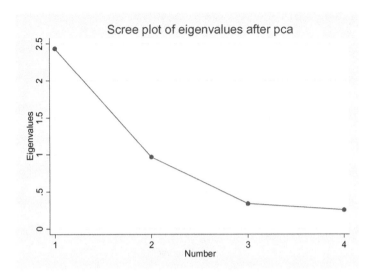

Figure A.1. This Graph Indicates the Variance Explained by the Different Factors

Table A.4. Principal Component Analysis for Composite IQ Index

Eigenvalues of Matrix				
Component	Eigenvalue	Difference	Proportion	Cumulative
1	4.26458	3.38597	0.7108	0.7108
2	0.878614	0.412208	0.1464	0.8572
3	0.466406	0.264734	0.0777	0.9349
4	0.201672	0.0934061	0.0336	0.9685
5	0.108266	0.0278053	0.0180	0.9866
6	0.0804605	—	0.0134	1.0000

Eigenvectors (loadings)						
Variables	Comp1	Comp2	Comp3	Comp4	Comp5	Comp6
COC	0.4523	−0.1388	−0.0766	−0.5890	−0.3663	0.5378
GOE	0.4506	−0.1361	−0.3084	0.0248	0.8167	0.1253
POS	0.3783	−0.0435	0.9055	0.1427	0.1163	0.0351
REQ	0.4428	−0.0234	−0.2598	0.7507	−0.3907	0.1406
ROL	0.4641	−0.0835	−0.1041	−0.2502	−0.1758	−0.8205
VOA	0.1943	0.9761	−0.0286	−0.0773	0.0426	0.0286

Note: COC is control of corruption, GOE represents government effectiveness, POS shows political stability and absence of violence, REQ denotes regulatory quality, ROL is the rule of law and VOA indicates voice and accountability.

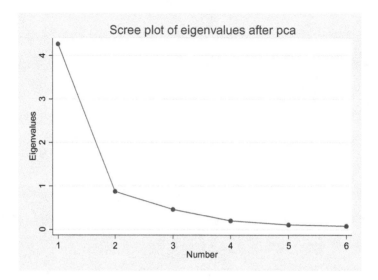

Figure A.2. This Graph Shows the Variance Described by the Different Components

References

Acemoglu, D and T Verdier (1998). Property rights, corruption and the allocation of talent: A general equilibrium approach. *The Economic Journal*, 108(450), 1381–1403. doi: 10.1111/1468-0297.00347.

Adeniyi, O, A Oyinlola, O Omisakin and FO Egwaikhide (2015). Financial development and economic growth in Nigeria: Evidence from threshold modelling. *Economic Analysis and Policy*, 47, 11–21.

Aduda, J and E Kalunda (2012). Financial inclusion and financial sector stability with reference to Kenya: A review of literature. *Journal of Applied Finance and Banking*, 2(6), 95–120.

Aggarwal, R and JW Goodell (2010). Financial markets versus institutions in European countries: Influence of culture and other national characteristics. *International Business Review*, 19(5), 502–520.

Aggarwal, R, A Demirgüç-Kunt and MSM Pería (2011). Do remittances promote financial development? *Journal of Development Economics*, 96(2), 255–264.

Aghion, P, R Blundell, R Griffith, P Howitt and S Prantl (2009). The effects of entry on incumbent innovation and productivity. *The Review of Economics and Statistics*, 91(1), 20–32.

Al-Yousif, YK (2002). Financial development and economic growth: Another look at the evidence from developing countries. *Review of Financial Economics*, 11(2), 131–150.

Anand, S and KS Chhikara (2013). A theoretical and quantitative analysis of financial inclusion and economic growth. *Management and Labour Studies*, 38(1–2), 103–133.

Anarfo, EB, JY Abor, KA Osei and A Gyeke-Dako (2019). Financial inclusion and financial sector development in Sub-Saharan Africa: A panel VAR approach. *International Journal of Managerial Finance*. https://doi.org/10.1108/IJMF-07-2018-0205.

Andrianova, S, P Demetriades and C Xu (2011). Political economy origins of financial markets in Europe and Asia. *World Development*, 39(5), 686–699.

Anwar, S and A Cooray (2012). Financial development, political rights, civil liberties and economic growth: Evidence from South Asia. *Economic Modelling*, 29(3), 974–981.

Arellano, M and S Bond (1991). Some tests of specification for panel data: Monte Carlo evidence and an application to employment equations. *The Review of Economic Studies*, 58(2), 277–297.

Arestis, P and P Demetriades (1997). Financial development and economic growth: Assessing the evidence. *The Economic Journal*, 107(442), 783–799.

Arora, RU (2010). Measuring financial access. *Discussiion Papers Economics*, 23. https://doi.org/10.1016/j.optlastec.2017.09.038.

Asyatun, I (2019). Regional and accessibility analysis of the banking system and their impacts toward regional financial inclusion in Indonesia. *Journal of Islamic Monetary Economics and Finance*. https://doi.org/10.21098/jimf.v4i2.1015.

Baltagi, BH, P Demetriades and SH Law (2009). Financial development and openness: Panel data evidence. *Journal of Development Economics*, 89(2), 285–296.

Banna, H and MR Alam (2020). Islamic banking efficiency and inclusive sustainable growth: The role of financial inclusion. *Journal of Islamic Monetary Economics and Finance*. https://doi.org/10.21098/jimf.v6i1.1089.

Batuo, M, K Mlambo and S Asongu (2018). Linkages between financial development, financial instability, financial liberalisation and economic growth in Africa. *Research in International Business and Finance*, 45, 168–179.

Beck, T, R Levine and N Loayza (2000). Finance and the sources of growth. *Journal of Financial Economics*, 58(1–2), 261–300.

Beck, T and A De La Torre (2006). *The Basic Analytics of Access to Financial Services*. The World Bank.

Beck, T, A Demirguc-Kunt and MS Martinez Peria (2008). Banking services for everyone? Barriers to bank access and use around the world. *World Bank Economic Review*, 22(3), 397–430.

Bhaskar, PV (2013). Financial inclusion in India — An assessment. Speech at the MFIN and Access-Assist Summit, New Delhi, 10.

Blundell, R and S Bond (1998). Initial conditions and moment restrictions in dynamic panel data models. *Journal of Econometrics*, 87(1), 115–143.

Bojanic, AN (2012). The impact of financial development and trade on the economic growth of Bolivia. *Journal of Applied Economics*, 15(1), 51–70.

Bonnal, M and ME Yaya (2015). Political institutions, trade openness, and economic growth: New evidence. *Emerging Markets Finance and Trade*, 51(6), 1276–1291.

Burgess, R and R Pande (2005). Do rural banks matter? Evidence from the Indian social banking experiment. *American Economic Review*, 95(3), 780–795.

[CGAP] Consultative Group to Assist the Poor (2013). *Financial Access 2012 Getting to a More Comprehensive Picture*. Washington, DC (USA): CGAP.

Chakravarty, SR and R Pal (2013). Financial inclusion in India: An axiomatic approach. *Journal of Policy Modeling*, 35(5), 813–837.

Cherif, M and K Gazdar (2010). Macroeconomic and institutional determinants of stock market development in MENA region: New results from a panel data analysis. *International Journal of Banking and Finance*, 7(1), 139–159.

Chibba, M (2009). Financial inclusion, poverty reduction and the millennium development goals. *The European Journal of Development Research*, 21(2), 213–230.

Christopoulos, DK and EG Tsionas (2004). Financial development and economic growth: Evidence from panel unit root and cointegration tests. *Journal of Development Economics*, 73(1), 55–74.

Collard, S (2007). Toward financial inclusion in the UK: Progress and challenges. *Public Money and Management*, 27(1), 13–20.

Creane, S, A Goyal, M Mushfiq and R Sab (2003). Financial development and growth in the Middle East and North Africa. IMF Working Paper, Washington, DC.

Demetriades, P and S Andrianova (2004). Finance and growth: What we know and what we need to know. In *Financial Development and Economic Growth*, pp. 38–65. London: Palgrave Macmillan.

Demirguc-Kunt, A and L Klapper (2012). *Measuring Financial Inclusion: The Global Findex Database*. The World Bank.

Dwumfour, RA and M Ntow-Gyamfi (2018). Natural resources, financial development and institutional quality in Africa: Is there a resource curse? *Resources Policy*, 59, 411–426.

Farooq, A and B Yasmin (2017). Fiscal policy uncertainty and economic growth in Pakistan: Role of financial development indicators. *Journal of Economic Cooperation and Development*, 38(2), 1.

Gantman ER and MP Dabos (2012). A fragile link? A new empirical analysis of the relationship between financial development and economic growth. *Oxford Development Studies*, 40(4), 517–532.

Ge, Y and J Qiu (2007). Financial development, bank discrimination and trade credit. *Journal of Banking and Finance*, 31(2), 513–530.

Giné, X and R Townsend (2004). Evaluation of financial liberalization: A general equilibrium model with constrained occupation choice. *Journal of Development Economics*, 74(2), 269–307.

Gokmenoglu, KK, MY Amin and N Taspinar (2015). The relationship among international trade, financial development and economic growth: The case of Pakistan. *Procedia Economics and Finance*, 25, 489–496.

Graff, M (2003). Financial development and economic growth in corporatist and liberal market economies. *Emerging Markets Finance and Trade*, 39(2), 47–69.

Girma, S and A Shortland (2008). The political economy of financial development. *Oxford Economic Papers*, 60(4), 567–596.

Gurley, JG and ES Shaw (1955). Financial aspects of economic development. *The American Economic Review*, 45(4), 515–538.

Hafer, RW (2013). Economic freedom and financial development: International evidence. *Cato Journal*, 33, 111.

Han, J and Y Shen (2015). Financial development and total factor productivity growth: Evidence from China. *Emerging Markets Finance and Trade*, 51(suppl. 1), S261–S274.

Harrison, A (1996). Openness and growth: A time-series, cross-country analysis for developing countries. *Journal of Development Economics*, 48(2), 419–447.

Hartmann, P, F Heider, E Papaioannou and M Lo Duca (2007). The role of financial markets and innovation in productivity and growth in Europe. ECB Occasional Paper, 72.

Hasan, I, P Wachtel and M Zhou (2009). Institutional development, financial deepening and economic growth: Evidence from China. *Journal of Banking and Finance*, 33(1), 157–170.

Huang, Y (2010). Political institutions and financial development: An empirical study. *World Development*, 38(12), 1667–1677.

Islam, R, CE Montenegro and R Islam (2002). *What Determines the Quality of Institutions?* The World Bank.

Jain, PK, E Kuvvet and MS Pagano (2017). Corruption's impact on foreign portfolio investment. *International Business Review*, 26(1), 23–35.

Jedidia, KB, T Boujelbène and K Helali (2014). Financial development and economic growth: New evidence from Tunisia. *Journal of Policy Modeling*, 36(5), 883–898.

Kendall, J (2012). Local financial development and growth. *Journal of Banking and Finance*, 36(5), 1548–1562.

Khan, HR (2011). Financial inclusion and financial stability: Are they two sides of the same coin? Address by Shri H.R. Khan, Deputy Governor of the Reserve Bank of India, at BANCON 2011, Organized by the Indian Bankers Association and Indian Overseas Bank, Chennai, 4 November. Available at www.bis.org/review/r111229f.pdf (accessed 20 August 2020).

Khan, MA, D Kong, J Xiang and J Zhang (2019). Impact of institutional quality on financial development: Cross-country evidence based on emerging and growth-leading economies. *Emerging Markets Finance and Trade*, 1–17.

Khmous, DF and M Besim (2020). Impact of Islamic banking share on financial inclusion: Evidence from MENA. *International Journal of Islamic Middle Eastern and Finance Management.* https://doi.org/10.1108/IMEFM-07-2019-0279.

Kim, DW, JS Yu and MK Hassan (2018). Financial inclusion and economic growth in OIC countries. *Research in International Business and Finance*, 43(October 2016), 1–14. https://doi.org/10.1016/j.ribaf.2017.07.178.

King, RG and R Levine (1993). Finance, entrepreneurship, and growth: Theory and evidence. *Journal of Monetary Economics*, 32(3), 513–542.

Klomp, J and J de Haan (2014). Bank regulation, the quality of institutions, and banking risk in emerging and developing countries: An empirical analysis. *Emerging Markets Finance and Trade*, 50(6), 19–40.

Kutan, AM, N Samargandi and K Sohag (2017). Does institutional quality matter for financial development and growth? Further evidence from MENA countries. *Australian Economic Papers*, 56(3), 228–248.

Law, SH and WNW Azman-Saini (2012). Institutional quality, governance, and financial development. *Economics of Governance*, 13(3), 217–236.

Law, SH, WNW Azman-Saini and MH Ibrahim (2013). Institutional quality thresholds and the finance–growth nexus. *Journal of Banking and Finance*, 37(12), 5373–5381.

Le, TH, J Kim and M Lee (2016). Institutional quality, trade openness, and financial sector development in Asia: An empirical investigation. *Emerging Markets Finance and Trade*, 52(5), 1047–1059.

Levine, R (1997). Financial development and economic growth: Views and agenda. *Journal of Economic Literature*, 35.

Levine, R (1998). The legal environment, banks, and long-run economic growth. *Journal of Money, Credit and Banking*, 30(3), 596–613, doi:10.2307/2601259.

Levine, R and S Zervos (1998). Stock markets, banks, and economic growth. *American Economic Review*, 88(3), 537–558. Retrieved June 30, 2020, from http://www.jstor.org/stable/116848.

Levine, R, N Loayza and T Beck (2000). Financial intermediation and growth: Causality and causes. *Journal of Monetary Economics*, 46(1), 31–77.

Mani, M (2016). Financial inclusion in South Asia — Relative standing, challenges and initiatives. *South Asian Survey*, 23(2), 158–179.

Mardan, M (2017). Why countries differ in thin capitalization rules: The role of financial development. *European Economic Review*, 91, 1–14. doi: 10.1016/j.euroecorev.2016.09.003.

Maruta, AA (2018). Can aid for financial sector buy financial development? *Journal of Macroeconomics*, 62, 103075.

McKinnon, RI (1973). *Money and Capital in Economic Development.* Washington, DC: Brookings Institution Press.

Mimir, Y (2016). On international consumption risk sharing, financial integration and financial development. *Emerging Markets Finance and Trade*, 52(5), 1241–1258.

Minea, A and P Villieu (2010). Financial development, institutional quality and maximizing-growth trade-off in government finance. *Economic Modelling*, 27(1), 324–335.

Mohieldin, M, Z Iqbal, A Rostom and X Fu (2011). *The Role of Islamic Finance in Enhancing Financial Inclusion in Organization of Islamic Cooperation (OIC) Countries.* The World Bank.

North, D (1981). *Structure and Change in Economic History.* New York, NY: Norton.

Odhiambo, NM (2011). Economic growth and carbon emissions in South Africa: An empirical investigation. *International Business and Economics Research Journal*, 10(7), 75–84.

Onaolapo, AR (2015). Effects of financial inclusion on the economic growth of Nigeria (1982–2012). *International Journal of Business and Management Review*, 3(8), 11–28.

Pradhan, RP, S Tripathy, S Pandey and SK Bele (2014). Banking sector development and economic growth in ARF countries: The role of stock markets. *Macroeconomics and Finance in Emerging Market Economies*, 7(2), 208–229.

Rachdi, H and S Mensi (2012, September). Does institutions quality matter for financial development and economic growth nexus? Another look at the evidence from MENA countries. In *Economic Research Forum/September, WP* (No. 705).

Rajan, RG (2015). A hundred small steps: Report of the committee on financial sector reforms.

Rashid, A and M Intartaglia (2017). Financial development — Does it lessen poverty? *Journal of Economic Studies*, 44(1), 69–86.

Ravikumar, T (2012). Role of banks in financial inclusion process in India. *International Journal of Marketing and Technology*, 2(2), 81–102.

Rillo, A (2014). Financial inclusion in Asia: Country surveys. Asian Development Bank Institute.

Rioja, F and N Valev (2004). Does one size fit all?: A reexamination of the finance and growth relationship. *Journal of Development Economics*, 74(2), 429–447.

Ro, YJ, IC Kim and JW Kim (2017). Financial development and investment in Korea. *Emerging Markets Finance and Trade*, 53(3), 534–543.

Rodrik, D, A Subramanian and F Trebbi (2002). Institutions rule: The primacy of institutions over integration and geography in economic development. International Monetary Fund (IMF) Working Paper No. 02/189. IMF, Washington DC.

Samargandi, N, J Fidrmuc and S Ghosh (2014). Financial development and economic growth in an oil-rich economy: The case of Saudi Arabia. *Economic Modelling*, 43, 267–278.

Saydaliyev, HB, L Chin and Y Oskenbayev (2020). The nexus of remittances, institutional quality, and financial inclusion. *Economic Research-Ekonomska Istraživanja*, 33(1), 3528–3544.

Sarma, M (2008). Index of financial inclusion. *Indian Council for Research on International Economic Relations Working Paper No.* 215 (215), pp. 1–26. https://doi.org/10.1007/978-81-322-1650-6_28.

Seetanah, B, R Sawkut, V Sannasee and B Seetanah (2008). Stock market development and economic growth in developing countries: Evidence from Panel VAR framework. Online. CSAE Working Paper, 41.

Schumpeter, JA (1912). *Theorie Derwirt-Schaftlichenentwicklung*. Leipzig: Duncker and Humblot.

Sharma, D (2016). Nexus between financial inclusion and economic growth: Evidence from the emerging Indian economy. *Journal of Financial Economic Policy*, 8(1), 13–36. https://doi.org/10.1108/JFEP-01-2015-0004.

Shaw, ES (1973). *Financial Deepening in Economic Development*. New York, NY: Oxford University Press.

Shihadeh, FH (2018). How individual's characteristics influence financial inclusion: Evidence from MENAP. *International Journal of Islamic Middle Eastern and Finance Management*. https://doi.org/10.1108/IMEFM-06-2017-0153.

Singh, D and A Delios (2017). Corporate governance, board networks and growth in domestic and international markets: Evidence from India. *Journal of World Business* 52(5), 615–627. doi: 10.1016/j.jwb.2017.02.002.

Svirydzenka, K (2016). *Introducing a New Broad-Based Index of Financial Development*. International Monetary Fund.

Tsoukas, S (2011). Firm survival and financial development: Evidence from a panel of emerging Asian economies. *Journal of Banking and Finance*, 35(7), 1736–1752.

Uddin, GS, B Sjö and M Shahbaz (2013). The causal nexus between financial development and economic growth in Kenya. *Economic Modelling*, 35, 701–707.

Yu, X, M Li and S Huang (2017). Financial functions and financial development in china: A spatial effect analysis. *Emerging Markets Finance and Trade*, 53(9), 2052–2062.

Zuleika, A (2010). Financial inclusion in Australia: Toward transformation policy. *Social Policy Working Paper No. 13*, Melbourne. Retrieved from www.bsl.org.in.

© 2025 World Scientific Publishing Company
https://doi.org/10.1142/9789819813735_0014

Chapter 14

Does Financial Inclusion Drive the Islamic Banking Efficiency? A Post-Financial Crisis Analysis[#]

Hasanul Banna[*,†,‖,§§], Md. Rabiul Alam[*,‡,§,**], Rubi Ahmad[†,††] and Norhanim Mat Sari[¶,‡‡]

[*]*Ungku Aziz Centre for Development Studies*
Faculty of Economics and Administration
University of Malaya, 50603 Kuala Lumpur, Malaysia

[†]*Department of Finance and Banking*
Faculty of Business and Accountancy
University of Malaya, 50603 Kuala Lumpur, Malaysia

[‡]*Department of Language and Literacy Education*
Faculty of Education, University of Malaya
50603 Kuala Lumpur, Malaysia

[§]*Department of English*
Asian University of Bangladesh, Dhaka, Bangladesh

[¶]*Putra Business School, University Putra Malaysia (UPM)*
43400 Serdang, Selangor, Malaysia
[‖]*bannaje@yahoo.com/banna@um.edu.my*
[**]*rabiulalam_84@yahoo.com*
[††]*rubi@um.edu.my*
[‡‡]*norhanim@putrabs.edu.my*

Considering the reverberations of financial crisis of 2007–09 that the banking industry terribly witnessed, this paper aims to estimate both the non-bias-corrected and bias-corrected efficiency by employing the data envelopment analysis and Simar–Wilson double bootstrapping regression techniques over the period of 2011–2017 and see how the financial inclusion impacts on Islamic banks. This study finds that most of the countries, except some Asian and Middle-Eastern countries, have inconsistent efficiency trends in Islamic banking sector. It also shows that financial inclusion is significantly allied with Islamic banking efficiency. Eventually, the results propose that Islamic banks are still bearing the consequence of that economic recession and, therefore, bank should focus more on financial inclusion since those banks having sound and inclusive financial environment are seen enjoying higher level of financial efficiency.

Keywords: Financial inclusion; bias-corrected efficiency; data envelopment analysis; Islamic banks; Asia; global financial crisis.

[§§] Corresponding author.
[#] This Chapter first appeared in the *Singapore Economic Review*, Vol. 67, No. 1, doi: 10.1142/S0217590819420050. © 2022 World Scientific Publishing.

1. Introduction

Does financial inclusion assist the attainment of Islamic banking efficiency in the aftershock of global financial crisis? This simple question brings many things into light. The global financial crisis (GFC) of 2007–09 broke the record of the past and the world is still bearing the consequences of that crisis. To overcome this devastating economic condition, the financial institutions, particularly the banking sector, have been investing their utmost effort by the inclusion of many services fascinating to the clients. Islamic banks, considered as one of the greater contributors to the overall economy of the world (Sole, 2007), have been spending their relentless endeavor too to overcome the aftermath of this crisis. In this regard, they are in the way of focusing many areas of their services to promote. Financial inclusion has been considered as their prime focussed area which includes many services such as mobile banking, SMS banking, ATM booth, free student account, short-term and long-term deposit schemes, SME loan facility and loan facilities to farmers (Jahan et al., 2019; Klein and Mayer, 2011). The stability, growth and efficiency of Islamic banking sector, in general, are contingent upon the easily reachable financial services in the form of financial inclusion they provide for the mass people. Financial inclusion has been an issue of great concern to scholars, stakeholders, researchers and financial organizations since the late 1990s (Collard, 2007; Leyshon and Thrift, 1995). Though it became the topic of research since the 1990s, the economic recession that the world witnessed in 2007–2009, which caused the collapse of conventional banking (Cullen, 2011), made the scholars ponder deeply of alternative solution to overcome the post-crisis period. Thus, Islamic finance was appreciated as an alternative solution which is practiced by Islamic banks.

From various aspects, Islamic banks are distinctive from their counterpart, conventional banks. The major characteristics of this banking system are zero tolerance to any sort of interest in any kind of transaction, no financial aid to illegal, anti-social, unethical and unlawful business sectors, like gambling, alcohol and pornography industry (Abdul-Majid et al., 2010). Islamic financial system does not promote any sorts of injustice, harmful, inhuman and destructive activities which ruin the society, hence, there is no place of interest payments, no speculation and no financing to unlawful transactions (Beck et al., 2010). Because of their Islamic-based interest-free financial transaction in every field, Islamic banks have seen more thrift and in leading position in many sectors compared with conventional banking (Sole, 2007).

Furthermore, Islamic finance has the power to overcome any shock because of its integral stability (Mirakhor, 2008) and the world will see a perfect alternative to overcome this collapsed situation if the banking and financial sectors are free from any kind of *riba* (usury) and *maysir* (gambling) (Siddiqi, 2009). According to Islamic Shari'ah, these are prohibited since they make businesses unsafe and unsecured. Not only Islam, but the fundamental sources of all the main religions of the world have forbidden the transaction of usury also as it breaches the harmony of human being which eventually leads them to the state of poverty. So, unlike their counterpart conventional banks which promote usury and consider it as a basic mean of financial thrift, Islamic banks have been looking for alternative and innovative services as means of their successful survival. Iqbal and Llewellyn

(2002) state that the global financial sector becomes flourished by many ways, like innovative financial products and individual risk-sharing features for all types of businesses that are seen in Islamic banking system. Banks are providing different sorts of financial services for the betterment of the human being where financial inclusion is the most remarkable one. In this cutting-edge era, they are coming up with a lot of attractive offers, innovative plans and easily accessible financial services for their clients with a very minimal or marginal service charge to ensure their own identity, growth, profit and stability.

Kim et al. (2018) show that financial inclusion leads to financial growth and both are very intrinsically related to each other. In the concept of globalization, it has occupied the most significant place to be contemplated deeply since banking efficiency is measured mostly depending on its financial services (Kim et al., 2018). Ahamed and Mallick (2019) state that those banks which ensured higher level of financial inclusion by providing various types of banking services to the customers with a very marginal and low service charge have the significant and enormous bank stability and financial sustainability. It is a means for an economy to attain comprehensive development. It refers to gathering all groups of people including disadvantaged and destitute under the umbrella of financial services and providing equal facilities to all (Sarma, 2008).

Banks which expand their services efficiently and productively to all attain the financial stability. Thus, financial inclusion endeavors to widen banking facilities to the people of all classes to keep the development flow rotating (Demirguc-Kunt et al., 2015) and build a very close bonding with their clients (Petersen and Rajan, 1995). Development in any sector is the result of a good rapport between the clients and the service providers from many viewpoints. Good relationship with all levels of customers enhances the market demand of the banking sector and high level of market demand allows bank to provide more loans to poor businessmen (Di Patti and Dell'Ariccia, 2001; Petersen and Rajan, 1995). Services to more clients prevent reliance on big and wholesale funding for their own existence and survival (Demirgüç-Kunt and Huizinga, 2010). For making their services reachable to the people of all classes, banks can expand their branches throughout the country which help in poverty alleviation. Analyzing the context of India (Burgess and Pande, 2005) and Mexico (Bruhn and Love, 2014), studies were conducted which show that more bank branches in village level and reachable financial services play a vital role in poverty eradication and hunger reduction (Owen and Pereira, 2018). According to Hannig and Jansen (2010), through the means of good term with the clients, banks are able to lessen information asymmetry, and by providing low-cost, easily accessible and innovative financial services, they become capable of reducing production's marginal costs too.

Apart from ensuring banking efficiency, growth and stability, financial inclusion also has a major role in the attainment of the sustainable development goals (SDGs). It has been given more focus by almost all the countries of the world. In connection with IMF, G20, AFI and CGAP, the central banks of Asian, African, American and European countries have highly considered the financial inclusion of the banking industry which results in socio-economic stability of the people at large (Demirguc-Kunt et al., 2019; Gebrehiwot and Makina, 2019). This socio-economic development is the prime target of achieving the

SDGs. Financial development is seen visible when people can save more money. And, savings is seen more when people have the easily accessible financial services (Allen *et al.*, 2016; Aportela, 1999) that lessen poverty and discrimination in earning (Ahamed and Mallick, 2019; Beck *et al.*, 2007a); develop mental stability by reducing stress (Ahamed and Mallick, 2019; Angelucci *et al.*, 2013); enhance job sectors (Prasad, 2010); accelerate the innovative concepts (Banerjee *et al.*, 2013, 2015; Klapper *et al.*, 2006); promote in decision making (Mani *et al.*, 2013) and create favorable environment for quality education (Flug *et al.*, 1998).

Ensuring financial inclusion basically means having a bank account by every individual. Without having a bank account, no individual can enjoy the services banks provide. Analyzing the context of Nepal, Prina (2012) shows that opening a bank account with free of charge or very poor charge increases the acceptance and usage of bank services. But as a matter of fact that still a lion portion of total population of the world is away from banking services. So, everybody should work collectively to gather this huge population under the umbrella of financial services.

> "The stark reality is that most poor people in the world still lack access to sustainable financial services, whether it is savings, credit or insurance. The great challenge before us is to address the constraints that exclude people from full participation in the financial sector. Together, we can and must build inclusive financial sectors that help people improve their lives."
> — Former United Nations Secretary General Kofi Annan.

Therefore, it is very evident that financial inclusion of banking sector is a way of leading to financial sustainability that helps achieve the SDGs; through financial sustainability the efficacy of banking sector can be measured. Based on the existing literature it is noted that the aftershock of the GFC was so severe and challenging period ever for all the banks to retain their existence where financial inclusion was thought to be a way of overcoming the crisis gradually; and Islamic banking system was regarded as an alternative solution to get rid of this critical period.

A good number of academics and policy-makers admit the advantages of financial services and products that are provided by Islamic banks, for example, the equity and risk-sharing elements mitigate the gap of short-term and long-term uncertain loan and demandable deposit contracts (Beck *et al.*, 2013) and other scholars have praised their smooth operation at the time of economic recession (Hasan and Dridi, 2010). The successful journey of Islamic banks made the researchers contemplate of Islamic finance realise the importance of it in the world financial market. Although many researchers started carrying out research to trace out the factors functioning behind their effective operations from various aspects, very few studies were conducted indicating the role of financial inclusion on the efficiency of Islamic banking sector in the post-GFC. Thus, this paper attempts to fill the gap by estimating the Islamic banks efficiency in the post-GFC and how financial inclusion influences this efficiency. Currently, Islamic banks are in operation in more than 50 countries throughout the world (Rosman *et al.*, 2014). However, we analyze the Islamic banks based on the data availability in the Orbis BankFocus (formerly known as Bankscope) database to estimate the actual performance of their smooth financial activities in the aftermath of the economic recession of 2007–2009 when most of the conventional banks were suffering.

This research contributes to the existing literature in the following ways. First of all, this paper estimates both the non-bias-corrected and bias-corrected efficiency of Islamic banks over 2011–2017 using more recent data. The aim is to see the bias-corrected efficiency trend of the Islamic banks after the GFC period. Secondly, we examine the relationship between financial inclusion and Islamic bank efficiency using diversified samples. This link helps to see how financial inclusion contributes a significant role in re-establishing a smooth economy like before by overcoming the crucial period through Islamic banking sector. Finally, the study adds value to the methodology by utilizing non-parametric data envelopment analysis (DEA) and Simar–Wilson (2007) double bootstrapping regression model to estimate bias-corrected efficiency and its determinants since tobit regression model, generalized method of moments (GMM), ordinary least square (OLS) and others are being severely criticized by the recent literature (Daraio *et al.*, 2018; Simar and Wilson, 2011) due to their biased estimation and misspecification in the second stage analysis.

The paper has two key findings. First, most of the countries have overall inconsistent efficiency trends in the Islamic banks over the period of study. This suggests that banks are still bearing the consequence of the GFC. Secondly, financial inclusion plays a significant role on improving Islamic banks efficiency in the post-GFC period. In line with previous studies, bank-specific, risk and macro-economic factors have significant contributions to improve efficiency. In addition, in the post-GFC period, Islamic banks were successfully running their operations and they have been proving their continuous efficiency through the implementation of financial inclusion. Furthermore, this study provides an insight to policy-makers, governments, regulators and bank management throughout the world to accelerate Islamic banking efficiency through the implementation of financial inclusion in a wider range since a positive relationship between banking efficiency and financial inclusion is shown by this study.

The remaining part of the paper is designed in the following structure. A detailed account of methodology is drawn in Section 2. Section 3 comprises findings of the study and their discussions, while Section 4 gives an overview of the concluding remarks.

2. Methodology

This study focuses on Islamic banks efficiency and the role of financial inclusion in improving their efficiencies. Therefore, in this section, this study presents the data envelopment analysis and Simar–Wilson double bootstrapping technique to find the relationship between Islamic banks efficiency and financial inclusion.

2.1. Methods

Although parametric and non-parametric approaches are considered as the two main techniques, this study uses merely non-parametric data envelopment analysis (DEA) approach to estimate the Islamic banks efficiency. In brief, Charnes *et al.* (1978) initiated the DEA, a non-parametric linear programming method (Farrell, 1957), to analyze the relative efficiency of a set of comparable decision-making units (DMUs) with a number of inputs and outputs. Later, Banker, Charnes and Cooper (BCC) (Banker et al., 1984) modified the first DEA model to estimate efficiency under variable returns to scale (VRS) assumption.

We choose the DEA over the stochastic frontier approach (SFA) for two key reasons. First, DEA, a linear-based approach, does not need to provide pre-specification of production function (Gardener et al., 2011). Thus, DEA needs less econometrics specifications than SFA and very user-friendly. Secondly, on the data generating process, it neither imposes any restrictive hypothesis nor requires so much assumptions about the technology. Therefore, it is even suitable for small sample size. Following Gardener et al. (2011) and Banna et al. (2019b), we, in order to determine the efficiency of Islamic banks, use the VRS input-oriented (cost minimization) model. The input-orientated DEA approach is used because it categorizes technical efficiency as a relative deterioration in the usage of input and to calculate technical efficiency as a relative growth in output or production. Besides, the choice of VRS over constant returns to scale (CRS) is suitable since the operation of all the banks is not at an optimum scale due to financial constraints and imperfect competition (Banna et al., 2019a, 2019b). The mathematical specification of DEA-VRS input-oriented model is as follows[1]:

$$\text{Min } \theta$$

Such that:

$$\sum_{j=1}^{n} \varphi_j B_{qj} \geq B_{q0}; \quad q = 1, 2, \ldots, y,$$

$$\sum_{j=1}^{n} \varphi_j A_{ij} \leq \theta A_{i0}; \quad i = 1, 2, \ldots, x, \quad (1)$$

$$\varphi_j \geq 0; \quad j \in 1, 2, \ldots, m,$$

$$\sum_{j=1}^{n} \varphi_j = 1,$$

where θ refers to the score of efficiency, B_{qj} and A_{ij} are shown as the value of the qth output generated and the value of the ith input consumed by the jth bank, respectively. The m index refers to the bank observations' number, x refers to three inputs (short-term funding and deposits, staff expenses and fixed assets) and y indicates two outputs (entire loans and other earning assets) and φ is constant. The first two constraints restrict the data to be enveloped from both the upper and lower. The third constraint is required to be non-negative of all inputs and outputs. The use of VRS is allowed by the fourth constraint.

---

[1] This study uses MaxDEA version 7 computer programming software and "teradial" command in Stata to estimate bias-uncorrected efficiency score. We estimated numerous variations of Equation (1) including more and less aggregated inputs, combining the output measures and dropping individual inputs. The inferences of the study remain unchanged across the different DEA specifications.

However, the conventional method of estimating the efficiency score and identifying the determinants of efficiency in a second stage has a severe flaw, that is, DEA efficiency scores are consecutively interrelated with an additional source of endogeneity which is the result of the measurement error in the efficiency estimates (Daraio et al., 2018; Simar and Wilson, 2007, 2011). Hence, Simar–Wilson (2007) double bootstrapping method is taken into consideration in the second stage analysis to explore the key determining factors of technical efficiency of the Islamic banks and how does financial inclusion effect on the efficiency.

Simar–Wilson (2007)[2] recommend two bootstrap techniques for the estimation problem related to two-stage efficiency. The primary step is intended to improve on inference, but not considering the bias-corrected estimation of efficiency which is called Algorithm 1. In the first-stage problem, a parametric bootstrap has been deployed to have bias-corrected estimates, which is called Algorithm 2. Algorithm 2 functions in two stages. In the first stage, a bias-corrected estimation related to the Shepard's distance function is estimated and for this, from the original distance function estimate, the bootstrap bias estimate is subtracted. This approach assists to restrict the problems caused by both endogeneity of outreach measure related to the efficiency score and autocorrelation of the non-observable components of efficiency (Banna et al., 2019b; Lépine et al., 2015). These bias-corrected efficiency scores are attempted to regress by means of bootstrapped truncated regression in the second stage. This method refers to the serial correlation in the DEA efficiency estimates as well as to fix the measurement error in technical efficiency scores used to examine the determining factors of technical efficiency.

To find the association between financial inclusion and Islamic banking efficiency, the subsequent baseline equation is specified[3]:

$$\theta_{ijt} = \gamma_0 + \gamma_1 \text{SIZE}_{ijt} + \gamma_2 \text{CAP}_{ijt} + \gamma_3 \text{ROAA}_{ijt} + \gamma_4 \text{CR}_{ijt} + \gamma_5 \text{GDP}_{jt} + \gamma_6 \text{FI}_{jt} + \varepsilon_{ijt}, \quad (2)$$

where

θ_{ijt} = DEA efficiency score of bank i of country j in year t;
SIZE_{ijt} = The natural logarithm of total assets of the bank i of country j in year t;
CAP_{ijt} = Total equity/total assets (capitalization) ratio of the bank i of country j in year t;
ROAA_{ijt} = Return on average assets of the bank i of country j in year t;
CR_{ijt} = Loan loss prov./net int. revenue (credit risk) of the bank i of country j in year t;
GDP_{jt} = Gross domestic product (GDP) growth of the country i and in year t;
FI_{jt} = Financial inclusion of country j in year t;
ε_{ijt} = Error term of the bank i of country j in year t.

2.2. Input and output variables selection

Two main approaches are seen in the existing literature to define the input–output variables for banks: the intermediation and production approaches (Gardener et al., 2011). In the

---

[2] The details can be found in Simar and Wilson (2007).
[3] "Simarwilson" command in Stata is used for operationalizing the first and second steps of Algorithm 2. The details of Stata procedure can be found in Badunenko and Tauchmann (2018).

intermediation approach, input variables include deposits, fixed assets and staff salaries of banks, whereas the loans and investments are seen as the output variables (Moffat and Valadkhani, 2008). However, in the production approach, physical variables are considered as input variables that include material, space, information systems and labor or the expenses associated to these and the banks' services to clients are considered as output variables (Das and Ghosh, 2006). The key dissimilarity between these two approaches is that the former considers deposits as inputs and estimates bank outputs with regard to money-based value, whereas the other uses deposits being the outputs and estimates bank outputs in the matter of the number of financial transactions/accounts. Although there is no exact theory and clear definition for the banks to determine the input–output variables, Berger and Humphrey (1997) suggested that production approach is suitable to compare efficiency of different branches of the same bank and intermediation approach is more suitable and authentic for assessing entire financial institutions. This is because banks do intermediary services between the demand and the supply of funds (Banna et al., 2019b; Rosman et al., 2014). More specifically, Islamic banks provide intermediation services by collecting deposits and other funds which are in turn invested in productive economic sectors that give profit free from usury (riba). Since this study aims to measure the efficiency of overall Islamic financial institutions rather than measuring the efficiency of branches, hence, this paper considers intermediation approach to select the input–output variables.

Accordingly, in order to measure Islamic banking efficiency from the period 2011 to 2017, three inputs: short-term funding and deposits, staff expenses and fixed assets; and two outputs: other earning assets and loans are taken into consideration. The year-wise efficiency frontier is created through the use of a balance of 154 Islamic banks sample from 32 countries over the period of 2011 to 2017, yielding 1078 bank-year observations.

2.3. Financial inclusion proxy

The basic feature of an inclusive financial sector is to see all the members of the economy with impartial eye regardless of their background and to consider all can have easy access and enjoy basic financial services effectively. From the regulator's point of view, the financial outreach and usage are the two dimensions of financial inclusion. Due to the constraint of data availability, proxies are needed for the two dimensions. Since the distance to avail financial services is considered as a big obstacle to financial inclusion, we use financial outreach dimension in order to justify the prevalence of the financial sector's outreach with regard to physical outlets of banks (Allen et al., 2014).

For automatic teller machine (ATM) services and bank branches, both the geographic and demographic penetrations are used in this study as these two are considered as main penetrations of bank services (Beck et al., 2007b). This study uses both the penetrations. As a part of geographic penetration, it sees the number of bank branches and ATM services per 1000 square kilometers, while it sees the number of bank branches and ATMs allocated for per 100,000 adults as a part of demographic penetration. Besides, as a part of usage dimension, this study also considers the number of bank accounts per 1000 adults to incorporate the penetration of the financial access.

Through the means of cross-country data, outreach and the determinants are investigated for determining common trends across the aforesaid indicators (Beck et al., 2007b). Therefore, a composite indicator across countries which is the combination of many interrelated indicators can be easily comprehended and compared by the average people (OECD, 2008). Hence, following Ahamed and Mallick (2019), both the composite index and its related determinates are considered to determine financial inclusion in this paper. The components that are used as parts of financial inclusion are closely connected to each other. To detect the common variation as a single measure from these interrelated determinants of financial inclusion, an index is developed by using principal components analysis (hereafter PCA). The financial inclusion index using PCA has been used to robust our results.

2.4. Data

Annual data of 154 Islamic banks of 32 countries from the year 2011 to 2017 have been taken from Orbis BankFocus database, the most authentic source of storing banking data of the whole world (Banna et al., 2017; Nguyen and Nghiem, 2017), for this study. The World Development Indicators (WDI) of World Bank and the Financial Access Survey (FAS) of International Monetary Fund (IMF) provide the macro-economic and financial inclusion data, respectively. We have excluded the banks having data missing for many years in the database. To find the missing data of those banks which have data missing for few years, we have searched their own website and tried to recover. Being failed to recover the data, we have measured the missing data by making an average when the data missing is for only one year.

The outliers of the variables are taken care of by using the winsorizing method of Hastings et al. (1947). This approach has been used to lessen the outcome of possible spurious outliers by limiting the extreme outliers in the data. More concretely, the top 1st and bottom 99th percentile of the variables is winsorized for the analysis (Banna et al., 2018; Barnett and Lewis, 1974; Mirzaei et al., 2013).

3. Results and Analysis

The findings of the analysis of Islamic bank efficiency are illustrated in this section. The efficiency measurement was carried out by the bias-corrected DEA based on Simar–Wilson method. This is because in the second stage analysis, the conventional DEA efficiency estimation techniques have endogeneity and measurement error problems, whereas the Simar–Wilson method is free from these flaws (Daraio et al., 2018; Simar and Wilson, 2007, 2011). Moreover, the findings of the relationship between Islamic bank efficiency and financial inclusion can be explained. Furthermore, the other factors pertinent to Islamic banking efficiency can be elucidated.

Constructing a yearly frontier is seen more flexible and more appropriate than constructing a single multi-year frontier for the banks (Rosman et al., 2014; Sufian and Noor, 2009). Therefore, for every year, this study uses a separate annual frontier for all the Islamic banks due to almost similar operational practice among them. Among many, the key benefit of utilizing panel data is to create scope of observing each bank several times in a given period (Isik and Hassan, 2002). However, its application is crucial for those business sectors which are having randomly changing atmosphere because of the technology banks use might not be equally effective for all the time (Sufian and Noor, 2009).

3.1. Descriptive statistics

Table 1 refers to the summary of banks' input–output variables for estimating efficiency. On average, the total deposits ($ 5277.185 million) of Islamic banks are more than their total loans ($ 3915.854 million). The pattern is similar with Doan *et al.* (2018) who studied

Table 1. Descriptive Statistics of Input–Output Variables (USD in Millions)

Variables	Obs.	Mean	Std. Dev.	Min	Max
2011					
Loans	154	3248.122	6393.093	4.856352	38,956.64
Other earning assets	154	1175.6	1954.113	0.729934	13,439.62
Deposits and short-term funding	154	4538.468	8476.247	5.75468	48,428.26
Fixed assets	154	146.8058	406.2705	0.0162	2708.945
Staff expenses	154	57.66877	124.0102	0.628434	786.6363
2012					
Loans	154	3724.274	6954.021	4.856352	38,956.64
Other earning assets	154	1334.258	2232.93	0.729934	13,439.62
Deposits and short-term funding	154	5130.742	9327.229	5.75468	48,428.26
Fixed assets	154	158.7875	433.0633	0.015	2708.945
Staff expenses	154	61.80917	131.1388	0.628434	786.6363
2013					
Loans	154	3384.973	5917.449	4.856352	38,956.64
Other earning assets	154	1269.73	2105.109	0.729934	13,439.62
Deposits and short-term funding	154	4765.765	8231.697	5.75468	48,428.26
Fixed assets	154	158.9363	450.0792	0.015	2708.945
Staff expenses	154	57.79285	115.9443	0.628434	706.7955
2014					
Loans	154	3760.113	6278.059	4.856352	38,956.64
Other earning assets	154	1265.026	2122.696	0.729934	13,439.62
Deposits and short-term funding	154	5171.674	8552.26	5.75468	48,428.26
Fixed assets	154	171.0471	485.3732	0.015	2708.945
Staff expenses	154	65.42144	129.6953	0.628434	786.6363
2015					
Loans	154	4100.46	6883.197	4.856352	38,956.64
Other earning assets	154	1316.901	2210.681	0.7764	13,439.62
Deposits and short-term funding	154	5525.811	9151.268	5.75468	48,428.26
Fixed assets	154	170.9143	459.2606	0.015	2708.945
Staff expenses	154	70.56168	141.2838	0.628434	786.6363

Table 1. (*Continued*)

Variables	Obs.	Mean	Std. Dev.	Min	Max
2016					
Loans	154	4415.131	7432.64	4.856352	38,956.64
Other earning assets	154	1282.57	2188.942	0.729934	13,439.62
Deposits and short-term funding	154	5645.111	9362.713	5.75468	48,428.26
Fixed assets	154	164.49	429.0565	0.015	2464.494
Staff expenses	154	73.57065	147.0907	0.628434	786.6363
2017					
Loans	154	4777.902	7869.303	4.856352	38,956.64
Other earning assets	154	1380.115	2319.865	0.729934	13,439.62
Deposits and short-term funding	154	6162.721	9955.548	5.75468	48,428.26
Fixed assets	154	163.8421	426.0033	0.015	2560.122
Staff expenses	154	76.62614	148.6239	0.628434	786.6363
All years					
Loans	1,078	3915.854	6847.284	4.856352	38,956.64
Other earning assets	1,078	1289.171	2159.513	0.7299335	13,439.62
Deposits and short-term funding	1,078	5277.185	9015.153	5.75468	48,428.26
Fixed assets	1,078	162.1176	440.7868	0.015	2708.945
Staff expenses	1,078	66.20724	134.2527	0.6284342	786.6363

Data Source: Orbis Bank focus, 2011–2017.

using the commercial banks sample and Rosman *et al.* (2014) who analyzed the Islamic banks. The mean other earning assets of the sample banks is $ 1289.171 million. The average values of the fixed assets and the staff expenses are about $ 162.118 and $ 66.207 million, respectively. It is noteworthy that high standard deviations visualize the large differences in the output variables among the sample countries.

The descriptive statistics of bank efficiency, bank size, capitalization, profitability, credit risk,[4] GDP growth and financial inclusion are produced in Table 2. The table reports the mean, standard deviation, along with maximum and minimum value for each variable in the sample. Few observations from this table are noteworthy for the DEA scores. First, the efficiency scores for the Islamic bank have a mean value of above 0.6 (mean = 0.652, standard deviation = 0.260), indicating the general tendency toward efficiency in Islamic banks. With these values, we infer that on average Islamic bank suffers from about 35% (i.e., 1–0.652) of the inefficiencies during the period of study. Moreover, the mean value of the logarithm of bank total assets and standard deviations are 7.58 and 1.74, respectively. Thus, a fairly low cross-country variation is suggested by these results. On average, the sample countries have 44 and 43 ATMs per 1000 km^2 and per 100,000 adults, respectively. The sample countries have about 16 and 14 commercial bank branches per 1000 km^2 and

---

[4] For both Islamic and conventional banks, the use of net interest revenue was standardized by the BankFocus, in which it compares the net profit of Islamic banks from financing. The total of the positive and negative flows of income, which is linked with the profit–loss sharing (PLS) arrangements, has been defined as Islamic banks' net interest revenue (Cihák and Hesse, 2008).

Table 2. Descriptive Statistics of Main Variables

Variables	Obs.	Mean	Std. Dev.	Min	Max
Efficiency	1078	0.652	0.260	0.034	1.000
Total assets (USD in millions)	971	6733.45	11,148.03	20.22	59,206.77
Size (log of total assets)	971	7.58	1.74	3.01	10.99
Capitalization (total equity/total assets) (%)	971	15.91	15.96	−27.18	82.28
Profitability (return on average assets) (%)	971	0.95	2.44	−10.88	7.17
Credit risk (loan loss prov/net int rev) (%)	655	26.21	72.80	−145.83	486.23
GDP growth (%)	1078	3.56	3.96	−13.62	13.40
Financial inclusion					
ATMs per 100 k adults	1078	42.81	31.81	1.88	129.57
Branches of commercial banks per 100 k adults	1078	14.10	8.56	1.70	31.83
ATMs per 1 k km^2	1078	43.36	58.58	0.31	289.42
Branches of commercial banks per 1 k km^2	1078	15.55	19.59	0.26	105.08
Number of bank account per 1000 adults	861	1127.56	832.88	120.39	3462.85

Note: Efficiency — Farrell input-oriented technical efficiency (TE) measure under variable return scale (VRS) using data envelopment analysis (DEA), ATMs — automated teller machines.
Source: Orbis bank focus, World Development Indicators (WDI), IMF Financial Access Survey (FAS).

per 100,000 adults, respectively. In addition, on average, the number of bank accounts per 1000 adults is 1128. In Appendix A, we report the pairwise correlation results between the independent variables used in our analysis.

3.2. *Efficiency of Islamic banks*

Table 3 summarizes the year-wise mean efficiency score of the Islamic banks. Our study mainly focuses on the post-crisis period. In 2014, the overall technical efficiency score touched the highest point while it was lower in 2011. However, it again fell down in 2015 and further relegated to the lowest score in 2017. The results note that Islamic banks showed an average technical efficiency of 65.2% during the study period. The results of

Table 3. Summary Statistics of Efficiency Scores of Islamic Banks

Year	Mean	Std. Dev.	Min	Max
2011	0.648	0.266	0.034	1
2012	0.653	0.260	0.062	1
2013	0.635	0.263	0.065	1
2014	0.673	0.256	0.053	1
2015	0.656	0.248	0.038	1
2016	0.650	0.258	0.054	1
2017	0.647	0.267	0.067	1
All years	0.652	0.260	0.034	1

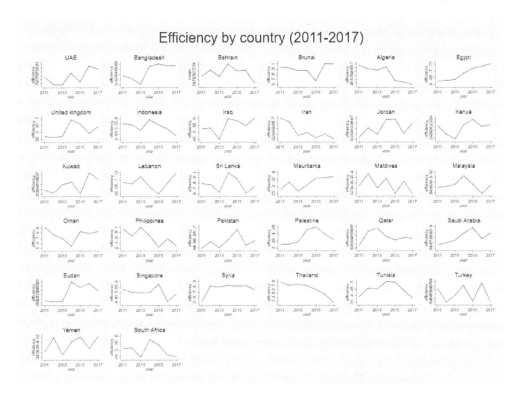

Figure 1. The Country-Wise Mean Efficiency of Islamic Banks (2011–2017)

this study advocate that to produce the same unit of outputs Islamic banks already produced, 34.8% of the inputs could have been saved by the banks. It can be said in other words as, by spending 65.2% of the inputs Islamic bank used, they could have made the same unit of outputs. The findings are quite similar with Rosman *et al.* (2014) who analyzed the Asian Islamic banks.

Figure 1 illustrates the country-wise trends of the Islamic banking efficiency. Most of the countries show fluctuating trends in the efficiency. Based on the findings, Egypt has upward trend in efficiency after 2012. Besides, Islamic banks in Bangladesh, Malaysia, Mauritia, Qatar, Tunisia and Sudan were performing efficiently than others. Interestingly, in spite of being war-affected countries, Islamic banks in Iraq and Palestine are performing well in terms of efficiency.

As the above efficiency scores are not bias-corrected (as criticized by the scholars), we consider the Simar–Wilson bias-corrected efficiency scores. Figure 2 shows both the non-bias-corrected and bias-corrected efficiency scores of the Islamic banks. The findings show that the bias-corrected efficiency scores (overall efficiency = 0.398) are lower than non-bias-corrected efficiency scores (overall efficiency = 0.652) of the Islamic banks. The result obtained through this technique suggests that to produce the same unit of outputs Islamic banks already produced, 60.2% of the inputs could have been saved by the banks. It can be said in other words as, by spending 39.8% of the inputs Islamic banks used, they could have made the same unit of outputs.

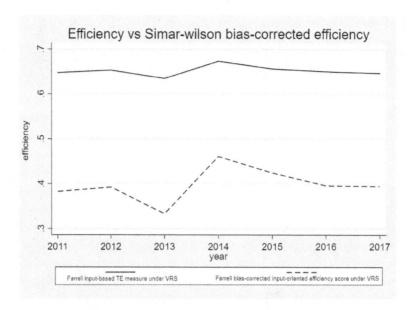

Figure 2. The Efficiency Versus Bias-Corrected Efficiency of the Islamic Banks (2011–2017)

3.3. *The financial inclusion and the efficiency of Islamic banks*

In order to see the association between Islamic banks' efficiency and financial inclusion, we consider Simar–Wilson (2007) double bootstrapping regression (Algorithm 1 and Algorithm 2) because of the criticism of Tobit regression. We control bank-specific factors such as bank size, capitalization, profitability and credit risk, as well as macro-economic factor such as the GDP per capita growth for the analysis.

In our analysis, the financial inclusion is divided into two main dimensions: financial outreach of the financial institutions (ATMs and branches) and usage of the clients (number of bank accounts). Financial outreach is classified into two penetrations: demographic and geographic. Models 1–4 show the relationship between Islamic banks efficiency and financial inclusion (financial outreach) in which models 1 and 2 demonstrate the demographic penetration and models 3 and 4 display the geographic penetration of financial outreach. Model 5 exhibits the relationship between Islamic banks' efficiency and financial inclusion (usage of the clients).

Table 4 exhibits the results of Simar–Wilson (2007) double bootstrapping regression (Algorithm 1) using the baseline Equation (2). Algorithm 1 only affects the estimated confidence intervals and standard errors, and it does not fully provide the bias-corrected efficiency score. In this stage, we could use the externally calculated efficiency score. However, in our analysis, we did not use the externally calculated efficiency scores to find the determinants of Islamic banks efficiency; rather, Simar–Wilson internally calculated efficiency scores have been used to find the relationship. This is because, Simar and Wilson (2007) argue that the externally calculated DEA efficiency estimates are seen to be serially correlated and to have measurement error which, in turn, lead to endogeneity problem.

Table 4. Bank Efficiency and Financial Inclusion (Simar and Wilson (2007): Algorithm 1)

Dep. Var: Efficiency Score	Exp. Sign	Model 1 (ATMs Per 100 k Adults)	Model 2 (Branch Per 100 k Adults)	Model 3 (ATMs Per 1 k km^2)	Model 4 (Branch Per 1 k km^2)	Model 5 (# of Bank Account Per 1 k Adults)
Size	+	0.099***	0.103***	0.084***	0.095***	0.094***
		(0.007)	(0.007)	(0.005)	(0.006)	(0.006)
Capitalization	+	0.004***	0.004***	0.003***	0.004***	0.003***
		(0.001)	(0.001)	(0.001)	(0.001)	(0.001)
Profitability	+	0.009**	0.008**	0.019***	0.017***	0.015***
		(0.004)	(0.004)	(0.004)	(0.004)	(0.004)
Credit risk	+/−	0.001	0.001	0.001*	0.001**	0.001*
		(0.001)	(0.001)	(0.001)	(0.001)	(0.001)
Financial inclusion	+	0.023***	0.028**	0.052***	0.055***	0.097***
		(0.009)	(0.013)	(0.004)	(0.005)	(0.011)
GDP	+	0.002	0.001	−0.002	−0.003*	−0.004*
		(0.002)	(0.002)	(0.002)	(0.002)	(0.002)
Year-fixed effect		Yes	Yes	Yes	Yes	Yes
Wald χ^2		289.480	306.300	495.690	461.930	495.390
Prob > χ^2		0.000	0.000	0.000	0.000	0.000
Observations		565	565	565	565	458
Efficient DMUs		90	90	90	90	76
Bootstr. reps		2000	2000	2000	2000	2000

Notes: Dependent variable, input-oriented technical efficiency score under VRS using DEA score. ***, ** and * represent significance at 1%, 5% and 10% level of confidence. Size, capitalization, profitability, credit risk, GDP and ATMs refer to log of total assets, equity/total assets, return on average assets (roaa), loan loss provision/net interest revenue, growth rate of gross domestic products, automated teller machines, respectively.

Hence, to obtain the bias-corrected DEA efficiency scores, these internally calculated DEA efficiency estimates are justified for this study.

The findings in Table 4 show that financial inclusion is significantly positively related with Islamic banks' efficiency based on all models. For all the cases, it is clearly evident that the greater efficiency of Islamic banks is associated with more financial inclusion as proved by its significant and positive (at 1% level) coefficients, regardless of penetrations and dimensions. Based on the mean efficiency score 65.2%, it is clear that the effect is both economically and statistically significant. The economic effect suggests that the soundness of individual banks can be enriched through the financial inclusion. Moreover, through the means of a sound inclusive financial sector, banks can bring in plenty of cheap retail deposits from a vast clientele ground. They can also remove the SME-related financing constraints, resolve the hazard seen in the post-financing period and mitigate problems pertinent to asset substitutions. Hence, banks having sound and inclusive financial environment enjoy higher level of financial efficiency.

Our findings on control variables are also supported by the existing studies. It is shown that size of the banks has a significant positive effect at 1% level for Islamic banks with regard to technical efficiency which is also supported by the study of Hauner (2005) and

Hassan (2006). It is also found that larger Islamic banks having skilled management team produce more outputs efficiently with their limited inputs.

Moreover, capitalization is positively related with the overall Islamic banks' technical efficiency at 1% level. The result is similar to the earlier studies (Banna et al., 2019b; Casu and Girardone, 2004; Sufian and Noor, 2009), which showed that more equity mitigate future losses. Thus, ceteris paribus, less leverage (i.e., more equity) has been used by more efficient banks than less efficient banks.

Further, profitability is positively and significantly related to Islamic banks' efficiency at 5% level while considering demographic penetration of financial outreach. Whereas, it is significant at 1% level while considering geographic penetration of financial outreach and financial inclusion's usage dimension which was clearly explained by the past studies (Banna et al., 2019b; Pasiouras, 2008; Sufian, 2009) where the scholars showed a significant positive relationship between profitability and bank efficiency. Thus, it is evident that by augmenting their profitability, banks become more efficient which was supported by Sufian (2009) as banks with more profitability are seen as more efficient than others with less profitability.

Furthermore, credit risk, surprisingly, has positive relation with Islamic banks' efficiency. Though credit risk is not significant while considering demographic penetration of financial outreach, but significant at 10% and 5% level while considering geographic penetration of financial outreach and financial inclusion's usage dimension. This finding seems to have a contradiction with the past studies (Kwan and Eisenbeis, 1997; Resti, 1997) in which the researchers obtained a negative association between bank efficiency and problem loans. In this regard, Ahmad and Hassan (2007) propose to keep this ratio as low as possible. However, the result is similar with Rosman et al. (2014) who observed a positive association after conducting a research on the Islamic banks of Asia and Middle East. They explained that it might be the possible reason behind the positive association between credit risk and efficiency that, during the research period, in order to be more careful in terms of dealing their finance-related affairs, financing is given more attention by those banks that are seen efficient. Therefore, credit risk and Islamic banking efficiency are positively linked.

Finally, the study shows an inconclusive effect of GDP growth on the efficiency of Islamic banking. We expected a positive relation between GDP growth and bank efficiency as growth might exalt the efficiency of the banking sector. But the finding is contradictory with the previous studies (Banna et al., 2019b; Grigorian and Manole, 2006). This could be the result of non-bias-corrected efficiency score in Algorithm 1.

As Algorithm 1 does not consider bias-corrected efficiency, we have run the Simar–Wilson (2007) double bootstrapping Algorithm 2 regression. In this process, we use bias-corrected efficiency score as a dependent variable. In this regression, externally calculated efficiency scores are not allowed to use as the regression estimates bias-corrected efficiency internally. In this procedure, we use 1500 replications in the bias correction bootstrap and 2000 replications in the bootstrap similar to Algorithm 1. Table 5 shows the results of Simar–Wilson (2007) efficiency analysis with Algorithm 2. In most cases, the significance and sign of the variables do not change in Algorithm 2. However, the bias-corrected

Table 5. Bank Efficiency and Financial Inclusion (Simar and Wilson (2007): Algorithm 2)

Dep. Var: Efficiency Score	Exp. Sign	Model 1 (ATMs Per 100k Adults)	Model 2 (Branch Per 100k Adults)	Model 3 (ATMs Per 1k km^2)	Model 4 (Branch Per 1k km^2)	Model 5 (# of Bank Account Per 1k Adults)
Size	+	0.098***	0.100***	0.085***	0.092***	0.103***
		(0.005)	(0.004)	(0.004)	(0.004)	(0.004)
Capitalization	+	0.004***	0.004***	0.004***	0.004***	0.004***
		(0.000)	(0.000)	(0.000)	(0.000)	(0.000)
Profitability	+	0.012***	0.012***	0.022***	0.020***	0.017***
		(0.003)	(0.003)	(0.003)	(0.003)	(0.003)
Credit risk	+/−	0.001	0.001	0.001	0.001*	0.001*
		(0.001)	(0.001)	(0.001)	(0.001)	(0.001)
Financial inclusion	+	0.017***	0.023***	0.041***	0.043***	0.080***
		(0.006)	(0.009)	(0.004)	(0.004)	(0.007)
GDP	+	0.004***	0.004***	0.001	0.000	0.000
		(0.001)	(0.001)	(0.001)	(0.001)	(0.001)
Year-fixed effect		Yes	Yes	Yes	Yes	Yes
Wald χ^2		824.580	814.430	1036.350	941.970	1663.230
Prob > χ^2		0.000	0.000	0.000	0.000	0.000
Observations		652	652	653	652	528
# of reps (bc)		1500	1500	1500	1500	1500
Bootstr. reps		2000	2000	2000	2000	2000

Notes: Dependent variable = bias-corrected Farrell input-oriented technical efficiency score under VRS using Simar–Wilson double bootstrapping regression. ***, ** and * represent significance at 1%, 5% and 10% level of confidence. Size, capitalization, profitability, credit risk, GDP, ATMs, bc refer to log of total assets, equity/total assets, return on average assets (roaa), loan loss provision/net interest revenue, growth rate of gross domestic products, automated teller machines and bias-corrected, respectively.

efficiency scores improve the estimated confidence intervals and the coefficients, as well as the significance of the models (based on the higher Wald χ^2 value). In Algorithm 2, the study finds a significant positive relation of financial inclusion and Islamic banks' efficiency. Interestingly, in this stage, the study shows a significantly positive relationship of Islamic banks efficiency and the GDP growth. Therefore, using the bias-corrected efficiency score, it is still clear that smooth and inclusive financial sector is positively connected with higher Islamic banking efficiency, regardless of penetrations and dimensions of financial inclusion.

We examine the robustness of the key results into two main ways. First, we use Algorithm 2 with invert[5] efficiency score to have the association between financial inclusion and bank inefficiency. Secondly, to construct a financial inclusion index by using dimensions of financial inclusion together, the PCA has been employed. Later, this financial inclusion index has been used to see the association of financial inclusion with bank efficiency in various dimensions.

---

[5] We use "invert" command in the option in "Simarwilson" command in Stata.

3.4. Robustness: Simar–Wilson (2007) double bootstrapping regression using inefficiency scores

So far, we have used Simar–Wilson (2007) double bootstrapping Algorithms 1 and 2 regressions and found a positive relation between Islamic banks' efficiency and financial inclusion. However, in order to robust the results, there is a need to see the alternative association between the bank inefficiency and financial inclusion by using invert efficiency scores in Simar–Wilson regression (in Algorithm 2). In this procedure, bias-corrected Shephard input-oriented technical inefficiency score under VRS is used as dependent variable. We use 1500 replications in the bias correction bootstrap and 2000 replications in the bootstrap similar with Algorithms 1 and 2.

The finding in Table 6 displays that financial inclusion has a negative impact on Islamic banks inefficiency regardless of dimensions. This suggests that financial exclusion can lead the Islamic bank to less efficient institution. Hence, these findings robust our previous results of positive link of bank efficiency and financial inclusion. Besides, the sign of all the control variables has changed as well.

Table 6. Bank Efficiency and Financial Inclusion (Simar and Wilson (2007), Algorithm 2 with Invert)

Dep. Var: Inefficiency Score	Exp. Sign	Model 1 (ATMs Per 100 k Adults)	Model 2 (Branch Per 100 k Adults)	Model 3 (ATMs Per 1 k km^2)	Model 4 (Branch Per 1 k km^2)	Model 5 (# of Bank Accounts Per 1 k Adults)
Size	−	−16.741**	−18.819**	−4.864***	−5.827***	−7.937***
		(8.494)	(9.602)	(1.417)	(1.747)	(2.514)
Capitalization	−	−0.732*	−0.805*	−0.318***	−0.352***	−0.432***
		(0.389)	(0.423)	(0.111)	(0.120)	(0.154)
Profitability	−	−0.195	−0.456	−0.988***	−0.895**	−0.070
		(0.970)	(1.104)	(0.376)	(0.366)	(0.398)
Credit risk	+/−	−0.014	−0.030	−0.008	−0.012	0.003
		(0.032)	(0.034)	(0.010)	(0.012)	(0.013)
Financial inclusion	−	−11.723*	−18.764*	−4.553***	−4.852***	−12.596***
		(6.631)	(10.183)	(1.310)	(1.436)	(4.090)
GDP	−	−1.016	−0.405	0.001	0.103	0.312
		(0.705)	(0.579)	(0.180)	(0.184)	(0.263)
Year-fixed effect		Yes	Yes	Yes	Yes	Yes
Observations		655	655	655	655	534
# of reps (bc)		1500	1500	1500	1500	1500
Bootstr. Reps		2000	2000	2000	2000	2000

Notes: Dependent variable = bias-corrected Shephard input-oriented technical inefficiency score under VRS using Simar–Wilson double bootstrapping regression. ***, ** and * represent significance at 1%, 5% and 10% level of confidence. Size, capitalization, profitability, credit risk, GDP, ATMs, bc refer to log of total assets, equity/total assets, return on average assets (roaa), loan loss provision/net interest revenue, growth rate of gross domestic products, automated teller machines and bias-corrected, respectively.

3.5. Robustness: Alternative measure of financial inclusion: PCA

Further, for observing the robustness of the main results, this study uses an alternative proxy of financial inclusion by the means of PCA. The PCA helps us get the single linear combination of the financial inclusion proxies from the first principal component that explicates majority of the variations which are visible in these proxies. Thus, this single index deals with the issue of over-parameterization and multicollinearity effectively. The four variables consist the financial outreach dimension and from which we, with the help of the PCA, capture common variation and formulate the single index of the financial outreach dimension. Then, we combine both the single index of the financial outreach dimension and usage dimension of financial inclusion to create a single financial inclusion by using PCA. Therefore, we consider two indices of financial inclusion; first index is comprised of financial outreach (both demographic and geographic penetrations) but

Table 7. Bank Efficiency and Financial Inclusion (Simar and Wilson (2007) Using Alternative Financial Inclusion Measure)

	Algorithm #1		Algorithm #2		Algorithm #2 With Invert	
Dep. Var: Efficiency/ Inefficiency Score	Model 1 (PCA Without Usage)	Model 2 (PCA With Usage)	Model 3 (PCA Without Usage)	Model 4 (PCA With Usage)	Model 5 (PCA Without Usage)	Model 6 (PCA With Usage)
Size	0.087***	0.092***	0.087***	0.101***	−7.286**	−6.713***
	(0.006)	(0.006)	(0.004)	(0.004)	(3.216)	(2.074)
Capitalization	0.003***	0.003***	0.004***	0.004***	−0.407**	−0.379***
	(0.001)	(0.001)	(0.000)	(0.000)	(0.199)	(0.137)
Profitability	0.017***	0.016***	0.019***	0.017***	−1.161*	−0.423
	(0.004)	(0.004)	(0.003)	(0.003)	(0.622)	(0.381)
Credit risk	0.001*	0.001*	0.001	0.001	−0.015	0.003
	(0.000)	(0.001)	(0.001)	(0.001)	(0.017)	(0.012)
Financial inclusion	0.039***	0.077***	0.031***	0.061***	−5.752**	−9.662***
	(0.005)	(0.008)	(0.004)	(0.005)	(2.563)	(2.989)
GDP	−0.001	−0.004*	0.002	0.001	0.064	0.308
	(0.002)	(0.002)	(0.001)	(0.001)	(0.282)	(0.229)
Year-fixed effect	Yes	Yes	Yes	Yes	Yes	Yes
Wald χ^2	384.640	488.680	925.930	1663.240		
Prob $> \chi^2$	0.000	0.000	0.000	0.000		
Observations	565	458	652	529	655	534
Efficient DMUs	90	76				
# of reps (bc)			1500	1500	1500	1500
Bootstr. reps	2000	2000	2000	2000	2000	2000

Notes: Dependent variable = Farrell input-oriented technical efficiency and bias-corrected Farrell (Shephard) input-oriented technical efficiency (inefficiency) score under VRS using Simar–Wilson double bootstrapping regression. ***, ** and * represent significance at 1%, 5% and 10% level of confidence. Size, capitalization, profitability, credit risk, GDP and bc refer to log of total assets, equity/total assets, return on average assets (roaa), loan loss provision/net interest revenue, growth rate of gross domestic products and bias-corrected, respectively.

without usage and second index is more comprehensive as it has included both financial outreach and usage dimensions.

In this analysis, we have used Simar–Wilson's Algorithms 1 and 2 and invert regressions. In these regressions, Farrell input-oriented technical efficiency, bias-corrected Farrell input-oriented technical efficiency, bias-corrected Shephard input-oriented technical inefficiency score under VRS have been used as dependent variables for Algorithm 1, Algorithm 2 and Algorithm 2 with invert, respectively.

In Table 7, the findings also suggest that financial inclusion is significantly related with Islamic banking efficiency by providing a positive link between them. Besides, we also consider Tobit regression, OLS and GMM for the robustness of the results and have found a positive relationship between financial inclusion and Islamic banking efficiency. However, we have not provided the results in this manuscript but the results are available upon request. It is found that our results are robust regardless of methods used in the study.

Therefore, it is clear from the various dimensions of analysis that the efficiency of Islamic banks is greatly influenced by the efficient and productive financial inclusion.

4. Conclusion

Although the financial inclusion has been a burning issue to scholars, stakeholders, researchers and financial organizations since the late 1990s, very few studies were carried out indicating the role of financial inclusion in the resilience and smooth operation of Islamic banks in the subsequent GFC period. Therefore, this paper mainly attempts to estimate both the non-bias-corrected and bias-corrected efficiency of Islamic banks in the post-GFC and how financial inclusion influences the efficiency improvement. DEA-based efficiency scores were first derived as a proxy to Islamic banking sector efficiency across the region to be evaluated through Simar–Wilson (2007) double bootstrapping method.

The findings show that most of the countries except some Asian and Middle-Eastern countries have overall inconsistent efficiency trends in the Islamic banking sector. So, it is suggested that banks are still bearing the consequence of the GFC. However, Islamic banks in Bangladesh, Malaysia, Mauritia, Qatar, Tunisia and Sudan are performing efficiently and more interestingly, in spite of being war-affected countries; Islamic banks in Iraq and Palestine have improvement trends in their efficiency. The results also exhibit that the Islamic banking efficiency is highly associated with financial inclusion which is significant both economically and statistically. This suggests that efficient and inclusive financial system accelerates Islamic banking efficiency regardless of penetrations and dimensions. Our results are robust from various analyses.

Policy-makers across the world have been craving for finding effective policies to enhance bank efficiency. Determining the push factors significantly related to banking efficiency eases the way of finding better policies in this regard. This study provides an insight into the policy-makers, bank management, regulators and governments how to accelerate the level of efficiency of the Islamic banking sector. They should focus more on financial inclusion for augmenting the banking efficiency. This is because, the soundness of individual banks becomes enriched through the financial inclusion. Moreover, through the means of a sound inclusive financial sector, banks are able to bring in plenty of cheap retail deposits from a vast clientele ground. They can also remove the SME-related financing constraints, resolve the hazard seen in the post-financing period and mitigate problems pertinent to asset substitutions. Hence, banks having sound and inclusive financial environment enjoy higher level of financial efficiency. In addition, Islamic banks can improve their level of financial inclusion by emerging the time-tested Shari'a-complaint financial product in both Islamic and non-Islamic countries. After all, the governments can achieve their SDGs by implementing time-demanding financial inclusion through Islamic banks.

This study has some limitations such as it has only considered Islamic banks as it samples over the period of 2011–2017 and it has not employed advanced DEA techniques (e.g., dynamic DEA and network DEA) for analyzing the data. This study has some limitations which, in turn, indicate opportunities and suggestions for further studies. The findings of this study can be expanded to compare the efficiency of conventional and Islamic banks from both country and regional perspectives by analyzing the data before and after the GFC. Besides, the DEA approach used in this study can be extended further to investigate the efficiency changes over time by employing dynamic DEA and network DEA as well as productivity changes over time by deploying the Malmquist productivity index.

Acknowledgments

The authors would like to thank the guest editor Prof. Dr M. Kabir Hassan, two anonymous reviewers, Dr Koh Hsieng Yang Eric, Dr Muhammad Mehedi Masud, Md Sohel Rana and Dr Aslam Mia for their critical review, precious comments and technical support. This research was partially funded by the Centre for Poverty and Development Studies (CPDS)/ Ungku Aziz Centre for Development Studies, Faculty of Economics and Administration, University of Malaya (Grant No. PD004-2018) and Faculty of Economics and Administration, University of Malaya (Grant No. GPF006P-2019).

Appendix A. Pairwise Correlation Among Variables

Appendix A.

	1	2	3	4	5	6	7	8	9	10	11	12	13
Efficiency score (1)	1												
Size (2)	0.4746*	1											
Capitalization (3)	0.0651*	−0.3941*	1										
Profitability (4)	−0.0196	0.0599	0.1189*	1									
Credit risk (5)	0.0226	−0.0108	0.0555	−0.2529*	1								
atms per 1k adults (6)	0.3518*	0.4197*	0.0139	−0.2988*	0.0765	1							
Branch per 1k adults (7)	0.1725*	0.3387*	−0.0640*	−0.2553*	0.0329	0.6635*	1						
Atms per 1 k km^2 (8)	0.1014*	0.0067	0.0719*	−0.2140*	0.0022	0.6483*	0.3213*	1					
Branch per 1 k km^2 (9)	−0.0021	−0.1229*	−0.0959*	−0.1857*	−0.0745	0.1539*	0.2002*	0.6688*	1				
Bank account per 1k adults (10)	0.4964*	0.4172*	−0.0558	−0.2264*	0.002	0.7497*	0.5720*	0.3536*	0.0133	1			
PCA without usage (11)	0.4179*	0.3576*	−0.1005*	−0.3659*	0.0323	0.7768*	0.7607*	0.5883*	0.4655*	0.6480*	1		
PCA with usage (12)	0.5573*	0.4162*	−0.0326	−0.3119*	0.026	0.8170*	0.7732*	0.5757*	0.2394*	0.9077*	0.9077*	1	
GDP growth (13)	0.0737*	−0.0069	0.0029	−0.0980*	−0.0971*	0.0411	−0.0136	0.0259	0.1399*	0.2684*	0.1537*	0.3353*	1

References

Abdul-Majid, M, DS Saal and G Battisti (2010). Efficiency in Islamic and conventional banking: An international comparison. *Journal of Productivity Analysis*, 34(1), 25–43.

Ahamed, MM and SK Mallick (2019). Is financial inclusion good for bank stability? International evidence. *Journal of Economic Behavior and Organization*, 157 (January 2019), 403–427. doi: 10.1016/j.jebo.2017.07.027.

Ahmad, AUF and MK Hassan (2007). Regulation and performance of Islamic banking in Bangladesh. *Thunderbird International Business Review*, 49(2), 251–277.

Allen, F, E Carletti, R Cull, JQ Qian, L Senbet and P Valenzuela (2014). The African financial development and financial inclusion gaps. *Journal of African Economies*, 23(5), 614–642.

Allen, F, A Demirguc-Kunt, L Klapper amd MS Martinez Peria (2016). The foundations of financial inclusion: Understanding ownership and use of formal accounts. *Journal of Financial Intermediation*, 27(C), 1–30.

Angelucci, M, D Karlan and J Zinman (2013). *Win Some Lose Some? Evidence from a Randomized Microcredit Program Placement Experiment by Compartamos Banco*. Retrieved from https://www.nber.org/papers/w19119.

Aportela, F (1999). Effects of financial access on savings by low-income people. MIT Department of Economics Dissertation.

Badunenko, O and H Tauchmann (2018). *Simar and Wilson Two-Stage Efficiency Analysis for Stata*. Retrieved from https://EconPapers.repec.org/RePEc:zbw:iwqwdp:082018.

Banerjee, A, E Duflo, R Glennerster and C Kinnan (2013). *The Miracle of Microfinance? Evidence from a Randomized Evaluation*. Retrieved from https://www.nber.org/papers/w18950.

Banerjee, A, E Duflo, R Glennerster and C Kinnan (2015). The miracle of microfinance? Evidence from a randomized evaluation. *American Economic Journal: Applied Economics*, 7(1), 22–53.

Banker, RD, A Charnes and WW Cooper (1984). Some models for estimating technical and scale inefficiencies in data envelopment analysis. *Management Science*, 30(9), 1078–1092.

Banna, H, R Ahmad and EH Koh (2017). Determinants of commercial banks' efficiency in Bangladesh: does crisis matter? *The Journal of Asian Finance, Economics and Business*, 4(3), 19–26.

Banna, H, R Ahmad and EHY Koh (2018). How does total quality management influence the loan quality of the bank? *Total Quality Management and Business Excellence*, 29(3–4), 287–300. doi: 10.1080/14783363.2016.1180954.

Banna, H, MS Rana, I Ismail and N Ismail (2019a). Quantifying the managerial ability of microfinance institutions: Evidence from Latin America. *Journal of International Development*. doi: 10.1002/jid.3419.

Banna, H, SKB Shah, AHM Noman, R Ahmad and MM Masud (2019b). Determinants of Sino-ASEAN banking efficiency: How do countries differ? *Economies*, 7(1), 13. doi: 10.3390/economies7010013.

Barnett, V and T Lewis (1974). *Outliers in Statistical Data*. New York: Wiley.

Beck, T, A Demirgüç-Kunt and R Levine (2007a). Finance, inequality and the poor. *Journal of Economic Growth*, 12(1), 27–49.

Beck, T, A Demirguc-Kunt and MS Martínez-Pería (2007b). Reaching out: Access to and use of banking services across countries. *Journal of Financial Economics*, 85(1), 234–266.

Beck, T, A Demirgüç-Kunt and O Merrouche (2010). *Islamic vs. Conventional Banking: Business Model, Efficiency and Stability*. Washington, D.C: The World Bank.

Beck, T, A Demirgüj-Kunt and O Merrouche (2013). Islamic vs. conventional banking: Business model, efficiency and stability. *Journal of Banking and Finance*, 37, 433–447.

Berger, AN and DB Humphrey (1997). Efficiency of financial institutions: International survey and directions for future research. *European Journal of Operational Research*, 98(2), 175–212.

Bruhn, M and I Love (2014). The real impact of improved access to finance: Evidence from Mexico. *The Journal of Finance*, 69(3), 1347–1376.

Burgess, R and R Pande (2005). Do rural banks matter? Evidence from the Indian social banking experiment. *American Economic Review*, 95(3), 780–795.

Casu, B and C Girardone (2004). Financial conglomeration: Efficiency, productivity and strategic drive. *Applied Financial Economics*, 14(10), 687–696.

Charnes, A, WW Cooper and E. Rhodes (1978). Measuring the efficiency of decision making units. *European Journal of Operational Research*, 2(6), 429–444.

Cihák, MM and H Hesse (2008). *Islamic Banks and Financial Stability: An Empirical Analysis*. Washington, D.C: International Monetary Fund.

Collard, S (2007). Toward financial inclusion in the UK: Progress and challenges. *Public Money and Management*, 27(1), 13–20.

Cullen, A (2011). *Why do banks fail? A look at characteristics of failed institutions from 2008 to 2010*. Retrieved from http://papers. ssrn. com/sol3/papers. cfm.

Daraio, C, L Simar and PW Wilson (2018). Central limit theorems for conditional efficiency measures and tests of the 'separability' condition in non-parametric, two-stage models of production. *The Econometrics Journal*, 21(2), 170–191.

Das, A and S Ghosh (2006). Financial deregulation and efficiency: An empirical analysis of Indian banks during the post reform period. *Review of Financial Economics*, 15(3), 193–221.

Demirgüç-Kunt, A and H Huizinga (2010). Bank activity and funding strategies: The impact on risk and returns. *Journal of Financial Economics*, 98(3), 626–650.

Demirgüç-Kunt, A, L Klapper, D Singer and P Van Oudheusden (2015). *The Global Findex Database 2014: Measuring Financial Inclusion Around the World*. Washington, D.C: The World Bank.

Demirguc-Kunt, A, B Hu and L Klapper (2019). Financial inclusion in the Europe and Central Asia region: Recent trends and a research agenda. The World Bank.

Di Patti, EB and G Dell'Ariccia (2001). *Bank Competition and Firm Creation*: International Monetary Fund.

Doan, A-T, K-L Lin and S-C Doong (2018). What drives bank efficiency? The interaction of bank income diversification and ownership. *International Review of Economics and Finance*, 55, 203–219.

Farrell, MJ (1957). The measurement of productive efficiency. *Journal of the Royal Statistical Society: Series A (General)*, 120(3), 253–281.

Flug, K, A Spilimbergo and E Wachtenheim (1998). Investment in education: Do economic volatility and credit constraints matter? *Journal of Development Economics*, 55(2), 465–481.

Gardener, E, P Molyneux and H Nguyen-Linh (2011). Determinants of efficiency in South East Asian banking. *The Service Industries Journal*, 31(16), 2693–2719.

Gebrehiwot, KG and D Makina (2019). Macroeconomic determinants of financial inclusion: Evidence using dynamic panel data analysis. In *Extending Financial Inclusion in Africa*, pp. 167–191. Cambridge, Massachusetts: Elsevier Academic Press.

Grigorian, DA and V Manole (2006). Determinants of commercial bank performance in transition: an application of data envelopment analysis. *Comparative Economic Studies*, 48(3), 497–522.

Hannig, A and S Jansen (2010). Financial inclusion and financial stability: Current policy issues.

Hasan, MM and J Dridi (2010). The effects of the global crisis on Islamic and conventional banks: A comparative study. *IMF Working Papers*, 1–46.

Hassan, MK (2006). The X-efficiency in Islamic banks. *Islamic Economic Studies*, 13, 50–78.

Hastings, C, F Mosteller, JW Tukey and CP Winsor (1947). Low moments for small samples: Acomparative study of order statistics. *The Annals of Mathematical Statistics*, 18(3), 413–426.

Hauner, D (2005). Explaining efficiency differences among large German and Austrian banks. *Applied Economics*, 37(9), 969–980.

Iqbal, M and DT Llewellyn (2002). *Islamic Banking and Finance: New Perspectives on Profit Sharing and Risk*. Camberley Surrey, UK: Edward Elgar Publishing.

Isik, I and MK Hassan (2002). Technical, scale and allocative efficiencies of Turkish banking industry. *Journal of Banking and Finance*, 26(4), 719–766.

Jahan, S, J De, F Jamaludin, P Sodsriwiboon and C Sullivan (2019). *The Financial Inclusion Landscape in the Asia-Pacific Region: A Dozen Key Findings*. Washington, D.C: International Monetary Fund.

Kim, D-W, J-S Yu and MK Hassan (2018). Financial inclusion and economic growth in OIC countries. *Research in International Business and Finance*, 43, 1–14.

Klapper, L, L Laeven and R Rajan (2006). Entry regulation as a barrier to entrepreneurship. *Journal of Financial Economics*, 82(3), 591–629.

Klein, M and C Mayer (2011). *Mobile Banking and Financial Inclusion: The Regulatory Lessons*. Washington, D.C: The World Bank.

Kwan, S and RA Eisenbeis (1997). Bank risk, capitalization, and operating efficiency. *Journal of Financial Services Research*, 12(2–3), 117–131.

Lépine, A, A Vassall, S Chandrashekar, E Blanc and A Le Nestour (2015). Estimating unbiased economies of scale of HIV prevention projects: A case study of Avahan. *Social Science and Medicine*, 131, 164–172.

Leyshon, A and N Thrift (1995). Geographies of financial exclusion: Financial abandonment in Britain and the United States. *Transactions of the Institute of British Geographers*, 312–341.

Mani, A, S Mullainathan, E Shafir and J Zhao (2013). Poverty impedes cognitive function. *Science*, 341(6149), 976–980.

Mirakhor, A (2008). Lesson of the recent crisis for Islamic finance. *IIUM Journal of Economics and Management*, 16(2), 132–138.

Mirzaei, A, T Moore and G Liu (2013). Does market structure matter on banks' profitability and stability? Emerging vs. advanced economies. *Journal of Banking and Finance*, 37(8), 2920–2937.

Moffat, B and A Valadkhani (2008). *Technical Efficiency in Botswana's Financial Institutions: A DEA Approach*. School of Economics, University of Wollongong, NSW, Australia. Retrieved from https://ideas.repec.org/p/uow/depec1/wp08-14.html.

Nguyen, TPT and SH Nghiem (2017). The effects of competition on efficiency: The Vietnamese banking industry experience. *The Singapore Economic Review*, 1–30.

OECD (2008). *Handbook on constructing composite indicators: Methodology and user guide*. Organisation for Economic Co-operation and Development (OECD), Paris.

Owen, AL and JM Pereira (2018). Bank concentration, competition, and financial inclusion. *Review of Development Finance*, 8(1), 1–17.

Pasiouras, F (2008). Estimating the technical and scale efficiency of Greek commercial banks: The impact of credit risk, off-balance sheet activities, and international operations. *Research in International Business and Finance*, 22(3), 301–318.

Petersen, MA and RG Rajan (1995). The effect of credit market competition on lending relationships. *The Quarterly Journal of Economics*, 110(2), 407–443.

Prasad, ES (2010). *Financial sector regulation and reforms in emerging markets: An overview*. Retrieved from https://www.nber.org/papers/w16428.

Prina, S (2012). Do basic savings accounts help the poor to save? Evidence from a field experiment in Nepal. Weatherhead School of Management, Case Western Reserve University, Cleveland, OH.

Resti, A (1997). Evaluating the cost-efficiency of the Italian banking system: What can be learned from the joint application of parametric and non-parametric techniques. *Journal of Banking and Finance*, 21(2), 221–250.

Rosman, R, NA Wahab and Z Zainol (2014). Efficiency of Islamic banks during the financial crisis: An analysis of Middle Eastern and Asian countries. *Pacific-Basin Finance Journal*, 28, 76–90.

Sarma, M (2008). *Index of Financial Inclusion*. East Asian Bureau of Economic Research. Retrieved from https://www.econstor.eu/handle/10419/176233.

Siddiqi, MN (2009). Current financial crisis and Islamic economics. *Insights*, 1(3).

Simar, L and PW Wilson (2007). Estimation and inference in two-stage, semi-parametric models of production processes. *Journal of Econometrics*, 136(1), 31–64.

Simar, L and PW Wilson (2011). Two-stage DEA: caveat emptor. *Journal of Productivity Analysis*, 36(2), 205.

Sole, MJ (2007). *Introducing Islamic Banks into Coventional Banking Systems (EPub)*. Washington, D.C: International Monetary Fund.

Sufian, F (2009). Determinants of bank efficiency during unstable macroeconomic environment: Empirical evidence from Malaysia. *Research in International Business and Finance*, 23(1), 54–77.

Sufian, F and MANM Noor (2009). The determinants of Islamic banks' efficiency changes: Empirical evidence from the MENA and Asian banking sectors. *International Journal of Islamic and Middle Eastern Finance and Management*, 2(2), 120–138.

Chapter 15

Low-Frequency Volatility and Macroeconomic Dynamics: Conventional Versus Islamic Stock Markets[#]

Hong-Bae Kim[*,‡] and A.S.M. Sohel Azad[†,§]

[*]Department of Business Administration
Dongseo University, Pusan, South Korea

[†]Department of Finance, Faculty of Business and Law
Deakin University, 221 Burwood Highway
Burwood, Vic-3125, Australia
[‡]rfctogether@gmail.com
[§]s.azad@deakin.edu.au

This study investigates the relationship between *macroeconomic risk* and low-frequency volatility of conventional and Islamic stock markets from around the world. Using a panel of 36 countries, representing developed, emerging and Islamic countries for the period from 2000 to 2016, the study finds that low-frequency market volatility is lower for Islamic countries and, markets with more number of listed companies, higher market capitalization relative to GDP and larger variability in industrial production. The study also finds that low-frequency component of volatility is greater when the macroeconomic factors of GDP, unemployment, short-term interest rates, inflation, money supply and foreign exchange rates are more volatile. The empirical results are robust to various alternative specifications and split sample analyses. The findings imply that religiosity has an influence on the correction of market volatility and investors may consider the Islamic stocks to diversify their risks.

Keywords: Low-frequency volatility; macroeconomic risk; conventional stock markets; Islamic stock markets.

1. Introduction

How different are Islamic stock markets from conventional stock markets in terms of their relationships with *macroeconomic risks*? Does Shariah-compliant Islamic markets decrease low-frequency volatility or only the developed markets that help correcting the market volatility? Does the global financial crisis (GFC) justify a closer look at the Islamic markets for portfolio diversification? This paper attempts to answer these research questions by combining the ideas of Engle and Rangel (2008), Rangel and Engle (2012), Beck *et al.* (2013), Abedifar *et al.* (2013) and Azad *et al.* (2018). While the first two studies provide theoretical justification and empirical proofs of decomposing market volatility and

---

[§] Corresponding author.
[#] This Chapter first appeared in the *Singapore Economic Review*, Vol. 67, No. 1, doi: 10.1142/S0217590819420049. © 2022 World Scientific Publishing.

the relationship between low-frequency volatility and stock market, the last three papers examine the risk and performance of conventional and Shariah-compliant stocks and business models both in tranquil and turmoil periods. Essentially, we combine the features from these two strands of literature in order to examine the relationship between low-frequency volatility of stock markets and *macroeconomic risk*.

Investigating the relationship between financial assets and macroeconomy helps one to identify precisely the macroeconomic sources that determine the exposure of financial assets to the macroeconomy as well as market portfolio (see, for instance, Wei *et al.*, 2019; González *et al.*, 2018; Kurov and Stan, 2018 and references therein). It would also allow one to directly relate macroeconomic effects to expected stock return and its volatility. This paper, thus, examines whether key macroeconomic variables namely, GDP, unemployment, short-term interest rates, inflation, money supply and foreign exchange rates affect the stock markets. However, this is the first paper that investigates whether, in contrast to conventional stock markets, Islamic stock markets have a different role in reducing (low-frequency) market volatility and perform well during a systemic crisis period. By doing so, we can gauge the distinguishing role of key macroeconomic variables in determining the stock return and its volatility. It is worth noting that while there are more points of similarities than distinctions, the relationship between macroeconomy and asset price volatility in two markets may not be similar due to some inherent characteristics of Islamic markets: (i) risk return preferences of investors in the presence of a salient religious identity (Benjamin *et al.*, 2016) and (ii) low debt feature of Islamic equities (Azad *et al.*, 2018). So, the first contribution of our paper is that we fill the research gap on the relationship between *macroeconomic risks* and stock price volatility in Islamic and conventional stock markets.

Second, Azad *et al.* (2011); Azad *et al.* (2012); Rangel and Engle (2012); Azad *et al.* (2015) and Lee *et al.* (2018) review a large number of literature that detects the weakness of aggregate volatility. This literature (see, for instance, Adrian and Rosenberg, 2008; Engle and Rangel, 2008) provides both the theoretical and empirical support of decomposing financial market volatility into (1) short-term or high-frequency volatility and (2) long-term or low-frequency volatility. While there are a limited number of studies that have used the Spline-GARCH model to extract the low-frequency volatility, there is no study that examines the link between macroeconomy and low-frequency volatility from the perspectives of religiosity.[1] This paper fills that gap using the data of mainstream and Islamic stock markets from around the world. Third, there is not study after Engle and Rangel (2008) on the relationship between low-frequency stock price volatility and *macroeconomic risk*. Thus, in addition to updating the results obtained by Engle and Rangel, we add Islamic markets and GFC period as well as various alternative specifications of models to extend the literature. Finally, our study corroborates the findings presented in the extant literature in relation to the performance of Islamic and conventional stock markets in various economic phases, like tranquil and turmoil period (for review of literature, see Azad *et al.*, 2018).

---

[1] Copula models have also got popularity recently and have been used in existing studies. See for instance, Kumar *et al.* (2019) and Boako *et al.* (2019), among others.

Our empirical analysis comprises a number of steps. First, using the Rangel and Engle (2012)'s asymmetric spline-GARCH (or factor spline-GARCH, hereafter ASP-GARCH or FSP-GARCH) we extract the low-frequency volatility from daily stock return of each market.[2] This low-frequency volatility is then annualized for every market. Second, to proxy the *macroeconomic risk* and uncertainty, we take the conditional volatility from GARCH (1,1) model or absolute values of the residuals from an AR(1) for a macroeconomic variable using the most available higher frequency data. These macroeconomic uncertainty measures are then used to compute their yearly average that results in a balanced panel of 36 cross-sections with 17 years data from 2000 to 2016 inclusive. Finally, low-frequency volatility is modeled as a function of macroeconomic variables (both volatility and changes in levels) as well as other financial and control variables. The estimation is done using different specifications, econometric approaches and sub-sample analysis.

For empirical investigation, we use a panel of 36 countries, representing developed, emerging and Islamic economies for the period from 2000 to 2016. To have an almost balanced panel, we select countries that have data of pre- and post- GFC crisis for at least three years and represent most continents, sub-continents and economically integrated and/or geographically close countries. This left us with a final sample of 20 non-Islamic or mainstream markets (includes developed and emerging) and 16 Islamic markets.

We find that, on one hand, low-frequency stock market volatility is lower for Islamic countries and, markets with a greater number of listed companies, higher market capitalization relative to GDP and higher variability in industrial production. On the other hand, low-frequency volatility is higher for emerging markets and when the macroeconomic factors of GDP, unemployment, short-term interest rates, inflation, money supply and foreign exchange rates are more volatile. Our empirical results are robust to alternative specifications of the regression models as well as sub-sample analyses. For example, using a number of econometric approaches including OLS, seemingly unrelated regression (SUR) and panel-data model that accounts for individual country random effects, keeping the time-fixed effects, we find that Islamic stocks have a major role in reducing market volatility and providing diversification benefits. This finding remains stable throughout various sub-sample analysis including the GFC of 2007 and is consistent with the existing literature (see for instance, Askari, 2012; Arouri *et al.*, 2013; Beck *et al.*, 2013; Jawadi *et al.*, 2014; Azad *et al.*, 2018). Since Azad *et al.* (2018) explain a number of reasons why Islamic markets outperformed conventional markets during the GFC period, we do not elaborate this discussion here. However, one can conclude that religiosity has an influence on the reduction of low-frequency market volatility. Such implication is somewhat akin to the Ramadan effect on the return volatility as observed by Białkowski *et al.* (2012) and Al-Khazali *et al.* (2017).

---

[2] The rationale behind using factor volatility model is well documented in Engle and Rangel (2008). They show that multiplicative decomposition of volatility in spline-GARCH model shows better power than additive decomposition of Engle and Lee (1999) and realized volatility model.

The remainder of this paper is structured as follows. Section 2 discusses data, variables and hypotheses. Section 3 describes the methodology, while Section 4 presents our empirical findings and related discussions. Section 5 is devoted to robustness analysis and Section 6 concludes.

2. Data, Variable Description and Hypothesis Development

2.1. *Data*

Data for the estimation of dependent variable, low-frequency volatilities of stock return, are collected from Thomson Reuters DataStream from January 1999 to December 2016. Daily low-frequency volatility is estimated from the log differences of daily stock indices of the selected countries. Global Financial Database (GFD) and respective stock market's websites are also used if the data for the benchmark indices are not available from Thomson Reuters DataStream. We include only the countries for which at least quarterly macroeconomic data are available. Macroeconomic variables are gathered from different sources including Global Insight/WRDS, Thomson Reuters DataStream, GFD, the Penn World Tables, Central Banks' websites, official websites of the stock exchanges and Federal Reserve Bank of St. Louis, etc. Data relating to market capitalization and the number of listed companies are also collected to reflect the size and diversification of each market associated with the countries listed in Table 1. These data are obtained from GFD, Thomson Reuters DataStream and official websites of the stock exchanges. Table 1 lists the countries, the names of the market indices, their country classification as developed, emerging and Islamic as well as other related information.

2.2. *Variable description and hypothesis development*

In this sub-section, we define a measure of our dependent and independent variables. The dependent variable low-frequency volatility is estimated on a daily frequency using the asymmetric spline-GARCH model of Rangel and Engle (2012). The daily low-frequency volatilities are then averaged for the respective year considering 252 trading days in a year.

The choice of our independent variables, i.e., *macroeconomic risk* proxies, is guided by financial economic theory and their importance and relevance supported by the prior literature. Moreover, as mentioned before, to have robust results, we consider those macroeconomic variables that are available in at least quarterly observations. To recall, there is no study that considers *macroeconomic risks* for analyzing the behavior of Islamic stock markets and their comparison with the conventional stock markets. Following the existing literature on volatility decomposition and on those that consider the impact of *macroeconomic risks* on financial markets, we take the levels as well as the volatilities of macroeconomic variables. Since macroeconomic variables are endogenous (Chen *et al.*, 1986; Engle and Rangel, 2008), we carefully select the *macroeconomic risk* proxies to reduce estimation bias. Moreover, we chose variables that are associated with fiscal and monetary policy decisions, which are expected to affect the low-frequency stock market volatility.

Table 1. A Summary of Equity Markets

Country	Market Classification	Name of the Index Used	Average Number of Listings (2000–2016)	Average Market Capitalization (in USD Millions)
Argentina	Emerging	IVBNG	103	45,839
Australia	Developed	ASX Ordinaries	1752	987,277
Bahrain	Islamic/Emerging	Bahrain All Share Price Index	40	16,202
Bangladesh	Islamic/Emerging	Bangladesh SE All Share Price Index/ Bangladesh DSE Broad Index	295	15,591
Brazil	Emerging	BOVESPA	372	747,251
Canada	Developed	S&P/TXS 300	3345	1,551,957
China	Emerging	SSE-180	1861	3,495,642
Egypt	Emerging	HERMES Financial Price Index	543	74,772
France	Developed	CAC-40	697	1,809,108
Germany	Developed	DAX	671	1,403,321
Hong Kong	Developed	Hang Seng Composite Index	1293	1,925,887
India	Emerging	Nifty 500 Price Index	5283	1,106,721
Indonesia	Islamic/Emerging	IDX Composite Price Index	401	216,474
Iran	Islamic/Emerging	TEPIX	337	75,639
Japan	Developed	Nikkei 225	2546	3,726,175
Jordan	Islamic/Emerging	Amman SE Financial Market Index	220	29,492
Kuwait	Islamic/Emerging	KIC General	55	799,683
Lebanon	Islamic/Emerging	BLOM	11	59,742
Malaysia	Islamic/Emerging	Bursa Malaysia KLSE	918	7658
Mexico	Emerging	IPC	142	287,839
Morocco	Islamic/Emerging	MASI (Morocco All Share Price Index)	67	315,768
Oman	Islamic/Emerging	Morocco All Share Price Index	151	55,972
Pakistan	Islamic/Emerging	Karachi SE 100 Price Index	626	45,016
Philippines	Emerging	Manila SE Composite Index	244	22,884
Qatar	Islamic/Emerging	Qatar SE Price Index	43	116,225
Russia	Emerging	Russia AKM Composite Index	359	134,642
Saudi Arabia	Islamic/Emerging	TASI (Tadawul All Share) Price Index	125	686,725

Table 1. (*Continued*)

Country	Market Classification	Name of the Index Used	Average Number of Listings (2000–2016)	Average Market Capitalization (in USD Millions)
Singapore	Developed	SES All Share Price Index	453	400,595
South Africa	Emerging	FTSE/JSE	377	438,307
South Korea	Emerging	KOSPI	1699	634,898
Switzerland	Developed	Switzerland Price Index	254	1,080,615
Thailand	Emerging	SET General Index	517	211,109
Turkey	Islamic/Emerging	Istanbul SE IMKB-100 Price Index	276	168,608
UAE	Islamic/Emerging	Dubai Financial Market Price Index	89	125,992
UK	Developed	FTSE-100	2307	2,708,732
USA	Developed	S&P500	4916	18,133,717

Notably, both the economic theories and the prior literature have been silent on the directional (positive or negative) hypothesis between *macroeconomic risk* proxies and the volatility of financial markets. Hence, the existing literature attempts largely to explore the key macroeconomic variables that significantly affect the financial markets. Following Black's (1987) hypothesis of positive association between *macroeconomic risk* and investment, later studies (see for instance, Lettau *et al.*, 2008; Genberg and Sulstarova, 2008; Beber and Brandt, 2009) attempt to establish theoretical and empirical links between *macroeconomic risk*/volatility and financial market volatility through firm's default probability. In line with these studies, we also expect a positive association, unless otherwise explained, between low-frequency stock volatility and *macroeconomic risk* variables. Table 2 shows the selected studies that find different results on *macroeconomic risk* and volatility of stock market.

The existing literature finds mixed results in regards to the impact of macroeconomic variables on financial markets. For example, Nowak *et al.* (2011) report mixed results for different economies. Moreover, while Officer (1973) and Diebold and Yilmaz (2008) find positive relationship between the variability of GDP growth rate or volatility of industrial production and the volatility of financial markets, others including Schwert (1989), Hamilton and Lin (1996), Adrian and Rosenberg (2008) and Engle and Rangel (2008) provide support of negative relationship. Those that view an inverse relationship argue that the higher the growth rate of GDP and variability in industrial production, the lower is the *macroeconomic risk* and firm's default risk.

Another important *macroeconomic risk* proxy we use is the unemployment rate, which bundles three types of primitive information: information about future interest rates, the equity risk premium, and corporate earnings and dividends (Boyd *et al.*, 2005).

Table 2. Low-Frequency Market Volatility and *Macroeconomic Risk*

Studies	Effect of Macroeconomic Variables on Low-Frequency Volatility							
	GDP	IP	IRs	CPI	PPI	UE	Ex	M2
Adrian and Rosenberg (2008)		−						
Diebold and Yilmaz (2008)	+			+				
Engle and Rangel (2008)	+		+	+			−	
Engle et al. (2013)		+/−			+			
Nowak et al. (2009)	+/−			+/−		+/−		
Azad et al. (2011)		+	+	+		−	+	+/−
Lee et al. (2018)	+	+	+	+			+	+/−

Notes: This table updates the summary presented in Azad *et al.* (2011) in regards to the relationship between low-frequency volatility and *macroeconomic risk*. IP = Industrial production; IRs = short-term interest rates; CPI = Consumer Price index; PPI = Producer Price Index; UE = Unemployment rate; Ex = Exchange rates. Most studies in this table use the second moments of the macroeconomic variables with the exception of unemployment rate.

Boyd *et al.* (2005) demonstrate that stock market responds positively to the news of rising unemployment in economic expansions and negatively in economic contractions. McQueen and Roley (1993) use both the industrial production and the unemployment to indicate the business conditions. Adrian and Rosenberg (2008) take the variability of industrial production as a proxy of business cycle risk. Since we regress the second moment of stock returns, we expect a positive association between low-frequency volatility and unemployment rate.

Proxies related to monetary policy shocks are also considered important determinants of financial market volatility. These policies play a major role in both inflationary and deflationary economic environment, and articulate the direction of future economic growth (Engle and Rangel, 2008). In an economic stagnation and deflationary environment, economists struggle to find optimal solutions and they often suggest conflicting and/or mistaken measures to tackle deflation and avoid recessions (see for instance, Azad *et al.*, 2011). Such consequences could arise due to the nature of countercyclical effects of monetary and fiscal policy decisions. An evaluation of the "policy implications hypothesis" or "anticipated liquidity effect hypothesis" and "inflationary expectation hypothesis" of Urich and Wachtel (1981, 1984) could give us some indication as to how these policies could result in conflicting outcomes. Both these hypotheses suggest that money supply, interest rate and inflation rate are key proxies of *macroeconomic risk* and, although the purpose of the restrictive monetary policy is to curb the inflation for the short-term, in the long run same policy could aggravate it. Consistent with the prior studies (Engle and Rangel, 2008; Azad *et al.*, 2011), we predict that changes in money supply, and volatility of interest rate and inflation rate increase the low-frequency stock volatility.

Our final proxy for *macroeconomic risk* is the exchange rate volatility which theoretically can influence firms' cash flow volatility and thus the required rate of return and its volatility (Shapiro, 1975; Dumas, 1978). Exchange rate volatility is highly linked to inflation, interest rates differential and foreign exchange carry trade (Andersen *et al.*, 2003; Simpson *et al.*, 2005), and is positively associated with the stock market volatility (Barclay *et al.*, 1990; Hamao *et al.*, 1990). We predict that low-frequency stock volatility will have a positive association with the exchange rate volatility. To make a proxy of the *macroeconomic risk* variable, following Engle and Rangel (2008) we take the residuals from an AR(1). We also take the conditional volatility from GARCH (1,1) process as robustness check.

Finally, we include financial variables namely, market capitalization and the number of listed companies, that reflect the size and diversification of each market. These variables are expected to suppress the low-frequency volatility (Engle and Rangel, 2008). Table 3 provides a summary of the independent variables that are used in this study.

Table 3. Explanatory Variables and Proxies / Transformations

Variables	Variables Details	Proxies / Transformations
Islamic	Islamic	Indicator of market type (1 represents for Islamic; 0 indicates non-Islamic)
Developed	Developed	Indicator of market development (1 represents developed; 0 for emerging markets including Islamic)
EM_NOIS	Emerging non-Islamic	Indicator of market development (1 represents for emerging non-Islamic; 0 for Islamic and developed)
LMCAP	Logarithm of market capitalization to GDP	Log of stock market capitalization relative to GDP
LGDP	Logarithm of GDP	Log of nominal GDP in current $US
LSTCOM	Listed companies	Number of listed companies in the exchange
UNEM	Unemployment rate	Changes in seasonally adjusted unemployment rate
M2VOL	Volatility of money supply (M2)	Absolute values of the residuals from an AR(1) model, obtained from average amounts outstanding/Money Stock
IPVOL	Volatility of industrial production	Absolute values of the residuals from an AR(1) model, obtained from industrial production index
CPIVOL	Volatility of inflation	Absolute values of the residuals from an AR(1) model, obtained from seasonally adjusted consumer price index
IRVOL	Volatility of interest rate	Absolute values of the residuals from an AR(1) model, obtained from three-months treasury rate
FXVOL	Volatility of foreign exchange rate	Absolute values of the residuals from an AR(1) model, obtained from real effective exchange rate against US dollar
GFC	Global financial crisis	1 represents GFC for the periods from 2007 to 2009 inclusive, 0 for other years

3. Estimation Methodology

In this section, we explain our methodologies to estimate and decompose the aggregate stock return volatility into two components, namely, high- and low-frequency volatility components. We then show how the low-frequency volatility is modeled as a function of *macroeconomic risk* proxies and other explanatory variables as explained above.

3.1. *Estimating and decomposing aggregate stock volatility*

To decompose aggregate stock return volatility into low-frequency (LF) and high-frequency (HF) volatility, we use the asymmetric factor spline-GARCH model of Rangel and Engle (2012). To illustrate Rangel and Engle's AFS-GARCH, let us start with the GARCH (1,1) model, which is used to extract the aggregate market volatility:

$$r_t - E_{t-1}(r_t) = \sqrt{h_t}\varepsilon_t \quad \varepsilon_t|\Phi_{t-1} \sim N(0,1). \quad (1)$$

Following Rangel and Engle (2012), h_t is decomposed into two components as follows:

$$h_t = LF_t \cdot HF_t, \quad (2)$$

$$LF_{,t} = \gamma_o \exp\left(\gamma_1 t + \sum_{j=1}^{k} \omega_j((t - t_{j-1})_+)^2\right), \quad (3)$$

$$HF_t = \left(1 - \alpha - \beta - \frac{c}{2}\right) + \alpha\left(\frac{\varepsilon_{t-1}^2}{LF_{t-1}}\right) + c\left(\frac{\varepsilon_{t-1}^2}{LF_{t-1}}\right)I_{r_{t-1}<0} + \beta HF_{t-1}, \quad (4)$$

where, r_t is the return on stock index (i.e., s&p500) on day t and $E_{t-1}(r_t)$ is the expected return at $t-1$. h_t is the conditional volatility. LF_t and HF_t characterize low-frequency and high-frequency volatility, respectively, on day t. Φ_{t-1} denotes an extended information set including the history of stock return changes up to day $t-1$. Given the estimates for $\gamma = (\gamma_o \gamma_1)'$ and $\omega_j (j = 1 \text{ to } k)$ a sequence of $\{t_j\}_{j=1}^{k}$ can be estimated (where $t_1 > 1$ and $t_k \leq T$, denotes a division of the time horizon T in k equally spaced intervals). This study estimates the following parameters for the above AFS-GARCH model: $\alpha, \beta, c, \gamma = (\gamma_o \gamma_1)'$ and $\omega_j (j = 1 \text{ to } k)$. The BIC (Bayesian Information Criteria) is used to choose the "optimal" number of knots k, where k governs the cyclical pattern in LF_t. Large values of k imply more frequent cycles, the "sharpness" (i.e., the duration and strength) of which is measured through coefficients $\{\omega_j\}$. The term $I_{r_{t-1}<0}$ in Equation (4) is an indicator function of negative shocks to accommodate the leverage effects (asymmetric volatility impact) on the high-frequency component. The presence of the leverage effect is judged through the significance of parameter c. We are mainly interested in the significance of parameters α, β, c and ω_j in Equations (3) and (4).

Once extracting daily low-frequency volatility from daily stock index volatility, we convert them into yearly average. The low-frequency volatility for a year can be computed as the following sample average:

$$\text{LFvol}_{i,t} = \sqrt{\frac{1}{N_{i,t}} \sum_{d=1}^{N_{i,t}} \tau_{i,d,t}}, \quad (5)$$

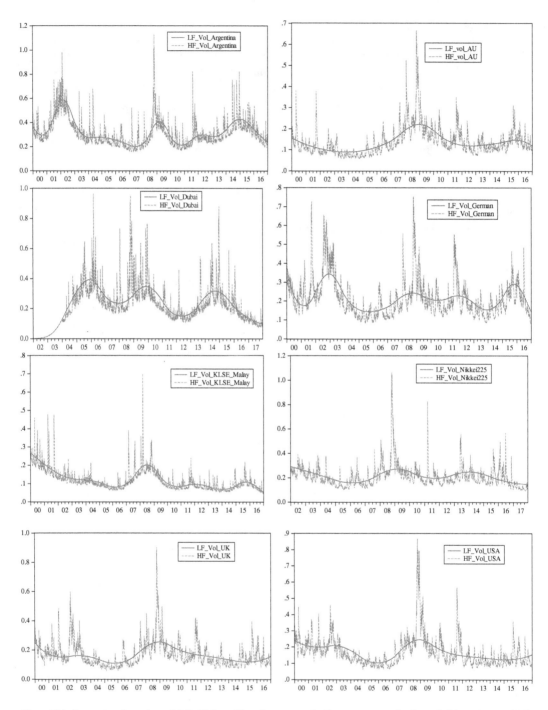

Notes: This figure plots the estimated daily high- and low-frequency volatility components for the period from January 2000 to December 2016 for the selected Islamic and conventional markets. The high-frequency component is estimated using Equation (4) and the low-frequency component is estimated using equation (3). The dotted line indicates the high-frequency component, while the solid line indicates the low-frequency component.

Figure 1. High- and Low-Frequency Volatility

where, LFvol$_{i,t}$ stands for the annualized low-frequency volatility for year t and country i. $N_{i,t}$ is the number of trading days in country i at year t. $\tau_{i,d,t}$ is the daily low-frequency volatility observed for country i at day d for year t in Equation (4).

A measure of yearly low-frequency volatility is needed to match our independent variables, which are also converted into yearly frequency as some of the independent variables, e.g., listed number of companies and market capitalization, are only available into yearly frequency.

3.2. Measure of macroeconomic risk

In order to explain how the low-frequency volatility is related to *macroeconomic risk* across conventional and Islamic stock markets, we need to construct a proxy for each of the six macroeconomic variables indicated in Table 3. Following Engle and Rangel (2008), we use conditional volatility from GARCH (1,1) model or the absolute values of the residuals from an AR(1) model. We compute the absolute values from an AR(1) using the following regression:

$$\Delta \log(Y_t) = \beta Y_{t-1} + u_t, \qquad (6)$$

where, Y_t is the relevant macroeconomic variable and $|\hat{u}_t|$ is the estimate of volatility/risk proxy for macroeconomic variable Y_t. Volatilities of industrial production, interest rates (without logs), exchange rates, inflation (CPI) rates and money supply are based on the residuals of fitted autoregressive models. Uncertainty regarding unemployment is measured as the changes in seasonally adjusted unemployment rate from the previous month or quarter and their yearly average.

3.3. Regression estimation

Finally, we model low-frequency stock volatility as a function of *macroeconomic risk* proxies and other control variables using the system of linear equations as specified in Equation (7):

$$\text{LFvol}_{i,t} = \alpha + \acute{v}_{i,t}\beta_t + \mu_{i,t}, \quad t=1,2,\ldots,T, \quad i=1,2,\ldots,N_t, \qquad (7)$$

where $\acute{v}_{i,t}$ is a vector of explanatory variables associated with country i and year t, and $\mu_{i,t}$ is the error term assumed to be contemporaneously uncorrelated with $\acute{v}_{i,t}$. It is to be noted that the assumption $[E(\acute{v}_{i,t}, \mu_{i,t}) = 0; t = 1, 2, \ldots, T, i = 1, 2, \ldots, N_t]$ does not rule out non-contemporaneous correlation. So, the error term at time t may be correlated with the regressors at time $t+1$. This setup is consistent with Schwert (1989)'s argument that financial volatility can cause macroeconomic volatility. However, when Equation (7) is estimated using SUR approach, the assumption of exogeneity is upheld (Engle and Rangel, 2008). Other econometric approaches including pooled regression (OLS), fixed effect (FE) and random effect (RE) are also used for robust results. Of the fixed and random effects, we put emphasis on random effects as we have several dummy variables that rarely change over time, namely, Islamic country, emerging country and GFC. By doing so, we corroborate our research findings with those of conventional and Islamic markets (Engle and Rangel, 2008; Abedifar *et al.*, 2013).

4. Estimation Results and Discussion

4.1. *ASP-GARCH estimation results*

For each stock market, we use its daily stock index and estimate the AFS-GARCH model of Rangel and Engle (2012). The estimation results are not reported to conserve the space. For all markets, the coefficients of the GARCH components (α and β) are statistically significant and standard in terms of magnitude. Also, the leverage effects (asymmetric volatility impact), which is judged through the significance of parameter c in high-frequency component, are observed for most except the following countries: Bangladesh, Brazil, Iran, Japan, Morocco, Saudi Arabia, South Africa, Singapore, Switzerland, South Korea, UAE and USA. As regards knot points, k, which indicate the cyclical effects in the series, we tried up to 20 knot points to determine the optimal knots for the ASP-GARCH. As stated before, we use the BIC to do this. Overall, developed countries are found to have less knot points than the emerging and Islamic markets.

Figure 1 provides a visual inspection of two volatility measures: daily high-frequency and low-frequency volatilities, respectively for some selected countries. The low-frequency component is associated with the slow-moving trend that characterizes the unconditional volatility and the high-frequency component is associated with the short-run conditional volatility. It is evident that volatilities were very high during the GFC period. Overall, the low-frequency component articulates the facts that the stock volatilities are highly related to business cycle fluctuations.

4.2. *Summary statistics*

Table 4 presents the summary statistics and univariate comparisons between Islamic and conventional markets (panel A) and between developed and emerging but non-Islamic markets (panel B) for each variable as well as the *p*-value of a two-sided *t*-test. All data are in yearly observations for the periods from 2000 to 2016. As shown in panel A of this table, the mean low-frequency volatility is higher for conventional stock markets (0.4472) than for Islamic stock markets (0.40). It is also found that (in panel B) the mean low-frequency volatility for Islamic markets is even lower than the developed markets (0.4211). The highest mean low-frequency volatility is associated with the emerging non-Islamic markets (0.4735). Islamic markets have higher variability in unemployment rate, interest rate and money supply, and slightly higher GDP than the conventional markets (panel A). Conventional markets have higher market capitalization, more number of listed companies and higher variability in industrial production (panel A), mostly led by developed economies (see panel B) except for industrial production volatility, which is led by emerging non-Islamic economies (panel B).

Table 4. Summary Statistics

Panel A

Variable	Full Sample (N = 599)				Non-Islamic (N = 339)				Islamic (N = 260)				Diff t-Test p-Value
	Mean	Std Dev	Min	Max	Mean	Std Dev	Min	Max	Mean	Std Dev	Min	Max	
Lvol	0.4272	0.1041	0.0174	0.7511	0.4472	0.0748	0.2902	0.7003	0.4010	0.1285	0.0174	0.7511	<0.0001
LMcap	4.1117	0.9363	0.5933	7.1345	4.3942	0.9012	1.8358	7.1345	3.7433	0.8505	0.5933	5.4362	<0.0001
LGDP	13.8294	3.5112	7.3036	26.1233	13.7599	2.0709	9.2336	18.6816	13.9200	4.7805	7.3036	26.1233	0.5805
Lstcom	946.00	1323.00	10.00	6917.00	1463.00	1556.00	21.00	6917.00	271.00	269.00	10.00	1150.00	<0.0001
Unem	0.0491	1.2837	−6.0000	10.7250	−0.0225	1.1861	−6.0000	10.7250	0.1424	1.3977	−5.1000	5.9000	0.1194
IRVol	0.2807	0.3700	0.0087	2.9046	0.2265	0.3270	0.0087	2.5507	0.3513	0.4095	0.0104	2.9046	<0.0001
IPVol	0.1698	0.7106	0.0020	9.1412	0.2691	0.9326	0.0020	9.1412	0.0404	0.0324	0.0027	0.1865	<0.0001
CPIVol	0.0188	0.0567	0.0006	0.5392	0.0194	0.0626	0.0006	0.5302	0.0180	0.0479	0.0006	0.5392	0.7678
FxVol	0.0171	0.0254	0.0000	0.2964	0.0170	0.0188	0.0001	0.2599	0.0171	0.0321	0.0000	0.2964	0.9645
M2Vol	0.0110	0.0090	0.0011	0.0917	0.0098	0.0092	0.0011	0.0917	0.0127	0.0085	0.0027	0.0590	<0.0001

Panel B

Variable	Developed (N = 170)				Emerging Non-Islamic (N = 169)				Diff t-Test p-Value
	Mean	Std Dev	Min	Max	Mean	Std Dev	Min	Max	
Lvol	0.4211	0.0647	0.2902	0.6557	0.4735	0.0752	0.3345	0.7003	<0.0001
LMcap	4.8645	0.7672	3.3878	7.1345	3.9211	0.7700	1.8358	5.7745	<0.0001
LGDP	12.9697	2.2812	9.2336	18.6816	14.5547	1.4583	11.5179	17.2531	<0.0001
Lstcom	1824.00	1484.00	227.00	6917.00	1101.00	1546.00	21.00	5853.00	<0.0001
Unem	−0.0692	0.6928	−1.8000	3.5000	0.0246	1.5308	−6.0000	10.7250	0.4673
IRVol	0.1072	0.1003	0.0087	0.6395	0.3465	0.4196	0.0197	2.5507	<0.0001
IPVol	0.0885	0.2202	0.0020	1.3596	0.4507	1.2786	0.0027	9.1412	0.0003
CPIVol	0.0310	0.0867	0.0007	0.5302	0.0077	0.0070	0.0006	0.0696	0.0006
FxVol	0.0165	0.0094	0.0001	0.0402	0.0175	0.0249	0.0009	0.2599	0.6502
M2Vol	0.0060	0.0042	0.0011	0.0290	0.0136	0.0110	0.0022	0.0917	<0.0001

Notes: This table shows descriptive statistics of low-frequency volatility (Lvol) and independent variables for full sample, Non-Islamic markets, Islamic markets, developed and non-Islamic emerging markets. Analysis covers the panel data for the years from 2000 to 2016.

Table 5 shows the sample correlation structure among low-frequency volatility and Islamic, developed, emerging non-Islamic countries as well as other financial and *macroeconomic risk* proxies. It suggests that low-frequency volatility is negatively correlated with Islamic countries, developed economies, market capitalization and the number of listed companies. However, the correlation coefficient is the highest for Islamic countries followed by the number of listed companies. The correlation coefficient between low-frequency volatility and developed countries is very small and statistically insignificant. The low-frequency volatility is positively associated with the remaining variables, namely, emerging non-Islamic countries and the volatilities of money supply, interest rate, industrial production, inflation, foreign exchange and unemployment rate. The highest positive correlation coefficient is observed between low-frequency volatility and emerging non-Islamic countries followed by the correlation of low-frequency volatility with interest rate volatility and GDP. Finally, GFC has a positive correlation with Islamic countries and negative correlation with emerging and developed countries, but both coefficients are very small and statistically insignificant.

4.3. Regression results: Full sample, Islamic and non-Islamic market sample

Table 6 presents the base regression results for the full sample as well as for Islamic and conventional stock markets using OLS, random effect (RE) and SUR estimation techniques. Results are fairly uniform throughout different estimation techniques. However, OLS and SUR provide more consistent results than random effect model. For the full sample and conventional markets, low-frequency volatility is lower when market capitalization and the number of listed companies are more and the volatility of industrial production is greater. Adrian and Rosenberg (2008) also report a negative coefficient of industrial production volatility, while Engle and Rangel find mixed results in relation to industrial production volatility. Low-frequency volatility is greater if the volatilities of GDP, interest rate, money supply and systematic crisis (GFC) are higher. To some extent, volatilities of unemployment and inflation also increase the low-frequency component of stock market volatility. Overall, these results are consistent with the existing findings of Engle and Rangel (2008).

Some different results are observed for Islamic markets. The coefficient of market capitalization is found to be positive and significant under random effect model but negative and insignificant under OLS and SUR techniques. The same goes to the coefficient of number of listed companies, which is found to be positive but only significant under SUR. The positive signs of the coefficients of market capitalization and listed companies could be due to the fact that Islamic market is smaller than the conventional market both in terms of market capitalization and the number of listed companies (see Table 4).

4.4. Regression results: Introduction of Islamic market dummy

We find some interesting yet consistent results with the above estimation when we introduce Islamic country dummy into the system and the results are more theoretically and practically appealing. It is to be noted that Islamic markets are mostly dominated by the Islamic banks, which have higher market capitalization and better asset quality than their

Table 5. Correlation Matrix

	Lvol	Islamic	Developed	Em_NoIs	LMcap	LGDP	Lstcom	Unem	IRVol	IPVol	CPIVol	FxVol	M2Vol	GFC
Lvol	1	−0.220	−0.007	0.283	−0.202	0.240	−0.002	0.056	0.273	0.027	0.032	0.069	0.150	0.175
Islamic	−0.220	1	−0.513	−0.464	−0.345	0.023	−0.447	0.064	0.167	−0.160	−0.012	0.002	0.163	0.010
Developed	−0.007	−0.513	1	−0.393	0.440	−0.107	0.456	−0.055	−0.277	−0.064	0.156	0.005	−0.343	−0.006
Em_NoIs	0.283	−0.464	−0.393	1	−0.170	0.124	0.046	−0.016	0.109	0.230	−0.131	0.039	0.174	−0.005
LMcap	−0.202	−0.345	0.440	−0.170	1	−0.457	0.255	−0.061	−0.346	0.117	−0.105	−0.172	−0.282	0.064
LGDP	0.240	0.023	−0.107	0.124	−0.457	1	0.011	−0.004	0.142	0.024	−0.009	0.189	0.099	−0.025
Lstcom	−0.002	−0.447	0.456	0.046	0.255	0.011	1	−0.023	−0.202	−0.080	−0.088	−0.062	−0.250	−0.008
Unem	0.056	0.064	−0.055	−0.016	−0.061	−0.004	−0.023	1	0.071	0.083	−0.020	−0.068	0.026	0.059
IRVol	0.273	0.167	−0.277	0.109	−0.346	0.142	−0.202	0.071	1	−0.062	−0.061	0.017	0.361	0.058
IPVol	0.027	−0.160	−0.064	0.230	0.117	0.024	−0.080	0.083	−0.062	1	−0.044	0.005	−0.054	0.065
CPIVol	0.032	−0.012	0.156	−0.131	−0.105	−0.009	−0.088	−0.020	−0.061	−0.044	1	−0.018	−0.033	0.063
FxVol	0.069	0.002	0.005	0.039	−0.172	0.189	−0.062	−0.068	0.017	0.005	−0.018	1	−0.034	0.012
M2Vol	0.150	0.163	−0.343	0.174	−0.282	0.099	−0.250	0.026	0.361	−0.054	−0.033	−0.034	1	0.068
GFC	0.175	0.010	−0.006	−0.005	0.064	−0.025	−0.008	0.059	0.058	0.065	0.063	0.012	0.068	1

Notes: This table shows Pearson correlation coefficients between low-frequency volatility (Lvol) and independent variables. Apart from the macroeconomic and financial variables, three other variables (i.e., Islamic, Developed and emerging non-Islamic countries) are also included to distinguish the correlation coefficients between Islamic and non-Islamic markets. Analysis covers a panel data of 599 observations for the years from 2000 to 2016 with a cross-section of 36 countries.

Table 6. Low-Frequency Volatility and Macroeconomic Risk

	Full Sample ($N = 599$)			Conventional Markets ($N = 339$)			Islamic Markets ($N = 260$)		
	OLS	RE	SUR	OLS	RE	SUR	OLS	RE	SUR
Intercept	0.3381***	0.3403***	0.3325***	0.4291***	0.5484***	0.4186***	0.3466**	0.1775***	0.3380***
	(0.0761)	(0.0597)	(0.0355)	(0.0777)	(0.1828)	(0.0343)	(0.1410)	(0.0589)	(0.0731)
LMcap	−0.0061	0.0007	−0.0039	−0.0132	−0.0127	−0.0111***	−0.0151	0.0194**	−0.0120
	(0.0131)	(0.0081)	(0.0054)	(0.0124)	(0.0165)	(0.0040)	(0.0276)	(0.0086)	(0.0124)
LGDP	0.0052*	0.0031	0.0052***	0.0028	−0.0050	0.0030**	0.0047	0.0055	0.0048**
	(0.0029)	(0.0037)	(0.0013)	(0.0026)	(0.0088)	(0.0016)	(0.0037)	(0.0039)	(0.0021)
Lstcom	−0.00001	−0.00001	−0.00001**	−0.00001	−0.00001	−0.00001**	0.0001	0.0000	0.0001**
	(0.0000)	(0.0000)	(0.0000)	(0.0000)	(0.0000)	(0.0000)	(0.0001)	(0.0000)	(0.0000)
Unem	0.0023	0.0015	0.0030	0.0036	0.0043	0.0062**	0.0000	−0.0028	−0.0007
	(0.0032)	(0.0022)	(0.0031)	(0.0029)	(0.0028)	(0.0026)	(0.0048)	(0.0024)	(0.0054)
IRVol	0.0620***	0.0479***	0.0654***	0.0666***	0.0442***	0.0704***	0.0461*	0.0425***	0.0494**
	(0.0225)	(0.0104)	(0.0120)	(0.0158)	(0.0145)	(0.0111)	(0.0268)	(0.0125)	(0.0195)
IPVol	−0.0060	−0.0021	−0.0074	−0.0026	−0.0028*	−0.0012	0.5639	0.7107***	0.5685**
	(0.0057)	(0.0026)	(0.0057)	(0.0034)	(0.0015)	(0.0034)	(0.3532)	(0.1551)	(0.2484)
CPIVol	0.0792	0.0578	0.1047	0.0877	0.0686	0.1120**	−0.0136	0.0282	0.0192
	(0.0997)	(0.0641)	(0.0710)	(0.0681)	(0.1120)	(0.0496)	(0.1408)	(0.0566)	(0.1572)
FxVol	0.1226	0.0828	0.1486	0.0459	−0.0239	0.1237	0.0808	0.0713	0.0910
	(0.3171)	(0.1132)	(0.1603)	(0.1966)	(0.1035)	(0.1661)	(0.2903)	(0.1657)	(0.2493)

Table 6. (Continued)

	Full Sample ($N = 599$)			Conventional Markets ($N = 339$)			Islamic Markets ($N = 260$)		
	OLS	RE	SUR	OLS	RE	SUR	OLS	RE	SUR
M2Vol	0.5730	1.9509***	0.7259	1.9952***	1.3046**	2.1644***	−1.5408	1.8148*	−1.4722
	(1.9755)	(0.7164)	(0.4887)	(0.6349)	(0.6719)	(0.3999)	(3.1338)	(1.1259)	(0.9047)
GFC	0.0433***	0.0443***	0.0011	0.0519***	0.0547	0.0057	0.0395***	0.0297***	0.0006
	(0.0080)	(0.0072)	(0.0038)	(0.0096)	(0.0670)	(0.0027)	(0.0135)	(0.0112)	(0.0030)
Adjusted R^2	0.155	0.1993	0.137	0.4761	0.1681	0.4174	0.1757	0.1942	0.1621

Notes: Results are based on the following regression model (see Equation (7) for details):

$$\text{LFvol}_{i,t} = \alpha + \acute{v}_{i,t}\beta_t + \mu_{i,t}, \quad t = 1, 2, \ldots, T, \quad i = 1, 2, \ldots, N_t,$$

where the dependent variable $\text{LFvol}_{i,t}$ stands for annualized low-frequency volatility for year t and country i and year t, and $\mu_{i,t}$ is the error term assumed to be contemporaneously uncorrelated with $\acute{v}_{i,t}$. See Table 3 for explanatory variable details. Equation (7) is estimated using OLS (ordinary least square), RE (random effect) and SUR (seemingly unrelated regression) techniques. Robust standard errors of the estimated coefficients are in parentheses. Sample covers the period from 2000 through 2016. *, ** and *** indicate level of significance at 10%, 5% and 1%, respectively.

Table 7. Low-Frequency Volatility and Macroeconomic Risk: Introducing Islamic and Other Dummies

	OLS	Seemingly Unrelated Regressions						Random Country Effects			
	I	II	III	IV	V	VI	VII	VIII	IX	X	XI
Intercept	0.3853***	0.4373***	0.4336***	0.4304***	0.4450***	0.4425***	0.4401***	0.3829***	0.3827***	0.3835***	0.3226***
	(0.0862)	(0.0356)	(0.0358)	(0.0360)	(0.0356)	(0.0357)	(0.0358)	(0.0654)	(0.0656)	(0.0671)	(0.0830)
Islamic	−0.0290	−0.0732***	−0.0717***	−0.0687***	−0.0713***	−0.0703***	−0.0683***	−0.0780*	−0.0742*	−0.0750*	−0.0187
	(0.0241)	(0.0088)	(0.0091)	(0.0100)	(0.0095)	(0.0097)	(0.0103)	(0.0434)	(0.0423)	(0.0451)	(0.0580)
Developed	0.0430**	—	—	0.0041	—	—	0.0027	—	—	−0.0020	0.0584
	(0.0185)			(0.0062)			(0.0052)			(0.0389)	(0.0652)
EM_NOIS	0.0510***	—	0.0025	0.0055	—	0.0016	0.0037	—	—	—	0.0667
	(0.0163)		(0.0035)	(0.0057)		(0.0029)	(0.0048)				(0.0560)
LMcap	−0.0139	−0.0151***	−0.0146***	−0.0146***	−0.0176***	−0.0173***	−0.0172***	−0.0004	−0.00002	−0.00002	0.0006
	(0.0135)	(0.0052)	(0.0052)	(0.0052)	(0.0052)	(0.0052)	(0.0052)	(0.0082)	(0.0083)	(0.0083)	(0.0083)
LGDP	0.0044*	0.0044***	0.0044***	0.0044***	0.0043***	0.0043***	0.0043***	0.0032	0.0030	0.0030	0.0029
	(0.0025)	(0.0012)	(0.0012)	(0.0012)	(0.0012)	(0.0012)	(0.0012)	(0.0039)	(0.0039)	(0.0039)	(0.0040)
Lstcom	−0.00001*	−0.00001	−0.000003	−0.000005	−0.000005*	0.00005*	−0.00005*	−0.00001	−0.00001	−0.00001	−0.00001
	(0.0000)	(0.0000)	(0.0000)	(0.0000)	(0.0000)	(0.0000)	(0.0000)	(0.0000)	(0.0000)	(0.0000)	(0.0000)
Unem	0.0034	0.0043	0.0043	0.0043	0.0031	0.0032	0.0032	0.0015	0.0011	0.0011	0.0011
	(0.0027)	(0.0029)	(0.0029)	(0.0029)	(0.0029)	(0.0029)	(0.0029)	(0.0021)	(0.0022)	(0.0022)	(0.0021)
IRVol	0.0611***	0.0637***	0.0636***	0.0636***	0.0605***	0.0604***	0.0604***	0.0481***	0.0484***	0.0484***	0.0484***
	(0.0189)	(0.0112)	(0.0111)	(0.0111)	(0.0112)	(0.0111)	(0.0111)	(0.0100)	(0.0101)	(0.0101)	(0.0101)
IPVol	−0.0051	−0.0012	−0.0015	−0.0015	−0.0031	−0.0033	−0.0033	−0.0027	−0.0033*	−0.0033*	−0.0034*
	(0.0037)	(0.0054)	(0.0054)	(0.0054)	(0.0054)	(0.0054)	(0.0054)	(0.0020)	(0.0019)	(0.0019)	(0.0019)
CPIVol	0.0306	0.0477	0.0512	0.0494	0.0204	0.0228	0.0219	0.0553	0.0580	0.0583	0.0592
	(0.0567)	(0.0662)	(0.0661)	(0.0660)	(0.0664)	(0.0663)	(0.0661)	(0.0631)	(0.0704)	(0.0701)	(0.0702)
FxVol	0.0126	0.0658	0.0663	0.0628	0.0340	0.0343	0.0321	0.0835	0.0744	0.0744	0.0707

Table 7. (Continued)

	OLS				Seemingly Unrelated Regressions				Random Country Effects			
	I	II	III	IV	V	VI	VII	VIII	IX	X	XI
	(0.1923)	(0.1491)	(0.1484)	(0.1480)	(0.1492)	(0.1485)	(0.1481)	(0.1148)	(0.1165)	(0.1165)	(0.1169)
M2Vol	0.3885	0.6025	0.5790	0.5829	0.4427	0.4271	0.4292	1.9742***	1.9539***	1.9528***	1.9507***
	(1.8139)	(0.4538)	(0.4528)	(0.4516)	(0.4549)	(0.4535)	(0.4522)	(0.6918)	(0.7107)	(0.7129)	(0.7105)
GFC	0.0567***	0.0048	0.0037	0.0053	0.0571***	0.0562***	0.0562***	0.0446***	0.0537***	0.0537***	0.0537***
	(0.0100)	(0.0069)	(0.0074)	(0.0075)	(0.0139)	(0.0140)	(0.0141)	(0.0071)	(0.0087)	(0.0087)	(0.0087)
GFC*Islamic	−0.0219	—	—	—	−0.0212	−0.0214	−0.0213	—	−0.0206	−0.0206	−0.0207
	(0.0176)	—	—	—	(0.0194)	(0.0193)	(0.0192)	—	(0.0145)	(0.0145)	(0.0145)
Year	No	Yes	Yes	Yes	Yes	Yes	Yes	Yes	Yes	Yes	Yes
Adjusted R^2	0.2576	0.2211	0.2224	0.2234	0.2482	0.249	0.2491	0.2085	0.2121	0.2121	0.2136

Notes: Results are based on the following regression model (see Equation (7) for details):

$$\text{LFvol}_{i,t} = \alpha + \acute{v}_{i,t}\beta_t + \mu_{i,t}, \quad t = 1, 2, \ldots, T, \quad i = 1, 2, \ldots, N_t,$$

where the dependent variable $\text{LFvol}_{i,t}$ stands for annualized low-frequency volatility for year t and country i. $\acute{v}_{i,t}$ is a vector of explanatory variables associated with country i and year t, and $\mu_{i,t}$ is the error term assumed to be contemporaneously uncorrelated with $\acute{v}_{i,t}$. See Table 3 for explanatory variable details. Equation (7) is estimated using OLS (ordinary least square), RE (random effect) and SUR (seemingly unrelated regression) techniques, where last four columns represent the results from the random country effects model using Equation (8). Robust standard errors of the estimated coefficients are in parentheses. Sample covers the period from 2000 through 2016. *, **, and *** indicate level of significance at 10%, 5% and 1%, respectively.

conventional counterparts in the same markets (Beck *et al.*, 2013). Moreover, Islamic markets and investments are characterized with (i) different risk return preferences (Benjamin *et al.*, 2016) and (ii) low-debt equities (Azad *et al.*, 2018). These features of Islamic markets helped them perform better than their conventional counterparts in terms of stability and resilience during the GFC period. In addition, due to the less number of Shariah compliant stocks and conservative approaches to the investments, Islamic markets are less volatile. Hence, it is practically appealing to examine the relationship between low-frequency volatility and the volatility of stock markets by including Islamic dummy.

When we introduce Islamic dummy and subsequently other dummies and controls, we observe some interesting results. Table 7, which presents the results of various combinations of the system of linear equations using Equation (7), indicates that low-frequency volatility is lower when Islamic markets are included. These results are consistent throughout different estimation techniques. The coefficients are also significant except with the pooled OLS model. It is to be noted that we replaced the Islamic dummy with the developed as well as emerging non-Islamic markets to compare our results with that of Engle and Rangel (2008). And similar to Engle and Rangel (2008), we find that low-frequency volatility is lower for developed markets and higher for emerging markets. When we include all types of country dummies (Islamic, developed, emerging non-Islamic) in OLS, we find that developed markets increase the low-frequency volatility. But neither of the SUR models exhibit significance of the coefficients for developed and emerging markets.

The SUR results are found to be robust than the OLS results. Islamic market dummy is significant throughout all models considered under SUR. Both developed and emerging non-Islamic markets turn out to be statistically insignificant though their coefficients are positive. Further to this, consistent with the base regression results in Table 6, market capitalization, number of listed companies, industrial production volatility and an interaction term between GFC and Islamic country dummy decrease the low-frequency volatility. An interaction term between GFC and Islamic market is included to corroborate the findings of Beck *et al.* (2013) and thus to examine the role of Islamic markets in times of crisis. The negative coefficient of the GFC*Islamic, which is consistent with Beck *et al.* (2013), implies that Islamic markets were less volatile during the GFC period and this helped to correct the market volatility in times of crisis. Prior studies suggest that the presence of ethical customer base in Islamic markets might have helped them to perform differently in times of crisis (for related literature review, see Azad *et al.*, 2018). The coefficients of log GDP, interest rate volatility and GFC period dummy are positive and significant for most of the regression models.

5. Robustness Checks: Country Heterogeneity and Sub-Sample Analysis

A natural question arises as to whether the above empirical findings are robust to alternative specifications. We start the robustness check by exploring the possibility of unobserved individual country effects in order to evaluate their possible impacts in our preceding results. In doing so, similar to Engle and Rangel (2008), we estimate a panel-data model that accounts for individual country random effects, keeping the time-fixed effects. That is, we model the error term in Equation (7) as follows:

$$\mu_{i,t} = \lambda_t + \eta_i + \vartheta_{i,t}, \tag{8}$$

where

λ_t indicates time-fixed effects
$\eta_i \sim iid(0, \sigma_\eta)$
$\vartheta_{i,t} = \rho \vartheta_{i,t-1} + \varepsilon_{i,t}$
$\varepsilon_{i,t} \sim iid(0, \sigma_\varepsilon)$
$\varepsilon_{i,t} \perp \eta_i$

Estimation results for Equation (8) are shown in the last 4 (four) columns of Table 7. Once again, different combinations of regressors along with year-fixed and random country effects are tried out. Islamic market dummy remains to be negative and significant for all but one model (last column), where it becomes insignificant. Developed country is also found to be negative but insignificant for one of the regressions. Coefficient signs for other variables remain to be consistent with the base regressions as well as OLS and SUR. The only exception is the varying degree of significance of the coefficients. For example, the volatilities of industrial production and money supply become significant in year-fixed and random country effects model.

Our final set of robustness checks include the base model plus types of market dummies with particular interest to Islamic market. The purpose is to examine the consistency of Islamic market's significance in split-sample analysis. Specifically, we conduct an analysis of the following sub-samples: (i) pre-GFC period between 2000 and 2006 (ii) GFC period between 2007 and 2009 (iii) post-GFC period between 2010 and 2016, and (iv) a normal or tranquil period that excludes the GFC period.

Table 8 presents sub-sample analysis results based on SUR technique and model with and without developed and emerging country dummies along with the key interest variable Islamic market dummy. The coefficient of Islamic market dummy is negative and significant at 1% level of significance for all periods. Consistent with the prior studies, interest rate volatility also remains to be significant (and positive) throughout all of the sub-sample analyses. During the tranquil economic environment, which excludes the GFC periods, the following variables are positive and significant: LGDP, IRVOL and M2VOL suggesting an increase of low-frequency volatility when those macroeconomic variables are highly volatile. Conversely, low-frequency stock volatility drops when the economies are associated with larger market capitalization, more number of listed companies and higher volatility in industrial production. Almost similar results are observed for pre-GFC, GFC and post-GFC analyses in terms of the sign and significance of coefficients except the sign of M2VOL, which becomes negative and significant for the GFC period. Azad et al. (2011) also find a negative coefficient of M2VOL during the GFC period. This suggests that an increase in money supply may dampen the market volatility in times of systemic crisis.

Table 8. Low-Frequency Volatility and Macroeconomic Risk: Robustness Check with Sub-sample (SUR)

	Normal Period				Pre-GFC		GFC		Post GFC	
	I	II	III	IV	V	VI	VII	VIII
Intercept	0.4503***	0.4498***	0.4126***	0.4098***	0.5073***	0.4989***	0.4977***	0.4963***
	(0.0392)	(0.0391)	(0.0590)	(0.0589)	(0.0992)	(0.0965)	(0.0522)	(0.0518)
Islamic	−0.0739***	−0.0735***	−0.0607***	−0.0598***	−0.0889***	−0.0837***	−0.0830***	−0.0817***
	(0.0099)	(0.0100)	(0.0149)	(0.0152)	(0.0225)	(0.0239)	(0.0130)	(0.0133)
Developed	—	0.0005	—	0.0003	—	0.0027	—	0.0018
	—	(0.0023)	—	(0.0052)	—	(0.0130)	—	(0.0045)
EM_NOIS	—	0.0005	—	0.0014	—	0.0079	—	0.0013
	—	(0.0021)	—	(0.0048)	—	(0.0120)	—	(0.0041)
LMcap	−0.0193***	−0.0193***	−0.0120	−0.0116	−0.0089	−0.0079	−0.0284***	−0.0284***
	(0.0058)	(0.0058)	(0.0086)	(0.0086)	(0.0133)	(0.0129)	(0.0079)	(0.0079)
LGDP	0.0042***	0.0042***	0.0056***	0.0056***	0.0039	0.0039	0.0041**	0.0041**
	(0.0013)	(0.0013)	(0.0020)	(0.0020)	(0.0033)	(0.0032)	(0.0017)	(0.0017)
Lstcom	−0.000005	−0.000005	−0.000006	−0.000006	−0.000007	−0.000007	−0.000006	−0.000006
	(0.0000)	(0.0000)	(0.0000)	(0.0000)	(0.0000)	(0.0000)	(0.0000)	(0.0000)
Unem	0.0032	0.0032	0.0033	0.0033	−0.0002	−0.0002	0.0020	0.0020
	(0.0036)	(0.0036)	(0.0048)	(0.0048)	(0.0057)	(0.0055)	(0.0053)	(0.0053)
IRVol	0.0540***	0.0540***	0.0539***	0.0538***	0.1045***	0.1040***	0.0207	0.0208
	(0.0123)	(0.0122)	(0.0157)	(0.0155)	(0.0318)	(0.0306)	(0.0206)	(0.0204)
IPVol	−0.0044	−0.0045	0.0055	0.0050	−0.0010	−0.0016	−0.0051	−0.0051

Table 8. (Continued)

	Normal Period		Pre-GFC		GFC		Post GFC	
	I	II	III	IV	V	VI	VII	VIII
CPIVol	(0.0069)	(0.0069)	(0.0231)	(0.0229)	(0.0095)	(0.0091)	(0.0067)	(0.0066)
	0.0476	0.0476	0.0371	0.0392	−0.0637	−0.0596	0.0359	0.0351
	(0.0849)	(0.0846)	(0.1327)	(0.1315)	(0.1147)	(0.1108)	(0.1057)	(0.1046)
FxVol	0.0715	0.0712	−0.1147	−0.1148	−0.0054	−0.0121	0.1202	0.1193
	(0.1653)	(0.1646)	(0.2497)	(0.2472)	(0.4126)	(0.3979)	(0.2119)	(0.2096)
M2Vol	0.9580**	0.9582**	1.3339**	1.3280**	−3.4223**	−3.4976**	−0.6769	−0.6718
	(0.4943)	(0.4923)	(0.6407)	(0.6343)	(1.3569)	(1.3116)	(0.7939)	(0.7860)
Adjusted R^2	0.2320	0.2321	0.2366	0.2371	0.2664	0.2711	0.2254	0.2259

Notes: Results are based on the following regression model (see Equation (7) for details):

$$\text{LFvol}_{i,t} = \alpha + \acute{v}_{i,t}\beta_t + \mu_{i,t}, \quad t = 1, 2, \ldots, T, \quad i = 1, 2, \ldots, N_t,$$

where the dependent variable $\text{LFvol}_{i,t}$ stands for annualized low-frequency volatility for year t and country i. $\acute{v}_{i,t}$ is a vector of explanatory variables associated with country i and year t, and $\mu_{i,t}$ is the error term assumed to be contemporaneously uncorrelated with $\acute{v}_{i,t}$. See Table 3 for explanatory variable details. Equation (7) is estimated using SUR (seemingly unrelated regression) technique. Robust standard errors of the estimated coefficients are in parentheses. Normal/tranquil period excludes the GFC period, pre-GFC period includes the analysis between 2000 and 2006, GFC period includes the data from 2007 to 2009 and post GFC data covers the period from 2010 to 2016. *, ** and *** indicate level of significance at 10%, 5% and 1%, respectively.

Table 9. Low-Frequency Volatility and Macroeconomic Risk: Robustness Check with Sub-sample (Country Heterogeneity)

	Normal Period		Pre-GFC		GFC		Post-GFC	
	I	II	III	IV	V	VI	VII	VIII
Intercept	0.3290***	0.3464***	0.4073***	0.2707**	0.5706***	0.3632***	0.3775***	0.4189***
	(0.0708)	(0.0860)	(0.1030)	(0.1247)	(0.0785)	(0.1290)	(0.0908)	(0.1294)
Islamic	−0.0623***	−0.0231	−0.0606**	−0.0205	−0.0934***	−0.0193	−0.0598**	−0.0345
	(0.0136)	(0.0596)	(0.0247)	(0.0268)	(0.0382)	(0.0229)	(0.0295)	(0.0229)
Developed	—	0.0560	—	0.0086	—	0.0319	—	0.0701***
	—	(0.0627)	—	(0.0211)	—	(0.0216)	—	(0.0210)
EM_NOIS	—	0.0598	—	0.0589***	—	0.1018***	—	0.0493***
	—	(0.0568)	—	(0.0200)	—	(0.0224)	—	(0.0183)
LMcap	0.0035	−0.0034	−0.0114	0.0054	−0.0210***	0.0100	−0.0075	−0.0283
	(0.0108)	(0.0094)	(0.0141)	(0.0180)	(0.0084)	(0.0186)	(0.0121)	(0.0203)
LGDP	0.0055*	0.0023	0.0056	0.0077**	0.0025	0.0049*	0.0038	0.0045*
	(0.0032)	(0.0042)	(0.0039)	(0.0039)	(0.0053)	(0.0028)	(0.0040)	(0.0025)
Lstcom	−0.000007	0.000001	−0.000006	−0.000005	−0.00001	−0.000006	−0.000001	−0.000008
	(0.0000)	(0.0000)	(0.0000)	(0.0000)	(0.0000)	(0.0000)	(0.0000)	(0.0000)
Unem	−0.0013	−0.0024	0.0039	0.0036	0.0054***	−0.0024	0.0028	0.0051
	(0.0025)	(0.0027)	(0.0054)	(0.0054)	(0.0020)	(0.0043)	(0.0028)	(0.0053)
IRVol	0.0409***	0.0471***	0.0583***	0.0571***	0.0551**	0.0914***	0.0304***	0.0291***
	(0.0121)	(0.0117)	(0.0212)	(0.0197)	(0.0233)	(0.0267)	(0.0117)	(0.0301)

Table 9. (Continued)

	Normal Period		Pre-GFC		GFC		Post-GFC	
	I	II	III	IV	V	VI	VII	VIII
IPVol	−0.0049*	−0.0070***	0.0065	−0.0159	0.0005	−0.0084	0.0012	−0.0052
	(0.0026)	(0.0024)	(0.0222)	(0.0270)	(0.0021)	(0.0056)	(0.0048)	(0.0039)
CPIVol	0.1486*	0.0871	0.0465	0.1458	0.0433	−0.0105	0.1211	0.0262
	(0.0887)	(0.0889)	(0.1084)	(0.1181)	(0.0366)	(0.0386)	(0.1138)	(0.0670)
FxVol	0.0416	0.1144	−0.1064	−0.1053	0.1636	0.0445	0.2787*	0.0636
	(0.1215)	(0.1130)	(0.2340)	(0.2650)	(0.3242)	(0.3180)	(0.1472)	(0.2182)
M2Vol	1.5591	2.2759***	1.2546	1.0154	−1.6850***	−4.3216	−1.0734	−0.7313
	(0.9678)	(0.7544)	(0.9203)	(0.9020)	(0.5784)	(2.9452)	(0.6656)	(2.8465)
Year	Yes	Yes	Yes	Yes	Yes	Yes	Yes	Yes
Adjusted R^2	0.1117	0.3008	0.2518	0.2759	0.2751	0.3421	0.0822	0.2979

Notes: This table reports the estimation results based on random country effects and year-fixed effects. Robust standard errors of the estimated coefficients are in parentheses. Normal/tranquil period excludes the GFC period, pre-GFC period includes the analysis between 2000 and 2006, GFC period includes the data from 2007 to 2009 and post-GFC data covers the period from 2010 to 2016. *, ** and *** indicate level of significance at 10%, 5% and 1%, respectively.

Table 9 presents the final set of robustness results based on year-fixed and random country effects. Consistent with the above findings, Islamic market dummy remains to be negative and significant for all sub-sample analysis when developed and emerging non-Islamic country dummies are excluded. The coefficient sign remains negative but becomes statistically insignificant when developed and emerging non-Islamic country dummies are included in the model. Non-Islamic emerging markets are positive and significant in the following sub-samples: pre-GFC, GFC and post-GFC periods. The coefficient of developed market also becomes positive and significant in post-GFC sample. The negative sign of market capitalization during GFC suggests that larger the market size, lower is the market volatility in times of economic crisis. The negative sign of M2VOL in times of crisis period, which is consistent with the SUR results in Table 8, implies that monetary insulation may help reducing the effects of market turbulence during system crisis period. Coefficient signs for other variables remain to be consistent with the base regressions as well as OLS and SUR.

To summarize, our results stimulate a new research agenda in analyzing the relationship between stock market volatility and macroeconomic volatilities/risks when conventional and Islamic markets are considered together for portfolio diversification. We document that candidate *macroeconomic risk* proxies have similar effects on conventional and Islamic stock markets. An interesting observation is that low-frequency market volatility is lower when Islamic stock markets are included. The results are fairly consistent throughout all estimation techniques, different sub-samples and random country effects.

6. Summary and Conclusions

We present, in this paper, a robust empirical result on the relationship between *macroeconomic risk* and low-frequency volatility of conventional and Islamic stock markets from around the world. Using a novel approach to extract "low-frequency" volatility from aggregate volatility shocks, we find that low-frequency component of volatility is greater when the macroeconomic factors of GDP, unemployment, short-term interest rates, inflation, money supply (in tranquil period) and foreign exchange rates are more volatile. Interestingly, however, low-frequency market volatility is lower for Islamic markets and markets with higher market capitalization relative to GDP, more number of listed companies, and larger variability in industrial production. A negative sign of Islamic market suggests that religiosity has an influence on the reduction of market volatility and thus, investors may consider Islamic markets for portfolio diversification when a systemic crisis shakes the stock market around the world. Lesser extent of low-frequency volatility in times of major financial crisis suggests that monetary authorities may decide to have expansionary monetary policy when a systemic crisis hits the financial markets. The empirical results are robust to various alternative specifications and split sample analyses.

Acknowledgment

This work was supported by the Ministry of Education of the Republic of Korea and the National Research Foundation of Korea (NRF-2017S1A5A2A01026973). We thank the editor and two anonymous referees for their valuable comments and suggestions.

References

Abedifar, P, P Molyneux and A Tarazi (2013). Risk in Islamic banking. *Review of Finance*, 17(6), 2035–2096.

Adrian, T and J Rosenberg (2008). Stock returns and volatility: Pricing the short-run and long-run components of market risk. *Journal of Finance*, 63(6), 2997–3030.

Andersen, T, T Bollerslev, F Diebold and P Labys (2003). Modeling and forecasting realized volatility. *Econometrica*, 71(2), 579–625.

Al-Khazali, O, E Bouri, D Roubaud and T Zoubi (2017). The impact of religious practice on stock returns and volatility. *International Review of Financial Analysis*, 52, 172–189.

Arouri, ME, H Ben Ameur, N Jawadi, F Jawadi and W Louhichi (2013). Are Islamic finance innovations enough for investors to escape from a financial downturn? Further evidence from portfolio simulations. *Applied Economics*, 45, 3412–3420.

Askari, H (2012). Islamic finance, risk sharing, and international financial stability. *Yale Journal of International Affairs*, 7, 1–8.

Azad, AS, S Azmat, A Chazi and A Ahsan (2018). Sailing with the non-conventional stocks when there is no place to hide. *Journal of International Financial Markets, Institutions and Money*, 57, 1–16.

Azad, AS, JA Batten, V Fang and J Wickramanayake (2015). International swap market contagion and volatility. *Economic Modelling*, 47, 355–371.

Azad, AS, V Fang and CH Hung (2012). Linking the interest rate swap markets to the macroeconomic risk: The UK and US evidence. *International Review of Financial Analysis*, 22, 38–47.

Azad, AS, V Fang and J Wickramanayake (2011). Low-frequency volatility of Yen interest rate swap market in relation to macroeconomic risk. *International Review of Finance*, 11(3), 353–390.

Barclay, MJ, RH Litzenberger and JB Warner (1990). Private information, trading volume, and stock-return variances. *The Review of Financial Studies*, 3(2), 233–253.

Beber, A and MW Brandt (2009). Resolving macroeconomic uncertainty in stock and bond markets. *Review of Finance*, 13(1), 1–45.

Beck, T, A Demirgüç-Kunt and O Merrouche (2013). Islamic vs. conventional banking: Business model, efficiency and stability. *Journal of Banking & Finance*, 37(2), 433–447.

Benjamin, DJ, JJ Choi and G Fisher (2016). Religious identity and economic behavior. *Review of Economics and Statistics*, 98, 617–637.

Białkowski, J, A Etebari and TP Wisniewski (2012). Fast profits: Investor sentiment and stock returns during Ramadan. *Journal of Banking & Finance*, 36(3), 835–845.

Black, F (1987). *Business Cycles and Equilibrium*. Cambridge, MA: Blackwell.

Boako, G, AK Tiwari, M Ibrahim and Q Ji (2019). Analysing dynamic dependence between gold and stock returns: Evidence using stochastic and full-range tail dependence copula models. *Finance Research Letters*, 31.

Boyd, JH, J Hu and R Jagannathan (2005). The stock market's reaction to unemployment news: Why bad news is usually good for stocks. *Journal of Finance*, 60(2), 649–672.

Chen, N-F, R Roll and SA Ross (1986). Economic forces and the stock market. *Journal of Business*, 59(3), 383–403.

Diebold, FX and K Yilmaz (2008). Macroeconomic volatility and stock market volatility, worldwide. National Bureau of Economic Research, Working Paper 14269.

Dumas, B (1978). The theory of the trading firm revisited. *The Journal of Finance*, 33(3), 1019–1030.

Engle, R and G Lee (1999). A permanent and transitory component model of stock return volatility. In *Cointegration, Causality, and Forecasting: A Festschrift in Honor of Clive*, WJ Granger, R Engle and H White (eds.), pp. 475–497. New York: Oxford University Press.

Engle, RF, E Ghysels and B Sohn (2013). Stock marekt volatility and macroeconomic fundamentals. *Review of Economics and Statistics*, 22(3), 776–797.

Engle, RF and JG Rangel (2008). The Spline-GARCH model for low-frequency volatility and its global macroeconomic causes. *Review of Financial Studies*, 21(3), 1187–1222.

Genberg, H and A Sulstarova (2008). Macroeconomic volatility, debt dynamics, and sovereign interest rate spreads. *Journal of International Money and Finance*, 27(1), 26–39.

González, M, J Nave and G Rubio (2018). Macroeconomic determinants of stock market betas. *Journal of Empirical Finance*, 45, 26–44.

Hamao, Y, RW Masulis and V Ng (1990). Correlations in price changes and volatility across international stock markets. *The Review of Financial Studies*, 3(2), 281–307.

Hamilton, J and G Lin (1996). Stockmarket volatility and the business cycle. *Journal of Applied Econometrics*, 5, 573–593.

Jawadi, F, N Jawadi and W Louhichi (2014). Conventional and Islamic stock price performance: An empirical investigation. *International Economics*, 137, 73–87.

Kumar, S, AK Tiwari, Y Chauhan and Q Ji (2019). Dependence structure between the BRICS foreign exchange and stock markets using the dependence-switching copula approach. *International Review of Financial Analysis*, 63, 273–284.

Kurov, A and R Stan (2018). Monetary policy uncertainty and the market reaction to macroeconomic news. *Journal of Banking & Finance*, 86, 127–142.

Lee, CL, S Stevenson and ML Lee (2018). Low-frequency volatility of real estate securities and macroeconomic risk. *Accounting & Finance*, 58, 311–342.

Lettau, M, SC Ludvigson and JA Wachter (2008). The declining equity premium: What role does macroeconomic risk play? *Review of Financial Studies*, 21(4), 1653–1687.

McQueen, G and V Roley (1993). Stock prices, news, and business conditions. *The Review of Financial Studies*, 6(3), 683–707.

Nowak, S, J Andritzky, A Jobst and N Tamirisa (2011). Macroeconomic fundamentals, price discovery, and volatility dynamics in emerging bond markets. *Journal of Banking & Finance*, 35(10), 2584–2597.

Officer, RF (1973). The variability of the market factor of the New York stock exchange. *Journal of Business*, 46, 434–453.

Rangel, JG and RF Engle (2012). The Factor–Spline–GARCH model for high and low frequency correlations. *Journal of Business & Economic Statistics*, 30(1), 109–124.

Schwert, GW (1989). Why does stock market volatility change over time? *Journal of Finance*, 44, 1115–1153.

Shapiro, AC (1975). Exchange rate changes, inflation, and the value of the multinational corporation. *The Journal of Finance*, 30(2), 485–502.

Simpson, MW, S Ramchander and M Chaudhry (2005). The impact of macroeconomic surprises on spot and forward foreign exchange markets. *Journal of International Money and Finance*, 24(5), 693–718.

Urich, T and P Wachtel (1981). Market response to the weekly money supply announcements in the 1970s. *Journal of Finance*, 36(5), 1063–1072.

Urich, T and P Wachtel (1984). The effects of inflation and money supply announcements on interest rates. *Journal of Finance*, 39(4), 1177–1188.

Wei, Y, S Qin, X Li, S Zhu and G Wei (2019). Oil price fluctuation, stock market and macroeconomic fundamentals: Evidence from China before and after the financial crisis. *Finance Research Letters*, 30, 23–29.

Chapter 16

Does Islamic Finance Follow Financial Hierarchy? Evidence from the Malaysian Firms[#]

Mamoru Nagano

Faculty of Economics, Seikei University
3-3-1 Kichijoji Kitamachi Musashino City, Tokyo 180-8633, Japan
mnagano@econ.seikei.ac.jp

Focusing on the *sukuk* market in Malaysia from 2000–2017, this study estimates the degree of each sample issuer information asymmetry and investigates how it influences *sukuk* issuance and how it differs by *sukuk* type. First, we find that a cost-plus-sales-based *Murabahah sukuk* is available for all *sukuk* issuers, even though the degree of information asymmetry is high. Second, a lease-based *Ijarah sukuk* can be chosen by high information asymmetric firms only when the firm has qualified collateral assets. Third, only a low information asymmetric firm can choose a profit-and-loss sharing-based *Musyarakah sukuk*. Therefore, we conclude that *sukuk* issuance also follows a financial hierarchy in accordance with the agency costs of each financial methodology required when a specific *sukuk* is chosen.

Keywords: Sukuk issuance; information asymmetry; *Murabahah sukuk*; *Ijarah sukuk*; *Musyarakah sukuk*.

1. Introduction

The Islamic bond (*sukuk*) primary market in Malaysia expanded dramatically from 2001 onwards. Its volume in 2016 was estimated to be USD 62 billion — the largest volume year during the 2001–2020 period — 946 times of what it was in 2000, according to Thomson Reuters. Following this trend, in recent years, an increasing number of studies reported evidence concerning *sukuk* issuance determinants. The recent research trend in this field focuses on the relationship between firm information asymmetry and *sukuk* issuance. Some studies reveal that *sukuk* issuance follows the pecking order theory (Hisham *et al.*, 2015; Halim *et al.*, 2017), and issuers perform poorly under the adverse selection mechanism (Godlewski *et al.*, 2013). In particular, Halim *et al.* (2017) analyze the differences in agency costs between *sukuk* and conventional bond issuance. Other recent studies examining the types of *sukuk* refer to different schemes to cope with the information asymmetry of issuers (Azmat *et al.*, 2014). The purpose of this study is to contribute to the literature by analyzing *sukuk* issuance determinants by type. We compare

---

[#]This Chapter first appeared in the *Singapore Economic Review*, Vol. 67, No. 1, doi: 10.1142/S0217590821420030. © 2022 World Scientific Publishing.

the agency costs of each type of *sukuk* and report the order of the funding methodology choices.[1]

We also contribute, to the existing literature, by reporting new empirical evidence. Specifically, this study focuses on three major types of *sukuk* schemes that account for more than 90% of the total schemes from 2000–2017: *Murabahah sukuk*, *Ijarah sukuk* and *Musyarakah sukuk*. We report which issuer chooses a specific *sukuk* scheme, depending on the size of the agency costs of each debt security. Here, we hypothesize that the pecking order effect influences not only the choice between *sukuk* and conventional debt, but also the choice of *sukuk* type. By comparing the relationship between the degree of issuer information asymmetry and each type of *sukuk* issuance choice, this study provides evidence that *Murabahah sukuk*, *Ijarah sukuk* and *Musyarakah sukuk* are chosen in ascending order of the final degree of agency costs for each financial methodology required when the specific *sukuk* is issued.

First, we suppose that a *sukuk* issuer, under high information asymmetry, can choose cost-plus-sales-based *Murabahah sukuk* when the firm increases the funding demand. This firm repeatedly issues a small, shorter maturity *sukuk* to satisfy the total funding demand. In this case, the information asymmetry of the firm is mitigated because the investors can monitor the debt service ability of the firm on each end of the short-maturity period and receive a fixed-income post-issuance regardless of the issuer's post-issuance performance. Therefore, this type of *sukuk* is available for highly information asymmetric issuers. Second, we posit that some eligible firms under financial constraint caused by high information asymmetry can choose *Ijarah sukuk*. This is because the debt financing mechanism of *Ijarah sukuk* structurally covers the agency costs of the issuer, even though the agency cost is large. Therefore, this financial methodology is available even for highly information asymmetric issuers. We also hypothesize that only a limited number of issuers, who can predict future high performance by external investors, choose *Musyarakah sukuk*. This is because, in the case of *Musyarakah sukuk*, both the issuer and the investors share the profit-and-loss distribution in the post-issuance period, but no debt financing mechanism in this scheme covers agency costs. Based on empirical evidence, we highlight the fact that each type of *sukuk* issuance is chosen depending on the final degree of agency costs of funding schemes. Accordingly, we show evidence that this order of *sukuk* choice is therefore consistent with the existing corporate financing theory.

In Section 2, we first present the trends in Islamic financing literature and, thereafter, introduce our hypotheses and their linkages with the existing literature. In the following sections, we present the empirical methodology and discuss the results. Based on the empirical results, we derive implications and present the conclusion in the last section.

2. Literature Review and Hypotheses

2.1. *Literature review*

While this field has recorded an increasing number of studies in recent years, most of them focus on the Islamic banking market. Although relatively few studies have traditionally

---

[1] Halim *et al.* (2017) compared agency costs of *sukuk* and conventional bond issuance. Azmat *et al.* (2014) reported that determinants of each type of *sukuk* are different.

examined the direct-financing *sukuk* issuance market, their number has increased in recent years (Table 1). Azmat *et al.* (2014), Godlewski *et al.* (2013), Halim *et al.* (2017), Naifar *et al.* (2016), Klein and Weill (2016) and Ahmed *et al.* (2018) have empirically studied the *sukuk* market using issuer data. Godlewski *et al.* (2013) compare the differences between the cumulative abnormal returns of *sukuk* issuers and conventional debt security issuers in Malaysia. They conclude that the stock market reacts to *sukuk* issuance announcements negatively, and that these poorly performing issuers are subject to an adverse selection mechanism.

Ahmed *et al.* (2018) also test the unique characteristics of *sukuk* issuers, and their conclusion is consistent with that of Godlewski *et al.* (2013). They conclude that *sukuk* issuers are financially unhealthy, risk tolerant and small. Hisham *et al.* (2015) also use *sukuk* and conventional debt security issuers' data and demonstrate two major conclusions. First, they show that *sukuk* issuers choose *sukuk* issuance to optimize the cost and benefit balance for issuers, and *sukuk* issuance is in accordance with the tradeoff theory in this regard. Second, they report that the degree of information asymmetry of issuers influences the choice of *sukuk* issuance as well, in accordance with the pecking order theory. Azmat *et al.* (2014) are the first to investigate issuance determinants by *sukuk* type. Following Azmat *et al.* (2014), Ashraf *et al.* (2020) examine the relationship between firm ownership structure and the *sukuk* issuance. They conclude that high government ownership ratio promotes *Murabahah* sukuk issuance.

Naifar *et al.* (2016) study the relationship between *sukuk* yields and stock market volatility and its transmission mechanism. They conclude that the relationship is asymmetric and that stock market volatility influences *sukuk* yield, but the *sukuk* market does not influence the condition of the stock market. Halim *et al.* (2017) and Klein and Weill (2016) also study the relationship between the degree of information asymmetry of issuers and *sukuk* issuance. They show evidence that the higher the degree of information asymmetry, the more frequently the firm issues *sukuk*. Hassan *et al.* (2018) examine volatility linkages among *sukuk* and other bond markets. They conclude that the volatility of the *sukuk* market is independent of other conventional markets.

We provide novel empirical results in the context of these recent research trends on*sukuk*. We show which *sukuk* issuer chooses which type of *sukuk*. We examine how the issuers' degree of information asymmetry and the degree of issuers' financial constraints influence the choice of *sukuk* type. Then, we theoretically explain how these empirical results may be interpreted in accordance with existing corporate financing theory.

2.2. Hypotheses development

Our first hypothesis focuses on the relationship between an issuers' degree of information asymmetry, the debt maturity length and the *Murabahah sukuk* issuance. *Murabahah sukuk* is essentially a cost-plus-sales-based debt security, as shown in Figure 1. A lead manager, or an arranger, first purchases the machinery and equipment demanded by the *sukuk* issuer. The lead manager and *sukuk* issuer then conclude the installment sales contracts for the machinery and equipment. Finally, the issuer issues the *sukuk* and redeems it at the

Table 1. Recent Empirical Literature on *Sukuk*

Study	Sample country	Sample period	Key conclusions
Godlewski et al. (2013)	Malaysia	2002–2009	(a) The stock market negatively reacts to *sukuk* issuance announcements, and these poorly performing issuers are under an adverse selection mechanism.
Hisham et al. (2015)	Malaysia	2002–2012	(b) *sukuk* issuers choose *sukuk* issuance to optimize the cost and benefit balance for the issuers, and *sukuk* is issued in accordance with the tradeoff theory.
Godlewski et al. (2016)	8 Islamic countries	2006–2013	(c) *Shari'a* board members' term length, nationality and reputation influence the post-issuance performance of issuers, as they contribute toward the mitigation of information asymmetry.
Halim et al. (2017)	Malaysia	2001–2014	(d) The higher the degree of information asymmetry, the more frequently the firm issues *sukuk*.
Klein and Weill (2016)	Malaysia	2004–2013	(e) The degree of information asymmetry of issuers influences the choice of *sukuk* issuance, and this issuance is also in accordance with the pecking order theory.
Naifar et al. (2016)	Malaysia, Saudi Arabia and UAE	2010–2014	(f) The relationship is asymmetric and the stock market volatility influences *sukuk* yield, but the *sukuk* market does not influence the condition of the stock market.
Ahmed et al. (2018)	All *sukuk* and conventional debt issuers	2001–2015	(g) *Sukuk* issuance announcement decreases the cumulative abnormal returns of the issuer.
Ashraf et al. (2020)	Malaysia	2008–2014	(h) Small and unhealthy firms are likely to issue *sukuk*.
			(i) High government ownership of firm promotes *Murabahah sukuk* issuance.
			(j) A board ethnicity influences and promotes *Musyarakah sukuk* issuance.

Notes: This table presents an overview of the recent literature on Islamic finance. The table summarizes studies focusing on the determinants of *sukuk* issuance.

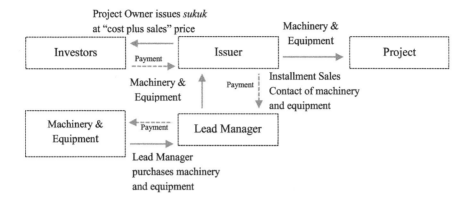

Figure 1. The Structure of *Murabahah sukuk*

"cost-plus-sales" price, in accordance with the market price of the machinery and equipment. Therefore, the characteristics here are similar to those of fixed-income debt security. Stohs (and Mauer), Ozkan (2002) and Pan *et al.* (2019) also assert that a firm with small information asymmetry and expected good corporate performance in the future can issue long-term maturity debt securities. This conversely implies that a firm with high information asymmetry is forced to frequently issue short maturity debt securities. Based on the literature, our first hypothesis is that short-term maturity, cost-plus-sales-based *Murabahah sukuk* do not require the issuer to have low information asymmetry, similarly to short-term conventional fixed-income debt security for external investors. Frequent, small issuances enable external investors to identify the debt repayment ability of the issuer at the end of every maturity period. Therefore, we suppose that *Murabahah sukuk* is preferred when the issuer has high information asymmetry.

Hypothesis 1. *A cost-plus-sales-based Murabahah sukuk can be chosen, even by highly information asymmetric issuers, because frequent debt issuance and the redemption mitigate investors' agency costs.*

Our second hypothesis is that a lease-based *Ijarah sukuk* is also preferred by highly information asymmetric issuers, when it has qualified collateral assets. In other words, we suppose that an issuer facing a high degree of financial constraint, and a firm with high information asymmetry, are encouraged to choose *Ijarah sukuk* as the collateral assets of the issuer covers the agency costs (Figure 2), which helps satisfy the funding demand. In the case of *Ijarah sukuk*, an original issuer first establishes a special purpose company (SPC) and sells the existing machinery and equipment to the SPC. The SPC and the issuer then conclude a contract to lease the machinery and equipment to continue the project's operation as planned. Finally, the SPC issues *sukuk* as a secured debt security to outside investors, and purchases and leases the new machinery and equipment. Here, the machinery and equipment sold to the SPC serve as collateral for debt security, and they are liquidated once the issuer becomes insolvent, post-issuance. Many studies note that the existence of some form of collateral reduces agency costs or friction with regard to the

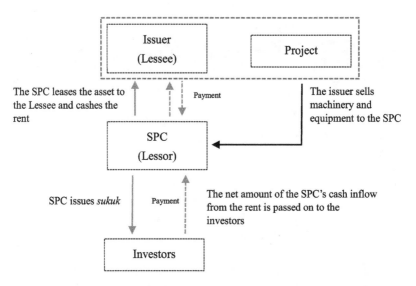

Figure 2. The Structure of *Ijarah sukuk*

contract when there is high information asymmetry between borrowers and investors (Bester, 1985, 1987; Chan and Thakor, 1987; Besanko and Thakor, 1987a,b; Boot *et al.*, 1991). Another stream of studies asserts that when the borrower's moral hazard is high, or the project is risky, the existence of the borrower's collateral encourages the drawing up of an optimal debt contract (Boot *et al.*, 1991; Cooley *et al.*, 2004; Almeida and Campello, 2010). Thus, following these studies, we hypothesize that a *sukuk* issuer under financial constraints, due to the information asymmetry of the issuer, prefers *Ijarah sukuk* over other types of *sukuk*. This is because the debt instrument of *Ijarah sukuk* covers agency costs via collateral assets.

Hypothesis 2a. *A lease-based Ijarah sukuk is preferred when the firm's information asymmetry is high.*

Hypothesis 2b. *A lease-based Ijarah sukuk is preferred when the firm has qualified tangible collateral assets.*

Our third hypothesis is that a firm's decision to choose profit-and-loss sharing-based *sukuk* is encouraged by the low degree of issuer's information asymmetry, as investors' returns are dependent on the firm's project performance. As shown in Figure 3, the structure of *Musyarakah sukuk* is similar to normal equity, as the investment return of the security varies depending on post-issuance project performance (Figure 3). In the past, many studies have focused on the choice between conventional debt and equity issuance. A series of studies on the pecking order hypothesis (Donaldson, 1961; Myers, 1984; Shyam-Sunder and Myers, 1999) assert that firms follow a financing hierarchy, where bank borrowing and fixed-income debt financing are given first preference, followed by equity financing. This order of funding methodology choice is consistent with the size of issuers' information asymmetry. Equity financing will only be used for firms with low information asymmetry, and fixed-income debt financing is chosen prior to equity financing. By

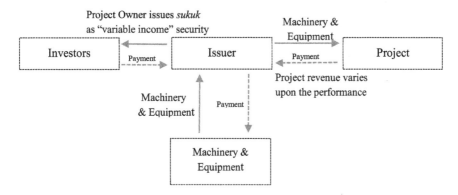

Figure 3. The Structure of *Musyarakah sukuk*

applying the above literature, Azmat *et al.* (2014) prove that the information asymmetry of issuers influences the funding methodology choice between *sukuk* issuance and conventional debt issuance. Halim *et al.* (2017) also assert that the determinants of a choice of *sukuk* type are different. We refer to these conclusions as well as the existing literature on pecking order theory, and posit the following hypothesis.

Hypothesis 3. A profit-and-loss sharing-based *Musyarakah sukuk* is preferred only when the issuer is a low information asymmetric firm.

3. Empirical Strategy

3.1. *Measuring information asymmetry*

To examine Hypotheses 1–3, we first calculate the degree of information asymmetry of each issuer, *Asymmetry*, using the data for publicly listed *sukuk* and conventional debt issuers in Malaysia. We estimate the degree of firm-level information asymmetry, between firm insiders and outsiders, following the methodology of Bharath *et al.* (2009), who suggest that market microstructure measures can help gauge the magnitude of information asymmetry facing outside investors in capital markets. First, we employ three variables that represent stock illiquidity measures. Then, we employ three other variables of adverse selection component measures. Using these six variables and the principal component analysis, we extract a common principal component of the cross-sectional level or annual change in the six variables, and the corresponding principal component scores as the main information asymmetry value of firm i, that is, *Asymmetry*, which represents the overall degree of information asymmetry of firm i in year t when the firm issues *sukuk*.

The first three illiquidity component measures mentioned above are *Illiquid_1*, *Illiquid_2* and *Illiquid_3*. *Illiquid_1*, developed by Amihud (2002), is calculated as the mean of the square root of the ratio of firm i's daily absolute stock return to the reported daily trading volume (in millions), over all days in fiscal year t with nonzero volume. *Illiquid_2*, developed by Cooper *et al.* (1985) and Amihud *et al.* (1997), is defined as the negative value of the mean of the square root of the ratio of firm i's reported daily stock volume (in millions) to its absolute stock return, over all days in fiscal year t with nonzero return.

According to Pastor and Stambaugh (2003), a stock's liquidity can be captured by the interaction between its returns and lagged order flow.

$$Stock\ Return_{T+1} = \phi_0 + Illiquid\_3_T \times sign(Stock\ Return_T - Index\ Return_T) \times v_T + \kappa, \quad (1)$$

where $Stock\ Return_T$ is the return on firm i's stock on day T, $Index\ Return_T$ is Kuala Lumpur Composite Index return on day T and v_T is firm i's stock turnover volume on day T. We follow this measure and estimate the absolute magnitude of such reversals for firm i's stock over each fiscal year t, and label it as *Illiquid_3*.

The second set includes the three adverse selection component measures: *Adverse_1*, *Adverse_2* and *Adverse_3*. We follow George et al. (1991), who have developed a measure allowing information-containing orders to generate differential impacts on the transaction price and quote midpoint. We obtain this adverse selection component of the spread by estimating the model indicated as follows:

$$2 \times Return\ Difference_T$$
$$= \pi_0 + \pi_1 \times Per\ Spread_T \times (Stock\ Return_T Stock\ Return_{T-1}) + \varepsilon$$
$$Adverse\_1_T = (1 - \pi_1) \times Per\ Spread_T, \quad (2)$$

where *Return Difference* is the difference between the traded stock price return and the quote midpoint return, and *Per Spread* is the spread percentage for firm i for day T. We compute the mean value for firm i's stock over each fiscal year t and label it as *Adverse_1*.

We also employ Roll's (1984) effective bid-ask spread of *Adverse_2*, measured by the square root of the first-order serial covariance of stock price changes for firm i for day T. We compute the mean value for firm i's stock over each fiscal year t and label it as *Adverse_2*.

$$Adverse\_2_T = 2 \times \sqrt{-cov_T}. \quad (3)$$

Last, we employ a variable that proxies the relative importance of information asymmetry considerations among all stocks in our sample, and we denote it as *Adverse_3*. Llorente et al. (2002), who empirically introduce *Adverse_3*, show that correspondence exists between the cross-sectional variation in stocks' volume-return dynamics and the relative importance of information-driven trading in stock price fluctuations. We estimate the parameter *Adverse_3* using ordinary least squares estimates of the empirical equation, as indicated as follows:

$$Stock\ Return_{T+1} = const + \beta \times Stock\ Return_T + Adverse\_3 \times Volume_T$$
$$\times Stock\ Return_T + \eta,$$
$$Volume_T = \log turnover_T - 1/200 \sum_{s=200}^{-1} \log turnover_{T+s}, \quad (4)$$

where the $\log turnover_T = \log(turnover_T + 0.00000255)$, and $Stock\ Return_T$ is the daily return of firm i's stock. We compute the value for firm i's stock over each fiscal year t and label it as *Adverse_3*.

Unlike some studies, we follow Gomes and Phillips (2012) and do not employ the PIN measure in addition to the above six measures. This is because these studies focus on publicly listed firms in major stock markets. Our study, however, focuses on firms in emerging economies that trade an extremely small number of stocks.

To consider the year effect in the six information asymmetry proxy variables, we standardize the measures by first taking the difference between the original value and the cross-sectional mean. Then, we divide this difference by the cross-sectional standard deviation. Next, we use principal component analysis to extract the first principal component as the main information asymmetry measure, which we denote as *Asymmetry*, an independent variable.

3.2. Sukuk type and choice of priority

By using the degree of information asymmetry of each sample firm, we estimate Model (5) to verify how *Asymmetry* and other determinants of firm i influence the choice of each type of *sukuk* issuance. We estimate Model (5) to verify the similarities and differences among the *Murabahah*, *Ijarah* and *Musyarakah sukuk* issuance determinants of firms. We used a multinomial probit model because security issuance under estimation fails to satisfy the so-called independence from the irrelevant alternatives property of the multinomial logit model. The dependent variables in Model (5) are the categorical variables of *SukukType*, which equals 1, 2, 3, 4, or 0 when firm i issues *Murabahah sukuk* ($=1$), *Ijara sukuk* ($=2$), *Musyarakah sukuk* ($=3$), other *sukuk* ($=4$), or *Debt* ($=0$). In addition to the four types of *sukuk* dependent categorical variables, we employ *Debt* as the categorical dependent variable. *Debt* is the base case dependent variable, which equals zero when firm i issues conventional straight debt security. After all, each dependent variable equals 0–4 when an issuer chooses a corresponding choice. This empirical model assumes that when the dependent variable equals 0, the result is the base outcome of the multinomial probit model estimation. Table 2 presents the definitions of all the dependent variables.

$$SukukType_i = const + \varphi_1 Asymmetry_i + \varphi_2 \ln KZindex_i + \varphi_3 Maturity_i + \varphi_4 MarketBook_i \\ + \varphi_5 Zscore_i + \varphi_6 \ln TotalAsset_i + \varphi_7 \ln FundSize_i + \varphi_8 TimeTrend_i + v_i. \tag{5}$$

Model (5) employs independent variable of *Asymmetry*. Model (5) also includes another independent variable, which proxies the measure of financial constraints (*KZindex*). We employ the Kaplan and Zingales (1997) index as a measure of the financial constraint of firm i. Following Lamont *et al.* (2001) and Baker *et al.* (2003), we estimate *KZindex* using the following equations:

$$KZindex_i = -1.002 \cdot \frac{CF_i}{TotalAsset_i} + 3.319 \cdot Lev_i - 39.368 \cdot \frac{DIV_i}{TotalAsset_i} \\ - 1.315 \cdot \frac{CASH_i}{TotalAsset_i}. \tag{6}$$

Table 2. Variable Definitions

Variables	Definition	Source
	Dependent variables	
Sukuk Type	Equals 1, 2, 3, 4 and 0 when firm i issues *Murabahah sukuk*, *Ijarah sukuk*, *Musyarakah sukuk*, other *sukuk* and conventional straight debt security, respectively for Model (5)	Thomson Reuters, *Thomson One*
Murabahah sukuk	Equals 1 when *sukuk* issuer i chooses *Murabahah sukuk*, and 0 otherwise for Model (5)	Thomson Reuters, *Thomson One*
Ijarah sukuk	Equals 1 when *sukuk* issuer i chooses *Ijarah sukuk*, and 0 otherwise for Model (5)	Thomson Reuters, *Thomson One*
Musyarakah sukuk	Equals one when *sukuk* issuer i chooses *Musyarakah sukuk*, and 0 otherwise for Model (5)	Thomson Reuters, *Thomson One*
CAR(+2, +60)	59-day event window cumulative abnormal returns around the *sukuk* issue dates for firm i in the post-issuance period	Thomson Reuters, *Thomson One*
	Independent Variables	
Asymmetry	Firm i's first principal component score in year t estimated from *Illiquid_1*, *Illiquid_2*, *Illiquid_3*, *Adverse_1*, *Adverse_2* and *Adverse_3*.	Thomson Reuters, *Thomson One*
Illiquid_1	Mean of the square root of the ratio of firm i's daily absolute stock return to the reported daily trading volume (in millions) over all days in financial year t with nonzero volume	Thomson Reuters, *Thomson One*
Illiquid_2	Negative value of the mean of the square root of the ratio of the reported daily volume of firm i's stock (in millions) to its absolute stock return, over all days in fiscal year t with nonzero return	Thomson Reuters, *Thomson One*
Illiquid_3	Parameter of the equation seen below; the dependent variable is Stock Return$_{T+1}$, that is, return on firm i's stock on day $T+1$, and the independent variable is Stock Return$_T$−Index Return$_T$, which is the return on firm i's stock minus each country's market index return on day T multiplied by firm i's stock turnover volume on day $T(v)$. $$\text{Stock Return}_{T+1} = \phi_0 + \textit{Illiquid\_3}_T \times \text{sign}(\text{Stock Return}_T - \text{Index Return}_T) \times v_T + \kappa.$$	Thomson Reuters, *Thomson One*

Table 2. (Continued)

Variables	Definition	Source
Adverse_1	Spread percentage multiplied by 1 minus a parameter that is estimated as the difference between the traded stock price return (Return Difference) and spread percentage (Per Spread) for firm i in day T. $2 \times Return\ Difference_T = \pi_0 + \pi_1 \times Per\ Spread_T \times (Stock\ Return_T - Stock\ Return_{T-1}) + \varepsilon$, $Adverse\_1_T = (1 - \pi_1) \times Per\ Spread_T$.	Thomson Reuters, *Thomson One*
Adverse_2	Square root of the first-order serial covariance of stock price changes for firm i in day T	Thomson Reuters, *Thomson One*
Adverse_3	Estimated parameter of the empirical equation seen as follows: $Stock\ Return_{T+1} = const + \beta \times Stock\ Return_T + Adverse\_3 \times Volume_T \times Stock\ Return_T + \eta$, $$Volume_T = \log turnover_T - 1/200 \sum_{s=200}^{-1} \log turnover_{T+s},$$ where $\log turnover_T = \log(turnover_T + 0.00000255)$, and R_T is the daily return of firm i's stock	Thomson Reuters, *Thomson One*
KZindex	$KZindex = -1.002 \times CF/TotalAsset + 3.319 \times Leverage - 39.368 \times DIV/Total\ Asset - 1.315 \times CASH/Total\ Asset$	Thomson Reuters, *Thomson One*
Maturity	Natural logarithm of maturity of *sukuk*/conventional debt in terms of years	Thomson Reuters, *Thomson One*
MarketBook	Market value of capital in year t plus book value of liability in year $t-1$ divided by book value of total assets of year $t-1$ for firm i	Thomson Reuters, *Thomson One*
CAR(−60, −2)	59-day event window cumulative abnormal returns around the *sukuk*, conventional debt, or equity issue dates for firm $i$in the pre-issuance period	Thomson Reuters, *Thomson One*

Table 2. (Continued)

Variables	Definition	Source
Zscore	Altman's Zscore of firm i in year t Zscore = 0.012 × (Current Asset − Current Liability) + 0.014 × (Retained Earnings) + 0.033 × (EBITDA/Total Asset) + 0.006 × (Market Value of Capital/Total Liability) + 0.999 × Total Sales/Total Assets	Thomson Reuters, *Thomson One*
CF	Sum of net income and depreciation of firm i in year t	Thomson Reuters, *Thomson One*
DIV	Cash dividends of firm i in year t	Thomson Reuters, *Thomson One*
CASH	Cash and short-term investment of firm i in year t	Thomson Reuters, *Thomson One*
Total Asset	Book value of total assets of firm i in year t	Thomson Reuters, *Thomson One*
FundSize	Total value of *sukuk*/debt issued by firm i in year t	Thomson Reuters, *Thomson One*

Notes: The variables defined here are employed to estimate the empirical model (E). Financial data on sample *sukuk* and debt issuers are sourced from Thomson Reuters' *Thomson One*. Data on firms' daily stock price returns, daily bid and ask stock prices, daily firm stock trading volumes and daily market index returns are also sourced from *Thomson One*. In this table, "year t" denotes the year in which firm i issues *sukuk* or conventional debt in the market.

CF is defined as net profit plus depreciation, *TotalAsset* is defined as the book value of total assets, *DIV* is dividend payable and *CASH* refers to cash and its equivalents. Model (E) employs *Maturity*, which is the natural logarithm of maturity of *sukuk* and conventional debt in terms of years.

Model (5) also employs *Maturity*, which is defined as natural logarithm of maturity of *sukuk* and conventional debt in terms of years. *MarketBook* is the book value of liability in year $t-1$ plus the market value of capital in year t, divided by the book value of total assets in year $t-1$ for firm i, when the firm issues *sukuk* in year t. Here, we define year t as the financial year of firm i when the firm issues *sukuk* or conventional debt. Other than *MarketBook*, this study also employs cumulative abnormal returns, $CAR(-60, -2)$, as proxies of firm i's market valuation to check the robustness of this variable. $CAR(-60, -2)$ is the independent variable of firm i's CARs around the *sukuk* or conventional debt issue date. Following Brown and Warner's (1985) methodology, we employ the results pertaining to the type of event window for *CARs*, namely a 59-day event window for $CAR(-60, -2)$. To calculate firm i's CARs, we estimate the predicted stock returns for the interval $(-250, -60)$. Model (E) also employs *Zscore*, which is Altman's *Zscore* of firm i. ln*TotalAsset* and ln*FundSize* are the natural logarithm values of the U.S. dollar-denominated book value of total assets and the value of *sukuk* issued by firm i, respectively.

4. Data

Our study uses data pertaining to *sukuk* deals and conventional debt securities for Malaysian firms, from 2000 to 2017, from *Thomson One* of Thomson Reuters. Our empirical analyzes use only publicly listed issuer data. Based on these dataset criteria, our sample data includes the following sample observations. A total of 144 firms are *sukuk* issuers, and the corresponding numbers for *Murabahah sukuk*, *Ijara sukuk* and *Musyarakah sukuk* issuers are 78, 19 and 34, respectively. There are 13 other types of *sukuk* issuing firms (i.e., *Istisna* (1), *Mudharabah* (2), *Al Wakala Bill Istithmar* (5) and others (5)). 39 *sukuk* issuance deals of unknown *sukuk* type in the *Thomson One* database are excluded from the sample. 123 firms are straight debt security issuers. In the case of straight debt security deal data, we employ only unsecured conventional debt security deals with a maturity length exceeding one year (Tables 3 and 4).

Component financial data of *KZindex* (i.e., firm cash flow (*CF*), dividend payable (*DIV*), cash and other equivalent assets (*CASH*)) are sourced from *Thomson One* of Thomson Reuters. To calculate MarketBook, we refer to Thomson Reuters for data pertaining to the market value of equity, book value of liability and book value of total assets of firm i in the year when the firm issues *sukuk*, or conventional straight debt securities. The daily stock price of firm i, and the domestic market index for $CAR(-60, -2)$, are also obtained from *Thomson One*. *Sukuk*, or conventional debt security issue values (*FundingSize*), book value of total assets (*TotalAsset*). Further details regarding data definitions and sources are provided in Table 2. The yearly and industrial distributions of *sukuk* issuance are presented in Tables 3 and 4, and the descriptive statistics of the sample data are shown in Tables 5 and 6, respectively. Tables 3 and 4 indicate that the number of

Table 3. Yearly Distribution of *sukuk* Issue by Type

	Murabahah sukuk	*Ijarah sukuk*	*Musyarakah sukuk*	Other *sukuk*	Conventional Debt
2000	0	0	0	0	5
2001	0	0	0	0	18
2002	0	0	0	0	0
2003	0	1	0	0	1
2004	1	2	0	0	3
2005	1	0	0	0	13
2006	0	1	0	0	10
2007	3	4	0	0	4
2008	4	2	6	0	5
2009	2	1	0	1	4
2010	5	0	1	0	5
2011	7	5	2	1	7
2012	6	3	4	1	4
2013	6	2	7	1	10
2014	13	0	5	5	9
2015	10	1	5	2	8
2016	9	1	2	0	9
2017	13	0	2	2	8
Total	78	19	34	13	123

Notes: The *sukuk* issuance sample is sourced from Thomson Reuters *Thomson One*, which covers the period from 2000 to 2017. The sample includes *Murabahah sukuk*, *Ijarah sukuk* and *Musyarakah sukuk* as well as other *sukuk* and conventional straight debt. "Other *sukuk*" is the sum of *Istisna*, *Mudharabah*, *Al Wakala Bill Istithmar* and others. *Sukuk* of types not described were excluded from the dataset. The numbers in the cells represent the number of issuers in a given year.
Source: *Thomson One*.

Table 4. Industrial Distribution of *sukuk* Issue by Type

SIC Code		*Murabahah sukuk*	*Ijarah sukuk*	*Musyarakah sukuk*	Other *sukuk*	Conventional Debt
01–14	Agriculture, Forestry, Fishering, and Mining	11	7	1	1	25
20–39	Manufacturing	22	0	12	0	27
40–49	Transportation, Communication, Electric, Gas, and Sanitary	10	12	10	10	32
50–59	Wholesale and Retail Trade	2	0	1	0	6

Table 4. (*Continued*)

SIC Code		Murabahah sukuk	Ijarah sukuk	Musyarakah sukuk	Other sukuk	Conventional Debt
60–67	Finance, Insurance, Real Estate,	28	0	5	1	19
15–17	and Construction					
70–89	Services	5	0	5	1	14
Total		78	19	34	13	123

Notes: The *sukuk* issuance sample is sourced from Thomson Reuters *Thomson One*, which covers the period from 2000 to 2017. The sample includes *Murabahah sukuk*, *Ijarah sukuk* and *Musyarakah sukuk* as well as other *sukuk* and conventional straight debt. "Other *sukuk*" is the sum of *Istisna*, *Mudharabah*, *Al Wakala Bill Istithmar* and other *sukuk*. *Sukuk* of types not described were excluded from the dataset. The numbers in the cells represent the number of issuers by SIC industrial codes.
Source: Thomson One.

conventional debt issuers was fifty firms, while that of *sukuk* was only four firms in 2002–2006. Afterwards, the number of conventional debt issuers was 60 issuers, while that of *sukuk* dramatically increased to 121 issuers between 2010–2017. In the latter period, most issuers chose either *Murabahah sukuk* or *Ijarah sukuk*. Tables 5 and 6 indicate that the *Asymmetry* of *Ijarah sukuk* issuers is significantly larger than that of *Musyarakah sukuk*.

5. Empirical Results

5.1. *Multinomial probit model results*

Table 7 shows the empirical results of Model (5). Equations (1)–(6) are estimated using the multinomial probit model. We omit the results of the base outcome estimation *SukukType* (=0). The sample data of empirical Equations (1)–(6) are *sukuk* issuers and conventional straight debt security issuers. We define five types of dependent variables in the equations. Equations (1) and (4) are the results of equations that *SukukType* equals 1, that is, firm i issues *Murabahah sukuk*. Equations (2) and (5) are the results of equations where *SukukType* equals 2; that is, firm i issues *Ijarah sukuk*, and Equations (3) and (6) are the results of equations where *SukukType* equals 3; namely, firm i issues *Musyarakah sukuk*. We omit the empirical results for *SukukType* equals 4, namely, the other types of *sukuk*, owing to space constraints (these results are available upon request). Equations (1)–(3) employ *MarketBook*, and Equations (4)–(6) employ $CAR(-60, -2)$ as a proxy of firm i's market valuation, respectively.

Table 7 shows that the parameters of *Asymmetry* are significantly negative for Equations (3) and (6), implying that a firm under low information asymmetry is likely to issue *Musyarakah sukuk*. The parameters of *Maturity* are significantly positive for equation (2), (3), (5) and (6) in Table 7. These results imply that the debt maturity period of *Ijarah sukuk* and *Musyarakah sukuk* are long compared to that of conventional debt. Regarding the

Table 5. Descriptive Statistics and Attributes of Sample Firms: Variables of Market Valuation and Deal Characteristics

	Asymmetry	KZindex	Maturity	Market Book	CAR (−60, −2)	CAR(+2,+60)
Murabahah sukuk						
Mean	0.568	9.053	5.666	1.513	0.003	−0.033
Median	0.574	6.798	5.192	1.516	−0.010	−0.034
N	42	43	43	78	78	78
Ijarah sukuk						
Mean	0.308	4.661	7.718	2.359	0.013	−0.009
Median	0.463	3.156	9.932	1.976	0.007	0.067
N	17	17	17	19	19	19
Musyarakah sukuk						
Mean	−0.181	8.7241	1.347	1.937	−0.012	0.027
Median	0.046	7.235	6.425	1.887	−0.002	0.006
N	18	18	20	34	34	34
Conventional Debt						
Mean	−0.118	7.518	4.614	1.611	−0.022	−0.038
Median	0.256	7.841	5.479	1.382	−0.008	−0.029
N	65	66	67	123	123	123
Total Mean	−0.009	7.143	6.072	1.681	−0.006	−0.021
Median	0.277	6.059	5.012	1.481	−0.006	−0.012
N	153	155	172	267	267	267
Difference Murabahah sukuk vs. other sukuk						
Student test	0.691	1.737**	−1.697*	−3.784***	0.031	−1.113
Wilcoxon test	0.684	2.613***	−2.512**	−2.844***	0.074	−2.224**

Table 5. (Continued)

	Asymmetry	KZindex	Maturity	Market Book	CAR (−60, −2)	CAR(+2,+60)
Difference *Ijarah sukuk* vs. other *sukuk*						
Student test	1.561*	−2.144**	0.275	2.710***	0.225	0.215
Wilcoxon test	1.933*	−2.335**	2.941***	2.499**	0.494	1.885*
Difference *Musyarakah sukuk* vs. other *sukuk*						
Student test	−2.696***	0.591	2.225**	0.862	−0.811	1.612*
Wilcoxon test	−2.241**	−0.595	0.713	−0.514	−0.735	1.584*

Notes: The sample includes *Murabahah sukuk*, *Ijarah sukuk* and *Musyarakah sukuk* as well as conventional debt issuers in Malaysia from 2000 to 2017. The mean, median and number of observations (*N*) relate to the pecking order variables (*Asymmetry*, *KZindex* and *Maturity*) and market valuation variables (*MarketBook*, *CAR* (−60, −2) and *CAR*(+2, +60)).
1. ***, ** and * indicate significance at the 1%, 5% and 10% levels of confidence, respectively.
2. The definitions of the variables are presented in Table 2.
Source: Thomson One.

Table 6. Descriptive Statistics and Attributes of Sample Firms: Issuers' Pecking Order Variables and Deals Characteristics Variables

	Zscore	ln*TotalAsset*	ln*FundSize*
Murabahah sukuk			
Mean	1.579	7.150	3.698
Median	1.266	7.118	4.025
N	78	78	78
Ijarah sukuk			
Mean	1.747	7.756	4.498
Median	1.441	8.841	4.247
N	19	19	19
Musyarakah sukuk			
Mean	1.748	7.513	4.273
Median	1.634	7.373	4.360
N	34	34	34
Conventional Debt			
Mean	1.658	7.189	4.281
Median	1.278	7.259	4.261
N	123	123	123
Total			
Mean	1.629	7.364	4.121
Median	1.482	7.284	4.146
N	267	267	267
Difference *Murabahah sukuk* vs. other *sukuk*			
Student test	−0.980	−0.359	−1.216*
Wilcoxon test	−1.894*	−1.511	−1.745*
Difference *Ijarah sukuk* vs. other *sukuk*			
Student test	0.743	0.841	1.536*
Wilcoxon test	0.877	1.099	0.446
Difference *Musyarakah sukuk* vs other *sukuk*			
Student test	0.910	−1.199	0.557
Wilcoxon test	1.112	−0.210	1.557

Notes: The sample includes *Murabahah sukuk, Ijarah sukuk, and Musyarakah sukuk* as well as conventional debt issuers in Malaysia from 2000 to 2017. The mean, median, and number of observations (N) relative to variables of issuers and deal characteristics (*Zscore*, ln*TotalAsset* and ln*FundSize*).
1. ***, ** and * indicate significance at the 1%, 5% and 10% levels of confidence, respectively.
2. The definitions of the variables are presented in Table 2.
Source: Thomson One.

relationship between *sukuk* and the variables pertaining to firm i's stock market valuation, the parameter *MarketBook* is significantly positive for empirical equation (2) in Table 7. The parameter of $CAR(-60, -2)$ is also significantly positive for equation (4) and (5) in Table 7. These results imply that the probability of choosing *Ijarah sukuk* is high when a firm is highly valued in the market and has a high growth opportunity as the parameters of

Table 7. Multinomial Probit Regression Results for Determinants of Choice of *sukuk* Type

Independent Variables	(1) SukukType: Murabahah sukuk (=1) vs. Debt (=0)	(2) SukukType: Ijarah sukuk (=2) vs. Debt (=0)	(3) SukukType: Musyarakah sukuk (=3) vs. Debt (=0)	(4) SukukType: Murabahah sukuk (=1) vs. Debt (=0)	(5) SukukType: Ijarah sukuk (=2) vs. Debt (=0)	(6) SukukType: Musyarakah sukuk (=3) vs. Debt (=0)
Specification	Multinominal Probit Model			Multinominal Probit Model		
Asymmetry	0.018	0.415	−0.588**	0.010	0.310	−0.310*
	(0.130)	(1.190)	(−2.240)	(0.070)	(1.120)	(−1.800)
KZindex	0.074	0.063	−0.059	−0.024	−0.461*	0.016
	(0.630)	(0.710)	(−0.470)	(−0.360)	(−1.840)	(0.170)
Maturity	0.070	0.793**	0.195**	0.020	0.450***	0.298**
	(0.940)	(2.090)	(2.150)	(0.940)	(3.100)	(2.110)
Market Book	1.110	3.944***	−1.414			
	(1.590)	(3.600)	(−0.920)			
CAR (−60,−2)				3.305*	4.171*	−0.631
				(1.780)	(1.860)	(−0.300)
Zscore (−1)	−0.747	−1.086***	0.315	−0.435	−0.364	−0.157
	(−1.450)	(−2.950)	(0.390)	(−0.640)	(−0.650)	(−0.260)
lnTotalAsset (−1)	−0.202	−0.496**	−0.031	−0.323	−0.694	−0.241
	(−1.360)	(−2.100)	(−0.100)	(−0.540)	(−1.510)	(−0.950)
lnFundSize	−0.150*	0.011	0.841	−0.695*	−0.097	0.307
	(−1.900)	(0.170)	(0.400)	(−1.910)	(−0.190)	(0.790)

Table 7. (Continued)

	(1)	(2)	(3)	(4)	(5)	(6)
Intercept	−1.212	−9.105***	−3.420	−0.044	−4.905**	−8.180
	(−0.880)	(−3.560)	(−1.400)	(−0.010)	(−2.110)	(−1.140)
Industrial Dummy	yes	yes	yes	yes	yes	yes
Time Trend	yes	yes	yes	yes	yes	yes
Time Trend Squared	yes	yes	yes	yes	yes	yes
Observations			248			248
Wald chi2			69.62**			71.46**
Log Likelihood			−133.4			−132.7

Notes: This table reports the results of the multinomial probit estimation for Model (5). The base dataset includes all the Malaysian sukuk and conventional debt issuers from 2000 to 2017. The dependent variables of equations (1), (2), and (3) are Murabahah sukuk or Debt, Ijarah sukuk or Debt, and Musyarakah sukuk or Debt. The base outcome dependent variable of equations (1)–(3) is Debt. The dependent variables of equations (4)–(6) are Murabahah sukuk or Debt, Ijarah sukuk or Debt, and Musyarakah sukuk or Debt, respectively. The base outcome dependent variable of equations (4)–(6) is Debt. We exclude sukuk issuer samples that do not have descriptions of sukuk type in the Thomson One database. The empirical results of other sukuk (Istisna, Mudharabah, and Al Wakala Bill Istithmar) vs. Debt are omitted. ***, **, and * indicate significance at the 1%, 5%, and 10% levels of confidence, respectively.

Ijarah sukuk are significantly positive both for Equations (2) and (5). Meanwhile, the parameters of *MarketBook* and $CAR(-60, -2)$ are insignificant for Equations (1), (3) and (6). These results also imply that a firm is unlikely to issue *Murabahah sukuk* and *Musyarakah sukuk* even when the pre-issuance stock price is high.

The parameter *Zscore* is significantly negative for Equation (2). This suggests that the higher the creditworthiness of firm i, the lower the probability of choosing *Ijarah sukuk*. Table 7 also shows that the parameters of ln *FundingSize* are significantly negative for Equations (1) and (4) but insignificant for Equations (2), (3), (5) and (6). These findings imply that a firm that demands a small-sized external fund is unlikely to issue *Ijarah sukuk* and *Musyarakah sukuk* and will issue *Murabahah sukuk* instead.

5.2. Binary probit model results

Table 8 shows the empirical results of the determinants of the choice of *sukuk* type. Equations (1)–(6) are estimated by a binary probit model with only *the sukuk* issuer sample. We exclude conventional straight debt security issuer data from the dataset and employ only *sukuk* issuer data for these estimations. For Equations (1) and (4), the dependent variable *Murabahah sukuk* equals 1 when firm i chooses *Murabahah sukuk*, and 0 otherwise. For Equations (2) and (5), the dependent variable *Ijarah sukuk* equals 1 when firm i chooses *Ijarah sukuk*, and 0 otherwise. For Equations (3) and (6), the dependent variable *Musyarakah sukuk* equals 1 when firm i chooses *Musyarakah sukuk*, and 0 otherwise.

Table 8 shows that the parameters of *Asymmetry* are significantly positive for Equations (1), (2), (4) and (5). The parameters of *Asymmetry* are significantly negative for Equations (3) and (6). These imply that a firm under high information asymmetry is most likely to issue *Murabahah sukuk* or *Ijarah sukuk*. These also imply that a firm under low information asymmetry is most likely to issue *Musyarakah sukuk*. Table 8 shows that the parameter of *Maturity* is significantly negative for Equations (1) and (4), while being significantly positive for Equations (2) and (5). These imply that maturity length of *Murabahah sukuk* is short, but *Ijarah sukuk* is significantly long. The parameter of MarketBook is significantly positive for Equation (2). The parameter of $CAR(-60, -2)$ is significantly positive for Equation (5). The parameters of ln*FundingSize* are significantly negative for Equations (1) and (4), while they are significantly positive for Equations (2), (3), (5) and (6).

5.3. Treatment effects model results

Table 9 shows the empirical results of the relationship between the choice of *sukuk* type and the post-issuance excess return of the issuer. Equations (1)–(6) are estimated by the treatment effects model. These two models are simultaneously estimated. For Equation (1), the dependent variable *Murabahah sukuk* equals 1 when firm i chooses *Murabahah sukuk*, and 0 otherwise. For Equation (3), the dependent variable *Ijarah sukuk* equals 1 when firm i chooses *Ijarah sukuk*, and 0 otherwise. For Equation (5), the dependent variable *Musyarakah sukuk* equals 1 when firm i chooses *Musyarakah sukuk*, and 0 otherwise. For

Table 8. Results of the Binary Probit Regression for Determinants of Choice of sukuk Type

Independent Variables	(1) Murabahah sukuk (=1) vs. other sukuk (=0) Binary Probit Model	(2) Ijara sukuk (=1) vs. other sukuk (=0) Binary Probit Model	(3) Musyarakah sukuk (=1) vs. other sukuk (=0) Binary Probit Model	(4) Murabahah sukuk (=1) vs. other sukuk (=0) Binary Probit Model	(5) Ijara sukuk (=1) vs. other sukuk (=0) Binary Probit Model	(6) Musyarakah sukuk (=1) vs. other sukuk (=0) Binary Probit Model
Specification						
Asymmetry	0.403**	0.731*	−0.396*	0.501**	0.714*	−0.394*
	(2.120)	(1.870)	(−1.890)	(2.110)	(1.880)	(−1.860)
KZindex	−0.078	−0.001	0.041	−0.079	−0.002	0.040
	(−0.710)	(−0.040)	(1.140)	(−0.690)	(−0.050)	(1.140)
Maturity	−0.112**	0.244***	0.401	−0.098**	0.234***	0.394
	(−2.210)	(3.350)	(0.950)	(−2.240)	(3.290)	(0.910)
Market Book	−1.486	2.114**	0.391			
	(−1.310)	(2.350)	(0.290)			
CAR (−60,−2)				1.394	2.080**	0.202
				(1.290)	(2.110)	(1.310)
Zscore(−1)	0.621	−0.484	0.088	0.664	−0.498	0.092
	(1.510)	(−1.300)	(0.440)	(1.450)	(−1.210)	(0.420)
lnTotalAsset (−1)	0.673***	−0.636*	−0.491	0.675**	−0.636*	−0.479
	(2.910)	(−1.790)	(−1.360)	(2.180)	(−1.790)	(−1.390)

Table 8. (*Continued*)

	(1)	(2)	(3)	(4)	(5)	(6)
ln*FundingSize*	−0.429***	0.419*	0.641**	−0.587***	0.421*	0.595**
	(−3.310)	(1.710)	(2.310)	(−2.710)	(1.710)	(2.310)
Intercept	4.899**	−5.965**	−4.576	4.792**	−5.825**	−4.130
	(2.450)	(−2.250)	(−1.390)	(2.440)	(−2.290)	(−1.380)
Industrial Dummy	yes	yes	no	yes	yes	no
Time Trend	yes	yes	yes	yes	yes	yes
Time Trend Squared	yes	yes	yes	yes	yes	yes
Observations	119	119	119	119	119	119
LR chi2	16.1**	32.3***	18.7**	14.5**	30.2***	16.9**
pseudo R^2	0.192	0.112	0.158	0.196	0.095	0.159

Notes: This table reports the results of the binary probit for Model (E). In contrast to Table 7, the base dataset excludes conventional straight bond issuers, but includes all the *sukuk* issuers in 2000–2017. The dependent variables of Equations (1) and (4) are *Murabahah sukuk* (= 1) or all the other *sukuk* (= 0), that of Equations (2) and (5) are *Ijarah sukuk* (=1) or all the other *sukuk* (= 0), and that of Equations (3) and (6) are *Musyarakah sukuk* (= 1) or all the other *sukuk* (= 0). All the dependent variable definitions are consistent with those in Table 7.
***, ** and * indicate significance at the 1%, 5% and 10% levels of confidence, respectively.

Table 9. Regression Results for the Relationship Between Post-Issuance Excess Returns and sukuk Issuer Characteristics

Independent Variables	Murabahah sukuk (=1) vs. other sukuk (=0)	CAR (+2,+60)	Ijara sukuk (=1) vs. other sukuk (=0)	CAR (+2,+60)	Musyarakah sukuk (=1) vs. other sukuk (=0)	CAR (+2,+60)
	(1)	(2)	(3)	(4)	(5)	(6)
Murabahah sukuk		0.014				
		(0.840)				
Ijara sukuk				0.089		
				(1.110)		
Musyarakah sukuk						0.056***
						(3.470)
Asymmetry	0.393**		0.699*		−0.399*	
	(2.100)		(1.910)		(−1.910)	
Maturity	−0.101**		0.247***		0.398	
	(−2.190)		(3.320)		(0.240)	
Zscore (−1)	0.558		−0.464		0.084	
	(1.440)		(−1.260)		(0.420)	
lnFundSize	−0.394***		0.397*		0.650**	
	(−2.990)		(1.860)		(2.200)	
lnTotalAsset (−1)	0.707***	0.152***	−0.639*	0.199***	−0.505	0.182***
	(3.140)	(3.560)	(−1.810)	(2.840)	(−1.330)	(4.460)
CAR (−60,−2)		0.011		0.144		0.090**
		(1.310)		(1.200)		(2.410)

Table 9. (Continued)

Independent Variables	Murabahah sukuk (=1) vs. other sukuk (=0)		Ijara sukuk (=1) vs. other sukuk (=0)		Musyarakah sukuk (=1) vs. other sukuk (=0)	
	(1)	CAR (+2,+60) (2)	(3)	CAR (+2,+60) (4)	(5)	CAR (+2,+60) (6)
KZindex		0.026**		0.052**	0.081	
		(2.220)		(2.370)		(1.700)
Intercept	3.926***	2.247	−6.112**	1.546**	−4.474**	1.664***
	(2.950)	(1.540)	(−2.210)	(2.260)	(−2.290)	(3.500)
Industrial Dummy		yes		yes		no
Time Trend		yes		yes		yes
Observations		119		119		119
Wald test of Indep. (rho0 = rho1 = 0): chi2		8.550**		8.390**		10.110**

Notes: This table presents the estimation results for the treatment effects model for Malaysian sukuk issuers from 2000 to 2017. We estimate two equations simultaneously. The dependent variables of Equations (1), (3) and (5) are Murabaha sukuk dummy, Ijara sukuk dummy, or Musyaraka sukuk dummy variable, which equals one when firm i chooses respective sukuk, otherwise zero. The dependent variables of Equations (2), (4), and (6) are the post-issuance market-adjusted stock return CAR(+2, +60).
***, **, and * indicate significance at the 1%, 5%, and 10% levels of confidence, respectively.

Equations (2), (4) and (6), the dependent variables are $CAR(+2, +60)$. For these empirical analyzes, we employ only *the sukuk* issuer sample. *Sukuk* deal data without descriptions of their type are also excluded. Table 9 shows that the parameter of *KZindex* is significantly positive for Equations (2) and (4). These imply that a firm under high information asymmetry, and therefore financial constraint, is likely to choose *Murabahah sukuk* or *Ijara sukuk* issuance, and the choice consequently increases the post-issuance return. Table 9 also shows that the $CAR(-60, -2)$ parameter is significantly positive for Equation (6). This implies that firms that issue *Musyarakah sukuk* under high market valuation in the pre-issuance period are more likely to increase the market valuation in the post-issuance period.

6. Discussion

A stream of literature concerning the pecking order hypothesis asserts that the different ways of raising capital are associated with different levels of agency costs. Our empirical evidence suggests that the *Murabahah sukuk*, *Ijarah sukuk*, or *Musyarakah sukuk* issuance is also chosen in descending order of the degree of information asymmetry of the issuer.

Specifically, Table 5 points out that the length of *Murabahah sukuk* maturity is significantly shorter than that of the other two *sukuk*s. Tables 8 and 9 also suggest that the degree of issuer information asymmetry is positively related to the issuance of *Murabahah sukuk*. A series of studies examining the relationship between debt maturity period and the agency costs of issuers, such as Stohs (and Mauer) and Ozkan (2002), commonly assert that these two are negatively related. Therefore, we interpret our empirical results to mean that the cost-plus-sales-based *Murabahah sukuk*, is chosen when the issuer has a high degree of information asymmetry and the debt maturity period is forced to be short-term. Therefore, our empirical evidence supports Hypothesis 1, and we conclude that cost-sales-based *Murabahah sukuk* is preferred when a highly information asymmetric firm increases funding demands and is allowed to issue it as short-term debt. Accordingly, this type of issuance is the most frequent as a result of meeting the total funding demand (Table 5). Table 9 also suggests that a firm under a high degree of financial constraint increases market valuation when the firm issues *Murabahah sukuk*. This result implies that *Murabahah sukuk* issuance mitigates the agency problem of the firm. Ashraf *et al.* (2020) conclude that high government ownership ratio promotes *Murabahah sukuk* issuance. Our empirical results are also consistent with this literature. To our best knowledge, few literature has empirically shown the relationship between the degree of information asymmetry of the issuer and *Murabahahsukuk* maturity period. We have first demonstrated the empirical evidence in this study.

Next, Table 7 suggests that the debt maturity periods of *Ijarah sukuk* and *Musyarakah sukuk* are significantly longer than those issued in 2000–2017. Table 7 also presents empirical evidence indicating that the *Ijarah sukuk* issuance probability and the market valuation of the firm are positively related. These positive relationships are confirmed for the independent variables *MarketBook* and $CAR(-60, -2)$ in Table 7. In addition, Table 8 indicates that the degree of issuer information asymmetry and the *Ijarah sukuk* issuance probability are positively related. Table 9 also shows that a firm under a high degree of financial constraint increases the post-issuance excess return once the firm issues *Ijarah sukuk*. This empirical evidence supports Hypothesis 2(a) and 2(b). Dong *et al.* (2011) prove empirically that the intersection of issuers' degree of financial constraint and market-to-book ratio positively influences conventional debt issuance. Consistent with the evidence of Dong *et al.* (2011), the third-party collateral of *Ijarah sukuk* mitigates the financial constraint, as Almeida and Campello (2010) and Bacha and Mirakhor (2018) assert that the issuance contributes to an increase in the post-issuance excess return of the issuer. Consequently, we conclude that an *Ijarah sukuk* issuer is a highly information asymmetric firm, but the tangible asset collateral mitigates the high financial constraint and helps achieve future high performance. A major difference between *Murabahah sukuk* and *Ijarah sukuk* issuances are funding size and issuance frequency. The funding size of *Ijarah sukuk* issuance is significantly larger than that of *Murabahah sukuk* (Table 6), and *Ijarah sukuk* issuance is less frequent than that of *Murabahah sukuk* (Table 3).

Last, our empirical results show that a *sukuk* issuer's information asymmetry is also a key factor in choosing *Musyarakah sukuk*. The results in Tables 7 and 8 indicate that *Musyarakah sukuk* are issued only when the issuer is under a low degree of information asymmetry. As Abedifar *et al.* (2015) and Khan *et al.* (2021) point out, this feature of *the Musyarakah sukuk* issuance closely resembles that of equity issuance, as both securities have profit-and-loss sharing structures and investors' returns, therefore, vary depending upon the future issuers' project performance. In other words, larger agency costs are imposed on external investors than in other types of *sukuk* issuance. Therefore, the required information asymmetry should be lower than that of conventional debt or lease-based *Ijarah sukuk* or cost-plus-sales-based *Murabahah sukuk*. Our empirical evidence supports Hypothesis 3. A series of existing literature in this field has empirically shown the significant relationship between a firm information asymmetry and the probability of *sukuk* issuance. Especially, Klein and Weill (2016) and Halim *et al.* (2017) have empirically shown the differences between *sukuk* issuance and the conventional debt issuance in this regard. Our conclusions are basically consistent with these literature conclusions. Meanwhile, our study has first shown that the choice of *Murabaha*, *Ijarah* and *Musyarakah sukuk* issuance is determined by the degree of firm information asymmetry.

7. Concluding Remarks

This paper provides empirical evidence that the choice of *sukuk* type within the *sukuk* market follows a financial hierarchy dependent upon the agency costs of each *sukuk* issuance imposed on external investors. We conclude that *Murabahah sukuk* is chosen preferentially when the firm decides to issue *sukuk*, no matter how high the issuer's information asymmetry is *Ijarah sukuk* is chosen by the highly information asymmetric firm as well, but it is chosen only when the firm has qualified tangible collateral assets. Here, *Ijarah sukuk* structurally covers agency costs. The choice of *Musyarakah sukuk* is preferred by the low degree of information asymmetric firms, as future profit-and-loss is shared by both issuers and investors. This study therefore concludes that the type of *sukuk* issuance choice also follows a financial hierarchy in ascending (descending) order of the agency costs (the degree of information asymmetry) of each funding methodology required when a specific *sukuk* is chosen.

The three major *sukuk* types, *Murabahah*, *Ijarah* and *Musyarakah sukuk* account for more than 90% of the total *sukuk* issuance deals in 2000–2017. Although this study provides significant insight into the determinants affecting the choice of these *sukuk* types, it unavoidably excludes other *sukuk* type issuance determinants. Our data do not allow us to identify the determinants of other types of *sukuk*, namely, *Istisna*, *Mudharabah* and *Al Wakala Bill Istithmar*, as the number of samples in such cases is extremely small. Therefore, we could not verify whether a *sukuk* issuer might prefer one of these types of *sukuk* over the three types of *sukuk* investigated primarily in this study. Future research can explore the factors affecting the choice of these types of *sukuk* in the *sukuk* primary market, as it is bound to expand in the future.

Acknowledgments

The author thanks various seminar participants for their helpful comments and suggestions. This study has been financially supported by JSPS Kakenhi, Grant No. JP18K01701.

References

Abedifar, P, SM Ebrahim, P Molyneux and A Tarazi (2015). Islamic banking and finance: Recent empirical literature and directions for future research. *Journal of Economic Surveys*, 29(4), 637–670.

Ahmed, H, M Kabir Hassan and B Rayfield (2018). When and why firms issue *Sukuk? Managerial Finance*, 44(6), 774–786.

Almeida, H and M Campello (2010). Financing frictions and the substitution between internal and external funds. *Journal of Financial and Quantitative Analysis*, 45, 589–622.

Amihud, Y (2002). Illiquidity and stock returns: Cross-section and time-series effects. *Journal of Financial Markets*, 5, 31–56.

Amihud, Y, H Mendelson and B Lauterbach (1997). Market microstructure and securities values: Evidence from the Tel Aviv stock exchange. *Journal of Financial Economics*, 45(3), 365–390.

Ashraf, D, MS Rizwan and S Azmat (2020). Not one but three decisions in *Sukuk* issuance: Understanding the role of ownership and governance. *Pacific-Basin Finance Journal*, forthcoming.

Azmat, S, M Skully and K Brown (2014). Issuer's choice of Islamic bond type. *Pacific-Basin Finance Journal*, 28, 122–135.

Bacha, OI and A Mirakhor (2018). Funding development infrastructure without leverage: A risk-sharing alternative using innovative Sukuk structure. *The World Economy*, 41, 752–762.

Baker, M, JC Stein and J Wurgler (2003). When does the market matter? Stock prices and the investment of equity-dependent firms. *The Quarterly Journal of Economics*, 118, 969–1005.

Bester, H (1985). Screening vs. rationing in credit markets with imperfect information. *American Economic Review*, 75(4), 850–855.

Bester, H (1987). The role of collateral in credit markets with imperfect information. *European Economic Review*, 31(4), 887–899.

Besanko, D and AV Thakor (1987a). Collateral and rationing: Sorting equilibria in monopolistic and competitive credit markets. *International Economic Review*, 28(3), 671–689.

Besanko, D and AV Thakor (1987b). Competitive equilibrium in the credit market under asymmetric information. *Journal of Economic Theory*, 42(1), 167–182.

Bharath, ST, P Pasquariello and G Wu (2009). Does asymmetric information drive capital structure decisions? *The Review of Financial Studies*, 22(9), 3212–3243.

Boot, A, AV Thakor and GF Udell (1991). Secured lending and default risk: Equilibrium analysis, policy implications and empirical results. *Economic Journal*, 101, 458–472.

Brown, SJ and JB Warner (1985). Using daily stock returns: The case of event studies. *Journal of Financial Economics*, 14, 3–31.

Chan, Y-S and AV Thakor (1987). Collateral and competitive equilibria with moral hazard and private information. *Journal of Finance*, 42(2), 345–363.

Cooley, TF, R Marimon and V Quadrini (2004). Aggregate consequences of limited contract enforceability. *Journal of Political Economy*, 112, 817–847.

Cooper, KS, JC Groth and WE Avera (1985). Liquidity, exchange listing, and common stock performance. *Journal of Economics and Business*, 37(1), 19–33.

Donaldson, G (1961). *Corporate Debt Capacity: A Study of Corporate Debt Policy and the Determination of Corporate Debt Capacity*. Boston, MA: Harvard Business School, Division of Research, Harvard University.

Dong, M, I Loncarski, J Horst and C Veld (2011). What drives security issuance decisions: Market timing, pecking order, or both? *Financial Management*, 41(3), 637–663.

George, TJ, G Kaul and M Nimalendran (1991). Estimation of the bid-ask spread and its components: A new approach. *Review of Financial Studies*, 4(4), 623–656.

Godlewski, CJ, R Turk-Ariss and L Weill (2013). Sukuk vs. conventional bonds: A stock market perspective. *Journal of Comparative Economics*, 41, 745–761.

Godlewski, CJ, R Turk-Ariss and L Weill (2016). Do the type of *sukuk* and choice of *Shari'a* scholar matter? *Journal of Economic Behavior and Organization*, 132, 63–76.

Gomes, A and G Phillips (2012). Why do public firms issue private and public securities? *Journal of Financial Intermediation*, 21(4), 549–722.

Halim, ZA, J How and P Verhoeven (2017). Agency costs and corporate *Sukuk* issuance. *Pacific-Basin Finance Journal*, 42, 83–95.

Hassan, MK, P Andrea, A Dreassi and A Sclip (2018). The determinants of co-movement dynamics between *Sukuk* and conventional bonds. *The Quarterly Review of Economics and Finance*, 68, 73–84.

Hisham, MH, M Masih and OI Bacha (2015). Why do issuers issue *sukuk* or conventioal bond? Evidence from Malaysian listed firms using partial adjustment models. *Pacific-Basin Finance Journal*, 34, 233–252.

Kaplan, SN and L Zingales (1997). Do investment-cash flow sensitivities provide useful measures of financing constraints? *Quarterly Journal of Economics*, 112(1), 169–215.

Khan, A, SAR Rizvi, M Ali and O Haroon (2021). A survey of Islamic finance research — Influences and influencers. *Pacific-Basin Finance Journal*, forthcoming.

Klein, P-O and L Weill (2016). Why do companies issue *Sukuk*? *Review of Financial Economics*, 31, 26–33.

Lamont, O, C Polk and J Saa-Requejo (2001). Financial constraints and stock returns. *The Review of Financial Studies*, 14(2), 529–554.

Llorente, G, G Saar and J Want (2002). Dynamic volume-return relation of individual stocks. *Review of Financial Studies*, 15(4), 1005–1047.

Myers, SC (1984). The capital structure puzzle. *Journal of Finance*, 39(3), 575–592.

Naifar, N, S Hammoudeh and MS Al dohaiman (2016). Dependence structure between *Sukuk* and stock market conditions: An empirical analysis with Archimedean Copulas. *Journal of International Financial Markets, Institutions and Money*, 44, 148–165.

Ozkan, A (2002). The determinants of corporate debt maturity: Evidence from UK firms. *Applied Financial Economics*, 12, 19–24.

Pan, W-F, X Wang and S Yang (2019). Debt maturity, leverage and political uncertainty. *North-American Journal of Economics and Finance*, 50, 100981.

Pastor, L and RF Stambaugh (2003). Liquidity risk and expected stock returns. *Journal of Political Economy*, 111(3), 642–685.

Roll, R (1984). A simple implicit measure of the effective bid-ask spread in an efficient market. *Journal of Finance*, 39(4), 1127–1139.

Shyam-Sunder, L and SC Myers (1999). Testing static tradeoff against pecking order models of capital structure. *Journal of Financial Economics*, 51, 219–244.

Chapter 17

The Economic Cost of Revolution: The Iranian Case. A Synthetic Control Analysis[#]

Serhat Hasancebi

Ph. D. student. Departamento de Fundamentos del Análisis Económico II
University of the Basque Country, UPV/EHU
Lehendakari Aguirre 83, 48015 Bilbao, Spain
shasancebi002@ikasle.ehu.eus

In 1978, a revolution in Iran succeeded in toppling Shah Mohammad Reza Pahlavi. After the Shah was forced to leave the country, Ayatollah Ruhollah Khomeini, one of the leaders of the revolution, returned from his exile in France to become the Supreme Leader of Iran. In this paper, we investigate the economic cost of the revolution using the synthetic control method. According to our estimates, we conclude that after the emergence of the revolution, the annual real gross domestic product (GDP) per capita in Iran declined by about 20.15% on average relative to its synthetic counterpart without the revolution in the period 1978–1980. If Iran had not faced such a revolution, the accumulated per capita GDP would have been $6,479 higher, which amounts to an average annual loss of about $2,159 over that period.

Keywords: Comparative case study; synthetic control method; Islamic revolution; Iran.

1. Introduction

The Islamic Revolution in Iran began on January 1978, overthrowing the Shah's regime. On 1 February 1979, Ayatollah Ruhollah Khomeini returned to Tehran from exile in Paris to be welcomed by several million Iranians. This occurred after series of popular protests had pushed the Shah, Mohammad Reza Pahlavi, to abandon the country (Moin, 1999). On 1 April 1979, following a national referendum (98.2% voted in favor), Iran was declared an "Islamic Republic". Iran's "Islamic Revolution" has had profound implications, domestically, across the Middle East and for wider Islamic–western relations. Khomeini's Islamic regime focused on a jihadhi approach to reorganize and reshape Iran's domestic and foreign policy priorities (Demirci, 2013).

Persia was ruled as a monarchy under a Shah starting in the 16th Century. The Qajar dynasty stayed in power until 1925 when the Shah was forced out in a military coup led by a Cossack officer, Reza Khan. He adopted the title Reza Shah Pahlavi, and in 1935 the country's name was changed to Iran (Arjomand, 1986). Iran's economy under the Shah

---

[#]This Chapter first appeared in the *Singapore Economic Review*, Vol. 67, No. 1, doi: 10.1142/S0217590820420072. © 2022 World Scientific Publishing.

regime exhibited steady growth. Industrialization, infrastructure investment, government aid for the private sector helped to set up a free market system which yielded sustainable growth for Iran's economy (Amuzegar, 1992). In 1963, Mohammad Reza Pahlavi promoted a so-called White Revolution which consisted of land reform, the sale of state factories to private entrepreneurs, and an extension of the vote to women. Thus, as reported by Demirci (2013), the White Revolution aimed to modernize society in the same mold as western countries, although the Shah administration's affairs with Unites States and European States were met with criticism from Khomeini's supporters.

With time, insufficient land reforms led the people to move to the cities from villages, and caused high unemployment rates in big cities. Increasing unemployment and widening inequality between the classes caused the people to start protests against the Shah's regime. Iran's high oil revenues were being transferred to the army budget in order to create a large and powerful army (Amuzegar, 1992). Meanwhile, public discontent with the regime's policies grew, and provoked a revolutionary movement that soon overthrew the monarchy, and resulted in the declaration of an Islamic Republic. The Islamic Revolution was the consequence of demands for change coming from different social groups within Iranian society (Esfahani and Pesaran, 2008).

By 1978, Iran had become the second largest OPEC producer and exporter of crude oil, and the fourth-largest producer in the world, churning out 5,242 billion barrels/day. However, due to the revolution, Iran endured a significant loss of around 39.56% in crude oil production, and reduced production to 3,168 billion barrels/day in 1979.[1] Economic growth and political stability are interconnected and, in particular, the uncertainty associated with an unstable political environment may have reduced investment and economic development (Alesina *et al.*, 1996). Therefore, analyzing the impact of the revolution on Iran's economy is crucial to understanding the role that political instability plays in economic growth.

There have been several papers that examine the economic consequences of the Iranian Revolution. Amuzegar (1992) investigates the Iranian economy before and after the revolution, and discusses socio-economic characteristics of the Shah regime, as well as examining the economic development of Iran. Amuzegar, *op. cit.*, highlights that after the revolution, the Iranian economy experienced a deep recession, and absolute poverty increased by 43% during the period from 1979 to 1985. Our paper, however, only studies the period 1978–1980. The reason for keeping the post-treatment period only until 1980 was due to the emergence of another treatment; otherwise, the results would have been biased as the effect of the Iran-Iraq war (1981–1988) would have coincided with the influence of the Iranian Revolution. Arjomand (1986) investigates the theoretical significance of the Islamic Revolution in Iran by focusing on the political dynamics of the radical change in Iran's societal structure of domination, along with the moral dynamics of re-integration and collective action. Maloney (2015) examines the complex process relating to the adoption of economic policies that has taken place since 1979. However, the studies carried out so far have not gone beyond in-depth analyses of the revolution, but have followed mainly descriptive approaches.

---

[1] Statistics have been obtained from OPEC dataset for oil production, *https://www.opec.org*

In this paper, we investigate the economic costs of the Islamic Revolution by using the synthetic control method (SCM) first introduced in Abadie and Gardeazabal (2003) as the analytical tool. The SCM has been implemented for comparative cases in order to measure the consequences of economic shocks, events or policy interventions. Abadie and Gardeazabal (2003) analyze the economic cost of terrorism in the Basque Country in terms of loss of gross domestic product (GDP). Horiuchi and Mayerson (2015) examine the influence of the 2000 Palestinian Intifada upon Israel's economy. Pinotti (2015) estimates the economic cost of organized crime in Southern Italy. Grier and Maynard (2016) study the impact of Hugo Chavez's regime on the Venezuelan economy. Gardeazabal and Vega-Bayo (2017) study the effect of the political and economic integration of Hong Kong with China. Bilgel and Karahasan (2017) analyze the cost of separatist conflict in Turkey in the case of terrorism. Echevarría and García-Enríquez (2019a) examine the economic consequences of the Libyan spring. Echevarría and García-Enríquez (2019b) analyze the economic cost of the Egyptian episode of the Arab Spring.

The main contribution of this paper is that, as far as we know, it represents the first study in which the SCM is used to evaluate the impact of the revolution on the Iranian economy. In addition, and as a by-product, we compare the performance of alternative computational procedures Matlab©, R, Stata©, and select the one providing the most accurate results. The evidence found in this study implies that after the Islamic Revolution the annual per capita GDP in Iran declined by about 20.15% on average, and by 47.70% in cumulative terms relative to its synthetic counterpart without the revolution in the period 1978–1980. This means that the cumulative per capita GDP loss in Iran was about 6,479 US dollars after the revolution, which amounts to an average annual loss of about $2,159 in the latter period.

The structure of the paper is as follows. Section 2 describes the SCM. Data and variables are described in Section 3. Section 4 shows the main results. Section 5 is devoted to the discussion of robustness checks on the results. Section 6 concludes. Two formal appendices are included at the end of the paper: Appendix A compares different computational methods to implement the SCM, and Appendix B describes technical details corresponding to Section 5.

2. Synthetic Control Method

Case studies usually purpose to observe the effect of a treatment in order to examine whether the effect is large or small according to the outcome of interest. Thus, case studies are feasible when some units are under the effect and others are not.

The SCM illustrates a hypothetical counterfactual unit by taking the weighted average of pre-intervention outcomes from selected donor units. The donor units that are combined to form the synthetic control are selected from a pool of potential candidates. Predictor variables that affect the outcome, and the outcome variable itself before the intervention is enacted, determine the selection of donor units and weights.

The following describes the SCM in comparative case studies.[2] Suppose that we observe $J + 1$ units. Without loss of generality, suppose also that only the first unit is exposed

---

[2] This heavily draws on Abadie *et al.* (2010, 2015), and Echevarría and García-Enríquez (2019a, 2019b).

to the intervention of interest, so that we have J remaining units as potential controls. Borrowing from the statistical matching literature, we refer to the set of potential controls as the "donor pool".

Let Y_{it}^0 be the outcome that would be observed for the unit i at time t in the absence of the intervention, for units $i = 1,\ldots,J+1$, and time periods $t = 1,\ldots,T$. Let T_0 be the number of the pre-intervention periods, with $t = 1,\ldots,T_0$. Let Y_{it}^1 be the outcome that would be observed for unit i at time t if unit i were exposed to the intervention periods $T_0 + 1$ to T. We assume that the intervention has no effect on the outcome before implementation period so, for $t = 1,\ldots,T_0$ and all $i = 1,\ldots,J+1$, we have that $Y_{it}^1 = Y_{it}^0$. In practice, interventions may have an impact prior to their implementation (e.g., via anticipation effects). In these cases, T_0 could be interpreted as the first period in which the outcome may possibly react to the intervention. Implicit in our notation is the usual assumption of no interference between units. That is, we assume that outcomes of the untreated units are not affected by the intervention implemented in the treated unit.

The treatment effect for the treated unit in period t is given by

$$\alpha_{1t} \equiv Y_{1t}^1 - Y_{1t}^0, \tag{1}$$

for $t = T_0 + 1, T_0 + 2,\ldots,T$ and where Y_{1t}^1 denotes the (observed) potential outcome under treatment, and Y_{1t}^0 denotes the (unobserved) potential outcome under the hypothesis of no treatment. The way to circumvent this difficulty was first suggested in Abadie and Gardeazabal (2003), which consisted of building up a synthetic treated unit: a weighted average conveniently obtained among the untreated units in such a manner that it mimics the pre-treatment periods as closely as possible. The payoff is an estimate of Y_{1t}^0 which allows one to obtain an estimate for α_{1t}.

Optimal weights are found by solving the following problem:

$$\min_{\{w\}_{j=2}^{J+1}} (\mathbf{X}_1 - \mathbf{X}_1^s)'\mathbf{V}(\mathbf{X}_1 - \mathbf{X}_1^s), \tag{2}$$

where $\mathbf{X}_1 - \mathbf{X}_1^s$ is the difference between the P-dimension pre-treatment characteristic vector of the treated unit, $\mathbf{X}_1$ denoting the vector of predictors of the outcome variable for the treated unit and $\mathbf{X}_1^s \equiv \sum_{j=2}^{J+1} \mathbf{X}_j w_j$ standing for the vector of predictors for the synthetic control. Optimal weights, $\{\mathbf{w}_j\}_{j=2}^{J+1}$, are restricted to being non-negative, and to add up to one. $\mathbf{V}$ is a diagonal, positive semidefinite matrix whose pth element, $V_p \geq 0$, represents a weight that reflects the relative importance assigned to the pth variable in vector $\mathbf{X}$ as a predictor of the outcome variable, $\mathbf{Y}$, and where $\sum_{p=1}^{P} V_p = 1$. The vector of optimal weights, $\mathbf{w} = \{w_2, w_3,\ldots,w_{J+1}\}$, will depend, of course, on the values of $\mathbf{V}$. This issue is thoroughly discussed in Appendix A.[3]

---

[3] See Appendix A for a technical discussion regarding the different computational procedures implemented in this paper to obtain the optimal weights, $\{w_j\}_{j=2}^{J+1}$, in Equation (2).

Once optimal weights, w_j^*, have been obtained, the effect of the intervention on the treated unit for period t is estimated as

$$\hat{\alpha}_{1t} \equiv Y_{1t}^1 - \sum_{j=2}^{J+1} w_j^* Y_{jt}^0, \quad (3)$$

for $t = T_0 + 1, T_0 + 2, \ldots, T$ and where (by construction and if the donor pool has been correctly specified) no Y_{jt}^0 is affected by the treatment or intervention experienced by unit 1.

A measure of the goodness of fit of the synthetic unit to the observed treated unit, and the one that we follow in this paper as a criterion to rank the alternative computational methods implemented, is the pre-treatment root mean squared prediction error (Pre–RMSPE), which is defined as

$$\text{Pre-RMSPE} \equiv \left(\frac{1}{T_0} \sum_{t=1}^{T_0} \left(Y_{1t} - \sum_{j=2}^{J+1} w_j^* Y_{jt} \right)^2 \right)^{1/2}. \quad (4)$$

Conversely, the post-treatment root mean squared prediction error (Post–RMSPE), defined as

$$\text{Post-RMSPE} \equiv \left(\frac{1}{T - T_0} \sum_{t=T_0+1}^{T} \left(Y_{1t} - \sum_{j=2}^{J+1} w_j^* Y_{jt} \right)^2 \right)^{1/2}, \quad (5)$$

provides us with an approximate measure of the effect (in absolute terms) of the treatment effect, so that the ratio of the latter to the former is interpreted as a natural assessment of the quantitative effect of the treatment.

3. Data and Variables

We use annual country-level data which results in a panel dataset consisting of 60 countries and 21 yearly observations for each country for the period 1960–1980. Due to the lack of data for periods prior to 1960, our sample starts in that year. The Islamic Revolution took place in 1978 which gives a 19-year pre-intervention period. As mentioned in the introduction, if there had been no other overlapping treatment such as the Iran-Iraq war (1981–1988), longer term analysis would have been feasible. It is not meaningful to mix the two treatments in the sample period, so that we finally set 1980 as the last post-treatment year.

First, as a tentative starting point, we used the Maddison Project Database as our data source which contains per capita GDP for 161 countries. As a next step, we excluded the countries which faced any armed conflict or civilian war during our sample period. If the potential control unit in the donor pool had experienced a sizeable strike, revolution, civilian war or any armed conflict during the same period, it would not have been possible to isolate the effect of the Islamic Revolution in the variable of interest. Nevertheless, structural breaks such as nationwide economic crises that affect both the treated country and the donor pool countries do not invalidate the synthetic control estimates. In addition, we also removed some countries from the sample due to the lack of data for the outcome variable and/or for the predictors which we discuss below.[4]

The donor pool finally consists of 59 control countries after omitting those that are significantly and sustainably affected by some sort of armed conflict. Remaining countries in the donor pool are: Albania, Angola, Australia, Austria, Bahrain, Belgium, Botswana, Cameroon, Canada, Cape Verde, China, Colombia, Costa Rica, Denmark, Djibouti, Egypt, Finland, France, Gabon, Germany, Hungary, India, Ireland, Israel, Italy, Jamaica, Japan, Jordan, Kenya, Kuwait, Lebanon, Madagascar, Malawi, Malaysia, Mauritius, Mexico, Mongolia, Morocco, Mozambique, Namibia, Netherlands, New Zealand, Norway, Philippines, Puerto Rico, Romania, São Tomé and Principe, Saudi Arabia, Senegal, Singapore, Spain, Sri Lanka, Sweden, Switzerland, Trinidad and Tobago, United Arab Emirates, United Kingdom, United States, and Venezuela.

The outcome variable in our case, Y_{jt}, is the per capita GDP in country j at time t [available at Maddison Project]. The per capita GDP is measured in 1990 international dollars which allows us to make international comparisons. Regarding the predictors, first, we use the average fertility rate (births per woman) for the period 1970–1977, and the average of gross capital formation to GDP ratio for the period 1973–1977. Data have been obtained from the World Bank and the United Nations Statistics Division respectively [World Bank].

Second, we also include the average of final consumption expenditure to GDP ratio for the period 1973–1977, and the average of retail trade to GDP ratio for the period 1972–1977. In addition, we include the average GDP share of exports of goods and services for the period 1972–1977. All the data have been obtained from the United Nations Statistics Division [available at UNSD].

Finally, we added some (but not all) lagged values of per capita GDP corresponding to 1960, 1963, 1965, 1971, 1974, 1976, and 1977. Otherwise, using all the lagged values of per capita GDP would make all other predictors irrelevant, as pointed out by Kaul *et al.* (2018). Initially, we also experimented with a wider set of additional predictors: population density (people per square km of land area), levels of educational attainment, changes in inventories (relative to GDP), population, total factor productivity, household consumption expenditure (relative to GDP), imports of goods and services to GDP ratio, exchange rate, human capital index based on years of schooling, price level of capital stock and, finally, manufacturing as a proportion of GDP. But, in all cases, their inclusion did not reduce the pre-treatment root mean square prediction error in Equation (4) which we have adopted as a measure of goodness of fit.

4. Results

The time paths of per capita GDP for Iran and the average of the countries in the donor pool between 1960 and 1980 are shown in Figure 1. The average per capita GDP among

---

[4] The whole list of the 48 excluded countries and the circumstance leading to exclusion in each case is shown in a table not included in this paper for the sake of space saving, but which can be obtained from the author upon request.

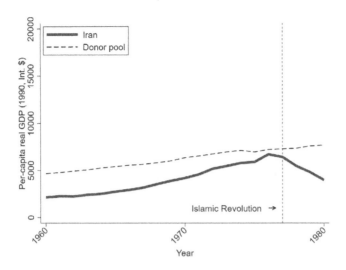

Notes: Time paths for per capita GDP for Iran and the average of the 59 countries in the donor pool.

Figure 1. Trends in Per Capita GDP: Iran and Donors

the donor countries approximately mimics Iran's until the Islamic Revolution. After the revolution, however, the difference between the two paths increases. Nevertheless, we will show that a synthetic control can more accurately resemble the pre-revolution per capita GDP path for the observed Iran than the simple average among control units.

The values of Pre−RMSPE, Post−RMSPE and the ratio of the latter to the former as a natural assessment of the quantitative effect of the treatment were obtained under the alternative computational procedures mentioned Footnote 3 (see Table A.1 in Appendix A). Note that, first, different procedures give rise to different control countries and, second, even to different weights for the same control countries.

To sum up the discussion in Appendix A, we conclude that the MSCMT package in R outperforms the other computational procedures in terms of goodness of fit and also in terms of computational speed (not reported for the sake of space saving). Therefore, all the results obtained in the sequel have been obtained using this package to compute synthetic countries. In particular, the synthetic Iran is obtained as a weighted average of five countries, namely: Botswana, Gabon, Japan, Saudi Arabia, and Singapore. The corresponding weights, w_j^*'s, are 30.19%, 9.81%, 15.12%, 0.40%, and 44.48%, respectively.

The pre-revolution characteristics for predictors and the outcome of interest for Iran, the synthetic Iran and the means for the 59 countries in the donor pool are shown in Table 1. As can be seen, the synthetic control resembles the treated country closely in terms of lagged per capita GDP values, gross capital formation, and retail trade quite remarkably. Regarding final consumption expenditure relative to GDP, exports of goods and services and fertility rate, the differences between Iran and its synthetic counterpart are higher. Despite such discrepancies, it can be concluded that, in general, both the observed Iran and its synthetic counterpart are very similar in terms of outcome predictors during the pre-revolutionary period. That is, the synthetic Iran provides a better fit for the pre-revolution

Table 1. Pre-Revolution Characteristics

Predictors	Iran	Synthetic Iran	Donor Pool	V
y_{1960}	2,156.48	2,176.94	4,693.88	28.49
y_{1963}	2,426.09	2,596.96	5,414.11	28.49
y_{1965}	2,753.15	2,713.95	6,350.74	28.49
y_{1971}	4,576.78	4,579.79	6,757.12	—
y_{1974}	5,777.71	5,854.13	6,971.01	—
y_{1976}	6,691.35	6,463.41	7,131.94	12.53
y_{1977}	6,402.08	6,433.52	6,969.99	—
$Fertility_I$	3.63	5.13	4.3	—
Gcf_{II}	29.65	28.69	28.3	0.25
Fce_{II}	89.48	83.73	76.1	0.44
$Retail_{III}$	9.9	10.03	14.0	1.16
$Export_{III}$	25.8	29.02	31.4	—

Notes: Economic predictors for the pre-revolution period for Iran, the synthetic Iran and donor countries, respectively. Predictors are as follows; y_t: per capita GDP at time t; Fertility: average fertility rate (total births per woman); Gcf: average gross capital formation (% GDP); Fce: average final consumption expenditure (% GDP); Retail: retail trade (% GDP); Export: average exports of goods and services (% GDP). Periods are denoted as follows I: 1970–1977; II: 1973–1977: III: 1972–1977. The last column shows the optimal predictor weights in per cent terms; weights below 0.1% are omitted.

period than the simple weighted average of the countries in the donor pool. As claimed in Botosaru and Ferman (2019), although the use of all covariates provides an advantage when balancing for constructing the synthetic control estimator, an accurate balance on covariates may not be required for the SCM, "as long as we have a good match on outcomes over an extended period of time prior to the treatment". Finally, the last column in Table 1 reports the values of the optimal matrix **V** in Equation (2). As expected, optimal predictors are higher for lagged values of per capita GDP than for the rest of predictors.

The trends in per capita GDP for Iran and its synthetic counterpart over the whole sample period 1960–1980 are displayed in Figure 2. The synthetic per capita GDP trajectory matches the actual GDP trajectory quite well in the pre-revolution period (1960–1977), which is the first sign of the success of the SCM. However, following the Islamic Revolution, the two paths start to diverge, the per capita GDP level of synthetic Iran following an upwards trend, while Iran's observed per capita GDP starts out on a heavily downward trajectory.

The estimate of the impact of the Islamic Revolution on economic development for Iran is given by the difference between the actual and the synthetic per capita GDP, as shown in Figure 3 which compliments Figure 2. The per capita GDP gap necessarily mimics the zero-gap line in the pre-revolution period (indicating good fit) and begins to depart from it after the exposure to the Islamic Revolution.

All in all, when looking at the numerical solutions, the results become more meaningful. Thus, Table 2 displays GDP and economic effects for Iran and its synthetic counterpart for

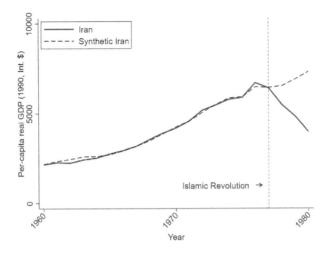

Notes: Time paths of per capita real GDP for Iran and the synthetic Iran for both the pre- and the post-treatment periods.

Figure 2. Trends in Per Capita GDP: Iran Versus the Synthetic Iran

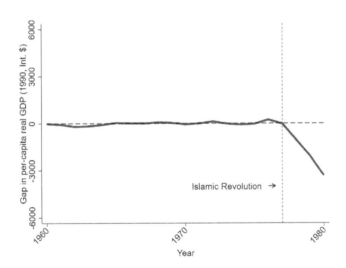

Notes: Time path for the gap of per capita real GDP.

Figure 3. Trends in Per Capita GDP Gap: Iran Versus the Synthetic Iran

each of the three years in the post-treatment period, along with the accumulated effects until 1980. The first column displays Iran's actual growth rate, while the second column indicates the growth rate of the synthetic Iran. For instance, the observed growth rate of per capita GDP in 1978 was −15.85%, while that of the synthetic Iran in the same year was 1.42%. Likewise, the observed growth rate of per capita GDP for Iran was −47.70% in the three year period, while that of the synthetic counterpart was 12.76%. The third column shows the difference in the growth rates between actual Iran and its counterfactual, thereby giving rise to a loss of 17.27% in the first year of the revolution, and 60.46% in the

Table 2. Growth and GDP Effects

Period	g	g^s	Δg	ΔpcGDP	ΔGDP (Billions)
1978	−15.849	1.420	−17.270	−1,061	−688.045
1979	−12.598	5.592	−18.190	−2,083	−1,383.656
1980	−19.249	5.748	−24.997	−3,335	−2,264.818
1978–1980	−47.696	12.760	−60.457	−6,479	−4,336.519
Annual average	−15.899	4.253	−20.152	−2,159	−1,445.506

Notes: g: growth rate (%) of per capita GDP for Iran; g^s: growth rate (%) of per capita GDP for the synthetic Iran; $\Delta g \equiv g - g^s$: difference in growth rates between Iran and its synthetic counterpart; ΔpcGDP: loss in per capita GDP; ΔGDP: loss in real GDP.

cumulative value of three years. The difference in the growth rates between actual Iran and its counterpart is indicative of the loss in per capita GDP. In the first year after the revolution, Iran's per capita GDP loss was $1,061. In the case of the cumulative effect, the forgone per capita GDP was 6,479 dollars (as measured in 1990 international dollars), that is, in the absence of the revolution Iran would have enjoyed $2,159 higher annual per capita GDP on average over a period of 3 years. Ultimately, in aggregate terms, the real GDP loss amounted to 4,336.519 billion dollars [see columns 4 and 5]. The reduction in Iranian oil production due to the Islamic Revolution caused a drop in national revenues. As mentioned before, Iran suffered a significant loss of crude oil production to the tune of roughly 39.56%, and fell to 3,168 billion barrels/day in 1979.

Summarizing, we conclude that after the outbreak of the Islamic Revolution the annual per capita GDP in Iran declined by about 20.15% on average relative to its synthetic counterpart without the revolution in the period 1978–1980.

5. Robustness Tests

In order to check the validity of our estimates, we run some robustness tests to check whether our results might have been driven by chance alone, or whether the SCM has detected a causality relationship between the Islamic Revolution in Iran and its economy. A summary of the results follows, the reader being referred to Appendix B for further details.

First, following Abadie and Gardeazabal (2003) and Abadie et al. (2010), we run the *in-space placebo test* by applying the SCM to each and every country in the set of control units (which, therefore, were not exposed to a revolution during the sample period of our study), shifting Iran to the donor pool in all cases. That is, we proceed *as if* each one of the countries in the donor pool had been affected by the revolution in 1978. If the placebo test had detected similar results for countries other than Iran, then the observed fall in growth and per capita GDP in Iran would have been driven by factors other than the Islamic Revolution.

We find that the probability of obtaining an average post-treatment gap less than or equal to Iran's would be $1/48 = 0.0208$. In other words, the null hypothesis of no treatment effect of the Islamic Revolution on Iran's per capita GDP would be rejected at a significance level of 5%. Complementary to this, we also computed the distribution of R, which is defined as $R \equiv (\text{Post}-\text{RMSPE}/\text{Pre}-\text{RMSPE})^2$ (see Equations (5) and (4)), for all the countries in the sample: intuition, confirmed by the results, says R should be the highest for Iran. We find that the probability of obtaining a value of R higher than or equal to that of Iran equals $1/60 = 0.0166$. That is to say, the null hypothesis of no treatment effect for Iran would be rejected at a significance level of 5%.

Second, we also run one *in-time placebo* test by shifting the intervention year as if Iran had hypothetically been treated in some generic period prior to 1978, for instance in 1968, which is the midpoint of our true pre-treatment period. Had the SCM properly implemented, no treatment effect should be detected before the revolution (Abadie *et al.*, 2015). We find that the time paths for the observed and the synthetic per capita GDP series are very close to each other both before and after 1968 (see Figure B.4 in Appendix B). In other words, the pretreatment fit is more than acceptable and, additionally, no treatment effect is detected. The conclusion is that the SCM has correctly detected the impact of the revolution on Iran's economy.

And, third, we implement a *leave-one-out* exercise in which we iteratively reestimate the baseline model to construct different counterfactuals, omitting in each iteration one of the five countries that received a positive weight in the synthetic Iran that we obtained in Section 4 (namely, Botswana, Gabon, Japan, Saudi Arabia and Singapore). By excluding countries that received a positive weight some goodness of fit is sacrificed, but this sensitivity check allows us to evaluate to what extent our results are driven by some particular control country. A similar exercise is conducted in Abadie *et al.* (2015) or Echevarría and García-Enríquez (2019a, 2019b) among others. Our results show that the smallest and the largest estimates of the effects of the revolution (in terms of accumulated loss of per capita GDP for the 1978–1980 period) correspond to cases where Singapore and Gabon are removed from the sample, respectively. In other words, leaving Gabon out of the donor pool leads to the highest estimate of the gap, while leaving out Singapore leads to the lowest (see Table B.1 in Appendix B).

Note that there is no monotonic relationship between (i) the size of the weight of the left-out unit (Singapore's weight equals 44.5%, the maximum) and (ii) the change in the estimated treatment effect after excluding that particular unit from the set of control units (omitting Singapore from the donor pool leads to a minimum effect). The intuition is as follows. For a given weight set obtained in the pre-treatment period, the consequence on the estimate of the treatment effect of leaving one specific unit out of the controls will trivially depend on the post-treatment time evolution of the outcome variable for that unit relative to the average among the rest of control units. Thus, removing a country with a high weight in the unconstrained synthetic country might have no significant effect on the estimated treatment effect provided that the post-treatment period evolution of the outcome variable happened to be close enough to the average for the unconstrained donor pool. However, and conversely, eliminating a country with a low (although not negligible) weight, but with a performance totally different from that of the rest of controls, might lead to a synthetic country completely distinct from the one obtained in the first instance. And, therefore, to a completely different estimate of the treatment effect. The conclusion drawn from the leave-one-out check is that no single control country seems to be driving the results or the estimates found in Section 4.

6. Conclusions

The Islamic Revolution, one of the most important conflicts in the history of Iran, began in 1978, overthrowing the Shah's administration. The following year, with the referendum held, Iran was declared an "Islamic Republic". This study was carried out to reveal the economic consequences of the Islamic Revolution in Iran by employing the SCM. The SCM creates a counterfactual unit with the weighted average of the best representative countries in the set of control units. Consequently, the comparison of the established counterfactual unit and the actual Iran allows us to assess the effect of the Islamic Revolution on Iran's economy. In addition, we attempted to achieve the best results by comparing alternative computational methods to obtain the synthetic or counterfactual Iran. Given that the root mean squared prediction error for the pre-treatment period attained with the MSCMT package in R was the lowest, thereby ensuring the best fit, such package turned out to be our choice.

According to our estimates, the numerical results are as follows. The per capita GDP growth rate achieved in the first year following the revolution was -15.85% for Iran, whereas for synthetic Iran it was 1.42%. The cumulative per capita GDP growth rate for the three-year period was -47.70%, while for the synthetic counterpart this rate was 12.7%. In other words, the loss in terms of the growth rate of per capita GDP in the three-year period was 60.46%. Furthermore, the average per capita GDP loss was \$2,159 per year, and the cumulative loss of the three-year period was \$6,479. That is, if Iran had not been faced with such a revolution, it would have benefited from an annual average of \$2,159 higher per capita GDP. Likewise, in aggregate terms, Iran would have seen an annual average of 1,445.5 billion dollars higher real GDP. This corresponds to a total of 4,336.5 billion dollars higher real GDP in the three-year period.

In order to check the statistical significance, we run some exercises. First, we tried an in-space placebo analysis by applying the SCM to all the countries in the donor pool as an attempt to assess the hypothetical effects that could emerge had all the countries been exposed to the revolution in 1978. Iran turned out to be the country most affected by the revolution, thereby rejecting the hypothesis of there being no treatment effect of the Islamic Revolution on Iran's economy. Second, we also performed an in-time placebo test by hypothetically shifting the intervention period to 1968, to conclude that the SCM did not find any treatment effect. Finally, we extend the sensitivity tests with a leave-one-out analysis: the results did not differ much from the results obtained in the benchmark case. In summary, all the robustness checks suggest that our conclusion is fairly robust in detecting the negative impact of the Islamic Revolution on Iran's economic development.

The evidence from this study suggests that the Islamic Revolution has a negative impact on the per capita GDP of Iran, and thereby on economic development. Most importantly, according to the results of our research, we have reinforced the importance of political stability in achieving economic development and prosperity in a country. We hope that our analysis will provide a contribution for future researchers.

Acknowledgments

I am deeply indebted to my advisors, Cruz A. Echevarría and Javier García-Enríquez, for their guidance, seminar participants in II Jornadas Doctorales de la UPV/EHU, Departamento Fundamentos del Análisis Económico II, Doctoriales Transfronterizos UPPA-UPV/EHU, and four anonymous referees for their valuable comments. The usual disclaimer applies.

Appendix A. Alternative Computational Methods

As mentioned in the Introduction, we compare the performance of alternative computational procedures to obtain the synthetic Iran based on two criteria. First, how matrix $\mathbf{V}$ is computed: **exogenous** [(i) researcher's choice or (ii) regression-based]; or **endogenous** [(i) nested minimization or (ii) Cross-Validation]. And second, the computer package implemented (R in its different alternatives synth-ipop, synth-LRQP and MSCMT), Matlab© and Stata©.

The optimal weights obtained upon solving the problem in Equation (2), $\mathbf{w}^*(\mathbf{V}) = \{w_j^*(\mathbf{V})\}_{j=2}^{J+1}$, will depend on the choice for matrix $\mathbf{V}$. Several alternatives have been considered in the literature (Ferman and Pinto, 2016; Firpo and Possebom, 2018; Echevarría and García-Enríquez, 2019a, 2019b). The first alternative is to choose the predictors weights according to the author's preference and knowledge from previous researches. As a second option, a data-driven method can be used to set matrix $\mathbf{V}$. After regressing the outcome $\mathbf{Y}$ on the set of predictors $\mathbf{X}$, the elements of matrix $\mathbf{V}$ are obtained by comparing the corresponding OLS coefficients (in modulus or squared) over the sum of all coefficients. We will refer to this alternative as the regression-based method.

The third option amounts to a *nested* (double minimization), where matrix $\mathbf{V}$ and control weights $\mathbf{w}^*$ are jointly obtained in such a way that $\mathbf{w}^*(\mathbf{V})$ solves the problem in Equation (2) and $\mathbf{V}$ minimizes the square distance of the outcome between the treated unit and the synthetic counterpart,

$$\min_{\{V_p\}_{p=1}^{P}} \sum_{t=1}^{T_0} (Y_{1t} - Y_{1t}^s)^2, \tag{A.1}$$

where $Y_{1t}^s = \sum_{j=2}^{J+1} Y_{jt} w_j(\mathbf{V})$ (see Equation (2)).

As a last alternative, the *cross-validation* option refers to the division of all pre-revolutionary years into two sub-periods: training and validation. In the training period, matrix $\mathbf{V}$ is minimized and used to obtain optimal $\mathbf{w}$ in the validation period (Abadie *et al.*, 2015; Becker and Klößner, 2017).

Table A.1. The Synthetic Iran: Alternative Computational Methods

---

1- Nested Optimization: R (Ipop-Synth)
Botswana: 0.318   Gabon: 0.103   Japan: 0.156   Saudi Arabia: 0.010   Singapore: 0.413
Pre–RMSPE: 96.918; Post–RMSPE: 2282.487 Ratio: 23.551

2- Nested optimization: R (LowRankQP-synth)
Botswana: 0.315   Gabon: 0.105   Japan: 0.155   Saudi Arabia: 0.008   Singapore: 0.417
Pre–RMSPE: 96.914; Post–RMSPE: 2284.461; Ratio: 23.572

3- Cross Validation: R (Ipop-synth)
Botswana: 0.288 Cameroon: 0.014 China: 0.020   Gabon: 0.156   Japan: 0.151   Singapore: 0.371
Pre–RMSPE: 120.723; Post–RMSPE: 2081.480; Ratio: 17.242

4- Cross Validation: R (LowRankQP-synth)
Botswana: 0.321   Gabon: 0.152   Japan: 0.169   Mongolia: 0.018   Singapore: 0.339
Pre–RMSPE: 118.224; Post–RMSPE: 2065.311; Ratio: 17.469

5- Nested optimization: R (MSCMT)
Botswana: 0.302   Gabon: 0.098   Japan: 0.151   Saudi Arabia: 0.004   Singapore: 0.445
Pre–RMSPE: 96.368; Post–RMSPE: 2351.978; Ratio: 24.406

6- Nested optimization: Matlab
Botswana: 0.276   Gabon: 0.137   Japan: 0.100   Singapore: 0.487
Pre–RMSPE: 121.197; Post–RMSPE: 2223.187; Ratio: 18.344

7- Regression-based: Stata
Botswana: 0.328   Gabon: 0.116   Japan: 0.155 Sao Tome and P.: 0.015   Senegal: 0.386
Pre–RMSPE: 98.588; Post–RMSPE: 2209.888; Ratio: 24.415

8- Nested optimization (Allopt): Stata
Botswana: 0.305   Gabon: 0.097   Japan: 0.151 Sao Tome and P.: 0.007   Senegal: 0.440
Pre–RMSPE: 96.375; Post–RMSPE: 2351.207; Ratio: 24.396;

Notes: Synthetic Iran (countries and weights) under alternative computational methods. See main text.

The results are shown in Table A.1. Regarding the choice of an appropriate computer package, we first tried the **synth** package in R, the *nested* minimization being the default option.[5] This package allows, in turn, the use of two different algorithms to minimize the Pre–RMSPE: Ipop and LowRankQP functions. The obtained Pre–RMSPEs were 96.918 and 96.914, respectively. Due to the long pre-treatment period, we also tried the *cross-validation* option (once again using the **synth** package in R) by dividing all pre-treatment period into two periods, training and validation. According to our choice, the training period occurs between 1960 and 1968 and the validation period between 1969 and 1977. The fit turned out to be worse in both cases (Ipop and LowRankQP) as the resulting Pre–RMSPEs were 120.723 and 118.224, respectively. Next, we also tried another package, MSCMT, implemented with R as well (Becker and Klößner, 2017, 2018). In this case, Pre–RMSPE turned out to equal 96.368.

---

[5] The synth packages for Matlab©, Stata© and R are available at http://www.mit.edu/~jhainm/synthpage.html.

Stata© has its own version of the synth package, which offers two options to compute matrix **V**. First, **V** can be exogenously obtained by means of a regression-based procedure, the default option, leading to a Pre–RMSPE equal to 98.588. Second, matrix **V** also can be endogenously obtained by implementing a *nested* minimization procedure (with respect to both **V** and **w**) which requires providing (up to three) initial or guessed values for **V**, returning the one which results in the lowest Pre–RMSPE. In this case, we obtained a value of Pre–RMSPE equal to 96.375. Performing this nested minimization, however, we found that Stata© was not robust to alternative ordering of predictors. That is, when the predictors' order is different, then the optimal weights change (McClelland and Gault, 2017).

As for the Matlab© package, it also implements a joint minimization with respect to both **V** and **w**, which needs the corresponding guessed solution as the starting values for **V**. Using a regression-based method to find such starting values, we obtained Pre–RMSPE equal to 121.197. Unfortunately, different starting values (which must be set by the researcher) led to very different solutions. Moreover, using alternative versions of Matlab© (and even different machines) again resulted in different optimal weights. All this makes Matlab© the least reliable computational method among those considered here. In summary, MSCMT, the R package, has proven to be the most effective tool to compute the synthetic control in this paper.

Appendix B. Robustness Tests

In-space placebo test. The graphical results are shown in Panel (a) in Figure B.1, where each gray line illustrates the estimated gap in per capita GDP for each of the 59 countries in the donor pool, while the blue line represents the estimated gap for Iran.

The estimated per capita GDP gap of Iran closely follows the zero gap line before the intervention which is one of the requirements for proper use of the SCM as an estimation method (Abadie, 2020). Notice also that the fit for some of the countries in the donor pool is not particularly precise. Therefore, confidence in the method is compromised in some instances. Thus, we discard those placebo runs for which the Pre–RMSPE [see Equation (4)] is more than twice that of Iran. As a result, the sample is reduced to Iran plus 47 control countries, so that 12 countries are excluded. The idea is that countries with a too high Pre–RMSPE (or, equivalently, with a poorer fit than Iran's) are not reliable, in the same way that a poor fit for Iran would also reduce our confidence in the validity of our results. This exercise can be found, amongst others, in Abadie *et al.* (2010) or Acemoglu *et al.* (2016).[6] The result is shown in Panel (b) in Figure B.1. As expected, now all the estimated gaps for the pre-treatment period are lower and closer to Iran's. And, additionally, after inspecting the plots of the estimated gaps for the post-treatment period for all countries, it becomes apparent that the Islamic Revolution had a negative impact on Iran that the 47 control countries did not experience.

---

[6] Acemoglu *et al.* (2016) follow a similar criterion as only control units with a Pre–RMSPE less than or equal to $3^{1/4}$ times that of the treated unit are considered to test the statistical significance of the treatment effect.

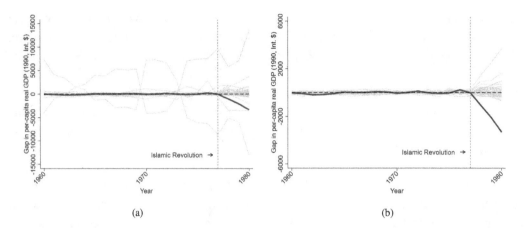

Notes: Per capita GDP gap in Iran and placebo gaps. Panel (a): Iran plus 59 control countries. Panel (b): Iran plus 47 control countries after excluding 12 countries whose Pre−RMSPE is at least twice Iran's.

Figure B.1. [Color online] In-space Placebo Tests

In order to formally test the statistical significance of the effect and go beyond a simple graphical analysis, we computed the distribution of the average post-treatment gap (AG) for the 48 countries represented in Panel (b) in Figure B.1. Since the difference between the observed outcome and its synthetic counterpart in the Iranian case will be (in absolute value) the largest amongst that set of countries, the average post-treatment gap in Iran is expected to be the lowest. More precisely, the AG of unit k is defined as

$$AG_k \equiv \frac{\sum_{t=T_0+1}^{T} \left(Y_{kt} - \sum_{q=1, q \neq k}^{K+1} Y_{qt} w_{kq}^* \right)}{T - T_0}, \quad (B.1)$$

where w_{kq}^* denotes the optimal weight for control unit q and for synthetic unit k, and where $\{1, 2, ..., k, ..., K+1\}$ denotes the set of countries in the sample left after removing those with a poor pre-treatment fit. Iran's AG was the lowest amongst the 48 countries, and the probability of obtaining an AG less than or equal to Iran's would be $1/48 = 0.0208$ (see Figure B.2). In other words, conditional on control countries resulting in Pre–RMSPE values less than twice that of Iran, the null hypothesis of no treatment effect of the Islamic Revolution on Iran's per capita GDP would be rejected at a significance level of 5%.

A complementary way to formally test the statistical significance of the impact of the Islamic Revolution on Iran's economy is to show the ratio of post-treatment mean square prediction error to pre-treatment mean square prediction error for all countries: intuitively, a sizeable impact should result in a high ratio. For this purpose, we obtained the entire distribution of ratios for all countries. More precisely, from Equations (4) and (5), the ratio for country j, R_j, is defined as

$$R_j \equiv \frac{\sum_{t=T_0+1}^{T} \left(Y_{jt} - \sum_{q=1, q \neq j}^{J+1} Y_{qt} w_{jq}^* \right)^2 / (T - T_0)}{\sum_{t=1}^{T_0} \left(Y_{jt} - \sum_{q=1, q \neq j}^{J+1} Y_{qt} w_{jq}^* \right)^2 / T_0} = \left[\frac{\text{Post−RMSPE}_j}{\text{Pre−RMSPE}_j} \right]^2. \quad (B.2)$$

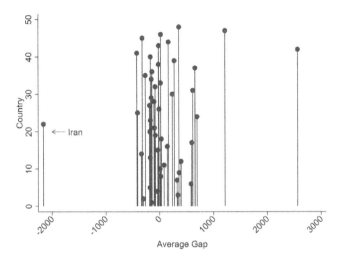

Notes: The average post-treatment gap of the 48 countries (including Iran) obtained in the last stage of the in-space placebo test. Numbers along the *y*-axis denote the country IDs.

Figure B.2. Average Post-treatment Gap Per Country

Figure B.3 displays the distribution of the ratio for the 60 countries in our sample. Formally, the probability of finding a ratio higher than or equal to Iran's is given by

$$p(R_1) \equiv \frac{\sum_{k=1}^{J+1}[R_k \geq R_1]}{J+1}. \tag{B.3}$$

In our case, $p(R_1)$ equals $1/60 = 0.0166$. That is to say, the null hypothesis of no treatment effect for Iran would be rejected at a significance level of 5%.

In-time placebo. In the case, we pose the treatment year in 1968 in order to see whether the SCM captures a treatment which did not take place. If that were the case, the SCM would have failed to find the exact effect of the Islamic Revolution. A similar exercise of out-of-sample validation is carried out in Abadie *et al.* (2015) where they set the hypothetical date of the German reunification in 1975, i.e. 15 years before reunification actually took place. The graphical result is shown in Figure B.4. We observe that the time paths for the observed per capita GDP and for the counterfactual follow the same pattern both before 1968 (so that the fit is remarkably good and the synthetic Iran is reliable as a counterfactual), and for the period 1968–1977 (so that no treatment effect is detected). We interpret this result as showing that the SCM has correctly detected the impact of the revolution on Iran's economy.

Leave-one-out. Here, we recalculate the synthetic Iran five times excluding alternatively Botswana, Gabon, Japan, Saudi Arabia and Singapore. Figure B.5 displays the results, where the blue solid line represents the observed Iranian per capita GDP in terms of evolution over time, the black dashed line represents the synthetic Iran with the above five controls (the same as in Figure 2), and the gray lines represent the five restricted counterfactuals.

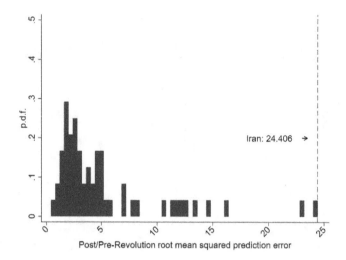

Notes: Ratio of the post-Islamic Revolution to the pre-Islamic Revolution *RMSPE*: Iran with 59 countries in the donor pool.

Figure B.3. Distribution of R

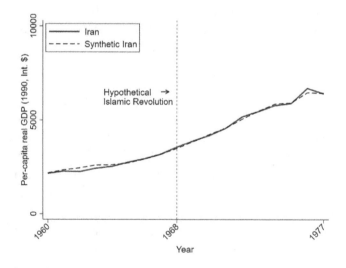

Notes: In-time placebo test under the counterfactual that the Islamic Revolution had occurred in 1968.

Figure B.4. In-time Placebo Test

The fit in the pre-treatment period (remarkably good) is quite similar in all cases. As for the post-treatment period, however, some small differences in the estimated counterfactuals (and, consequently, in the estimated gaps) appear. Thus, the exercise provides a sort of confidence band for the estimated post-treatment gap which contains, by construction, the estimate obtained in Section 4.

The numerical results of the exercise (the quantitative counterpart to Figure B.5) are shown in Table B.1. More precisely, the Table presents the smallest and the largest

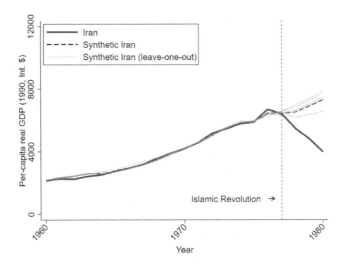

Notes: Time paths of per capita GDP for Iran, the synthetic Iran with all donor pool countries with positive weights and the synthetic Iran dropping one country at a time.

Figure B.5. [Color online] Leave-One-Out

Table B.1. Leave-One-Out Analysis

| | | Leaving Out Gabon | | | | Leaving Out Singapore | | | |
| | | (Maximum Effect) | | | | (Minimum Effect) | | | |
Period	g	g^s	Δg	ΔpcGDP	ΔGDP (Billions)	g^s	Δg	ΔpcGDP	ΔGDP (Billions)
1978	−15.85	5.93	−21.78	−1,517.2	−983.2	−1.66	−14.19	−744.7	−482.6
1979	−12.60	5.75	−18.35	−2,576.9	−1,711.1	2.34	−14.44	−1,538.4	−1,021.5
1980	−19.25	6.31	−25.56	−3,901.7	−2,649.3	3.20	−22.45	−2,588.6	−1,757.7
1978–1980	−47.70	17.98	−65.68	−7,995.9	−5,343.6	3.88	−51.58	−4,871.8	−3,261.9
Annual average	−15.90	5.99	−21.89	−2,665.3	−1,782.2	1.29	−17.19	−1,623.9	−1,087.3

Notes: See Key to Table 2.

estimates of the effects of the revolution (in terms of accumulated loss of per capita GDP for the period 1978–1980). These are obtained when Gabon and Singapore respectively are left out of the sample: i.e. leaving Gabon out of the donor pool leads to the highest estimate, while leaving out Singapore leads to the lowest. For instance, the (post-treatment) average annual growth rate of per capita GDP of the synthetic unit formed when Gabon is removed from the donor pool is 17.98%, while that of the synthetic Iran formed when Singapore is taken out of the donor pool is 3.88% [see columns 2 and 6]. For completeness, columns 4 and 8 display the estimated losses of per capita GDP when Gabon and Singapore are left out of the donor pool respectively.

Thus, the removal of Gabon would result in an annual average loss of per capita GDP of $2,665, while leaving out Singapore would imply a loss of $1,624.

References

Abadie, A (2020). Using synthetic controls: Feasibility, data requirements, and methodological aspects. *Journal of Economic Literature*, forthcoming.

Abadie, A, A Diamond and J Hainmueller (2010). Synthetic control methods for comparative case studies: Estimating the effect of California's tobacco control program. *Journal of the American Statistical Association*, 105(490), 493–505.

Abadie, A, A Diamond and J Hainmueller (2015). Comparative politics and the synthetic control method. *American Journal of Political Science*, 59(2), 495–510.

Abadie, A and J Gardeazabal (2003). The economic costs of conflict: A case study of the Basque Country. *American Economic Review*, 93(1), 113–132.

Acemoglu, D, S Johnson, A Kermani, J Kwak and T Mitton (2016). The value of connections in turbulent times: Evidence from the United States. *Journal of Financial Economics*, 121(2), 368–391.

Alesina, A, S Ozler, N Roubini and P Swagel (1996). Political instability and economic growth. *Journal of Economic Growth*, 1(2), 189–211.

Amuzegar, J (1992). The Iranian economy before and after the revolution. *Middle East Journal*, 46, 413–442.

Arjomand, SA (1986). Iran's Islamic Revolution in comparative perspective. *World Politics*, 38, 383–414.

Becker, M and S Klößner (2017). Estimating the economic costs of organized crime by synthetic control methods. *Journal of Applied Econometrics*, 32(7), 1367–1369.

Becker, M and S Klößner (2018). Fast and reliable computation of generalized synthetic controls. *Econometrics and Statistics*, 5, 1–19.

Bilgel, F and BC Karahasan (2017). The economic costs of separatist terrorism in Turkey. *Journal of Conflict Resolution*, 61(2), 457–479.

Botosaru, I and B Ferman (2019). On the role of covariates in the synthetic control method. *Econometrics Journal*, 22(2), 117–130.

Demirci, S (2013). The Iranian Revolution and Shia Islam: The role of Islam in the Iranian Revolution. *International Journal of History*, 1(2), 37–48.

Echevarría, CA and J García-Enríquez (2019a). The economic consequences of the Libyan spring: A synthetic control analysis. *Defence and Peace Economics*, 30(5), 592–608.

Echevarría, CA and J García-Enríquez (2019b). The economic cost of the Arab Spring: The case of the Egyptian revolution. *Empirical Economics*.

Esfahani, H and H. Pesaran (2008). The Iranian economy in the twentieth century: A global perspective. *Iranian Studies*, 42, 177–211.

Ferman, B and C Pinto (2016). Synthetic controls with imperfect pre-treatment fit. Munich Personal RePEc Archive.

Firpo, S and V Possebom (2018). Synthetic control method: Inference, sensitivity analysis and confidence sets. *Journal of Causal Inference*, 6(2), 1–26.

Gardeazabal, J and A Vega-Bayo (2017). An empirical comparison between the synthetic control method and Hsiao *et al.*'s panel data approach to program evaluation. *Journal of Applied Econometrics*, 32, 983–1002.

Grier, K and N Maynard (2016). The economic consequences of Hugo Chavez: A synthetic control analysis. *Journal of Applied Econometrics*, 125, 1–21.

Horiuchi, Y and A Mayerson (2015). The opportunity cost of conflict: Statistically comparing Israel and synthetic Israel. *Political Science Research and Methods*, 3(3), 609–618.

Kaul, A, S Klößner, G Pfeifer and M Schieler (2018). Synthetic control methods: Never use all pre-intervention outcomes together with covariates. Working Paper.

Maloney, S (2015). Iran political economy since the revolution. *Contemporary Review of the Middle East*, 3(2), 223–225.

McClelland, R and S Gault (2017). The synthetic control method as a tool to understand state policy. State and Local Finance Initiative. Urban Institute.

Moin, B (1999). *Khomeini. Life of the Ayatollah*. London: I.B. Tauris.

Pinotti, P (2015). The economic costs of organised crime: Evidence from Southern Italy. *The Economic Journal*, 125, F203–F232.

© 2025 World Scientific Publishing Company
https://doi.org/10.1142/9789819813735_0018

Chapter 18

Islamic Blended Finance for Circular Economy Impactful SMEs to Achieve SDGs[#]

Tariqullah Khan[*]

Hamad Bin Khalifa University
Education City, Ar-Rayyan, Qatar
tkhan@hbku.edu.qa

Fatou Badjie

University of The Gambia
Serrekunda, Gambia
fatimahbadjie@gmail.com

In this research, we present a framework for blended Islamic finance for impactful small and medium enterprises (SMEs) to achieve sustainable development goals (SDGs). The blend results from discussing the pertinent perspectives that underlie the motives of philanthropy, private sector activities and public sector facilitation. The consensus of these three stakeholders on the impact criteria is an essential precondition for the blend to happen. Therefore, we first developed the consensus-based impact criteria for SMEs, namely, 4Zeros & SS (zero-waste, zero-emissions, zero-interest, zero-foreclosures and service to society). After that, we adopted a financial engineering approach to design products by blending the three motives. Financial contracts could be incentive compatible and effective if these three motivations are recognized and brought together. The purpose of our research is to offer such incentive-compatible structures that can mobilize funding for impactful SMEs, save cost as well as generate revenue for self-sustainability. In the contract design, the private sector provides finance, the philanthropist pays the costs of funds, the public sector facilitates, and the impactful SME gets subsidized financing. Since the blended nature of the contract provides a social subsidy to fund the cost element of the financing, the proposed structure creates a win–win result for the blending parties. While financial institutions expand into the SMEs sector for profitability, blended Islamic finance will attract additional resources toward enhancing development impact. Through the philanthropic component, SMEs, on the other hand, will access the source of social subsidy that will relieve the burden of the exorbitant commercial rates. The funding structure will reduce risk perception and spur growth.

Consequently, this collaborative and innovative contract design will contribute to achieving multidimensional human development, as enshrined in the *Maqasid al-Shariah*, and the SDGs. Impactful businesses must integrate environmental, social and governance best practices as well as national development goals. Hence, the proposal offers several benefits and prospects of extended use for other consensus-based purposes such as low-cost housing, solar paneling, health, education, etc.

Keywords: Islamic social finance; blended Islamic finance; sustainable human development; Zakah; Waqf; Sadaqa; sustainable development goals; circular economy.

---

[*]Corresponding author.
[#]This Chapter first appeared in the *Singapore Economic Review*, Vol. 67, No. 1, doi: 10.1142/S0217590820420060. © 2022 World Scientific Publishing.

1. Introduction

We assume it to be a common knowledge that small and medium enterprises (SMEs) are an effective and sustainable means for achieving multidimensional development (MD). The MD concept enshrines in the *Maqasid Al-Shariah* (local aspirations in Muslim societies), the Qatar National Vision 2030 (as an example of national priorities) and the sustainable development goals (SDGs) (aspired global targets). However, there are also concerns about funding costs and collateral requirements as barriers to accessing financing by SMEs. This paper aims to address the barriers of SMEs in accessing finance through a blended Islamic structure. Blended finance is not a new concept. However, recently, in the context of the SDGs, its importance has increased. The basic idea is simple. Profits motivate activities of the private sector. The basis of the philanthropic work is compassion. Proactive governments must play an effective facilitating role. The three motivations working together and jointly can put economies and societies on the track of healthy transformation.

Agreement on a joint agenda by the *three key stakeholders requires a common purpose based on consensus.* In this paper, we argue that achieving the SDGs and MD could be the sought common purpose. In Section 2, we discuss this consensus framework. We adopt the well-established argument that SMEs can play an important role in MD. We also recognize that the high cost of funding impairs the growth of SMEs. To address these concerns, the three stakeholders could develop a consensus criteria for impactful SMEs. We discuss this point in Section 3. Then the three stakeholders can jointly develop institutional arrangements to provide sustainable social subsidy to such impactful SMEs. This social subsidy is achieved effectively through the design of blended Islamic finance. We discuss this prospect in Section 4. Finally, in Section 5, we conclude and suggest implications.

2. Multidimensional Development: Framework For Consensus

Historically, there are extensive intellectual efforts to promote multidimensional approaches where human development is addressed comprehensively. An effective policy framework must recognize at least three broad perspectives and ensure harmony between these for policy success. Figure 1(a) summarizes these perspectives.

(a) Local aspirations: Preferences and cultural values drive the motivations of individuals, families, firms, civil society organizations and local and municipal political and governance structures. In the context of the Muslim societies, at the local level, the *Maqasid Al-Shariah* framework addresses the subject of comprehensive human development through its five components — religion, progeny, intellect, life and wealth. The framework was developed during the 12th–14th centuries by scholars like al-Shatibi, al-Ghazali, Ibn Taimiyyah, Ibn al-Qayyim and others. Chapra (2008) formally presented the Islamic vision of development based on the framework. Since then, a large set of literature has been developed by different writers discussing different aspects and implications of the framework.

(b) National priorities: At the national level, each sovereign state must have its long-term vision and transformation targets. National initiatives, for example, the Qatar National

Islamic Blended Finance 439

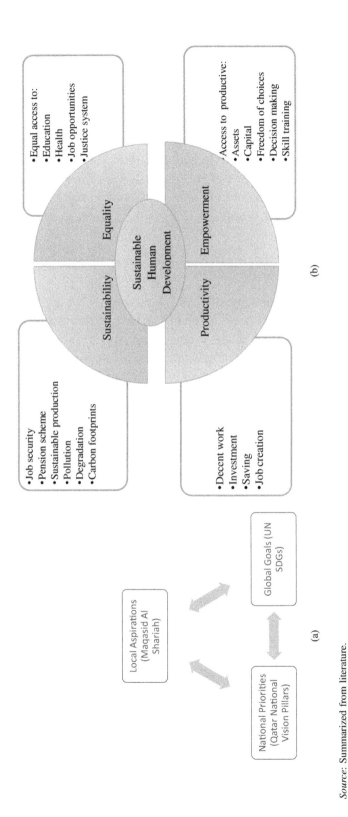

Source: Summarized from literature.

Figure 1. (a). Comprehensive Human Development Policy Framework. (b). Components of Sustainable Human Development

Vision (QNV) 2030, address the subject of MD with their four-pillar approach — people, economy, society and environment. Likewise, in African context for example, in the Gambia National Development Plan 2018–2021 sets eight critical priorities.

(c) Global goals: The UN framework for human development has a long history. The ultimate purpose is to enhance wellbeing, safeguard human dignity and broaden choices to achieve sustainable human development through its four pillars — equality, productivity, sustainability and empowerment UNDP (2018) and (Haq, 1995). It means putting people at the heart of business models and economic development process. Since 2005 under the umbrella of the United Nations, first, the millennium development goals were introduced and then since 2016, SDGs have been introduced. In the global framework, the SDGs address the same subject of comprehensive human development through the 17 global goals.

Based on the review of work done at different UN bodies, especially UNDP and research of other scholars, in Figure 1(b), we summarize the pillars and preconditions of MD.

The new trend is not about a shortage of physical resources rather is about rethinking impact to finance SDGs. The way business is conducted, from sourcing resources, to final, the consumption has to be revisited. Positive impact initiative by Société Générale and UNEP FI (2018) argued that strategic thinking, collaboration and policy integration and investment in mindset especially the positive approach to business is the productive way forward to achieve 2030 agenda. Impactful and socially responsible SMEs in this perspective means alignment of business models with the mapped objective (sustainable human development),[1] integration of social, environment and governance (ESG) principles, in addition to other global initiatives such as the circular economy and zero-waste movement.

Barriers to accessing finance impinge the proper functioning of SMEs. Financial hurdle for SMEs is a global phenomenon. According to Organization for Economic Co-operation and Development (OECD) scoreboard highlights 2018, the rate of lending to SMEs has declined drastically since 2016 due to high default rate in some countries and unfavorable macroeconomic policies in others. For example, in Greece, Slovenia and Portugal, lending to SMEs decreased as a result of high non-performing loans, while in Brazil and Russian Federation, the decrease is triggered by unfavorable macroeconomic policies (OECD, 2018a) and World Bank (2018).

In the context of Muslim societies whose local aspirations are summarized above, the thoughtful question then is how to define impactful and socially responsible SMEs? Furthermore, and how to empower and unlock their potentials to achieve the objectives? The growing literature on Islamic finance presents it as an instrument to promote financial inclusion. We explore the prospects of a two-pronged approach; (a) first to discuss and set

---

[1] Note that sustainable human development, multidimensional human development and comprehensive human development are used interchangeable in this paper.

criteria for socially responsible and impactful SMEs and (b) to sustainably fund such businesses using blended Islamic finance.

In the past, local preferences, national priorities, and global goals have conflicted, for success, the three must converge. However, a careful study of *Maqasid*, SDGs and sustainable human development in Figure 2 revealed an interesting convergence between the three. This convergence suggests the following prospects:

(a) The synchronization of local aspirations, national development targets and global goals is a potential opportunity to resolve policy confusion and conflict that exists in the Muslim countries,

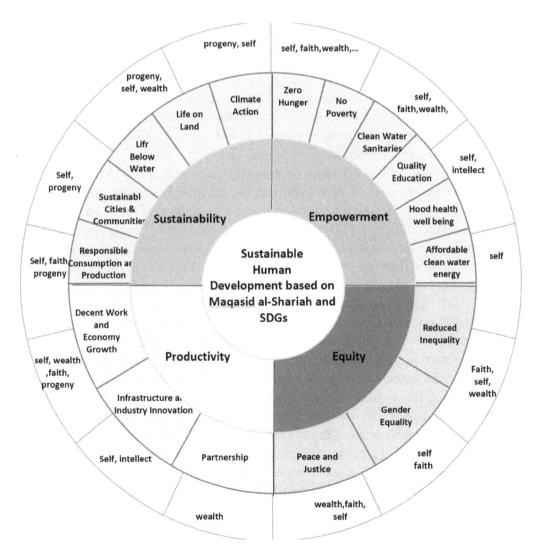

Source: Authors' Own 2019.

Figure 2. Mapping of Maqasid al-Shariah, SDGs and SHD

(b) One can suggest a holistic development tool to achieve the mapped goals through stimulating active participation of the compassionate motive of society, blending it with the Shariah-compliant profit motive to mobilize the required resources, especially provide a social subsidy on the cost of funding and

(c) SMEs could play the most important and sustainable role in achieving the seven most critical and intertwined SDGs[2] as confirmed by many researchers: Husson (2015), Izhar and Dikmener (2017), BNP Paribas (2018), Kamal-Chaoui (2019), Dariah et al. (2016).[3] SMEs are also the engine of economic development worldwide and their importance in job creation, innovation and human development is also globally acknowledged (World Bank Group, 2017). The blending can be achieved through consensus criteria about impactful and socially responsible SMEs in view of the three perspectives summarized above.

3. Islamic Impactful Business Criteria

Within the framework of our three stakeholder perspective summarized above and the motivations behind Islamic compassion and Shariah-compliant profit incentive, in this section, we define and describe consensus criteria for impactful Islamic investment — a criterion that is mutually agreeable to philanthropists, commercial entities and the government and regulatory authorities.

While there is no unified definition of impactful investment and so does its measurement criteria, the objective of investment and the effect of business's operation on its ecosystem (environment, society and stakeholders) is a fundamental start point to define what an impactful business is. GIIN defined impact investments as "investments made into companies, organizations and funds with the intention to generate social and environmental impact alongside a financial return" (Garmendia and Olszewski, 2014, p. 5). Seeking financial returns as well as social impact in concurrence with global initiatives means thinking broadly, and acting locally to strike a balance between financial and non-financial benefits. Hence any realistic criteria should be reflective of this fact, especially for SMEs as the driver of economic development worldwide (World Bank Group, 2017).

It is important to craft measurement criteria that are broad and accommodative of diverse investment appetites. Although impact investment is aiming for both environmental and social alongside a financial return, the levels of the affinity of different impact, investors should not be an oversight. Bearing in mind that some investors "invest for impact" and others with impact. The differences lie in the willingness to forgo or take higher risk in exchange of greater social impact (Gianoncelli and Boiardi, 2018). This is of critical importance to initiate positive, impactful business criteria to aligned business activities with development agenda targeting four components of multidimensional human

---

[2] SDG1, eradicating poverty; SDG 2 ending hunger, achieving food security and promoting sustainable agriculture; SDG 3 promoting health and well-being; SDG 5 achieving gender equality and economic empowerment of women; SDG 8 promoting economic growth and jobs; SDG 9 on supporting industry, innovation and infrastructure; and SDG 10 on reducing inequality.

[3] Referred to these seven goals as end goals of development and representative of human well-being.

development, ESG, SDGs and circular economy (Reduce, Redesign, Reuse, Recycle). This is because all frameworks envisioned to achieve sustainable human development. Integration of ESG and circular economy will ensure business sustainability as well as attainment of development agenda (Société Générale and UNEP FI, 2018). One will notice that even though halal is essential as the foundation, it is not sufficient to make businesses socially responsible.

For setting the consensus criteria, we use (a) Maqasid al-Shariah, (b) the pillars of sustainable human development (equality, productivity, empowerment and sustainability) and (c) ESG and circular economy concerns. Thus, more comprehensive steps in this screening are shown in Figure 3.

3.1. *Equity component screens*

Criteria under equity will look at the impact of the business in awarding equitable opportunities during sourcing quality human resource through hiring, promotion and training opportunities for employees. Measures will evaluate

(a) Recruitment and hiring procedures in the human resources department to evaluate equitable access to positions including managerial positions irrespective of gender, tribe or religion.
(b) Remuneration and benefits packages for staff in the same position, executive management, and junior staff, and basis of promotions, maternity, and sick leave will be assessed.
(c) Equitable access to on-job training opportunities both internal and external training, is ensured.
(d) The number of women and minority employees and number in a leadership position is given proper weight.
(e) Equitable access to justice within and outside the business.

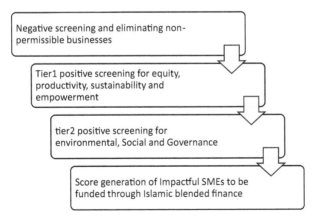

Source: Authors' Own 2019.

Figure 3. Screening Steps for Positive Islamic Impactful Business Criteria

3.2. Productivity component screen

This screen is based on the level of business investment in its employees to enhance well-being and the full realization of their potentials. While equity screens evaluate the accessibility of opportunities in the organization, productivity screens focus on the investment in employee to spur their maximum functioning. Thus, the screen evaluates

(a) Educational opportunities and skill development to elevate skills and knowledge of employees (internal and external training).
(b) The business is supporting employee wellbeing through health insurance scheme and protection against health hazard related job with risk allowance.

3.3. Empowerment component screen

This screen is looking at the decision-making process and level of employee participation and decentralization of governance in the business. Thus, it evaluates

(a) The level of employee participation in the decision making the process in both job related and non-job-related issues.
(b) Level of freedom of expression/disclosure of employees, the existence of collective bargaining rights with matters directly or indirectly affecting them.
(c) Screening for an employer–employee relationship in governance and freedom of choice
(d) The level of support and motivation for employees to realize self-set targets and innovation.
(e) The number of job creation and available opportunities especially in countries with the high unemployment rate and lack of private-sector job creation is reported. Thus, any business that opens up job opportunities and facilitates self-employment will be impactful (for example, allowing employees to start-up their own businesses from work experience and supporting business diversification).

3.4. Sustainability component screen

The criteria for this measure are based on the argument that future generations deserve equal privileges like the present generation. Though this concept is dynamic and fits into almost all modern issues (Haq, 1995). In the context of Impactful Business Criteria (IBC), in addition to environmental issues, it refers to business action in facilitating factors that affect the life of employees during and after employment, e.g., after retirement. The screen will evaluate

(a) The job security of employees, alteration rate and anti-turnover measures in the company.
(b) The pension scheme contribution for the employees from the employer and the employee is reported.
(c) Sustainable production will be assessed in light of energy efficiency and adaptation of renewable energy depending on the line of business, and financial sustainability for both short term and long term profitability.

(d) Business supplier–customer relationship.
(e) Business innovation through the use of technology will also be considered.
(f) Environmental pollution, degradation and carbon footprints will screen.
(g) Waste disposal and management mechanism will screen.
(h) Business in Countries challenged with the limited or undiversified economy can be impactful if their operation enhances innovation, widen the market and leads to a diversified income source.

3.5. Criteria from global initiatives towards impactful business

The screening criteria in this section are derived from the global description of impactful business using principles such as ESG and Circular economy. It is worth highlighting that most of the impact measurement metrics are already captured in the mapped frameworks.

ESG framework serves as a guide in investment decision-making processes. Kell (2018) described ESG as the use of "environmental, social and governance factors to evaluate companies and countries on how far advanced they are with sustainability." ESG has now become an important buzzword in the business ecosystem. Meaning, firms wanting to excel and capitalize on current market opportunities should incorporate ESG factors in their business models. Unlike traditional financial analysis, ESG considers a wide range of issues that have environmental, social and financial consequence ignored in traditional financial system (Kell, 2018). For example, a hospital operating in a remote area rendering affordable health services to the poor communities but in turn dumps its waste into the river. This has a pollution effect on the environment, health hazard on the people, and reputational and financial risk to the business, leading to more harm than good. Such institutions cannot be impactful in our perspective. A good example is the case of BP's Deepwater Horizon 2010 oil spill in the Gulf of Mexico which exposes the company not to only financial loss of $90 billion as estimated by Financial Times but also result to reputational damage and a fall in company's share prices (Garmendia and Olszewski, 2014).

ESG screening is gaining prominence with the emergence of millennial and women investors. A recent survey conducted by Izhar and Dikmener (2017) shows that over 80% of the millennial and more than three-quarter of women have a strong interest in ESG investing. Similarly, an increasing number of funder managers are committed to integrating ESG criteria in their portfolio allocation process (Freiburghaus *et al.*, 2016). Integrating ESG in business model ensures sustainability, profitability and cost minimization. Clark *et al.* (2015) investigated the economic importance of ESG practice in business using over 200 high standard academic studies and sources on sustainability. Their result revealed that 90% shows cost-saving and 88% shows efficient operational performance. They concluded that firms who want to "do well while doing good" should integrate ESG in their business (Clark *et al.*, 2015, p. 9).

The circular economy (achieving zero-waste and zero-emissions) is an emerging and important area for economies in severe scarcity as well as climate change. Circular economy paradigm holds great potentials for sustainability and efficient usage of limited

Table 1. A Summary of Factors Considers under Each Element of Environmental, Social and Governance.

Environmental ("E")	Social ("S")	Governance ("G")
Biodiversity	Community relations	Accountability
Carbon emissions	Controversial business	Anti-takeover measures
Climate change risks	Customer relations/product	Board structure/size
Energy usage	Diversity issues	Bribery and corruption
Raw material sourcing	Employee relations	CEO duality
Regulatory/legal risks	Health and safety	Executive compensation schemes
Supply chain management	Human capital management	Ownership structure
Waste and recycling	Human rights	Shareholder rights
Water management	Responsible marketing and R&D	Transparency
Weather events	Union relationships	Voting procedures

Source: Clark *et al.* (2015).

resources to create a huge societal and environmental impact in realizing developmental objectives. Lacy and Rutqvist (2016) defined Circular Economy as "the decoupling of economic growth from extraction and consumption of constrained natural resources, i.e., scarce resources with negative footprints." According to Khan (2019), circular economy paradigm attempts to replicate the cycle of science and natural laws in which waste is zero. The waste product of plants (oxygen) becomes the input for a human being likewise the waste product (carbon dioxide) of human is inevitably the input for plants. The water cycle and photosynthesis are other examples. From Islamic finance perspectives, we can add zero-interest and zero-foreclosures to zero-waste and zero-emissions targets and get the 4Zeros circular Islamic finance and economy paradigm.

The replication of the natural cycle in business is achieved through reducing, reuse, recycle and redesign to avoid extraction, production, consumption and wastage like in linear paradigm. Accordingly, businesses that operate within the framework of *Maqasid al-Shariah*, SDGs, and Circular economic will have full preservative of ecology and can ensure sustainable human development (Khan, 2019). In this screening, great emphasis will be on the three fundamental Rs (reduce, reuse and redesign) because some countries are yet to recycle. Furthermore, successful implementation of these three Rs will lead to minimal need for recycle except in rare cases. Consequently, businesses will be screened based on their ability to effectively use minimal resources to generate high output and ability to reuse the waste of one activity as an input for another activity.

A flow chart of the impactful Shariah-compliant business criteria is provided in Figure 4. It is obvious that due to significant screening considerations, the cost of doing the business may initially be higher than the market rate. Since the long-term social benefits of such projects are expected to be higher, the society needs to give preference to such businesses. Governments cannot meet the required cost subsidy requirements. However, governments can facilitate to establish an institutional framework for creating social subsidy by harnessing the power of the institutions of compassion in a Muslim society.

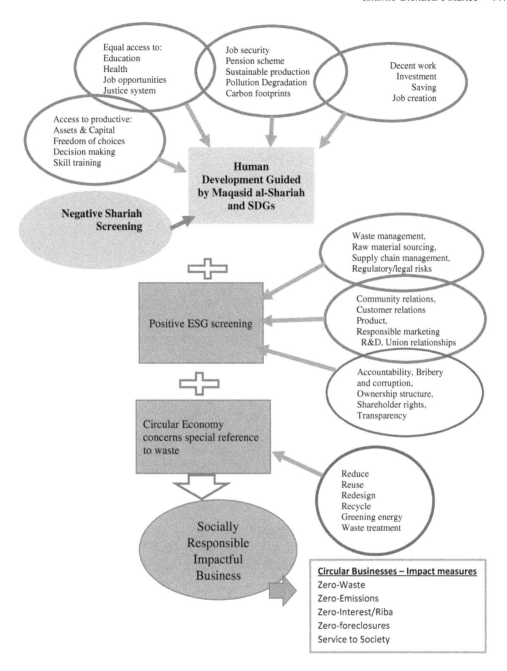

Source: Authors' Own 2019.

Figure 4. Impactful Shariah-Compliant Business Criteria

These institutions of compassion are interest-free loans, Zakah, Awqaf, Sadaqa, forbearance, compassionate guarantees, takaful and transfer of debts, etc. By reorganizing and strengthening these institutions of compassion, the governments can facilitate the creation of a sustainable social subsidy for the impactful businesses based on the consensus criteria.

4. Islamic Blended Finance

4.1. *Conventional blended finance definition*

There is no standardized definition for blended financed due to high fragmentation in blending ecosystem. While some definitions have an explicit focus on resources mobilization for SDGs in emerging markets (WEF & OECD, 2015; Blended Finance Task Force, 2017), other definitions are reflective of the objectives of the blended institution. OECD defined Blended Finance as "the strategic use of development finance for the mobilization of additional finance towards sustainable development in developing countries" (OECD, 2018b, p. 13).

Blended finance is the use of grant and in most cases, concessionary development finance to attract commercial finance into unattractive development activities. This is supported by Samans and Solheim's definition of blended finance. They defined blended finance as "the strategic used of development finance and philanthropic funds to mobilize private capital flows to emerging and frontier market" (Samans and Solheim, 2015, p. 4). It is obvious from these definitions that the common and overarching objective of blending is to utilize limited development finance in a manner that incentivises private sector participation in development impact project.

Another potential of blended finance is overcoming market barriers by adjusting risk-return relation to catalyse capital flows to projects with high development impact, which could otherwise be impossible. Shifting the risk-return profile, sharing local knowledge, building local capacity and shaping policy and regulatory reforms are some of the characteristics of blended finance that attracts private players to sectors with explicit social impact, financially viability and sustainable but are shying away due to market barriers (Samans and Solheim, 2015). Overcoming these barriers is extremely important to bridge development gaps, especially in SMEs sectors in dire need of resources.

In addition to the direct mobilization of commercial capital, the ambition of blended finance is to be catalytic, i.e., to spur the replication of similar projects via demonstration and build functioning markets that can result in larger volumes of commercial capital for development. According to WEF & OECD (2015), blending finance is characterized by three interconnected pillars as follows:

- Leverage: the strategic utilization of development and philanthropic funds to attract more private investment into development impact projects. This increases the capacity of limited development finance.
- Impact: blending development funds should yield sustainable social, environmental and economic impact that would otherwise be impossible.
- Returns: ensuring an attractive risk-adjusted return for private players to encourage them and sustainable value creation.

From the above, blended finance can be described as a platform that creates a win–win result for the blending parties. Its flexibility, according to IFC (2018), enables players to pool varieties of capital with different motives, maturity and risk appetite into a single investment portfolio. Development funds could either be used as a subsidy to provide a supportive mechanism, grant and concessional loan or to provide risk cushion in the form of subordinate equity, flexible debt or guarantee. This choice ultimately depends on the type of blending facilities and desired outcome for development actors (Pereira, 2017). Regarding geographies, sectors and instruments, blended finance can be used in a range of sectors and structures.

4.1.1. *The rationale of blended finance*

Blended finance creates a platform in which development funds mitigate and adjust risk-return, thereby levelling the playground for private investment, including the removal of investment barriers in development sectors. Through blended finance, all players obtain maximum benefits that could otherwise be impossible by individual efforts. The collaboration among blended parties, on the one hand, enable development finance to augment capacity from external sources while relaxing the pressure on ODA or aid, and revitalization of dormant markets. Creation of new jobs and wages increases government revenue through tax payment from staff and shareholders.

Private investors, on the other hand, are provided with risk cushion and roadway to access untapped and highly promising markets which could otherwise be impossible too. Oxfam in their paper "Private-Financing Blending for Development" described blending as an officially development assistance that can be used to remove investment 'barriers', allowing private finance to invest in developing countries when purely commercial motives would have precluded this, and at the same time improve the development focus and outcomes of private investment (both domestic and multinational). The economic viability and sustainability, and the fact that replication of projects is possible without development finance helps investors to diversify an investment portfolio and accurately match risk-return of investment to enjoy flourishing markets and attractive return (IFC, 2018).

Society is the most benefiting party of blended finance. Job creation, knowledge and skills transfer and most importantly, access to essential facilities that could otherwise be impossible under limited-pressurised donors and government budget can be met by blended finance. These, according to OECD, are the immense benefits that society could derive from any successful blending. Accordingly, effective blending focuses on key priorities of the immediate need to the society but unserved due to market barriers. However, it should be noted that such projects must be financially feasible and potentially viable overtime to attract commercial capital (IFC, 2018). Thus, blended finance is a "happy marriage" (Bosch, 2018, p. 2) that gives "Win–Win" result to all blended parties.

4.1.2. *Challenges of blended finance*

The phenomenon of blended finance is a new area in development finance, aiming at blending social funds or grants with loans for impact financing. The concept has been used by international organizations and donor partners to stimulate economic development at the same time gets returns on investments. Its potential in mobilizing impact financing is no doubt gaining prominence. However, the ecosystem of blended finance in most cases are one-sided giving the financier the right to dictate terms. Besides, the most critic is its target for the middle class and overlooking or precluding the pro-poor. Recently, the report by OECD DAC (2018) and Convergence (2018) shows only 9% blended facilities in low income for the past years of blending. These countries have the highest possibilities of being left behind in 2030, according to SDG[4] 2017 progress and prospects report. Yet, the main sources of development finance are being shifted to countries that are better off. Traditional blending may also result in misallocation of resources hence thrusting countries into more unsustainable debt, likewise, lack of transparency and accountability (Gavas *et al.*, 2014). Until now, the amount leveraged from the private sector through blending cannot be accurately articulated (Eurodad, 2013). Furthermore, balancing between financial and development incentives is sometimes challenging, especially when blending structure is dominated by financially motivated investors. Also, the likelihood of excluding faith-inclined entrepreneurs is high due to the interest element and inherent shortcomings of the conventional *riba*-based system. Although this is perceived as voluntary exclusion, Obaidullah and Khan (2008) argued that exclusion due to religion is, in fact, involuntary given Sariah conviction on economic activities of Muslims.

4.2. Islamic blended finance

In Section 2, we set a consensus-based policy framework given local, national and global realities and expectations. Considering the synergy between these three perspectives, in Section 3, we developed the impactful SME criteria, *4Zeros (zero-waste, zero-emissions, zero-interest, zero-foreclosures) and service to society*. The SMEs adhering to this impactful criteria may incur additional costs of doing the business.

The philanthropic and the profit motivations facilitated by the public sector can jointly structure a blended finance facility. We can define blended Islamic finance as "an optimal mixture of Islamic social funds like Zakah, Waqf, Sadaqa, Qard and grants, etc. with financial instruments to finance impactful SMEs for SDGs." Based on the consensus impact criteria, conventional philanthropists can also participate and contribute. In the broad contract design discussed in Figure 5(b) and discussed in detail later, the private sector provides finance, the philanthropist pays the costs of funds, the public sector facilitates and the impactful SME gets subsidized financing. Since the blended nature of the contract provides a social subsidy to fund the cost element of the financing, the proposed structure creates a win–win result for the blending parties.

Instead of using limited development funds to attract private capital, Islamic social funds are used to mitigate diversion of funds to unproductive activities and high default risk by providing safety-net, skills training and startup capital for the economically active poor and low-income entrepreneurs to create socially responsible businesses. Islamic microfinance can be used to attract private capital into the blended structure.

The logic is to reinforce the inherent nature of Islamic finance and also to unveil commercially viable markets such as financing the poorest and pro-poor entrepreneur,

---

[4] See Financing For Development Progress and Prospects: Report of the Inter-agency Task Force on Financing for Development (United Nation, 2017).

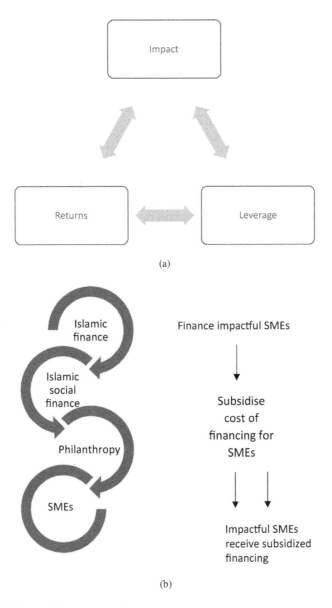

Sources: (a) OECD (2018b), and (b) drawn by authors.

Figure 5. (a). Pillars of Blended Finance (b). Summary Structure of Blended Islamic Finance

adjust the risk-return profile for commercial investors, and increase development resources for SDGs. Most importantly, to ensure the environmental, social, governance and financial sustainability of businesses. Gavas *et al.* (2014) assert that the philosophical concept of blended finance is to create and ensure the financial sustainability of businesses and their replication without development assistance. Blended finance has catalyst potentials to private investment into critical markets to support global goals. However, its success to a high degree depends on its application as a tool (Tonkonogy *et al.*, 2018).

4.2.1. The rationale of Islamic blended finance

The rationale is to create a win–win for all blended parties and to mobilize more commercial capital through financially viable projects. The outcome of the blended transaction is a benevolent loan (*qard*) to the SMEs, Murabahah for a financial institution and partial grant for the blended entity. The win–win for the three entity is

Financial Institutions: expanding into untapped and scalable market segments which were impossible due to high perceived risk and market barriers. Blending *Murabahah* adjust the risk-return profile, the lower operating cost compared to sharing contracts, guaranteed a fixed stream of cash flow through *Murabahah* contract[5] and most importantly, portfolio diversification and profitability for the commercial investor.

Small Medium Enterprises: blended Murabahah is beneficial to SMEs because it smoothens access to finance by overcoming key bottlenecks such as cost of funds, information symmetry,[6] and high operating cost. The provision of social subsidy does not only eliminate the cost of funding but also incentivise commercial investors into SMEs financing.

Philanthropic/blended entity: also save funds by just financing the markup component instead of providing full grant which could have to consume more resources. Murabahah blended unlike another financing mechanism, minimizes the utilization of limited development funds.

4.2.2. Conceptual framework of Islamic blended finance

The role of philanthropic Funds and Islamic Social Funds: In the context of blended Islamic finance, the Islamic social funds by default are meant to create value and enhance wellbeing without any expected financial return, especially for *Zakah* funds. In this regard, ISF will be used to de-risk the market and mitigate default risk through the provision of safety net, skills training and social subsidy for economically active poor and startups. According to Addae-Korankye (2014), high-interest rate and improper monitoring among other factors are the cause of high default rate in Microfinance. Thus, the provision of social subsidy eases the burden of high-cost finance on SMEs and reduces the risk perception. Besides, guarantee and technical support using ISF will attract commercial investors to Islamic blended finance.

In Fig. 6, we propose an Islamic model of blended finance with different components and stakeholders. The *Waqf* funds will be co-invested as flexible debt (longer duration) or subordinate equity (lower share of profit) or as seed capital with private capital to provide risk cushion. The *Waqf* proceeds will be distributed accordingly with excess *Zakah* funds to provide *Marabahah* subsidies, Kafala, *qard* and Technical Assistance (TA) in the blended structure. The capital will be reinvested to generate perpetual cash flow. Likewise, the penalty funds received as charity from financial institutions will be utilized for these purposes. In summary, only the Waqf funds from ISF will be used for commercial purposes.

---

[5] The price in *Murabahah* (both cost and markup), payment mode and dates are agreed at the beginning of the contract which in this context is paid by the blended entity hence the stream of cash flows are known and fixed.

[6] The direct involvement of blended entity to pay markup reduces the information and risk profile of SMEs.

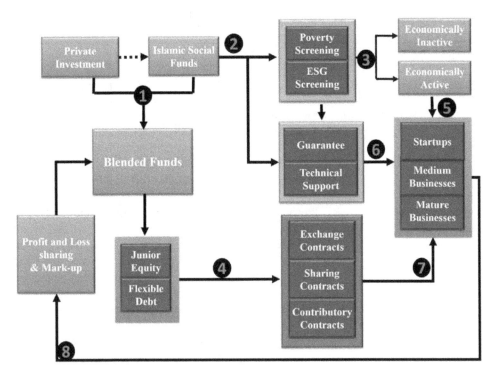

Source: Authors' Own 2019.

Figure 6. Proposed Islamic Blended Finance Model (IBFM)

The role of Private investment in Islamic blended finance: It is important to highlight that this category of blended finance constitutes of diverse investors. Ranging from purely commercially motivated investors, social investors and impact investors as discussed earlier. Their individual interest dictates their roles in the blended structure. For example, some investors are socially motivated and always motivated to create substantial development impact through good loans. Hence, what they require is a guarantee of capital through Kafala using IFSs. Others may be interested in both (impact and financial gains); thus their capital has to be invested in the revenue-generating avenue. Finally, investors motivated by commercial factors and risk cushion to attract their funds into blended portfolio requires a higher share of profit, guarantees, subsidies or even TA through ISFs.

The role of Government in Islamic blended finance: It is apparent that government have the mandate to craft sound policies that foster the conducive business environment and coexistence. In Islamic blended finance, the role of government is to craft flexible policies that smoothen SMEs financing in a transparent and accountable manner. The isolated efforts of development institutions can hardly bear any fruits. For instance, ISFs are sometimes perceived as free money makes them difficult for collectors to create substantial impact especially in countries where such collection is not institutionalized. Similarly, institutions responsible for businesses, e.g., Chambers of Commerce cannot afford

Table 2. Conventional Blended (CB) Instruments and Replication in Islamic Blended (IB).

CB Instruments & Structure	IB Instruments	Market Segment	Additional Information
Grants	Waqf, Sadaqah, Zakah penalty fees	Preparing Pioneering	In Islamic blended instead of using the limited development assistance, the society faith-based is tapped to prepare the economically active of society through skills training, Capital to start a business.
Repayable Grants	Qard	Preparing Pioneering Facilitating	It is used to support business startup, existing small businesses and even medium business. The loan can be spent on working capital, purchase of a fixed asset to smoothen business operation and growth.
Guarantees	Kafala (third party quarantee)	Pioneering, Facilitating Anchoring	The use of guarantees dominated blended finance market for the past years. Kafala can be used for the same. However, the amount to be guaranteed is subjected to controversy.
Debt (concessional loans)	Murabahah line of credit, Sukuk, Salam, Istina	Preparing Pioneering Facilitating Anchoring	It should be noted that the interest payment is replaced with a make-up/return lower than the market rate for Islamic Blended Funds. This is suitable to support the start-up and growth of existing firms.
Debt (market rate)	Murabahah line of credit, Sukuk, Salam, Istina	Anchoring Transitioning	The make-up/returns are at par with prevailing market rates and conditions. Usually, this type of loan is suitable for a mature company
Equity (first loss absorber/ risk capital)	Unrestricted Mudarabah, Musharakah, Muzarah	Preparing Pioneering	In Islamic finance, this is based on profit and loss sharing. Therefore, the different contract can be depending on the preferences of the investors. Mudarabah capital is unguaranteed, but Mudrib can give hibah to mitigate displaced commercial risk.
Market-based equity	Musharakah (diminishing), Mudarabah	Anchoring Transitioning	Similarly, equity can be provided at a market rate depending on the company life cycle. For example, a mature company that has already crowd-in commercial can be funded on market-rate equal to private investors.
Technical Assistance	Waqf, Sadaqah, Zakat	All stages of the life cycle	Similar but differs in sources of funding.

singlehanded tackle the myriad challenges of businesses. In addition, financial institutions acting on fiduciary duty are restricted to the level of compassion and the type of investment. Portfolios with explicit high risk are avoided to avoid negligence in explicit risky investment even though; such investment might be commercially viable. Coordination and corporation of these bodies by the government can help strike a balance, create efficiency and huge development impact through regulatory legal frameworks and policies that empower independent bodies to engage in ISF. For instance, the creation of a blended entity that pools obligatory private collection of Zakah, legal frameworks that allows the usage of ISF to provide social subsidy by independent organizations. Also to give the privilege to receive and direct the donations from State-owned enterprises.

Role of Conventional Philanthropists: Since the consensus framework setting in section two included SDGs and since the impact criteria discussed in section three included ESG considerations, it can be expected that conventional philanthropic organizations will participate with Islamic finance and social finance institutions. In fact, in 2012, the Bill & Milinda Gates Foundation (BMGF) worked with the Islamic Development Bank (IsDB) to develop an Islamic blended finance facility. The IsDB extended $200 million Murabaha financing of Polio vaccines for Pakistan. The BMGF paid the cost of financing (mark-up). The facility became for Pakistan cost-free financing (reference link https://bit.ly/35gmtz6).

(1) The Blended body is responsible for the pooling of funds from private sources and compassionate funds (Zakah, Waqf, Sadaqah, a penalty from delinquency charity, donations, etc.). The Blended entity can equally provide incentives to attract private investors who may want to invest directly to the SMEs and need to benefit from the blended finance incentives. In this case, the blended finance is able to attract the needed investment. This will have a higher impact in terms of scope as private investors may not want to pool their funds.
(2) The screening process to determine the economically active poor and the inactive.
(3) A permanent safety net for economically inactive poor and skill training, proper bookkeeping and ESG principles the economically active poor. In addition, IBC screening and for existing firms and borrowers to assess the risk of default.
(4) The Waqf funds will be co-investment with private capital in income-generating activities and the return to be distributed as prescribed by the *Wakil*. The funds can be invested in sharing contracts or financing depending on the suitable contract. It should be noted that ISFs (except for Waqf) are not co-mingled with private for transparency and accountability purposes.
(5) The economically active are provided with startup capital after acquiring enough entrepreneur skills, bookkeeping and ESG factors to graduate from poverty.
(6) Existing SMEs depending on GIBC screening scores, they are either provided with a guarantee (*Kafala*) or technical support through feasibility studies, etc. Firms can be trained to integrate ESG and ensure proper bookkeeping and accounting.
(7) They are investing in existing SMEs. It worth highlighting that the blended entity is not only providing social subsidies but also investing to be financially sustainable and

commercially viable. Although the main focus is to ease funding hurdles for SMEs, some mature businesses may only need equity or flexible financing and not subsidies, bearing in mind that subsidies are only permanent at the incubation stage.

(8) Finally, the share of profit and loss or markup from SMEs depending on the contract used. This investment is made into mature and established SMEs.

4.2.3. Blended Murabahah

In Fig. 7, we present a structure for the proposed blended Murabahah. *Murabahah* financing has three components: (a) principal amount of finance which is the price of the asset purchased, (b) opportunity cost of finance that the financier faces; it is benchmarked with the LIBOR or any other money market rate and (c) profit that the financier is expected to earn determined by the credit risk of the finance user.

The components (b) plus (c) determine the cost for the finance user. For micro and medium enterprises, this cost is exorbitant because of the perceived risk that financial institutions face by stepping out from their business culture and engaging in financing SMEs. The governments cannot provide subsidy to the SMEs due to limited resources. Provision of social subsidy to fund markup is possible through blended finance.

The government and regulatory authority can develop an institutional framework whereby the social institutions of Islamic economies namely *Zakah, Awqaf, Sadaqa, Qard*, grants, etc. are reorganized through an Islamic social finance fund (ISFF).

In a blended *Murabahah,* the component (a) of finance, namely, principal amount of financing will be paid by the financial institution and components (b) plus (c) will be paid

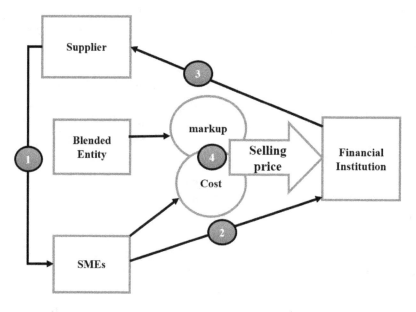

Source: Authors' Own 2019.

Figure 7. Blended *Murabahah*

by the ISFF. In this way, the *Murabahah* financing will serve as an interest-free loan for the beneficiary SME.

4.2.4. Blended Murabahah line of credit

In Fig. 8, we develop a blended Murabahah line of credit. *Murabahah* line of credit[7] is suitable funding for repetitive transactions such as working capital for SMEs. It has similar components and logic as blended *Murabahah*, however, in blended *Murabahah* line of credit, the blending entity instead of providing social subsidies will directly engage with private entities such as multilateral and bilateral banks using Master *Murabahah* line of credit. The logic is to eliminate component (c) (profit that the financier is expected to earn determined by the credit risk of the finance user) and secure funding at interbank labor which in this case is a markup lower than the market rate.

Currently, IDB is using this approach to fund SMEs in The Gambia through the Arab Gambian Islamic Bank (AGIB). IDB provided $5million worth of *Murabahah* funding to (AGIB) in the first quarter of 2017 at a markup of 6.5%. AGIB charges a fluctuating rate of 17–20% depending on the risk profile of the SMEs. The difference between the two markups is the profit of AGIB. In order to save cost and become self-financial sustainable, the blended entity can opt for wholesale *Murabahah* as well. Depending on the beneficiary SMEs, the blended entity can finance the purchase orders using market rate, or at par

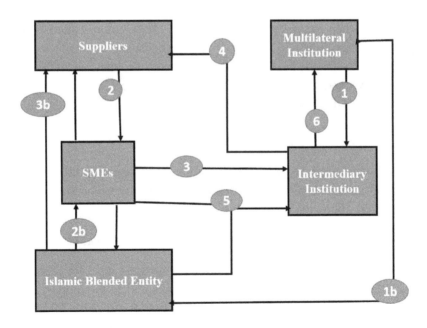

Source: Authors' Own 2019.

Figure 8. Blended *Murabahah* Line of Credit

---

[7] For line of credit of Murabahah, see Kahf (2013) Islamic Financial Contracts 2013, p. 392 for detail understanding.

known as *Tawliyah* sale or even at a discount known as *Hatitah*. Of course, the choice of financing will depend on the objective and business status of the SMEs (whether startup, medium or mature). It should be noted that these two contracts are independent of each other. The master contract between the banks and the blended entity is separate from each other. Thus, the blended entity can equally include *Wakala* to enable the SMEs to take delivery on behalf of the entity.

The outcome is to broaden funding sources for SMEs as conventional financial institutions can equally be tapped into through this approach. Blended *Muarabahah* is replicable in other exchange contracts as well. In *Ijarah*, *Salam* and *Istisna* contract, the entity can pay the rent and markup element, respectively. SMEs can use the asset for free except for Ijarah ending with ownership in which SMEs will contribute toward the purchase. In sharing contracts such as *Musharakah*, *Muz'arah*, etc., the Blended entity assumes lower profit sharing. For *Mudarabah* capital, the Islamic Social Funds can provide *Kafala* for *Mudarabah* capital in socially responsible and impactful SMEs.

Explanation of the Blended Murabahah line of credit

(1) The intermediary sign mater Murabahah contract with the multilateral bank at the makeup of 6.5% for example.
(2) The intermediary bank also enters into another Murabahah with SMEs who collect the invoice from the Supplier.
(3) The banks buy from the supplier and SMEs on *Wakala* takes delivery on behalf of the bank. The bank then charges the makeup base on the Libor and the desired profit, for example, 17–20%.
(4) The mark-up (17–20%) is paid by the Blended Entity and the cost by the SMEs. 1b) to be cost-effective and efficient in the fund's management, the Blended Entity may directly deal with multilateral banks to pay a makeup of 6.5% instead of 20%.

5. Conclusions and Policy Framework

In this research, we used comprehensive human development, MD and sustainable development inter-changeably. We contextualized these concepts for Muslim societies and now recapitulate the following conclusions:

(a) *The synergy between local aspirations, national priorities and global goals*

These are not new concepts. Islamic scholars during the 12th–14th century developed the Maqasid al-Shariah framework which now represents local aspirations of individuals, families, businesses, compassionate organizations. Countries utilize the MD framework for nation-building; a good example of this is the Qatar National Vision 2030. In international context specially within the UN institutions significantly work is ongoing for decades now taking the form of the UN SDGs. It is a healthy sign for policy making and implementation that a synergy between the three perspectives exists. A consensus understanding of the concepts is emerging. This can be utilized as a target for resource mobilization.

(b) *The synergy between the motivations of philanthropy, profits and government facilitation*

Our second conclusion is the direct result of the first conclusion. In any society, including Muslim societies, three motivations play an important role. The motive of compassion drives the actions of philanthropic organizations. Commercial entities work for profits. Governments have to be proactive in facilitating the institutional framework for development. If these three motivations are blended, the outcome can be more effective. We argued in the paper that impactful SMEs that promote MD could be a shared goal of the three motivations.

(c) *Impact criteria for SMEs*

In this paper, we developed potential consensus criteria for SMEs that the three groups of stakeholders will agree as to their common purpose. These are 4Zeros — zero-waste, zero-emissions, zero-interest and zero-foreclosures and service to society.

(d) *Islamic blended finance*

The first and second conclusions and derived the impact criteria enable us to suggest an engineered financial product for financing the impactful SMEs. The cost of funding for SMEs is most of the times high. Some additional cost may be added for impactful SMEs because these may be based on new modalities. Governments cannot offer subsidies on the cost of funding. In blended Islamic finance, the principal amount of finance is contributed by a commercial entity, and the cost of finance is fully or partially met by the compassionate and philanthropic entity. We characterized this as a win–win arrangement to finance impactful SMEs that contribute to MD.

(e) *Policy framework*

The research suggested a definition and criteria for impactful businesses. The businesses must be cognizant of environmental, social and governance issues and other global initiatives if we are to attain sustainability. Evidence in the literature shows that integration of ESG principles in businesses has proven to increase profitability, mitigate environmental risk, reduces cost and guarantees sustainability. Besides, ESGs integration has global opportunities to tap into divergent funding sources and attract investors who want to do well while doing good and philanthropists who are mainly persuaded by social and environmental factors.

However, one of the major challenges is the funding these types of SMEs, due to the incompatibility of their business model with current banking culture and functions. Hence the funding costs are exorbitant for them to bear. The governments' resources are limited and under pressure, and no public subsidy could be sustainable.

In this paper, an institutional framework for social subsidy is proposed using the concept of blending finance. The study discussed the concept of conventional blending finance and built on its shortcomings to present the idea of Islamic blended finance, potentially using the Islamic social institutions of compassion such as Zakah, Sadaqah, Waqf, etc. Integration of Islamic to incentivises private sector participation and economically active of the society to facilitate wealth creation and resources mobilization.

The study expects that this framework of blended Islamic finance could be instrumental in providing funding for the SMEs. Proposed Blended *Murabahah* and Blended *Murabahah* line of credit model in which the Blending charitable entity provides a social subsidy to pay the markup while the SMEs pays the cost only results into a win–win for all parties. While the financial institutions tap into SMEs sector through Blended contracts to increase profitability, the Blended entity minimizes the amount of grant by providing a partial grant to fund the markup only. The SMEs' have interest free loans to increase productivity.

Islamic blended finance unlike other not for profit organizations reinforces market-based financing to leverage commercial capital to SDGs related projects. Overcoming market barriers, adjusting the risk-returns profile, lowering the aid-dependent rate and the ability to attract commercial capital into projects with explicit development impact which could otherwise be impossible are the reasons for blended finance prominence and featuring in the global agenda. Besides, Islamic blended finance through Islamic Social Funds has the magic power to overcome the shortcomings of conventional blended finance such as; poor local ownership, lack of transparency and accountability, lack of specific strategies for poverty alleviation and shifting ODA to middle-income countries at the detriment of the developing countries.

Given the need for funds for comprehensive human development Islamic blended finance is expected to have a wide range of applications including such a low-cost housing, impactful SMEs, health and educational services, water and sanitation, climate-related initiatives, etc. Our research offers a potential framework for formulating specific national policies in these and other critical areas.

References

Addae-Korankye, Alex (2014). Causes of poverty in Africa: A review of literature. *American International Journal of Social Science*, 3(7), 147.
BNP Paribas (2018). Microfinance Barometer 2018: Is microfinance profitable? *Microfinance Barometer*, pp. 1–4. https://group.bnpparibas/en/news/microfinance-barometer-2018-microfinance-profitable.
Blended Finance Task Force (2017). *Better Finance Better World Better World*. London: Business & Sustainable Development Commission.
Bosch, FVD (2018). A recipe for blended finance. *SME Finance Forum*, 11 November, pp. 1–4.
Chapra, MU (2008). *The Islamic Vision of Development in the Light of Maqasid al-Shariah*. Jeddah, KSA: Islamic Research and Training Institute, Islamic Development Bank.
Clark, GL, A Feiner and M Viehs (2015). From the Stockholder to the Stakeholder: How Sustainability Can Drive Financial Outperformance. In *SSRN*, pp. 1–62. https://arabesque.com/research/From_the_stockholder_to_the_stakeholder_web.pdf.
Convergence (2018). *The State of Blended Finance*. Convergence Blending Global Finance.
Dariah, AR, MS Sallah and HM Shafiai (2016). New approach for sustainable development goals in Islamic perspective. *Procedia-Social and Behavioral Sciences*, 219, 159–166.

Eurodad (2013). *A Dangerous Blend? The EU's Agenda to 'Blend' Public Development Finance with Private Finance*. Belgium: Eurodad.

Freiburghaus, L, F Tinner, J Varonier and F Wenk (2016). Blended Finance: How blended finance can close the prevailing investment gap and allow social enterprises to grow. *University of St. Gallen*, pp. 1–45. http://www.msdconsult.ch/wp-content/uploads/2017/07/blended-finance.pdf.

Garmendia, C and A Olszewski (2014). *Impact Investing in Development*, s.l.: IIPC network.

Gavas, M, A Prizzon and S Mustapha (2014). *TOPIC GUIDE: Blended Finance for Infrastructure and Low Carbon Development*. UK: Evidence on Demand.

Gianoncelli, A and P Boiardi (2018). *Impact Strategies – How Investors Drive Social*. Brussels: The European Venture Philanthropy Association.

Haq, MU (1995). *Reflections on Human Development*. Oxford University Press.

Husson, T (2015). *Green Microfinance: A Solution for Access to Essential Services*. Available at: https://ideas4development.org/en/green-microfinance-solution-access-essential-services/ [Accessed 16 October 2018].

IFC (2018). *Blended Finance — A Stepping Stone to Creating Markets*. International Finance Corporation.

Izhar, H and G Dikmener (2017). I for impact: Blending Islamic Finance and impact investing for the global goals. *Islamic Economic Studies*, 130, 1–8.

Kahf, Monzer (2013). Islamic Financial Contracts (author's self publication on Amazon) ISBN-13: 978-1514682951.

Kamal-Chaoui, L (2019). *Unlocking the Potential of SMEs for the SDGs*. Available at: https://oecd-development-matters.org/2017/04/03/unlocking-the-potential-of-smes-for-the-sdgs/.

Khan, T (2019). Reforming Islamic Finance for Achieving Sustainable Development Goals. *JKAU: Islamic Economics*, 32(1), 3–21.

Lacy, P and J Rutqvist (2016). *Waste to Wealth: The Circular Economy Advantage*. Palgrave Macmillan.

Obaidullah, M and T Khan (2008). *Islamic Microfinance Development: Challenges and Initiatives*. Jeddah: Islamic Development Bank.

OECD DAC (2018). *Amounts Mobilised from the Private Sector by Official Development Finance Interventions 2016 OECD-DAC Survey – Preliminary Analysis*. OECD.

OECD (2018a). *Financing SMEs and Entrepreneurs 2016: An OECD Scoreboard*. Paris: OECD Publishing.

OECD (2018b). *Making Blended Finance Work for the Sustainable Development Goals*. Paris: OECD Publishing.

Pereira, J (2017). *Blended Finance What it is, How It Works and How It Is Used*. Eurodad and Oxfarm.

Samans, R and E Solheim (2015). *A How-To Guide for Blended Finance A Practical Guide for Development Finance and Philanthropic Funders to Integrate Blended Finance Best Practices into their Organizations*. World Economic Forum.

Société Générale and UNEP FI (2018). *Rethinking Impact to Finance the SDGs*. s.l.: s.n. https://www.unepfi.org/wordpress/wp-content/uploads/2018/11/Rethinking-Impact-to-Finance-the-SDGs.pdf.

Tonkonogy, B et al. (2018). *Blended Finance in Clean Energy: Experiences and Opportunities*. Commission and the Blended Finance Taskforce.

UNDP (2018). *Human Development Report*. Available at: http://hdr.undp.org/en/humandev [Accessed 25 January 2019].

United Nations (2017) Financing For Development Progress and Prospects: Report of the Interagency Task Force on Financing for Development.

WEF & OECD (2015). *Blended Finance Vol. 1: A Primer for Development Finance and Philanthropic Funders*. WORLD ECONOMIC FORUM.

World Bank Group (2017). *What's Happening in the Missing Middle*. Washington: International Bank for Reconstruction and Development/The World Bank.

World Bank Group (2018). *Improving Access to Finance for SMEs Opportunities through Credit Reporting, Secured Lending and Insolvency Practices*. World Bank.

Chapter 19

Hybrid Review of Islamic Pricing Literature[#]

Md. Abdullah Al Mamun[*,§], M. Kabir Hassan[†,¶],
Md. Abul Kalam Azad[*,||] and Mamunur Rashid[‡,**]

[*]*Department of Business and Technology Management
Islamic University of Technology, Gazipur 1704, Bangladesh*

[†]*Department of Economics and Finance
University of New Orleans, New Orleans, LA 70148, USA*

[‡]*Universiti Brunei Darussalam
Brunei Darussalam*
[§]*mamunr@iut-dhaka.edu*
[¶]*mhassan@uno.edu*
[||]*kalam@iut-dhaka.edu*
[**]*mamunur.rashid@ubd.edu.bn*

During the last decade, studies on Islamic pricing (IP) have received considerable attention from researchers and academicians. Given the growing popularity of IP, this study critically examines IP literature using a hybrid review — bibliometric analysis with content analysis. In addition to that the Islamic view of pricing based on the principles of Quran and Sunnah is also examined. The bibliometric results show that IP literature demonstrates a low productivity, low citations ratio, and high research collaboration. The content analysis identifies that the pricing methods, mechanisms, considerations and other industries except Islamic finance industry, are still under-researched. This study is of critical importance because it simultaneously shows the evolution of IP and explores new dimensions of it.

Keywords: Islamic pricing; Islamic marketing mix; bibliometric analysis; content analysis; Islam.

1. Introduction

The term "Price" refers to the amount of money paid by customers for the purpose of having or using a product or service (Hamid *et al.*, 2014). The Islamic perspective of pricing requires it to be Shariah compliant to ensure greater benefits to society through the satisfaction of Almighty Allah (Saeed *et al.*, 2001; Kusuma, 2019). Islam does not allow businessmen to be greedy (Saeed *et al.*, 2001; Saleh and Salsabila, 2018). Ibn Taymiyah uses two terminologies to refer to IP — "*equal compensation*" and "*equal price*", where the first one focuses on the essence of justice, the second one focuses on the standard price

---

[||]Corresponding author.
[#]This Chapter first appeared in the *Singapore Economic Review*, Vol. 67, No. 1, doi: 10.1142/S0217590821420029. © 2022 World Scientific Publishing.

for a particular place and time (Kusuma, 2019). IP focuses on both sellers and buyers; and on method and brand for setting a fair price to serve a community (Hashim *et al.*, 2014; Kabiraj *et al.*, 2014; Haque *et al.*, 2017). Pricing in Islam must not exploit consumers' psychology by creating false impressions and businessmen should not create difficulties for customers to access the products and services (Shaw, 1996; Koku, 2011; Hamid *et al.*, 2014; Kabiraj *et al.*, 2014). Profit margin in IP should be just and it should encourage healthy competition (Kabiraj *et al.*, 2014). Islam strongly discourages and prohibits deceptive pricing, inconsistent pricing, unjustified price changing, corner market, hoarding, usury, riba, coercion, distortion, predatory pricing, dumping, cartels, and price discrimination (Saeed *et al.*, 2001; Abdullah, 2008; Arham, 2010; Hashim *et al.*, 2014; Kabiraj *et al.*, 2014; Yousaf, 2016; Haque *et al.*, 2017; Saleh and Salsabila, 2018).

During the last decade, many papers review Islamic marketing (IM) and Islamic finance literature with a variety of focus. Examples include the study of CSR practices and marketing mix (Hamid *et al.*, 2014; Hashim and Hamzah, 2014; Haque *et al.*, 2017; Saleh and Salsabila, 2018) and the Muslim consumer or market segment (Rajasakran *et al.*, 2017; Salam *et al.*, 2019). Tournois and Aoun (2012) explore Islamic market-oriented cultural approach for non-Muslim businessmen. Sandıkçı (2011) identifies the reasons behind growing interest in Islamic marketing. Mamun *et al.* (2020) critically review Islamic marketing literature to identify research trends. Jafari (2012) emphasizes the importance of self-critique and reflexivity in advancing knowledge in IM; whereas, Hossain *et al.* (2018) focus on linking the gap between researches and practices in IM. Cader (2015) discovers the challenges of Islamic advertising. A review of Islamic finance and accounting literature to provide a contemporary outlook of Islamic finance industry is completed by Hassan *et al.* (2019). However, till today, no review papers have been published specifically focusing on IP demonstrating its development over time. Considering this limitation, this study attempts to consolidate, review, and integrate IP literature using a hybrid research approach based on 140 documents from Scopus[1] database (1990–2020). The purposes of this study are

(1) To demonstrate how IP literature has evolved over time and which authors, countries, and sources have contributed the most to its development.
(2) To demonstrate the topic relevance over time and describe key insights from recent trending papers and the most cited documents.
(3) To explore new dimensions of IP based on a comprehensive discussion of the guidelines of the Quran and Sunnah about pricing.

---

[1] SCOPUS database is one of the largest databases of peer-reviewed articles in the fields of science, social science, arts, humanities and medicine. It covers more than 20,000 peer- reviewed journals. The Scopus database provides access to tens of millions of published articles found at http://www.info.sciverse.com/scopus/scopus-in-detail/facts. In comparison with Web-of-Science database, the Scopus database is more comprehensive in nature because it provides more title coverage (http://wokinfo.com/media/pdf/WoSFS_08_7050.pdf). Many renowned scholars recommend and apply SCOPUS database for bibliometric review (Chicksand *et al.*, 2012; Randhawa *et al.*, 2016). With the hope of searching the major influential and peer reviewed articles, SCOPUS database is hoped to capture most of it.

The analysis reveals that IP literature has been entering into an exponential growth phase, and it can be characterized by high collaborations but a low citation ratio. Mohammad Kabir Hassan, Malaysia, and *Journal of Islamic Accounting and Business Research (JIABR)* are the most eminent author, country, and source respectively in IP literature. Content analysis from recent trending papers suggests that pricing in Islamic banking and finance industry is the core focus among researchers. The three-field plot analysis and a comprehensive discussion of the guidelines from the Quran and sunnah explore various perspectives and dimensions of IP. This study is not only timely but also of critical importance because it simultaneously shows the development of IP literature, explores new dimensions of IP, and identifies future research agenda for theoretical and policy implications.

The remaining of the paper is presented in six sections. Section 2 explains the review techniques we use, followed by the results of the bibliometric analysis in Section 3. The most relevant documents are carefully examined in Section 4. Discussion and exploration of new dimensions are included in Section 5. Section 6 concludes the study.

2. Methodology

Several techniques are available for a critical literature review. Examples include (1) structured systematic review, (2) review for framework development, (3) meta-analysis, (4) theory-based review, (5) hybrid review, and (6) bibliometric review. This study employs a two-stage hybrid review process to provide an in-depth understanding of IP literature.

In the first stage, "bibliometric review technique" is used to study scientific links among authors, keywords, countries, and journals. The search process for this study is conducted in April 2020 using the search, appraisal, Synthesis, and Analysis (SALSA) framework in the Scopus database (Papaioannou *et al.*, 2010). The Scopus database is selected because it is the largest database for peer-reviewed papers in social science disciplines and it is widely recognized for qualitative study (Norris and Oppenheim, 2007; Bartol *et al.*, 2014; Guerrero-Baena *et al.*, 2014; Durán-Sánchez *et al.*, 2019). Several keywords are used when searching for published papers, including Islamic Price, Halal Price, Religious Pricing, Islamic Pricing, Halal Pricing, Religious Price, Ethical Pricing, and Ethical price. The search covers the years of 1990–2019. Next, the search is limited to the subject-areas of Business or Economics and document type of journal or book. The search returns a total of 140 documents on which bibliometric analysis is completed.

In the second stage, this study analyzes the contents of the 34 selected documents — 14 are recently published and 20 are the most cited documents to identify widely used methods and widely studied topics within Islamic pricing literature. Additionally, the abstracts of all 140 documents are carefully scrutinized to demonstrate the topic relevance over time. Finally, the guidelines from the Quran and Sunnah are studied to explore new dimensions of IP. The whole methodological approach is shown in Figure 1. Islamic books, such as the Holy Quran and Hadith, present ideas on practices involving finance. The hybrid research approach provides a synthesis of the arguments from a literature review with those ideas on mind. Also, this approach helps readers get a comparative view of pricing policies in theory and practice. Future research agenda are summarized based on these two stages.

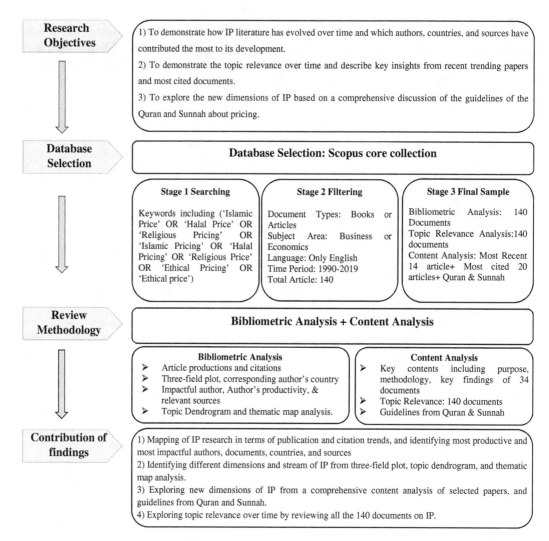

Figure 1. Methodological Approach

3. Results and Discussion

In general, the Islamic pricing (IP) literature can be characterized with a low level of productivity, below average citations per document, and high collaboration among researchers. During the last three decades, only 140 documents are written by 337 authors. The average citations per document appear to be low when the entire time span of thirty years is taken into consideration. Collaboration among the researchers appears to be dominant as more than 80% of the studies are co-authored.

3.1. Publication and citation trends

The trend of IP literature publication is shown through historical series analysis in Figure 2. The earliest document in IP literature can be traced back to 1990, and since then, a relatively inferior quantity of annual publications has been observed until 2006. During 2002–2003, there are no publication at all. The number, nonetheless, has picked up after 2007 with the highest peak in 2017 and an annual growth of 9.65%. The exponential growth that starts in 2010 coincides surprisingly with the emergence of the Journal of Islamic Marketing. The average article citations per year appear to be less homogenous. Documents published in 1996 and 2008 possess the highest average citations followed by the documents published in 2007 and 1991 respectively. Documents published during 2008 dominate the list of average per year citations. In 2008, only 5 documents are published, each of which has received 52 citations on average in the following 12 years, which stands at 4.33 citations annually. However, the mean citations per year remains steady over time.

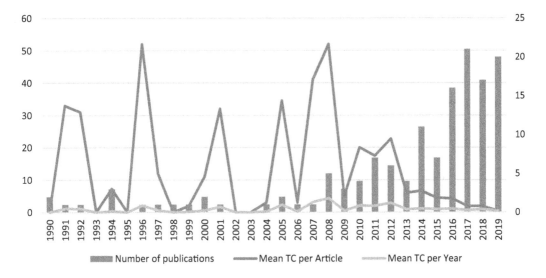

Figure 2. Publication and Citation Trends

3.2. Three-field plot

Authors approach IP literature from five perspectives: (1) spirituality, (2) products (market offerings), (3) pricing, (4) pricing models, and (5) market structure. Figure 3 demonstrates the three-field plot with prolific researchers on the left field, authors' keywords in the center, and sources on the right field. Spirituality is found to be one of the core dimensions of IP that conceptualizes pricing strategies and procedures from an Islamic perspective. Discussions on the second dimension, products, focus on the need for a clearer understanding of the product types, including-banking, finance, and sukuk while integrating perceived knowledge from the literature on spirituality. Alongside these two dimensions, existing pricing strategies, theories, models, concepts, and practices play an important role in setting prices by Muslim marketers. While preferring the fundamental factors over the emotional or religious factors as determinants of Islamic prices, it is found that market structure, market dynamics, market types, and geographic location have a significant impact on setting pricing strategies from an Islamic perspective.

468 *Introduction to Islamic Economics and Finance*

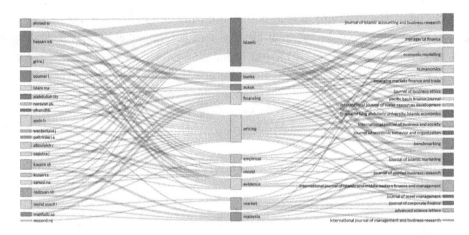

Figure 3. Three-Field Plot

3.3. *Corresponding author's country*

Figure 4 demonstrates the IP related documents in terms of single (SCP) and multiple publications (MCP) for each country. Malaysia leads this list with 19 documents, of which 15 are single country documents leaving 4 to be multiple country documents. Several researchers from Saudi Arabia, Morocco, Egypt, Indonesia, Qatar, Algeria, Austria, Germany, and Jordan publish single author papers. Researchers from Brunei, Ghana, and Greece are found in active collaboration with researchers from other countries. It is interesting to note that among the listed 20 countries, 3 are within D-8 (developing 8 countries with Muslim majority people). These countries are moving towards a preferential trade agreement for a better economic co-operation (Othman *et al.*, 2013). The results of the SCP and MCP reveal that researchers are more interested in collaborating and publishing their documents in a single country rather than multiple countries. This signifies that Islamic pricing is impacted by a strong country- or region-specific factor.

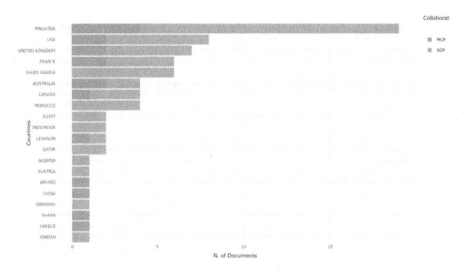

Figure 4. Corresponding Author's Country

3.4. *Most relevant authors and authors' impact*

The list of the most prolific authors in IP literature is presented in Table 1. The table also presents the corresponding value for the number of documents, total citations, g-index, h-index, and m-index. It is observed that the top 20 authors contributed to 35.7% (50 documents) of the total published documents and only 4 authors contributed to more than two documents each. With a total of eight documents, Mohammad Kabir Hassan appears to be the most productive author in IP literature, followed by Aboulaich Rajae (4 documents) and Essia Ries Ahmed (3 documents). While most authors are from academia, relative lesser impact of IP literature has resulted in poorer h-index. Hanudin Amin has the highest h-index of 3, with ninety-eight citations from his three documents. Comparing the growth of impact of each researcher (g-index and h-index), Mohammad Kabir Hassan is easily the top researcher in IP literature.

Table 1. Most Relevant Authors and Author Impact

Author	h-index	g-index	m-index	Total Citations	Number of Publications
Mohammad Kabir Hassan	2	4	0.4	25	8
Aboulaich Rajae	1	1	0.167	2	4
Essia Ries Ahmed	2	3	0.333	10	3
Hanudin Amin	3	3	0.25	98	3
Walid A. Abderrahman	2	2	0.095	22	2
Tariq Tawfeeq Yousif Alabdullah	1	1	0.333	3	2
Faisal Alqahtani	2	2	0.333	15	2
Nathan Berg	2	2	0.286	16	2
M. Shahid Ebrahim	2	2	0.091	16	2
Jocelyn Grira	2	2	0.4	16	2
Zarinah Hamid	2	2	0.2	22	2
Md. Aminul Islam	1	1	0.333	3	2
Salina Hj Kassim	1	2	0.1	18	2
Jeong-Yoo Kim	2	2	0.286	16	2
Suhal Kusairi	1	1	0.25	1	2
Akhmad Affandi Mahfudz	1	2	0.2	4	2
Micheal J. Mccord	1	2	0.125	7	2
Rosylin Mohd Yusof	1	2	0.2	4	2
Na Mohr	1	1	0.037	2	2
Nader Naifar	2	2	0.25	14	2

Notes: h-index = h-index means that a particular author has "h" articles published, each of which has received "h" or more number of citations; g-index = it means top g articles cited on an average g number of times, m-index = it is an individual's h index divided by the number of years since his or her first publication.

3.5. Authors' productivity pattern and Lotka's Law

Table 2 shows the authors' productivity pattern using Lotka's law. It is observed that during 1990–2019, 308 authors (91.4%) contribute to only one paper, twenty-five (7.4%) authors contribute to two papers each, and only four authors contribute to more than two papers each. Lotka's law generates a number of authors by comparing with the observed number of authors. The observed percentage of authors who contribute to one document is much higher than the expected percentage found by applying Lotka's law. It indicates the domination of single documents emanating from an individual author who publish only one document in IP literature. The authors' productivity pattern does comply with Lotka's law and the dataset also fits quite well when viewed as a distribution.

Table 2. Authors' Productivity

Number of Documents	Number of Authors (Observed)	Observed (%)	Number of Authors (Expected)	Expected (%)
1	308	91.4	308	69.4
2	25	7.4	77	17.3
3	2	0.6	34	7.7
4	1	0.3	20	4.5
8	1	0.3	5	1.1

3.6. Most relevant sources and their impacts

All 140 Scopus-indexed IP documents are published in 96 sources. Table 3 shows that the top 20 journals published 63 (45%) documents. IP is relatively a new field of study. About 88% of the sources have published no more than two documents each and only five sources have printed more than five documents. The documents in IP literature are widely scattered as they have not yet formed a systematic hierarchy. *Journal of Islamic Accounting and Business Research (JIABR)* publishes the maximum number of documents (9), followed by *International Journal of Islamic and Middle Eastern Finance and Management (IMEFM)*. JIABR also holds the dominant position with the highest citations of 139 from its nine documents. Even in terms of the h-index, it occupies the top position. However, as the h-index comes under criticism because it is influenced by self-citations and additional publications do not increase h-index if they are not cited an appropriate number of times, researchers suggest the use of m-index and g-index (Choudhri et al., 2015). The g-index for JIABR is also high. Both *International Journal of Environmental Science and Technology* and *International Journal of Management and Business Research* have received no citations and thus demonstrate low impact on IP literature. Documents published in these journals are relatively recent and citations usually take time.

Table 3. Most Relevant Sources and their Impact

Sources	h-index	g-index	m-index	TC	NP
Journal of Islamic Accounting and Business Research	5	9	0.45	139	9
International Journal of Islamic and Middle Eastern Finance and Management	3	5	0.25	26	6
Humanomics	2	4	0.09	72	4
Journal of Islamic Marketing	2	4	0.20	31	4
Managerial Finance	1	4	0.08	45	4
Benchmarking	2	3	0.20	24	3
Economic Modelling	3	3	0.60	38	3
International Journal of Business and Society	1	3	0.09	19	3
Journal of Business Ethics	3	3	0.33	63	3
Journal of Economic Behavior and Organization	3	3	0.19	30	3
Journal of King Abdul Aziz University, Islamic Economics	1	2	0.20	4	3
Advanced Science Letters	1	1	0.25	1	2
Emerging Markets Finance and Trade	1	1	0.50	2	2
International Journal of Environmental Science and Technology	0	0	0	0	2
International Journal of Management and Business Research	0	0	0	0	2
International Journal of Water Resources Development	2	2	0.10	47	2
Journal of Applied Business Research	1	2	0.14	7	2
Journal of Asset Management	1	1	0.11	1	2
Journal of Corporate Finance	1	1	0.50	1	2
Pacific Basin Finance Journal	2	2	0.40	15	2

Note: TC = total citations; NP = number of publications.

3.7. Topic dendrogram

The hierarchical cluster relationship between keywords is presented in the topic dendrogram in Figure 5. The figure demonstrates that two relatively small and one large cluster have emerged for illustrating the keywords used by the researchers while describing the Islamic perspective of pricing. Derivatives, Shari'ah compliance, Islamic risk management, financial engineering, and call options are presented in the first cluster. Signaling, piety, devout, norms, marketing, layout, and Islamic banking appear in the second cluster. The house pricing, hedonic pricing, segregation, and religion are different branches from price discovery, Islamic stock, and financing. Researchers separate both areas of research in their scholarly works from the broader context of the third cluster. Meanwhile, asset pricing, Shari'ah, stock market, pricing model, deposit rate, and portfolio management, from a price setting point of view, are related to setting prices of tangible and intangible products and property. The list of keywords, near the center of the dendrogram, appears to be discriminant enough to form different clusters. Researchers are able to form distinctive clusters among those keywords. It appears that a separate body of knowledge is developed by combining those concepts and methods when researchers demonstrate their work in IP literature. However, the keywords in cluster one and cluster two are not discriminant enough to form further clusters, indicating the possibility of discovering new clusters in the near future.

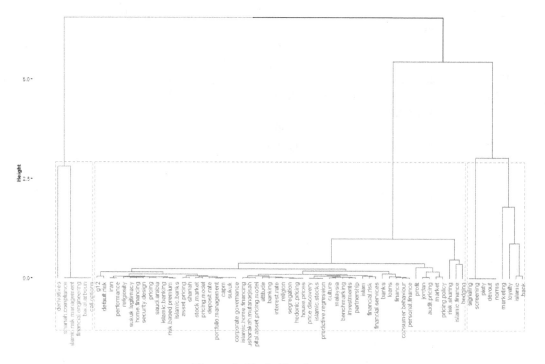

Figure 5. Topic Dendrogram

3.8. *Thematic map analysis*

The thematic map in Figure 6 demonstrates that Islamic finance and marketing appear to be the motor keywords and the most developed themes in Islamic pricing literature (upper right quadrant). In addition to that, some developments are noticed in pricing policies and strategies. These keywords are frequently used in Islamic finance and Islamic marketing literature. The transversal theme, representing the lower right quadrant of the thematic map, demonstrates that the sukuk, religiosity, and spiritual perspective of prices are appearing as new trends that demand scholarly discoveries. The lower-left quadrant shows that hedonic pricing is under-researched and IP practices in Iran can be a potential future research area. Although the upper left quadrant is theoretically less important to IP, it is possible to find the real implications of pricing model, default risk, and performance from a practical standpoint.

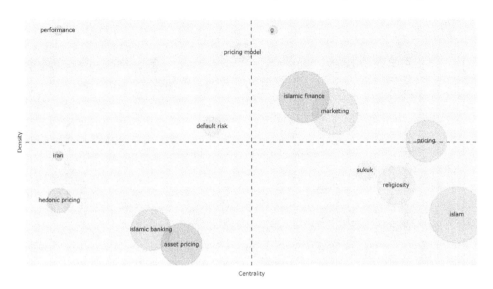

Figure 6. Thematic Map Analysis

4. Overview of the Most Recent Published Documents

Table 4 summarizes 14 of the most recent documents on IP published in Scopus indexed Journals. This selected list offers a clear outline of the methodologies being used and topics being studied in recent times. Regression analysis and SEM (structural Equation Modelling) analysis are found as the most widely used methodologies. Almost all researchers focus on the "Islamic finance and banking" industry in their recent documents (Aysan *et al.*, 2015; Ahmad and Prentice, 2019; Ahmed *et al.*, 2019; Charag *et al.*, 2019; Dharani *et al.*, 2019; Grira *et al.*, 2019; Shaikh *et al.*, 2019). Meaning all other industries have not received sufficient attention from the researchers; however, within this industry, areas of focus vary significantly. Some focus on studying the impact of religiosity (Alhomaidi *et al.*, 2019; Blau and Crane, 2019), while others focus on Islamic sukuk (Ahmed *et al.*, 2019; Razak *et al.*, 2019). Lastly is a focus on consumer behavior (Anouze *et al.*, 2019; Charag *et al.*, 2019; Xu and Leung, 2019). Alhomaidi *et al.* (2019) attempts to determine the impact of religious compliance on stock prices. Islamic stocks face lower idiosyncratic risk, but macroeconomic factors, such as religiosity, influence Islamic stock returns. Due to this loss-averse tendency, religiosity results in the positive skewness of returns (Blau and Crane, 2019). It may seem surprising that in banking industry, mixed banks perform much better than both conventional and purely Islamic banks (Ahmad and Prentice, 2019). Ahmed *et al.* (2019) explore a positive relationship between pricing and sukuk legitimacy. Razak *et al.* (2019) examine structure, critical issues, contracts, and pricing mechanisms of sukuk. Anouze *et al.* (2019) identify pricing as one of the most important factors determining customer satisfaction; Xu and Leung (2019) show that a belief in the afterlife encourages people to spend more. Other researchers focus on equity and asset pricing; Islamic mortgage; and the performance of Islamic banks (Dharani *et al.*, 2019; Grira *et al.*, 2019; Hanif, 2019; Shafron, 2019; Shaikh *et al.*, 2019). However, industry specific pricing processes, models, and mechanisms are yet to be discussed in IP literature. Further study can be undertaken in these areas.

Table 4. Most Recent Published Documents in IP Literature

Paper	Purpose	Methodology	Key Findings
(Alhomaidi et al., 2019)	Determine the impact of religious compliance on stock prices and market segmentation.	Regression Analysis.	• Islamic stocks exhibit lower idiosyncratic risk and higher liquidity due to shariah certification. • Local and global macroeconomic factors influence Islamic stock returns in the Saudi market.
(Ahmed et al., 2019)	Investigate influence of different determinants on sukuk legitimacy.	Semi-structured Interview.	• There is a positive significant relationship between different determinants (pricing, type of structure, etc.) and sukuk legitimacy.
(Anouze et al., 2019)	Determine factors of customer satisfaction for Islamic and conventional banks.	SEM Analysis.	• Pricing, convenience, and shariah compliance are most important factors for customer satisfaction and the impact of those factors differ between Islamic and conventional banks.
(Blau and Crane, 2019)	Determine the influence of local religiosity on the normality of return distribution.	Multivariate Analysis.	• Loss-averse tendency of more religious culture ultimately results in the positive skewness of stock returns.
(Charag et al., 2019)	Investigate the factors that influence the intention to adopt Islamic banking.	SEM Analysis.	• Attitudes, culture, religiosity, perceived risk, government support collectively determine the intention of consumer to use Islamic Banking. • The effects of religiosity are mediated by attitudes.
(Dharani et al., 2019)	Investigate the performance of conventional and shariah stock portfolios in India.	Regression Analysis	• The effect of shariah on stock returns is positive and shariah portfolios offer higher returns because they have lower risk and lower volatility during crisis time.

Table 4. (*Continued*)

Paper	Purpose	Methodology	Key Findings
(Grira et al., 2019)	Assess and compare the ex-ante cost of equity between Islamic and conventional banks.	Regression Analysis	• Institutional quality improves the cost of equity with more impact for Islamic banks. • Islamic banks have higher financing cost and face less effective competition.
(Hanif, 2019)	Analyze current Islamic mortgage' practices develop Islamic mortgage model (IMM).	Descriptive Research	• Ignorance of market pricing, trading of equity units, transfer of all ownership risks to one partner are some divergences in existing practice of Islamic mortgages. • IMM has been developed based on musharakah principles.
(Nawaiseh et al., 2019)	Measure the effects of ownership structure on audit fees in Jordan.	Regression Analysis.	• Family and govt. ownership have negative impact on audit fees of conventional banks, and controlled family and institutional ownership have negative impact on audit fees. • Ownership variable has a dominant impact on audit fees.
(Razak et al., 2019)	Examine structure, critical issues, contracts and pricing mechanism of sukuk.	Review Paper	• Sukuk is better than conventional bonds because the return of sukuk is expected from principal asset and it is less volatile. • The application of bay al-dayn and bay al-inah in the sukuk and debate over the volatility are the main issues in sukuk.

Table 4. (*Continued*)

Paper	Purpose	Methodology	Key Findings
(Sabah and Hassan, 2019)	Develop a simple Islamic Deposit Insurance Scheme model using a shariah complaint contract.	Descriptive Research	• Deposit insurance based on actuarially fair pricing creates moral hazards for Islamic banks because they hold undue systematic risk. • Selection of pro-cyclical loans will increase shareholders' equity. • Private issuers can charge higher price without offering any subsidy.
(Shaikh et al., 2019)	Examine the cross-section of expected returns on *Shari'ah*-compliant stocks using single-factor or multi-factor asset pricing models.	Quantitative Research	• Size premium is significant and positive that explain the cross section returns of small size stocks and value premium is significant and positive that explain the cross-section of returns of high value stocks.
(Xu and Leung, 2019)	Advance the relationship between a particular religious belief and buyer behavior.	Experimental Research	• If the afterlife belief is salient among people, they become more willing to pay. This effect can be mediated by positive product thoughts.
(Shafron, 2019)	Determine whether investor tastes affect asset pricing.	Regression Analysis.	• The taste of an investor for shariah compliant bonds affects bond pricing significantly. • Investors with a taste for shariah compliant bonds have different demand distributions than investors without that taste. Investor tastes affect cost of capital.

5. Discussions and Exploring New Dimensions

5.1. *Islamic principles by Quran and Sunnah on pricing*

According to Islamic ideology, the holy Quran is known to be the supreme and complete guidelines, which covers all aspects of human life, including pricing aspects of business. Allah states in the holy Quran that man is vicious about his love of wealth (Quran: 100:8). Even after having everything, man is prone to be greedy for more (Quran: 74:14-15). Extreme love for wealth sometimes encourages businessmen to engage in malice like *riba*, usury, bribery, gambling, hoarding, cheating, and selfishness. However, Muslim businessmen should not forget that money or wealth is a test from Allah as evidenced in the holy Quran (2:155; 3:116; 8:28; 9:55; 18:46; 23:55; 64:15; 71:21; 74:12; 89:20). Money is a worldly success; that's why, businessmen should not be greedy.

Islam strongly discourages cheating in all forms (Quran: 4:161; 7:85; 9:34; 11:84; 11:85; 26:181; 26:183; 83:1; 83:3). The Quranic view of gambling is to get something without doing any work for it or without hard labor (Quran: 2: 219). Islam discourages gambling of all forms (Quran: 5:90-91) and encourages hard labor (Quran: 2:177; 3: 134; 22: 78). This is also true in case of pricing from Islamic perspectives. Marketers can create false impressions about demand and supply through hoarding and charge higher prices. Islam prohibits not only hoarding (Quran: 9:35; 3:157; 4:37-38; 10:11; 43:32; 57:20; 70:21; 102:1; 104: 2-3), but also usury (riba) (Quran: 2:278; 4:161; 3:130), corruption (Quran: 28:83), selfishness (Quran: 4:128), bribery, and dishonesty (Quran: 2:188; 4:29; 5:8; 5:63; 6:152). Muslim businessmen should not be so extravagant that they are distracted by profit or business, keeping them away from the remembrance of Allah (Quran: 9:28; 24:37; 62:9, 11; 63:9).

Islam encourages a self-operating mechanism of price adjustments and healthy competition (Quran: 83:26). In Islam, the businessmen are assumed to be charging a fair price if their product quality are equivalent to their promise. A Muslim can never break his promise in business dealings. They cannot abuse their oaths for their business purpose (Quran: 12:20; 16:94, 95). Ultimately, money will not help any person on the Day of Judgment; so, he/she must not make any false promises about the quality and quantity of the products. Muslim marketers must remember that wealth and profit are just worldly possessions and disbelievers may possess more than the believers (Quran: 43:33–35; 111:2). Muslim businessmen engage in business activities in order to satisfy Allah, and they set the prices of their products accordingly. By Allah, this belief is recognized as the most profitable investment for a Muslim (Quran: 9:111).

Prophet Mohammad (*peace be upon him*) states that-*"Nine-tenths of the benefits come from trade compared to job/service"* (Munawi, Faydul-Qadir, 3:220). However, in business dealings, it must be remembered that wealth is also a source of *fitnah* for Muslim businessmen (Tirmidhi, Zuhd, 19). Prophet Mohammad (*pbuh*) said, *"By Allah, I do not fear poverty and starvation overtaking you, but I fear that you will have abundant wealth at your disposal as it had been at the disposal of the nations before you. You will then become* extremely greedy in accumulating this wealth just as the previous nations had done. This (greed) will be the cause of your ruin and destruction as it destroyed the people before you" (Bukhari: 3158; Muslim: 2961). Even after having two valleys of money, it is not uncommon for a person to demand for a third one (Bukhari, Riqaq, 10; Muslim, Zakah, 116). Because of this greed, many businessmen set incalculable tricks and get involved in deceptions, hoarding, false oaths, cheating, usury, interests, and gambling that eventually raise the prices of products. According to the holy Prophet (*pbuh*), *"A time will come upon the people when one will not care how one gains one's money, legally or illegally"* (Bukhari: 2059). During that time, people will not bother about whether they are following lawful or unlawful ways for earning money (Bukhari: 2083).

Honest Muslim businessmen will be under the shade of the Allah's Throne on the Day of Judgment alongside prophets, loyal people, and martyrs (Ibn Majah, Tijarat 1; Tirmidhi, Buyu, 4); so, businessmen must not be greedy in setting prices for their products. The prophet (pbuh) said *"Guard yourself from greed, for greed destroyed those before you. It caused them to shed blood and to make lawful what was unlawful"* (Muslim: 2578). Muslim businessmen must not deceive any customer by overcharging, creating black-markets, practicing usury, cheating while weighting, charging interests, hoarding, or making false promise. To deceive people in business dealings is a big crime in the eye of Islam (Bukhari, Riqaq, 10; Jihad, 70; Ibn Majah, Zuhd, 8). Businessmen will be sinners if they do not practice honesty in their business (Tirmidhi, Buyu, 4; Ibn Majah, Tijarat, 3). Umar (R) states that the true character of a man is understood in business dealings and traveling (Kharaiti, Makarimul-Akhlaq, 1:185). We cannot anticipate the true face of a person until he is tested for his material interest. Prophet Mohammad (*pbuh*) says *"Allah does not look at your prayers and fasting but at your financial relationships"* (Kanzul-Ummal: 8435, 8436). While prayers are important, Muslim businessmen must not overlook their financial objectives, activities, and relationships.

The price of a product must not be raised by making false promises and creating artificial crises. Unnecessary and false promise about the quality of a product is the act of devil (Abu Dawud, Buyu 1; Tirmidhi, Buyu 4; Nasai, Ayman 7). Allah will not speak to them on the day of resurrection (Muslim, Iman, 171). Muslim businessmen must not be involved in taking usury because they will be under divine threat from Allah and the Prophet (*pbuh*) (Muslim, Musaqat, 106; Darimi, Manasik 34). Creating black markets or stocking goods in order to raise prices is a great sin because it exploits the community. Prophet Mohammad (*pbuh*) says, *"He who supplies to the market gains; he who waits in order to sell at a higher price is damned by Allah"* (Ibn Majah, Tijarat, 6). Stocking a good to raise its price is a crime in the eye of Islam. Prophet Mohammad (*pbuh*) says, *"No one withholds goods till their prices rise but a sinner"* (Sunan abu-dawud, hadith no: 3440, 980). Even during competition, Islam does not allow the raising or lowing of prices of particular commodities. Prophet Mohammad (*pbuh*) points out, *"Do not raise prices in competition"* (An-Nawawi 2:270). Selling a product at a lower price than the market price is also not allowed. For instance, once Khalifah Umar (*R*) passes by Hatib ibn Abi Balta'ah and finds him selling his product at a much lower price to draw the attention of customers. Umar (*R*) told him- *"Either enhance your rate or get away from our market"* (Ibn Kathir, 1991/1411, I, p. 350).

Islam always promotes free markets, moderate profits, and self-adjustment mechanisms for price setting because they increase the efficiency of trade systems and ensure the welfare of society. This means demand and supply will determine the prices of commodities. Islam promotes co-operation among the marketers rather than competition. During the Ottoman Empire (1300–1922), a person goes to a grocer. He suggests the man to go to the next grocer saying *"I have made my first sale today. Go to my neighbor who has not sold anything this morning"*.

Prices should be just and it should reflect the quality of products. If there is any change in quality, there will be changes in the price to avoid cheating and gambling. If there is any uncertainty about the products, it is prohibited to conduct transactions with them (Muwatta: 31.34:75; Muslim: 3615). Muslim customers have the right to check the products before they purchase them (Muwatta: 31.35:76) and the contents of the products must be consistent with the description provided by the seller (Muwatta: 31.36.79). If weight is the most important factor in setting price, then the weight of the product must be precisely known to the buyer (Muslim: 3654–3655). The weight of products should be accurate; otherwise, it will be considered a form of cheating (Muwatta: 31.45.100). In such situations, the responsibility of measuring the goods to be sold rests on the seller. The Prophet (*pbuh*) says, *"If you are the seller, you have to measure, and if you are the buyer, then let the seller measure for you."* (Bukhari: 34:51). However, both parties involved in a transaction should share the defects and qualities of goods because a lie causes the blessings from Allah to be lost (Bukhari: 2079, 2082). Both the buyer and seller should be free from fraud (Muwatta: 31.45:99) and they will be generous to each other (Muwatta: 31.45.101). Moreover, Islam permits canceling transactions by any party before they separate (Bukhari: 2108, 2110; Muwatta: 31.37:80; Muslim: 3656–3658).

Islam encourages hard labor. Prophet Mohammad (*pbuh*) says: *"Nobody has ever eaten a better meal than that which one has earned by working with one's own hands."* (Bukhari: 2072). Islam believes in forgiveness in business dealings. Prophet Mohammad (*pbuh*) says, *"There was a merchant who used to lend the people, and whenever his debtor was in straitened circumstances, he would say to his employees, 'Forgive him so that Allah may forgive us.' So, Allah forgave him."*(Bukhari: 2078). Islam also encourages charity. Prophet Mohammad (*pbuh*) says *"the hand that gives is superior to the hand that takes."* (Muslim, Zakah, 106). Trade must not divert people from the worship of Allah. As Qatada (R) says, *"The people used to do sale and trade; but whenever they were to perform any of Allah's obligations, then trade and sale would not divert them from Allah's worship, but they would rather fulfill that obligation (to Allah)"* (Muwatta: 31: 57).

Islam does not support hoarding or stockpiling to raise prices (Muwatta: 31.24.56-58). Prophet Mohammad (*pbuh*) says: *"he who hoards is a sinner"* (Muslim: 3910-3912). Islam prohibits re-selling goods before the resellers get delivery and have possession of the products (Muwatta: 31.19:40-44; Muslim: 3640-3645). Two sales in one transaction is not permitted in Islam (Muwatta: 31.33.72-73). Interest is also prohibited in Islam and should not be included in a product's price. Prophet Mohammad (*pbuh*) curses the person who accepts and pays interest (Muslim: 3880-3881). Outbidding, that is entering into a transaction on which another Muslim brother is already negotiating, in order to raise price is prohibited in Islam (Muwatta: 31.44.97; Muslim: 3617-3618). A Muslim marketer or a Muslim customer cannot create a trade which results in any undue advantages at the time of purchasing the product (Muslim: 3623, 3625-3626). Prophet Mohammad (*pbuh*) forbids some types of transactions; such as- *mulamasa, munabadha,* and *habal al-habala* (Muslim: 3608, 3615; Bukhari: 2146). Taking oaths in business transactions is dangerous because it blots out the blessings from Allah (Bukhari: 2087). As Prophet Mohammad (*pbuh*) states, *"Swearing produces a ready sale for a commodity but blots out the blessing"* (Muslim: 3913). Deception is a crime. A businessman was selling wheat by keeping wet part under the normal part. Prophet Mohammad (*pbuh*) checks it and says *"Why did you not put the wet part on top so that people would see it? He who deceives us is not one of us"*(Muslim, Iman, 164). Prophet Mohammad (*pbuh*) says, *"When he buys, he should say: There should be no attempt to deceive"* (Muslim: 3663). If a product has two owners, the product cannot be sold without the full consent of both owners (Muslim: 3915).

Islam also has specific guidelines for insolvency, delay payment, and advance buying. The seller has the right to take his goods back if he finds that the buyer is insolvent (Muslim: 3782-3784). But if the buyer is solvent, he must pay the price as soon as possible, because in this case, any kind of delay will be considered an injustice in the eye of Islam (Muslim: 3796). The price can be paid in advance; but, in this case, there should be a specified weight, measure, a definite time period, and guarantor (Muslim: 3906-3908; Bukhari: 2239, 2241, 2251). Islam also allows setting prices based on estimations if the benefits of the product are evident (Bukhari: 2188, 2193; Muslim: 3665-3666). Islam has specific instructions about return policies. It is not good to urge somebody to return the goods they have already purchased (Bukhari: 2139-2140). In the case of delayed payment, Muslim customers must mortgage an asset or property. Once Prophet Mohammad (*pbuh*) buys food from a Jew on credit and mortgages his iron armor to him (Bukhari: 2252, 2068-2069).

Muslims need to engage in business for the sake of Allah, and they should spend a share of their earning in the cause of Allah (Quran: 2:26). This is considered the best form of business dealings (Quran: 61:11). Moreover, in the holy Quran, it is stated that – *"All the human beings are at loss except those who do believe, do good deeds, guide people to the truth, and have patience"* (Quran:103:1-3). These good deeds in business can be implemented through giving charity and zakat from the wealth of people. In many versus of the holy Quran, Allah encourages people to provide charity (2:3, 195, 254, 267; 4:39; 5:45; 8:3; 13:22; 14:31; 22:35; 28:54, 57; 32:16; 33:35; 42:38; 63:10; 64:16; 108:2) and zakat (5:55; 8:72; 9:71; 2:188; 24:37). Allah tests human with some loss of money (Quran: 2:155), but the loss of money in business, in some incidences, is not a real loss in the eye of Islam, it is a test. Rather, the real losers are those who lose their souls and their families on the day of resurrection (Quran: 39:15).

5.2. *Discussion of extant Islamic pricing literature*

Islamic pricing studies are divided into five-year intervals to investigate the evolution of research topics over time (see Table 5). In this case, words highlighted with grey background indicate the similarity of topics from previous time-periods and words without any grey background denote emerging topics of research. During the first period, from 1990 to 1995, only a few documents are published; in which the topics- "marketing and Islamic banking" and "political economy" appear frequently. IP is rarely discussed. During the second stage (1996–2000), a growing attention is observed in the discussion of "water management and water pricing", "efficiency of participating growth model", and "stock pricing". The discussion of water management and water pricing is extended to the third period (2001–2005). During this period, "Islamic pricing ethics", "financial markets and future contracts", and "seasonality on stock returns" were the areas of focus among researchers (Saeed *et al.*, 2001; Seyyed *et al.*, 2005; Ebrahim and Rahman, 2005). As the IP literature during the first three periods is overly unsophisticated, we find this period to be less meaningful than the rest.

During the fourth period (2006–2020), IP literature gathers momentum. The majority of the studies focus on "Islamic finance and banking industry". Selim (2008) discusses the Islamic capital asset pricing model. Amin *et al.* (2010) demonstrate that pricing is one of the most important factors that affects the acceptance of *Qard ul Hassan* financing among the bank customers of Malaysia. Amin *et al.* (2009) explore that price influences the choice of Islamic mortgage. Other price relevant factors gradually pop-up (Magdelaine *et al.*, 2008; Mojaver, 2009). This period is pointed out as the introduction stage.

During the last two periods (2011–2015 and 2016–2020), many topics are researched that are relevant to Islamic pricing. Many new topics for research are introduced during this time and the focus on the previous stage's topics increases both in depth and breadth. The discussions of using the capital asset pricing model are extended from the fourth period to the last period. However, Islamic home financing, religious tourism, equity pricing, pricing of different Islamic finance and banking commodities, and comparative pricing analysis between Islamic and conventional banks are some hot topics during the last two periods. Due to their growing importance, these two periods are identified as the emerging periods of IP.

Table 5. Relevant Topics (Dimensions) Over Time

Topics 1990–2005	Topics 2006–2010	Topics 2011–2015	Topics 2016–2019
Topics 1990–1995	Water Pricing and Ethics (1)	Islamic Personal Financing (2)	Idiosyncratic risk and stock returns (2)
Marketing, Islamic Banking andFinance (1)	Response to Financial Incentives (1)	Lending Behavior and deposit rates (1)	Pricing bounded value based salam (1)
Health beliefs and Attitudes (1)	Faith-Based Investment (1)	Religious tourism (1)	Market segmentation and Islamic Finance (1)
Political Economy (1)	Perception and knowledge of Islamic finance (1)	Islamic home financing (3)	Islamic Home financing and Musharakah Mutanaqisah (9)
Underground Finance: Arms Black Market (1)	CAPM (2)	CAPM (2)	CAPM (2)
Tuition Rate Policies (1)	Modes of Finance and Performance of Banks (1)	Equity Pricing (1)	Compatibility to reporting standards (1)
	Poultry Meat Market (1)	Livestock and Meat Market (1)	Pricing beliefs: cost of deposit insurance for Islamic banks (1)
Topics 1996–2000	Islamic mortgages (1)	Islamic Investing (1)	Islamic Mortgages (1)
Seasonality, culture and Pricing of Stocks (1)	Economic growth and Stagnation (1)	Value premium of the place of worship (1)	Social relationships and Health Conditions (1)
Water Management, Market and Pricing (3)	Pricing and Qard ul Hassan Financing (1)	Taboo Trade-offs in Pharmaceutical Marketing (1)	Faith based performance finance (1)
Political Economy (1)	Profit sharing Investment Accounts (1)	Performance of equity Investments (1)	Price discovery and asset pricing (1)
Efficiency of Participating Growth Model (1)	Conventional VS Islamic Banks: credit risk (1)	"Peace walls" and Pricing in housing market (1)	Islamic Life insurance (1)
	Islamic Sukuk (1)	Islamic Sukuk (3)	Islamic Sukuk (4)
Topics 2001–2005		Efficiency of Islamic banks (1)	Pricing of By-salam (1)
Water Pricing (1)		Risk sharing: Islamic Finance (1)	Contingent Premium Option (1)

Table 5. (Continued)

Topics 1990–2005	Topics 2006–2010	Topics 2011–2015	Topics 2016–2019
Marketing Ethics (1)		Persistence of performance (Dow Jones): Pricing Model (3)	Islamic Banks' Pricing practices (1)
Genomics Patents (1)		Perceived price fairness and satisfaction (1): tourism	Islamic banking: customer adaptation (1)
Financial Markets and Futures Contracts (1)		Water Management (1)	Ecosystem services trade-offs (1)
By-Salam contract (1)		Riba and Gharar: Islamic Banking (1)	Stock market: shariah compliant equities (1)
Stock Returns and Stock Volatility (1)		Worship Houses and Housing Prices (1)	Islamic Equity performance and Equity Pricing (2)
		Culture-specific number symbolism (1)	Political cost Islamic house pricing, peace walls (1)
		Factors affecting Islamic market mechanisms (1)	Islamic VS conventional banks: competition, deposit rate, intermediation margins, satisfaction, risk-sharing, asset pricing and ownership structure (6)
		Islamic financial product pricing (1)	Pricing Islamic banking products (1)
		Islamic IPO Pricing (1)	Islamic IPO Pricing (1)
		Islamic down payment policy (1)	Islamic down payment policy (1)
			Prices of Islamic Commodity, deposit insurance, finance, medicines and gas (5)
			Sharing contracts' marginalization, and markup calculation (1)
			Religious tourism (1)

Table 5. (*Continued*)

Topics 1990–2005	Topics 2006–2010	Topics 2011–2015	Topics 2016–2019
			Religiosity: cost of debt, audit pricing, bond outcomes, stock return, segmentation, buying Behavior (7)
			Attitude and Islamic finance (1)
			Price discovery and future markets (1)
			Mudharabah Contract in Islamic banks (1)
			Performances of wind farms (1)
			Price adaptation strategy (1)
			Commercial Organizations and Marketing (1)

Notes: Words without gray background denote the new topics of research. Words highlighted with gray background refer to the similarity of the topics from previous time-period. Number of papers is in the parenthesis.

5.3. Criticism of existing literature and review findings

Our review reveals that the majority of IP documents have positioned their focus around the "Islamic finance and banking" industry. Other industries have not received much attention from researchers. There are some documents in IP literature that do not have strong relationship with Islamic pricing (Adetunji, 1991; Hansen, 1991; Brown, 1994; Lindrooth and Weisbrod, 2007; Magdelaine et al., 2008; Siddiqui, 2008; Peter McGraw et al., 2012; Ashta and Hannam, 2014; Demessinova et al., 2018; Aghajani et al., 2019; Al-Ansari et al., 2019). Even the most cited documents (Magdelaine et al., 2008) included in the IP literature do not have any relationship with Islamic pricing. This document (Magdelaine et al., 2008) receives 80 citations, which is the most; however, it discusses factors that determine poultry meat consumption. Although competitive pricing has been recognized as an important factor that affects poultry meat consumption, no relationship has been demonstrated between Islam and poultry meat consumption. Naylor (1994), another most cited document, discusses the arms black market, which is not related to Islamic pricing. As shown in Appendix A, some of the highly cited documents carry very little insights for Islamic pricing.

Some titles are confusing. Abakah (2020) discusses about Christianity and bond outcomes but the title of the document is "Local religious beliefs and municipal bond market outcomes". At first glance, it may seem relevant to Islamic pricing; but in reality, it demonstrates no relationship with Islamic pricing. The literature also lacks the focus on discussing the relevant commandments from the holy Quran and Hadith in support of their arguments in their documents. Moreover, pricing mechanisms, pricing methods, and pricing considerations receive very limited attention from researchers. Only a few topics are studied in-depth, such as the Islamic home financing, stock price, bond outcomes, capital asset pricing models, Islamic securities, and Islamic sukuk. Future studies may extend their scope to different industries and different product categories; and may emphasize on the commandments of the Quran and Sunnah.

6. Conclusions

This study examines 140 manuscripts on IP which are published on the Scopus indexed journals using a hybrid review (bibliometric and content analysis) technique. The results from the bibliometric analysis reveals that Islamic pricing literature can be categorized as having a low level of productivity, low average citations per document, and high collaboration among researchers. As the Islamic and halal industries grow, more cross-country collaborations are expected, which signifies the emergence of comparative (cross-industry and cross-cultural) pricing tools. As most literature on IP is still emerging, overall citation counts are noticeably low. A significant geographic density of the researchers is found, resulting in most literature coming from the United States, Middle East, North African countries, and Southeast Asian countries. Overall, Malaysia tops the list of countries producing a significant proportion of resources on IP. Content analysis reveals that topics on IP consider studies from Islamic finance, which broadly covers topics on Islamic banking products, sukuk, and pricing of other Shari'ah compliant financial products. This review reveals that managers, who are in charge of pricing strategy, will have to deal with a plethora of cross-cultural, country- and region-specific factors.

However, this study suffers from some critical limitations. First, only the Scopus-indexed database is accessed to extract documents on IP. Albeit, the Scopus database is comprehensive in nature, considering other databases will provide a more complete picture of IP literature. Second, this study only considers recently published and the most cited papers, the Quran, and Sunnah for comprehensive review, other kinds of documents are overlooked. Finally, this study reviews IP literature covering a long range of time. Despite these shortcomings, this study is both timely and of critical importance because it simultaneously discusses the evolution of IP literature over time and explores new dimensions of IP through a comprehensive review of published papers and the guidelines from the Quran and Sunnah.

Limited connection to theory of pricing and dominance of religious factors are worthy of special notes for future researchers. Future research may include a comparative pricing analysis between conventional and Islamic products, Islamic financial and non-financial products, and pricing in Muslim dominant and non-Muslim dominant countries. These comparisons will help gaining in-depth insights into the pricing strategies of Islamic marketers.

Appendix A. Most Cited Documents in IP Literature

Table A.1.

Paper	TC	TC/Y	Purpose	Methodology	Key Findings
(Magdelaine et al., 2008)	80	6.153	Determine Factors that affect consumption of Poultry Meat.	Descriptive and Trend Analysis	Competitive pricing, absence of cultural/religious obstacle, nutritional qualities explain attractiveness. Main trends of Poultry consumption have not changed due to Avian Influenza.
(Amin et al., 2009)	66	6.600	Investigate effects of different factors on intention to use personal financing.	Correlation and Regression Analysis	Attitude, social influence, and pricing influence intention to use personal home financing. Religious obligation and Govt. Support are significant predictors.
	64	4.923	Review attitude, perception and	Synoptic Survey	Bank reputation, service quality, pricing, and

Table A.1. (*Continued*)

Paper	TC	TC/Y	Purpose	Methodology	Key Findings
(Gait and Worthington, 2008)			knowledge of Islamic financial products.		religious convictions are main factors to influence the use of Islamic finance. Risk sharing concept is a substantial barrier to Islamic method of financing.
(Wilson, 2008)	60	4.615	Analyze different sukuk structures from financial perspective and explore sukuk pricing issues.	Flow Charts are used to illustrate financial transfers	Special purpose vehicles are a prerequisite for the successful issuance and management of sukuk. GDP-based pricing benchmarks would result in greater payments stability for sovereign debt in Saudi Arabia.
(Seyyed *et al.*, 2005)	55	3.438	Examine the effects of Ramadan on weekly stock returns and volatility of the overall Saudi Stock market.	Time Series Analysis	Systematic decline of volatility in Ramadan has significant implications for pricing of securities and asset allocation decisions. Anomaly appears to be consistent with a decline in trading activity during Ramadan.
(Chan *et al.*, 1996)	55	3.438	Use daily returns to identify seasonality on 4 stock markets.	OLS Analysis	Day-of-the-week effects, Month-of-the-year effects exist on Kuala Lumpur stock exchange and the stock exchange of Singapore. Week holiday effects concerning several Indian lunar holidays are evident on the stock exchange of Bombay. Results confirm the importance of cultural influences in the pricing of stocks.
(Peter McGraw *et al.*, 2012)	47	5.222	Determine how overtly commercial marketing	Descriptive Research	For need-based product communal justifications are effective. But, if

Table A.1. (*Continued*)

Paper	TC	TC/Y	Purpose	Methodology	Key Findings
			strategies create moral distress and investigate when communal-sharing reduces distress.		consumers are attuned to the persuasive intentions of the organization, Market-pricing justifications become more effective.
(El Ghoul et al., 2012)	45	5.000	Determine whether religion matter to equity pricing.	Sensitivity Tests	Equity financing costs are cheaper for firms located in more religious counties. Religion plays a role in equity pricing predominantly mainline protestants. But, the importance of religion to equity pricing is concentrated in firms with lower visibility
(Siddiqui, 2008)	45	3.462	Examine risks of various modes of Islamic finance and other characteristics.	Descriptive Research	Those Islamic banks that engage in little long long-term project financing show good performance with respect to the returns on their assets and equity and demonstrate better risk management.
(Lindrooth and Weisbrod, 2007)	41	2.929	Determine the response of religious for-profit and non-profit hospices to Medicare reimbursement incentive.	Empirical Research and Descriptive statistics.	For-profit hospices are significantly less likely to admit patients with shorter, less profitable, expected lengths of stay. Incentives for efficiency could be strengthened by a Medicare pricing system that replaced the current flat per diem payment.
(Walkshäusl and Lobe, 2012)	38	4.222	Determine whether Islamic indices exhibit a different performance to	Sharpe Ratio Tests Time-Series, Factor Regression Tests.	No compelling evidence of performance differences is noticed after controlling for market risk. Islamic indices invest

Table A.1. (*Continued*)

Paper	TC	TC/Y	Purpose	Methodology	Key Findings
			conventional benchmarks		mainly in growth stocks and positive momentum stocks. This outperformance is largely attributed to the exclusion of financial stocks in Sharia-screened portfolios.
(Adetunji, 1991)	33	1.100	Examine the ways in which adults' health beliefs and attitudes affect their response to five killer diseases during childhood.	In-depth Interview	Majority of those diseases were believed to be caused by teething and food related factors. Herbal tea was most commonly prescribed treatments. Parents' location during their children' sickness, access to good advisors, seriousness of the sickness and religious beliefs were important determinants of their response.
(Abu-Zeid, 2001)	32	1.600	Determine criteria for equitable cost sharing and discuss elements of agricultural water pricing.	Mixed Method	The cost of water services, the value of water and the cost recovery mechanisms are measures to implement agreed upon policies to value water. Water pricing is a good mean to cover initial costs and sustain resources should reflect the economic, social, environmental, cultural and religious values of society. The pricing of irrigation involves 3 things: the cost of the water system infrastructure and the cost of operating and maintaining that system
(Hansen, 1991)	31	1.069	Study the political economy of	Mixed Method	After independence, both countries followed an

Table A.1. (*Continued*)

Paper	TC	TC/Y	Purpose	Methodology	Key Findings
			development in modern Egypt and turkey compares these with secular countries		statist development strategy to base their industrialization on import substitution and to expand their public sectors. As a result of that strategy, the growth of productivity has been constrained in both countries
(Archer *et al.*, 2010)	28	2.546	Present a value-at-risk approach to the estimation of displaced commercial risk and the associated adjustments in capital requirements.	Empirical Econometric Study	The characteristics of profit-sharing investment accounts can vary Displaced commercial risk has a major impact on Islamic bank's economic and regulatory capital requirements, asset-liability management, and product pricing An econometric approach to estimating displaced commercial risk is proposed but report that individual Islamic banks generally lack the data needed to apply this approach,
(Hassan *et al.*, 2010)	25	2.273	Analyze Unit Trust funds' performance, and address risk tolerance and diversity issues.	Comparative Study	No convincing performance differences are found between Islamic and non-Islamic Malaysian unit trust funds. Non-Islamic unit trust funds in Malaysia are value-focused while Islamic unit trust funds are small cap oriented
(Razak, 2011)	20	2.000	Determine customers' perception of two modes of home financing.	Survey-Method	Diminishing partnership home financing mode is more preferred to bai bithaman ajil mode of financing because profit

Table A.1. (*Continued*)

Paper	TC	TC/Y	Purpose	Methodology	Key Findings
					and risk is shared between the customer and bank resulting in greater fairness, justice and equity.
(Naylor, 1994)	20	0.741	Explains the contradiction between the amount of human, social and political damage weapons do and the ease with which weapons are acquired.	Mixed Method	International arms transfers can be pessimistic way because of black market Demand for weapons drives more buyers into the black market and changes on the supply side. Broad structural changes in the machinery of black market are outlined with asserting the role of unconventional currencies.
(Amin *et al.*, 2009)	19	1.727	Analyze the factors that determine "qard ul hassan financing" acceptance among bank customers.	Factor and Regression Analysis	"Attitude" and "subjective norm" are important factors that influence customers' perception of accepting "qard ul hassan financing".
(Ben Nasr *et al.*, 2014)	18	2.571	Model the volatility of the Dow Jones Islamic Market World Index (DJIM) using FITVGARCH model	Econometric Study	FITVGARCH model performs better than FIGARCH model in explaining conditional volatility of DJIM in terms of information criteria, portfolio allocation and model diagnostics.

Note: TC = total citations; TC/Y = total citations per year.

References

Abakah, AA (2020). Local religious beliefs and municipal bond market outcomes. *Financial Management*, 49(2), 447–471, doi: 10.1111/fima.12271.

Abdullah, K (2008). *Marketing Mix from an ISLAMIC PERSPECTIVE: A Guide for Marketing Courses*. London: Pearson/Prentice Hall.

Abu-Zeid, M (2001). Water pricing in irrigated agriculture. *International Journal of Water Resources Development*, 17(4), 527–538, doi: 10.1080/07900620120094109.

Adetunji, JA (1991). Response of parents to five killer diseases among children in a Yoruba community, Nigeria. *Social Science and Medicine*, 32(12), 1379–1387, doi: 10.1016/0277-9536(91)90198-L.

Aghajani, D, M Abbaspour, R Radfar and A Mohammadi (2019). Using Web-GIS technology as a smart tool for resiliency management to monitor wind farms performances (Ganjeh site, Iran). *International Journal of Environmental Science and Technology*, 16(9), 5011–5022.

Ahmad, W and D Prentice (2019). How large are productivity differences between Islamic and Conventional Banks? *The Singapore Economic Review*, 64(5), 1–20.

Ahmed, ER, MA Islam, TTY Alabdullah and AB Amran (2019). A qualitative analysis on the determinants of legitimacy of sukuk. *Journal of Islamic Accounting and Business Research*, 10 (3), 342–368, doi: 10.1108/JIABR-01-2016-0005.

Al-Ansari, B, A-M Thow, M Mirzaie, CA Day and KM Conigrave (2019). Alcohol policy in Iran: Policy content analysis. *International Journal of Drug Policy*, 73, 185–198, doi: 10.1016/j.drugpo.2019.07.032.

Alhomaidi, A, MK Hassan, WJ Hippler and A Mamun (2019). The impact of religious certification on market segmentation and investor recognition. *Journal of Corporate Finance*, 55, 28–48, doi: 10.1016/j.jcorpfin.2018.08.012.

Amin, H, M Ghazali and R Supinah (2010). Determinants of Qardhul Hassan financing acceptance among Malaysian bank customers: An empirical analysis. *International Journal of Business and Society*, 11(1), 1–16.

Amin, H, MRA Hamid, S Lada and R Baba (2009). Cluster analysis for bank customers' selection of Islamic mortgages in Eastern Malaysia. *International Journal of Islamic and Middle Eastern Finance and Management*, 2(3), 213–234, doi: 10.1108/17538390910986344.

Anouze, ALM, AS Alamro and AS Awwad (2019). Customer satisfaction and its measurement in Islamic banking sector: a revisit and update. *Journal of Islamic Marketing*, 10(2), 565–588, doi: 10.1108/JIMA-07-2017-0080.

Archer, S, RAA Karim and V Sundararajan (2010). Supervisory, regulatory, and capital adequacy implications of profit-sharing investment accounts in Islamic finance. *Journal of Islamic Accounting and Business Research*, 1(1), 10–31, doi: 10.1108/17590811011033389.

Arham, M (2010). Islamic perspectives on marketing. *Journal of Islamic Marketing*, 1(2), 149–164, doi: 10.1108/17590831011055888.

Ashta, A and M Hannam (2014). Hinduism and microcredit. *Journal of Management Development*, 33(8/9), 891–904.

Aysan, AF, M Disli, H Ozturk and IM Turhan (2015). Are Islamic banks subject to depositor discipline? *The Singapore Economic Review*, 60(01), 1550007.

Bartol, T, Budimir, G, Dekleva-Smrekar, D, Pusnik, M and Juznic, P (2014). Assessment of research fields in Scopus and Web of Science in the view of national research evaluation in Slovenia. *Scientometrics*, 98(2), 1491–1504, doi: 10.1007/s11192-013-1148-8.

Ben Nasr, A, AN Ajmi and R Gupta (2014). Modelling the volatility of the Dow Jones Islamic Market World Index using a fractionally integrated time-varying GARCH (FITVGARCH) model. *Applied Financial Economics*, 24(14), 993–1004, doi: 10.1080/09603107.2014.920476.

Blau, BM and BD Crane (2019). Religiosity and loss aversion: Does local religiosity influence the skewness of stock returns? *International Review of Finance*, doi: 10.1111/irfi.12287.

Brown, KW (1994). Private-college financial results and their effect on tuition-rate policies. *Journal of Accounting and Public Policy*, 13(1), 1–29, doi: 10.1016/0278-4254(94)90010-8.

Cader, AA (2015). Islamic challenges to advertising: a Saudi Arabian perspective. *Journal of Islamic Marketing*, 6(2), 166–187, doi: 10.1108/JIMA-03-2014-0028.

Chan, ML, A Khanthavit and H Thomas (1996). Seasonality and cultural influences on four Asian stock markets. *Asia Pacific Journal of Management*, 13(2), 1–24.

Charag, AH, AI Fazili and I Bashir (2019). Determinants of consumer's readiness to adopt Islamic banking in Kashmir. *Journal of Islamic Marketing*, 11(5), 1125–1154, doi: 10.1108/JIMA-10-2018–0182.

Chicksand, D, G Watson, H Walker, Z Radnor and R Johnston (2012). Theoretical perspectives in purchasing and supply chain management: an analysis of the literature. *Supply Chain Management: An International Journal*, 17(4), 454–472, doi: 10.1108/13598541211246611.

Choudhri, AF, A Siddiqui, NR Khan and HL Cohen (2015). Understanding bibliometric parameters and analysis. *Radiographics*, 35(3), 736–746, doi: 10.1148/rg.2015140036.

Demessinova, A, A Saparbayev, M Seidakhmetov, Z Kydyrova, E Onlasynov, A Shadiyeva, *et al.* (2018). Renewable energy sector of Kazakhstan: Factors of its sustainable development. *International Journal of Management and Business Research*, 8(1), 34–51.

Dharani, M, MK Hassan and A Paltrinieri (2019). Faith-based norms and portfolio performance: Evidence from India. *Global Finance Journal*, 41, 79–89, doi: 10.1016/j.gfj.2019.02.001.

Durán-Sánchez, A, MdlC Del Río, J Álvarez-García and DF García-Vélez (2019). Mapping of scientific coverage on education for entrepreneurship in higher education. *Journal of Enterprising Communities: People and Places in the Global Economy*, 13(1/2), 84–104, doi: 10.1108/JEC-10-2018-0072.

Ebrahim, MS and S Rahman (2005). On the pareto-optimality of futures contracts over Islamic forward contracts: implications for the emerging Muslim economies. *Journal of Economic Behavior and Organization*, 56(2), 273–295, doi: 10.1016/j.jebo.2003.09.007.

El Ghoul, S, O Guedhami, Y Ni, J Pittman and S Saadi (2012). Does religion matter to equity pricing? *Journal of Business Ethics*, 111(4), 491–518.

Gait, A and A Worthington (2008). An empirical survey of individual consumer, business firm and financial institution attitudes towards Islamic methods of finance. *International Journal of Social Economics*, 35(11), 783–808, doi: 10.1108/03068290810905423.

Grira, J, MK Hassan, C Labidi and I Soumaré (2019). Equity pricing in Islamic banks: International evidence. *Emerging Markets Finance and Trade*, 55(3), 613–633, doi: 10.1080/1540496X.2018.1451323.

Guerrero-Baena, MD, JA Gómez-Limón and JV Fruet Cardozo (2014). Are multi-criteria decision making techniques useful for solving corporate finance problems? A bibliometric analysis. *Revista de Metodos Cuantitativos para la Economia y la Empresa*, 17, 60–79.

Hamid, ABA, MS Ab Talib and N Mohamad (2014). Halal logistics: A marketing mix perspective. *Intellectual Discourse*, 22(2), 191–214.

Hanif, M (2019). Islamic mortgages: principles and practice. *International Journal of Emerging Markets*, 14(5), 967–987, doi: 10.1108/IJOEM-02-2018-0088.

Hansen, B (1991). *The political economy of poverty, equity, and growth: Egypt and Turkey*: Oxford University Press.

Haque, A, A Shafiq and S Maulan (2017). An approach to Islamic consumerism and its implications on marketing mix. *Intellectual Discourse*, 25(1), 135–152.

Hashim, H, SR Hussin and NN Zainal (2014). Exploring islamic retailer store attributes from consumers perspectives: An empirical investigation. *International Journal of Economics and Management*, 8(S1), 117–136.

Hashim, N and MI Hamzah (2014). 7P's: A Literature review of islamic marketing and contemporary marketing mix. *Procedia–Social and Behavioral Sciences*, 130(2014), 155–159, doi: 10.1016/j.sbspro.2014.04.019.

Hassan, MK, ANF Khan and T Ngow (2010). Is faith-based investing rewarding? The case for Malaysian Islamic unit trust funds. *Journal of Islamic Accounting and Business Research*, 1(2), 148–171, doi: 10.1108/17590811011086732.

Hassan, MK, S Aliyu and M Hussain (2019). A contemporary review of Islamic finance and accounting Literature. *The Singapore Economic Review*, 64(3), 1–38.

Hossain, MS, SB Yahya and S Kiumarsi (2018). Islamic marketing: bridging the gap between research and practice. *Journal of Islamic Marketing*, 9(4), 901–912, doi: 10.1108/JIMA-09-2017-0100.

Jafari, A (2012). Islamic marketing: Insights from a critical perspective. *Journal of Islamic Marketing*, 3(1), 22–34, doi: 10.1108/17590831211206563.

Kabiraj, S, R Walke and S Yousaf (2014). The need for new service innovation in halal marketing. *Indian Journal of Marketing*, 44(2), 5–14, doi: 10.17010/ijom/2014/v44/i2/80442.

Koku, PS (2011). Natural market segments: Religion and identity–the case of "zongos" in Ghana. *Journal of Islamic Marketing*, 2(2), 177–185, doi: 10.1108/17590831111139884.

Kusuma, KA (2019). The Concept of Just Price in Islam: The Philosophy of Pricing and Reasons for Applying It in Islamic Market Operation. *5th Int. Conf. Accounting and Finance 2019 (ICAF 2019)*. pp. 116–123. Atlantis Press

Lindrooth, RC and BA Weisbrod (2007). Do religious nonprofit and for-profit organizations respond differently to financial incentives? The hospice industry. *Journal of Health Economics*, 26(2), 342–357, doi: 10.1016/j.jhealeco.2006.09.003.

Magdelaine, P, M Spiess and E Valceschini (2008). Poultry meat consumption trends in Europe. *World's Poultry Science Journal*, 64(1), 53–64, doi: 10.1017/S0043933907001717.

Mamun, MAA, CA Strong and MAK Azad (2020). Islamic marketing: A literature review and research agenda. *International Journal of Consumer Studies*, doi: 10.1111/ijcs.12625.

Mojaver, F (2009). Sources of economic growth and stagnation in Iran. *The Journal of International Trade and Economic Development*, 18(2), 275–295, doi: 10.1080/09638190902916519.

Nawaiseh, ME, A Bader and HN Nawaiseh (2019). Ownership structure and audit pricing: Conventional versus Islamic banks in Jordan. *Academy of Accounting and Financial Studies Journal*, 23(2), 1–20.

Naylor, R (1994). Loose cannons: Covert commerce and underground finance in the modern arms black market. *Crime, Law and Social Change*, 22(1), 1–57.

Norris, M and C Oppenheim, (2007). Comparing alternatives to the Web of Science for coverage of the social sciences' literature. *Journal of Informetrics*, 1(2), 161–169, doi: 10.1016/j.joi.2006.12.001.

Othman, J, M Acar and Y Jafari, (2013). Towards OIC economic cooperation: Impact of developing 8 (D-8) preferential trade agreement. *The Singapore Economic Review*, 58(2), 1–18, doi: 10.1142/S0217590813500094.

Papaioannou, D, A Sutton, C Carroll, A Booth and R Wong (2010). Literature searching for social science systematic reviews: consideration of a range of search techniques. *Health Information and Libraries Journal*, 27(2), 114–122, doi: 10.1111/j.1471-1842.2009.00863.x.

Peter McGraw, A, JA Schwartz and PE Tetlock (2012). From the commercial to the communal: Reframing taboo trade-offs in religious and pharmaceutical marketing. *Journal of Consumer Research*, 39(1), 157–173, doi: 10.1086/662070.

Rajasakran, T, S Sinnappan, T Periyayya and S Balakrishnan, (2017). Muslim male segmentation: the male gaze and girl power in Malaysian vampire movies. *Journal of Islamic Marketing*, 8(1), 95–106, doi: 10.1108/JIMA-01-2015-0007.

Randhawa, K, R Wilden and J Hohberger, (2016). A bibliometric review of open innovation: Setting a research agenda. *Journal of Product Innovation Management*, 33(6), 750–772, doi: 10.1111/jpim.12312.

Razak, DA (2011). Consumers' perception on Islamic home financing:Empirical evidences on Bai Bithaman Ajil (BBA) and diminishing partnership (DP) modes of financing in Malaysia. *Journal of Islamic Marketing*, 2(2), 165–176, doi: 10.1108/17590831111139875.

Razak, SS, B Saiti and Y Dinç, (2019). The contracts, structures and pricing mechanisms of sukuk: A critical assessment. *Borsa Istanbul Review*, 19, S21–S33, doi: 10.1016/j.bir.2018.10.001.

Sabah, N and MK Hassan (2019). Pricing of Islamic deposit insurance. *Economics Letters*, 178, 91–94, doi: 10.1016/j.econlet.2019.01.013.

Saeed, M, ZU Ahmed and S-M Mukhtar, (2001). International Marketing Ethics from an Islamic Perspective: A Value-Maximization Approach. *Journal of Business Ethics*, 32(2), 127–142, doi: 10.1023/A:1010718817155.

Salam, MT, N Muhamad and VS Leong (2019). Measuring religiosity among Muslim consumers: observations and recommendations. *Journal of Islamic Marketing*, 10(2), 633–652, doi: 10.1108/JIMA-02-2018-0038.

Saleh, C and K Salsabila (2018). Success factors in halal marketing mix. *Journal of Engineering and Applied Sciences*, 13, 5308–5312.

Sandıkçı, Ö (2011). Researching Islamic marketing: past and future perspectives. *Journal of Islamic Marketing*, 2(3), 246–258, doi: 10.1108/17590831111164778.

Selim, TH (2008). An Islamic capital asset pricing model. *Humanomics*, 24(2), 122–129, doi: 10.1108/08288660810876831.

Seyyed, FJ, A Abraham and M Al-Hajji (2005). Seasonality in stock returns and volatility: The Ramadan effect. *Research in International Business and Finance*, 19(3), 374–383, doi: 10.1016/j.ribaf.2004.12.010.

Shafron, E (2019). Investor tastes: Implications for asset pricing in the public debt market. *Journal of Corporate Finance*, 55, 6–27, doi: 10.1016/j.jcorpfin.2018.08.006.

Shaikh, SA, MA Ismail, AG Ismail, S Shahimi and MHM Shafiai (2019). Cross section of stock returns on Shari'ah-compliant stocks: Evidence from Pakistan. *International Journal of Islamic and Middle Eastern Finance and Management*, 12(2), 282–302, doi: 10.1108/IMEFM-04-2017-0100.

Shaw, WH (1996). Business ethics today: a survey. *Journal of Business Ethics*, 15(5), 489–500.

Siddiqui, A (2008). Financial contracts, risk and performance of Islamic banking. *Managerial Finance*, 34(10), 680–694, doi: 10.1108/03074350810891001.

Tournois, L and I Aoun (2012). From traditional to Islamic marketing strategies. *Education, Business and Society: Contemporary Middle Eastern Issues*, 5(2), 134–140, doi: 10.1108/17537981211251179.

Walkshäusl, C and Lobe, S (2012). Islamic investing. *Review of Financial Economics*, 21(2), 53–62, doi: 10.1016/j.rfe.2012.03.002.

Wilson, R (2008). Innovation in the structuring of Islamic sukuk securities. *Humanomics*, 24(3), 170–181, doi: 10.1108/08288660810899340.

Xu, H and A Leung (2019). Ever after: a price story–afterlife belief salience's effect on willingness to pay. *Journal of Consumer Marketing*, 37(1), 99–109, doi: 10.1108/JCM-05-2017-2192.

Yousaf, S (2016). Promotion mix management: A consumer focused Islamic perspective. *Journal of Marketing Communications*, 22(2), 215–231, doi: 10.1080/13527266.2014.888575.

Chapter 20

A Contemporary Review of Islamic Finance and Accounting Literature[#]

M. Kabir Hassan[*,§], Sirajo Aliyu[†,¶] and Mumtaz Hussain[‡,∥]

[*]*Department of Economics and Finance*
University of New Orleans
New Orleans, LA 70148, United States

[†]*Department of Banking and Finance*
RM 20 Annex New Building — School of Business Studies
Federal Polytechnic, Bauchi, Nigeria

[‡]*Policy Development and Review Department International Monetary Fund (IMF)*
700 19th St. NW, Washington, DC 20431, United States
[§]*mhassan@uno.edu*
[¶]*sirajoaliyu@yahoo.com*
[∥]*mhussain@imf.org*

This paper reviews empirical studies with a particular interest in Islamic finance literature and highlights future research directions. The earlier literature on Islamic finance was built on the Islamic economic foundation of social justice and fairness, which was formed theoretically from the primary sources of Sharia coupled with some analytical frameworks. Subsequent studies emphasized the empirical investigations without including far-reaching analytical and theoretical postulations in the area. Although empirical studies on Islamic banking are plenty, there is a new body of emerging empirical literature on Islamic finance focusing on corporate finance and *Takaful*, whereas Islamic accounting studies are mostly qualitative. The literature provides a mixed picture of Islamic financial markets and instruments, showing that the Islamic ones perform better most of the time but also perform worse at times than their conventional counterparts. This paper discusses issues that are relevant to Islamic finance and identifies avenues for future research and policy implications.

Keywords: Islamic Capital Markets, Islamic Corporate Finance, Islamic Accounting, Insurance.

1. Introduction

In the 1950s, conventional financial studies became an independent subset discipline of economics (Fama, 2011). However, Islamic finance is a sub-topic in Islamic economics (Hassan and Aldayel, 1998), and the emergence of the former is concurrently discussed within the context of the latter in the earlier period of its development. The founding

---

[¶]Corresponding author.
[#]This Chapter first appeared in the *Singapore Economic Review*, Vol. 67, No. 1, doi: 10.1142/S0217590819420013. © 2022 World Scientific Publishing.

principles of Islamic economics and financial studies developed in response to the failure of socioeconomic justice, which continues to exploit the weak in society. For instance, the ironic rationality in this context can be seen from demanding extra costs as usury when the borrower has insufficient capital to establish a small business. As conceded in the earlier studies on corporate finance (Modigliani and Miller, 1958), the cost of borrowing capital stands as one of the cardinal arguments that drove previous discussions in conventional corporate finance, which were challenged by Islamic financial doctrines later.

Islamic finance was built on the Sharia compliance regulations that restrict or prohibit gambling, excessive speculation, and complex derivatives. The Islamic financial system is expected to exhibit evidence of decoupling from the effects of conventional contagion risk and uncertainties that can be spread by prohibited activities within the system. In contrast to the conventional corporate firm, which is inclined towards debt financing, the Islamic capital structure is explained by a tendency towards equity financing tied to the company's tangible asset value (Ahmed, 2007). The Islamic financial mode of transaction is less prone to the complex market crises that are linked to debt settlement. For instance, Islamic equity portfolios are characterized by low leverage and higher real asset investments (Ashraf *et al.*, 2017). As a consequence, asset-backed contracts of Islamic finance may provide sustainable solutions to the unenforceable problem of the sovereign debt crisis (Önder, 2016). Indeed, this can be true when the system upholds its foundational theoretical postulations on the risk-sharing paradigm, which set to achieve optimal resource allocation for more significant social well-being enhancement.

However, the earlier critics of Islamic economics and financial theories indicate some impossibilities of the system to uphold its fundamental assumptions of a shared economy being compatible with the contemporary financial market structure (Kuran, 1983). Some scholars have argued in contrast to these assertions and support the possibility of achieving the desired goal(s) under the condition of certainty (Bashir, 1983) and even in uncertain situations (Haque and Mirakhor, 1986; Ebrahim and Safadi, 1995). In this regard, the empirical evidence supports the viability of Islamic finance as being more stable and less prone to financial shocks because of its asset-backed finance and various prohibitions (Khan, 1986; Darrat, 1988; Bashir and Darrat, 1992; Bashir *et al.*, 1993; Hassan and Aldayel, 1998). A decade later, some empirical findings have reported that there is no difference in business modalities between conventional and Islamic banks (Rosly, 1999; Chong and Liu, 2009; Kassim *et al.*, 2009; Khan, 2010; Sukmana and Kassim, 2010; Zainol and Kassim, 2010; Ergeç and Arslan, 2013; Ergec and Kaytanci, 2014; Saraç and Zeren, 2014; Akhatova *et al.*, 2016; Al-Jarrah *et al.*, 2016). Additionally, El-Gamal (2006) argues beyond banking institutions by attacking contemporary practices regarding Sharia arbitrage issues, Islamic mortgage finance modalities, reliance on debt-based *Sukuk*, and divergence from mutuality principles in *Takaful* among others. It is within these arguments that the author claims that the system is disentangling the legal form of its transactions from economic substance, which may lead to inefficient service by adding unnecessary underwriting costs. Thus, these can undermine the ultimate social justice that should be achieved through Islamic financial transactions and may revert to the former situation of exploitation that the system hoped to provide alternative solutions for.

However, some recent findings provide evidence that Islamic banks' transactions are not mimicking the similar trends of their conventional peers (Abedifar *et al.*, 2013; Asbeig and Kassim, 2015; Yusof *et al.*, 2015; Sukmana and Ibrahim, 2017). Nevertheless, it is not clear whether the decoupling hypothesis will remain valid for the Islamic capital market since some instruments in the industry are formally designed to operate in a manner that is less prone to ambiguity.[1] Despite other Islamic financial instruments being an emerging hybrid structure, reviewing the empirical findings on these instruments can increase our understanding regarding the current market status. Regardless of the fact that the majority of the current Islamic finance transactions are dominated by debt-based contracts rather than risk and reward sharing contracts (World Bank and Islamic Development Bank Group, 2017), the system can achieve its ultimate goals when the Islamic finance growth is found to be positively enhancing socioeconomic well-being. However, a tendency towards avoiding risks-and-rewards business and relying on debt-based finance that is expanding the credit size of an economy has repercussions, particularly in this period of anticipating a future financial crisis (Chapra, 2017). Islamic finance is not shielded from the adverse effects of a crisis, as some studies claimed that a few years after the turmoil, Islamic banks were affected (Alqahtani *et al.*, 2016) and also the Islamic capital market in some cases (Mohieldin, 2012). Thus, extending our in-depth survey of the empirical literature will provide insights beyond the surface outcomes of several studies and this will allow us to draw strong conclusions for future decisions.

Periodical reviews of Islamic financial research are required because of business complexity, which necessitates behavioral changes in transactions. This human behavioral change can easily cause a disparity between the foundational theories of the discipline and their real-world application, which may, in turn, hinder the objectives an Islamic financial system aims to achieve. Thus, the recent struggle to sustain Islamic finance in competing for growth in the market leads to a paradigm shift towards a debt-based structure, and the complexity of accepting innovative hybrid products may tend to refute earlier claims of becoming more resilient during financial shocks. Recent concerns about these issues raised by scholars (Chapra, 2017; Hassan and Aliyu, 2018) and policymakers (Shabsigh *et al.*, 2017; World Bank and Islamic Development Bank Group, 2017) on the paradigm shift to debt-based finance, the performance of the system on modern finance platform, and the prioritization of the form above substance motivate us to also review the empirical findings on some Islamic financial transactions. We will focus on highlighting the insights into the industry that will increase our understanding of having a clear direction for future decisions. The review does not claim to cover all the thematic issues regarding Islamic finance; instead, it emphasizes selected topics that touch on the concern of policymakers, academics, and practitioners in the industry.

Moreover, an empirical survey of this type is informative for detecting the gaps in the Islamic finance literature regarding the samples, geographical locations, findings, and data. There has been an overwhelming emphasis on Islamic banking in most of the previous

---

[1] The ideal principles to some Islamic finance contracts (such as mutual funds and equity investment) are formed with less ambiguity, though we are witnessing hybrid nature to some Islamic financial instruments (*Sukuk, Takaful*, and real estate finance).

survey papers on Islamic finance (Zaher and Hassan, 2001; Alam and Rizvi, 2017; Aliyu *et al.*, 2017; Hassan *et al.*, 2018). This review, however, tackles empirical studies of Islamic finance with an emphasis on Islamic corporate finance, *Takaful*, and Islamic accounting, which are neglected from recent empirical survey (Abedifar *et al.*, 2015; Narayan and Phan, 2017). The goal of this article is not only to present the different findings of Islamic financial empirical research but also to highlight areas of debate that have not been integrated into a single study. Thus, this paper summarizes major findings and presents future research directions in conclusion.

The remaining sections discuss Islamic finance topics regarding its principles and practice. The next section presents Islamic financial principles, the capital market, the current status, and performance comparisons. Section 3 reviews Islamic corporate finance, while Section 4 focuses on the Islamic insurance, and accounting literature are discussed in Section 5. The last section concludes the paper with suggestions for future research.

2. Islamic Finance

This section unveiled the fundamental paradigm and its shift in the system. Similarly, it has linked the principles of Islamic capital market with its current status that delves into the need for standard setters and ends with the global comparison between Islamic and conventional indices performance. Therefore, the epistemology of Islamic finance and economics go back to Sharia (Islamic law) principles which are deduced from the guidance of the Quran (the sacred book of Islam), *Sunnah* (the tradition of the Prophet), the scholars' consensus (*Ijma*), analogy (*Qiyas*), and exertion (*Ijtihad*) (Maghrebi *et al.*, 2016; Pervez, 1990).[2] The primary transactional modalities used to build Islamic finance paradigm are on the promotion of social well-being that is associated to the risk-sharing perspective rather than risk-shifting or transfer. The system therefore is aimed towards efficient risk allocation to influence the participation of all economic agents on the participation in real economic activities. Despite the fact that contemporary Islamic finance system was developed on the platform of modern finance, the former has other restrictions that make the system differ from the latter (Maghrebi *et al.*, 2016). Moreover, establishing truthfulness among the contract parties is intrinsic to risks and rewards system. Thus, the functional pillars that are expected to guide this frame are nested within the moral and justice system, which is also found in the earlier works of conventional philosophers. The work of Adam Smith on the moral sentiment is one of the literature that shares common perspectives with Islamic financial economics towards establishing social justice. In the particular context of Islamic finance, the primary sources of Sharia permit transactional exchanges and prohibit dealings

---

[2] Sharia (Islamic law) principles are deduced from the guidance of the Quran (the sacred book of Islam), *Sunnah* (the tradition of the Prophet), the scholars' consensus (*Ijma*), analogy (*Qiyas*), and exertion (*Ijtihad*). The Quran is the book that Muslims hold as central guidance for their life and they believe that it has been revealed by Allah. The *Sunnah* is the way of life, tradition, and custom, and is technically is regarded as the sayings, actions or approval-by-silence of the Prophet Muhammad (peace be upon him) that are reported in the Hadith. *Ijma* refers to the resolution on Sharia issues that is acceptable among scholars: the consensus of the holy Prophet's companions was very important for deriving the Islamic laws of the generation after them. *Qiyas* is another source of Islamic law derived from existing laws through analogy, when the two cases share the same basis (*illah*). *Ijtihad* is a formulation of certain Islamic rules by qualified jurists to explicitly ascertain the actual interpretation of divine ruling based on the pieces of evidence from the Quran and *Sunnah*.

with interest, ambiguity, and gambling, among others. Thus, all forms of transactions have an inherent risk, but deferred contracts involve a time interval that is liable to other risks and requires the parties involved to record the transaction (Aliyu et al., 2017). The risk element of financial transactions emerged from the probability of outcomes in contractual relationships which necessitated risk and profit sharing under the Islamic concept of financial transactions. Although Islamic finance is asset-backed, sharing risk and profit is one of the major tools used to achieve the targeted enhancement of social well-being. The Islamic financial model is directly participatory in contrast to the conventional one and tends to require intensive management and regulatory functions that can result in higher transaction costs than its counterpart (El-Gamal, 2006).

The growth of the Islamic capital market and its corporate institutions can be seen in a review of its current status, even though present developments of the system have a close link with its earlier status. Nonetheless, scholars and practitioners should not neglect the existing shift in the industry from the initial paradigm of risk and reward sharing to debt-based finance. It is often documented in the literature that Islamic finance aims to offer an alternative medium to the conventional financial system, which aims to foster the economic growth and development of the practicing countries through profit and loss sharing finance.

However, the paradigm in the system has shifted from asset-backed to asset-based financing.[3] Within this system, the Islamic capital market provides a range of instruments for transactions, some of which are consistent with earlier notions such as mutual funds, equity investments, and stock trading, whereas other instruments like *Sukuk*, real estate finance, and insurance have developed hybrid and debt-based models within the system. As a result, the sources of Islamic corporate finance that were expected to be equity-based are now hybrid through various means that are compatible with Sharia principles. Consequently, part of the capital structure and other segments of Islamic corporate finance are not very different from conventional practices. Therefore, some conventional theories may be suitable for explaining the behavioral norms of the Islamic managers and firms owners' agency conflicts. As such, the services rendered by the managers are sometimes contrary to the interests of the shareholders. However, there are other services in the Islamic finance industry that, some scholars claim, violate the international norms and practices of the profession (such as Islamic accounting procedures and treatment). Given this, it is pertinent that Sharia principles may contradict the conventional arrangements for accounting processes, but the reconciliation between form and economic substance is the duty of the standard setters. In some cases, the inconclusive debate leaves the issue of the time value of money unresolved. Similarly, in the case of *Takaful*, some scholars strongly prefer mutuality contracts rather than hybrid contracts. All of these aim to contribute towards improving social well-being. The Islamic finance paradigm was first developed with the aim of promoting social welfare. Therefore, achieving Islamic finance growth that is socio-centric may tend to improve the system.

---

[3] The difference between asset-based and asset-backed holding contracts is not in the financing capital value of the assets, but the return and repayment of the contract holder of the former is not directly determined by assets, whereas the assets direct the latter.

2.1. *The principles of the islamic capital market*

The general principles of Islamic finance are consistent with the other guidelines of Islamic law, which prohibits activities related to social life (immorality, alcohol, fraud, corruption, gambling, pork, speculations, and pornography among others), and economic gain (interest, gambling, speculation, fraud, and corruption, etc.). In the particular context of Islamic finance, Hussain *et al.* (2015) enumerated three major principles (equity, participation, and ownership) that guide the ideal Islamic financial transactions. First, the emphasis is on the equity principle that eliminates the unproductive accumulation of wealth through interest and excessive risk-taking by the entrepreneur that might end in squandering the entire business capital in seeking higher returns, and on wealth distribution, which is basically *zakat* and other forms of charity. Therefore, supporting one another will eliminate the vast disparity between rich and poor, and the parties involved in a particular contract have a duty to disclose truthful information between them. Second, participation is in line with reward and risk sharing contracts that are opposed to interest-based financing and promote direct investment in the productive sectors of the economy. The third principle denounces disposing of property that is not owned by the seller such as short selling. Therefore, the rights of ownership prevail in this situation and stand as the foundation for linking financial transactions with a real sector of the economy. The first generation of theorists on Islamic economics and finance emphasized participating contracts based on profit and loss sharing, which mostly take the form of *Mudarabah* and *Musharaka* contracts. However, more recent developments in the system have shifted towards lease and sale-based contracts, while fee-based contracts stand as an auxiliary to some financial products (*Mudarabah* and *Murabaha*) (Hussain *et al.*, 2015). Most of these financial transactions are possibly becoming hybrids rather than adhering to the foundational principles that form a transactional relationship and prioritizing the legal form above economics substance (El-Gamal, 2006).

The Islamic capital market represents another segment of Islamic finance that contributes to the development of the Islamic economic and financial system. Within Islamic capital market practices, Sharia-compliant indices must pass a certain screening process. As such, Dusuki (2012) illustrates how the selection process of the Dow Jones, Standard & Poor (S&P) and Financial Times Stock Exchange (FTSE) Sharia-compliant indices are slightly different, though they have other consistent similarities to non-permissible activities. They share the same prohibitions of activities such as investment in institutions dealing in pork production, non-halal food, alcohol, interest-based transactions, and gambling among others. Meanwhile, the leverage position must be less than 33% which is measured using slightly different ratios: Dow Jones uses total debt to the yearly moving average of market capitalization, S&P uses total debt to the market value of equity, and FTSE uses total debts to total assets. Additionally, the accounts receivable in proportion to assets for Dow Jones and FTSE is less than 45%, whereas the share market value of equity is less than 49% in the case of S&P. Therefore, indices that are not able to pass the screening criteria are excluded to provide a definite standard for measuring the performance of Islamic stock indices (Ashraf, 2016; Dow Jones, 2003; Hassan *et al.*, 2018). Thus, instruments that are deemed to have passed the screening process are selected as being valid for Sharia-based transactions.

2.2. Current status of the islamic finance industry

Our understanding of the contemporary status of Islamic finance is incomplete without a review of its progress and trends. Nowadays, the overwhelming growth in Islamic financial services has attracted the attention of academics, practitioners, investors, and policymakers. The development of Islamic finance in this millennium can be traced back to its historical background. For instance, the concept of mutuality embedded in the system influenced the socioeconomic and religious performance of Malaysian citizens and led to the development of an Islamic investment company (*Tabung Hajj*). The *Lembaga Tabung Hajj* (Pilgrim Management and Fund Board) in Malaysia was established in 1963 to facilitate pilgrimage services; the board accepted deposits (they now have up to 9 million customers) and empowered Malaysian citizens through their 124 branches.[4] The establishment of the Islamic Development Bank (IsDB) in 1975 was timely for fostering the economic and social well-being of the member countries through the medium of Islamic finance. From its inception to the second quarter of 2017, the IsDB approved the sum of US$128.8 billion for the development needs of its member countries.[5] The IsDB has five supporting member institutions helping to achieve its ultimate goals of using Sharia-compliant products and financing,[6] and it also awards an annual prize to those contributing to Islamic economics, finance, and banking.[7]

---

[4] The board claimed to one of largest investment companies in Malaysia that touch on social well-being. The company invests in construction, Islamic finance, property development, information technology, hospitality, and oil and gas (http://www.tabunghaji.gov.my/maklumat, accessed 26 June 2017). The current Malaysian Islamic financial market is operating in parallel with the conventional system, where 74% of its listed stocks are Sharia-compliant, whereas Islamic banks and *Sukuk* dominate the Islamic finance industry (Zeidane et al., 2017).

[5] The IsDB divided the member countries into four groups and allocated the funds according to their respective needs: The Middle East and North Africa ($49.1 billion), Asia and Latin America ($37.2 billion), Sub-Saharan Africa ($21.3 billion), and Europe and Central Asia ($19.1 billion). The funds were disbursed to finance: energy, transport, finance sector, agriculture, health, information technology, industry and mining, water and sanitation, and education sectors, among others. The bank's modes of finance are in line with Islamic finance practices, in which the projects are funded by either *Istisna'a* or leasing, and *Murabaha* is used for trade financing. http://www.isdb.org/irj/portal/anonymous?NavigationTarget=navurl://fe68ebaa6541fcf4c62134ea6d389185, accessed 18 August 2017.

[6] The IsDB has five member institutions. (1) The Islamic Research and Training Institute (IRTI) (established 1981) to help the bank by providing research, training, and information regarding economics, finance, and banking. The IRTI became a reservoir of Islamic finance literature through its various programs: in-house research, Islamic finance country reports, thematic workshops, fellowships, policy papers, research grants, and conferences. The institution publishes books on Islamic economics, finance and banking, and maintains a free database for finance and banking (http://islamicfinancedata.org/ActionResult.aspx?e=1, accessed 6 September 2017). As part of their support to Islamic finance, they provide scholarships for PhD and Masters students in this area, and grants for book publication, etc. (2) The Islamic Corporation for Insurance of Investments for Export Credits (ICIEC) (established 1994) to enlarge the flow of transactions and investments among the members of the Organization of Islamic Cooperation (OIC), and provides services to banks, exporters and investors. (3) The Islamic Corporation for Development of the Private Sector (ICD) (established 1999) aims to complement the IsDB's mission of enhancing the economic development of the member countries. The ICD is tasked with identifying investment opportunities and accelerating growth in the IsDB member countries. (4) The International Islamic Trade Finance Corporation (ITFC) (established 2005/2006) was established to promote trade in the IsDB member states through providing finance and facilitating inter-member trade and international trade. (5) The World *Waqf* Foundation (WWF) (established 2001) is a global entity for *waqf* that liaises with governments, philanthropists, and non-governmental organizations in promoting *waqf* activities that contribute to the socioeconomic and cultural events of the member countries and other Muslim communities around the globe. Their programs include poverty alleviation, supporting *waqf* institutions, and projects relating to education, health, studies on *waqf*, and drafting legislation, among others. (http://www.isdb.org/irj/portal/anonymous?NavigationTarget=navurl:///a72aee4111f842adddabfe81158fd365&LightDTNKnobID=-1946185670, accessed 18 August 2017).

[7] To date, the IsDB awarded 36 laureate prizes, which are usually given to a selected scholar(s) or institution(s) and present these during the bank's annual meeting, which began in 1988 to date (http://www.irti.org/English/Awards/Documents/IDBPRIZE/List%20of%20IDB%20Prize%20Winners.pdf, accessed 18 August 2017).

The first international Islamic economics and finance conference was another achievement of 1976 that ignited knowledge sharing in this area.[8] Besides the Sharia-based commercial banks inaugurated in the 1970s, the subsequent decades witnessed other Islamic financial products and institutions. For instance, it is documented that property finance and syndication coupled with Islamic insurance (*Takaful*) companies began during this period. Ayub (2007) outlined the history and showed that the first *Takaful* company was the Islamic insurance company of Sudan established in 1979 and the Malaysian corporation took effect in 1984; later other countries from the Middle East adopted the practice. Nowadays, virtually almost all countries practicing Islamic finance have Islamic insurance companies. Similarly, the countries' (such as Pakistan, Sudan, and Iran) declaration to accommodate Islamic finance increased the system's strength in the 1980s.[9] Meanwhile, the International Islamic *Fiqh* Academy rectified a ruling on *Takaful* based on solidarity donations as being an acceptable contract for Islamic finance (Hayat and Malik, 2014). In the 1980s, the use of *Mudarabah* certificates and participatory term certificates became current practice, and in 1992 *Sukuk*-based modes of issuance gained popularity (Ayub, 2007). In the early 2000s, the two *Sukuk* issued in dollar denominations in Malaysia ($600 million) and the IsDB's solidarity trust *Sukuk* ($400 million) triggered sovereign and corporate Islamic bond issuance in different jurisdictions (Ayub, 2007).[10] Despite the overwhelming growth of the Islamic financial and capital market in particular across many countries, including those in Africa, *Takaful* companies, private pensions, and the *Sukuk* market are not present in Djibouti but in Kenya, which has two licensed Islamic funds (Zeidane *et al.*, 2017).[11]

Demand for the establishment of the Islamic financial standard setting bodies (standard setters) intensified in the late 1980s (Abdel Karim, 1990), and the formation of the Accounting and Auditing Organization for Islamic Financial Institutions (AAOIFI) was realized in 1991.[12] Other bodies were established in 2002: the Islamic Financial Service Board (IFSB) and the International Islamic Financial Market, both of which provide standards for Islamic financial institutions. The former considers the financial soundness and stability, while the latter stresses the contractual documentation process such as

---

[8] The conference invites scholars to contribute towards the development of the discipline, and the conference series continues to take place at intervals. The first conference in 1976 was held at Makkah; in 2016, the International Islamic University Malaysia hosted the event. The 2017 event is planned to be hosted at Makkah by Umm Al-Qura University. The conference is usually organized in collaboration with the IRTIof the IsDB, the International Association of Islamic Economics, any other interestedpartners and the hosting institution.

[9] An IMF report (Zeidane *et al.*, 2017) revealed that Pakistan and Sudan are reported to have considerable growth in Islamic finance industry. For instance, their financial market witnessed the presence of successfully performing Islamic banks, *Takaful*, *Sukuk*, Islamic micro-finance, and the stock exchange. Although sovereign issuance dominates their *Sukuk* market, Pakistan also has an Islamic real estate investment trust.

[10] Many countries and corporations issued *Sukuk*, and these include Malaysia, Saudi Arabia, Bahrain, UAE, Qatar, Germany, Pakistan, Indonesia, Brunei, Egypt, Gambia, Iran, Kazakhstan, Kuwait, Singapore, Somalia, Turkey, the UK, and Hong Kong, among others.

[11] This refers to Islamic investment companies and *Takaful* companies. The African Islamic financial market is developing: Nigeria established an Islamic microfinance bank in 2010, an interest-free bank in 2012, and the first *Sukuk* in 2013 (Zeidane *et al.*, 2017).

[12] At present, the AAOIFI has issued 94 standards which comprise 54 on Sharia, 26 on accounting, five on auditing, seven on governance, and two on ethics; these are published in two volumes.

templates and agreements among other issues. More recently, the IFSB issued guidelines on Islamic capital market products and the principle of "re-*Takaful*" (Islamic reinsurance). Nowadays, the Islamic standard setters are trying to harmonize their standards with other internationally acceptable standards that deal with similar issues.

Apart from the AAOIFI, which provides standards for accounting and auditing procedures for Islamic financial institutions, other Islamic finance-practicing countries have adopted the International Financial Reporting Standards (IFRS). Another regional standard body (the Asia–Oceania Standard-Setters Group (AOSSG)) is working with the International Accounting Standard Board (IASB) towards the uniformity of standards since their meeting in 2009.[13] In 2011, the IASB initiated a consultation group to focus on the Islamic finance topics that need to be included as part of its technical agenda; in 2013, the meeting of the consultative group was held in Malaysia (IFRS, 2014; Pacter, 2016). Similarly, the joint report of Klynveld Peat Marwick Goerdeler (KPMG) and the Association of Chartered Certified Accountants (ACCA) disclosed some reasons for the inclusion of Islamic finance topics in models of the AACA exams (KPMG and ACCA, 2012). The reason for this inclusion is the rapid growth of Islamic finance in some of the ACCA member countries/regions where most jurisdictions prefer to adopt the IFRS standards in most of their financial reporting.[14] The joint report of the KPMG and ACCA (2012) also cited the conclusion of the Dubai roundtable, where they requested IFRS to provide other standards that suit Islamic financial transactions.[15] Sharing knowledge on Islamic finance contracts is beyond the capacity of institutions in emerging Muslim-majority countries, so European universities are offering programs up to postgraduate degree level.[16] Conventional considerations of economic substance rather than prioritizing legal form and the issues regarding the time value of money are the major opposing arguments within the Islamic reporting standards (AOSS, 2010). The standard setters are not the only segment required for Islamic financial transactions; other institutional infrastructure is essential for proper and smooth financial transactions within the industry. For instance, liquidity management infrastructure is a prerequisite for integrating a sound Islamic financial system.

The establishment of a liquidity management center in 2002 constituted four equal shareholders and aimed to contribute towards Islamic capital market growth by providing

---

[13] In November 2009, the AOSSG pursued IASB to address the issues relating Islamic financial accounting reporting standards, which is a step towards the inclusion of Sharia-compliant instruments and transactions in the mainstream IFRS (http://www.accaglobal.com/content/dam/acca/global/PDF-technical/financial-reporting/pol-afb-gabc.pdf, accessed 12 August 2017).

[14] In the forward address of the ACCA, the chief executive (Helen Brand) explained that the association is keen to foster the growing track of Islamic finance by incorporating topics in the area, which the system is practiced in some of their members' regions/countries, which include Malaysia, Pakistan, Indonesia, UK, Middle-East, and Ireland.

[15] Page 7 of the report cited the Malaysian Accounting Standards Board (MASB)'s chairman: "*We feel that we can use the International Financial Reporting Standards (IFRS) unless someone can show us that there is a clear prohibition in the Sharia, and then we will amend it accordingly. Until such a time, we will use the IFRS*" (http://www.accaglobal.com/content/dam/acca/global/PDF-technical/financial-reporting/pol-afb-gabc.pdf, accessed 12 August 2017).

[16] Some of the institutions offer Islamic finance in the Gulf, Malaysia, Pakistan, and Indonesia. Universities in the UK — Durham, Aston, Bangor, Cass Business School, and Salford among more than 60 institutions in the country — are offering Islamic finance courses (https://www.ft.com/content/2fcf979a-96d2-11e6-a80e-bcd69f323a8b, accessed 19 August 2017).

optimal financing solutions, advisory services, and portfolio management.[17] Financial liquidity management is a functional activity that goes beyond private organizations. Another corporation was established within the members of financial authorities and regulators of different countries. Thus, the International Islamic Liquidity Management Corporation (IILM) was inaugurated in 2010, and various central banks and monetary authorities became members.[18] The IILM is a cross-border corporation that creates liquidity according to Sharia-compliant standards for Islamic financial institutions. As such, the $490 million dollar A-1 S&P-rated *Sukuk* in 2013 marked their inaugural issuance. This multi-jurisdictional primary dealer network handles a highly rated Sharia-compliant money market backed by sovereign assets that are traded in US dollars.[19] Indeed the functional role of the IILM is greatly required to enhance the liquidity management of Islamic financial institutions (especially banks) within short-term Sharia-compliant instruments.

Although Islamic banks possessions make up an asset proportion (80%) of all the Islamic financial institutions, the contribution of the remaining segment to Islamic finance cannot be neglected. Thus, the need for an efficient and effective capital market is required to support long-term financial intermediation. A recent report characterized the Islamic capital market as underdeveloped compared with the established conventional system since the former is relatively new compared with the latter (World Bank and Islamic Development Bank Group, 2017). The country overview indicates that Bahrain plays a major role in Islamic financial development, which includes hosting the infrastructural institutions of AAOIFI, IIFM, and the Islamic International Rating Agency. The Islamic financial institutions in this country are dominated by the activities of Islamic banks, which make up 97%, although other segments such as *Sukuk*, Islamic funds, and *Takaful* are performing well, since they serve as a medium of financial transactions (Zeidane *et al.*, 2017). The same report indicates the dominance of Islamic capital market products in Indonesia rather than Islamic banks in which Islamic stock, mutual funds, and *Sukuk* account for 83%, which is the same percentage of participatory banks in Turkey. It is clear that the Islamic capital market is not developed in Turkey compared with Indonesia, which is the most populous Muslim nation on the earth, where Islamic finance has high potential in the country, as well as Malaysia.

Sukuk issuance appreciated immediately after the recent global financial crisis. Figure 1 shows clear evidence of global *Sukuk* issuance after the crisis, when it performed above the linear issue trend. Even with the below-linear trend of performance before and during the financial crisis period, global *Sukuk* issuance appreciated in all years, except in 2006.

The global *Sukuk* issuance persistently increased until 2015, when it had a decrease of 80 issues, though it decreased by 25 issues a year before (i.e., between 2013 and 2014).

---

[17] The equal proportion of shares held by Bahrain's Islamic bank, the Dubai Islamic bank, the IsDB, and Kuwait Finance House Investment Company covered authorized capital of $200 million and paid out capital of $53.550 million. The liquidity management center engaged in a primary market arrangement in 2003 and has a track record in Bahrain, UAE, Kuwait, and Sudan (for details; see http://www.lmcbahrain.com, accessed 6 September 2017). The corporation recorded other secondary activities that include Islamic unit trust, syndicated investment facilities, *Sukuk* (*Musharakah*, *Istisna*, *Ijarah*, and investment agencies) among others (for details, see http://www.lmcbahrain.com/banking-track-record.aspx, accessed 6 September 2017).
[18] The present member countries include Indonesia, Luxemburg, Kuwait, Mauritania, Malaysia, Nigeria, Qatar, Turkey, the UAE, and the ICD. These countries are represented by either central banks, government ministries, financial regulators, or monetary authorities (http://www.iilm.com/about-us/, accessed 6 September 2017).
[19] For details, see http://www.iilm.com/the-issuance-programme/(accessed 6 September 2017).

Thomson Reuters

Figure 1. Global *Sukuk*

This reflects adverse changes in *Sukuk* issuance, which is expected to be a temporary shock. The recent slowdown of Islamic financial services improved in 2016, albeit, *Sukuk*, Islamic funds, and *Takaful* were in second place behind Islamic banking in the industry (Islamic Financial Services Board, 2017). For instance, the global *Sukuk* issuance rose to $88.3 billion in 2016 compared with $60.7 billion in 2015; the market realized the impact of issuance from Africa, the Gulf Corporation Council-GCC, and Asia, which is dominated by Malaysia (IIFM, 2016). Although Islamic finance indicates appreciative growth across emerging, developing and developed nations, the performance trend of its instruments compared with their conventional equivalents will highlight other insights into the trends in the market.

2.2.1. Performance comparison: Islamic and conventional indices

Sharia-compliant companies receive Islamic indices if they derive a high proportion of their revenue from permissible (*halal*) transactions. As a result, the screening process for selecting Sharia-compliant companies exclude all those involved in alcohol, tobacco, pornography, gambling, pork, and other prohibited businesses, alongside companies with high liquid assets and lending sources from interest-based institutions (Ashraf, 2016).[20] Islamic equity investors purchase portfolio through a public offer of mutual funds, unit trusts, or exchange-traded funds.

Figure 2 depicts the global performance of the S&P conventional gross total returns versus the Sharia index. The Sharia index performed slightly higher than the conventional property index in the very beginning of 2012, and the trend continues with almost similar performance between the two indices.

---

[20] Ashraf (2016) detailed the ethics required for the screening of major index providers such as S&P, FTSE, Dow Jones, and Morgan Stanley Capital International (MSCI). Although our discussion concentrates on S&P, this does not differ greatly from the others.

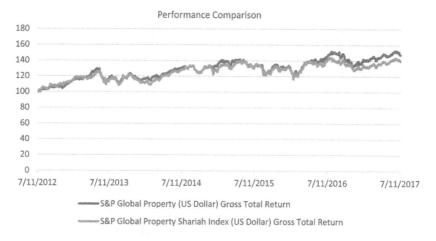

Sources: S&P and Dow Jones indices (http://eu.spindices.com/).
S&P: Standard and Poor's.

Figure 2. Global Property Comparison

Meanwhile, a significant margin between the two indices can be identified immediately after the first quarter of 2016, where the gross total return performs above the Sharia index.

Figure 3 compares the S&P Global 1200 performance between Sharia-compliant and conventional indices. Our sample revealed that from July to September 2012, Sharia-compliant S&P 1200 performed slightly higher than the conventional index of the same brand, then the conventional index outperformed the Sharia-based index up to around October 2015, when Sharia index outpaced the conventional one for most of the remaining period. However, the panel section of our trend analysis considers regional performances, which include indices from the United States (USA), Europe, Pan-Asia, and Pan Arab

Sources: S&P and Dow Jones indices (http://eu.spindices.com/).
S&P: Standard and Poor's.

Figure 3. S&P 1200-Global Comparison

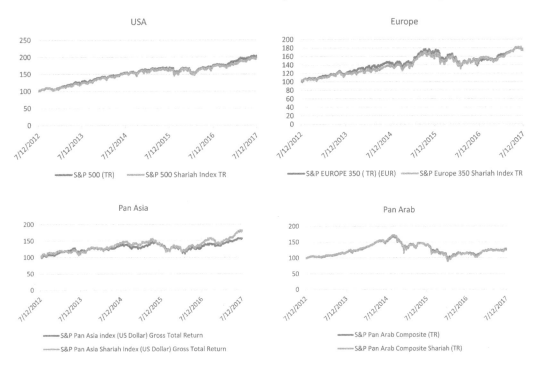

Sources: S&P and Dow Jones indices (http://eu.spindices.com/).
S&P: Standard and Poor's.

Figure 4. Panel Comparisons by Region

markets. Figure 4 shows the different indices by regions with a similar type (i.e., Sharia-compliant and conventional indices). The USA's performance comparison indicates insignificant differences between the Sharia-compliant index (S&P 500) and the conventional (S&P 500). Despite this, the Sharia-compliant index indicates higher performance only in the first 3 months, but the conventional index took over after this.

A similar case is seen for the European market, where the Sharia index (S&P Europe 350) outperformed the conventional one (S&P Europe 350) for the first two months of our sample, whereas it switched to the conventional index (S&P Europe 350) leading until June–October 2016. After that, the conventional index outstripped the Sharia index for most of the remaining periods of the sample. A different situation is found in the case of the Pan-Asian index, where the Sharia-compliant index outperformed the conventional one throughout almost all the periods, and the gap started widening at the third quarter of 2016 until the end of our sample. The Pan-Asian trend is consistent with the joint report on the status of Islamic finance (World Bank and Islamic Development Bank Group, 2017). The same report shared similar findings for the Pan-Arab index. The Pan-Arab Sharia index performed strongly before January 2014. The index also indicates weak performance between November 2014 and May 2015, despite the insignificant differences between the two types of indices (Sharia-compliant and conventional).

Figure 5 depicts another index comparison for the Middle East and North Africa (MENA) *Sukuk*. Although from the first three months of the *Sukuk* index performance is

Sources: S&P and Dow Jones indices (http://eu.spindices.com/).
S&P: Standard and Poor's.

Figure 5. Middle East and North Africa Region

above the bond index, the remaining period of the illustrated return performance revealed a lag behind conventional bonds.[21] Although the current status of the MENA *Sukuk* exhibits lower performance, it closely follows the conventional bond's trend movement, which supports another argument in the Islamic finance literature. The contemporary literature on Islamic finance claims that despite the screening process of *Sukuk*, its rate of return and that of conventional interest bonds does not seem to be different (Ayub, 2007; Hussain *et al.*, 2015).

Islamic finance records concerned international scholars and practitioners in the early period, which resulted in many publications, including those published in the 1980s by International Monetary Fund staff (Karsten, 1982; Khan, 1986; Haque and Mirakhor, 1986). The system was not free from criticism, which ranged from disentangling form from substance (El-Gamal, 2006), convergence with conventional products (Ayub, 2007), the high cost of operations and inefficiency (El-Gamal, 2006), poor accounting procedures, and neglecting the socioeconomic and environmental objective (Kamla and Rammal, 2013; Kamla and Haque, 2017) as a priority (Karsten, 1982; Kuran, 1983, 1995). The paradigm shift from reward and loss sharing to debt-based finance generated other concerns in the literature and in practice. Although support for the debt-based *Murabaha* contracts within Islamic finance emerged in the mid-1970s (El-Gamal, 2006), its dominance as a prominent product in contemporary Islamic financial business strengthened the opinions of many Islamic scholars. The use of debt-based instruments in Islamic financial institutions outweighs that of profit and loss sharing. For instance, 70% of Islamic banks' financing is based on *Murabaha* and *Ijara* contracts (Shabsigh *et al.*, 2017). Likewise, a recent report acknowledges the massive issuance of debt-based *Sukuk* despite scholars' lamentation that it contributes little to the economy apart from liquidity management (World Bank and

---

[21] A similar outcome was documented by Leung (November 2015) (https://www.indexologyblog.com/2015/11/19/the-mena-*Sukuk*-market-expanded-14-ytd/, accessed 17 August 2017).

Islamic Development Bank Group, 2017). Therefore, the current status of Islamic finance is characterized as follows:

(a) Islamic finance is growing beyond the Muslim majority countries.
(b) Islamic investment corporations improve the well-being of their immediate society.
(c) A multinational corporation (like the IsDB) supports Islamic financial development in various ways.
(d) The IFRS recognizes Islamic financial transactions; its topics are incorporated as part of the ACCA modules and various degree courses in developed countries.
(e) The disentangling of substance from form and the time value of money are the major differences between Islamic and conventional reporting standards.
(f) The trend of Sharia-compliant indices exhibits insignificant differences from conventional indices except in the Pan-Asian region.
(g) *Murabaha* and *Ijara* contracts dominate the current practices within Islamic financial transactions.

3. Islamic Corporate Finance

Corporate finance deals with the capital structure, sources of funds, and management functions for maximizing the value of capital owners, among others. However, the section emphasized the sources of capital which dominate a higher proportion of studies in this area and finally suggests for future studies other undiscussed topics. As shown in Table 1, Islamic corporate finance may differ from conventional corporate finance because of Sharia and other restrictions on prohibited transactions. The theoretical foundation of Islamic financial institutions contains the assumption of lower leverage than their conventional peers. Therefore, in principle, the capital structure of Islamic financial institutions is largely equity-based rather than debt-based, a conclusion that is consistent with recent studies (Sorwar *et al.*, 2016). Thus, the financial risk attached to the conventional capital structure is not found in Islamic financial institutions since they share profit and loss, and give quasi-ownership to investment account holders (Al-deehani *et al.*, 1999). Furthermore, mobilizing funds through investment account holders can increase the market and shareholder value of Islamic financial institutions and reduce their potential risks. Nonetheless, a factual analysis of the real data reveals that the capital structure of the 263 Sharia-compliant firms listed in Bursa Malaysia between 2006 and 2011 was determined by risk, portability, and non-debt tax shields (Thabet *et al.*, 2017). The first two determinants support the predicted priority of pecking order prediction towards leverage and the last one supports the assertion of a trade-off from leverage. However, Pratomo and Ismail (2007) found that higher leverage is associated with high profitability, which supports the agency hypothesis. In contrast, a sample of 85 banks covering 19 countries revealed that an increase in equity positively influences profitability, which supports the signaling theory (Al-Kayed *et al.*, 2014).

Conventionally, a deductible allowance is a debt-incentive for corporate taxable income that stands as a shield against interest on loans. Conversely, Islamic finance prohibits

Table 1. Summary of Studies on Islamic Corporate Finance

Authors	Period	Sample and Country (ies)	Methodology	Main Findings
Al-deehani et al. (1999)	1989–1993	12 Islamic banks	Propositional construct with panel analysis	The Islamic capital structure is different from that of conventional debt-based structures based on financial risk. The shareholders and investment account holders of Islamic financial institutions are obliged to share profit and loss. In the case of Islamic banks, an increase in investment accounts will correspondingly increase the value of the firm and the shareholders without extra financial risk.
Pratomo and Ismail (2007)	1997–2004	15 Malaysian Islamic banks	Fixed effect model	The finding of this study supports the fact that higher leverage is associated with higher profit, which supports the agency hypothesis of capital structure.
Al-Kayed et al. (2014)	2003–2008	85 Islamic banks in 19 countries	Two-stage least squares	The performance of Islamic banks increases as the capital ratio (equity) positively increases, which supports signaling theory. However, the study concludes that the optimal capital structure of Islamic banks is non-monotonic between profitability and the capital–asset ratio.
Sorwar et al. (2016)	14-year period from 3 January 2000–31 December 2013	65 Islamic banks and 65 conventional banks from 20 groups of countries	Value-at-Risk (VaR) and Expected Shortfall (ES)	Market risk was similar for Islamic and conventional financial institutions, whereas dynamic correlation concludes that Islamic institutions experience lower market risk for both VaR and ES, particularly during the financial crisis. Consequently, Islamic corporations are less leveraged than conventional ones, which calls for developing a different capital structure for Islamic financial institutions.

Table 1. (Continued)

Authors	Period	Sample and Country (ies)	Methodology	Main Findings
Ebrahim et al. (2016)	No data	Mathematical model	Modified Lucas tree model	The theoretical propositions for enhancing securitization of debt contracts are provided for under Islamic cultural tenets. The study argues that information asymmetry and the agency costs of debt will be alleviated through the Islamic classical principles of tangibility and intangibility exchange, moderately adverse selection, and risk management. Thus, stability in the system and economic growth will be promoted.
Alsaadi et al. (2016)	2003–2013	Belgium, Denmark, Finland, France, Germany, Italy, Netherlands, Spain, Sweden, and the UK	Fixed effects	The findings characterize Sharia members' firms as having a low rating towards corporate social responsibility and a likelihood to manipulate their earnings. Non-Sharia compliant firms were found to have higher corporate responsibility ratings and a lower possibility of manipulating their earnings.
Elnahas et al. (2016b)	1980–2013	404 bankrupt firms and 2107 non-bankrupt firms	Logistic regression model, multiple discriminant analysis Z-score and fixed-effect model	It is argued that some of the traditional corporate financial ratios used for evaluating Sharia-compliant firms contradict Sharia rulings on Islamic finance, such as prohibiting interest, uncertainty, and undervaluation, among others. Therefore, the study provides a modified measure of the corporate liquidity ratio and validates it via empirical applications.

Table 1. (*Continued*)

Authors	Period	Sample and Country (ies)	Methodology	Main Findings
Thabet *et al.* (2017)	2006–2011	263 Sharia-compliant firms in Malaysia	Fixed-effect model	Non-debt tax shields, profitability, and risk influence the capital structure choice of Sharia-compliant firms in Malaysia. Meanwhile, there is insufficient evidence that the capital structure choice is determined by tax and the tangibility of Sharia-compliant firms.
Zaman *et al.* (2017)	Conceptual mathematical model	Model calibration	Scenario-based simulation technique	This study proposes a shift from an interest tax shield to a dividend tax shield and uses simulation to justify the viability of their proposed corporate financing policy that follows Islamic financial tenets, formulated to reduce indebtedness, promote risk and profit sharing, reduce the cost of financing, and provide stability in the system.
Elnahas *et al.* (2017)	1984–2014	103 mergers and acquisitions	Regression and difference-in-difference method	Contractual agreements on mergers and acquisitions that are based on earn-out clauses contradict Sharia guidelines. They find that contractual agreements under earn-out conditions lead to lower abnormal returns than non-earn-out clauses.
Naz *et al.* (2017)	2001–2014	Pakistan (42 firms) and the UK (132 firms)	Fixed effects	There is a significant difference in the individual effect of managers who move from conventional firms to Sharia-compliant firms towards their financial decisions on working capital, dividend payouts, and leverage. In contrast, those who transfer their services from one Sharia-compliant firm to another do not differ in their financial decisions.

Table 1. (*Continued*)

Authors	Period	Sample and Country (ies)	Methodology	Main Findings
Ebrahim *et al.* (2016)	No data	Mathematical model	Modified Lucas tree model	The theoretical propositions for enhancing securitization of debt contracts are provided for under Islamic cultural tenets. The study argues that information asymmetry and the agency costs of debt will be alleviated through the Islamic classical principles of tangibility and intangibility exchange, moderately adverse selection, and risk management. Thus, stability in the system and economic growth will be promoted.
Alsaadi *et al.* (2016)	2003–2013	Belgium, Denmark, Finland, France, Germany, Italy, Netherlands, Spain, Sweden, and the UK	Fixed effects	The findings characterize Sharia members' firms as having a low rating towards corporate social responsibility and a likelihood to manipulate their earnings. Non-Sharia compliant firms were found to have higher corporate responsibility ratings and a lower possibility of manipulating their earnings.
Elnahas *et al.* (2016b)	1980–2013	404 bankrupt firms and 2107 non-bankrupt firms	Logistic regression model, multiple discriminant analysis Z-score and fixed-effect model	It is argued that some of the traditional corporate financial ratios used for evaluating Sharia-compliant firms contradict Sharia rulings on Islamic finance, such as prohibiting interest, uncertainty, and undervaluation, among others. Therefore, the study provides a modified measure of the corporate liquidity ratio and validates it via empirical applications.

Table 1. (Continued)

Authors	Period	Sample and Country(ies)	Methodology	Main Findings
Thabet et al. (2017)	2006–2011	263 Sharia-compliant firms in Malaysia	Fixed-effect model	Non-debt tax shields, profitability, and risk influence the capital structure choice of Sharia-compliant firms in Malaysia. Meanwhile, there is insufficient evidence that the capital structure choice is determined by tax and the tangibility of Sharia-compliant firms.
Zaman et al. (2017)	Conceptual mathematical model	Model calibration	Scenario-based simulation technique	This study proposes a shift from an interest tax shield to a dividend tax shield and uses simulation to justify the viability of their proposed corporate financing policy that follows Islamic financial tenets, formulated to reduce indebtedness, promote risk and profit sharing, reduce the cost of financing, and provide stability in the system.
Elnahas et al. (2017)	1984–2014	103 mergers and acquisitions	Regression and difference-in-difference method	Contractual agreements on mergers and acquisitions that are based on earn-out clauses contradict Sharia guidelines. They find that contractual agreements under earn-out conditions lead to lower abnormal returns than non-earn-out clauses.
Naz et al. (2017)	2001–2014	Pakistan (42 firms) and the UK (132 firms)	Fixed effects	There is a significant difference in the individual effect of managers who move from conventional firms to Sharia-compliant firms towards their financial decisions on working capital, dividend payouts, and leverage. In contrast, those who transfer their services from one Sharia-compliant firm to another do not differ in their financial decisions.

interest and interest-bearing transactions while promoting trade through sharing returns and risk. Therefore, the corporate financing policy of Islamic firms proclaims to be sustainable and prone to wealth creation and redistribution through real economic activities. Thus, the proponents of a shift from an interest tax shield to a dividend tax shield conducted a policy experiment using a simulation technique and found that Islamic financial principles can control corporate indebtedness, reduce financing cost and instability, and promote profit and loss sharing coupled with value orientation (Zaman *et al.*, 2017). Alongside this, it has been argued that the Islamic financing structure can promote a stable financial system, so long as the fundamental ethical and regulatory guidelines are strictly followed. Thus, Amran *et al.* (2017) concluded that initial public offer earnings increase because of enforcement of regulations on disclosure. Consequently, the viability of Islamic corporate finance to mitigate the agency costs of debt and asymmetry of information, apart from interest-related issues, will strengthen the industry. Thus, Ebrahim *et al.* (2016) showed that Islamic corporate finance provisions dealing with the agency costs of debt and information asymmetry provide help through tangibility (Ayn) and intangibility (Dayn) exchanges, risk management, and moderately adverse selection to promote stability, fairness, and social justice in the system. In view of this, Islamic financial regulators should strengthen enforcement towards ethical and prudential compliance. Sharia-compliant firms in 10 European countries tend to be earning manipulators with lower corporate social responsibility than their conventional counterparts (Alsaadi *et al.*, 2016). This underscores the necessity of adhering to fundamental Islamic financial principles to improve the system towards attaining social justice, and fairness, and aiming to fulfill the objectives of Sharia.

However, Elnahas *et al.* (2017) found the existence of a gap between the theoretical and practical compliance of Islamic financial corporations to Islamic laws regarding performance realization assessments. Thus, Elnahas *et al.* (2016) argued within this frame that some financial ratios used in assessing the state of corporate firms' financial positions violate other commands of Sharia which denounce transactional relations related to interest bearing, undervaluation, and uncertainty. Therefore, they propose an alternative Sharia-compliant modified ratio for corporate liquidity. Some financial agreements about mergers and acquisitions contradict the primary guidelines of Islamic financial transactions. Firm acquisitions are conventionally settled through earn-out agreements which contradict the tenets of Islamic financial laws. The earn-out contracts violate the Sharia rule on transactions, since the settlement of the acquired entity is subject to its future performance, which is uncertain.

Thus, Elnahas *et al.* (2017) used a comparative analysis with the difference-in-difference technique to conclude that mergers and acquisitions with earn-out clauses yielding lower long-term abnormal returns than contracts without earn-out agreements. Regardless of the findings concerning the economic benefits to the firm, the legal and policy implications are important for achieving the stated objectives of Islamic financial corporations.

A firm's performance depends on the ability of the top management to make financial decisions efficiently. Given this, Islamic financial institutions are hiring personnel within and outside the industry to support their financial and non-financial decisions. Nonetheless, the decision style of staff migrating from conventional to Islamic financial institutions could be different from those transferring within the industry. In this regard, Naz et al. (2017) found that the effects of managers who move from conventional to Sharia-compliant firms are significantly different regarding their financial decisions on working capital, dividend payouts, and leverage. However, those who transfer their services from one Sharia-compliant firm to another do not differ in their financial decisions. Although the findings are informative regarding the managers' mobility within and outside the Islamic financial industry, the study highlights the need for future studies to explore whether this significant difference in the managers' financial decisions influences the value and efficiency of the firm.

4. Islamic Insurance

This section discourses the issues relating to the operational definition of Islamic insurance, the feasibility of its operations, and other experimental findings on the contract. As such, contemporary business and other aspects of life are indemnified with an insurance cover to mitigate the catastrophes that arise from risks and losses attached to lives, property, and commercial activities. Like every segment of life, financial institutions are mandated to have insurance cover against unwanted calamity. As Sharia scholars prohibited conventional insurance at a time when the demand for insurance was increasing among Islamic financial institutions, Islamic insurance (*Takaful*) emerged in the late 1970s (Ayub, 2007). The prohibition of conventional insurance is because of the risk transfer to another party, and the inclusion of *Riba* (interest), uncertainty and gambling therein. *Takaful* is considered to be the Sharia-based alternative to conventional insurance through the reciprocated guarantee of repayment in a cooperative manner which takes place in the event of loss (Siddiqi, 2006). As a matter of principle, *Takaful* is regarded as mutual assistance derived from the *Kafala* (guarantee), which provides mutual solidarity and risk-sharing between or among the group members (World Bank and Islamic Development Bank Group, 2017). The idea of conventional insurance is transformed into an arrangement of contributing donations (*Tabarru*) to cover the losses of the members through mutual assistance. The members sacrifice to share the responsibility through payment of a subscription by each participating policyholder. That is, the cooperators in this arrangement agree to share the losses of their co-member in need of help based on a risk-sharing formula.

However, the Islamic Financial Services Board (2009) highlight from experience that the mutual form of conventional insurance companies has problems implementing effective governance as their size increases above a certain threshold. Nevertheless, empirical studies are inadequate for verifying the position of real mutual *Takaful* entities. As a result of particular difficulties in their operations, most *Takaful* arrangements are based on a hybrid structure. Hayat and Malik (2014) highlighted that most of the countries offering *Takaful* are not complying with mutuality contracts but instead prefer the formation of an entity through sharing capital. They highlighted this issue as a result of the difficulty of the entity in meeting the required regulatory capital through mutual cooperative donations, which leads the corporation to take on hybrid mutuality form.[22] As such, Ayub (2007) identified other difficulties relating to the *Takaful* industry, including the capital requirements, having the operational efficiency to compete favorably in the market, the legal framework, capacity development, and the perceptions of the public about insurance.

However, Khan (2015) suggested that *Takaful* corporations should give incentives to their contributors based on surplus-sharing (i.e., based on a *Mudarabah* contract) in all *Takaful* contracts, since they are considered to be cooperative ventures. In this scenario, the author neglected the fact that other contracts such as *wadiah* and *wakalah* have different effects on the level of acceptance, information asymmetry, risk coverage, and efficiency. Nonetheless, Ayub (2007) argued that *Takaful* cannot be feasible under the *Mudaraba* and *Mudarabah–Wakala* hybrid model, although the relationship is the best practice under a *Tabarru* arrangement. Islamic insurance has wide ranging acceptance in Malaysia and other countries practicing Islamic finance. For instance, in Bangladesh, *Takaful* has experienced enough successful growth to require a separate regulatory authority from the government to strengthen its activities (Khan *et al.*, 2016).

Table 2 summarizes the significant findings on *Takaful* transactions. An empirical investigation on *Takaful* in Malaysia reveals that demand for the *Takaful* products positively depends on individual income, education, development of Islamic banks, and the proportion of the Muslim population (Sheriff and Shaairi, 2013). However, another investigation did not find sufficient evidence that strict Sharia compliance measures reduce underpricing of insurance offers (Boulanouar and Alqahtani, 2016). Therefore, it is clear that even highly regulated industries are not free from the effect of information asymmetry, which mostly plays a role in the initial public offer of Islamic insurance. Operationally, cost efficiency in the *Takaful* industry is an essential ingredient that will lead to self-sufficiency. Thus, the size of the board and firm coupled with product specialization has been found to influence cost efficiency, but splitting the top management does not have any effect. Therefore, the need to understand the economic efficiency of the *Takaful* industry goes beyond evaluating the costs, since the expectation is for the industry to compete favorably in terms of quality coverage, timely delivery, price, and avoiding malpractice. This is a growth area of empirical research, as more and more data will help us answer other important questions about the insurance industry as it relates to the *Takaful* industry (Hala *et al.*, 2010). Similarly, Hala *et al.* (2014) reaffirmed the influence of board size and composition on cost efficiency in the *Takaful* industry of 17 countries across the globe. There is a need for further empirical studies in the area of *Takaful* insurance, especially on ascertaining their performance, solvency, and benefit distribution. Since the origin and specification of *Takaful* contracts differ from those of conventional insurance, there is a need for an adequate methodology that will consider the situation where a contributor is not at risk for a long period.

---

[22] Paragraph 19 of the IFSB-8 described *Takaful* business as being similar to conventional insurance with a few exceptions that must adhere to *Tabarru* and *Ta'awun*, and the prohibition of *Riba*. However, *Takaful* industries are based on a hybrid of mutual and proprietary entities, which are subject to conflicts of interest (Islamic Financial Services Board, 2009, p. 7).

Table 2. Summary of Studies on Islamic Insurance

Authors	Period	Sample and country(ies)	Methodology	Main Findings
Hala et al. (2010)	2004–2006	26 Takaful non-life insurance companies	DEA and second-stage logit transformation regression model	The separation of the CEO, NED, and Chairman functions has no significant effect on cost efficiency, whereas board size and regulatory environment positively affect cost efficiency.
Sheriff and Shaairi (2013)	1986–2010	Malaysia	Ordinary least squares (OLS) and GMM	Income, Islamic banking development, level of education, dependency ratio, and Muslim population influence the demand for Takaful. Meanwhile, family Takaful consumption is affected by macroeconomic indicators such as inflation, real interest rate, life expectancy, and ?nancial development.
Hala et al. (2010)	2004–2007	17 Islamic countries	DEA and logistic regression	The efficiency of developed non-life insurance reflects the cost efficiency of the Takaful market. The relationship of board composition with cost efficiency is influenced by the board size, whereas the relationship of the corporate governance system to cost efficiency is affected by the other firm variables.
Boulanouar and Alqahtani (2016)	2007 and 2013	33 insurance firms listed in Saudi Arabia	OLS regressions	Sharia compliance is not a determining factor for reducing underpricing in Saudi Arabia's insurance companies.

Note: DEA, data envelopment analysis; GMM, generalized method of moment (GMM); Chief Executive Officer, CEO; Non-Executive Directors NED.

5. Islamic Accounting

Although Islamic accounting studies are mostly qualitative, the section uncovers the concept of Islamic accounting that links between the need for recording transaction, establishment of standards setter, and the issues arising from international and local practices. Thus, the process of identifying, measuring, and communicating information for decision-making is considered to be an accounting procedure. The information, in this regard, must be documented in a systematic manner that can be recognized and interpreted as the decision-making process. The concept of recording financial contracts is supported in the primary sources of the Islamic law of transactions (Qur'an 2:282). The Islamic view of accounting and accountability emphasizes other values beyond just recording transactions. For instance, in the case of borrowing between two parties, the scribe shall be a third party who does not have a direct influence on the fund's ownership (Aliyu *et al.*, 2017). Therefore, Islamic accounting has to be in accordance with Sharia principles without distorting the technical content or misguiding policymakers and investors on their decisions.

The AAOIFI was established to fill the gap between the theory of Islamic finance and other international accounting standards, which include, for instance, the issues of *zakat* treatment and distribution (Abdel Karim, 1995). Despite the AAOIFI enactment, some jurisdictions still prefer to use the IFRS, whereas others adhere to local generally accepted accounting principles (GAAP). For instance, a report on Islamic financial institutions' reporting indicated that 48 companies in 14 out of 31 sample countries comply with IFRS regulations (AOSS, 2015).[23] The use of IFRS standards become apparent where Islamic financial standards do not cover certain provisions even in the host country (Bahrain), where the AAOIFI was established (Zeidane *et al.*, 2017). Similarly, the AOSSG report highlighted that 46 Islamic financial institutions in Bangladesh, Egypt, Indonesia, Pakistan, and Yemen complied with local GAAP. However, these countries supplement Islamic financial guidelines with other transactions. Meanwhile, Islamic financial institutions from Brunei, India, Thailand, Philippines, Sri Lanka, Turkey, Iran, the US, and part of Bangladesh failed to indicate their compliance with Islamic financing needs for transactions. The findings of the AOSS (2015) survey revealed the preferences adopted for recording transactions, and indicated that most of the sample institutions do not strictly comply with the Islamic financial accounting standards issued by AAOIFI. Nonetheless, the report listed some Islamic financial institutions from six countries (Sudan, Qatar, Oman, Lebanon, Jordan, and Bahrain) that comply with the Financial Accounting Standards (FAS) issued by the AAOIFI.

It is clear that despite the announcement by the AAOIFI to have common standards for Islamic financial transactions, some differences in the accounting process still exist across different jurisdictions. Perhaps the absence of globally acceptable Islamic financial accounting standards is undermining uniformity in the system. This arises from having

---

[23] Countries with 10 Islamic financial institutions adopting IFRS within the AOSSG sample are Saudi Arabia, the UAE, and Malaysia; those with five, Qatar; those with two, Bahrain, Kuwait, and Turkey; those with one, South Africa, Sudan, Switzerland, Kazakhstan, Australia, and Albania (AOSSG, 2015, p. 6) (https://www.asb.or.jp/en/wp-content/uploads/pressrelease_20150311_01_e.pdf, accessed 12 August 2017).

divergent views on some Sharia rulings concerning transactions that must be approved by the Sharia board of each institution. As such, the Sharia board of a particular corporation can approve an operation that can be nullified by another institution's board which can lead to other distortions that have an economic effect. Future challenges will lie in the areas of the accounting treatments for some Islamic financial contracts in the recent edition of the IASB-IFRS standards. For instance, IFRS 9 has other implications for *Ijara* contracts, and other issues related to the classification of *Murabaha* and *Musharaka* contracts as compliance with the standard must be accomplished by early 2018.[24] For instance, IFRS 9 allows recognition of expected loss; however, Islamic finance (AAOIFI) does not permit a party to charge the customers for future losses but recognizes incurred losses. The substance over form issue is regarded as a significant concern for the application of IFRS standards which impact Islamic financial contracts. As a result, the IASB formed a consultative group to deliberate on the issues regarding the application of IFRS 9 regarding the Islamic financial contracts, and present a report thereafter (IFRS, 2014, 2015, 2016). Although the proceedings are not meant to convince Islamic finance institutions to adopt the IFRS, they highlight other areas of disagreement and attempt to clarify some provisions and present other matters for comments.[25]

The IFRS (2016) disclosed that *Sukuk* is referred to as a Islamic bond, but some types of the instrument differ slightly from the conventional features of a similar contract, which make it complicated to classify some of the transactions appropriately. In summary, the report concluded that some Islamic financial contracts meet the IFRS-9 criteria of amortization costs, especially when it comes to classification and measurement. Despite this, some contracts can be disqualified if they do not meet the lending requirements to use the amortized cost. Thus the need for thorough analysis that looks beyond the form of the contracts to their substance is required for Islamic financial products.

However, most Islamic accounting literature is qualitative. Table 3 presents the available empirical studies in the area. For instance, Gharbi (2016) argued that the AAOIFI should consider providing alternative benchmarks to interest-based valuation techniques for Sharia-compliant transactions. Likewise, recent findings have identified the unsuitability of using traditional liquidity measures for Islamic corporate firms as a yardstick for

---

[24] In 2009, the draft version of IFRS 9 was issued, and the final version of the financial instrument was added on the 24 July 2014 and is determined to take effect on 1 January 2018. (https://www.iasplus.com/en/events/effective-dates/2018, accessed 13 August 2017).

[25] Regarding the application of IFRS 9; the proceedings identified that some instruments of Islamic finance are trade-based and were developed to fund the buying and selling of tangible and intangible things that can be accommodated by the application of IFRS 15 'Revenue from Contracts with Customers', and does not strictly relate to financial assets. Despite that, the subsequent receivables from the customer can be treated using IFRS 9. Another issue is the one relating to 'principal and interest', which highlights another debate on the time value of money: it does not contradict Islamic financial principles of deferment (*ajal*) as long as Sharia ordinance is adhered to it (i.e., not including *riba*). Consequently, the proceedings are less concerned with the presentation of "finance income" instead of "interest income", but the issue is on the measuring standards. Some Islamic financial institutions fulfill the IFRS standards by applying the constant effective yield for outstanding amounts, while others adopt a "time apportioned method". Detailed investigation of these practices reveals that Malaysia recognizes finance income based on IFRS standards using the straight line method, but in the UAE, different methods apply to various institutions, including the time apportioned basis, the effective interest method, and the declining value method, whereas the UK uses a time apportioned basis and South Africa uses either the reducing balance or straight line method for *Murabaha* (AOSS, 2015).

Table 3. Summary of Studies on Islamic Accounting

Authors	Period	Sample and Country(ies)	Methodology	Main Findings
Suhaimi and Yaacob (2011)	2000–2005	Malaysian cash *waqf* (Islamic)	Triangulation approach	Despite the improvement in accounting procedures and reporting practices of the cash *waqf* in Malaysia, there is a need for further enhancement to ensure accountability.
Farooq and AbdelBari (2015)	2005–2009	Middle East and North Africa (MENA): Morocco, Egypt, Saudi Arabia, United Arab Emirates, Jordan, Kuwait, and Bahrain	Regression analysis	The non-Sharia compliant firms of the MENA region have greater earning management than Sharia-compliant companies, and external governance is recommended to improve the disclosure performance of conventional institutions.
Wan Ismail et al. (2015)	2003–2008	508 companies in Malaysia	Fixed effect	The earning quality of Malaysian firms was found to be associated with Sharia-compliant firms rather than non-compliant ones. The high-quality Sharia-compliant companies attract foreign investors. Likewise, the higher scrutiny of the Sharia-based companies induced them to provide high quality reports.
Gharbi (2016)			CAPM theory; Proposed modified CAPM Theory	Conventional interest-based techniques are inappropriate for Islamic finance. Therefore, adoption of conventional accounting practices may lead to incorrect conclusions. Consequently, the nominal gross domestic product growth rate is proposed to be used as a benchmark rather than the interest rate.

Table 3. (Continued)

Authors	Period	Sample and Country(ies)	Methodology	Main Findings
Elnahas et al. (2016b)	1980–2013	404 bankrupt firms and 2107 non-bankrupt firms	Logistic regression model, multiple discriminant analysis Z-score and fixed effect model	Some of the traditional corporate financial ratios used in evaluating Sharia-compliant firms contradict Sharia rulings on Islamic finance such as the prohibition of interest, uncertainty, and undervaluation, among others. Therefore, the study provides some modified measures of the corporate liquidity ratio and validates them via empirical applications.
Abdelsalam et al. (2016)	2008–2013	The Middle East and North Africa region	Logit regression model; fixed-effect; OLS regression model	Despite the strict accounting policies adopted by Sharia-compliant institutions, they were found to be less likely to manage their earnings efficiently. Therefore, religious norms and moral accountability hinder organizations' ability to have a substantial impact on their reporting quality and agency cost.
Amran et al. (2017)	1 January 2004–29 February 2012	111 Malaysian IPOs	Univariate and multivariate statistical analyses	Enforcement of disclosure regulations influences the earnings management forecast of the initial public offer. When the regulators enforce disclosure, then the quality of the initial public offer earnings forecast can be determined and vice versa.
Yasmin and Haniffa (2017)	2008–2010	123 Muslim charity organizations in England and Wales	Content and descriptive analysis	Muslim charity organizations need to increase awareness of the necessity to emphasize reporting and ensure transparent accounting activities in accordance with the required standards.

Note: Capital asset pricing model, CAPM; Ordinary least square, OLS; initial public offer, IPO.

performance assessment; instead, the study proposes a modified version (Elnahas *et al.*, 2016). Kamla (2009) claimed that Islamic accounting diverges from the social and moral considerations that form the core of Islamic economics, banking, and finance. Therefore, social, moral, and Sharia considerations are paramount in the accounting process and product development.

Similarly, the recent move towards restructuring Islamic financial products through developing a hybrid system without much consideration to socioeconomic well-being and *Maqasid* may end by distorting the requirements of Islamic accounting standards, especially when treating the transactions for accounting records. In view of this, Atmeh and Maali (2017) extended their investigation of a combination of contract techniques and *Tabarru* and concluded that the ambiguity of such innovations is responsible for a tendency to misclassify assets or liabilities, earning management issues, and having insufficient reports for decision-making. In a similar debate, Shafii and Abdul Rahman (2016) argued that adopting fair value treatment in the accounting procedure tends to create avenues for *gharar* and inaccurate valuations of assets and liabilities, which may lead to deception, misapplication, and manipulation of financial statements. In another version of the treatment of *Murabaha* contracts, Ahmed *et al.* (2016) criticized the accounting procedures of the product using both the AAOIFI straight-line method and that of the IFRS that is based on the amortization cost of profit allocation. Despite the contentious debates on some of the techniques adopted by the AAOIFI regarding Sharia-compliant transactions, another study calls for regulators to enforce the standards and work towards having a unified rule of accounting procedures that is Sharia-compliant (Sarea and Hanefah, 2013).

However, Azmi and Hanifa (2015) found that the majority of *waqf* institutions apply different accounting procedures, though they are within the Sharia requirements except for disclosure on Sharia-based investment since *waqf* funds should be used as directed by the donor. Thus, the AAOIFI guidelines on *waqf* can serve as a benchmark for assessing organizational compliance with the *waqf* disclosure requirements in organizational financial reports. Although the present managerial accounting for *waqf* is within the AAOIFI guiding principles, improvements are required to ensure that proper accountability is being upheld (Suhaimi and Yaacob, 2011). In a similar view, Yasmin and Haniffa (2017) highlighted the need for Muslim charity organizations to be transparent in their activities and transactions in accordance with standard accounting requirements for reporting. Therefore, regulatory agencies should enforce reporting standards for proper scrutiny and accountability. Thus, Amran *et al.* (2017) concluded that initial public offer earnings should increase because of enforcement of regulations on disclosure. Therefore, regulators have to enforce firms to comply with strict disclosure reporting.

Despite the immense need for regulators to enforce Islamic financial firms to include Sharia-related content in their financial reports, the firms' professionals affirm that they easily understand and identify such information when it is published as part of the corporate financial statement (Azmi *et al.*, 2016). Meanwhile, understanding the relevant accounting information highlights other insightful accounting practices in the industry such as earning management manipulation and corporate social responsibility. As such, the non-Sharia compliant firms of the MENA region have greater earning management than

Sharia-compliant companies, and external governance is suggested as the best mechanism of improving the disclosure performance of conventional institutions (Farooq and AbdelBari, 2015). Nonetheless, high earning quality is associated with Sharia-based companies in Malaysia, which they use as a strategy for attracting foreign investors besides their Sharia status and close regulatory scrutiny (Wan Ismail *et al.*, 2015). Therefore, Abdelsalam *et al.* (2016) identified that if strict accounting policies are adopted by Islamic banks, this reduces their likelihood of manipulating fund management, which highlights that religious norms have a greater influence on agency costs and the quality of accounting information. Therefore, this determines that adherence to religious norms tends to influence managers to improve the quality of their financial reports and reduce the agency costs to the stakeholders.

6. Conclusion and Future Research

The focus of this survey is to review the empirical literature on Islamic finance and accounting. It is noted that Islamic finance was established with the aim to provide the social justice that is lacking in the self-centered ideology of the conventional system. Therefore, the Islamic financial system is centered within the paradigm of achieving socioeconomic and environmental objectives via capital allocation and financial decisions. Islamic finance and accounting is a subset of Islamic economics that focuses on transactional relations, some thematic blocks of which are discussed in this review. These include the Islamic finance (principles and current status), Islamic corporate finance, Islamic insurance, and accounting. Figure 6 depicts the distribution of studies (with replication) reviewed per section (see detailed table in the appendix). The introduction part of this paper cited 45(32%) studies, 44(31%) studies focus on the Islamic finance section, Islamic accounting records 25(18%) publications, while Islamic corporate finance and Islamic insurance covers 13(9%) studies, respectively. Consequently, this review revolves around empirical literature that is shown in Figure 6. Figure 6 depicts that 11(48%) of the empirically tabulated papers used are for Islamic corporate finance, 4(17%) of the Islamic insurance studies also appeared in Table 2, while Table 3 presents 8(35%) of Islamic

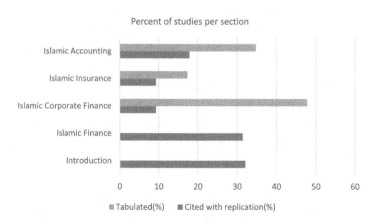

Figure 6. The Distribution of Studies Cited per Section

Table 4. Directions for future research

Themes	Lessons Learned	Policy Implications	Future Research Directions
Islamic finance	• It is noticeable that Islamic finance is growing faster in this millennium with debt-driven contracts, but it has to expand beyond the banking sector, which dominates 80% of its assets. Non-banking institutions such as *Takaful* have an immediate benefit towards increasing the financial access of the micro-sector (e.g., households and firms), whereas capital market instruments are utilized for infrastructure and sovereign finance, which has an impact on overall economic growth and development (World Bank and Islamic Development Bank Group, 2017). • Islamic financial institutions are moving towards debts driving contracts. • Disentangling of substance from form and time value of money are the significant differences between the conventional and Islamic financial reporting standards. • The earlier paradigm of the Islamic finance is based on risk-sharing principles, now the industry is focusing on debt-based finance	• Therefore, regulators have to turn their focus towards the non-banking sector by allowing avenues for developing new risk and reward sharing products, and functional incentives that will give a chance for Islamic finance to realize its actual potential through linking with the real economy. For instance, some jurisdictions allow for some segments of Islamic finance (like banking) to exist, but neglect to provide provisions for others such as Islamic social finance (zakat, sadaqat charity, and waqf), which claim to have a direct impact on poverty reduction, increasing inclusion, and prospering social well-being. • Regulators have to set a benchmark regarding risk minimization on these debts permissible contracts. • Islamic financial standards setters have to emphasis on the substance while designing products. Similarly, regulators have to increase enforcement of the practitioners towards adhering to guiding principles. • Islamic finance regulators have to restructure their focus towards accommodating Islamic finance within modern finance practice without deterring Sharia principles.	• The last three decades of Islamic finance studies have concentrated on adding value to the literature based on empirical findings without in-depth deductions and analogical development of the analytical framework. Failure to continue developing normative Islamic financial theories, analytical and conceptual frameworks stagnate other innovations and expansion in Islamic finance. Thus, this will increase our understanding towards discovering other avenues to model future empirical studies. • Empirical investigation and surveys of literature regarding Islamic social finance legislations are limited to the academic cycle. • The extent to which Islamic financial institutions are minimizing risk on their permissible debt contracts is limited in the literature. • Empirical studies relating to modalities that will factually present other evidence relating to Islamic finance emphasis. • The empirical investigation regarding the form above substance is limited in the Islamic finance literature. • Future studies have to extend investigations regarding the paradigm shift in the Islamic finance.

Table 4. (Continued)

Themes	Lessons Learned	Policy Implications	Future Research Directions
Islamic corporate finance	• The empirical Islamic corporate finance literature is less developed than other segments of Islamic financial institutions. It is documented that the composition of the Islamic capital structure differs from that of conventional firms. Islamic financial institutions are designed to share profit and loss with a broad range of transactional restrictions which include interest, gambling, complex derivatives, and extreme uncertainty. Therefore, the Sharia-compliant firms are largely asset-based, with an ownership legitimacy share of the investment account holder in other cases.	• The proposed Islamic corporate financing policy claims to be sustainable with the aim of wealth creation and redistribution through real economic activities. Thus, Islamic finance principles are believed to control corporate indebtedness, promote profit and loss sharing, and reduce financing costs and instability in the system. Meanwhile, for this funding policy to be successful, holistic support is required from all the stakeholders of the financial system. Apart from financing policy, Islamic corporate finance has the necessary strategies of controlling the agency costs of debt and information asymmetry through tangibility and intangibility exchanges coupled with risk management and moderate portfolio selection, which can provide stability, fairness, and social justice in the system. • Nonetheless, regulators of Sharia-compliant firms' efforts must control earnings manipulation and promote corporate social responsibility, which was found to be insufficient in one of the regional studies. Consequently, some of the financial ratios used to assess Sharia-compliant firms are not in accordance with Sharia principles. One example is the corporate liability ratio. Further investigation is required in this area. • Earn-out agreements consistently contradict the principles of Islamic finance. This demands the attention of regulators and Sharia advisors, and Islamic financial corporations should refrain from such contracts. • The transfer of managers' services within and outside the Islamic financial industry affects individual financial decisions.	• Islamic financial studies have another vacuum in the literature which requires further investigation to bridge the gap that remains open. For instance, the Islamic corporate finance of recent times has exposed issues regarding the corporate liabilities ratio and earn-out agreements, which suggests the need for alternative measurements and contractual agreements, respectively. Apart from these two issues, further studies can extend investigations to other suitable corporate measurements and contractual procedures complying with Sharia law. Consequently, the capital structure of Islamic corporate finance differs from conventional debt-based finance. For instance, Islamic corporate financing policies aim to promote profit and risk sharing, sustainable wealth creation and redistribution, and reducing financing costs and instability in the system. Therefore, other studies are required to validate further the proposed dividend tax shield for equitable, sustainable wealth creation using real-life data. Again, one could explore the assertion that attaining an equilibrium position between the level of dividends and the cost of equity will optimize the corporate capital structure (Zaman et al., 2017). Consistently, other studies believe that the Islamic capital structure is decoupled from that of its conventional counterpart, a conclusion which demands the development of a new capital structure that will form the basis for an Islamic corporate capital structure (Sorwar et al., 2016). • Future studies could explore more about managers' movements and their effect on the value and efficiency maximization of a firm. • There is a need for studies relating to corporate financial structure, capital budgeting, cost of capital, and working capital management among others.

Table 4. (*Continued*)

Themes	Lessons Learned	Policy Implications	Future Research Directions
Takaful	• Though there are many constructive arguments regarding the surplus-sharing incentives offered to *Takaful* corporations, studies in this area have not sufficiently tackled the different effects of these contracts, such as the level of acceptance, information asymmetry, risk coverage, and efficiency. In various explorations, empirical research has shown that the level of income and education, the proportion of the Muslim population, and Islamic financial development all influence *Takaful* insurance demand. The cost efficiency of the *Takaful* industry is an essential ingredient that will lead to self-sufficiency. The size of the board and firm has been found to influence cost efficiency, whereas splitting the top management does not affect. • *Takaful* capital structure is nevertheless similar to other firms' arrangement that does not strictly comply mutual contributions. • The few Takaful empirical literature informed us about its determinant, efficiency, and performance in some countries.	• The present growth in *Takaful* investments requires efficient services that can compete with conventional insurance companies. Despite the recent development of the *Takaful* business guidelines, standard setters have more work to do on hybrid practices. For instance, the regulators have to explain in detail the percentage of acceptable product combinations between mutuality and proprietary entities to avoid conflicts of interest. At the same time, supervisors have to ensure that the *Takaful* industry competes comparatively and efficiently regarding price, delivery time, and quality of coverage. Additionally, human capacity enhancement is required on a timely basis, as hiring professional personnel tends to improve efficient performance. • Policy arrangement is required to reverse the system to its ideal practices. • The corporate governance structure of the *Takaful* may tend to be different compared with other Islamic financial institutions. Regulators have to consider the uniqueness of Takaful arrangement and design a mechanism that will protect all stakeholders.	• Another section of this review describes the acceptability of *Takaful* in countries offering Islamic financial services. Nonetheless, the current empirical performance studies on *Takaful* corporations are not enough to uncover other avenues that might require the funds to adopt the Solvency II framework. Similarly, empirical studies are necessary to investigate whether a conflict of interest exists in the *Takaful* industry, as their hybrid structure between mutuality and proprietary entities has different interests to protect. Similarly, empirical studies on *Takaful* mutuality lack in the literature, despite its direct impacts on society. • Available empirical studies on Takaful are sufficiently discovered the effect of deviating from mutuality principle in capital structure as well as the policyholders' benefits. • We are not aware whether the majority of Islamic financial firms are insured through *Takaful* companies or not. • The few empirical literatures on *Takaful* neglect their other areas such as corporate structure, accountability, consumer protections, insolvency, disclosure, and capital regulations.

Table 4. (*Continued*)

Themes	Lessons Learned	Policy Implications	Future Research Directions
Islamic accounting	• Islamic accounting is another growing area which is relevant to the Islamic financial system since recording transactions is part of the fundamental Islamic legal principles of deferred contracts. However, Islamic accounting techniques are expected to be consistent with Sharia, which considers truthfulness and transparency, coupled with disclosure of information, to be of paramount importance. • It is noticeable that most countries are practicing Islamic finance adopting IFRS standards rather than FAS for Islamic financial institutions. The significant differences between conventional and Islamic accounting treatment lie in the "form above substance" claim and the reflection of the time value of money in some Sharia-based transactions. • Consequently, the complexity of some Islamic instruments leaves an inconclusive vacuum for product classification and measurement to be addressed.	• Therefore, regulators and standards setter have to engage in providing a comprehensive procedure for Islamic accounting if at all differ significantly with conventional principles.	• Studies on Islamic accounting are qualitative with few empirical investigations. Thus, this gap in the empirical literature on Islamic accounting hinders further suggestions on potential ways to improve accounting practices to conform to earlier theoretical postulations. Likewise, there is a need for future studies to increase our understanding by exploring the form and substance issues regarding accounting techniques for treating unresolved Islamic financial transactions.
Data and Methodology	• Few of the Islamic finance studies include sample countries outside the GCC region, MENA, and Southeast Asia.	• Extending grants, conferences and seminars to the Muslim minority countries will contribute toward understanding the nature of the Islamic finance practices particularly in the financially developed nations.	• Empirical studies that cover other regions are required.

accounting empirical studies. Finally, the major issues and directions for future research based on each section are highlighted in Table 4.

Appendix A

Table A.1. Summary of Studies per Section

S/N	Section	Cited with Replication	Percent	Tabulated	Percent
1	Introduction	45	32	0	0
2	Islamic Finance	44	31	0	0
3	Islamic Corporate Finance	13	9	11	48
4	Islamic Insurance	13	9	4	17
5	Islamic Accounting	25	18	8	35
	Total	140	100	23	100

References

Abdel Karim, RA (1995). The nature and rationale of a conceptual framework for financial reporting by Islamic Banks. *Accounting and Business Research*, 25(100), 285–300. http://doi.org/10.1080/00014788.1995.9729916.

Abdelsalam, O, P Dimitropoulos, M Elnahass and S Leventis (2016). Earnings management behaviors under different monitoring mechanisms: The case of Islamic and conventional banks. *Journal of Economic Behavior & Organization*. http://doi.org/10.1016/j.jebo.2016.04.022.

Abedifar, P, SM Ebrahim, P Molyneux and A Tarazi (2015). Islamic banking and finance: Recent empirical literature and directions for future research. *Journal of Economic Surveys*, 29(4), 637–670. http://doi.org/10.1111/joes.12113.

Abedifar, P, P Molyneux and A Tarazi (2013). Risk in islamic banking. *Review of Finance*, 17(6), 2035–2096. http://doi.org/10.1093/rof/rfs041.

Ahmed, H (2007). *Issues in Islamic Corporate Finance — Capital Structure in Firms. IRTI Research Paper Series* (1st ed.). Jiddah, Saudi Arabia: Islamic Research and Training Institute (IRTI) or the Islamic Development Bank Group (IDBG).

Ahmed, MU, R Sabirzyanov and R Rosman (2016). A critique on accounting for murabaha contract. *Journal of Islamic Accounting and Business Research*, 7(3), 190–201. http://doi.org/10.1108/JIABR-04-2016-0041.

Akhatova, M, MP Zainal and MH Ibrahim (2016). Banking models and monetary transmission mechanisms in Malaysia: Are Islamic banks different? *Economic Papers: A Journal of Applied Economics and Policy*, 35(2), n/a-n/a. http://doi.org/10.1111/1759-3441.12131.

Al-deehani, T, RAA Karim and V Murinde (1999). The capital structure of Islamic banks under the contractual obligation of profit sharing. *International Journal of Theoretical and Applied Finance*, 2(3), 243–283. https://doi.org/10.1142/S0219024999000157.

Al-Jarrah, IM, KS Al-Abdulqader and S Hammoudeh (2016). Cost-efficiency and financial and geographical characteristics of banking sectors in the MENA countries. *Applied Economics*, 1–15. http://doi.org/10.1080/00036846.2016.1262524.

Al-Kayed, LT, SRSM Zain and J Duasa (2014). The relationship between capital structure and performance of Islamic banks. *Journal of Islamic Accounting and Business Research*, 5(2), 158–181. http://doi.org/10.1108/JIABR-04-2012-0024.

Alam, N and SAR Rizvi (2017). Empirical research in Islamic banking: Past, present, and future. In *Islamic Banking*, Alam, N and SAR Rizvi (eds.), 1st ed., pp. 1–13. Cham: Springer International Publishing. http://doi.org/10.1007/978-3-319-45910-3_1.

Aliyu, S, MK Hassan, R Mohd Yusof and N Naiimi (2017). Islamic banking sustainability: A review of literature and directions for future research. *Emerging Markets Finance and Trade*, 53(2), 1–31. http://doi.org/10.1080/1540496X.2016.1262761.

Alqahtani, F, DG Mayes and K Brown (2016). Economic turmoil and Islamic banking: Evidence from the Gulf Cooperation Council. *Pacific-Basin Finance Journal*, 39(January), 44–56. http://doi.org/10.1016/j.pacfin.2016.05.017.

Alsaadi, A, MS Ebrahim and A Jaafar (2017). Corporate social responsibility, shariah-compliance, and earnings quality. *Journal of Financial Services Research*, 51(2), 169–194. http://doi.org/10.1007/s10693-016-0263-0.

Amran, A *et al.* (2017). Social responsibility disclosure in Islamic banks: A comparative study of Indonesia and Malaysia. *Journal of Financial Reporting and Accounting*, 15(1), 1–33. http://doi.org/10.1108/JFRA-01-2015-0016.

AOSSG (2010). *Financial Reporting Issues relating to Islamic Finance: Working Group on Financial Reporting Issues relating to Islamic*. Kuala Lumpur, Malaysia: Asian-Oceanian Standard-Setters Group. Retrieved from http://www.aossg.org/docs/AOSSG_IF_WG-Research_Paper_11Oct2010.pdf.

AOSSG (2015). *Financial Reporting by Islamic Financial Institutions: A Study of Financial Statements of Islamic Financial Institutions*. Kuala Lumpur, Malaysia.

Asbeig, HI and SH Kassim (2015). Monetary transmission during low interest rate environment in a dual banking system: Evidence from Malaysia. *Macroeconomics and Finance in Emerging Market Economies*, 8(3), 275–285. http://doi.org/10.1080/17520843.2015.1060248.

Ashraf, D (2016). Does Shari'ah screening cause abnormal returns? Empirical evidence from Islamic equity indices. *Journal of Business Ethics*, 134(2), 209–228. http://doi.org/10.1007/s10551-014-2422-2.

Ashraf, D, K Felixson, M Khawaja and SM Hussain (2017). Do constraints on financial and operating leverage affect the performance of Islamic equity portfolios? *Pacific-Basin Finance Journal*, 42, 171–182. http://doi.org/10.1016/j.pacfin.2017.02.009.

Atmeh, MA and B Maali (2017). An accounting perspective on the use of combined contracts and donations in Islamic financial transactions. *Journal of Islamic Accounting and Business Research*, 8(1), 54–69. http://doi.org/10.1108/JIABR-07-2014-0024.

Ayub, M (2007). *Understanding Islamic Finance. The Atrium, Southern Gate, Chichester: John Wiley & Sons Ltd*. West Sussex, England: ohn Wiley & Sons Ltd, The Atrium, Southern Gate, Chichester,. Retrieved from http://books.google.com/books?id=-3eZcL_kAkMC.

Azmi, CA, N Ab Aziz, N Non and R Muhamad (2016). Sharia disclosures. *Journal of Islamic Accounting and Business Research*, 7(3), 237–252. http://doi.org/10.1108/JIABR-03-2016-0029.

Azmi, CA and MH Hanifa (2015). The Sharia-compliance of financial reporting practices: A case study on waqf. *Journal of Islamic Accounting and Business Research*, 6(1), 55–72. http://doi.org/10.1108/JIABR-10-2012-0069.

Bashir, A-HM and AF Darrat (1992). Equity participation contracts and investment some theoretical and empirical result. *The American Journal of Islamic Social Sciences*, 9(2), 219–232.

Bashir, A, AF Darrat and MO Suliman (1993). Equity capital, profit sharing contracts, and investment: Theory and evidence. *Journal of Business Finance & Accounting*, 20(5), 639–651. http://doi.org/10.1111/j.1468-5957.1993.tb00281.x.

Bashir, BA (1983). Portfolio management of islamic banks. *Journal of Banking & Finance*, 7(3), 339–354. http://doi.org/10.1016/0378-4266(83)90043-2.

Boulanouar, Z and F Alqahtani (2016). IPO underpricing in the insurance industry and the effect of Sharia compliance. *International Journal of Islamic and Middle Eastern Finance and Management*, 9(3), 314–332. http://doi.org/10.1108/IMEFM-12-2014-0118.

Chapra, MU (2017). The looming international financial crisis: Can the introduction of risk sharing in the financial system as required by Islamic finance, play a positive role in reducing its severity? *Islamic Economic Studies*, 25(2), 1–13. http://doi.org/10.12816/0038220.

Chong, BS and MH Liu (2009). Islamic banking: Interest-free or interest-based? *Pacific Basin Finance Journal*, 17(1), 125–144. http://doi.org/10.1016/j.pacfin.2007.12.003.

Darrat, AF (1988). The Islamic interest-free banking system: Some empirical evidence. *Applied Economics*, 20(3), 417–425. http://doi.org/10.1080/00036848800000054.

Dow Jones (2003). *Guide to the Dow Jones Islamic Market Index*. Retrieved from http://www.kantakji.com/media/7653/dj.pdf.

Dusuki, AW (2012). *Islamic Financial System: Principles & Operations* (1st ed.). Kuala Lumpur, Malaysia: International Shari'ah Research Academy for Islamic Finance (ISRA).

Ebrahim, M-S and A Safadi (1995). Behavioral norms in the Islamic doctrine of economics: A comment. *Journal of Economic Behavior & Organization*, 27(1), 151–157. http://doi.org/10.1016/0167-2681(94)00029-E.

Ebrahim, MS, A Jaafar, FA Omar and MO Salleh (2016). Can Islamic injunctions indemnify the structural flaws of securitized debt? *Journal of Corporate Finance*, 37, 271–286. http://doi.org/10.1016/j.jcorpfin.2016.01.002.

El-Gamal, MA (2006). *Islamic Finance. Islamic Finance: Law, Economics, and Practice*. New York, United State of America: Cambridge University Press. Retrieved from www.cambridge.org/9780521864145.

Elnahas, AM, MK Hassan and GM Ismail (2016). Religion and ratio analysis: Towards an Islamic corporate liquidity measure. *Emerging Markets Review*. http://doi.org/10.1016/j.ememar.2016.09.001.

Elnahas, AM, M Kabir Hassan and GM Ismail (2017). Religion and mergers and acquisitions contracting: The case of earnout agreements. *Journal of Corporate Finance*, 42, 221–246. http://doi.org/10.1016/j.jcorpfin.2016.11.012.

Ergeç, EH and BG Arslan (2013). Impact of interest rates on Islamic and conventional banks: The case of Turkey. *Applied Economics*, 45, 2381–2388. http://doi.org/10.1080/00036846.2012.665598.

Fama, EF (2011). My life in finance. *Annual Review of Financial Economics*, 3, 1–15. http://doi.org/10.1146/annurev-financial-102710-144858.

Farooq, O and A AbdelBari (2015). Earnings management behaviour of Shariah-compliant firms and non-Shariah-compliant firms. *Journal of Islamic Accounting and Business Research*, 6(2), 173–188. http://doi.org/10.1108/JIABR-07-2013-0021.

Gharbi, L (2016). A critical analysis of the use of fair value by Islamic Financial Institutions. *Journal of Islamic Accounting and Business Research*, 7(2), 170–183. http://doi.org/10.1108/JIABR-10-2013-0037.

Hakan Ergec, E and B Gülümser Kaytanci (2014). The causality between returns of interest-based banks and Islamic banks: The case of Turkey. *International Journal of Islamic and Middle Eastern Finance and Management*, 7(4), 443–456. http://doi.org/10.1108/IMEFM-07-2014-0072.

Haque, NU and A Mirakhor (1986). *Optimal Profit-Sharing Contracts and Investment in an Interest-Free Islamic Economy*. Washington, D.C., USA. Retrieved from http://documents.worldbank.org/curated/en/843891468152707289/Optimal-profit-sharing-contracts-and-investment-in-an-interest-free-Islamic-economy.

Hassan, MK and AQ Aldayel (1998). Stability of money demand under interest-free versus interest-based banking system. *Humanomics*, 14(4), 166–185. http://doi.org/10.1108/eb018821.

Hassan, MK and S Aliyu (2018). A contemporary survey of islamic banking literature. *Journal of Financial Stability*, 34, 12–43. http://doi.org/10.1016/j.jfs.2017.11.006.

Hassan, MK, S Aliyu, A Paltrinieri and A Khan (2018). A review of Islamic investment literature. *Economic Papers: A Journal of Applied Economics and Policy*, 1–36. http://doi.org/10.1111/1759-3441.12230.

Hayat, U and A Malik (2014). *Islamic Finance: Ethics, Concepts, Practice (Literature Review)*. Charlottesville, Virginia: CFA Institute Research Foundation. Retrieved from http://www.cfapubs.org/doi/pdf/10.2470/rflr.v9.n3.1.

Hussain, M, A Shahmoradi and R Turk (2015). An Overview of Islamic Finance. *IMF Working Papers*, No. 15-120. http://doi.org/10.1142/S1793993316500034.

IFRS (2014). *Consultative Group on Shariah-Compliant Instruments and Transactions: Issues in the application of IFRS 9 to Islamic Finance*. Retrieved from http://archive.ifrs.org/Meetings/MeetingDocs/Other Meeting/2014/September/IFRS-9-Discussion-paper-September-2014.pdf.

IFRS (2015). *Outreach on Shariah-Compliant Instruments and Transactions: Issues in the Application of IFRS 9 to Islamic Finance*. London: International Accounting Standards Board. Retrieved from http://archive.ifrs.org/Meetings/MeetingDocs/OtherMeeting/2015/June/IFRS9-outreach-paper-V2.pdf.

IFRS (2016). *Outreach on Shariah-Compliant Instruments and Transactions: Issues in the Application of IFRS 9 to Islamic Finance*. London. Retrieved from http://archive.ifrs.org/About-us/IASB/Advisory-bodies/Working-groups/Documents/Issues-in-the-application-of-IFRS-9-to-Islamic-Finance.pdf.

IIFM (2016). *A comprehensive study of the Global Sukuk Market*. Manama, Bahrain.

Islamic Financial Services Board (2009). *Guiding Principles on Governance for Takāful (Islamic Insurance) Undertakings*. Kuala Lumpur, Malaysia: Islamic Financial Services Board.

Islamic Financial Services Board (2017). *Islamic Financial Services Industry Stability Report 2017*. Kuala Lumpur, Malaysia.

Kader, HA, MB Adams and P Hardwick (2010). The cost efficiency of Takaful insurance companies. *The Geneva Papers on Risk and Insurance Issues and Practice*, 35(1), 161–181. http://doi.org/10.1057/gpp.2009.33.

Kader, HA, M Adams, P Hardwick and WJ Kwon (2014). Cost efficiency and board composition under different takaful insurance business models. *International Review of Financial Analysis*, 32, 60–70. http://doi.org/10.1016/j.irfa.2013.12.008.

Kamla, R (2009). Critical insights into contemporary Islamic accounting. *Critical Perspectives on Accounting*, 20(8), 921–932. http://doi.org/10.1016/j.cpa.2009.01.002.

Kamla, RG and H Rammal (2013). Social reporting by Islamic banks: does social justice matter? *Accounting, Auditing & Accountability Journal*, 26(6), 911–945. http://doi.org/10.1108/AAAJ-03-2013-1268.

Kamla, R and F Haque (2017). Islamic accounting, neo-imperialism and identity staging: The accounting and auditing organization for Islamic financial institutions. *Critical Perspectives on Accounting*, 1–20. http://doi.org/10.1016/j.cpa.2017.06.001.

Karsten, I (1982). Islam and financial intermediation (L'Islam et l'intermediation financiere) (Islamiso e intermediacion financiera). *Palgrave Macmillan Journals*, 29(1), 108–142. http://doi.org/10.2307/3866946.

Kassim, SH, M Shabri, A Majid and RM Yusof (2009). Impact of monetary policy shocks on the conventional and islamic banks in a dual banking system: Evidence from malaysia. *Journal of Economic Cooperation and Development*, 30(1), 41–58.

Khan, F (2010). How "Islamic" is Islamic Banking? *Journal of Economic Behavior and Organization*, 76(3), 805–820. http://doi.org/10.1016/j.jebo.2010.09.015.

Khan, H (2015). Optimal incentives for takaful (Islamic insurance) operators. *Journal of Economic Behavior and Organization*, 109, 135–144. http://doi.org/10.1016/j.jebo.2014.11.001.

Khan, I, NNBA Rahman, MYZBM Yusoff and MRBM Nor (2016). History, problems, and prospects of Islamic insurance (Takaful) in Bangladesh. *SpringerPlus*, 5(1), 1–7. http://doi.org/10.1186/s40064-016-2400-5.

Khan, MS (1986). Islamic interest-free banking: A theoretical analysis. *Palgrave Macmillan Journals*, 33(1), 1–27.

KPMG and ACCA (2012). *Global Alignment: Bringing Consistency to Reporting of Islamic Finance through IFRS*. Retrieved from http://www.accaglobal.com/content/dam/acca/global/PDF-technical/financial-reporting/pol-afb-gabc.pdf.

Kuran, T (1983). Behavioral norms in the Islamic doctrine of economics. *Journal of Economic Behavior & Organization*, 4(4), 353–379. http://doi.org/10.1016/0167-2681(83)90014-8.

Kuran, T (1995). Further reflections on the behavioral norms of Islamic economics. *Journal of Economic Behavior and Organization*, 27(1), 159–163. http://doi.org/10.1016/0167-2681(94)00030-I.

Maghrebi, N, A Mirakhor and Z Iqbal (2016). *Intermediate Islamic finance* (1st edn.). Solaris South Tower, Singapore: John Wiley & Sons (Asia) Pte Ltd. Retrieved from http://www.columbia.edu/cgi-bin/cul/resolve?clio11889320.003.

Modigliani, F and MH Miller (1958). The cost of capital, corporation finance and the theory of investment. *American Economic Review*, 48(3), 261–297. http://doi.org/10.4013/base.20082.07.

Mohieldin, M (2012). *Realizing the Potential of Islamic Finance*. Washington, D.C. USA. Retrieved from http://documents.worldbank.org/curated/en/987991468171844534/Realizing-the-potential-of-Islamic-finance.

Narayan, PK and DHB Phan (2019). A survey of Islamic banking and finance literature: Issues, challenges and future directions. *Pacific-Basin Finance Journal*, 53, 484–496. http://doi.org/10.1016/j.pacfin.2017.06.006.

Naz, I, SMA Shah and AM Kutan (2017). Do managers of sharia-compliant firms have distinctive financial styles? *Journal of International Financial Markets, Institutions and Money*, 46, 174–187. http://doi.org/10.1016/j.intfin.2016.05.005.

Önder, YK (2016). Asset backed contracts and sovereign risk. *Journal of Economic Behavior & Organization*. http://doi.org/10.1016/j.jebo.2016.10.006.

Pacter, P (2016). IASB Corner. *The International Journal of Accounting*, 51(4), 525–536. http://doi.org/10.1016/j.intacc.2016.10.003.

Pervez, IA (1990). Islamic finance. *Arab Law Quarterly*, 5(4), 259. http://doi.org/10.2307/3381929.

Pratomo, WA and AG Ismail (2007). Islamic bank performance and capital structure. *Munich Personal RePEc Archive*, 60(12), 1–7. Retrieved from http://mpra.ub.uni-muenchen.de/6012/.

Rosly, SA (1999). Al-Bay' Bithaman Ajil financing: Impacts on Islamic banking performance. *Thunderbird International Business Review*, 41(4–5), 461–480. http://doi.org/10.1002/tie.4270410410.

Saraç, M and F Zeren (2014). The dependency of Islamic bank rates on conventional bank interest rates: Further evidence from Turkey. *Applied Economics*, 47(7), 669–679. http://doi.org/10.1080/00036846.2014.978076.

Sarea, MA and MM Hanefah (2013). The need of accounting standards for Islamic financial institutions: Evidence from AAOIFI. *Journal of Islamic Accounting and Business Research*, 4(1), 64–76. http://doi.org/10.1108/17590811311314294.

Shabsigh, G et al. (2017). *Ensuring Financial Stability in Countries with Islamic Banking*. New York, United State of America. Retrieved from https://www.imf.org/en/Publications/Policy-Papers/Issues/2017/02/21/PP-Ensuring-Financial-Stability-in-Countries-with-Islamic-Banking.

Shafii, Z and AR Abdul Rahman (2016). Issues on the application of IFRS9 and fair value measurement for Islamic financial instruments. *Journal of Islamic Accounting and Business Research*, 7(3), 202–214. http://doi.org/10.1108/JIABR-03-2016-0031.

Sheriff, M and NA Shaairi (2013). Determinants of demand on family Takaful in Malaysia. *Journal of Islamic Accounting and Business Research*, 4(1), 1759–0817. http://doi.org/10.5465/amj.2013.0599.

Siddiqi, MN (2006). Islamic banking and finance in theory and practice: A survey of state of the art. *Islamic Economic Studies*, 13(2), 1–48. http://doi.org/10.4197/islec.17-1.4.

Sorwar, G, V Pappas, J Pereira and M Nurullah (2016). To debt or not to debt: Are Islamic banks less risky than conventional banks? *Journal of Economic Behavior & Organization*. http://doi.org/10.1016/j.jebo.2016.10.012.

Suhaimi, NH and H Yaacob (2011). Accountability in the sacred context. *Journal of Islamic Accounting and Business Research*, 2(2), 87–113. http://doi.org/10.1108/17590811111170520.

Sukmana, R and MH Ibrahim (2017). How Islamic are Islamic banks? A non-linear assessment of Islamic rate — conventional rate relations. *Economic Modelling*, (February), 0–1. http://doi.org/10.1016/j.econmod.2017.02.025.

Sukmana, R and SH Kassim (2010). Roles of the Islamic banks in the monetary transmission process in Malaysia. *International Journal of Islamic and Middle Eastern Finance and Management*, 3(1), 7–19. http://doi.org/10.1108/17538391011033834.

Thabet, O, F Shawtari, A Ayedh and F Shawtari (2017). Capital structure of Malaysian shariah-compliant firms, *Journal of King Abdulaziz University-Islamic Economics*, 30(1), 105–116. https://doi.org/10.4197/Islec.30-1.10

Wan Ismail, WA, KA Kamarudin and SR Sarman (2015). The quality of earnings in Shariah-compliant companies: Evidence from Malaysia. *Journal of Islamic Accounting and Business Research*, 6(1), 19–41. http://doi.org/10.1108/JIABR-03-2013-0005.

World Bank and Islamic Development Bank Group (2017). *Global Report on Islamic Finance 2016: A Catalyst for Shared Prosperity?* Washington, DC: World Bank and IDBG: The World Bank. http://doi.org/10.1596/978-1-4648-0926-2.

Yasmin, S and R Haniffa (2017). Accountability and narrative disclosure by Muslim charity organisations in the UK. *Journal of Islamic Accounting and Business Research*, 8(1), 70–86.

Yusof, RM, M Bahlous and H Tursunov (2015). Are profit sharing rates of mudharabah account linked to interest rates? An investigation on Islamic banks in GCC Countries. *Jurnal Ekonomi Malaysia*, 49(2), 77–86. http://doi.org/10.17576/JEM-2015-4902-07.

Zaher, T and M Hassan (2001). A comparative literature survey of Islamic finance and banking. *Financial Markets, Institutions & Instruments*, 10(4), 155–199. http://doi.org/doi: 10.1111/1468-0416.00044.

Zainol, Z and SH Kassim (2010). An analysis of Islamic banks' exposure to rate of return risk. *Journal of Economic Cooperation and Development*, 31, 59–84.

Zaman, QU, MK Hassan, M Akhtar and MA Meraj (2018). From interest tax shield to dividend tax shield: A corporate financing policy for equitable and sustainable wealth creation. *Pacific-Basin Finance Journal*, 52, 144–162. http://doi.org/10.1016/j.pacfin.2017.01.003.

Zeidane, Z et al. (2017). *Multi-Country Report Ensuring Financial Stability in Countries with Islamic Banking — Case Studies — Press Release; Staff Report* (Vol. June). Washington, D.C. USA. Retrieved from https://www.imf.org/~/media/Files/Publications/CR/2017/cr17145.ashx.

www.ingramcontent.com/pod-product-compliance
Lightning Source LLC
Chambersburg PA
CBHW080708300625
28794CB00003B/3